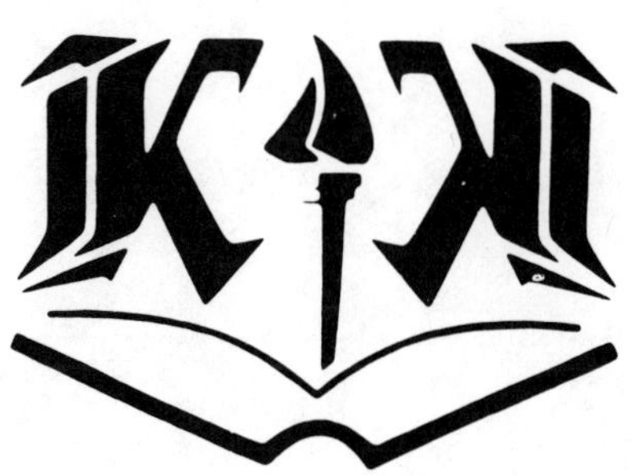

Limited Classical Reprint Library

STUDIES IN THE EPISTLE TO THE ROMANS

by

Hermann Olshausen, D.D.

Foreword by Dr. Cyril J. Barber

Klock & Klock Christian Publishers, Inc.
2527 Girard Avenue North
Minneapolis, Minnesota 55411

Originally published by
T. & T. Clark
Edinburgh, 1849

Copy from the personal library of
Dr. Cyril J. Barber

ISBN: 0-86524-163-5

Printed by Klock & Klock in the U.S.A.
1983 Reprint

FOREWORD

Hermann Olshausen (1796-1839) was a famous Lutheran theologian and New Testament exegete. He studied at the Universities of Kiel and Berlin. At the latter institution he sat under Friederick Schleiermacher and Johann Neander. Upon graduation, he served successively on the faculties of the Universities of Berlin (1820), Konigsberg (1821-34) and Erlangen (1834-39). He died of tuberculosis at age 43.

While at Konigsberg, Dr. Olshausen began his commentary on the New Testament. A staunch evangelical, he approached the text as the "living Word of God." Although he lived only long enough to expound the gospels, Acts and Epistles of Paul through I & II Thessalonians, he left behind him a rich heritage for all students of the New Testament. His works were translated into English and were published in Edinburgh in six volumes between 1847-1860.

It is a testimony to the erudition of Professor Olshausen that his works are still being eagerly sought after by evangelicals more than a century and a half after their first appearance.

This study of Paul's letter to the believers in Rome is well deserving of repeated consultation.

Cyril J. Barber
Author, *The Minister's Library*

ADVERTISEMENT.

A translation of Olshausen's valuable Commentary on the New Testament was projected by some members of the English Church in the end of the year 1845, and the Epistle to the Romans was selected as the portion which should be first executed.

Before this part of the work was completed, however, the whole Commentary was announced for speedy publication in the Foreign Theological Library; and, as it was evident that a competition between two translations would not be desirable, the translators of the Commentary on the Epistle to the Romans resolved to offer their version to Messrs Clark, and to abandon the rest of their original design. Hence it is that the contents of the present volume appear as a part of the Publishers' series.

If the translators had brought out the work on their own account, and on their own responsibility, they would have endeavoured to adapt it to English use, by considerable omissions of matter which relates to merely German opinions and controversies, by condensation of the language, and by intimating their own occasional differences from the respected author. Under the actual circumstances, however, such a process of editing would manifestly be out of place. The book, therefore, is intended to represent the original as faithfully as possible, although the translators are fully sensible that their task has been very inadequately performed. Their own very few additions are marked by brackets.

Olshausen's Commentary extends to the Gospels, the Acts, and the Epistles to the Romans, Corinthians, Galatians, Ephesians, Colossians, and Thessalonians. In the following pages there will be found frequent references to portions which the author did not live to execute It has seemed well to retain these, as they may be useful in directing the reader to a comparison of other commentaries; and it appears better to mention here, once for all, the limits of the actually existing work, than to append to every such reference a statement that the design is incomplete.

Four persons have been concerned in the translation; their respective portions are as follows:

General Introduction, (pp. 1–24),	. . .	A.
Introduction to the Epistle (25–58),	. . .	B.
Commentary chap. i. 1, to v. 11 (59–183)	. .	A.
,,	v. 12, to viii. 39 (184–304) . .	C.
,,	ix. 1, to ix. 30 (304–342) . .	D.
,,	ix. 30 to the end (342–431) . .	B.

B.

January 23, 1849.

CONTENTS.

GENERAL INTRODUCTION TO THE EPISTLES OF ST PAUL.

Page.

§ 1. Of the Life and Ministry of St Paul in general, ... 1
2. The peculiarities of St Paul's character, ... 8
3. Order of succession of St Paul's Epistles, ... 14

THE EPISTLE TO THE ROMANS—INTRODUCTION.

§ 1. Of the Genuineness and the Integrity of the Epistle, ... 26
2. Time and place of the composition, ... 33
3. Of the Roman Church, ... 35
4. Argument of the Epistle, ... 48
5. The value and the peculiar character of the Epistle, ... 51
6. Literature, ... 56

PART I.

THE INTRODUCTION.

(i. 1—17.)

§ 1. The Salutation (i. 1-7). ... 59
2. Introduction (i. 8-17), ... 70

PART II.

THE DOCTRINAL EXPOSITION.

(i. 18—xi. 36.)

A. SECTION I.

OF THE SINFULNESS OF THE HUMAN RACE.

(i. 18—iii. 20.)

§ 3. Condition of the heathen world (i. 18-32), ... 79
4. Condition of the Jews (ii. 1-29), ... 93
5. Comparison of the Jews and Gentiles (iii. 1-20), ... 119

B. SECTION II.

THE DESCRIPTION OF THE NEW WAY OF SALVATION IN CHRIST.

(iii. 21—v. 11.)

§ 6. The doctrine of free grace in Christ (iii. 21-31), ... 132
7. Abraham justified by faith (iv. 1-25), ... 158
8. Of the fruits of faith (v. 1-11), ... 174

C. SECTION III.

OF THE VICARIOUS OFFICE OF CHRIST.

(v. 12—vii. 6.)

§ 9. Parallel between Adam and Christ (v. 12, 21), ... 184
10. The believer is dead to sin (vi. 1—vii. 6), ... 207

D. SECTION IV.

OF THE STAGES OF THE DEVELOPMENT AS WELL OF INDIVIDUALS AS OF THE UNIVERSE.

(vii. 7—viii. 39.)

§ 11. Of the Development of the Individual until his Experience of Redemption (vii. 7—24), ... 236
12. Of the Experience of Redemption until the Perfection of the Individual Life (vii. 25—viii. 17), ... 257
13. Of the Perfection of the whole Creation with the Children of God (viii. 18—39), ... 281

E. SECTION V.

THE RELATION OF ISRAEL AND OF THE GENTILE WORLD TO THE NEW WAY OF SALVATION.

(ix. 1—xi. 36.)

§ 14. Of the Election of Grace (ix. 1—29), ... 305
15. Israel's guilt (ix. 30—x. 21), ... 342
16. Israel's Salvation (xi. 1—36), ... 355

PART III.

THE ETHICAL EXPOSITION.

A. SECTION I.

EXHORTATIONS TO LOVE AND OBEDIENCE.

(xii. 1—xiii. 14.)

§ 17. Of Love (xii. 1—21), ... 387
18. Of Obedience (xiii. 1—14), ... 396

B. SECTION II.

OF BEHAVIOUR AS TO THINGS INDIFFERENT.

(xiv. 1—xv. 3.)

§ 19. Of bearing with the Weak (xiv. 1—23), ... 406
20. Christ an example of bearing with the Weak (xv. 1—13), ... 414

C. SECTION III.

PERSONAL COMMUNICATIONS.

(xv. 14—33.)

§ 21. Apology (xv. 14—21), ... 418
22. Notice of Journeys (xv. 22—33), ... 421

PART IV.

SALUTATIONS AND CONCLUSION.

(xvi. 1—27.)

§ 23. Salutations (xvi. 1—20), ... 425
24. Conclusion (xvi. 21—27), ... 429

GENERAL INTRODUCTION

TO THE

EPISTLES OF ST PAUL.

§. 2. OF THE LIFE* AND MINISTRY OF ST PAUL IN GENERAL.

The connected consideration of the Epistles of St Paul calls for a summary view of his personal character in all its grandeur, as well as of the ways in which the Lord of the Church prepared this distinguished instrument for the execution of His purposes. For so entirely are St Paul's writings the proper growth of his own mind and spirit, almost, so to speak, living parts of his very self, that it would be most difficult to understand their peculiar nature without a clear perception of these points.

St Paul was called, for the further spread of the gospel, to form the connecting link between the Roman-Grecian and the Jewish world; it was necessary therefore that both heathen and Jewish habits of life and thought should bear a part in his education, in order that he might be able to understand and sympathise with both. Born of Jewish parents, and in later life brought up at the feet of Gamaliel, in the principles of the Pharisees, Jewish views and feelings certainly formed the *ground-work and substance* of his education. But, as his birth-place was Tarsus, where Grecian

* On the life of St Paul, besides the older works of Pearson (Annales Paulini) and Paley (Horæ Paulinæ), there have more recently appeared the writings of Menken, "Blicke in das Leben des Apostels Paulus." (Bremen, 1828), of Hemsen (Göttingen, 1830), of Schrader (Leipz. 1830–32, iii. vols.), and of Schott (Jena, 1832). The work of Schrader is rich in new results, which, however, cannot bear the test of an impartial

art and science flourished in a high degree,* this could not fail to exert an immediate effect upon the outward form which his Jewish principles assumed; indeed, that it did so, is still evident from the quotations made in his writings from Grecian poets. (Acts xvii. 28, 1 Cor. xv. 33, Tit. i. 12.) So that it is at least more than probable that, in the later part of his life, when he had escaped from the stern bondage of the narrow-minded system of the Pharisees, the views he had gained in his youth of the nobler aspects of Grecian life rose up again before his mind, and gave him that just appreciation of Gentile life, which is discernible in his writings.

For just as Philo, and other Jews, who lived entirely amongst Greeks, as well as the earlier Fathers of the Church (as, for instance, Justin Martyr), regarded the better men amongst the Gentiles as by no means excluded from the blessings of the Divine Word, the Giver of the heavenly powers of holiness and the knowledge of God; even so did St Paul recognise within the heathen world a spiritual Israel; that is, spirits nobler than the rest, who thirsted after truth and righteousness (Rom. ii. 14, 15); and whom he sought, through the preaching of the gospel, to lead to the covenants of promise. Even the birth, therefore, of the Apcstle, and the influences under which he grew up, were all so ordered by the providence of God, as best to train him for the teacher of the Gentiles (Galat. i. 15.) For though at first sight it might appear that his connexion with the sect of the Pharisees would not conduce to that freedom of spirit which he afterwards attained to, yet, on closer consideration, we shall discern in this very circumstance the wisdom of a directing Providence.

In the first place, there were found in this sect many elements of truth, more especially moral earnestness and strictness of life; for it was in *many* only, but by no means in all, that these became hypocrisy. And, besides this, just such a nature as that of St Paul needed the full experience of *all* that one system had to offer, before he would become fully conscious of what was erroneous and one-sided in it, and embrace with complete devotion, and all the

criticism.—Very interesting and instructive are the remarks of Tholuck in the "Studien und Kritiken" of 1835. P. ii. p. 364, &c.

* Strabo (Geogr. xiv. p. 991, ed. Almelov.) places Tarsus, in this respect, on a level with Athens and Alexandria.

powers of his being, the complementary truth which that system obscured or denied. The energy and determination of his will made him carry out his principles as a Pharisee to a fanatical extreme against the Christians; and it was not till he had done this, that he was possessed by that deep longing which this system of life could not satisfy, and which led him to perceive the state into which he had fallen. The miraculous vision which was imparted to St Paul, and the startling nature of the announcement, that he who was still the raging opposer of the Crucified, was henceforth to be His messenger to the Gentiles, are of course to be considered as the decisive causes of the sudden change in his spiritual state; at the same time, we cannot doubt that his sincere striving after righteousness by the mere works of the law had already, though perhaps without his own consciousness, awakened in the depth of his soul the conviction, that his own strength could not attain to the fulfilment of righteousness; nay, that it might even lead him, when his intention was good, into the most fearful errors. This conviction brought with it that which, though not the *cause*, was a necessary *condition* of his passing into the new life;—namely, the longing after something higher, and the power of appreciating such moral phenomena, as the ministry and death of Stephen, in which that for which he longed was presented to him in actual life.

Without entering more at length, in this place, into the consideration of that event which made St Paul into that great instrument in the kingdom of God, as which we honour him, let us notice, in the next place, the position which he obtained with respect to the Twelve and the Seventy, after his conversion. His relation to the Twelve it is of particular importance to determine; for though the Seventy seem to come nearest him, in respect of their ministry, which, like his, was directed to the Gentile world,* yet these so entirely disappear as a body from the history after the resurrection of the Lord, that no trace of them remains. The separate members of it might indeed have been afterwards actively engaged in preaching the gospel, but no rivalry could have arisen between them as such and St Paul, since no one could doubt that St Paul was at least equal to them. But the case was quite different with respect to the twelve. These

* See in this Comm. the Notes to Luke x. i.

formed a strictly defined and limited body; so that, even after the Ascension, the vacancy* which was occasioned in their number by the apostacy of Judas Iscariot was immediately filled up by the express command of the Lord. (Acts i. 15, &c.) This body was, in fact, to contain within itself the pillars and supports of the Church, in proof of which we find the twelve Apostles spoken of as the spiritual Fathers of the spiritual Israel. (Matth. xix. 28; Revel. iv. 10, xxi. 14.) So that this question is immediately forced upon us:—in what relation did St Paul stand, according to the mind of the Lord, to this sacred Body of Twelve? Now, if we regard this question entirely apart from the individuals, as a matter determined by outward circumstances, it cannot be denied that the Twelve stand higher than St Paul, as those who had been with the Lord throughout this earthly pilgrimage (which St Peter considers as requisite in a true Apostle, Acts i. 21), and the special witnesses of the whole progress of the Redeemer's life on earth. They are, and must continue to be, the real foundations of the New Jerusalem (Revel. xxi. 14), so to speak, the roots of the whole tree, those who received from the Lord the first-fruits of the Spirit. St Paul might indeed justly call himself a witness of the Resurrection,† since he had beheld the crucified Jesus as the risen Lord, and had experienced in his own person His divine power; but he plainly had not the privilege of having seen the whole course of the life of Christ, and in this respect he stood, as it were, one step further from that throne of glory which was immediately surrounded by the Twelve. But if we turn our eyes from this view of the relation as it is in itself, and look at the men themselves as they appear in history, we must confess, on the other hand, that the Apostle Paul left all the Twelve far behind him, in that "he (that is, the grace of God in him) laboured more abundantly than they all." (1 Cor. xv. 10; 2 Cor. xi. 23.) And this arose by no means from his personal devotedness alone, but also in a great measure from circum-

* It would help us to understand the important position which we find James, the brother of the Lord, afterwards occupying, if we might assume that he was taken into the number of the Twelve in the place of James, who, we learn (from Acts xii. 1), was beheaded. At the same time, we have no distinct historical evidence on this point; and, besides, he does not appear to have left Jerusalem, whilst the Apostles were to travel.

† It would indeed appear probable, from 2 Cor. v. 16, that St Paul had seen our Lord before His resurrection, on the occasion of his presence at the Passover in Jerusalem; but certainly no nearer connection had subsisted between him and the Saviour.

stances. For, since the vineyard of God's kingdom was taken away from the Jews, and opened to the Gentiles, and St Paul was called to labour especially amongst the latter, as the Twelve in the first instance amongst the former, it was natural that the ministry of St Paul should bear much richer fruit, and that all the other Apostles should in comparison with him fall into the back-ground. From this we may likewise easily perceive how the relation of the gospel to the outward institutions of the Old Testament, and the admission of the Gentiles into the Church without observing these, should have become plain to the Apostle Paul, at an earlier period, and more completely than to any of the other Apostles—more especially than to St Peter, who was called to labour immediately amongst the Jews, and who was designed to represent, as it were, the element of stability in the Church. In consequence, therefore, of this state of things, the Apostle, whilst standing on a level with the Twelve, was also entirely independent of them, and occupied a position of his own, as called immediately by the Lord to be the Apostle to the Gentiles. (Acts xxvi. 17.) And this is a point on which St Paul often found it necessary to insist in his arguments with his opponents, who wished to impugn his authority as an Apostle. (See notes on Galat. ii. 9.) In doing so he laid particular stress upon the fact, that he did not in any way receive his knowledge of the gospel from the Twelve, or from any other Christian, but immediately from the Lord Himself. (See the notes on Galat. i. 12.) Now, as regards the purely spiritual part of the gospel, there is no difficulty in conceiving how St Paul could have made this his own without any instruction from man. For the Holy Ghost, who was imparted to him, filled his inner man as an all-pervading light, and made plain to him, through his belief in Jesus as the Messiah, the whole of the Old Testament, in which all the germs of the New were already laid down. In the Spirit, who is absolute truth (1 John v. 6), was given the assured conviction of the truth of the gospel, and insight into its meaning, in details. With regard, however, to the ***historical*** side of Christianity, the case appears to be different; and yet there are points connected apparently altogether with this (as, for example, the institution of the Lord's Supper, 1 Cor. xi. 23, &c.), of which the Apostle asserts that he had received them immediately from the Lord. Now, we should undoubtedly be running into an erroneous extreme, if we were to assume that *all* historical particulars in the life of our Lord were imparted to him by revelation. The general outlines of Christ's outward life, the history of His miracles, of His journeys, and what belongs to them, were no doubt related to him by Ananias or other Christians. But whatever in that life was necessarily connected with the peculiar doctrines of the gospel, as, for instance, the institution of the Sacraments, the Resurrection, and similar points, came, no doubt, to the Apostle in an extraordinary manner, by immediate revelation of the Lord;* so as to accredit him as an independent witness, not only before the world, but also to believers. No one could come forward and say, that what St Paul knew of the gospel had been received through him. For it was from no man, but from the highest Teacher Himself, that he had received as well the commission to preach, as also the essential facts of the gospel, and the Holy Spirit who gives light and life to those facts.

By this, however, it is not intended to deny that there was a development in the new life of St Paul; though assuredly (as will be shown more at length in the following paragraphs), no further change of doctrinal views could have taken place in him. But he himself doubtless advanced gradually from childhood to youth, and then to manhood in Christ. And so, when the Apostle came forward as a teacher at Damascus immediately after his conversion (Acts ix. 19), it was but the expression of the true feeling of the necessity which lay upon him at once to bear open witness to the change which, through God's grace, had taken place in him. But he himself, no doubt, soon began to perceive that, before he could labour with a blessing, it was very necessary that his inner life should be much deepened, and more thoroughly worked out. In consequence of his perception of this truth, he retired into Arabia for three years—a time which, it is probable, he spent chiefly in a thorough study of the Scriptures.† In the midst of these studies, probably, the enlightening of the Holy Ghost first revealed to him, as a connected whole, the great purpose of the

* According to the account given in the Acts, St Paul was more than once graciously honoured with a vision of the Lord. (See Acts xxii. 17, xxiii. 11.)

† See, on this point, the remarks on Acts ix. 20, etc. St Paul himself enjoins Timothy (1 Tim. iii. 6,) that no new convert shall be a bishop. Is it, then, likely that he would have acted in opposition to his own rule? or would his wonderful conversion have exempted him from a rule to which even the Twelve were subject?

Lord with respect to the human race; and now inwardly ripened, and firmly established in true principles of doctrine and life, he went forth into the great field of labour which the Lord had appointed him. As the waters of a stream are spread abroad, so did he spread abroad, beyond the narrow depths in which they had hitherto been gathered together, the quickening powers contained in the new doctrine; and the whole heathen world, which, left to itself, had come nigh to entire corruption, was made fruitful as by the fresh springs of an heavenly life. Now, as an energetic character, as one whose whole work lay out of himself, the Apostle was in danger of forgetting himself in his care for others; or, at least, of letting his incessant labours drain and exhaust his inward life. In order to prevent this, we perceive, on the one hand, the grace of God effectually renewing him with the powers of the higher world (2 Cor. xii.), since the mighty labours in which he was engaged had not been undertaken by him on his own impulse, but had been expressly assigned to him by the Lord. And, on the other hand, God so ordered his circumstances as to afford seasons of rest to his spirit; to which belong, for instance, the imprisonments which he had to undergo. In such times of lonely stillness his spiritual life was more fully developed within itself, so that the preacher of the world might not preach to others and be himself a castaway.

The last step in the Apostle Paul's progress towards perfection must finally have been taken on the occasion of his martyrdom. That which St John experienced inwardly in the spirit, St Peter and St Paul were to experience also in the body.* It was in the centre of the heathen world, in Rome, during the first great persecution which befel the Church of God, that St Paul died, beheaded, as a Roman citizen, with the sword. The fact itself of his death is established by so many and ancient witnesses, (amongst whom the presbyter Gaius, and the bishop Dionysius of Corinth, are the oldest. See Euseb. H. E. ii. 25.), that it cannot be questioned. There remains, however, an uncertainty as to the year of his death, because in this is involved the doubtful question concerning St Paul's second imprisonment at Rome.† This question must not

* See more on this subject in the notes on John xxi. 20, etc.

† Compare on this point, in Hemsen's Life of St Paul, the concluding considerations on his death.

occupy us till later; and I only here remark, in passing, that I think it necessary to assume a second imprisonment of St Paul in Rome, and cannot therefore place his death earlier than the last year of the reign of Nero (A.D. 67 or 68.)

§ 2. THE PECULIARITIES OF ST PAUL'S CHARACTER.*

That St Paul was one of those energetic characters of whom, in different ages of the Church, the Lord has taken so many in some marked manner to Himself, is so evident that no one can well fail to perceive it. Whatever a man may think of the truths taught by the Apostle, even the sceptic must confess that a powerful and earnest spirit† breathes through his writings, full of the glow of enthusiasm for that which he held as true, and of burning zeal to communicate what he knew to all. But it is of the greatest consequence to obtain a more accurate knowledge of the peculiarities of St Paul's mind; because the nature of his writings and doctrine will be much more easily comprehended if we keep before our minds a clear image of their author.

Now the simplest way of obtaining an insight into the peculiarities of St Paul's character is by comparing him with St John, the Evangelist. Contemplation (*Γνῶσις*), in the highest sense of that word, we found to be the peculiar feature of St John's life.‡ The whole bent of his mind was inward and meditative. His soul was entirely receptive, wholly occupied with gazing upon the eternal ideas of truth. Thus outward labours were not so prominent in his case, and the flower of his life was prophecy. The image presented to us by St Paul is very different from this. He was not, of course, without that living knowledge of the truth

* On the subject of the following paragraphs, compare the essay of Neander on the Apostle St Paul, in his History of the Apostolic Age (Geschichte des Apostolischen Zeitalters, vol. ii. pp. 501, sqq.)

† We are easily tempted to picture to ourselves St Paul's personal appearance, as very powerful, or even colossal; but, according to 2 Cor. x. 10, just the contrary was the case: In the dialogue Philopatris (which, however, to be sure, was not written earlier than the fourth century), St Paul is called, "The Galilean with the bald head, and the hooked nose." (See Tholuck's Remarks, noticed at the beginning of this Introduction, in which he describes the temperament of the Apostle as the cholerico-melancholic.)

‡ See the Introduction to the Gospel of St John.

which comes by contemplation; but in his way of treating religion he gives a prominence, as St John never does, to the exercise of the intellect, and exhibits the characteristic acuteness of his understanding in working out the ideas received by the spiritual sense into distinct conceptions. It was through this talent for reasoning that St Paul became the author of a precisely defined doctrinal language, and the founder of Theology, as a science, in the Church of Christ. In him is represented the necessity of science for the Church, even in the very narrow circle of those on whom the Holy Spirit was first poured forth.* And the same character of mind, which made him express his religious ideas in a scientific form, made him also, in the fruitful labours of his outward life, develop especially the gift of wisdom (1 Cor. xii. 8). In addition to the energy which belonged to him as a man of action, we may discern in his activity the peculiar faculty of using the most difficult and complicated worldly relations for the purest and noblest purposes of the kingdom of God, so that we must distinctly recognise in this a distinguishing feature of his character. This is very clear, if we compare him with St Peter; for in the latter there was no less energy, but it seems in him to be fettered with a stiffness which hindered its adapting itself to circumstances; and though this was quite in keeping with his character, which was firm as a rock, yet we cannot mistake the contrast it affords to St Paul's.

This bent of St Paul's mind influenced, as we might have expected, his whole apprehension of the gospel. While St John received it more, as it is in itself, as an object of contemplation, and so made what is revealed to us of God and Christ the centre of his doctrine; St Paul, on the other hand, looked at the gospel more directly in its bearing upon himself, and so made what is told us of man's nature, and of the method of his salvation, the prominent

* It is in this dialectic character of St Paul's discourse that we may find the reason that Longinus places the Apostle on a level with the famous Greek orators, if, at least, the famous passage of that rhetorician, in which he makes mention of the Apostle, is really genuine. Besides vigorous powers of reasoning, the might of deep conviction, and the glow of enthusiasm, manifest themselves in St Paul's writings, so that Jerome (in his work against Jovinian) declares "quotiescunque Paulum apostolum lego, non verba audire mihi videor, sed tonitrua." (See Flacii clav. S. S. Basil, 1567, p. 387, sqq., and the works of Bauer, Philologia Thucydideo-Paulina (Halæ 1773), Logica Paulina (ib. 1774), Rhetorica Paulina (ib. 1782). Also Tzschirner's treatise in his opusc. acad., edited by Winzer. Leips. 1829. Lastly, Tholuck's Remarks, pp. 387, sqq., as noticed at p. 1 of this Introduction.

points of his theology. In the experience of his own life he had seen the sinful state of the human heart, as well as man's inability to deliver himself from it, and the consequent need of a remedy which should come from God, such as was realized in Christ; and from this living source his whole system of doctrine springs forth and spreads itself. The *Western* character of St Paul's mind is seen in this conception of the gospel as clearly as in the bent of those two great kindred spirits to his, St Augustin and Luther, in whom indeed his own course of education was repeated. In St John, on the other hand, is shown the *Eastern* spirit, which loses sight of itself in the contemplation of that which is presented to it of God, and which, through all the developments of doctrine in later ages, ever dwelt by preference on what is revealed to us of God and Christ. So that though there is no specific difference, no actual contradiction between the teaching of St Paul and St John, yet these two Apostles do already exhibit in themselves the two chief tendencies of the later development of doctrine. As the grain of corn, though one, opens itself into two halves on the unfolding of the germ, or as the magnet, from one middle point, discharges, at the same time, a positive and a negative power; so the two chief tendencies of the Church, the Eastern and the Western, which mutually complete each other, are represented in the earliest ages by the two great Apostles, St John and St Paul.

From the vigorous and decided manner in which the Apostle both taught and acted, we might at once conclude that it was not likely that any considerable change would take place in his convictions, after that first great spiritual conversion, by which the fierce opponent of Jesus Christ became his fearless witness. After his admission into the Church of Christ, he no doubt early formed for himself a consistent view of Christian truth, and therefore expresses himself, even in his latest epistles, in the same way as in his earliest; from the Epistles to the Thessalonians down to those to Timothy and Titus, we find the same fundamental truths ever recurring. In one single point only can we discern in his later writings a different form of doctrinal statement from that contained in his earlier epistles; that is, in his views concerning the second coming of Christ. In his earliest epistles St Paul expresses a hope that he may himself live until the time of the Lord's return (see 1 Thess. iv.; 2 Cor. v.), but in the latter he has renounced this hope, and longs to depart and to be with Christ (Phil. i. 23). The modification of his views in this point may, however, be easily explained, if we consider the peculiar nature of the subject. The time of Christ's second coming was, according to our Lord's own teaching, to remain uncertain (see Matth. xxiv. 1, and the remarks on the passage); St Paul himself, therefore, neither knew nor could know this time (Acts i. 7). Whilst, therefore, the fervour of his love made him at first regard all things as near, and long after the kingdom of God upon earth as the highest good; at a later period the great crisis of the Advent retreated, in his apprehension, to a greater distance. We cannot therefore say that St Paul's convictions on this point of doctrine underwent any change; but only that his own individual position with respect to the object presented in this doctrine was altered. If, however, the above observations show that the *substance* of St Paul's doctrine remained unchanged, yet we may certainly observe a constant progress in the merely *formal* development of it; for we cannot fail to perceive, that his theological language is more full, and his conceptions more complete and symmetrical, in the later epistles, especially those to the Philippians and Colossians, than in the earlier.

St Paul not only kept aloof from the *gnostical* tendency (the relative truth of which is represented by St John), and vigorously combated the errors into which, as is plain from the Epistles to the Colossians, to Timothy, and Titus, it soon led some of its followers; but also from that *judaico-materialist* tendency, which showed itself in so many of those who had left the sect of the Pharisees to join the Christian Church. As a tree torn from its original soil, and transplanted with all its roots and fibres into other ground, such had been the change effected in St Paul at his conversion; and he therefore transferred nothing of the one-sidedness and narrowness of the system of the Pharisees into his views of Christian doctrine. The attempts which have been made to explain many leading features of his system from his Jewish views of life,* show just as little knowledge of the human

* We need hardly remark that we do not therefore mean to deny that the history of Jewish doctrine furnishes us with a key to the further understanding of many particular statements in St Paul's writings; we only wish to maintain, that the essential points of his system are the results of his own inward experience; the views which he entertained at an earlier period of his life at most only affected the form in which he presented the truth.

heart, as those which seek to account for Augustin's doctrine by his former Manichæan errors, and for Luther's by his education as a monk. We find, on the contrary, that men of energetic character are generally inclined after such transitions to despise too much the systems from which they have escaped, and to reject even what is true in them, rather than to transfer any thing belonging to them into their new line of thought and life. But from this error, into which Marcion and his disciples fell, St Paul was preserved by that fundamental Christian view, of which the Holy Spirit had led him to see the importance, and which regards the Old Testament as divine in its nature, and containing, under a typical and prophetical veil, all the essential truths of Christianity in the germ. He perceived that the error lay entirely in the rigid spirit of the Pharisees, who wished to have the husk of the letter regarded as the substance of the spirit itself. St Paul therefore represented that true and just mean, which lies between the false spiritualism of the Gnostics on the one hand, and the materialism of the Jews on the other, whilst he held the true Scriptural doctrine of the reality and importance of both spirit and matter, in their proper relations to each other; and this in such a manner as fully to maintain his balance, without leaning to either error. In the theology of St John likewise, the same correct views of the relation of matter and spirit cannot be mistaken, although in his gospel and epistles we find an inclination towards genuine spiritualism, of course without making any concession to Gnostic errors: it was only in the Apocalypse that St John found the opportunity of bringing forward in greater prominence that side of the gospel which presents to us the material and spiritual in their connection; and therefore any future author who wishes to give a just view of St John's doctrine, must consider the ideas of the Apocalypse as complementary of those of his remaining works.

This well-balanced character of St Paul's whole disposition, as well as of his theology, is also the reason why the feeling of the Church, guided in this matter also into the truth by the Spirit of Christ working in her, has regarded the collection of his epistles, in which every thought is expressive of that correct mean which he preserved in his doctrine, as the crown of the canon of the New Testament. Whilst every separate gospel found its necessary complement in the other gospels, and altogether form the roots of the

New Testament, whilst the Acts of the Apostles only constitutes, so to speak, the stem, which unites the roots with the crown of the tree,—St Paul, without laying claim to any authority in point of doctrine independent of the rest, stands before us in all the riches of his personal endowments, spreading around on all sides the fruitfulness of his inward life. He was the first, in whom was reflected on all sides, as far as was possible in *one* man, not of course the person of the Lord himself, but that Spirit which he had bestowed upon the Church; and this universality of character and gifts of grace made him capable, through the powers of the same Spirit, of so unfolding the peculiar nature of the principles of Christianity both in his doctrine and in his life, as to represent it to the Gentile world almost in his sole person. Whatsoever, therefore, appeared in the gospels as a bud but partially disclosed, and indeed in the synoptical evangelists manifestly engrafted upon Old Testament principles,—that the Apostle displays before our minds openly and freely, and in some parts of his writings, for instance, in the Epistles to the Romans and Galatians, in so strictly didactic a form, that it commends itself as much *by the cogency of the arguments to the thoughtful, as to the feeling mind* by that glow of enthusiasm which breathes throughout his statements. If, however, we compare the collection of the Catholic epistles (with which we must also class the Epistle to the Hebrews, as proceeding from the same starting point), with the Epistles of St Paul, we shall perceive that the latter are more calculated for the beginning of the spiritual life, whilst the concluding writings of the New Testament tend more directly to the perfection of the fruits of regeneration in holiness and sanctification. Accordingly, if in the epistles of St Paul the central ideas, around which he considers everything to move, are *faith* in opposition to the works of the law, *justification* and *atonement*, and we cannot fail to perceive the earnestness with which he labours to impress these deeply on the minds of his hearers and readers; the Epistle to the Hebrews and the Catholic epistles, on the other hand, setting out with these doctrines as their admitted foundation, teach from them how the man is to perfect holiness in the fear of God The latter epistles, therefore, seem to bear more of a legal character, and on that account found much less access to the mind of the Church than those of St Paul. They demand, however, also for their right comprehension a higher degree of development of the regenerate soul; and because this was often deficient, a correct perception of the difficulties of those writings deterred many expositors from attempting to explain them. The different collections therefore which compose the New Testament canon, each proceed from a different point of view, and on this very account mutually complete each other, furnishing satisfaction for every stage of advancement, and excitement to press forward to higher perfection. (See Comm. P. I. Introd. § 2)

§ 3. ORDER OF SUCCESSION OF ST PAUL'S EPISTLES.

From the thoroughly practical character of St Paul's life, we might at once expect that his productions as an author would have nothing of an abstract form about them. And in fact we neither possess any treatises by him on religious subjects, nor have we any reason to suppose that he ever wrote any. His letters are all suggested by existing circumstances, and are therefore adapted to the most particular occasions of actual life. On this account, everything in them is individual, marked, traced with strong and definite outlines, and yet, by means of that spiritual principle which animated the Apostle, truths of the most universal bearing are reflected in those special cases, and give to all his remarks and counsel a meaning and importance for every age. In what manner those epistles of the Apostle which have come down to us were formed into one collection, it is now impossible to make out on satisfactory historical grounds. We find, however, in the hands of Marcion the Gnostic, a collection of ten epistles of St Paul, the three pastoral epistles to Timothy and Titus being wanting, whilst in the Catholic Church the collection consisted of thirteen epistles (that to the Hebrews not being included): this might then be regarded as the original nucleus of the collection of epistles, to which the pastoral epistles were added at a later period. And yet if we consider the matter more closely, this does not appear probable, and we may therefore suppose that the pastoral epistles were only accidentally omitted from the canon of Marcion. For we find that the order of succession of the epistles, according to Marcion's arrangement, was an entirely different one from that of the collection sanctioned by the Catholic Church; but if the latter had only inserted the pastoral epistles into Marcion's collection, the order would have remained unaltered. The cause of the discrepancy of the order was, moreover, occasioned by the adoption of an entirely distinct principle of arrangement; the Marcionites arranging the epistles, as we shall soon prove, according to their chronological succession; the Catholics, in the first place, according to the importance of the churches to which the writings were addressed, and then according to the dignity of the private persons who had received them. This appears most plainly in the case of the Epistle to Philemon; this letter would seem, at first sight, to belong to the Epistle to the Colossians, where Marcion has also placed it, but in the collection of the Catholic canon, it followed last of all, as being the shortest epistle directed to a private person. The Marcionite collection was most probably first formed in Asia Minor. In its composition, the framers of it either proceeded on the principle of omitting letters to private persons, and only admitting epistles to whole communities (the letter to Philemon finding a place in the collection merely as an appendage to the epistle to the Colossians), or they were unacquainted with the pastoral epistles. On the other hand, the Catholic collection of St Paul's epistles probably had its rise in Rome; and the authors of it followed the order of importance of the communities to which the epistles were addressed, and also admitted such private letters as seemed to be of value for the Church at large. The tendency of the Roman community to pay considerable attention to matters relating to the outward constitution of the Church answers remarkably well to this supposition with respect to the pastoral letters, and therefore also increases the probability that the Catholic canon of St Paul's epistles was formed at this place.

In our investigation of the order of succession of St Paul's epistles, we shall, however, not only exclude the Epistle to the Hebrews (which does not proceed from the Apostle himself, although it was composed under his sanction*), but also the epistles to Timothy and Titus; for in these such complicated relations require

* See the two critical treatises on the subject of the Epistle to the Hebrews in Olshausen's Opuscula Theologica.—[The author's theory is, that it was written by the clergy of some church in which St Paul was sojourning, and that the Apostle approved it when finished. Thus he thinks to account at once for the connection of St Paul's name with the epistle, and for the difference from the style of his undoubted compositions. (Opuscula Berol., 1834, pp. 91–122.) The reader may be referred to Dr Mill's remarks, Prælectio Theologica, Cantabr., 1843, pp. 6–7, and note p. 32. B.]

to be discussed, that they require a distinct consideration. We have therefore, in the first place, only to do with the order of succession of those ten epistles of St Paul, which even Marcion included in his collection. With respect to the years in which these are supposed to have been composed, a great discrepancy doubtless exists in the dates assigned by the learned, because the chronology of the history of the apostles in general, and of St Paul's life in particular, is so very uncertain. But our present subject is properly only the order in which the epistles follow upon one another; and in the determination of this point, the views taken are by no means so widely different, as in deciding the years under which every single epistle ought to be arranged, because this last question must always depend upon the chronological system adopted by the particular investigation, a circumstance, however, which affords much assistance in judging of the accuracy of any theory as to the order of succession of the epistles in general. In order to facilitate our survey of the different views which have been taken on this subject, we give, in the following tabular form, the opinions of three scholars belonging respectively to the earliest, modern, and most recent times.

*Marcion.**	*Eichhorn.*	*Schrader.*
Galatians	I. Thessalonians	I. Corinthians
I. Corinthians	II. Thessalonians	II. Corinthians
II. Corinthians	Galatians	Romans
Romans	I. Corinthians	I. Thessalonians
I. Thessalonians	II. Corinthians	II. Thessalonians
II. Thessalonians	Romans	Ephesians
Ephesians	Ephesians	Colossians
Colossians	Colossians	Philemon
Philemon	Philemon	Philippians
Philippians	Philippians	Galatians

In the first place, from this table we cannot but perceive that, as we have already mentioned above, Marcion could not have placed the epistles in this order *accidentally;* it corresponds too exactly with the results of the most industrious critical researches, not to have proceeded from the *design* of arranging the epistles according to the date of their composition. The conclusions of the most recent examiner, Schrader, coincide exactly with Marcion's

* See Epiphanius. *hær.* xlii., c. 9.

scheme, except with respect to the epistle to the Galatians. Certainly, with respect to this composition, the discrepancy is so much the greater; for whilst Marcion assigns to it the first place, Schrader places it last. Eichhorn, in this case, agrees rather with Marcion than with Schrader, in that he places the epistle to the Galatians, in point of time, before those to the Corinthians and Romans; at the same time, he differs from both in respect to the epistles to the Thessalonians, for whilst they put these letters immediately after the epistle to the Romans, Eichhorn considers them to have been written first of all. Since more exact information, with regard to the dates of the composition of the separate epistles, may best be prefixed to the special introductions devoted to each, we will only briefly consider in this place the epistles of which the date is questionable, those to the Thessalonians and Galatians, in respect of the time of their composition, in order to advance a *preliminary* justification of our adoption of the order assigned by Eichhorn, in favour of which Hemsen and the majority of modern scholars have also decided.

The peculiarity of Schrader's arrangement of the epistles of St Paul is founded on a theory propounded by this scholar, according to which the Apostle made a journey to Jerusalem after leaving Ephesus, (where, according to Acts xix., he passed more than two years). He thinks that this journey took place in the interval between the events recorded in the 20th and 21st verses of this chapter. In consequence of this journey, in which he supposes St Paul to have visited Thessalonica, Schrader places the composition of the epistles to the Thessalonians at a period subsequent to that of those to the Romans and Corinthians. Schott has, however, already proved at length,* that nothing can be found in the epistles to the Thessalonians which speaks of their having been written at this later time, but rather that every thing indicates that they were written in Corinth immediately after the first visit of St Paul to Thessalonica (Acts xvii.), on the occasion of the first planting of that church. The epistles to the Thessalonians must, therefore, necessarily be reckoned amongst the earliest, and it is a decided mistake to place them after the epistle to the Romans, if

* See Schott's Programm, "Isagoge historico-critica in utramque Pauli ad Thessalonicenses epistolam." Jenæ, 1830. And the same author's "Erörterung einiger wichtigen chronolog. Punkte im Leben Pauli," (Jena, 1832), p. 48, etc.

only for this reason, that Paul did not write the latter until he was at Corinth on his third missionary journey. But Schrader's hypothesis, with respect to the epistles to the Galatians, is even more capricious. His assumed journey from Ephesus to Jerusalem is in fact supposed to be that mentioned, Galat. ii. 1, from which it would no doubt follow that the composition of the letter belongs to a much later period, since the Apostle, in the course of that chapter, mentions many other occurrences in his life. But the very circumstance that Barnabas accompanied the Apostle to Jerusalem, in the journey alluded to, Galat. ii. 1, whilst it is certain from the account in Acts xv. 36, etc., that they had parted from one another long before St Paul went to Ephesus, is a convincing argument against this wholly unfounded theory; and Schrader's assertion that the difference between St Paul and Barnabas had previously been made up is likewise founded upon mere hypothesis. For though I am very far from accounting for this separation, as Scholt appears to do (Erörterung, p. 64, etc.) by supposing a discrepancy in their views, and am much rather inclined to assume merely outward reasons as the cause of its continuance, yet the circumstance, that after Acts xv. 36, etc., Barnabas is no more mentioned in connection with St Paul, is decisive against Schrader's assumption.* But the arguments, which Schrader thinks he can adduce from the contents of the Epistle to the Galatians in favour of his hypothesis, are so completely overthrown by Scholt in detail (p. 65, etc.) that it is enough in this place to refer to the latter writer's treatise. Schrader thinks especially that he discovers in the passage, Galat. vi. 17, a declaration of the Apostle, that he is looking forward to the sentence of death, and, therefore, concludes that the composition of this letter must be referred to quite the end of St Paul's life. But how entirely unfounded is such an explanation of the text will appear hereafter from our commentary upon it. Köhler † also has made a similar attempt to refer the composition of the Epistle to the Galatians to a later period; but he does not understand the jour-

* The passage 1 Cor. ix. 6, is the only one which appears to support a later coming together of Barnabas and St Paul; if we are not willing to admit that Barnabas was separated from St Paul in Corinth. He must, however, at all events have visited this city, according to the passage above quoted, after the foundation of the Christian community there.

† "Uber die Abfassungszeit der epistolischen Schriften des N. T." Leipz. 1830.

ney to Jerusalem mentioned in Galat. ii. 1, like Schrader, of a separate journey made from Ephesus, but thinks that he discovers in it the journey recorded in Acts xviii. 22. No doubt, as I have already endeavoured to represent as probable in my commentary on the passage, St Paul did visit Jerusalem about that time, (which Scholt is mistaken in denying, p. 37); but for the assumption that this journey is meant in Galat. ii. 1, there is not a shadow of proof; it is much more certain that it was that made from Antioch to the council of the Apostles, Acts xv. Much less however can we assent to Köhler's view, that St Paul first preached the gospel in Galatia on his journey through that province mentioned in Acts xviii. 23, since the words added in that passage, ἐπιστηρίζων τοὺς μαθητάς, plainly express that the Apostle wished to confirm in the faith the churches which he had already founded in Galatia. (See Acts xvi. 6.) Since, moreover, this scholar can only give even a shadow of probability to his postponement of the composition of the epistle to the Galatians to the latest period of St Paul's life, by means of a conjecture and hypothesis heaped upon his first assumption, we cannot feel ourselves called upon by his arguments to depart from that order of succession of the epistles of St Paul, which is now almost universally received. This is connected in the following manner with the principal events of St Paul's life, according to the chronology which we have adopted from Hug; in this account, we must however, as we have already remarked, leave the pastoral epistles again untouched, because they present peculiar difficulties as regards their insertion into the history of St Paul's life, and on that account demand a separate consideration.

After St Paul's conversion on the road to Damascus, (about the year 36 after the birth of Christ), he went to Arabia, where he remained three years. (Galat. i. 17). After this he returned to Damascus, but in this city he was persecuted by the Jews, and only escaped to Jerusalem with extreme difficulty (2 Cor. xi, 32. Acts ix. 24, 25). On this visit of St Paul to Jerusalem, Barnabas introduced the Apostle to St Peter and St James (Galat. i. 18, 19); he however only remained there fourteen days. On leaving Jerusalem, the Apostle repaired first to his native city Tarsus (Acts ix. 25, etc.), from whence Barnabas, who it appears was the first to discover his wonderful gift of teaching, fetched him away to Antioch, at which place, in the meantime, Christianity had also begun to spread amongst the heathen. (Acts xi. 19). This happened about A.D. 42. St Paul and Barnabas had been teaching together about a year in Antioch when the great famine made its appearance in Palestine, in consequence of which they were both sent to Jerusalem (St Paul for the second time) as the bearers of a contribution to the necessities of the poor brethren at that place. Acts xi. 30. Perhaps, however, Paul himself did not go to Jerusalem, for it is not stated in the Acts that he did, and that difficult passage Galat. ii. 1, would render the supposition probable. After the accomplishment of this business, the people of Antioch expressed a wish that the Gospel might be preached to the Gentiles in other countries also. The elders of the church thereupon chose St Paul and Barnabas as their messengers to the heathen, and they accordingly entered upon their *first missionary journey* (about A.D. 45). Their journey went first by Cyprus, through Pamphylia and Pisidia, and they then returned to Antioch by sea (Acts xiii. 5; xiv. 26). The time of their return it is just as impossible to determine with any certainty, as the length of their subsequent stay at Antioch (Acts xiv. 28). At the same time there can be no doubt that the *third* journey of St Paul to Jerusalem, occasioned by the disputes concerning the reception of Gentile converts into the Church, formed the conclusion of this residence (Galat. ii. 1). The apostles and the presbyters of the Church at Jerusalem examined into this question together, and, after hearing the reports of St Paul and Barnabas, decided in favour of the milder course, according to which the heathen were not obliged to submit to circumcision and observe the whole law. This important transaction, the so-called apostolic council (Acts xv.), happened A.D. 52 or 53. Immediately after the return of St Paul from Jerusalem to Antioch, about A.D. 53, he entered upon his *second missionary journey*, which he undertook in company with Silas. On this journey he first of all visited again the churches he had already planted, and then proceeded to Galatia, and by Troas to Macedonia (Acts xvi. 9). Philippi was the first city of this country in which St Paul taught, but this place he was soon obliged to leave in consequence of a tumult stirred up against him by the employers of a female ventriloquist, and to betake himself to Thessalonica (Acts xvi. 12, etc.). The Apostle was only able to preach here a few weeks, yet even in this short time a Christian community was formed there. But a tumult occasioned by the Jews compelled St Paul soon to fly from Thessalonica, and to go to Athens by Berea, to which latter place his enemies continued to follow him (Acts xvii. 1). His companions, Silas and Timothy, he had left behind him at Berea, but soon called upon them to follow him to Athens, probably that he might obtain intelligence of the churches in Macedonia (Acts xvii. 15). However, he immediately despatched Timothy to Thessalonica, in order that he might establish in the faith that young and hardly pressed community (1 Thess. iii. 1). In the meantime the Apostle, after the dismissal of Timothy, left Athens, where he does not appear to have laboured long, and repaired to Corinth (Acts xviii. 1). Here he met with the famous Jewish family of Aquila and Priscilla, which had been expelled from Rome by Claudius; and as Aquila practised the same handicraft which St Paul had learnt, the latter undertook to work with him, and since his preaching produced great effect, remained there a year and a half. By means of the fact here mentioned, the expulsion of the Jews from Rome by Claudius, we also obtain pretty exact information with respect to the date of St Paul's residence at Corinth; it must have been in the year of our Lord 54 and 55. During this his stay at Corinth, it would appear that the Apostle commenced his labours as a writer, at least nothing remains to us of any letters which he may previously have indited. In fact, when Timothy had returned from his mission to Thessalonica, St Paul wrote his *First Epistle to the Thessalonians*, and soon afterwards *the Second*, likewise from Corinth. All his apostolical epistles belong, therefore, to the later and more mature period of his life, a circumstance which is certainly not to be regarded as accidental.

After the lapse af a year and a half St Paul left Corinth in the company of Aquila and Priscilla, in order to go up to Jerusalem to keep a vow (Acts xviii. 18). In his voyage he touched at Ephesus, without, however, being able to make any long stay there, as he wished to be at Jerusalem for the feast of Pentecost. At the same time he promised to return thither as soon as possible; and, in accordance with this promise, immediately after a brief sojourn in Jerusalem (his *fourth* visit to that city, see Commentary on Acts xviii. 22) and in Antioch, he set off again to proceed to Ephesus; this forms the commencement of his *third missionary journey* (about A.D. 57). The Apostle continued in this important city two years and three months, and wrote from hence in the first place to the Galatians (perhaps as early as A.D. 57, certainly not later than the beginning of 58) ; he had visited them on his journey to Ephesus, and had perhaps, even on this occasion, remarked sundry errors, or at all events had soon after heard of such. Next the Apostle began his correspondence with the Corinthian Church, writing likewise from Ephesus, in consequence of the unfavourable accounts which he had received of them also. The First Epistle of St Paul to the Corinthians is lost (1 Cor. v. 9), but after it was sent, new reports arrived from Corinth, which caused the Apostle to send thither Timothy and Erastus (1 Cor. iv. 17, etc., Acts xix. 22), and immediately afterwards he composed that *first epistle to the Corinthians* which is yet extant. The writing of this letter may be referred to A.D. 59, or the commencement of 60. Scarcely, however, had St Paul finished this letter, when the goldsmith Demetrius stirred up a tumult against him in Ephesus, in consequence of which he was obliged to fly. The Apostle proceeded by Troas to Macedonia, full of desire to receive more exact information concerning the state of things in Corinth. When he had received this from Timothy and Titus, who came directly from Corinth, he wrote, about A.D. 60, the *second epistle to the Corinthians.* Titus conveyed this letter to Corinth ; and the Apostle himself journeyed after him slowly, through Achaia, to the same city. During this his second stay in Corinth, St Paul found occasion to write to the Romans, which he must have done as early as in the year 60, shortly before his departure from Corinth, since, in Romans xv. 25, 26, he makes mention of the charitable collections made for the Christians in Jerusalem, as well as of the journey he had in prospect. This journey to Jerusalem, his *fifth,* the Apostle accomplished by sailing from Philippi in Macedonia to the coasts of Asia Minor, then proceeding to Syria, and from thence visiting Jerusalem (Acts xx. 3, etc.) As early as the tenth day after his arrival there, he was taken into custody, on the occasion of an uproar of the people, and remained (from A.D. 60 to 62) two years in prison at Cæsarea. When, however, Portius Festus was made Proconsul of Syria in the room of Felix, he sent the Apostle to Rome, on his appealing to Cæsar. On his voyage to Rome, St Paul was shipwrecked upon the island of Malta, and did not reach Rome, in consequence, until the beginning of the year 63 (Acts xxv–xxvii.) Here he remained two years (from 63 to 65) in a mild imprisonment (Acts xxviii. 30), and composed in this period the epistles to the Ephesians, Colossians, Philemon, and the Philippians.*

The question concerning the date of the composition of the three pastoral epistles, as well as the investigation concerning the Apostle's second imprisonment and the time of his death at Rome,† which is so closely connected with it, we leave here, as already remarked, untouched ; inasmuch as the special introduction to these epistles, which form, as it were, a little whole of themselves, will furnish us with a more suitable opportunity for the discussion of these points. We reserve also the more detailed exposition of our reasons for the place which we have assigned to each of the epistles for the special introductory observations on those epistles ; and, finally, we explain them in the order followed by the ordinary editions, since the plan of beginning with the epistle to the Romans affords many advantages towards the dogmatical exposition of the rest, and if any one should prefer to study St Paul's epistles in their chronological order, nothing would interfere with his thus submitting them to his more accurate consideration, because every composition, with its commentary, forms a little whole. If any important changes could be pointed out in the course of St Paul's spiritual advancement, it would certainly be the preferable plan to expound his epistles in their chronological order ; but as this, as we have already seen, is not the case, it appears to us much better to follow the ordinary arrangement. In observing this order, we have, first of all, the opportunity, in the epistle to the Romans, of considering in their connection the central ideas of St Paul's doctrinal system, presented, so to speak, in a dogmatical compendium. A number of passages in St Paul's other epistles thus receive their explanation by anticipation, whilst it would be difficult to explain

* The view which has quite recently been put forward by several scholars, and especially by Böttger (Beiträge, ii.), that those epistles which have hitherto been attributed to the period of St Paul's first captivity at Rome might have been written during his captivity at Cæsarea, we shall consider more at length in our introductions to these epistles, adducing the reasons by which it is supported, and our own objections to it.

† Amongst the most recent investigators, Bleek declares himself decidedly for the assumption of a second imprisonment, in his review of Mayerhoff's work, in the Studien, 1836. H. iv. p. 1028.

them at all if the epistle to the Romans had not previously been interpreted. On the other hand, in the epistles to the Corinthians St Paul's principles of practice are developed, and the external relations of the apostolical church are discussed with so much accuracy that, by their help, much light is thrown upon many passages in the smaller epistles, Such being the peculiar nature of the larger epistles of St Paul, we are persuaded that every connected exposition of the apostolical writings will best begin with them, because only on this plan can the riches of St Paul's ideas be properly unfolded in all their different relations, and without repetition.

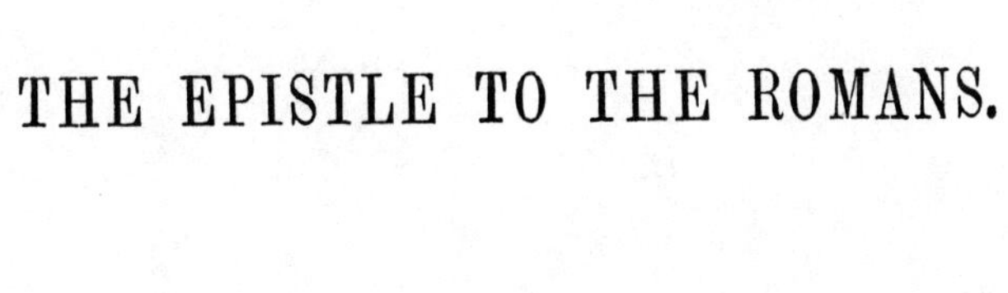

THE EPISTLE TO THE ROMANS.

INTRODUCTION.*

§ 1. OF THE GENUINENESS AND THE INTEGRITY OF THE EPISTLE.

THE authority of St Paul's Epistle to the Christians of Rome is warranted by such a completeness of evidence, both internal and external, that no one could think of denying, on any system of impartial criticism, its claim to be the composition of the Apostle. Nor, indeed, did any one in all antiquity dispute the genuineness of the Epistle ; for, while it is true that the Judaists and all Judaising sects make no use of St Paul's Epistle to the Romans (as is also the case with his other epistles), the reason is not that they consider it spurious, but, on the contrary, that they see in it a genuine production of *that* apostle whom they regard as the greatest enemy of Judaism, and an apostate from the truth. Even the searching criticism of later German theology has left this epistle altogether unassailed ; an Englishman of the name of Evanson alone has, in his work against the Gospels, cursorily expressed his doubts as to the genuineness of the Epistle to the Romans also. His grounds, however, are of such a kind that no better testimony *in favour of* the genuineness need be desired than the fact that arguments of this quality are the only ones which can be brought *against* it. The silence of the Acts of the Apostles as to this Epistle, the existence of a great Christian community at Rome before an apostle had been there, and the numerous greetings to the Church of Rome at a time when St Paul had not yet visited it,—such are the chief

* For the Introduction to the Epistle to the Romans, compare, among earlier writers, J. L. Rambach's Introductio Hist. Theologica in Ep. Pauli ad Romanos. Halæ, 1730. In the most recent times, it has been most fully and learnedly treated by Reiche, in his Commentary, pp. 1–106.

points which appear to Evanson to render the genuineness of the Epistle questionable. (Compare Reiche's Comm. p. 20, seqq.)

The case is different as to the integrity of the Epistle; while its genuineness has been generally acknowledged, this has been very often called in question, and especially in modern times. All the more ancient witnesses, however—fathers of the church, versions, and MSS.—regard the Epistle as a connected whole; for Marcion's copies cannot be made to tell on the other side, inasmuch as he treated the Epistles no less capriciously than the Gospels; and Tertullian's quotation of the passage xiv. 10, as contained in the "clausula epistolæ" (Adv. Marcion v. 14) cannot possibly be used as evidence that he was not acquainted with the 15th and 16th chapters, since the expression *clausula* is so general that it need not be strictly limited to the last two chapters. The scholars of later times, consequently, found themselves altogether restricted to the department of what is styled the higher criticism—a department in which it is not often that any very trustworthy results are to be obtained.

Heumann* led the way, by asserting that the Epistle to the Romans properly ends with the xith chapter, and that c. xii. is the beginning of a new letter, which extends to c. xv. This letter he supposes to have been likewise addressed to the Romans, but not to have been composed by St Paul until after the completion of the first and longer epistle, on occasion of reports which had in the meantime reached him as to the moral laxity of the Romans. In the sixteenth chapter, according to this view, are contained some further postscripts, which had been originally intended to accompany the first letter. These, it is supposed, were written on the same parchment with the two epistles, and thus the various parts came to be united. This hypothesis, however, is so improbable that it has not been able to make any way. Heumann's process of dividing this epistle might, with equal reason, be applied in separating the doctrinal from the ethical part in every other of St Paul's writings. In the passage xii. 1, the particle *οὖν* is evidently a mark of transition from the preceding to the following portion; and so the *ἀμήν* at the end of c. xi. is clearly not the termination of the epistle, but merely of the doxology with which St Paul very appropriately concludes the doctrinal portion.

* Comp. Heumann's Erkl. des N. Test. vol. vii. pp. 537, seqq.

The antiquity of the epistle was attacked in a different way by J. F. Semler, according to whom it is only in the xvth and xvith chapters that a diversity of subject from the Epistle to the Romans is to be traced.* The grounds on which he relies, however, are, for the most part, of no greater weight than those which had been advanced by Heumann. Still, there is some plausibility in Semler's manner of turning to account the mention of Aquila and Priscilla's family (xvi. 3, seqq.) These persons, it is observed, were still at Ephesus when the first Epistle to the Corinthians was written (1 Cor. xvi. 19) ; since, then, St Paul wrote to the Romans soon after the date of his Epistle to the Corinthians, there cannot, in Semler's opinion, have been time enough for Aquila first to travel to Rome, and afterwards to send accounts of himself to the Apostle at Corinth,—which he must be supposed to have done, as we find St Paul informed that Aquila had again a church in his house. (Rom. xvi. 6.) The case, however, is quite intelligible, if we only suppose that Aquila left Ephesus suddenly, and that he sent an early report of his new circumstances in Rome to the Apostle at Corinth ; for it is impossible to determine exactly by months the dates of the epistles in question, while, even with the slow means of communication which the ancients possessed, a few months would be sufficient for the journey from Ephesus to Rome and back. In any case, a circumstance of this nature cannot be a sufficient argument to justify Semler's theory. But when we find this learned writer go on to make it a difficulty that several places of Christian assembly are mentioned as existing in Rome (xvi. 4, 14, 15), it appears to us that an exactly opposite inference would be more legitimate ; in a vast capital, the resort of all the world, such as Rome was, the necessity of places of assembly in various quarters of the city would surely become manifest on the very first formation of a church ; and, in like manner, the numerous salutations (c. xvi.) to a church which St Paul had not yet visited, may be easily explained from the character of the city, which was continually receiving visitors from every corner of the world, and in turn sending out travellers into all countries. Hence the Apostle may not have been acquainted, except by reputation,

* Semler de duplici appendice epistolae Pauli ad Romanos, Halæ, 1767. He supposes c. xvi. to be a list of persons to be saluted by the bearer of the letter *on his way from Corinth to Rome*, and c. xv. in like manner to be a separate writing, intended not so much for the Romans as for all brethren who might be met with on the way.

with many of the persons who are named; and yet may have sent his greeting to them, because he felt himself most intimately connected with them by the bond of the same faith.

These objections to Semler's hypothesis hold good also against the kindred view of Dr Paulus,* who is of opinion that c. xv. is a special epistle to the more enlightened Christians of Rome, and that c. xvi. is addressed to the governors of the church only Every letter to a church, he observes, would, as a matter of course, in the first instance, be put into the hands of the presbyters, who read it in public, and delivered the greetings which it contained: it could not be at once given to the whole community. But it does not necessarily follow from this remark that the portion which contains the greetings was addressed to the presbyters *exclusively of the church in general*, and that, consequently, it cannot be regarded as an integral part of the epistle; and while, in like manner, we allow that in c. xv. the Apostle writes *in part* with an especial regard to the more advanced members of the Roman church, still this circumstance by no means obliges us to consider that chapter a letter by itself, inasmuch as the less advanced believers are not excluded from a share in its instruction.

In the most recent times, the genuineness of the last two chapters has been again denied by Baur, (Studien, 1836. No. iii.) He supposes that a later writer of St Paul's school attempted to effect a compromise between his party and the Judaizers, who were predominant in Rome; and that, with this view, he endeavours, by annexing these two chapters, to soften what was offensive in the epistle. The only evidence offered for the theory is of the internal kind—*e.g.*, that c. xv. 1–13 contains matter which has already been far better expressed in cc. xii.–xiv. But against this it has already been remarked, by Klinge, (Stud., 1837. No. ii. p. 309,) that, while in c. xv. 1–13 there is a recurrence of ideas similar to some which had before been treated, they are reproduced with ingenious and spirited modifications, in a way which quite accords with the Apostle's usual practice. It is alleged further, that the phrase διάκονος τῆς περιτομῆς, (xv. 8,) is not in St Paul's manner; that, in xv. 14, seqq., the *captatio benevolentiæ* seems unworthy of an Apostle; and, lastly, that the

* First set forth in a programme (Jena 1801); afterwards in his Erklärung des Römer und Galaterbriefs, (Heidelberg 1831.)

mention of Illyria and Spain, in xv. 17–24, must be a spurious insertion. These points I have already discussed at length in my essay against Baur, (Stud. 1838. No. iv.) and they will be more particularly considered in the commentary on the several passages. I shall only observe further, that the first words of c. xv. are of themselves sufficient to render Baur's supposition altogether improbable. The expression *ἡμεῖς οἱ δυνατοὶ* characterizes the Gentile Christians as the more liberal and enlightened party; surely a follower of St Paul, writing for the purpose of conciliating the Judaizers, could not have made choice of a more inappropriate phrase. Moreover, Baur's idea of a Judaizing tendency in the Roman church requires us to assume that the presbyters too were members of the Judaizing party; but how can it be supposed that, in such circumstances, a disciple of St Paul could add a forged appendage to the Apostle's letter? Baur's hypothesis, then, appears to be nothing else than the work of a misdirected acuteness and an unrestrained hyper-criticism, and will, therefore, never be able to establish itself.*

We must notice, in the last place, the attempts of Eichhorn, Griesbach, and Flatt,† to explain the different positions of the concluding doxology, and its relation to the various forms of conclusion which occur after xiv. 23. These writers assume, although with a variety of modifications, that St Paul ended his epistle on the large parchment at xiv. 23, and that the rest was written on smaller pieces, which were afterwards shifted and arranged in different ways. This hypothesis, it must be allowed—especially as it is stated by Eichhorn—explains all the critical difficulties which occur in the last chapters. Still, it is not to be denied that it has somewhat of a far-fetched and strained character, and therefore we could wish for the means of disposing of these difficulties by some easier and simpler solution. J. E. Chr. Schmidt (in his Introduction) supposed that an easier explanation of this kind might be found by assuming the spuriousness of the doxo-

* Böttger, in his Beiträge, Supplem. Göttingen 1838, pp. 17 seqq., also declares himself against Baur's theory.

† Eichhorn, Einleit. ins N. T. vol. iii. Griesbach, Curæ in historiam textus Gr. epistolarum Pauli, p 45. Flatt, in the appendix to his Erklärung des Römerbriefs. Schulz has lately maintained that c. xvi. does not properly belong to the Epistle to the Romans, but may have been perhaps intended for Ephesus. (Comp. Stud. und Kritiken, for 1829, No. iii. pp. 309 seqq.)

logy; and this supposition has lately been stated by Reiche in a manner which really seems to render it very plausible. If, he observes, the circumstances of the case be closely examined, the difficulties of the last chapters are all in reality to be traced to this doxology. But, in the first place, it is altogether wanting in some MSS. (especially in F); while in others, such as D and G, it is struck out by a later hand. Then, in the copies which are of critical authority, it is found in three different places; (1) at the end, in B, C, E, and several other critical authorities; (2) after xiv. 23, in the codex J, and in almost all such MSS. as are written in small letters; and, (3) in *both* places, as particularly in the codex A. That such differences are very ancient, is remarked by Origen in his commentary on the epistle; only he does not state that he was acquainted with copies which had the doxology in *both* places. On the other hand, Jerome (on Ephes. iii. 5) knew of copies in which the doxology was altogether wanting. Reiche, then, supposes that the reading of the epistle in the public assemblies of the early Christians probably extended only as far as xvi. 23, since little that is of an edifying kind follows in the after part of the epistle. In order that the conclusion in this place might not be without a benediction, he supposes that the doxology was first added in copies which were used in church; that it was originally moulded after the doxology at the end of St Jude's epistle, and was afterwards gradually extended, until at length it was placed, as a full-sounding form, at the conclusion of the whole epistle. In order to give this view additional support, its learned author endeavours to show that the substance of the doxology itself does not point to St Paul as the writer. He considers it inflated, overladen, obscure as to the connection of the ideas, and merely made up from Pauline forms. But it is precisely this which seems to me to be the weak side of Reiche's theory. The supposition that the doxology is spurious would indeed appear to me probable in the highest degree, if the nature of the passage were different from what it is. In this opinion Schott agrees (Einl. p. 250), as also Köllner and Fritzsche in their commentaries; the last-named expositor, in particular, may be considered to have settled the question by his excellent defence of the doxology (vol. i. pp. 38 seqq.). The very commencement, τῷ δὲ δυναμένῳ ὑμᾶς στηρίξαι κατὰ τὸ εὐαγγέλιόν μου, κ. τ. λ. is enough to make the assumption of its spuriousness exceedingly questionable. If the passage had originated in the way which Reiche points out, we might expect to find it a simple doxology, and in all likelihood a short one; but here the personal circumstances of St Paul and of his readers are distinctly marked. He addresses them, speaks of himself in the first person, expresses ideas peculiar to himself exactly in the manner usual with him, and yet so that the doxology as a whole appears altogether new, and without a parallel in the Pauline epistles. Such an addition would hardly have been ventured on by one of the clergy who had no other object than to supply a good conclusion for the public reading.

I am therefore unable to determine that the doxology is spurious, and am rather disposed to adopt Eichhorn's view,* although not insensible to its partly far-fetched character; it has, however, the merit of solving the difficulties, and on this account is to be adhered to until something more deserving of commendation shall be discovered. But in any case it is established that the various *position* of the doxology is the only subject to be discussed, and that this subject has no connection with any question as to the *matter* of the last two chapters. The Epistle to the Romans, consequently, is not only genuine, but it has also descended to us in a state of completeness, without mutilation or addition.

§ 2. TIME AND PLACE OF THE COMPOSITION.

The Epistle to the Romans, dictated by St Paul to a person of the name of Tertius (xvi. 21), and sent by the hands of the deaconess Phoebe (xvi. 1), contains such decisive indications as to the time and the place of its composition, that there has been little difference of opinion on these points, whether in earlier or in more modern times. The only difference which can be properly said to affect the subject, is that as to the general chronology of the

* The opinion of Koppe and Gabler, that the transposition of the concluding doxology is to be traced to the ecclesiastical use of the epistle, would not be undeserving of attention, if only a sufficient probability could be made out for the annexation of the doxology to c. xiv. While c. xv. has a good termination, it must still be very forced to suppose the final doxology transferred from the end of the epistle, not to c. xv. but to c. xiv. If c. xvi. were once omitted, it is most likely that the doxology would also have been given up with it.

Apostle's life. Dr Paulus, of Heidelberg, indeed, has (in the two publications already referred to) proposed the novel opinion, that the epistle must have been written in Illyria, because the writer states in c. xv. 19, that he had travelled "from Jerusalem, and round about unto Illyricum;" but it is very evident that the Apostle, in that passage, intends to name Illyricum only as the furthest point westward to which he had at the time penetrated, and not as the country in which he was at the moment of writing. An equally extravagant view as to the *time* when the epistle was written has been proposed by Tobler,* who maintains, on the ground of the Apostle's extensive acquaintance with the Christians of Rome, that it ought probably to be referred to a date later than his first imprisonment. But it is at once manifest what a violent construction this supposition would require us to put on such passages as i. 9, and xv. 23, in which the Apostle plainly declares that he had not yet been at Rome. The ordinary view, then,—according to which the epistle was written from Corinth, during the visit which St Paul paid to that city after having been driven from Ephesus, and having travelled through Macedonia,—is the only one which has the advantage of accounting easily and naturally for all the passages in which he speaks of himself, his journeys, and his undertakings. Thus, in 1 Cor. xvi. 1, he mentions an intention of going from Corinth to Jerusalem with a collection; and we find from Rom. xv. 25, that he purposed to set out on this journey immediately after despatching his epistle to Rome. Aquila and Priscilla, who were still at Ephesus when St Paul thence wrote his first epistle to the Corinthians, had, at the date of the present epistle, again arrived at Rome. (1 Cor. xvi. 19; Rom. xvi. 3.) We find from Acts xix. 21, that the Apostle intended to visit Rome after he should have accomplished his journey to Jerusalem about the business of the collection; and in Rom. xv. 28, he speaks of the same design, only with the difference, that his plan had been extended to the extremity of the west (τέρμα τῆς δύσεως), so as to embrace a visit to Spain. If, in addition to these chief grounds, we take into consideration some coincidences in detail with what we know otherwise of St Paul's history, *e. g.*, that he sends greetings to the Christians of Rome from Caius (xvi. 23), a person mentioned in 1 Cor.

* Compare Tholuck's Comment. Introd. P. x. Tobler's view is refuted by Flatt in a programme which is inserted in Pott's Sylloge Comment. vol. ii.

i. 14, as then resident at Corinth; that Erastus, from whom he in like manner conveys greetings (xvi. 23), and whom he styles *οἰκόνομος τῆς πόλεως* (*i.e.* of the city in which he was writing) is also mentioned elsewhere as an inhabitant of Corinth (2 Tim. iv. 20); that Phoebe, the bearer of the epistle, was a deaconess of the church at Cenchrea, the port of Corinth—and other circumstances of a like kind—there can be no further doubt that the Epistle of St Paul to the Romans was written from Corinth during his second visit to that city. And consequently, according to the system of chronology which we have adopted, the time of its composition is to be referred to about A.D. 59.

The circumstance that the epistle was written in Greece, and in an entirely Greek city, would at once render it highly probable that it was composed in Greek; and this idea is confirmed by the universal tradition of the ancient church, and by the style of the composition, which throughout appears to indicate an original. Indeed both earlier and later writers have been almost unanimous in the opinion that it was originally written in Greek, since St Paul, as a native of Tarsus, must have had the command of that language, while in Rome it was sufficiently diffused to be generally intelligible. (Comp. Sueton. *Claud.* c. 4. *Dialog. de Orator.* c. 29. Juvenal, *Satyr.* iv. 185, seqq.) Bolten, however, (whose views have been adopted by Bertholdt), has here, as in other cases, misapplied his acuteness, with a view of shewing that St Paul probably composed the epistle in Aramean—a notion which is surely, from the nature of the case, the most improbable that could well be conceived. We might even rather suppose with Hardouin, that it was originally written in Latin, and that it is still preserved to us in this ancient form in the Vulgate, if it were not too evident that this supposition is intended merely to enhance the glory of the version received in the [Roman] Catholic Church. So manifest is this, that the futility of the opinion has been shown even by some more liberal members of the author's own communion.

§ 3. OF THE ROMAN CHURCH.

The circumstances under which the Roman church was formed, and the date of its origin, are involved in a darkness which could only be dissipated by the discovery of ancient documents hitherto unknown—a discovery which we can now hardly venture to hope for. At the time when St Paul wrote to the Romans, there already existed in the capital of the world which then was, a church so considerable that it was spoken of throughout the world (i. 8), and required several places of assembly in the various quarters of the city, (xvi.) The Church of Rome cannot have been founded by an apostle; for in that case St Paul would neither have addressed it by letter nor have visited it in person, since it was a general principle with him, and is expressly stated as such in this very epistle, (xv. 20), to avoid interference with the work which had been already begun by another apostle: and when, in addition to this, we find in the Acts no mention of an apostle's having been at Rome, we may fairly reject the assertion, which originated early and has long been maintained by the [Roman] Catholic Church, that St Peter was the *founder* of the Church of Rome.* On the other hand, the presence of St Peter in Rome at a later time, and his martyrdom there, are facts so well attested by historical evidence that they ought never to have been questioned.† In the first place, Caius, the well-known Roman presbyter and zealous opponent of the Montanists, states that in his time, (towards the end of the second century), the graves of the apostles were pointed out at Rome. When it is considered that he wrote in Rome itself,and that he is particular in mentioning the localities (viz., on the Vatican, and on the road to Ostia), it is inconceivable that there should be a mistake in this statement, since thousands must at once have confuted him. If the apostles died at Rome, and that by public execution, their death, and the place where their bodies rested, could not possibly have remained concealed; if they did not die there, it is impossible to account for so early an origin of the tradition that they died

* It is suprising that even some Protestant writers, such as Bertholdt and Mynster, can have acquiesced in this altogether unsupported notion of the *founding* of the Romish Church by Peter.

† The question has lately been again raised by Baur, in his essay on the party "of Christ" at Corinth (*Tübing. Zeitschr.* 1831, No. iv.), and even Neander appears to have been shaken by his reasoning, (Apost. Zeitalter, ii. 459 seqq.) To me, however, Baur's grounds seem altogether insufficient, and I consider the death of St Peter at Rome a fact not to be denied. In this judgment Bleek agrees (*Stud.* for 1836, No. iv. pp. 1061, seqq.) I have examined the matter more fully in a separate essay against Baur's hypothesis, (*Stud.* 1838, No. iv.) Winer, on the other hand, (*Real. lexicon*, new ed. Art. *Petrus*) considers the accounts to be at least doubtful.

there, unless we suppose the whole church to have consisted of mere deceivers; and, moreover, *there must, in that case, have been some other discoverable statement as to the place of St Peter's death,* since it is not to be supposed that the most celebrated of the apostles could disappear without leaving some trace. But even allowing Caius to be no valid witness, because he was a Roman presbyter, and might have been desirous to enhance the lustre of his church by the alleged fact, no such exception can be taken to Dionysius, Bishop of Corinth, who lived half a century earlier, and, although interested in like manner for the church of Corinth, yet plainly witnesses that the two great apostles died, not in his own city, but in Rome. (Comp. the passages of both authorities in Euseb. *Hist. Eccl.* ii. 25.) To these testimonials are to be added those of Irenæus (*adv. Haer.* iii. 1, in Euseb. *Hist. Eccl.* v. 8), Clement of Alexandria, (in Euseb. *Hist. Eccl.* ii. 14, 15; vi. 14), and of the critical Origen, who, like the others, refers the martyrdom of St Peter and St Paul to Rome.* (Euseb. *H. E.* iii. 1.)

As, then, the apostles must have died somewhere, and no other city of antiquity claims the honour of their death, there is really no sufficient ground for doubting the account which is thus accredited.

Still, however, we do not from this get any light as to the *origin* of the Roman church. For, even although the Apostle Peter be styled by Caius and Dionysius the *founder* of the church of Rome, it will naturally be understood that the expression is not to be referred to the *original* foundation of the community, but to its enlargement *and more complete establishment* by him; and in this sense St Paul also is always named with him as joint founder of the church in Rome. We are, therefore, wholly left to conjecture on this point; and perhaps the most likely way of accounting for the formation of the community may be, to suppose that a knowledge of Christianity was early conveyed to the capital by travellers, if not even by the Romans who were present at the Feast of Pente-

* Reiche, (*loc. cit.* p. 40,) Note 8, doubts whether the account in Eusebius ought to be referred to Origen; but the concluding words of the chapter, ταῦτα Ὠριγένει κατὰ λέξιν, κ. τ. λ. evidently apply to the whole relation. We could, at the utmost, only doubt (with Valesius), whether the words from Θωμᾶς μέν, κ. τ. λ. be Origen's; from Πέτρος δέ κ. τ. λ. they are certainly his.

cost, (Acts ii. 10,) and that through the influence of these persons a church was gradually formed there. For if any one strongly prominent individual had been the only agent in the foundation of the Roman church, it is more than probable that his name would have been preserved. And, again, the lively intercourse which Rome kept up with all parts of the empire, renders it equally inconceivable that Christians should not early have come to the capital from Antioch or Jerusalem; and if they came, their zeal would have also led them to preach the word there.

We have not, however, any certain trace of the existence of a Christian community in Rome *earlier* than the present epistle. For whether (as many have supposed, and as appears to myself *probable*), Aquila and Priscilla were already Christians at the time of their banishment from Rome by the edict of Claudius, is a point incapable of proof, since the passage, Acts xviii. 1–3, does not expressly state it; although, if we consider that otherwise their conversion would surely have been related, it can hardly be well doubted that this family brought its belief in Christianity from Rome with it.

But, even if it were not so, still it is evident that a community so considerable as that of Rome appears from St Paul's epistle to have been, could not have come into existence all at once, but required some time for its formation; and for this reason, if for no other, we must refer the foundation of the church to a period much earlier than the date of the epistle.

There is, however, a difficulty in reconciling this supposition (which the contents of the epistle to the Romans oblige us to adopt,) with the narrative of St Luke at the end of the Acts, where it is stated that St Paul, on arriving in Rome, sent for the elders of the Jews who lived there, and related to them the cause of his being a prisoner; to which they are represented as answering, that they had not received any letters concerning him; but that, as to the sect of the Christians, they begged him to give them some information, since they had heard no more of it than it was everywhere spoken against (Acts xxviii. 17–22.) From this it would appear that no church could then have existed in Rome, since otherwise it would seem inconceivable that the Jews should not have been aware of its existence. This conclusion was actually drawn by Tobler (*Theol. Aufs.* Zürich, 1796), who, in consequence of it, referred the composition of the epistle to the latest period of St Paul's life—an opinion which is, of course, altogether untenable, (as has already been observed,) but which has some excuse in the difficulties of this yet unexplained passage, since it is certainly sufficient to remove them. If it be said (as Tholuck and Reiche suppose) that the Jews may have concealed their knowledge of the matter, it is impossible to see why they should have done so. A man so dangerous as St Paul must have appeared from the Jewish point of view, would surely have at once been met by them with open opposition. But this supposition becomes yet more improbable on a more particular consideration of the sequel, as related in the Acts. For we find that at their next meeting with St Paul, the chiefs of the Roman Jews appear really unacquainted with the subject of the gospel; it is evident that they hear it for the first time, and the announcement of it raises, as was usual, a contention among their own number—some assenting to it, and others opposing it; and surely it is impossible to suppose this contention feigned. Hence we might suppose that the church may have been entirely broken up by the persecution of Claudius (Sueton. Claud. c. 25), and that its subsequent gathering may have been so gradual that the few Christians who were at Rome when St Paul arrived there were unknown to the Jews of the capital.* I had myself formerly declared in favour of this opinion (Comm. on Acts xxviii. 17 seqq., 1st ed.); but it cannot well serve as a way of escape from the difficulty, since the date of the Epistle to the Romans falls in the interval between the persecution of the Jews under Claudius, and St Paul's visit to Rome, and the epistle supposes the existence of a *flourishing* church; it is, therefore, impossible that at the later period there can have been but a small number of Christians in Rome, as the community was already so numerous at an earlier time.

There is, however, the greater reason for desiring a solution of the difficulty, because thus light would be thrown on the relative circumstances of the Jewish and the Gentile Christians in Rome—a subject which is of so great importance for the explanation of the

* There had been an expulsion of the Jews from Rome as early as the reign of Tiberius. (Cf. Sueton Tib. c. 36. Tacit. Ann. ii. 85; Joseph. Arch. xviii. 4, 15.) Perhaps the passage of Suetonius about the expulsion of the Jews in the time of Claudius may indicate also an expulsion of the Christians, who would not at first be sufficiently distinguished from the Jews.

whole epistle. For that there were Christians in Rome when St Paul arrived there, appears (if indeed it yet require any proof), from Acts xxviii. 15, where it is related that brethren went as far as Forum Appium and Tres Tabernae to meet the Apostle; nor is there any conceivable reason why the Christians of Rome should have become fewer at the time of St Paul's arrival than they were at the date of the epistle, since (in so far as we know) nothing had happened in the meantime to disturb them; and yet it would appear that the chiefs of the Jewish community in Rome knew nothing of the Christians. This indicates a peculiar relation between Gentiles and Jews, Gentile and Jewish Christians, in Rome, and so leads to the important question—*What was the nature of the Church of Rome, or what may have been the tendencies existing in it* when St Paul wrote? a question closely coinciding with the inquiry as to the *occasion and object of the epistle,* since the epistle is the only source from which we can derive our information as to the tendencies which, in the earliest times, were prevalent in that church.

Now in the Epistle to the Romans itself there is no special cause assigned for its being written.* St Paul merely mentions (i. 9 seqq.; xv. 15 seqq.) his desire to preach the gospel, as to the Gentiles in general, so especially to the inhabitants of Rome, as being the capital of the heathen world; whence it would simply appear that his object in writing his epistle was of quite a general kind. Notwithstanding this, it has often been attempted to point out particular causes, and particular objects in connection with these, for the sending of the epistle to the Romans. It has been supposed by many writers, and some of them highly distinguished, that the only, or, at least, the most important, object was to mediate between contending parties in Rome, especially the Gentile and the Jewish Christians. Others find in the epistle a controversial design against Jews or Jewish Christians; while others again suppose that St Paul wished to guard against the abuse of his doctrine as to grace, or that he meant to oppose the Jewish spirit of insurrection. All these views, however (as to which more particular in-

* Dr Paulus takes a naïf view of the matter, inferring from xv. 19 that the beautiful appearance of Italy from the high coast of Illyria awaked in the Apostle's mind a longing for Rome. This aesthetic motive, however, is very problematical, inasmuch as (not to mention other objections) it is well known that Italy cannot be seen across the Adriatic.

formation may be gathered from Reiche, pp. 75 seqq.), on closer consideration, appear untenable; the whole exhibition of doctrine* in the epistle is purely objective in its character, nor is there, except in passing, any intentional and conscious regard to anything save the truth of the gospel. But it is, of course, in the very nature of truth that it forms oppositions against all errors, and thus far such oppositions appear in the Epistle to the Romans, as elsewhere; and, moreover, it was a part of the Apostle's wisdom as a teacher, that he all along represents the doctrine of the gospel in such a manner that the statement itself may be a safeguard against the errors which could not but fall in the way of the Christians; but besides the endeavour to exhibit the gospel to the Christians of Rome in its natural relation to the law, and in its practical results on life, it is quite impossible to discover in the Epistle to the Romans a further design to oppose the Jews, and to keep differences with them in view, such as is clearly expressed in the Epistle to the Galatians.

The idea of differences between the Gentile and the Jewish Christians at Rome, for the appeasing of which it is supposed that the Apostle's letter was intended, is, however, so widely prevalent, that it is necessary for us to go into a more particular inquiry as to this point.† This opinion may probably have at first been occasioned by the obvious parallel between the Epistle to the Romans and that

* [Darstellung.]

† It has very recently been again proposed in a peculiar form by Baur (Stud. 1836, No. 3), and Kling (Stud. 1837, No. 2) partly agrees with him. I have more fully considered the treatises of these two writers in an essay (Stud. 1838, No. 4), to which I must here refer the reader, contenting myself with shortly characterizing the views of Baur and Kling. Baur supposes the main part of the epistle to be, not cc. iii.–viii., but the section cc. ix.–xi. This portion, he argues, is intended to assert against the Jewish Christians the universality of the Christian dispensation; and he supposes that cc. iii.–viii. were intended to lead to this conclusion, the object of those chapters being to quench the jealousy of the Jews at the influx of Gentiles into the church, by showing that Jews and Gentiles stand in the same relation with respect to Christianity. Thus it is supposed that a Judaizing spirit, opposed to St Paul, had prevailed in Rome. Baur had previously endeavoured to prove this in the Tübinger Zeitschrift, 1831, No. 4, and he now attempts to bring further evidence of it from the Acts, which book he supposes to have been composed at Rome, for the purpose of defending St Paul's course of operation against the antipauline party; a view of which I have already given my opinion in commenting on the Acts. Kling is inclined to adopt Baur's views, to the extent of recognising in the epistle a controversial design against Jewish opinions; but finds fault with him for considering the mass of the Roman Church as Judaistic, instead of regarding the Judaizers as only one element in it. In the mass, he says (p. 320), the Roman Church might rather be considered as animated by a Gentile-Christian tendency.

to the Galatians; and next by the idea, that on account of the large body of Jews in Rome, there must also have been there a great number of Jewish Christians; and that if so, it is not to be supposed but that the Roman community came in for a share of the all-pervading contentions between Gentile and Jewish Christians. But plausible as this conclusion may appear, it is evident that it ought in the first place to be capable of historical proof; not only, however, is there an utter absence of such proof, but there are very important reasons to the contrary. In the whole Epistle to the Romans *there is not a syllable which mentions disputes as to the relations of the law and the gospel*, such as those which prevailed in Galatia. In xv. 7 seqq., there is a faint hint that in the case of the ascetics, towards whom the Apostle had recommended a tender course of dealing (c. xiv.), the difference of Jewish Christians also came into question; and again, in xvi. 17–18, there is a warning against such as *might* cause divisions; but in v. 19 the Romans are plainly described as *yet free* from such errors, so that it is only the *possibility* of a disturbance of their peace that is contemplated. All that could be said, therefore, is this, that, while the Apostle's argument is not *openly* directed to the subject of divisions, it is yet so managed as to make us feel through it that he has a covert regard to the two opposite systems.

If, however, the matter be so understood, it must also be allowed that this feeling may very easily deceive, and by so much the more because these possible divisions are not expressly represented as originating with the Judaizing party. Where such differences actually existed, as in Galatia, St Paul speaks out plainly respecting them; why then should he not do so in this case? If he wished, independently of any possible or existing errors, to set forth the nature of the evangelical doctrine of salvation, he could not do so otherwise than by representing the relation of this new element to the two old systems of the Gentile and the Jewish life; both must, of course, fall into the background in comparison with the gospel, and therefore his view* *appears* to be polemical. But that it is not so, even in a covert intentionally-concealed manner, is shown by the notice in the Acts of St Paul's appearance at Rome, which has not been at all sufficiently brought to bear on the inquiry as

* [Auffassung.]

to the object of the Epistle to the Romans. If we conceive the state of the church in Rome at the date of the epistle according to the common view, the history of St Paul in that capital is utterly incomprehensible. It is supposed that the Roman Church was divided into two parties; that the strict Jewish-Christians wished still to observe the Law of Moses even outwardly, with circumcision, keeping of the Sabbath, and the like; that the Gentile Christians, on the other hand, had freed themselves from it. Must we not, on this supposition, necessarily assume that the Roman Jewish Christians adhered to the synagogue in Rome? As the Jewish Christians of Jerusalem remained attached to the Temple, and did not renounce the Jewish polity, so, too, the Jewish-Christians of Rome could not have separated themselves from the Synagogue. But now let us read the narrative in Acts xxviii. 17, seqq., which represents the Christians as quite unknown to the rulers of the Roman synagogue, and let us ask whether, according to this, the supposition just stated has any appearance whatever of probability? There is in that passage (as has already been remarked) no ground at all for supposing an intentional concealment; and if this cannot be assumed, there remains nothing else but to say that the chiefs of the Jews really knew nothing of the Christians in Rome. The speech of St Paul (Acts xxviii. 17–20) is evidently reported in an abridged form; he had spoken in it of his belief in Christ, as is still indicated by the mention of the ἔλπις τοῦ Ἰσραήλ. On this, then, the Jews declare περὶ τῆς αἱρέσεως ταύτης γνωστόν ἐστιν ἡμῖν ὅτι πανταχοῦ ἀντιλέγεται. Do people speak thus of a sect which is before their eyes—on whose struggles and contentions they are looking? This can hardly be made to seem likely. And to this is to be added the discussion which follows with St Paul (xxviii. 23 seqq.), in which for a whole day he expounds the Scriptures to them, in order to prove the Messiahship of Jesus, whereupon there arises a contention among the Jews themselves:—all which would, according to the common view, have been a mere mockery,* since by that view the Jews must be supposed to have known of Christ long before, and to have decided against Him.† It

* [Gaukelspiel.]

† This is decisive against the supposition of Meyer, that the Jews spoke only as officials, and in this capacity shewed an official reserve—that they merely meant to say that nothing had been *officially* announced to them. But—besides that this is an evident

is only in the towns where there were not as yet any churches that we find the Jews so free from prejudice as they here appear in Rome; where, on the other hand, they were already acquainted with the Gospel through the formation of a church, they do not admit of any expositions of doctrine by Christians. As, however, there must yet have been a church in Rome, the question is, how we are to explain this remarkable position of the Jews towards it?

The only possible explanation of this phenomenon—and it is one which at the same time indicates the origin of the tendency which we afterwards find in the Roman Church— appears to be this.* It must be assumed that the Christians of Rome were induced, by the persecutions directed against the Jews under Claudius in the ninth year of his reign, to make their differences from the Jews clearly and strongly apparent—perhaps in consequence of the influence which even at that early time some disciples of St Paul already exercised on the Roman Church; exactly as at a later date the Christians of Jerusalem separated themselves from the Jews, that they might not be confounded with them, and might be allowed to live in Aelia. If disciples of St Paul early acquired a decisive influence in Rome, we shall also understand how it was that the Apostle

transferring of modern circumstances to the ancient world—the disputes which arose among the Jews themselves in consequence of St Paul's preaching will not allow us to explain the phenomena before us by the character of the official body of the Roman Jews.

* For the further establishment of this view, and the justification of it against the attacks of Baur, I refer to my essay, already cited above, in the Studien for 1838, No. 4. This only I remark here, that his appeal to Tacitus (Ann. xiv. 44), by way of proof that the Christians were quite well known in Rome, is by no means adapted to decide the question before us, since it is the Jews who are here spoken of as unacquainted with the Christians, while Tacitus speaks of heathens; moreover, it was only by means of the rack that the heathens extorted the names of the members of the Christian community in Rome: which evidently speaks for their concealed and retired condition Kling (Stud. 1837, No, 2, pp. 307 seqq.) refutes, indeed, the capricious fancies of Baur, but himself reverts to the old untenable view, that the Jews of Rome only pretended to know nothing of Christians there, in order to avoid disputes with them. That they wished to hear St Paul, is explained by Kling merely from the forward curiosity* of Jews, which led them to seek for an opportunity of hearing a discourse from a famous rabbi. But it is unnecessary to shew how unsatisfactory this representation is. The Jews of Rome evidently hear of Christ for the first time; they fall into disputes among themselves; this, surely, cannot be pretence! Unless we suppose the Acts of the Apostles to be tinged with fiction† (as Baur maintains), there remains no other explanation than that here proposed. Böttger's explanation of the case is also extremely unsatisfactory. He supposes that the difficulties are all of my own creation, and that in reality there are none. (Comp. Beiträge, Supplem. pp. 27 seqq.)

* Vorwitz. † [Soll die Apostelgeshichte keine romanhafte Farbe tragen.]

could regard the Roman Church as his own, and could open his correspondence with it without invading another's field of labour. In consequence of this persecution of the Jews, Aquila and Priscilla took refuge at Corinth; and there they were found by the Apostle Paul (Acts xviii. 2), who, without doubt, became even at that time acquainted, by means of these fugitives, with the Roman Church and its circumstances. On this knowledge St Paul, four or five years later, at the beginning of Nero's reign, on his third missionary journey, wrote from Corinth his epistle to Rome. There is little likelihood that any great number of Jews can have ventured so early to return to Rome; those who returned were obliged to keep themselves in concealment, and it was naturally the interest of the Christian community there to remain as far as possible from them. Even three years later, when St Paul himself appeared in Rome, the body of Jews there may still not have been considerable,—in part, too, it may not have been composed of its old members, who had lived there before the persecution by Claudius, but of altogether new settlers, who were unacquainted with the earlier existence of a Christian community. And thus it might come to pass within eight or ten years that the Christian community at Rome appears entirely separated from the body of Jews in that city; and in such a state of separation we find it, according to the notice at the end of the Acts. As, according to the same narration, the Jews did not receive St Paul, so that here also he found himself obliged to turn to the Gentiles, this separateness continued to subsist, and thus by degrees there was developed at Rome a directly anti-Judaic tendency, which caused a prohibition of celebrating the Sabbath, and of everything Jewish.* According, then, to this representation, it is altogether unlikely that there should have been Jewish-Christians in Rome from whom contentions with the Gentile Christians could proceed. Christians of the former kind were in the habit of keeping up the connection with the synagogue, and if so, the chief persons of the synagogues could not be unacquainted with the existence of

* The latest expositor of the epistle, Dr Köllner, supposes that St Paul, during his imprisonment, sent for the chief of the Jews for the purpose of gaining them, and that St Luke did not intend to give an account of his intercourse with the Christians. This, however, is but an evasion of the difficulty: the real point is,—how the *behaviour of the Jews* which is in question can be conceivable, if in Rome itself there existed a Christian community, in which there were Judaizing Christians. Köllner has not advanced anything towards the solution of the difficulty.

a community which declared Him who was crucified to be the Messias. There might still have been Jews by birth or proselytes among the members of the Roman church, but these would, in that case, have altogether taken up the freer Pauline view of the law, and have detached themselves from the connexion of the synagogue. If, indeed, there were any decided testimony for the fact that in Rome, as in Galatia, there existed within the church itself a party of gross Jewish-Christians, the view which has just been given, and which rests on the evidence of history, might still be combated with some appearance of justice; but there is no such testimony whatever. There is, as has been observed, an utter absence of clear statements on the subject in the Epistle to the Romans; for (as I have above remarked) xvi. 17 seqq. points only to a *possible* danger, and the proper doctrinal body of the epistle (chap. iii.–viii.) treats the relation between law and Gospel in a purely objective way, without any reference to differences in the bosom of the church itself. Chapters ix.–xi. are evidently intended for Gentile Christians only, who also are throughout exclusively addressed, and, lastly, chapters xii. and xiii. contain wholly objective admonitions. There remain, consequently, only the first and last chapters; and in these very chapters the hints of such contentions have been supposed to be found. In c. ii., it is said, the subject is quite clearly the Jews, who are expressly addressed (ii. 17, 27), so that the epistle must also necessarily be supposed to have been written to Jewish-Christians; in iii. 1, seqq. the advantages of the Jews are discussed, and, although in c. xiv. the mistaken freedom of Gentiles is reproved, yet it is in contrast with Jewish scrupulousness, which must, therefore, necessarily be also supposed to have had certain representatives in the Roman church. To the observations from the opening chapters, however, it is to be answered, that still St Paul assuredly did not write to Jews, and yet it is *Jews*, and not *Jewish-Christians*, who are addressed in the passages ii. 17, 27; the address, therefore, is evidently not to be used as a foundation for inferences as to the character of the readers, but is rather to be regarded as merely a rhetorical figure. St Paul's object in the first chapters is only to prove of both Gentiles and Jews that they had need of Christ the Saviour; but into these two elements the whole world was divided, when regarded from the theocratic point of view; and thus, in as far as

St Paul has an universal purpose in writing his epistle, in so far was he obliged to contemplate Christianity in its relation to the previously-existing systems,* without giving us a ground for thence deducing anything as to the composition of the Roman Church. Hence it was quite necessary that the advantages of the Jews also should be discussed, (iii. 1 seqq.,) inasmuch as it was necessary for the Gentiles, even if they embraced Christianity without any intermediate step, to know how they stood with relation to the Old Testament economy and to the people of Israel; and, consequently, from a discussion on these points nothing can be inferred for the existence in Rome of Jewish Christians in the proper sense of the term,—*i.e.* of persons who not only were of Jewish descent, (for in that sense St Paul himself would be a Jewish Christian,) but who attached an exaggerated value to Jewish views, and adhered to the connexion with the synagogue and the temple. A more plausible evidence for the existence of such a party at Rome is c. xiv.,—according to which, undoubtedly, there must have been in Rome a class of persons scrupulous as to the law. It is, however, extremely improbable that these were Judaizers of the ordinary kind, such as were found in Galatia; for the latter had no scruple as to the eating of flesh in general, but only as to the flesh of unclean animals; whereas the Roman ascetics, on the other hand, disapproved of *all use of animal food*, and lived wholly on herbs and fruits, (xiv. 2.) The whole question as to the character of these persons, therefore, requires a closer examination, which we shall institute in the exposition of the passage; in any case, however, we must say that c. xiv. is not adapted to prove the existence of Judaizers in Rome, since the description is not at all suitable to them.

We regard, consequently, the hypothesis of an intended settlement of dispute between Gentile and Jewish Christians in Rome as wholly untenable; and we find in the epistle to the Romans *a purely objective statement of the nature of the Gospel, grounded only on the general opposition between Jews and Gentiles, and not on the more special opposition existing in the church itself, between Judaizing and non-Judaizing Christians.*†

* [Lebensstufen, degrees of life.]

† It were to be desired that the terms *Jewish* and *Gentile* Christians were more carefully distinguished than they usually are from *Judaizing* and *non-Judaizing Christians.* It is, indeed, certainly to be supposed that most of those who were Jews by birth con-

§ 4. ARGUMENT OF THE EPISTLE.

With respect to the plan of the epistle to the Romans, two extremes are to be avoided : *first*, the view which represents the Apostle as having written according to a most exactly elaborated logical scheme ; and, *secondly*, the supposition that, without having any settled design, he merely abandoned himself to his inward impulses. Between the two views, the following appears to come out as the true and correct idea—that certainly St Paul had designed a general plan for the epistle, but without having carried it into detail. His epistle, consequently, has not the precision of a theological treatise, but preserves the freer form of a letter ; still, there is expressed in it so determined and clear a train of thought that St Paul cannot have written it without any plan, and in mere obedience to the current of his feelings. For how different a shape such an absolutely free and unpremeditated effusion takes, we see, among other instances, in the Epistle to the Ephesians. *One* leading idea, *the relation of Law and Gospel*, is carried out so carefully by the Apostle, with the necessary preliminaries for understanding it, and the most important consequences which result, that nothing whatever of essential importance can be pointed out as missing in his statement.*

The whole epistle falls under four divisions. The *first* part contains the *opening*, (i. 1–17,) in which, after the *salutation*, (1–7,) is given the *Introduction* to the following discussion, (8–17.) The last two verses expressly state the theme for the

tinued, even as Christians, to keep up a great attachment to the Jewish law, and that most of those who were Gentiles by birth remained free from it as Christians; yet doubtless, there were also many Jews by birth (and consequently Jewish Christians) who, as Christians, did not Judaize ; and, in like manner, many of Gentile birth might have already, as proselytes, been so strongly implicated in Judaism, that, even after becoming members of the Christian church, they continued to follow a Judaizing tendency. The names of *Jewish* and *Gentile Christians*, therefore, ought to be used only to signify *descent*, and the erroneous spiritual tendency to be denoted by the epithet *Judaizing*.

* The view proposed by Baur, (Stud. 1836. No. 3,) that the main part of the epistle consists, not of the section cc. iii.-viii., but of cc. ix.-xi., has been already noticed above. The untenable character of this supposition has been shown in my essay, already more than once cited, (Stud. 1838. No. 4,) to which I now refer the reader.

whole epistle, viz., that *the Gospel is a power of God, and in it the righteousness from faith is revealed.**

This idea is developed in the *Second Part* (i. 18—xi. 36), which, as being the *doctrinal* portion of the epistle, is that which gives it its great importance. It falls into *five sections*, of which the *first*, (i. 18—iii. 20,) is a preparation for the deduction properly so called; being devoted to proving the universal sinfulness of all mankind, in order to manifest the insufficiency of the law, both moral and ceremonial, and the necessity of another way of salvation, the righteousness of faith. First of all, the Apostle proves the sinfulness of the Gentile world, (i. 18–32); next, he treats of the Jews *more especially*, (ii. 1–29); lastly, he further considers the relation of the Jews to the Gentiles, and allows to the former great advantages in their calling, but declares that they have forfeited these by their unfaithfulness, wherefore there is now no difference between Jews and Gentiles in their position with respect to the gospel, (iii. 1–20.)

With the *second section* (iii. 21—v. 11), the Apostle then enters on the doctrinal exposition itself. Since the law, whether ceremonial or moral, was not sufficient to render men righteous and holy before God, He has opened another way, namely this, that men should become righteous and blessed through faith in Jesus, who is set forth as a mercy-seat,† (iii. 21–31.) St Paul indicates the germs of this righteousness by faith in the Old Testament, as far back as the life of Abraham, who pleased God, not by works of the law, but by faith, which was imputed to him for righteousness, (iv. 1–25.) This holy way, then, by which alone man in his sinful state can attain to peace with God, has, through the love of Christ, been manifested to all men; for which cause we may not now glory save in Christ only, (ver. 1–11.)

The *third section* indicates the internal necessary connexion of this way of faith with the nature of man. As from Adam the stream of sin poured itself forth over mankind, and hence every one who is descended from him has fallen under sin,—so from Christ does righteousness proceed, which He imparts to the faithful in the new birth. The law, therefore, is intended only to make sin

* It will be seen in the commentary that the author takes the words differently from the English version.

† Ἱλαστήριον, ver. 25. *Propitiation*, Eng. version.

powerful, in order that grace may become more powerful, (ver. 12–21.) The same, therefore, which took place in Christ, has been accomplished in his people also, seeing that all are in him, as they were in Adam. For this cause, also, must not any one who has been incorporated into Christ any longer serve sin; for he has died in the old man, and, like a woman who has been set free by the death of her husband, he has become married to another husband, even Christ, (vi. 1—vii. 6.)

After this follows, in the *fourth section,* the description of the course of conversion in man, (vii. 7—viii. 39.) From the first movements of grace and the quickening of sin, the Apostle proceeds to depict the process by which the inner life is evolved, to the fully developed contest between light and darkness in the soul, which at last is triumphantly ended by experience of the power of the grace of Christ, (vii. 7–24.) With this is connected the description of the life in grace itself, and in the continual growth therein, to the consummation of the whole personality in God, (vii. 25—viii. 17.) Lastly, the Apostle passes from the consummation of the individual to the consummation of the whole, which is represented and assured in it; and with this is attained the purpose of the course of the world, since thus all that was corrupted by the fall will be restored to its original purity, (viii. 18–39)

In the fifth section, (ix. 1—xi. 36,) the Apostle leads back his readers to the peculiar relation in which the Jews stand towards the Christian system of salvation. It is primarily intended for *them;* and, nevertheless, *they* appear as if expressly shut out from it, and the Gentiles as if called before the Jews. In consequence of this relation, the Apostle first unfolds the doctrine of election in general, agreeably to the indications in the Old Testament, and shows that the holiness and blessedness of the creature are solely the work of God's gracious election, and that the unholiness and damnation of the creature are no less to be regarded as solely his own work (ix. 1–29). He then shews that it is the unfaithfulness of the Jews which has hindered them from laying hold on the righteousness which is by faith; they had obstinately clung to the law as the way of salvation, whereas Christ is the end of the law, and in Him alone dwelleth peace for Jews and Gentiles (ix. 30—x. 21). And, lastly, St Paul opens the prospect, that even for the Jews a conversion to Christ is yet to be expected.

He points to the fact that a holy seed has yet remained in the people, which will not be lost; and then, in bold prophetic glances, he passes on to the end of days, when Israel shall again be engrafted into the olive tree, in whose roots the Gentiles only have at first been set as wild shoots. This contemplation incites the Apostle at last to an enthusiastic* glorification of God, with which he concludes this second and most important part of the epistle (xi. 1–36.)

The *third part,* the hortatory (xii. 1—xv. 33), may be divided into three sections. In the *first* (xii. 1—xiii. 14), St Paul gives general admonitions to brotherly love, and to obedience. In the *second section* (xiv. 1—xv. 13), he treats of the regard to be paid to such as are weak in faith, and suppose themselves obliged to an exact observance of some altogether unessential practices or precepts. The Apostle exhorts the stronger members of the Church to treat these with a forbearing consideration, and prays them rather, after their Lord's example, to refrain from using their liberty than to offend a brother. In the *third section,* St Paul communicates notices respecting himself and his intended journeys.

The *fourth* and concluding *part* forms the epilogue, and contains greetings and good wishes for the readers (xvi. 1–27).

According to this summary of the contents, the nine chapters from the third to the eleventh form unquestionably the most essential part of the epistle. They furnish a careful doctrinal exposition of the nature of the Christian scheme of salvation,† by no means, as Reiche says, (p. 66), apologetico-polemical considerations on it. But the peculiar character of the epistle still requires a special consideration, on which we intend to enter in the following paragraphs.

§. 5. THE VALUE AND THE PECULIAR CHARACTER OF THE EPISTLE.

Among the epistles of St Paul, three classes may be distinguished; first, epistles of *doctrinal* instruction; next, epistles of

* [Begeisterten.]

† So, with substantial correctness, Höpfner, De consecutione sententiarum in Pauli epistola ad Romanos; Lips. 1828. Compare also Fuhrmam's Essay, De Concinnitate in Ep. ad Rom. in Velthusen, &c., *Sylloge,* vol. i. 461, seqq.

practical instruction; and, lastly, friendly outpourings of the heart. To the last class belong the Epistles to the Ephesians, the Philippians, the Colossians, and Philemon. All these presuppose the common faith as known, and aim only at perfecting of believers in it, and confirming them in brotherly love. Those which I have styled epistles of practical instruction are especially occupied with the external side of the ecclesiastical life. The Epistles to the Corinthians, to Timothy, and to Titus, are those which, while they touch on individual points of doctrine, set especially before our view the ecclesiastical circumstances of the apostolic age. But the Epistle to the Romans, with those to the Galatians and Thessalonians, belongs, beyond the possibility of mistake, to the first class—the epistles of doctrinal instruction. In respect of subject, it is most nearly akin to that to the Galatians; both treat of the relations of law and gospel: while, however, as has been shown above, this relation is treated altogether *objectively* in the Epistle to the Romans, the Epistle to the Galatians represents it *polemically*, in opposition to the Judaizing Christians. The Epistle to the Galatians, moreover, limits itself exclusively to this relation, and discusses it more briefly than is the case in the Epistle to the Romans. In this, on the other hand, the relation of law and gospel is set forth didactically, in the proper sense of the word, nay, scientifically, so that the doctrine of the sinfulness of human nature, which is essential to its foundation, and the doctrine of the divine decree, which furnishes the key to the passing of the gospel from the people of Israel to the Gentiles, are also set forth in connection with it. *

Hence we may say that in the Epistle to the Romans is contained, as it were, a system of Pauline doctrine, inasmuch as all the essential points which the Apostle was accustomed to bring forward with essential prominence, in treating of the gospel, are here unfolded in detail. It is very appropriate that he, the Apostle of the Gentiles, set forth this in an epistle of instruction to the Christians of Rome in particular, since that city represented, as it were, the whole Gentile world, in like manner as Jerusalem represented the

* That in the Epistle to the Galatians the relation between law and gospel alone is treated, while in that to the Romans the doctrine of election is also considered, may be regarded as the reason why Luther commented on the Galatians only; he wished undoubtedly to avoid declaring himself on predestination.

Jewish. The Epistle to the Romans is thus far a letter to all Gentiles and Gentile-Christians collectively (as the Epistle to the Hebrews is addressed to all Jews and Jewish-Christians, with a view of bringing them nearer to the more comprehensive Pauline position);—and in consequence of this significancy, its contents have also, in perfect accordance with the process of the Church's development, became the basis of all the doctrinal development of the Western Church. There is in human nature an inclination to deviate ever again and again from the essential character of the gospel, and to sink back into the law. The difficulty of overcoming the law, and of enforcing the gospel truth in its peculiarity, shewed itself, even as early as during the foundation of the Church. Even those who had experienced the power of the gospel, like the Christians of Galatia, might be again led astray, and drawn back to the Old Testament position of the law. Afterwards, during the medieval period, a new legal character was developed in the bosom of the Church itself, and the righteousness of faith, without the works of the law, was altogether misapprehended. By the light of the Word of God, and especially by the careful, profound, and experimental statement of the doctrine in the Epistle to the Romans, the Reformers again discovered the original doctrine of the righteousness which comes of faith, and so they built the church anew on its eternal, indestructible foundation. Since the middle of the eighteenth century, lastly, the Church again sank down to the legal position, in the rationalistic-neological tendency which, from that period, became prevalent; and if the most recent time has been able once more to find the jewel of faith under the ruins of the demolished Church, it is mainly indebted for this to the comprehensive, and, to every yearning heart, convincing statement, of the Apostle Paul, in his Epistle to the Romans. * And as the Church, altogether, has always been in danger of losing the evangelical truth, and sinking back to the position of the law, so is the same to be observed in the development of the life of the individual also. Every awaking of sin, and of the striving after deliverance from it, proceeds from the endeavour to fulfil the

* That after this the Apostle's fundamental suppositions are the only part of the epistle to which Reiche (vol. i. p. 91) is even now able to attach a value, is intelligible from this learned writer's doctrinal position. Köllner (p. 58) considers it necessary to extract the kernel from the husk before we can get at abiding truths in the epistle; he, too, regards its significance as a whole as only temporary.

law of God, whether the inward law of the conscience, or the outwardly given law of revelation. The vanity of the struggle which arises from this striving is the first thing which brings to the conviction that there must be another way which leadeth unto life. From this feeling of the need of salvation, arises, by means of the preaching of Christ, faith, and in it regeneration, the changing of the whole inward man, and the filling with the power of divine life. As, however, the old man, in whom sin dwells, still remains alive in the individual after this has taken place, there remains also for him the danger of relapsing into the law, which becomes so much the more threatening, if he is obliged to own that he has not avoided the opposite extreme, relaxing in the struggle against sin, and falsely taking comfort from the merits of Christ. And as this danger of relaxing in the struggle threatens the individual, so again does it threaten the aggregate also, and to the avoiding of it are directed (as has been already observed) the catholic epistles, with the Epistle to the Hebrews, which, in this respect, form a necessary complement to the body of St Paul's epistles in general, and to the Epistle of the Romans in particular.*

A writing of such penetrative significancy—which in the course of centuries has been the regulating authority for the Church in the most critical moments of her development—which has already been, is, and to the end of time will continue to be, the regulating authority for persons without number, as to the training of their individual life—must have had the deepest foundation in the life of its author. It was only from lively experience that the Apostle could treat a relation of such uncommon difficulty in such a manner that his words still, after thousands of years, tell as profoundest truth in the hearts of millions, and in the collective consciousness of great ecclesiastical communities. Indeed the whole substance of the vast experiences through which St Paul had passed in his own life may be traced back to the relation between law and gospel. Before his conversion, he knew no other way than that of fulfilment of the law, and with all the ardour of his noble soul he threw himself on the mass of inward and outward precepts which the Mosaic law and the tradition of the

* [Olshausen's views as to the authorship of the Epistle to the Hebrews have already been mentioned in a note on the General Introduction, § 3.]

Pharisees presented to him, with the intention of fulfilling them all. His zeal was honest, and he advanced far; he was regarded by those around him as pious and God-fearing. In the depth of his soul, however, the Divine Spirit testified the contrary to him; the life of the believers, whom in his zeal for the law he persecuted unto blood, shewed him something in which he was lacking. To the stirrings of this inward craving the power of grace attached itself, and the appearance of the Lord near Damascus darted like a ray from a higher world into his darkness. He was now penetrated by a feeling at once of the infinite impotence of man, and of the abounding power of grace. All his exertion in fulfilment of the law had resulted in a fighting against God and His holiest working; him, the fighter *against* God, grace in a moment changed into an instrument *for* His purposes. Hence the Apostle, after this experience, knew not how to preach anything save the grace of God in Christ, whereby man is enabled to accomplish whatever the rigid law can require, and still infinitely more, without becoming high-minded, void of love, or contemptuous towards the weak, inasmuch, namely, as it is grace that works all in him, not he himself by his own might. The words of Augustine—*Da quod jubes, Deus meus, et jube quod vis,*—contain, therefore, the whole system of the Apostle Paul.

Such being the nature of the contents of the Epistle to the Romans, it may be understood why it is usually regarded as very difficult. Indeed it may be said that where there is wanting in the reader's own life an experience analogous to that of the Apostle, it is utterly unintelligible. Everything in the epistle wears so strongly the impress of the greatest originality, liveliness, and freshness of experience; the Apostle casts so sure and clear a glance into the most delicate circumstances of the inward life in the regenerate; he contrives with such genius to place all that is individual in connexion with that which is most general, that the reader who stands on the limited, inferior ground of natural knowledge of the world, must at one time become dizzy at the vast prospects into the periods of development of the universe which St Paul discloses, and at croscopically exhibited circumstances which the Apostle unveils with respect to the most secret processes in the depth of the soul. Where, however, analogous inward experience, and the spiritual eye sharpened thereby, draw near, there theessential purport of the epistle makes itself clear, even to the simplest mind, as Luther has shown in the most popular manner in his celebrated preface to the Epistle to the Romans. It is not, however, my intention by this to deny that, even where experience is pre-supposed, there still remain considerable difficulties in the execution and form of the statement, and likewise in particular parts of the epistle—*e.g.*, in the dissertation on election; but these are still only the subordinate parts of the epistle, as compared with the leading main ideas respecting law and gospel. It would, however, be a great mistake to suppose from what has been said that it is intended to represent the study of the Epistle to the Romans as useless in cases where the transition from law to gospel has not yet been experienced; rather the thorough and laborious study of its profound contents is often the very means by which a yet defective experience trains itself. My intention is much more to warn against the employment of guides who, without a glimmering of the true sense of the Apostolic letter, can only hinder the beneficial effect of the study of it by their erroneous explanations.

§ 6. LITERATURE.

There is hardly any book of the New Testament which has been so frequently and fully treated as the Epistle to the Romans—a circumstance which is sufficiently explained by the significance of its contents. A comprehensive survey of the literature connected with this epistle is furnished by Reiche (pp. 95 seqq.); the following appear to be the principal works.

First, as to the Fathers of the Church—we have no commentary from that doctor who would have been qualified above all others for a deeply-grounded exposition of the epistle—Augustine. We possess by him only a fragmentary exposition of some passages, under the title, Expositio quarundam propositionum ex Epistola ad Romanos, and the commencement of a work on too extensive a plan, and therefore left incomplete. This does not embrace more than the greeting (i. 1–7), and is entitled Inchoata expositio epistolae ad Romanos. On the other hand, a commentary on the Epistle to the Romans by his celebrated opponent Pelagius is preserved among the works of Jerome and in the revision of Cassiodorus. The work of Origen on this book we possess only in Rufinus' translation, by which it has lost much of its value for us. Besides these, we have commentaries by Chrysostom and Theodoret, executed in their usual manner. The exposition by the so-called Ambrosiaster is peculiar; but his exposition of St Paul's Epistles is of more importance with reference to history than to doctrine. In later times Oecumenius and Theophylact employed themselves on the Epistles of St Paul, and also on the Catholic Epistles; their commentaries, however, contain but little of their own. But the Greek Fathers altogether have, in consequence of their Pelagianizing tendency, been very far from successful in the exposition of the Epistle to the Romans; the whole purport of the epistle was too remote from them to admit of their mastering it.

The middle ages were especially unfitted by the prevailing tendency to a legal system for the profitable illustration of the Epistle to the Romans. It was not until the Reformation that a new period for the interpretation of it commenced. Luther, indeed, was in the same case with Augustine; he left no commentary on this epistle. On the other hand, besides Calvin's profound work, the most intimate associate of Luther, Melanchthon, has presented us with an exposition in which we clearly trace the spirit of the great reformer. He published in 1522 a shorter exposition, under the title of Annotationes in Epistolam ad Romanos, Viteb. 1522, 4to. A more detailed commentary afterwards appeared under the title of Commentarii in Epist. ad Romanos, 1540, 8vo. Expositions of the Epistle to the Romans also appeared by Bugenhagen, Zwingli, Oecolampadius, Musculus, Bucer, in all which, however, as is easily accounted for, controversy against the Romish Church predominates. In the seventeenth century, and in the earlier half of the eighteenth, many additional commentaries appeared, in which the same polemical reference was prominent. Among the better of the expositors who took this direction is Sebastian Schmidt, (Commentarius in Ep. ad Romanos, Hamburg 1644); Abraham Calov, in his Biblia Illustrata, combats Grotius, and his often (especially in the exposition of the Epistle to the Romans) very shallow views. Among the [Roman] Catholics, Cornelius a Lapide wrote in the seventeenth century a commentary on this, and also on all the rest of St Paul's Epistles, which is still, at this day, not wholly without use. (Antwerp, 1614.)

From the middle of the last century until near its end, special expositions of the Epistle to the Romans were written by Baumgarten, (Halle, 1747.) Mosheim (whose work was edited by Boysen, 1770), Koppe (first in 1783, the latest edition, under the care of Von Ammon., appeared in 1824), Andr. Cramer (Kiel, 1784), and Morus (edited by Holzapfel, 1794).

After this, for about a quarter of a century,* no labour of any importance was bestowed on the epistle, until since 1820 the activity of literary men has again been directed to it. The latest expositions † are by Böckel, (Greifswalde, 1821), Tholuck (first edition, 1824 ; third edition, 1830), Flatt, (edited by Hoffmann, Tübingen, 1825), Stier, in the second Sammlung der Andeutungen (Leipzig, 1828, pp. 205–451) Klee ([Roman] Catholic in his view, Mainz, 1830), Rückert, (Leipzig, 1831), Benecke, (Heidelberg, 1831), Dr Paulus, (Heidelberg, 1831), Reiche, (2 vols., Göttingen, 1833–4), Glöckler, (Frankfort O. M., 1834) Köllner, (Göttingen, 1834), and Fritzsche, (Halle, 1836, vol. i.) A work very important for the doctrinal part of the exposition is Leonhard Usteri's Entwicklung des Paulinischen Lehrbegriffs (Zürich, 1833, fourth edition), Dähne's Paulinischer Lehrbegriff, (Halle, 1835), may also be compared. Earlier works of this kind, such as Meyer's Entwicklung der Paulinischer Lehrbegriffs, (Göttingen, 1801), are but little adapted for use according to the present standard of theological science.

* [Mehrere Decennien Hindurch.]

† Compare Kling's essay, Der Brief an die Römer und dessen neuere Baarbeitungen, in Klaiber's Stud. vol. iv., No. 2, pp. 59 seqq.; vol. v. No. i., pp. 1 seqq., and his review of Reiche and Köllner in the Stud. for 1836. No. 3.

EXPOSITION OF THE EPISTLE.

PART I.

(I. 1—I. 17.)

THE INTRODUCTION.

The Apostle opens the first part of his great doctrinal epistle, according to his usual practice in all his epistles, with a *salutation* (i. 1–7); but the fulness of the ideas which he brings before his readers even on his first address, is such as he seldom (and perhaps never in such a degree) thus early presents to them, and shows how entirely full his heart was with his subject; he hastens as it were even in the salutation to give a sketch of the whole contents of the composition which is to follow. With the salutation is immediately connected some introductory matter, concluding with the introduction of the theme, of which he designs to treat, (ver. 8–17.) We shall, therefore, consider the first part of the epistle, according to these two divisions.

§ 1. THE SALUTATION.

(I. 1–7.)

We find an entirely distinct character impressed upon the forms of salutation in St Paul's Epistles, in that they contain, instead of the χαίρειν (James i. 1) customary amongst the Greeks, a benediction accompanying the name, the calling, and the designation of those to whom the letter is addressed. The blessing thus added has the same tenor in all the epistles, except that in those to Timothy, besides *χάρις* and *εἰρήνη*, *ἔλεος* is also mentioned : the same phrase is used in the Second Epistle of St John, and a similar in the Epistle of St Jude—viz., *χάρις, εἰρήνη καὶ ἀγάπη πληθυνθέιη*, which last word is also found in the two Epistles of St Peter. Peculiar, however, to the salutation of the present epistle is the addition of intervening doctrinal statements, by means of which it is converted into a small self-contained whole ; in the Epistles to the Galatians and to Titus a similar peculiarity may be observed, but existing in a very inferior degree. In three parentheses, which may be distinguished by the usual marks, the Apostle directs attention in the salutation of his Epistle to the Romans—1, To the pre-announcement of the gospel by the prophets ; 2, to the dignity of the Redeemer; and, 3, to his own calling to the office of apostle; by means of these he would lead his readers to remark the nature of the gospel, as well as its historical connection with the Old Testament, and the personal relation in which the Apostle himself stood to it.

Ver. 1. St Paul generally calls himself at the beginning of his epistles simply *ἀπόστολος Ἰησοῦ Χρίστοῦ*, only in this place and Phil. i. 1, *δοῦλος Ἰησοῦ Χριστοῦ*, and in Tit. i. 1, *δοῦλος Θεοῦ*. The term *δοῦλος* designates here the spiritual condition of the Apostle in general, whilst *ἀπόστολος* defines it more exactly. He had been overcome by the Redeemer, conquered and subdued by His higher *δύναμις*, (i. 4.) But as one not merely outwardly conquered and still disposed to resist, but inwardly subdued, St Paul had at the same time become a willing instrument for executing the purposes of his Lord, as an Apostle. Since the article is wanting both to this word and to *δοῦλος*, we may observe that St Paul places himself upon a level with other servants and apostles of Christ, without, however, in this place (as in Galat. i. 1) defending his apostolical dignity with especial emphasis, since it had never been impugned by the Roman Christians. Only the epithet *κλητός* designates his office as not chosen by his own will, but one to which he was ordained by the will of God, (cf. Acts xxii. 21.) *Κλητός* has not, therefore, here the general meaning (Matt. xxii. 14), according to which every member of the Christian Church, to whom in any way the divine *κλῆσις* has come, is so designated, (as in ver. 6 below,) but that special meaning, according to which it is synonymous with *ἐκλεκτός*. From the general number of the *κλητόι*, a new and more exclusive κλῆσις (*i.e.* the ἐκλογή), called St Paul to be an Apostle. Consequently ἀπόστολος cannot here mean any itinerant teacher of the gospel whatsoever (as in Acts xiv. 4, 14, Rom. xvi. 7; 1 Cor. xii. 29), but it denotes (as Galat. i. 1, where the Apostle himself lays stress upon the word) a teacher chosen by Christ himself, and standing upon a level with the body of the Twelve. Besides St Paul, the only one whom we find in this high position, standing entirely parallel with the Twelve, is St James, the brother of the Lord, the Bishop of Jerusalem (cf. Notes on Galat. i. 19. ii. 9), who filled up that vacancy which occurred by the death of St James, the son of Zebedee (Acts xii. 1), without, however, having been formally elected, as St Matthias. In κλητός, therefore, the same thought is implied, as is expressed, 2 Cor. i. 1, by διὰ θελήματος Θεοῦ, or negatively in Galat. i. 1, by ὀυκ ἀπ' ἀνθρώπων. The words ἀφωρισμένος εἰς ἐυαγγέλιον Θεοῦ, appear therefore to be tautological if we refer them also, as is commonly done, to Θεος, as the Separator. Besides, if the Apostle had meant to say this of God, he would scarcely have added, Θεοῦ to ἐυαγγέλιον. It is therefore much better to regard this addition as a nearer definition of ἀπόστολος, and we may then, no doubt, see in them an obvious reference to the account given in Acts xiii. 2, where the *Holy Ghost* says, ἀφορίσατε δή μοι τὸν Βαρνάβαν καὶ τὸν Σαῦλον εἰς τὸ ἔργον, ὅ προσκέκλημαι αὐτόυς. Even Theodoret, amongst the Fathers, appears to have thought of this reference (as later Turretinus), in that he bids us remark how, not only the Father and the Son, but also the Holy Ghost, had sent forth the Apostle. The explanation of ἀφωρισμένος (in Hebrew, פָּרוּשׁ), by referring it to the former state of St Paul as a Pharisee, must be rejected altogether as a mere play upon words; neither is the element from which St Paul was separated to be regarded as the κόσμος, but as the Christian Church herself, to which he already belonged, when his original calling of God to be an Apostle was outwardly confirmed by the choice of the Church at Antioch. In the words ἐυαγγέλιον Θεοῦ, the genitive does not denote the object, for that is Chirst (ver. 3), but the author of the gospel. The words εἰς ἐυαγγέλιον are rightly resolved into εἰς τὸ κήρυγμα εὐαγγελίου, for unto the gospel in itself, *i. e.*, to the personal enjoyment and use of the gospel, every Christian is separated, but not every one is commissioned to teach it. (James iii. 1.)

Ver. 2. The first parenthesis* refers, as already remarked, to the relation of the gospel to the Old Testament Scriptures; it is intended thereby to declare that the former was not a thing entirely disconnected with the previous history of the world, but the blossom which had grown out of the roots of the Old Testament (cf. Acts xxvi. 22). St Paul does not, however, subjoin this remark, in order to encounter Jewish opponents, for such did not exist in Rome, but to impress upon his hearers from the very first that truth which he proves at greater length in a subsequent part of his epistle,—viz. that the Old and New Testaments are closely connected. It was needful that the relation of the two dispensations should be made not less plain to Gentiles than to Jews; we are not therefore, from such allusions to the Old Testament, to form any conclusion concerning the position of the Jews, and Judaizing Christians in Rome. *Θεός* is to be supplied as the subject of *προεπηγγείλατο* from the preceding *ἐυαγγέλιον Θεοῦ*. The prophets appear as the instruments of the divine will, and their communications are considered to be contained in the Holy Scriptures, whose divine authority is pre-supposed as a matter of course. The *προφῆται* are not, however, those persons merely who are called prophets in the more confined sense, but all the sacred writers, inasmuch as they were filled by God's Spirit. All the passages, therefore, which refer to the Messiah are included in these words, from Genes. iii. 25, to Malach. iv. 2; for wherever a prophecy was uttered concerning Christ, it was uttered concerning the gospel, for He is Himself the gospel.

Προεπαγγέλλεσθαι, "to promise or grant anything beforehand (before one's appearance)" is only found in this passage in the N. T.—*'Εν γραφαῖς ἁγίαις* we cannot take with Dr Paulus as signifying "in passages of holy Scripture." The reason of the omission of the article is simply this, that the expression is taken as denoting a well-known whole; the words are therefore to be translated, "in the collection of sacred writings with which you are so well acquainted." The O. T. was naturally introduced at once even into communities consisting of Gentile converts.

* Fritzsche wishes to connect *περὶ τοῦ υἱοῦ ἀυτοῦ*, not with *ἐυαγγέλιον Θεοῦ*, but with *προεπηγγείλατο*, so as to avoid making ver. 2 a parenthesis, and to consider it quite as part of the principal thought; but the position of *περὶ τ. υ. α.* does not appear suitable to this view. At the same time, we must allow that the parenthetical nature of the clauses in vers. 3, 5, is much more strongly marked than here.

Ver 3. The gospel of God treats of *His* Son, it is therefore most nearly connected with Himself, and a special object of His care. But the Apostle cannot mention the sacred person of the Son of God without entering into a closer definition of His nature; he describes Him, therefore, according to the two relations of His being, the human and the divine. The connection of *περὶ τοῦ υἱοῦ ἀυτοῦ* with *ἐυαγγελιον Θεοῦ* is no doubt the most natural, since *Ἰησοῦ Χριστοῦ* in the 4th verse evidently has regard in the same way to *υἱοῦ ἀυτοῦ*, passing over the second parenthesis. Of this latter sentence the first half *τοῦ γενομένου ἐκ σπέρματος Δαβὶδ κατὰ σάρκα* presents no difficulty. The meaning of *κατὰ σάρκα* can hardly be mistaken, if we define it by the help of the words in opposition to it *κατὰ πνεῦμα*; it will then signify the earthly human side of our Lord's being, that by which he was subject to birth and growth, that in which he appeared to the world. (*Γένεσθαι* is opposed to *εἶναι*. See Notes to St John, i. 1.) *Σάρξ* is, in fact, employed not merely to denote the substance of the flesh (see Notes vii., 14), but also the human soul and spirit, that is to say, a complete human nature, which is here designated by the word *σάρξ* only in order to express more strongly its identity with universal human nature (see Notes to viii. 3). The special reference to the *σπέρμα Δαβὶδ* is evidently occasioned by the mention of the prophecies in the preceding verse, which represent the Redeemer as being of the family of David according to His human nature.* It might, however, at first sight appear as if the Apostle used the name *ὁ υἱὸς τοῦ Θεοῦ* not only of the divine, but also of the human nature of Christ, that is of His whole Person, since *τοῦ γενομένου* is immediately connected with *υἱοῦ ἀυτοῦ*. But since, in the very next verse, the fourth, *υἱὸς Θεοῦ* is expressly applied to the divine nature, we must acknowledge that this connection of *γενομένου* with *υἱοῦ* can only be explained by supposing that reference is made to the *unity of the Person* in which the human and

* The supposition that St Paul here expresses his adoption of the Ebionite view of the generation of Christ by the words *ἐκ σπέρματος Δαβὶδ* is altogether inadmissible. Christ's descent from David through the Virgin Mary entirely justifies this expression. The Apostle's object did not the least call upon him to specify how Jesus was begotten of the Virgin Mary. Nothing but that rage for scepticism, which announces itself in the assertion that Christ was not at all descended from David's family, but that this descent was only attributed to Him on account of certain passages in the Old Testament, can believe itself warranted in using this passage as if it denied the generation of Christ by the Holy Spirit.

divine natures are so united that it is in general impossible to separate them expressly. That the application of this expression to the God-Man is admissible, is founded upon the fact, that the Lord as man is and may be called the Son of God just as well as He is so as God. When, however, we consciously separate the divine in Him from the human, the term υἱὸς Θεοῦ can *only* be applied to the divine nature of Christ, to the eternal Logos. (See this more fully discussed in the Notes to Luke i. 35.) On this account there is no tautology in the words of this and the fourth verse, υἱοῦ ἀυτοῦ—ὁρισθέντος υἱοῦ Θεοῦ, for the υἱοῦ Θεοῦ (ver. 4,) is to be taken in opposition to the υἱοῦ Δαβὶδ in ver. 3, or the υἱοῦ ἀνθρώπου which is implied in the first part of verse 4.

Ver. 4. He did not, therefore, also *become* such. He only manifested Himself as such in His eternal power. The words υἱὸς Θεοῦ form, therefore, in this place, an opposition and climax to the υἱὸς Δαβὶδ. Christ was both at the same time, the Son of God from eternity, the son of David in time. Amongst modern exegetical commentators, Rückert explains the passage in this manner with especial force and clearness. On account of the choice made of the word ὁρίζεσθαι, however, several ancient and modern commentators have understood the words in an entirely different sense. This word, namely, in the language of the N. T., means "to fix, to determine, to choose for some purpose." (Luke xxii. 22, Acts ii. 23, x. 42, xvii. 26.) From this was derived the translation, "God has chosen and appointed Him to be the Son of God," which would at once lead to the Jewish view of Christ's subordinate character, viz., that he was not the Son of God according to His being, but only by God's election (ἐκλογή). (Justin Martyr. Dial. c. Tryph. Jud., p. 267.) In close connection with the above stands another interpretation, which makes ὁρισθέντος to mean the same thing as προορισθέντος, a word which Epiphanius has even admitted into the text. Accordingly the expression is translated *prædestinatus est,* and referred to God's decree with respect to the incarnation. (Iren. adv. hær. iii. 22, 32. August. de prædestin. sanct., c. 15.) But both views, to say nothing of the untenableness of the former on doctrinal grounds, must be rejected, because rom the connection it is manifestly not the decree of God, but the *proof* before men of Christ's divine Sonship, that is here in question. No other course, therefore, remains but to take ὁρίζεσθαι in the sense "to declare, to exhibit as something," as Chrysostom has already rightly done. This explanation of the expression is, as far as the thought contained in it goes, sufficiently supported by passages such as Acts ii. 22, in which Christ is called "ἀνὴρ ἀπὸ τοῦ Θεοῦ ἀποδεδειγμένος δυνάμεσι καὶ τέρασι." We may therefore render ὁρισθέντος, with Chrysostom, by δειχθέντος, αναφανθέντος. Only there is some difficulty in proving that ὁρίζεσθαι is ever used in this sense. For ὁρίζω always means originally "to define the boundaries," ὁρίζεσθαι, "to determine or mark out for one's self," *i.e.*, to decree. No passage in which it means directly "declarare, ostendere," is to be found either in profane or scriptural writers. At the same time, the notion that Christ was decreed to be the Son of God by His resurrection, is so entirely at variance with every doctrinal system, and the whole range of scriptural ideas, as well as with the language of the Bible, (for, even supposing that υἱὸς Θεοῦ meant nothing more than "Messiah," yet Christ was not first appointed or made Messiah by His resurrection), that nothing remains but to decide that the Apostle has here used the word in a rather wider sense, since it must mean in the present passage, in accordance with the connection, "to prove, or present." It can, after all, only be regarded as an accidental circumstance, that a convincing example of this use of the word is wanting; for when a man is defined as to his character by means of some public act, such as the resurrection, he is at once thereby declared to be that which he really is. Thus only too can ἐν δυνάμει be fitly connected with ὁρίζεσθαι; the resurrection is in fact considered as an expression of the almighty power of God, as it is also usually represented in other places of the N. T., (Acts xvii. 32; Rom. iv. 24; 1 Cor. xv. 3, 17.) But that expression could not be employed of the divine decree, and any other connection whatsoever of the words ἐν δυνάμει is totally untenable. But if it has ever been held, as even Tholuck believes, that the resurrection of Christ was not adapted to prove the higher nature of Christ, it is because men have started in this assertion with the supposition that the resurrection of Christ, like the resurrection of Lazarus, was nothing but the revival of his mortal body; but in our exposition of the history of the resurrection we have proved at length, that the resurrection was the glorification of the humanity of Christ, a view which gives to this event an importance such as the N. T. attributes to it. We have already remarked, in our observations on Matth. xxii. 29, that this is the only passage in which *ἀνάστασις νεκρῶν* stands instead of *ἐκ νεκρῶν*.* But no doubt it is only the preceding *ἐκ* which has caused the omission of that preposition before *νεκρῶν*. To understand this formula as having the same signification as *ἐξ οὗ ἀνέστη*, and to refer it to the work of the glorified Redeemer by means of His Spirit in the Church, would not be objectionable with respect to the idea; the fact of the resurrection is always presented to us in the N. T. as that from which the ascension and all the operations of the Spirit in the Church proceed as simple consequences. But *κατὰ πνεῦμα* can only form in this place, according to the context, the opposition to *κατὰ σάρκα*, and cannot, therefore, be referred to the operations of the Spirit; and, moreover, if this reference were not admitted, that is to say, if we took *ἐξ ἀναστάσεως* as merely indicating the time at which the operations of Christ began to manifest themselves, no stress would be laid upon the resurrection as especially declaring Him to be the Son of God. Finally, with respect to the expression *κατὰ πνεῦμα ἁγιωσύνης*, the indeterminateness of the word *ἁγιωσύνη* in the language of the N. T. prevents us from gaining any certain clue to its meaning, and we must therefore be guided entirely by the context. For which *ἁγιότης* signifies the state of holiness (Hebr. xii. 10; 2 Maccab. xv. 2), and *ἁγιασμὸς* denotes the becoming holy or sanctification (Rom. vi. 19; 1 Thess. iv. 3; 2 Thess. ii. 13), *ἁγιωσύνη* is sometimes taken as synonymous with *ἁγιασμὸς* (2 Cor. vii. 1; 1 Thess. iii. 13), and sometimes appears to be equivalent to *ἁγιότης*. In a mere question of language it might be considered, therefore, equivalent to *πνεῦμα ἅγιον*. But if resting on this grammatical possibility we were to apply the expression of the text to those prophecies of the O. T. which were given by the Holy Ghost, (as if

* The expression *ἀνάστασις νεκρῶν* has so fixed an usage as signifying the resurrection of the *body*, that we cannot suppose there is in this any reference to that *spiritual* resurrection, which Christ brought into the world; perhaps, however, St Paul here chose an expression which does not so emphatically designate the resurrection of Jesus alone, *ἀνάστασις ἐκ νεκρῶν*, in order to intimate, that with Him the saints of the Old Testament had also risen (Matth. xxvii. 53.) At the same time this also was but a partial *ἀνάστασις*, and it was therefore necessary to distinguish the *ἀνάστασις νεκρῶν* once more from the *ἀνάστασις τῶν νεκρῶν*.

the words stood *καθὼς τὸ πνεῦμα ἅγιον προείρηκε*), or to that Spirit who was imparted to Christ at His baptism, both interpretations would be inadmissible, according to the context, which must here alone decide. The opposition to *κατὰ σάρκα* requires it to refer to the Person of the Redeemer Himself, and therefore the third Person of the Godhead cannot here be meant, though certainly the divine nature of Christ may be. In order to denote this the expression *πνεῦμα* is chosen on account of the *σάρξ* which has gone before, just in the same way as in 1 Pet. iii. 18, compared with Rom. ix. 5. The divine nature of the *υἱὸς Θεοῦ* is therefore here very properly said to consist in the *πνεῦμα*, which is the substance of God (John iv. 24), and forms an opposition to the *σάρξ*, in which the eternal Word veiled Himself (John i. 14). (See also 1 Tim. iii. 16, 1 John iv. 2, 2 John *v.* 7, Heb. ii. 14.) But this Spirit, as the absolute Spirit, is not only in Himself the Holy One, but also the Sanctifier of collective humanity, *i. e.*, He who communicates His nature to the creatures; this last sense, however, does not come prominently forward in this place, which is occupied more particularly with the description of the person of the Lord himself.

Ver. 5. At the naming of the holy name of Jesus Christ, the common Lord of all believers, the Apostle feels himself constrained to expatiate in another parenthesis on that which this bountiful Lord had done for him, who was so undeserving of it. We must not think that any polemical allusion is intended (as in Galat. i. 1), and therefore suppose an implied contrast of *ὸν δι' ἀνφρώπων* with *δι' οὗ*. St Paul mentions this grace of the Lord out of a pure feeling of thankfulness for the mercy which had been shown to him. *Χάρις καὶ ἀποστολή* is not to be taken as *ἕν διὰ δυοῖν*, but as a designation of the general grace (that of calling and forgiveness of sins), and of the particular grace (his election to be an Apostle). Augustin says justly, "gratiam cum omnibus fidelibus, apostolatum non cum omnibus communem habet." On account of the *αποστολή*, and the nearer definition added to it, *ἐλάβομεν* can only refer to the Apostle. The whole following sentence, *εἰς ὑπακοὴν πίστεως ἐν πᾶσι τοῖς ἔθνεσιν ὑπὲρ τοῦ ὀνόματος αὐτοῦ* is Hebraistic, and answers to the words חָאֱמוּנָה בְּכֹל הַגּוֹיִם עַל שְׁכוּר לְהִשָּׁמוּעַ.
In pure Greek this must have run, *ἵνα ὑπακούωσι δι' ἐμοῦ*

πάντα τὰ ἔθνη τῇ πίστει κ. τ. λ. St Paul often uses the word *ὑπακοή* (the opposite to *παρακοή*, "neglect of hearing, the turning a deaf ear," 2 Cor. x. 6), for instance, Rom. xv. 18, xvi. 19, (also found 1 Pet. i. 2), in the sense of "obedience to the influences of divine grace," properly the listening to anything, giving earnest heed to it. *Πίστις* (see this subject treated more at length in the Notes on Rom. iii. 21) does not mean the doctrines of the faith, but the disposition of faith which necessarily supposes the *ὑπακοή*. But the operations of the Apostle were to extend to the whole Gentile world, and therefore the Romans could not be excluded from them, since their city was the centre of all Gentile life. (cf. ver. 11.) Of the words *ὑπὲρ τοῦ ὀνόματος αὐτοῦ* we must certainly regard the most important meaning to be "for the honour and glory of His name" (cf. Acts xv. 26, xxi. 13), where *ὄνομα* = שֵׁם, stands for the being, the personality itself (cf. Comm. on Matth. xviii. 21, 22, John xiv. 11–14). At the same time we must not overlook the fact, that in the language of St Paul, as in the discourse of all persons of comprehensive minds, especially when their style is not perfectly formed, sentences often occur which are loosely and indeterminately connected, and therefore allow of manifold applications. Such instances of grand indefiniteness a considerate expositor will not dare to sweep away with a single hasty explanation ; he will take them just as they present themselves. The wide range and bearing of single thoughts gives, in fact, a peculiar charm to the language ; it enables us to take a view of the world of the author's ideas, even though it did not permit him, on account of its very riches, to express at one time all that filled his mind as he desired. Thus, in this very instance, it cannot be denied that the connection, which Tholuck has defended, of these words with *ὑπακοὴ πίστεως*, so as to give the meaning, "ut obediatur fidei ob ejus nomen," is just as unstrained as the above ; *all things in all both are and shall be for God and for the execution of His will,* whether it be St Paul's apostolical office, or the faith of the whole heathen world, or that of every individual member of the Church.

Vers. 6, 7. The Christians in Rome therefore are also members of that great Gentile world which was committed to him ; and in that place the Gentile element from the very beginning assumed considerable prominence in the Church. The glory of their calling to be members of the kingdom of God, the Apostle represents by means of several commendatory epithets ; he styles them called, beloved of God, holy. The name ἀγαπητοὶ Θεοῦ is not found in any other place in the N. T. It answers to the Hebrew יָחִיד or דוֹד. This name, as well as the following, ἅγιοι, denotes Christians to be the spiritual Israel of the new covenant ; for what is called Israel after the flesh in the N. T. also bears the name קְדשִׁים, Deuter. xxxiii. 3, 1 Sam. ii. 9, Ps. iv. 4. With regard to ἅγιος, ἁγιάζειν, see the observations on John xvii. 17, and Acts ix. 13. The word, in its proximate meaning, denotes no degree of moral perfection (the Corinthians, who were in so many respects deserving of blame, are called ἅγιοι), but refers to the separation of believers from the great mass of the κόσμος, the Gentile world. But doubtless the idea is also implied, that Christians have been made partakers of the principle of a higher moral life, which, as in a course of development, is gradually to pervade the whole man, and produce perfect holiness. Now this principle is the Spirit of Christ, so that St Paul's idea, ἐχαρίτωσεν ἡμᾶς ἐν τῷ ἠγαπημένῳ, is also to be applied to the conception of ἅγιος. Christians are holy on account of Christ, who lives in them, and who is their true self. The very juxtaposition of κλητοί and ἅγιοι, which we find here, points to the gradual development of holiness ; for, as Augustin justly observes, " non ideo vocati sunt, quia sancti erant, sed ideo sancti effecti, quia vocati sunt."

The words χάρις ὑμῖν καὶ εἰρήνη, finally, contain the special form of salutation. Χάρις is no doubt the Latin *salus*, which was also the customary form of greeting in letters ; but in the mouth of the Apostle this expression, as well as εἰρήνη, which is the Eastern form, receives a deeper significance. Χάρις and εἰρήνη are related to one another as cause and effect ; χάρις is the divine ἀγάπη manifesting itself towards sinful humanity, εἰρήνη is that state of inward harmony of life which arises in the man from the reception of the χάρις. Grace, however, does not merely begin the new life ; it also supports it every moment, and is capable of an infinite increase, as a consequence of which the εἰρήνη is also perfected in its turn. The *source* of grace is God, the Father of all men ; the *organ* by which it is communicated is the Son, the eternal Word (John i. 1), by whom all things were originally made, and by whom the fallen creature must be again restored. And nothing, we may observe, speaks more decisively for the divinity of Christ, than these juxtapositions of Christ with the eternal God, which run through the whole language of Scripture, and the derivation of purely divine influences from Him also. The name of no man can be placed at the side of that of the Almighty. He only, in whom the Word of the Father, who is himself God, became flesh, may be named beside Him; for men are commanded to honour Him, even as they honour the Father. (John v. 23.)

§ 2. INTRODUCTION.

(I. 8-17.)

The Apostle begins the letter itself with the expression of his hearty joy for the faith of the Romans, and with the mention of his desire to be permitted to visit them. For, since his commission was directed to all Greeks and barbarians, he naturally entertained the wish to preach the gospel at Rome also. The essence of this gospel St Paul immediately points out to be *that righteousness of God by faith* which is revealed in it; he thus then propounds the subject, which he intends to treat more at length in the epistle itself.

Ver 8. St Paul opens most of his epistles with giving thanks to God for the faith of his readers; it is only in the second Epistle to the Corinthians, and in that to the Galatians, where he was obliged to find decided fault, that this thanksgiving is wanting. But as in the life of the believer every thing is received through his relation to the Redeemer, so also here the Apostle thanks God διὰ Ἰησοῦ Χριστοῦ. We must not regard this as a mere phrase, but as a true expression of the Apostle's deepest consciousness. Thanksgiving and prayer are only pleasing to God when offered through the Spirit of Christ dwelling in the heart. The object of these thanks is, however, the Roman Christians themselves, not anything in them, for the life of faith is a matter of the deepest inward personality; by means of this life St Paul had, as it were, himself gained them, and could therefore return thanks for them as brothers given to him. It followed from the very nature of the case, that the faith of the Roman Christians would be known generally amongst believers, since Rome, as the capital of the world, had connections with all parts of it, hence Irenæus (iii. 3) designates the Roman Church as that, "in quâ fideles undique conveniunt." In the faith of the capital city, therefore, was contained, in the Apostle's view, the pledge that this faith would soon spread itself universally over the Gentile world.

St Paul had in his mind at first a *δεύτερον δέ* to correspond to the preceding *πρῶτον μέν*, but left the second half of the sentence uncompleted. Instead of *ὑπέρ* A.B.C.D., read *περί*, which is indeed often interchanged with *ὑπέρ*; at the same time we may very well prefer *ὑπέρ* in this place, as it seems to express the more uncommon thought, that the Romans themselves are the object of the Apostle's thanks. That no stress is to be laid upon *ἐν ὅλῳ τῷ κόσμῳ*, is self-evident; we must refer it to the countries in which the gospel had already spread itself; beyond the limits of the Christian Church little was as yet known of Christianity.

Ver 9. As the reason of the thanks, which *he* presented to God on their behalf, the Apostle appeals to his continual prayers for them, prayers which he no doubt offered up to God, as for the Roman community, so also for all the churches in the world. This calling God to witness is not here intended to obviate any mistrust on the part of his readers, but only to give the thought more emphasis. But if St Paul here calls himself the servant of God, as he above called himself the servant of Christ, it is plain that he only served God through Christ, and in Christ only served God. The expression *λατρεύω*, however, represents more the spiritual aspect of the relation, than *δουλεύω* (see Phil. iii. 3). And therefore in this place (as well as in the passage cited) the worship is referred to the *πνεῦμα*, without, however, any antithesis to the Jewish religion being intended. Against Theodoret's interpretation of these words as designating a spiritual gift, on account of which the Apostle rejoiced, it is sufficient to adduce the *μοῦ*; but it is also inadmissible to take *πνεῦμα μου* as a mere designation of personality. Both *σῶμα* and *ψυχή* can be put to represent personality, by no means, however, promiscuously, but under such conditions as are supplied by the context. (See on this subject Olshausen opusc. theol. p 156, seqq.) With regard to the addition, *ἐν τῷ ἐυαγγελιῳ*, we are not to think merely of St Paul's activity as a teacher, the words denote also that element in which his own personal religious life was exercised, and his worship of God performed. That strong form of affirmation, which has something of the nature of an adjuration, *μάρτυς μου ὁ Θεός*, is often found in St Paul's writings. See 2 Cor. i. 23, xi. 31; Phil. i. 8; 1 Thess. ii. 5. The *ὡς* before *ἀδιαλείπτως* is here rightly taken by Fritzsche as equivalent to *ὅτι*; Calvin, Heumann, Flatt, Reiche, take it erroneously in the sense *quam*.—(The form *ἀδιαλείπτως μνέιαν ποιοῦμαι* is one of the favourite expressions of St Paul, see Ephes. i. 15; Phil. i. 3; Col. i. 3; 1 Thess. i. 2.)

Ver. 10. As the subject of his prayers, St Paul now mentions his wish to reach Rome, by which visit the Romans would receive the surest pledge of his frequent thoughts of them. This desire, with respect to which the Apostle expatiates at some length in what follows, doubtless proceeded from his longing to preach the word of reconciliation at the very centre of the Gentile world. He could not think that he had fulfilled the command which the Lord had laid upon him before he had preached the gospel in Rome, the mistress of the world.

Ἔιπως ἤδη ποτε must be rendered, "if not at length at some time." See on the use of *ἤδη* in the sense "at length," Hartung's Partikellehre. vol. i., p. 283.—*Εὐοδοῦν* means strictly "to prepare a good way for some one," and then generally "to further, to favour," and therefore *ἐνοδοῦσθαι* must signify "to proceed favourably, to succeed." (See 1 Cor. xvi. 2; 3 John ver. 2.) The Apostle has learnt to place himself and his plans entirely under God's guidance and superintendence.

Ver. 11. Entirely possessed with the great object of his calling, St Paul longs to communicate to others out of the fulness of his own spiritual life in Rome also, and to strengthen the believers there. We are not to think, as Reiche justly remarks, of any of the extraordinary gifts of the Spirit (1 Cor. xii.) as intended by this *χάρισμα πνευματικόν*, for St Paul did not estimate these so highly as to consider the communication of them the business of his life; but we are to understand by it the spiritual renewal of faith, and love, and hope, in short of the Christian life in general. (*Χάρισμα* = *δώρημα*, Rom. v. 16, 17.) The Apostle therefore presupposes that the spark of the divine life has been kindled in his readers, and only contemplates the increase of the same.

Στηριχθηναι = *βεβαιοῦσθαι*, Rom. xvi. 25; 1 Thess. iii. 2, 13;

2 Thess, ii. 17. As to εἰς τὸ with an infinitive following, see Winer's Grammar, p. 304.

Ver. 12. Far, however, from wishing to intrude himself upon the Roman Christians as a teacher, the humble-minded Apostle only places himself upon a level with them as a brother; he desires to establish himself together with them in the faith.

The compound word συμπαρακαλεῖσθαι is only found in this passage in the N. T. in the sense, "mutually to strengthen one another in spirit." The infinitive is to be taken as standing in opposition to στηριχθῆναι, not, as Tholuck asserts, to be referred back to ἐπιποθῶ, in fact it explains στηριχθῆναι only. The words ἐν ἀλλήλοις must, as Reiche well observes, denote that which is *reciprocally* strengthening and quickening in the life of faith. On the other hand, that which is *common* to all in the possession of faith is expressly declared, and more distinctly brought before the consciousness, in the words ὑμῶν τε καὶ ἐμοῦ.

Ver. 13. St Paul's *wish* to go to Rome had already several times grown into a distinct resolution,* but at the same time he had always been prevented from carrying his resolution into effect. Nothing at all is known of the causes which hindered him; whatever, therefore, may be said on this subject can only rest upon mere conjecture. St Paul represents as the object of his journey to Rome, "that he might have some fruit there also," such as he had already gathered amongst the other Gentiles. That, by this fruit, he meant nothing for himself, but only acquisitions for the kingdom of God, is manifest; at the same time, under the influence of pure love he regards this as his own gain, according to the principle, "all things are yours."

St Paul frequently uses the formula, οὐ θέλω ὑμᾶς ἀγνοεῖν, see 1 Cor. x. 1, 2 Cor. i. 8. For this very reason, the reading οὐκ οἶμαι, furnished by DEG, is perhaps to be preferred, because the alteration of so common a form of expression is scarcely to be expected. This is the only passage in the N.T. in which δεῦρο denotes time, it is elsewhere constantly used of place. The reading τινὰ καρπὸν is by all means to be preferred, as well on account of its MSS. authority, as for the sake of the sense; καρπόν τινα would

* According to Act xxiii. 11, the Apostle St Paul had a vision of Christ, in which it was expressly said to him, "Thou must bear witness of me at Rome also." But this vision did not take place until *after* the composition of the Epistle to the Romans.

imply a doubt whether any fruit of his labours would ever be seen, and to doubt this were to doubt the power of Christ. The image of the sower lies at the bottom of the expression καρπός in the Apostle's mind.

Ver. 14. St Paul regards his relation to the Gentile world as that of a debtor who has to pay his creditors. In the gospel an infinite treasure had been committed to him, out of which he considered himself bound to impart to all Gentiles, without exception. The expression, Ἕλλησί τε καὶ βαρβάροις signifies, therefore, nothing more than the universal heathen world; the Jews, whom even Philo (*vit. Mos.* p. 685) reckons amongst the barbarians, are not mentioned at all here, since St Paul did not consider himself as their debtor. (See Notes to Galat. ii. 7.) The Romans, however, inasmuch as they partook of the general civilization of the world at that time, are naturally to be reckoned amongst the Greeks, which expression in the Apostle's time had lost, to a certain degree, its merely national application, and had obtained this wider meaning, merely because the culture of the old world had proceeded from the Greeks. The second contrast, σοφοῖς τε καὶ ἀνοήτοις is not, however, by any means parallel to the first; amongst the Greeks there were many ἀνόητοι, and amongst the barbarians were to be found individual σοφόι. Whilst, therefore, the first contrast is founded upon a general distinction, the second refers to particular, individual differences; but the gospel is equally well calculated for all differences of national and personal character, and therefore St Paul regards himself as a debtor to the whole of the vast Gentile world. These expressions would, however, have a very startling effect in the Epistle to the Romans, if, as Baur supposes, the Church in Rome had indulged in a Judaizing tendency, and was therefore composed for the greater part of Jews. But the supposition, either that St Paul was entirely silent about his readers, or else (if we consider the Jews included in this expression), counted them amongst the barbarians, cannot certainly be admitted.

Ver. 15. From this his general spiritual relation, St Paul then deduces his readiness to serve the Romans also.

With respect to the grammatical connection of this verse with the preceding, we may best consider οὕτω as elicited by a καθώς, to be understood in verse 14. To connect it with the καθώς so far back as verse 13, only increases the difficulty. At the same time it is not absolutely necessary to supply *καθώς*; for the sentences may be much better taken merely consecutively according to the analogy of Acts xvii. 33, xxvii. 17, 44, 1 Cor. xi. 28, xiv. 25. "I am debtor to all the Gentiles—so, as such, I am ready to preach to you also." Thus in profane writers also *ὅυτως* stands directly for *ὅυτος*. (See Matthiœ's Gr. Gramm. vol. ii. p. 1235.) The words *τὸ κατ' ἐμὲ πρόθυμον* are best taken in the sense, "my inclination, my readiness." *Πρόθυμον*, as substantive, is found in the best authors, *e. g.* Eurip. Medea. v. 178; Iphig. Taur. v. 989. And *κατ' ἐμέ* is a circumlocution for *ἐμοῦ*, this form of expression being chosen to point more distinctly to *καθ' ὑμᾶς* on the other side.—*Εὐαγγελίζω* and *εσθαι* = בִּשֵּׂר is construed in the N. T.either with *τινί* or *τινά*.

Ver. 16. With a sudden, but, as far as the thought is concerned, well-managed transition, St Paul now comes to the nature of the gospel itself. Both the doctrine of Christ crucified, and the circumstances under which it must be preached in Rome, seemed to the eye of man to render a successful result of St Paul's preaching there very improbable. In the magnificent capital of the earthly potentate of the then world,* in a city where all the schools of Grecian philosophy had their representatives, it might well appear hopeless to the natural man to preach the crucified Son of God, a Master who could only promise his disciples death and suffering as far as this world was concerned. Nevertheless, under the conviction of that divine power which resided in the gospel, St Paul utters his *οὐκ επαισχύνομαι*. This must be considered as a Litotes, inasmuch as the preaching of the gospel was to him the subject of his highest glory (1 Tim. i. 8, etc.) In order to show plainly how little cause there was for him to be ashamed of the gospel, he terms it a *δύναμις Θεοῦ*. The expression combines a reference to the exalted source, and to the almighty power of the gospel, which stand in strange contrast with its insignificant, yea strange, startling outward appearance, at which both Jews and Gentiles stumbled. (1 Cor. ii. 2, &c.) It is not, however, the *doctrine* in itself which is regarded as this *δύναμις*, but the doctrine in living unity with the

* Alexander Morus says very strikingly on this subject, "audax facinus ad crucem vocare terrarum dominos." See Reiche on this passage.

events to which it is related. The gospel is a *divine act*, which continues to operate through all ages of the world, and that not in the first place outwardly, but inwardly, in the depths of the soul, and for eternal purposes. (Σωτηρία is the opposite to ἀπώλεια. See Matth. xviii. 11. Because salvation from temporal and eternal ruin is the highest end of Christianity, the gospel itself is called εὐαγγέλιον τῆς σωτηρίας, and Christ ἀρχηγὸς τῆς σωτηρίας.) The condition of its operation in man is only πίστις. (With respect to the conception of πίστις, see the notes to Rom. iii. 21.) The medicine only works when it is taken by the patient, and, in like manner, the gospel is only effectual when the man receives it in faith. But this faith is of God's grace possible to every one, the time of whose calling has arrived; the Jews have, however, the first claim to this calling, The contradistinction of Jews and Greeks has nothing in common with that of Greeks and barbarians in ver. 14. There the Apostle was speaking of his personal relation to all classes of the Gentile world, here he is speaking of the purely objective relation of the gospel to the human race. Looking at mankind as presented to us in the divine economy of the world, he considers it divided into two halves, the Jewish and the Gentile world, and ascribes to all the privilege of being called to believe, whilst he recognizes a certain prerogative on the part of the Jews (see also ii. 9, 10.) This prerogative was no mere pretension advanced on the part of that people from pride and blindness,* but a divine ordinance, which had the design of erecting amongst the people of Israel a hearth and an altar for God,† from which, as a centre, the sacred fire might then be more easily spread over the whole earth. (See notes to John iv. 22.) How the Jews lost the advantage thus assigned to them, by their unbelief, is mentioned later, in chapter x.

Ver. 17. The Apostle again, by means of the particle γάρ, annexes the reason, why the gospel could be thus effectual as a

* From the general prevalence of this view arose, no doubt, the omission of πρῶτον, observable in some MSS., viz., B, G, which is, however, certainly quite erroneous. No doubt, in the case of the Jews, there was frequently connected with the consciousness of their election, arrogance and contempt of the Gentiles, instead of humility; but the conviction of their election was not, on that account, by any means, itself an error.

† Πρῶτον is therefore not merely to be referred, as is done by the Greek Fathers, to the earlier calling, but also to their larger endowment with the gifts and fulness of grace. Theodoret erroneously asserts that πρῶτον designates merely τάξεως τιμὴν, οὐ χάριτος πλεονασμόν.

divine power unto eternal salvation; namely, because in it a new way of salvation is discovered, "*the righteousness of God, proceeding from faith.*" The explanation of the leading ideas in the theme which the Apostle thus proposes, *i.e.*, the *δικαιοσύνη Θεοῦ*, and *πίστις*, will be found in the introductory observations on iii. 21. I will only make this preliminary remark, that the former word does not here signify the divine attribute of righteousness, or goodness, or faithfulness, as has been supposed, but that the Apostle opposes the *δικαιοσύνη Θεοῦ* (or *εκ Θεοῦ*, Phil. iii. 9), to the *δικαιοσύνη ἐκ νόμου* (or *ἐξ ἀνθρώπου. i.e., ἰδία*), and regards the whole peculiar influence of the gospel as determined by this difference. The realization of absolute perfection (Matth. v. 18) is the highest end of man's existence; the law could not effect this any further than the bringing forth of an outward legality, but by regeneration an inward condition is through grace produced in believers, the *δικαιοσύνη Θεοῦ*, which answers the highest requirements. This new way of salvation was hidden from all eternity (Ephes. iii. 9; 1 Cor. ii. 7), it needed therefore to be *revealed* by Christ in His actual accomplishment of the work of redemption; St Paul's business was simply to communicate this information. From the connection with ver. 16, which exalts the gospel as the *power* of God, it is plain, that *δικαιοσύνη Θεοῦ* cannot signify the mere declaring a person righteous, but the real making him righteous. This St Paul declares not only of those who were then living, but also of all later generations, because he considered the righteousness of all as absolutely realized in Christ. That which in Him was perfected once for all, is gradually transmitted to individual men in proportion to the degree of their renewal, and is received by them in faith, and reckoned to their account. Peculiar in the present passage is the addition of *εἰς πίστιν*. But doubtless this is not so to be understood, as if in this place an increase of faith were intended, an inward development of faith from a lower degree to a higher, the advance from a more external mode of personally appropriating salvation to an inward mode. There was plainly no occasion whatsoever here for St Paul to allude to the development of faith, which in itself must by all means be acknowledged to be a fact; on the contrary, if we were to adopt this interpretation, the principal point connected with the mention of the righteousness of God, namely, that it proceeded (on man's part) *from* faith, would remain entirely untouched, Ἐκ does not therefore indicate in this place, as Reiche has justly remarked, the *point of departure* with respect to an *advance*, but the *ground of obtaining* righteousness, the personal appropriation of the divine benefit, which becomes also particularly clear, if we for a moment leave εἰς πίστιν out of sight.

In the same way that the Apostle proves in a subsequent part of his Epistle (chap. iv.) by the example of Abraham, that, even in the case of the pious men who lived before Christ, it was faith which made them righteous; so also in this place he describes the new way of salvation in its historical connection. We must not consider this a mere accommodation, and application of Old Testament expressions to entirely different relations; this retrospective use of the O. T. is rather to be derived from that scriptural fundamental view of it, which supposes that in it all the germs of the N. T. are already really contained, and that, therefore, the N. T. is only the πλήρωσις of the Old. (See notes to Matth. v. 17.) The quotation from Habak. ii. 4, is also made use of in Galat. iii. 11, and Hebr. x. 38, in both with reference to faith, and the righteousness of the N. T., and we must acknowledge with justice, since it is but *one* faith at different stages of its development which is represented in both the Old and New Testament. (See Hebr. xi. 1, etc.) Eternal life (ζήσεται is used in a pregnant sense = ζωὴν αἰώνιον ἕξει) is never obtained otherwise than by means of faith. According to the Hebrew text, צַדִּיק בֶּאֱמוּנָתוֹ יִחְיֶה, ἐκ πίστεως cannot be connected with δίκαιος, yet it must be thus taken according to the sense in which it is used by St Paul. We frequently meet with such free interpretations of the O. T. text, and it has already been remarked, that the indeterminateness of the connections in the Hebrew very much favours such a proceeding.* Applied in a profane spirit, as by the Rabbinical writers, this method perverts the Scripture; but when exercised in the Holy Spirit, this liberty is a means of manifesting the infinite fulness of its contents. (The LXX. must have read בֶּאֱמוּנָתִי, for they translate it ἐκ πίστεώς μου, and ascribe faith, *i.e.*, faithfulness, to God. But the faithfulness of God is doubtless manifested in sending the Messiah, and in his work, so that this way of taking the passage leads us back to the right thought again.)

* See the notes to Luke iv. 18, 19.

PART II.

(I. 18—XI. 36.)

THE DOCTRINAL EXPOSITION.

SECTION I.

OF THE SINFULNESS OF THE HUMAN RACE.

(I. 18—III. 20.)

THE very nature of the Apostle's undertaking required that he should prove the necessity that existed for a new method of salvation for man, before he entered upon his account of the true nature of that method. It was further requisite that this necessity should be pointed out in both those great divisions, under which the human race is considered according to the idea of the kingdom of God, that is to say, amongst Jews as well as Gentiles or Greeks ; in order that it might plainly appear that such a new and complete way was needed by both in common. St Paul, therefore, from the 18th to the 32nd verse of the first chapter, treats exclusively of the condition of the Gentiles; from the 1st to the 29th verses of the 2nd chapter, the Jews principally occupy his attention ; and lastly, from the 1st to the 20th verse of the 3d chapter, he draws a parallel between the two, in which he considers the different relations in which they stand to the remedy provided by the mercy of God. We will treat this first section according to these three divisions.

§ 3.—CONDITION OF THE HEATHEN WORLD.

(I. 18–32).

In describing the necessity of a new way of salvation for the heathen world, the Apostle naturally set out with considering their depraved moral condition.* But it was also required that this state of alienation from God should be traced to its origin. Even the Gentile world was not without some knowledge of God, and in con-

* See Usteri's Paulinischer Lehrbegriff, 4th ed. p. 15, sqq., and the passages there quoted.

sequence some insight into the divine law; but the knowledge which was thus within their reach, the Gentiles lost by their own fault, and with their theoretical errors, the stream of their practical transgressions rose to a most fearful height. The mere recovery of that general knowledge of God, which they once possessed, could, of course, effect nothing in this evil case, for if it had not been effectual in preventing them from sinking into vice, still less could it raise the mass from the slough of iniquity into which it had fallen; it was therefore necessary that a new element of life, a *δύναμις Θεοῦ* should be introduced into the world, and that by its means the possibility should be given of a new beginning for man; such the gospel proved itself to be.

Ver. 18. The Apostle had already used *γὰρ* three times in succession in the 16th-17th verses, and uses it yet a fourth time, in order to connect this verse with the preceding, as (1 Cor. ix. 16, &c.) For he is contrasting the revelation of God's righteousness in the gospel with the revelation of his wrath in the law, as the former comes *εἰς πίστιν. i. e., εἰς πάντας πιστεύοντας*, so the latter *ἐπὶ πᾶσαν ἀσέβειαν.* But the last *γὰρ* connects what follows in such a manner with what has gone before, as to direct attention to the life which is by faith: "Those only who are just by faith shall live, for God's wrath reveals itself against all unrighteousness" (which cannot be avoided by him who lives not by faith.) Looking upon *γὰρ* as intended to connect, or explain the clauses of an argument (see Hartung's Partikellehre, i. 363, &c.), we may here translate it by "yea;" it points back to the well-known truth of God's justice in punishing sin, which the life of faith alone can satisfy. In this general idea, therefore, that God punishes sin, on which the Apostle Paul grounds his whole argument, he already brings distinctly forward the contrasts between the two dispensations; for vers. 17, 18, exactly correspond to one another. Sinful man has the most pressing need of the revelation of the *δικαιοσύνη Θεοῦ*, for without this he is subject to the *ὀργὴ Θεοῦ*. (The endeavours to force another meaning upon *γὰρ*, "but," for instance, are altogether to be rejected. Comp. Winer Gramm. § 423, &c.) The divine anger we of course consider as merely signifying the manifestation of God's justice against sin; this is here represented in its two principal forms, as alienation from God

* See Notes to Matth. xviii. 34, 35, Joh. iii. 35, 36.

(ἀσέβεια), and discord in earthly relations (ἀδικία), and these in all possible cases, greater as well as smaller (πᾶσα). The only separate question is this, how are the words ἀποκαλύπτεται ἀπ' οὐρανοῦ to be taken? Great stress has been laid upon the expression ἀπ' οὐρανοῦ, and some have interpreted it of some particular judgment of God by lightning and so on, or have referred it to the last judgment. But the general character of the whole passage by no means admits of such special applications. Each and every, outward as well as inward, present as well as future, utterance of God's punitive justice is here designed; they are for this reason only represented as coming ἀπ' οὐρανοῦ, inasmuch as that eternal harmony which reigns in the heavenly world of spirit, from which alone all pure manifestations of the divine proceed,—even those of holy and just punishment is opposed to the sin of the earth.

In the opposition τῶν τὴν ἀλήθειαν ἐν ἀδικίᾳ κατεχόντων, truth, as the principle of every thing good, is set against falsehood, as the mother of all sin (as well of ἀσέβεια as of ἀδικία), and the former is represented as oppressed by the latter by means of the ἀδικίᾳ. (We are not to take ἐν αδικίᾳ as equivalent to ἀδικῶς, or ἀνομῶς, since it needs no words to prove that the suppression of the truth is criminal; the thought expressed is rather this, that unrighteousness = ἀνομία, departure from the divine law, stifles the truth, and gives birth to error and lies.) (Κατέχειν, in the sense "to keep under, to restrain the activity of," is found also in 2 Thess. ii. 6, Acts xxvii. 40.) Here, moreover, the truth that is kept under is to be referred neither altogether to its inward effects, nor altogether to its outward, but to both together. This pernicious energy of sin naturally begins in the hearts of individual men, but extends itself gradually more and more, and darkens the conscience of whole nations and ages, in that it makes it incapable of perceiving the voice of truth and duty. Thus, in the case of the Romans, from the total obscuration of conscience, wickedness reached such a pitch, that the gladiatorial games, one of the most horrible outgrowths of sin which has ever appeared in the history of mankind, were the general custom.* Accordingly there is con-

* It may be said that the practice of causing thousands of their fellow men to be slaughtered merely to feed their eyes with a sight of shows, was almost worse even than that of eating human flesh, which appears to have proceeded at first only out of the un-

tained in this passage an assertion, that ever since the fall, and in the state of hereditary sin, there was and is a truth in human nature, which by constant active sin may be kept under and finally stifled. St Paul does not represent man as being, in consequence of hereditary sin, in such a state that he can sink no deeper, but much rather as having a light in himself; by the extinguishing of which light he may become at length wholly blind.

Ver. 19. The Gentile world was not, however, excusable in these its errors, from what might be thought the impossibility of its attaining to the knowledge of God—God, on the contrary, revealed Himself to it. This thought is expressed in the 19th ver., where it is stated that the knowledge of God is founded upon the manifestations of the divine energy; God, in fact, is spoken of as He who Himself manifests Himself to men. And it is just on this account that their knowledge of God is so undeniable, viz., because it is conveyed by the beams of the original source of light, God Himself. The expression *τὸ γνωστὸν τοῦ Θεοῦ*, is peculiar to this passage; the word *γνωστὸν* may mean either that which *is* known, or that which *may be* known; according to the first meaning, the phrase would mean the same as *γνῶσις τοῦ Θεοῦ*; according to the latter, it would, on the other hand, distinguish that which may be known of God from that which may not. (1 Tim. vi. 16.) In our choice between these two interpretations, we can be guided only by the whole connection of the passage, according to which (as will soon be shown more at length), the absolute incapacity of the heathen for the knowledge of God, is just as strongly denied, as the possibility of their unlimited knowledge of him. The expressions *γνῶσις*, or *ἐπίγνωσις τοῦ Θεοῦ* denote, however, in the language of the New Testament, that absolute knowledge of God which is conveyed to man by means of the manifestation of God in Christ; from which we may assume that the form *τὸ γνωστὸν τοῦ Θεοῦ* was purposely chosen by the Apostle, in order to designate that lower degree of acquaintance with God, which was given to men on the footing of the Gentiles, and which was only gradually obscured by sin.

bridled fury of battle. That the gladiatorial games were not only maintained at the time of the highest civilization of the ancient world, but then first attained a definite form, shows how little the education of the head without the real reformation of the heart humanizes the manners.

However, it is plain that the knowledge of God, which is here spoken of, is not to be referred merely to His government of the world, and His works in it, but also particularly to Himself.

Γνωστός in the N. T. generally means recognised, known, (Acts i. 19, ii. 14, iv. 10, &c., Luke ii. 44, xxiii. 49), for which in classical Greek the form *γνωτός* is usual. The N. T. affords no example of the word used in the sense, "which may be known," to support that interpretation here; the usage is however abundantly supported by passages of the Classics.* The words *ἐν ἀυτοῖς* refer to the internal nature of the knowledge of God; the meaning of the Apostle is, that the nature of God is represented in the soul as in a mirror, so as not to be mistaken. It gives quite an erroneous view of the passage to suppose with some that this expression is used only of the philosophers who lived in the Gentile world, for the Apostle is here treating of an universal character of human nature, and what is here said of the heathen, it is needless to say, refers to Jews also.

Ver. 20. Once more with a fresh *γάρ* (the seventh, which follows without interruption from ver. 16, for *διότι*, ver. 19, is in meaning exactly the same as *γάρ*) the Apostle annexes a thought in which that energy, by means of which God reveals himself, is described more closely. We can point to no manifestations of Deity either immediate or by means of angels to the Gentile world, such as were vouchsafed to the Jews; but God revealed Himself to them by His creation from the very beginning—*'Απὸ κτίσεως κόσμου*, can only refer to *time*, as Rückert and Reiche justly observe; (on which account, also, *ἐφανέρωσε* stands in the past tense at ver. 19); otherwise the use of *ποιήματα* immediately afterwards, by which is denoted the created world, could not but be tautological.† The determination of the time is besides particularly important here, because the Apostle has the express intention of proving, that at no time, and under no circumstances, was there any excuse for the deep moral depravity of the Gentiles, since the knowledge of God in the works of nature was always within their reach. At the same time, *what*

* See Herrmann's note on the Oedip. Rex. of Sophocles, v. 362. Even the general analogy of the verbals in *τος* also supports this interpretation.

† On the word *κτίσις*, see the remarks on viii. 19: It denotes properly and primarily the *act* of creation, whilst *κτίσμα* is used for *that which is created;* in the N. T., on the other hand, *κτίσις* denotes commonly what is created.

God was pleased to reveal concerning himself, is more exactly declared in the words τὰ ἀόρατα ἀυτοῦ, which expression is explained and limited at the end of the verse by ἥ τε ἀΐδιος ἀυτοῦ δύναμις καὶ θειότης. The ἀΐδιος δύναμις is very definite and easy to understand. In the contemplation of the creation, the infinite *power*, which this presupposes, first impresses itself upon the spirit (see Wisdom, ch. xiii.) ; and as compared with the merely temporal evolutions of the physical powers, creative power comes forward as eternal. On the other hand, the expression θειότης is both striking and obscure, since Θεοῦ is necessarily added to it. But doubtless the Apostle by this word, as above, by choosing γνώστὸν, intended to mark the incompleteness of their knowledge. The divinity of God, *i. e.*, his higher nature in general, the dominion of a mighty power over the elements of the world, and of a condescending benevolence in the care of all the creatures,—all this may be recognised in the mere contemplation of nature ; but by no means the true θειότης of God, His personal existence as the absolute Spirit, as well as His justice and holiness. But, after all, the most remarkable part of this passage is the ἀόρατα ἀυτοῦ ; it appears from this that there is an ὁρατὸν Θεοῦ. And doubtless this is just the meaning of the Apostle. The world is the mirror in which the inward nature and being of God is displayed ;* the garment which clothes His very Self (Ps. civ. 2). Therefore, also the world, in order to lead man to the knowledge of God, needs to be contemplated with a *spiritual* eye (νοούμενα καθορᾶται = ἐν τῷ νῷ καθορᾶται) ; as only the spirit can comprehend the spiritual expression of the human countenance, because in this case, likewise, the invisible being of the man is mirrored in his visible form, so also nature speaks of God's might and goodness to him alone, who beholds her with more than the mere bodily eye; the latter finds only disorder in her.

Κτισις κόσμου (see Notes viii. 18) cannot mean the world, that which was created, but only the power that was put forth to create it. If we take it in the former sense, the connection with καθορᾶται by means of ἀπό would present a difficulty ; if this had been intended, ἐκ would have been chosen, as it is in an entirely paral-

* Calvin justly observes on this passage, Deus per se invisibilis est, sed quia elucet ejus majestas in operibus et creaturis universis, debuerunt illico homines agnoscere, nam artificem suum perspicue declarant.

lel passage in Wisdom xiii. 5. Meyer, to be sure, refers to Matt. vii. 16, where is found ἀπὸ τῶν καρπῶν ἐπιγνώσεσθε (Berl. Jahrb. 1836, N. 113). But the construction καθορᾶται with ἀπό would never be found.—Ἀΐδιος from ἀεί, everlasting, eternal; ἀϊδής, invisible.—The expressions θεότης and θειότης differ from one another as Θεός, and θεῖος, of which they are the abstract nouns. The fulness of the θειότης resides in the world, the fulness of the θεότης in Christ (Coloss. ii. 9); in Him alone can the Father be contemplated as a Person.

And now, at this remarkable passage, the question arises, what does St Paul wish particularly to impress upon us by this thought? For we might think it necessary to understand by the passage, that men in earlier times, when they stood nearer to the first age of the world, might have been able to acquaint themselves with God through nature, but that, by continual unfaithfulness, they had all of them, without exception, lost this knowledge, and were abandoned to idol-worship. But this is plainly not the meaning of the Apostle, rather is he speaking here of human nature, as it manifests itself at all times and places, so that he conceives, the knowledge of God might always have developed itself afresh from the contemplation of the world, whether by reflection on its phenomena, or through immediate impressions on the mind, or through awakenings of the conscience. The germ of sin, which existed in all men, would not indeed have been done away with, but certainly checked in its development, by obedience to that knowledge of God which was thus within their reach. But instead of this, men gave themselves up to the evil desires of their hearts, darkened thereby the knowledge of God which yet remained to them, increased thereby, in return, their lusts to such a pitch as to violate the laws of physical nature, and thus first fell away into idolatry, which is the violation of the laws of the spirit. But there were at all times individuals who proved, by leading a nobler life, even in the most depraved state of the heathen world, that it was at all times possible for man, by the earnest contemplation of nature, to raise himself to a certain knowledge of God. This power given to sinful man of acquainting himself with God in nature, is brought forward by the Apostle in other places also, for instance, Acts xiv. 15, &c., xvii. 23, &c. The Redeemer himself assumes such a power in passages like Matt. vi. 22, 23, John viii. 47. (Comp. Usteri's Paul Lehrbegriffe § 21.

There is, therefore, nothing in the passage we are now considering that is not found elsewhere. But as this passage is found in the Apostle's proof of the sinfulness of human nature, the impression has been produced upon many minds, that the idea expressed in it concerning the capability of man to raise himself to the knowledge of God, limits the greatness of man's depravity. But in this the truth has been overlooked, that moral depravity has not its immediate ground in the understanding, but in the will, and presupposes the want of real love, on which account even the morally evil spirits are said to have the knowledge of God. (James ii. 19.) In fact, the capability of knowing God heightens the moral depravity of man; for that they, notwithstanding this knowledge, can go on further and further in sin, supposes a higher degree of aversion of the will from the law than if they had sinned without this knowledge. But the [Roman] Catholic Church, as well as Rationalists, take an entirely false view of this verse, whilst they understand by the simple *γνωστὸν τοῦ Θεοῦ*, true love and obedience together. But, at the same time, as we have already observed, the Apostle restricts that knowledge of God to which man can attain by means of the mere contemplation of nature, to the knowledge of the might and goodness of God. For the proper nature of God, as the Supreme Spirit, and pure Love, *i. e.*, communication of self, remained unknown to the heathen, as well as to most of the Jews themselves; on which account Christ is so often obliged to tell the Jews, that they know not God. Accordingly, St Paul might, with the same justice, have here brought out the idea (if it had happened to suit his argument), that man, from the mere contemplation of nature, could never arrive at the *true* knowledge of God; passages, therefore, such as Ephes. ii. 12, are by no means inconsistent with the present. Even the best of the heathen, with their weak glimmering of the knowledge of God, remained without hope, because it was able to awaken in their minds only fear, at most a *longing* after the unknown God. But when Schneckenburger says that St Paul might have derived this view from the Alexandrian Gnostics, he brings forward a very unnecessary hypothesis; it is much simpler to suppose that it arose independently in his own mind, as it did also in that of the Alexandrians, from the immediate contemplation of the nobler moral *phenomena* amongst the Gentiles. Even supposing that St Paul had heard of the doctrine of the Alexandrians, yet he did not adopt it from them, but only propounded it on account of the deep truth which he recognised in it by the light of the Spirit.

Ver. 21. St Paul points out the unfaithfulness of the Gentiles to the measure of the knowledge of God which they possessed as the beginning of their errors. (The *γνόντες τὸν Θεόν* is not inconsistent with the more general term *θειότης* which has gone before, for here he is only speaking historically of that true knowledge of God which existed in men originally, and which they gradually lost.) God, as the absolutely highest Being, claims man entirely, with all his adoration and all his gratitude; and indeed, since God is Spirit and Love, and man is so likewise according to his true nature, *spiritual* adoration, and *spiritual* gratitude, *i. e.*, the complete surrender of self, and the obedience of the inmost powers of life. *Thus*, as the highest Spirit, and the purest Love (*ὡς Θεόν*), they honoured Him *not*, even if they did not fail in outward homage likewise. The consequence of their forsaking the truth was then their sinking into vanity (*ματαιοῦσθαι* = הִסְכִּיל, Jerem. ii. 5), of their forsaking the Light, the sinking into darkness, the element of sin.

The *διαλογισμοι* are the actions of the *νοῦς* (see Olshausen's *opuscula theologica*, p. 157), hence both *νοῦς* and *καρδία*, the two principal powers of the man, are drawn down deeper into sin. With the *νοῦς* begins also the restoration of the man in the new birth (See Comm. vii. 25.)

Ver. 22, 23. Gradually the Gentile world became more and more degenerate, till the idea of God was entirely obliterated, so that men, and even beasts of the meanest and most disgusting forms, received divine honours. Amongst modern expositors, Reiche has contested this profound derivation of idol-worship from sin, which is yet undeniably expressed in the Old Testament. (Jerem. ii. 11; Ps. cvi. 20.) His opinion is rather (p. 158), that the deification of the powers of nature, and individual created things, preceded Monotheism, because all the conditions for the highest development of the religious feeling were wanting. But in this Reiche has set out with the quite unscriptural, and in every respect untenable view, that the course of the development of humanity begins with the completest rudeness, and proceeds to the gradual perfection of the inward as well as outward life. But the doctrine of the Apostle is founded on the opposite view of a gradual sinking out of a nobler state into sin, parallel with which degradation appears the restoration of man to his original glory, by means of a succession of manifestations of God's grace. He does not, therefore, mean to say, that the degradation of the human race showed itself suddenly in the fearful form of the worship of created powers and images, but that this indicated a continual succession of transgressions, and developments of sin.* In consequence of these the higher power of man's life (the *πνεῦμα*) vanished almost entirely, and only the brutal inclinations and instincts remained, without a ruler. In this way man, of course, fell a prey to the powers of nature, in which he perceived that working on a mighty scale which he felt to be active in himself. It was especially the generative and receptive powers of nature which were recognised by men as the most powerful in themselves, and in external things, and these were, on that account, in all nature-worship honoured with all kinds of cruel and impure services. Where holy love to the Highest Good was lost, another love must necessarily have occupied the heart, for *without* love man cannot exist; but according to the object of his love does the man himself become, for love implies self-surrender. The speculative reason of man could not free him from this bondage of the powers of nature, for it awakened no higher love, and led at best to a hylozoistic Pantheism. The wisdom of man was foolishness (1 Cor. iii. 9.) The law, at the same time, could only awaken the feeling of bondage, and the longing after freedom; but freedom itself, and the raising of the spirit to communion with God the Spirit, could only be wrought by the imparting of a higher principle of love through Christ, wherefore it is the Son alone who makes free.

Ἤλλαξαν δόξαν, κ. τ. λ., answers exactly to Ps. cvi. 20, where the LXX. have *ἠλλάξαντο τὴν δόξαν αὐτῶν*, (*i.e.*, Jehovah), *ἐν ὁμοιώματι μόσχου*. In *ἐν ὁμοιώματι εἰκόνος*† is, no doubt, an

* The necessity of a preaching of the name of the Lord (Genes. iv. 26) is the first indication of that falling away from the true God, which it was the object of the preaching of the successive patriarchs to prevent.

† The expressions *κατ' εἰκόνα καὶ καθ' ὁμοίωσιν* (Genes. i. 26), which there form a Hendiadys, are here compounded into one expression, *ὁμοίωμα εἰκόνος*,—God will be worshipped only in the perfect image of His Son, not in Adam, and his children.

allusion to Gen. i. 26. Man, according to God's will, is certainly intended to present an image of Himself in holiness and righteousness, but this image is not to be misused as if it were for adoration; since he, as *φθαρτός*, is separated from the *ἄφθαρτος* by an infinite chasm. With respect to *ὁμοίωμα* and *ὁμοίωσις*, see Com. on Rom. viii. 3.

The worship of beasts had developed itself in Egypt into the rudest forms, and had issued in the most hideous errors, so that even bestiality came forward as part of their worship, as in the service of Mendes. The expressions used by the Apostle are applicable to the worship of the Ibis, Apis, Crocodile, &c. &c.

Vers. 24, 25. God punishes sin by sin, that sin may bring with it those fearful consequences which first tend to lead man to the consciousness of his alienation from God. He, therefore, withdrawing the influences of His grace, now left men in their blindness to their own evil lusts, which shewed themselves especially in the unchecked dominion of the most powerful of their natural instincts, viz., the desire of the sexes, and to the power and Prince of darkness, who is the Lord of sin and all its manifestations. By *ἀτιμάζεσθαι τὰ σώματα ἐν ἑαυτοῖς* unnatural lust is not yet meant, but simply lust in general, which always in its sinful exercise defiles the body, whilst other sins are without the body. (1 Cor. vi. 18. The opposite is *κτᾶσθαι σκεῦος ἐν τιμῇ*. 1 Thess. iv. 4.) Such abominations, which were not only considered lawful, but the proper service of their gods, proceeded from the wandering away from truth into falsehood.

Ἀλήθεια and *ψεῦδος* are here to be taken absolutely, not as *logical*, or simply formal, mathematical truth and falsehood, but as substantial, real truth. God himself is the Being, and the Truth (cf. John i. 14); sin is the absence or perversion of the real, is nothingness and lie. *Σεβάζεσθαι* = *προσκυνεῖν* is only found in this place in the N. T. The words *παρὰ τὸν κτίσαντα* are best taken as meaning, putting into the back ground, passing over the true God, or being hostile, opposed to Him. The doxology is intended to give prominence to the contrast between the heathen's forgetfulness of God, and the honour which was due to Him.

Ver. 26, 27. God let the Gentiles sink to yet lower degradation, in permitting them to fall into unnatural lusts. Here humanity appears degraded below the beasts; in the indulgence of natural passions, man falls under the power of a very strong appetite, and has in that a certain excuse, but sins of unnatural lewdness are sheer abominations of unmixed wickedness. That they were so much in vogue in the Roman and Grecian world, is a convincing proof of the depravity of the age, notwithstanding all its outward polish of cultivation. (Compare Tholuck's Abhaudlung über den sittlichen Zustand der Heidenwelt, at the beginning of Neander's Denkwürdigkeiten, B. I.)

Ver 28. The punishment of such abominations was the complete spiritual ruin which accompanied it (*ἀντιμισθίαν ἐν ἑαυτοῖς, i.e., ἐν τῷ νῷ ἀπολαμβάνοντες*, ver. 27), in consequence of which the relations of men to one another, as members of a state and neighbourhood, must further have been destroyed. God permitted them to fall into this condition, to bring the consequences of their sin completely home to their consciences.

As the *knowledge* of God is eternal life (John xvii. 3), so St Paul rightly finds in the absence of it the source of all sins, and their results. The expression *ἀδόκιμος νοῦς* contains a play upon the words *οὐκ ἐδοκίμασαν*. The fact that they did not consider God, who is the Good itself, as good, made them reprobates; in rejecting *Him*, as they supposed, He cast *them* away, and they cast themselves away. The corruption is represented as having penetrated to the deepest spring of life, in that the *ἀδοκιμία* has reference to the *νοῦς* itself; the *νοῦς* was intended to govern both body and soul, how great then must be the ruin, if the highest principle, the power by which man receives the divine, is itself destroyed. (Matt. vi. 22.) Sexual impurities are set forth as the source of all other vices, because they destroy the most sacred and delicate relations of human nature.

29–31. In the following catalogue of sins (a similar list is found Galat. v. 19, &c., 2 Tim. iii. 3) by which the mind that is estranged from God discovers its enmity, no very distinct succession can certainly be traced out, and occasionally the Apostle is guided in the connection by the similarity of sound of the words; at the same time it cannot be denied that, setting out with the more general forms of sin, he rises to its more special manifestations.*

* Glöckler's attempt only confirms me in my view, that we must not attempt to go further in demonstrating the order of the words in the following catalogue of the mani-

The reading *πορνείᾳ* is not found in A.B.C. and several other MSS. and documents of critical authority. Without doubt this reading is not here genuine, as St Paul had already treated at length of sins relating to the sexes. Copiers, who thought that this very sin was here missing, added this expression instead of *πονηρία*. *Πονηρία* and *κακία* are certainly nearly allied, at the same time the idea of producing mischief and evil is more prominent in the former; *πονηρός* is more the corrupting, *κακός* the corrupted. *Φθόνου* and *φόνου* are connected in the same way on account of the sound in Euripides Troad, v. 763. *Κακοήθεια* denotes depravity of mind, inclination to evil, the opposite to *εὐήθεια*. *Ψιθυριστὴς*, a secret calumniator, back-biter; *κατάλαλος*, every slanderer, even the common, public evil-speaker. According to the latest investigations, the distinction between *θεοστύγης*, God-hating, and *θεοστυγής*, God-hated, is unfounded.* The active meaning, despisers of God, is probably to be here preferred, since all evil-doers, as such, are without exception displeasing to God, but sin does not rise in all to the actual despising of God. The ancients also mention the particular sin of *Θεοσεχθρία*. See Aristoph. Vesp. v. 416. By *ὑβριστής* is meant the violent and insulting, whilst *ὑπερήφανος* marks him who is proud of his personal dignity, &c. *Ασυνέτους* is wanting in several documents of authority, but still it is to be retained as genuine on account of the Paranomasia with *ἀσυνθέτους*. It is most suitably taken as "foolhardy, rash in wicked enterprizes," whilst *ασυνθέτους* denotes the covenant-breaker.—*Ασπόνδους* is not found in A.B.D.E.G. and several other copies of authority, at the same time it was probably only omitted by the copyists on account of its similarity in form to the other words, if at least it has not found its way into this passage from 2 Tim. iii. 3. As to its meaning, it differs from the kindred *ἀσύνθετος* in this, that it marks not the breaking of the covenant, but the refusal to enter into one, and therefore implies implacableness, want of love.

festations of sin. He wishes to regard *ἀδικία*, *κακία*, and *κακοήθεια* as the general expressions, and all that follows upon them, as the special manifestations of these. But against this so much may be urged in almost every particular expression, that it is better to consider the order of succession as more free.

* The accentuation of the word as an oxytone is to be preferred, in conformity with the rule, that compound adjectives in *ης* are always oxytones. See Buttmann's Larger Grammar, B. II. p. 317.

Ver. 32. Into this flood of sins the holy God permitted unholy men to sink; not by means of any special influence tending to make them bad, but according to the necessary law of the moral order of the world. For where God and His holy Being is not, and therefore the vanity of the creature's self is the ruling power, there sin begets sin, and punishes itself by sin. In this law divine love shews itself as plainly as divine justice; for the frightful consequences of sin are intended to awaken in the man the germ of those better feelings that slumber there. And if even within the Christian world instances of all these manifold forms of vice present themselves, this is only a proof how carefully the visible Church of Christ is to be distinguished from its invisible reality; indeed, if even in the heart of the believer traces of some of the sins which are here denounced as heathen are to be found, this only declares the truth, that in him too the "old man" is living, who, as such, carries with him that alienation from God which is the mother of all sin. But as in the new man, in the case of the individual believer, so also in the invisible Church, in the case of that community of Christ on earth to which so much is yet lacking, there is, by means of the Spirit which fills her, a new principle active, which recognizes the true character of all these abominations, corrects them in itself and others, and contains within itself the power gradually to overcome them. But it is just this, *truth existing in the very state of sinfulness, i. e.*, true repentance, which the Apostle so painfully feels the lack of in the heathen world. It knows the commandment of God, it knows how deserving of death are its transgressions, and yet it not only practises them itself, but praises others also who practice them.

Δικάιωμα is used here in the sense of *ἐντολή*, חֹק, ordinance. See notes on Rom. iii. 21, and on the thought itself notes on Rom. ii. 14, 15. The MSS. D.E.G. and several versions contain after *ἐπιγνόντες* the words *οὐκ ἐνόησαν*, or *οὐκ ἔγνωσαν, οὐ συνῆκαν*. These additions have, however, only arisen from a misapprehension of the thought here expressed; the meaning of the Apostle is just this, that they not only recognized sin, but also punishment as its just desert. In *ἄξιος θανάτου* is implied the idea, that death is the consequence of sin from its very nature, in the same way that life is the consequence of righteousness. (See Rom. viii. 13.) The Apostle had mentioned many fruits of the sinfulness of the heart, which, considered by themselves, could not be punished with death by the civil power; but in the individual they never appear isolated, and in the sight of God, who knows the inmost disposition of the heart, the lesser outward transgression is considered as just as culpable, if it has been committed under aggravating circumstances, as the grosser outward offence committed under circumstances of palliation. A man's own sinful deed commonly disturbs, by the increased force it gives to the lusts, his power of clear judgment; and therefore to take pleasure in the sins of others when one's own evil desires are more subdued, and therefore the voice of conscience is more easily heard, indicates a higher degree of sinful development, than the sinful action itself.

§ 4. THE CONDITION OF THE JEWS.

(II. 1-29.)

That condition of moral depravity amongst the Gentiles, which was depicted in the first chapter, made apparent the necessity of a new way of salvation; but previous to describing the nature of this way, the Apostle also directs his attention to the second great division of the human race, as considered from the theocratic point of view, that is to the Jews. It is, however, only in ver. 11 that St Paul expressly begins to treat of the Jews; for in the first verses he is still speaking of Gentiles, of those, namely, who had been preserved from the grosser forms of vice. He represents these as excusing themselves, and declaring the gross sinners to be alone culpable. This denial of the charge of sinfulness lay also in the spirit of the Jewish people, who were accustomed to look down upon the whole Gentile world as sinners compared with themselves; therefore the Apostle, in these verses which form a transition to the other subject, amalgamates this part of the Gentile world with the Jewish world, which must have recognized its share in the rebuke, in order that he might in the first place exhibit the degradation of the latter the more plainly, by contrasting it with the excellencies of some really noble spirits amongst the Gentiles. The Apostle, therefore, first proves that the state of sinfulness does not the less exist, in cases where it even produces no such outward evil fruits.

The manifestations of sin only assume a less gross and prominent appearance, without being on that account really different. None should therefore judge his neighbour, but rather judge himself, and let the goodness of God lead him to repentance, knowing that the just God punishes without fail all sin, whether refined or coarse, whether outward or inward, and only rewards the good. Now if this principle was applicable to all men, it was so in an especial manner to the Jews, who had received an express law; but on this very account they would but be more strictly punished if they had not observed this holy law, and put to deep shame before many heathens, who had walked according to their inferior knowledge more faithfully than many Jews had followed their deeper acquaintance with God. Even circumcision, the seal of their election to be God's people, had then only any significance, when it was recognised as an obligation to a faithful observance of the law. The real character of the Jew was not therefore something outward but inward, and depended upon the circumcision of the heart.

Ver. 1. The view, that the Apostle addresses himself to the Jews alone from the very first verse, has been supported by Flatt, Tholuck, Rückert, and Reiche, besides other expositors; this view, however, appears to be altogether untenable from the general character of the expressions which the Apostle makes use of. For instance, ὦ ἄνθρωπε πᾶς (in ver. 1) in connection with πᾶσα ψυχὴ ἀνθρώπου (ver. 9) is so general, that Jews *alone* cannot well be meant by it.* Besides, αὐτὰ πράσσεις (ver. 1) if it is taken according to the usual explanation, that is, if it is spoken of the outward practice of *all* Jews, receives no proper sense, inasmuch as the Jewish people collectively were actually much more free from gross vices than the Gentile world. At the same time it is quite true that *those* Gentiles, whose condition is depicted in the first chapter, cannot be spoken of in the second, (though some older commentators, for instance Calovius, have supported this view); for the persons, who outwardly indulged in all the vices there delineated, certainly would not dare to judge others under the sense of their

* Glöckler recognizes the *general* character of these expressions, but supposes still that St Paul is merely speaking of the Jews; he does not, however, shew how these two views can co-exist. The first passage ὦ ἄνθρωπε πᾶς might still be construed as is done by Fritzsche, ' whosoever thou art, even if thou shouldest belong to the people of God." But ver. 9 is clearly to be taken quite generally.

own innocence. Such persons could only be either hypocrites or idiots, with whom further argument would be useless. The connection appears then only to be natural and complete, when we assume that St Paul is speaking to Gentiles indeed, but only to such as lived in outward respectability, addicted to no such flagrant vices. These considered themselves to be better than their degraded fellow-countrymen, and therefore sat in judgment upon their sins. The Jews too stood in a similar position. In general, they were more free from gross viciousness than the Gentiles, and this made them inclined to condemn them; in this manner, then, the Apostle obtains an easy transition to the consideration of the condition of the Jews, in that he points out how the germ of all those vices is also slumbering in their hearts, as well as in those of the better Gentiles.* Augustin rightly understood the passage in this manner, and it is only thus that the argument of the Apostle receives its full truth. All the Gentiles did not actually live in the commission of the crimes painted in such glaring colours in chapter i., and but few of the Jews especially; nevertheless, they are all, both Jews and Gentiles, sinners without exception, because they all bear in their hearts the seed which is able to produce all vices. The Gentiles, who are commended in chapter ii. 14, 15, only receive this commendation because they assent to this truth. The Apostle therefore distinguishes in his description *three classes of men*,† who indeed are all, without exception, sinners, but yet stand in a different relation to sin. The *first* class consists of all those who live unconcerned in flagrant vices; to this class belonged the great mass of the Gentile world, and some few individuals amongst the Jews. The *second* class consists of those who check the grosser outbreaks of sin, but nevertheless bear in their hearts the germ of sinfulness, and with it all its subtler manifestations, but without recognising their sinful condition, and without longing for something better. To this

* Very instructive for the right understanding of this passage is Galat. ii. 15, where it is written, *ἡμεῖς φύσει Ἰουδαῖοι, καὶ οὐκ ἐξ ἐθνῶν ἁμαρτωλοί.* Here then also the Gentiles are called *κατ' εξοχήν* the *αμαρτωλοί*, as the most morally sunken, according to which the Jews as a body must be conceived of as the *δίκαιοι*, *i. e.* of course as the righteous after the law.

† These three classes we meet with again in all places and at all times, and therefore the Apostle's statement has not merely a temporary import, but depicts in an entirely objective manner the nature of man's heart in and by itself.

class belonged the great mass of the Jews and individual Gentiles. Their condition is only apparently better than that of those belonging to the first class, since, whilst they lacked the latter's coarse sensuality and vice, they suffered from spiritual blindness and want of love, so that their apparent virtues were in fact but "splendida vitia." To the *third* class, lastly, belong those who not only have avoided the grosser outbreaks of sin, but at the same time also recognise, with penitent sorrow, their inward sinfulness, and entertain a longing for a more perfect condition. Of these alone can it be said, that they keep that law (ii. 14, 15, 26, 27) which demands love and truth. They fulfil the law of love in that humility which will not permit them to judge their weak fellow-creatures; they fulfil the truth in that repentance which teaches them to condemn their own sins, even when they do not break out into gross iniquity. A picture of this genuine Gentile piety is presented to us in Cornelius (Acts x.); and St Paul can only have meant such, according to his fundamental principles, in chapter ii. 14, 15, 26, 27.*

Accordingly the person mentioned in ii. 1, as judging others, is a man who has not indeed outwardly indulged in the same grosser sins, which he condemns in others, but who is in fact inwardly living after a subtler form in the same corrupt frame of mind; and it is just this which is expressed by the words τὰ γὰρ αὐτὰ πράσσεις. According to the usual interpretation, it must be *e.g.* a murderer who condemns another for murder, an assumption which has altogether something unnatural about it, as we have already observed. According to our view, on the other hand, the man who judges the murderer does the same things if he hates his brother. It is, however, very conceivable, that a man may not recognise the same sin in the hatred as in the murder, and will therefore set himself above his fellow-creature. Just in the same way, therefore, as our Lord, in the Sermon on the Mount, is the Apostle here en-

* The greater number of modern expositors have misunderstood the Apostle's representation in this place. Benecke comes the nearest to the truth, but at the same time he has not accurately and pointedly conceived the character of the pious Gentiles described in ii. 14, 15, inasmuch as he also only understands by these persons men outwardly faithful to the law, without recognising in them the elements of repentance and faith. The manner in which he approximates to the view taken by us, shows itself especially in his remarks on ver. 33, where he calls attention to the fact, that in the very act of condemning others, that very sin is incurred which in its turn condemns the condemner.

engaged in bringing to men's consciousness their sins in their root.

Διό refers to i. 32, where the knowledge of God's law is attributed to sinners. On account of this knowledge, even he who transgresses the law in a less obvious manner, and judges his fellow-man, has no excuse, for the law requires also humility and compassionate love. *'Εν ᾧ* is not to be explained by means of בַּאֲשֶׁר, but as the following words *τὰ αὐτά* shew, by supplying *ἐν τούτῳ*. The stress is laid upon the fact, that the person judging commits the same sin as the person condemned.

Ver. 2. The Apostle illustrates the foregoing thought by the idea of the divine justice. God's judgment is an absolutely true one, and therefore punishes sin as well in its subtler as in its grosser manifestations, since the law demands its perfect fulfilment.

Κατὰ ἀλήθειαν is to be construed with *κρίμα,* as designating the nature of the divine agency in the work of judgment. The verdict of men is often erroneous, God's judgment alone can judge hidden sins according to truth.

Vers. 3, 4. In order to awaken the consciousness of sin in these persons, the Apostle next points out that the impunity they had hitherto enjoyed in their sinful state was not to be considered a sign of God's grace towards them, since the only object of God's long-suffering was to lead them to repentance. That therefore which the law was intended to produce, *μετάνοια,* was just the thing which was still wanting in them, whilst those who are depicted afterwards (ii. 14, 15.) had obtained this blessing.

In ver 3 *λογίζῃ δέ τοῦτο* is to be understood, "But canst thou suppose or dream?" Ver. 4. The expressions *χρηστότης, ἀνοχή* and *μακροθυμία* contain a climax describing the relation of God to this class of sinners, who are often with the most difficulty convinced of their guilt. *Χρηστότης* namely denotes goodness in general, *ἀνοχή* its exercise in postponing punishment, *μακροθυμία* again signifies continued *ἀνοχή*. To all three St Paul applies the expression *πλοῦτος,* which he frequently uses as synonymous with *πλήρωμα.* (See Rom. ix. 23, xi. 23; Ephes. i. 7, ii. 7, iii. 16; Coloss. i. 27.) *Μετάνοια* denotes in this place, exactly as in the gospels (see notes to Matth. iii. 2), the painful conviction of sin, accompanied with a longing hope of help from above. Repentance is the mother of compassion, and covers a brother's sin, instead of judging it. This expression is not however one of those in current use with St Paul; it is only found besides 2 Cor. vii. 9; 2 Tim. ii. 25.

Ver. 5. The abuse of the long-suffering of God only leaves therefore in the mind of the impenitent a fearful looking for of future judgment which is ever becoming more oppressive.

Σκληρότης denotes that state in which a man has no power, *i.e.*, no desire of receiving spiritual things, by which the influences of divine grace are rendered ineffectual, and the exercise of repentance prevented. The form ἀμετανόητος is only found in this place in the N. T. Κατὰ is here to be taken in the sense of "according to the proportion," but not, as Koppe suggests, as if it stood for the *dativus instrumenti.* The ἡμέρα ὀργῆς is to be understood of the general day of decision, of the judgment of the world, on which the manifestation of the righteousness of God so long deferred will infallibly take place. Now the man who despises the goodness of God is increasing his guilt against this day of decision, and therefore increasing that punishment which proceeds from God's punitive justice. In the expression treasured up ὀργή, therefore, the cause is put for the effect. The substantive δικαιοκρισία is only found in this passage of the N. T.; the only other place in which it is used is in a Greek translation of Hosea, vi. 5. Δικαιοκρίτης is found 2 Maccab. xii. 41. Instead of ἀποκαλύψεως some MSS. read ἀνταποδόσεως, at the same time the preponderance of evidence of critical authority requires us to retain the common reading. A considerable number of MSS. read καὶ after ἀποκαλύψεως, and Mill, Wetstein, and Knapp have approved of this reading; at the same time καὶ, it is plain, has only been inserted on account of the three consecutive genitives, and therefore it is better with Griesbach to erase καὶ. The passage loses all appearance of singularity, if we only consider δικαιοκρισία τοῦ Θεοῦ as one conception, and the subject of the ἀποκάλυψις.

Vers. 6–8. This passage, which describes so simply the course of retributive justice, has been misunderstood on the part of the [Roman] Catholics, and used as evidence against the Protestant doctrine of justification by faith; it has in consequence been interpreted with an excess of caution on the part of Protestants. We cannot in fact agree with them in thinking that the Apostle intended to speak merely objectively of the judgment of God, and that he wished to assert, not that any one would actually on account of his works, receive eternal life, but only that *if any one had these to shew*, he would receive it; the fact being that no one has them, because all without exception are sinful, and therefore no one can, on account of his works, obtain everlasting life. Now, there is no doubt that this argument is in perfect harmony with St Paul's principles, but if he had intended to use it in this place, surely he would not immediately afterwards have spoken of Gentiles, who did the works of the law (ii. 14, 15). The key to the interpretation of this passage is rather to be found in the definition given in ver. 7 of a true *ἔργον ἀγαθόν*, by means of which the words *ποιεῖν τὰ τοῦ νόμου* will likewise receive their correct meaning. From the whole tenor of the Apostle's argument, it is plain that the term *ἔργον ἀγαθόν* cannot be understood merely of an outward work done in obedience to an outward law, which work might be combined with inward self-conceit and pride, but only of works proceeding from a genuine state of penitence, of which state faith always forms an element. As Abraham and other saints, before the coming of Christ, lived a life of faith, so individual pious Gentiles had also those germs of faith in their hearts, without which no *ἔργα ἀγαθά* are possible, because where they are wanting the best actions to outward appearance remain *ἔργα νεκρά*. We may therefore affirm, that God always judges men according to their works, as well those who lived *before* Christ, as those who live *after* Him, because, in fact, the inward man must ever be manifested in certain outward appearances, and the latter bear testimony to the character of the former. We may, however, also say, *vice versâ*, that as well before as after Christ, men are always judged according to their faith, because it alone is the principle of good works; indeed, we might call faith itself the greatest and most important work (see Notes to John vi. 29), inasmuch as it is the mother of all good works. The faith of men before and after Christ is not therefore something specifically different, but only different in degree and in object. (See notes Rom. iii. 21, etc., Hebr. xi. 1, etc.) But as faith in its highest exercise causes men to judge themselves, in so far are believers under the New Covenant not judged at all (John iii. 18), and thus the difficulty of the present passage vanishes when viewed on this side also. The remark, therefore, which Höpfner and Usteri make, that St Paul is here considering the subject from a merely legal point of view, is so far well founded, as, that if this had not been the case, St Paul would not have so expressed himself.* At the same time, the thought, although the Apostle proceeds from legal premises, has acquired such an universal application, that it has its truth, with regard to God's judicial dealings, for all stages of spiritual development. The distinction between the *blessedness* of heaven and the *degrees* of this blessedness, which latter depend upon the man's works, whilst faith is the condition of the former, is no doubt in itself correct and scriptural (see notes to 1 Cor. iii. 11, etc.), but it has nothing whatever to do with the present passage. Reiche's interpretation of this text is quite a mistaken one. He wishes namely, that a distinction should be made between the moral order of the world and the limitation of this order by the grace which is in Christ; in this case the former is alone spoken of, and the latter left entirely out of sight. But he considers the latter to be merely an amnesty once allowed for certain circumstances, and which admits of no farther extension so as to embrace the world after Christ. It is manifest, however, that the very nature of Christianity, as a means of salvation, as an institution calculated for all men in all ages, would be entirely destroyed by such an assumption. The grace of God in Christ does not contract the range of the general moral order of the world, but establishes it upon its real principles, and gives it the fullest scope. Finally, this and similar passages (as *e. g.* iii. 6, xiv. 10, 1 Cor. v. 13) on the subject of the last judgment, are particularly important as coming from St Paul, inasmuch as we may conclude from them that St Paul did not entertain any discrepant views with respect to the damnation and the resurrection of the wicked. He expresses himself openly, in fact, on neither subject (only in 2 Thess. i. 9, we find the words "eternal destruction"), and much in his epistles seems to speak to the contrary. (See notes to Rom. xi. 32, 1 Cor. xv. 24, etc.) But from his description of the day of judgment it is yet probable that, whilst St Paul kept that side of the question in the

* At the same time we find, even in 1 Sam. xxvi. 23, "The Lord recompenses every man according to his righteousness and his *faith*. On the other hand, in Ps. xxviii. 4; Eccles. xii. 14; Jerem. xvii. 10, as well as in Matth. xvi. 17, mention is made of *works* only.

back-ground, he fundamentally entertained the same views as the other writers of the N. T.

As regards the construction, Reiche has tried to connect once more, *ζητοῦσι* with *ζωὴν αἰώνιον*, and, on the other hand, to attach *δόξαν κ. τ. λ.* to *ἀποδώσει*; but, although this connection is not altogether impossible, we prefer, in common with almost all other expositors, the connection of *ζωὴν αἰώνιον* with *ἀποδώσει*, in which case *δόξαν ζητοῦσι* stands in opposition to *τοῖς μὲν κ. τ. λ.* Yet it is still undeniably a very forced construction to connect *ζητοῦσι ζωὴν αἰώνιον* with *τοῖς δέ*, and then to let the accusative, which is governed by *ἀποδώσει*, come between. In the conception of the *ἔργον ἀγαθόν* we are to have respect, as has been already observed, not merely to the lawfulness of the deed, but especially to the sincerity of the motive, which can be nothing but faith, without which it is impossible to please God in any stage whatsoever of spiritual life; it stands therefore opposed, not only to the *ἔργον πονηρόν*, but also especially to the *ἔργον νεκρόν*. The addition, *καθ' ὑπομονήν* (see Rom. xv. 4; 1 Thess. i. 3; 2 Cor. i. 6), refers to the continuance of activity in well-doing, and forms the contrast with those transient ebullitions of better feelings in the heart, of which even the wicked are not entirely destitute, but which disappear as quickly as they arise. The expression may be resolved into *πᾶσι τοῖς ὑπομένουσιν ἐν ἔργῳ ἀγαθῷ*. The sense of spiritual need which belongs to those who receive eternal life is pointed out in the opposition, in which *ζητεῖν* denotes the hungering and thirsting after righteousness. *Δόξα, τιμή* and *ἀφθαρσία* are to be regarded as forming a climax. The future glory is contrasted with the present shame, which is often the lot of the humble man here below; the *τιμή* with that *ἀτιμία* which he recognises as his desert; the *ἀφθαρσία* with that *ματαιότης* and *φθορά* with which he feels himself now burdened.

Ver. 8. The accusatives *ὀργὴν καὶ θυμόν* ought to have followed the preceding *ζωὴν αἰώνιον*. The Apostle, however, drops that construction, and finishes the sentence as if *ἀποδοθήσεται* had gone before. *Θάνατος* should also, properly speaking, have been opposed to the idea of *life* in the preceding clause; the words *ὀργὴ καὶ θυμός*, however, denote the cause instead of the effect, just as in verse 5. With respect to the expression *οἱ ἐξ ἐριθείας*, we may remark, that it is founded upon the figure of the being born of a certain element, an idea which is elsewhere expressed by *υἱὸς* or *τέκνον*. (See Phil. i. 16, 17, 1 John iv. 5.) The word *ἐριθεία** is only found amongst classical writers in the works of Aristotle (Polit. v. 2, 3); he uses it in the sense of " faction, party." The etymology of the word is doubtful; it may come from *ἐριθεύω* (from *ἔριον*, " wool,") which means " to work in wool," and then " to work " in general, " to work at a person, to seek to bring a person over to one's own side;" or it may come from *ἔρις*, " strife," and from the verb *ἐρίζειν*, when it would signify " love of strife." This meaning is best suited to the use made of the word in the language of the N. T. (See 2 Cor. xii. 20; Galat. v. 20; Phil. i. 17, ii. 3; James iii. 14.) Since, in this place, *ἐριθεία* is opposed to *ἔργον ἀγαθόν*, it can naturally only denote rebellion against God, which is the contrary to self-surrender to Him, and devotion towards Him. In this condition the man believes himself to possess all that is necessary for him, and is, therefore, without spiritual desires and aspirations. The opposition *καὶ ἀπειθοῦσι κ. τ. λ.* gives here a more exact description of the state of the godless, as the opposition above *ζητοῦσι κ. τ. λ.*, of the condition of the righteous. The root of their sin is disobedience to the truth. The lie should properly be set against the truth in this passage; the Apostle, however, puts for it *ἀδικία*, inasmuch as this word, which forms the contrary to *δικαιοσύνη*, contains in itself the idea of the lie.

Ver. 9, 10. The Apostle repeats once more the same thought for the sake of greater emphasis, but, in the first place, with that modification which is usually found in the accounts of the divine judgments given in the N. T., namely, that the gracious acceptance of believers, and not the just rejection of unbelievers, is mentioned *last*, so as to leave upon the mind the cheerful impression of that redemption which has been accomplished (see notes to Matth. xxv. 41–46); and, in the second place, with a more distinct reference to the Jews, whose condition alone he considers in fuller detail in what follows. In fact, in the case of the Jews, both blessing and curse must necessarily manifest themselves with increased intensity, since they had much fuller means of becoming acquainted with God, as the following representation proves. The Jews, therefore, are so far from being exempt from the general judgment as the

* With respect to *ἐριθεία* see the Excursus of Fritzsche, vol. i. p. 143 sqq.

chosen people of God, that it visits them the more severely in case of unfaithfulness.

The opposite to *στενοχωρία*, that is to say *ἐυρυχωρία*, is not found in the N. T., though it is used by classical writers. The word denotes, like *θλίψις*, the *spiritual* punishment of sin, since, in this place, it is not the earthly consequences of wickedness that are spoken of, but the punishments inflicted at the *ἡμέρα ὀργῆς* (ver. 5), on which account also it is said *πᾶσα ψυχὴ ἀνθρώπου*, which cannot be said of earthly punishments, since many wicked men escape them altogether. In the same way the expressions *δόξα*, *τιμή*, and *εἰρήνη*, in this passage, only refer to the inward aspects of man's life (see ver. 16), for to all outward appearance the contrary is the case in this world, on which account the natural man, in his false security, supposes that he shall be able to escape the judgment of God, (ver. 3.) The more special definitions of ver. 7, 8, are here resolved into the abstract terms *κακόν* and *ἀγαθόν*. The verb *ἔρχεται* or *ἔστι* must be supplied.

Ver. 11. The higher position of the Jews, *simply* on account of their descent from Abraham after the flesh, a prerogative which they were always so ready to assert against the Gentiles, is denied by the Apostle on the grounds of the impartiality of God; the free improvement and application of those means to which each man has access, is that which alone determines his character in the sight of God; (see notes Matth. xv. 14, etc.) The privileges of the Jews therefore only heightened their *responsibility*; it was the faithful use of them which alone raised the worth of the possessors. We are not however to think that the converts from Judaism are alluded to in this text; the Apostle is rather treating the subject, as well as regards the Jews as the Gentiles, entirely irrespectively of individuals, in order to demonstrate from it the necessity of some other way of salvation than that which the law presented. (The substantive *προσωποληψία* is also found Ephes. vi. 9; Coloss. iii. 25; James ii. 1.)

Vers. 12, 13. As the cause of the greater responsibility of the Jews, and the lesser of the Gentiles, the Apostle brings forward the law of Moses which the Gentiles did not possess. But the grace of God always supposes the exercise of free will in man, and therefore wherever this grace is at work, the guilt of man may be increased through the abuse of his freedom.

'Ανόμως is not intended to express here the absolute absence of

all law,* as ver. 15 shows, but only the want of the positive law of Moses. In 1 Cor. ix. 21, ἔννομος is found as the opposite to ἄνομος. The opposite terms διὰ νόμου and ἀνόμως are naturally to be understood as signifying, "with or without reference to the law of Moses." The words ἀνόμως καὶ ἀπολοῦνται are startling, we might expect that they would not be judged at all. But because no one is absolutely without law, he shall be judged according to his knowledge. The ἀπώλεια cannot therefore either be considered as something absolute. In the same way we find Luke xii. 48, that he who knew not his Lord's will received *few* stripes, but by no means *none at all*. We shall reserve for the notes on Rom. iii. 21, the more exact determination of the meaning of δίκαιοι, and δικαιωθήσονται, and only in this place observe with respect to them that they stand opposed to ἀπολοῦνται and κριθήσονται. In this passage, σώζεσθαι might have been substituted for δίκαιος εἶναι or δικαιοῦσθαι, since it is only the divine acknowledgment of the existing δικαιοσύνη which is intended; but of course, God, who is eternal truth, cannot recognize anything which does not exist. The ποιηταὶ τοῦ νομοῦ have therefore in St Paul's opinion a certain δικαιοσύνη at all stages of their spiritual life. But since the performance of the law before regeneration is that which is here spoken of, the δικαιοσύνη, which God recognizes in the doers of the law, can of course only be understood of the ἰδία δικαιοσύνη. This must however be recognised as far as it goes; it is by no means, in consequence of hereditary sin, a matter of indifference, whether a man endeavours to observe the law or not. The righteousness of the law in its genuine form, that is to say, when the man retains the consciousness of his own need, prepares the way for the reception of that righteousness which is by faith, whilst unfaithfulness renders it more difficult. For that opinion, of which we have already spoken in our observations on ver. 6, which affirms that the Apostle is here only speaking *hypothetically* of the performance of the law, since that was altogether beyond the power of sinful man, is plainly inadmissible, since he speaks in the verses immediately following of Gentiles who do perform the works of the law. That this however does not deny the truth, that man in his natural state is unable to keep the law, will be shown in the following remarks.

* In classical writers ἀνόμως is only found in the signification of "contrary to law;" even in Isocrates Panegyr. p. 28, edit. Mori, this meaning is to be retained, although in this passage the other meaning "without law," is also interwoven. (See Alberti observatt. in N. T., p. 473.)

De Wette's interpretation of the passage is entirely wrong; for he asserts that ver. 13 refers altogether to the Jews, and that St Paul only returns to the mention of the Gentiles in ver. 14. Rather does ver. 13 refer to all who keep the law, whether they be Jews or Gentiles; but since the possibility of observing the law might appear to be inconceivable in the case of the Gentiles, it is explained in ver. 14 how far this might be predicated of them also.

Vers. 14, 15. In order to prove that it might be said of Gentiles also that they performed the law, the Apostle proceeds to demonstrate, in *the first place*, that a law was in fact also given to the Gentiles. He defines this law as a *νόμος γραπτὸς ἐν ταῖς καρδίαις*, which expression forms a contrast with the law of the O. T., which was engraven on tables of stone (see 2 Cor. iii. 2, 3), and obviously means by this term the voice of God in the conscience, which makes itself heard, in however indistinct a manner, even in the most degraded state of the heathen world. But with respect to the relation which this inward law bears to the outwardly given law of Moses, we must allow that the latter is not only more clear and definite, and much more exact in its demands, but also that it stands much higher on this account especially, that it claims most expressly to be the law of *God himself*. The want of this distinct reference of the law to God, in the case of the inward law of the heathen, manifests itself most clearly by the inward struggle of their thoughts; for the language of lust and sin always succeeds in making itself heard in conflict with this better voice, because the latter is not expressly recognised as that, which it really is, the voice of the Most High God; at the same time, the more indistinct the inward law appears, the more exalted is the faithfulness of those who yield obedience to its weak and confused admonitions. The difference, therefore, between the law of the heathen, and the clear law of Moses, invested as it is with undoubted divine authority, is immense, and, in consequence, the advantage of the Jews in the possession of this law was very great also. At the same time, this difference appears to be somewhat diminished by the fact, that the Mosaic law with all its definiteness, required for any particular case an application determined by the manner of its exposition and interpretation; and this naturally depended as much upon the whole state of mind of the individual Jew, as the interpretation of the inward law upon that of the individual Gentile. However, the number of the purely external commandments was so great, that, by means of them, even in those characters, amongst the Jews, in which the moral feeling was but little developed, there was continually preserved alive the consciousness of a God, who came to men with inexorably strict requirements. But even more important than the information, that even the Gentiles were not absolutely without law, is, in the *second place*, the express assertion of the Apostle, that they were also in a condition to follow this law, to keep its commandments, and to fulfil it (see ver. 26, 27). It has already been remarked (on ver. 1), that this is not to be understood merely of an external and legal observance of it, in that this would by no means deserve to be called the fulfilment of the law (ἔργον αγαθόν, ver. 7), but that the necessary condition of every good work, *faith and love*,* which never exist without one another, must also be pre-supposed in the case of the pious Gentiles. But now the question arises, how is this assertion to be reconciled with the doctrine, that it is only through the grace of Christ that really good works can be produced? Through Christ a pure and holy principle of life has been acquired for man, the σπέρμα τοῦ Θεοῦ, which is absolutely without sin, even as God. The regenerate, in whom this principle dwells, cannot sin (1 John iii. 8); the sins of the regenerate are in fact only the utterances of the sinful old man, who at some moments forces back the new, but the inmost centre of their life remains untouched by sin. (See more on this subject in the notes to Rom. vii. 25.) Such an absolutely pure principle wrought neither in the Gentiles, nor in the time before Christ in general; it was first made possible for men to receive it on the completion of the work of Christ. (See the notes on John vii. 39.) Therefore also the doctrine of the sinfulness of all men without exception, even of those who do the work of the law, retains its full truth; for in the first place, not only is he under sin, who commits it *constantly* or *often*, but also he who commits it only once, or only transgresses the law on one side. (See notes to Galat. iii. 10.) If, therefore, the devout Gentiles sometimes, or even often, followed their better motions, yet they did not always do so, and therefore they remained

* With respect to the sense in which it may be said of the Gentiles also, that they have faith and love, further remarks will be found in the notes to Matt. xxv. 31, etc., Rom. iii. 21, etc., Heb. xi. 1, etc.

sinners. But again, the conception which men have of sin, is very different according to the degree of their spiritual knowledge. Even the better Gentiles were in this respect but little advanced, and their performance of the law could never, therefore, be anything but a *relative* one ; only that man, who fails not even in a single word, can be reckoned entirely perfect and without sin. (James iii. 2.) The possibility of a *relative* fulfilment of the law is however in contradiction neither to the Scriptural nor Church doctrine of the sinfulness of human nature ; both Scripture and Church only deny the possibility of an *absolute* fulfilment of the law.* On this account also the *relative* obedience of the Gentiles cannot of course *as such* be taken as the foundation of their eternal blessedness, this could only be supplied by such an absolute holiness as is possible to no mere man ; but in connection with that whole frame of mind, which even a merely relative fulfilment of the law presupposes in a Gentile, it could form such a foundation, in that this state of mind would render him capable of receiving, in penitent faith, that salvation which is offered in Christ. As, therefore, the true children of Abraham are the children of promise in Christ, so also are the devout Gentiles, because they also are true children of Abraham. (See ii. 28, 29.) This appropriation of the salvation which is in Christ on the part of the Gentile world, is recognised in Scripture as possible in the doctrine of the " descensus Christi ad inferos."

A limitation of the conception of a fulfilment of the law, on the part of the Gentiles, is therefore by all means required ; at the same time, notwithstanding this necessary restriction, there is still contained in this passage a most consolatory truth. Even in the wilderness of the heathen world, does the Apostle teach us, the λόγος σπερματικός had scattered his precious seed ; there were Gentiles, who, by means of a certain conviction of their sins, had become humble and contrite, who had an earnest desire to be faithful to the light which was vouchsafed them, who cherished longings for a better spiritual state, and therefore possessed the capacity for apprehending Christ, when He presented Himself to them, wherever it might be. These elements were sufficient, according to their particular stage of spiritual development, to constitute a foundation for eternal blessedness ; in fact, that which did not accrue to them

* This manifests itself particularly in the doctrines of the *gratia universalis*, and of the *actus manuductorii ad conversionem*.

here, they received in the regions of the dead, after Christ's manifestation there. (See notes to 1 Pet. iii. 18.) Humble faithfulness to that knowledge of the Divine which a person possesses, however small it is, *if at least this ignorance is not self-incurred*, will, the Apostle means then to say, receive its reward in whatever stage of spiritual development it may exist. Unfaithfulness, on the other hand, even when accompanied by the greatest privileges, receives at all times its deserved punishment. But the reward of the Gentile world, so far as it was well-pleasing to God, was this, that it was capable of being led to Christ, because it possessed in *μετάνοια* the capacity for apprehending Him. It was not, therefore, even in the case of the pious Gentiles, *works as such*, which were the condition of their salvation, but the germ of faith from which they proceeded. That which they retain of undiscovered sin is forgiven them without works, through the merits of Christ, as they inherited the same without conscious guilt from Adam. Christ appears, therefore, as the Redeemer of all those who do not positively reject Him, and retain the capacity for receiving Him into their hearts. (See notes to Acts x. 34–36.)

It is quite wrong to understand *ὅταν ποιῇ* of a merely ideal *possibility*, the Apostle plainly speaks of an *actual* reality (vers. 26, 27); because there do really exist pious Gentiles, St Paul concludes they must have some law or other which they follow. *Ὅταν*, with the subjunctive mood after it, no doubt denotes a merely possible, but also a frequently recurring circumstance, with respect to which it is only left indeterminate *where* and *when* it actually occurs. St Paul does not wish to designate any particular persons, but certainly to affirm *that such exist*. (See Matthiæ's Greek Gr. § 521, Winer's Gram. p. 255.) Bengel, whom Rückert has in this point followed, takes *φύσει* with *ἔχοντα*, but the collocation of the words as well as the sense demand that it should be connected with what follows. It was, in fact, unnecessary to remark that the Gentiles had *not* any thing by nature, since the Jews especially already rated their condition low enough; but it was very needful to call attention to the fact, that they could without higher support obey the law in a certain measure. *Φύσις*, namely, has here a dogmatical meaning. It denotes in the N. T., 1°. The natural constitution of anything (it is thus used Rom. i. 26, xi. 21–24, Galat. iv. 8) or else the natural descent after the flesh, as in Galat.

ii. 15. 2°. The condition of man without the grace of God, as he is flesh born of the flesh. (John iii. 6.) In this sense it is found Rom. ii. 27, and especially in Ephes. ii. 3, 4. St Paul, therefore, manifestly supposes that in the fallen nature of man the seeds of something better still remain, which, in particular persons, will sometimes succeed in developing themselves in a surprising degree, so as to produce complete receptivity for the grace of God. So, for instance, in the Canaanitish woman. (See notes to Matth. xv. 32, etc.) The natural man finds himself indeed burdened with a "proclivitas peccandi," but no "necessitas peccandi," so far at least as *action* is concerned; in respect, however, of evil desires, and an inward conformity to the divine law, man appears altogether incapable. By the words *ἑαυτοῖς εἰσι νόμος* it is not intended to deny that God is the author of this inward law also, but only to call attention to the fact that the Gentiles are not *conscious* of this connection, and, therefore, in so far appear as if they were a law to themselves. The inward law of God, which exists indeed constantly in man, and makes itself known to him, so that he cannot mistake it, by means of the motions of his conscience and the inward conflict of his thoughts, will hereafter at length *become manifest to all* in the actual *consequences* of obedience or disobedience to this law, *ἐνδείκνυνται ἐν ἡμέρᾳ κ.τ.λ.*, in that many will wonder that so many heathens have been thought worthy to sit down with Abraham, and Isaac, and Jacob, in the kingdom of heaven, whilst so many *Jews* are excluded. *Ἔργον τοῦ νόμου*, I cannot consider with Tholuck to be pleonastic, nor can I regard it with Reiche to be synonymous with the plural *τὰ ἔργα*, for particular *ἔργα* are not written in the heart of the man, since they are elicited by circumstances. The Apostle's intention is rather to declare that there is not merely a knowledge of the law in the *minds* of the Gentiles, but also that their *will* has the power of observing this law to a certain degree. On this account the man's thoughts may accuse him with justice, because he actually had the power to abstain from the sinful *deed*. And, therefore, *ἔργον* is to be considered equivalent to *τὸ ἐργαζεσθαι*. Glöckler takes it similarly as that which the law is intended to produce, that is to say, righteousness. In the same way that St Paul speaks of a *νόμος γραπτός ἐν ταῖς καρδίαις*, so also Plutarch (Moral. vol. v. p. 11, edit. Tauchm. ad princ. in erud. c. 3) of a *νόμος οὐκ ἐν βιβλίοις ἔξω γεγραμμένος*, ἀλλ' ἔμψυχος ὢν ἀνθρώπῳ. It is that νόμος τοῦ νόος, of which St Paul treats, Rom. vii. 23, and of which we shall speak at greater length at that place. But συνείδησις possesses always, in addition to the knowledge of the law, the consciousness in itself of being able and bound somehow or other to observe that law. At the same time, this original law must be accurately distinguished from that which, according to Jerem. xxxi. 32, Hebr. ix. 10, is written in the hearts of the regenerate by the Spirit of Christ. This latter is the absolutely perfect law, which communicates at the same time the highest power for its fulfilment, and, therefore, also strengthens the will; the former is a weak glimmer of that light which filled the heart of the first man.* Συμμαρτυρεῖσθαι is only a stronger form of μαρτυρεῖσθαι, *i.e.* to testify, and thereby bring before the consciousness. Λογισμός is also found 2 Cor. x. 4. More common expressions are διαλογισμός (i. 21), διανόημα, νόημα, to denote the operations of the λόγος or νοῦς. The accusing principle is that of the Divine Spirit, the excusing that of the natural life; this inward heaving and tossing of the thoughts is wanting in those who are wholly dead, but also in those who are perfectly sanctified, whose souls enjoy peace like that of the unruffled mirror of the ocean. This inward conflict, then, as more fully described by St Paul in the 7th chapter, is but a melancholy advantage, a consequence of the awakening of the inner life, a witness of that original holiness which man has lost, and yet this is better than death.

Ver. 16. With an implied reference to ver. 5, the Apostle declares that this manifestation of the state of the Gentile world, of which the Jews in particular would know nothing, will be deferred till the decisive day of judment.

Reiche has defended the old way of connecting ver. 16 with ver. 12, so that vers. 13–15 form a parenthesis. However, this connection has its difficulties, not only on account of the length of the parenthesis, but also on account of the contents of vers. 13–15. For the subject of these verses stands in the closest connection with ver. 12, and forms the foundation of the ideas expressed in the last verse; it is impossible, therefore, to place them in a parenthesis.

* In the Rabbinical writers the law in the conscience is called דָּת טִבְעִיית, or also תּוֹרָה טִבְעִית from טֶבַע nature. (See Buxtorf. lex. rabb. et talmud. p. 352, and 1349.) The opposite to this is formed by the תּוֹרָה שֶׁבִּכְתָב. lex quæ scripta est scil. in tabulis lapideis.

The whole difficulty of the passage disappears if we only, as Bengel has done, lay the emphasis upon ἐνδείκνυνται in ver. 15. Conscience and the accusing and excusing thoughts are no doubt always at work in the heart of man, but are not manifested in conjunction with their consequences. This shall only take place in the case of all, as well of those who have followed the admonitions of the inner voice, as of those who have neglected them, at the day of judgment. (See notes to Matth. xxv. 31, etc.) It is only by this construction too, that ἐνδείκνυνται forms a suitable opposition to τὰ κρυπτά; those inward transactions which take place in the depths of the soul generally remain quite indiscernible, on which account the Apostle deems it necessary in this place to bring them before the consciousness of his readers in general, and of the Jews amongst them in particular. They remain indeed hidden not merely to others, but also, as regards their real nature, to the man's own self, in that the *good* principle considers itself worse, and the *evil* principle better than it is. The parable in Matth. xxv. 31, etc., is therefore in this respect an excellent commentary on the present passage. It is intended that we should here take notice of both the acquitting and condemning voice of conscience on the day of judgment. Other explanations of the relation of ver. 16 to what has gone before, such as Heumann's view, that vers. 13–15 might have been written afterwards by the Apostle on the margin, or Koppe's opinion, that μεταξὺ is to be taken in the sense of μετέπειτα, are altogether untenable. In itself μεταξὺ can indeed signify "afterwards," (see notes to Acts xiii. 42), but here the connection with ἀλλήλων will not allow of this meaning. Christ is here, as ever in the N. T., represented and conceived of as carrying into effect the last judgment of the world. (See notes on Matth. xxv. 31, etc.; Acts vii. 17, 31.) The addition κατὰ τὸ εὐαγγέλιον μου does not refer, as was erroneously supposed by the ancients, to a written gospel of St Paul's, but designates merely the spirit and substance of his preaching of the gospel.

Vers. 17–20.* St Paul now finally directs himself to the Jews in a distinct address, and in the first place brings forward prominently all those advantages which had been vouchsafed them, in order then to make them perceive, how little they had shewn themselves worthy of them, and how therefore they could make no boast

* On the passage ii. 17–29, see Augustin. de spir. et litt. c. 8.

of being in a better condition than the Gentiles, amongst whom noble natures were to be found. It has been erroneously concluded, as already remarked in the Introduction, from this address, that there must have been in Rome a party of rank Jew-Christians. St Paul however speaks, as already observed in the Introduction, not of Jew-Christians, but quite generally of all the Jews and all the Gentiles in the world, and this distinct address can therefore only be regarded as a rhetorical figure. If therefore there were even amongst the Roman Christians, as is probable, those who had formerly been Jews, yet these were not affected with a Judaizing tendency; but the only concern that we have with this circumstance is in the question respecting the composition of the Roman community.

The reading of the textus receptus *ἰδέ* has been rightly rejected by the greater number of modern critics and exegetical commentators, *ἐι δέ* has not only the most important MSS. of critical authority in its favour, especially A. B. D. E. and others, but is also preferable on account of the connection. To be sure an anacoluthon is occasioned by it, but it is probably only to the endeavour to get rid of this that *ἰδέ* owes its origin. *'Επονομάζειν, ἐπαναπάνειν* are sonorous words chosen on purpose to mark distinctly the excessive self-conceit of the Jews. With respect to the form *καυχᾶσαι*, see Winer's Gr. p. 72. In the words *ἐν Θεῷ* is contained a reference to the special relation in which God stood to Israel as its covenant God. The objective law of God is taken as the rule of self-examination. In consequence of this position of privilege, the Jews, blind as to their own glaring unfaithfulness, arrogated to themselves the most decided spiritual authority over the Gentiles, whom they regarded as altogether blind in comparison of themselves. In *ὁδηγὸς τυφλῶν* there is no doubt an allusion to Matth. xv. 14. This tendency in Judaism to overrate their mere outward calling had developed itself most strongly amongst the Pharisees. The expressions *ἄφρονες* and *νήπιοι* have this difference, that the former denotes a low degree of knowledge, in this case of divine things, the latter a low degree of spiritual development in general. If the law is described as a *μόρφωσις τῆς γνώσεως καὶ ἀληθείας*, it is plain that this expression still indicates an advantage on the side of the Jews; the Gentiles had not even a typical representation of essential truth. At the same time, in the choice of the word *μορφωσις* it is implied, that in the O. T. the substance itself was not yet given. *Μόρφωσις* is used here in the sense of picture, outline (see 2 Tim. i. 13, iii. 5), like the *σκία* as contrasted with the *σῶμα*. (Coloss. ii. 17.) Knowledge (John xvii. 3) and truth (John i. 17) are *really* imparted in the N. T., and not merely typically.

Vers. 21–24. In what follows, the unfaithfulness of the Jews is presented in the most glaring contrast with their assumptions. Notwithstanding their possession of the divine law, the Jews transgressed its holy commandments in particular cases outwardly, and the great mass of them inwardly, in cherishing evil desires; and thus, by their openly immoral or arrogant conduct, and that want of real self-knowledge which it betrayed even to the pious Gentiles, they injured the cause of truth, instead of promoting it according to God's will by their faithfulness and humility. And whilst in such a condition themselves, they wished yet to teach others, from a feeling of their proper vocation, that they were mainly intended to be the teachers of the world; but to them may be applied those words of the Psalmist (Ps. l. 16, 17), "What hast thou to do to declare my statutes, or that thou shouldest take my covenant in thy mouth, seeing thou hatest instruction and castest my words behind thee?"

The second clause of the sentence should properly have followed in ver. 21, connected with the first clause by *διατί*, or some such word, but instead of this, the Apostle drops the construction. I would rather not take the following sentences interrogatively, as Knapp does; the address becomes more emphatic by the use of the decided declarations, You are unfaithful. In the mere external sense, it is impossible to understand these sins as committed by all the Jews; for as now, so also then, the great mass of the Jews lived outwardly with morality, especially in respect of sexual intercourse. *Βδελύσσεσθαι*, to entertain abhorrence, particularly against idolatrous practices; therefore *βδέλυγμα* = שִׁקּוּץ, an idol. (1 Kings xi. 5, Isaiah ii. 8.) With this, however, *ἱεροσυλεῖν* forms no proper contrast, for the latter word can only mean to plunder or rob the sanctuary. But no doubt covetousness, the national sin of the Jews, was present to the Apostle's mind, when he made choice of this expression; covetousness he always regards as an inward idolatry (Col. iii. 5), so that in this way the contradiction between the profession and practice of the Jews is plainly expressed, as if he had said: "Thou abhorrest idols, and yet, in thy covetousness, thou practisest idolatry."* No doubt ἱεροσυλεῖν cannot in itself mean, "to indulge covetousness," but inasmuch as ἱεροσυλεῖν is the most daring manifestation of the covetous spirit, this crime may be used to express that which is the motive to it.† Israel was in God's purpose intended to exhibit to the Gentiles a picture of truly holy national life; its unfaithfulness therefore dishonours God himself; it causes the Gentiles to say, "The God of this nation cannot be the true God!" This fearful operation of Israel's sin (which is repeated in the case of all, who are called upon at any period to be the focus of divine life, and by unfaithfulness fall away from their vocation), is already rebuked by the prophets of the Old Testament. See Isaiah lii. 5, Ezek. xxxvi. 20; another parallel is, 2 Sam. xii. 14.

Ver. 25. St Paul, however, by no means loses sight of the prerogatives of Israel (see iii. 1, etc., where he considers them at greater length); he only shows that they demand faithfulness to those responsibilities which are connected with them by God, if they are not to turn out to the deeper condemnation of their possessors. The Apostle, therefore, pre-supposes, in all stages of spiritual life, the possibility of a certain measure of faithfulness and moral earnestness, corresponding to the degree of knowledge; and the personal condition of the individual is determined by his exercise of this faithfulness.

The περιτομή is here regarded as the seal of the divine election, so that in it all theocratical privileges are considered as concentrated. The Jews therefore, with their materialistic tendencies, attributed the greatest value to the outwardly accomplished operation of circumcision. In consequence of this view, it is declared in the Talmudic treatise Schemoth (see Schöttgen on the passage), that in the case of Jews who are damned, the foreskin must first be outwardly re-

* Stier, in his "Andeutungen" (part ii. p. 267), follows Luther, who says on this passage, "Thou art a thief towards God, for honour belongeth unto God, and this all self-righteous persons take from Him." The connection, however, points to actual sin, not to mere self-righteousness.

† An example of such sacrilege is related by Josephus (Arch. xxii. 6, 2), who tells us that the presents of the rich proselyte Fulvia were pilfered by the Jews, to whom they had been entrusted.

stored. The Gentile world is therefore also called at once *ἀκροβυστία* = עָרְלָה, as unclean, lacking the sign of the covenant.* *Ἐάν* in ver. 25 as well as in ver. 26 is not used conditionally, for St Paul does not overlook the transgressions of the Jews, and the faithfulness of many Gentiles; but in the same way as *ὅταν* in ver. 14, where the fact is regarded as certain, whilst however it remains uncertain in what particular case it occurs.

Vers. 26, 27. If such a degradation of the Jew to a lower station as to privilege and honour was conceivable to him, from the dreadful threatenings under which the O. T. demanded obedience (see Deut. xxviii. 15, etc.); yet the reception of the Gentiles to grace was to him inconceivable. And yet the Apostle asserts this also, and sets the Gentiles before the eyes of the Jews as rebuking the latter by their good conduct.

Δικαίωμα = *ἐντολή*, the particular command of the general *νόμος*. In the phrase *λογίζεσθαι εἰς περιτομήν* there is evidently an allusion to the *λογίζεσθαι εἰς δικαιοσύνην* (in iv. 3); that which they have not is imputed to them as if they had it. Now the ground of this imputation is this, that though they have not indeed the sign, they have instead of it the germ of that reality which the sign represents, *i. e.* a good conscience, which they maintain faithfully, according to the small measure of knowledge which God has given them, is their bond with God; and therefore they may not untruly be regarded as such as have the sign also, ver. 27. *Καὶ* is best taken as carrying on the question with *οὐχί* understood. In *κρίνειν* that rebuke is of course only intended, which unrighteousness is constantly receiving from righteousness from its very nature. (Matth. xii. 42, Hebr. xi. 7.) The connection of *ἐκ φύσεως* is uncertain; at first sight, on account of the arrangement of the words, the only one which seems admissible, is that with *ἀκροβυστία*, so that it would mean the natural circumcision as opposed to circumcision in a spiritual sense. Thus Tholuck, Rückert, and Reiche. At the same time, however much may apparently be in favour of this construction, I cannot hold it to be the right one. For in the first place the addition of *ἐκ φύσεως* to *ἀκροβυστία* is quite unnecessary; if St Paul had thereby wished to distinguish born Gentiles from Jews with Gentile sentiments, and

* The form of the word in pure Greek was *ἀκροποσθία*. See on this point Fritzsche. vol. i., p. 136.

such is the meaning of ἀκροβυστία in ver. 25, he would have been obliged to add ἐκ φύσεως to ἀκροβυστία at once in ver. 26; but since he twice uses ἀκροβυστία in ver. 26, without this addition, it appears to be unsuitable in ver. 27. On the other hand, the opposition to ὁ διὰ γράμματος καὶ περιτομῆς παραβάτης, imperatively demands that ἐκ φύσεως be referred to human nature left to itself, whilst γράμμα (= νόμος, or νόμος γραπτός, 2. Tim. iii. 15, in so far as it is contemplated amongst the Jews as something externally given, and standing over against the man) and περιτομή denote the grace of God, in which the Israelities made their boast. Koppe observed this quite rightly, but made this mistake, that he wanted to refer ἐκ φύσεως immediately to τελοῦσα, to which course however the order of the words offers too much resistance. But the case is otherwise, if we take ἀκροβυστία τὸν νόμον τελοῦσα as making up *one* conception; ἐκ φύσεως then becomes related to this one collective thought, and the whole idea comes out clearly, whilst the reference of the words to ἀκροβυστία alone always introduces some awkwardness. The meaning of the words is then "that Gentile world, which, without special help from above, observed the law, judgeth thee who, in the possession of this special help from above, transgressest the law." Beza's interpretation of διὰ in its instrumental sense, so that the sense becomes, "the law and circumcision were to the Jews *occasions* of sin," expresses a thought in itself correct; but it is improbable that St Paul should have so far anticipated the course of his argument as to introduce it here; he only enters upon that topic later (vii. 14). Rückert rightly derives the application of διὰ in question from its local signification, according to which it may mean, "with, during, under the circumstances." See Rom. iv. 11, xiv. 20. The meaning, "notwithstanding, in spite of," which Glöckler supports, is unprecedented. The way in which Meyer endeavours to justify this meaning, "breaking through as it were its limits," has manifestly something very strained about it.

Vers. 28, 29. In these verses is contained the key to the whole of the Apostle's argument in the two first chapters of the Epistle to the Romans. St Paul exhibits to us the contrast of Jews and Gentiles in a manner full of deep meaning. It is not the bodily physical descent, or the circumcision of the flesh, which constitutes the true son of Abraham, but conformity to Abraham's life of faith, (for their ancestor, Abraham, had also sons, who were not partakers of the promise, Rom. ix. 7, Galat. iv. 22), and that circumcision of the heart, by which the sinful προσαρτήματα τῆς ψυχῆς are removed. In the outward Israel, *i. e.*, after the flesh, there exists therefore a heathen world, which God, in that great judgment which visited the Jews at the destruction of Jerusalem, condemned, whilst the few genuine Israelites were either received into the Christian Church, or preserved for later times as the germs of a new generation (Rom. xi.) But in the Gentile world also there is to be discovered an Israel,—that is to say, a number of noble souls, truly capable of receiving every thing of a higher nature, for whom the divine promises are not less intended than for Israel after the flesh, for those at least of it who belong also to the spiritual Israel; at the same time, however, it is not to be denied that, *ceteris paribus*, the children of Abraham after the flesh had a more comprehensive vocation, so that, for instance, Gentiles could not have been numbered amongst the Twelve, nor could Christ have been born with the same propriety of a Gentile mother. (See notes to John iv. 22.) This view is not found merely amongst the later Rabbinical writers,* who might have adopted it from the effects of Christian influence, but also in the O.T. Scriptures. These demand not only the circumcision of the heart (Deut. x. 16, xxx. 6; Jerem. iv. 4, compared with Coloss. ii. 11, Phil. iii. 2), but also represent the true children of God as scattered throughout all the world, and amongst all nations. Thus especially in Isaiah xliii. 5, etc. Here the Lord commands that His children be brought from the ends of the world, " even every one that is called by His name, and whom He has created for his glory." The dispersion of Israel after the flesh amongst all nations is not spoken of in this passage; by these, then, can only be meant those nobler souls scattered amongst all nations, those in whose hearts the λόγος σπερματικός has planted his seeds. In the same sense the Re-

* Compare the remarkable words of Rabbi Lipmann, in the Nizzachon, p. 19. "Irrisit nos Christianus quidam dicendo: mulieres quæ circumcidi non possunt, pro Judæis non sunt habendæ; verum illi nesciunt, quod fides non posita sit in circumcisione, sed in corde. Quicunque vero non credit, illum circumcisio Judæum non facit; qui vero recte credit, is Judæus est, etiam si non circumcisus." Reiche adduces a very striking passage from Plutarch (de Isid. et Osir. p. 352), where, on the principles of the heathen religions, the same is said of the genuine worshippers of the gods.

deemer speaks of other sheep, which are not of this fold, *i. e.*, of the community of Israel after the flesh. (See the notes to John x. 16, xi. 52, and in the O.T. the passage of Micah ii. 12.) According to this scriptural exposition, therefore, the election of God appears in complete harmony with the free self-determination of man. In the case of every man, whether much or little have been entrusted to him, all depends upon the personal faithfulness with which he improves the privileges to which he has been called, and by the faithful employment of that which has been vouchsafed to him the most insignificant individual may outstrip the man to whom the greatest gifts have been entrusted, if the latter shows himself unfaithful. The difficulty returns upon us, however, with increased strength, when, penetrating deeper into the subject, we come to regard faithfulness itself as a fruit of grace; we shall not, however, arrive at this before we consider Rom. ix. The whole passage, moreover, is in so far remarkable, that it exhibits the manner in which the Apostles and writers of the N. T. explained the O. T.; *verbally* indeed, but by no means *literally*.

Ver. 28. The *γὰρ* in this verse is to be explained by the thought which is implied in ver. 27, "Jews can also be rejected." To this, then, as its reason, is annexed the thought, that the true idea of the Jew as a member of the theocratic nation, and of circumcision as the seal of the theocratic covenant, is not an outward but an inward one. The external descent from Abraham, the external operation of circumcision, has no real meaning without the inward foundation of a right disposition. *Κρυπτός*, as the opposite of *φανερός*, used of the moral disposition, is also found 1 Pet. iii. 4.

Ver. 29. There is a difficulty in the words *οὐ γράμματι*, on account of the indefinite character of the connection of *ἐν πνεύματι* with what precedes. The contrast of *γράμμα* and *πνεῦμα* is not very different from that of *σάρξ* and *πνεῦμα*. In the same way that the body is the clothing of the spirit, so constituted that by it the spirit presents its own impress, and without it cannot manifest itself as a personal being here below,—so also in Scripture, the letter is the transparent veil of the spirit, without which the spirit cannot be fixed. In this way, then, we should arrive at the exact contrast of *φανερόν* and *κρυπτόν*. But because these last expressions have already occurred, *γράμμα* and *πνεῦμα* cannot well, without tautology, express this same contrast;

and, on this account, it is no doubt better in this place, with Beza, Heumann, Morus, and Reiche, to understand *γράμμα*, as in ver. 27, of the law, but of course of the law in so far as it is considered on the side of the letter. For, regarded as to its inward nature, there was the *πνεῦμα* also in the law. And therefore Rückert is right in understanding *πνεῦμα* of the New, *γράμμα* of the O. T., for the spirit in the O. T. is just the New Testament in its *πλήρωσις*. (Matth. v. 17.) Ver. 29 is therefore to be understood thus: "but the inward Jew and the circumcision of the heart is the *true* circumcision, in that it contains the reality of the thing represented by the outward sign, after the spirit and not after the mere letter." The concluding sentence, *οὗ ὁ ἔπαινος, κ. τ. λ.*, refers, of course, to the leading idea, that is to the true Jew, though it may also refer to *πνεῦμα*, which, as far as the sense goes, comes to the same thing; the judgment of God on the man, as the true judgment, is opposed to the false judgment of man, which is determined by outward appearances. The preposition *ἐκ* is very suitable, for a commendation pronounced *by* man can also be *from* God, if it is a just one.

§ 5. COMPARISON OF THE JEWS AND GENTILES.

(III. 1-20.)

This spiritual view of the relation between the Jews and the Gentiles might, however, as the Apostle, not without reason, feared, be easily misunderstood. St Paul, therefore, finds it necessary to call attention to the fact, that by this representation of the relation it was by no means intended to depreciate in themselves those advantages which the Jews possessed above the Gentile world; on the contrary, he confesses that they were of the greatest importance. Only these advantages had annexed to them the *condition of faith*, and this condition had not been fulfilled by the mass of the nation; although, therefore, the promises of God had been accomplished notwithstanding their unbelief, yet the people of Israel, as such, had lost their theocratical prerogative, and the spiritual Israel alone, composed of Jews and Gentiles, had received the promise, as the true children of faithful Abraham. According to this view of the connection, those difficulties disappear, which have been supposed to embarrass this portion of the Epistle to the Romans. The Apostle does not at all lose the thread of his argument (so that it were necessary to assume, as even Reiche still proposes, that it is only at Rom. ix. 4 that the same is resumed), but he completely obviates an objection, so far, at least, as it was needful. For that no δεύτερον follows the πρῶτον in ver. 2, is naturally accounted for by the fact, that this *first* which is adduced includes in it everything else which could have any claim to be mentioned besides. The passage iii. 9 stands, however, in no contradiction with ver. 2; for, whilst this passage treats of the original calling of the Jews, the former speaks of the actual state of their relations to God which had been introduced by their unbelief. All the promises of the Old, as well as the New Testament, are, in fact, conferred upon the *condition* of believing obedience; if this does not exist, they are, *eo ipso*, annulled, nay more, the blessing is converted into its direct opposite, the curse. (See Deut. xxviii. 1 etc. 15 etc.) St Paul might therefore have expressed himself even more strongly than he does in iii. 9, he might have said, "the Jews have not only no advantages over the Gentiles, but the Gentiles are now preferred to them, they have been grafted into the olive tree instead of those branches which have been hewn off. But, according to Rom. xi. 20 etc., the same condition holds good also of the Gentiles, and they may through unbelief just as well forfeit their calling to privileges, as the Jews did before them. Chapters ix.–xi. are therefore a kind of extended commentary upon this passage, but without being a continuation of what is here begun.

Vers. 1, 2. With a glance back at the foregoing deduction of the sinfulness of the Jews, the Apostle now asks, what then has become of the privileges of the Jews? Their sinfulness had placed them on a level with the Gentiles, for the law had not attained its exalted object in their case at all. The law was intended to produce the ἐπίγνωσις ἁμαρτίας (iii. 20), that is to say, true repentance, instead of which, on account of their unbelief and the unfaithfulness which this gave rise to, it only produced sin itself, and indeed the very worst form of sin, the exact contrary to repentance, the arrogant opinion that they were without sin, and as the descendants of Abraham after the flesh, were already inheritors of the kingdom of heaven. Nevertheless, the divine promise retained its objective reality; those Jews, who apprehended in faith the salvation offered to them in Christ, received also His full blessing, notwithstanding the great body of the nation forfeited it.

Τὸ περισσὸν is to be taken as a substantive, just as *τὸ γνωστὸν* in i. 19, in the sense of "advantage or prerogative." We are not to suppose that in this passage either, as Reiche justly remarks, St Paul was disputing with actual personages; the matter is treated quite objectively. The opposite to *κατὰ πάντα τρόπον* is found 2 Maccab. xi. 31, *κατ' ὀυδένα τρόπον.* No doubt *πρῶτον μέν* points as far as *form* is concerned to other advantages, which St Paul intended to name. But he felt quite rightly, that all was in *reality* contained in that one which he had adduced. In the interpretation of *ἐπιστεύθησαν*, Reiche is inclined to adopt the view of Koppe and Cramer, according to which it is translated, "the divine promises were confirmed to them." But the usual meaning of the word, "were confided to them," is plainly more suitable to the connection, since in what follows it is just their *ἀπιστία* in the possession of these promises which is spoken of. Mention is made of the divine *πίστις* only in consequence of this *ἀπιστία.* (On the well-known construction of the passive see Winer's Gram. p. 237.) The *λόγια τοῦ Θεοῦ* are no doubt in the first place the promises (Acts vii. 38; 1 Pet. iv. 11; Hebr. v. 12), and indeed especially those of the Messiah and the kingdom of God, to which all the others were related. But inasmuch as these promises constituted the most important part of Holy Scripture, the whole Word of God is also indicated by this expression.

Ver. 3. It is not altogether easy to follow the course of the Apostle's thoughts in this transition; Tholuck has, however, already rightly supplied the links which are wanting. The Apostle namely presupposes the notorious fact of the unbelief of the Jews, just at the time when the promises were being fulfilled, and deduces from thence that even if the blessing was lost to the nation collectively, it yet, according to God's faithfulness, remained even now confirmed to individual believers, and should hereafter also belong to the whole of Israel when God should have led them back by wondrous ways. (Rom. xi. 25.) He forbearingly calls the unbelievers *τινές* in the hope that many in Israel might yet turn to Christ. See ix. 1, etc.

For *ἠπίστησαν* the M.S. A. reads *ἠπείθησαν*, because the λό για were taken as synonymous with the law. The matter is understood more in accordance with St Paul's views, by regarding unbelief as the root of disobedience. (See notes to John xvi. 9.) With regard to πίστις, πιστεύω and its opposite ἀπιστέω, see notes to Rom. iii. 21. With respect to the word καταργεῖν, which occurs so frequently in St Paul's language, see notes to Luke xiii. 7, the only place in the N. T. in which it is found except in St Paul's writings. In the LXX. also it occurs but four times.

Ver. 4. With man's unfaithfulness is now contrasted the unchangeable faithfulness of God, who knows how to form for Himself, in spite of sin, the inheritors of His promises. For God's promises cannot be fulfilled without the existence of persons to accept them; He is therefore not only true in giving and keeping His promises for His own part, but He is also faithful in creating such as are worthy to receive them, so that if *all* men were to be unfaithful *they* would not be unfulfilled. In chap. ix. this idea is carried out more at length, and it is only when thus understood that the words, "if we believe not yet He remaineth faithful, He cannot deny himself," receive their full meaning. The streams of the divine grace, when impeded on the one side, turn themselves to the other, and form for themselves amongst Jews and Gentiles organs for the kingdom of God, without, however, operating by constraint, without any prejudice to man's freedom, rather by really establishing and completing it.

Μὴ γένοιτο answers to the Hebrew חָלִילָה, which latter word is thus translated by the LXX. (See Gesenius' Lexicon under חָלִיל.) It is also frequently found in Polybius, Arrian, and others, and particularly often in St Paul's writings in the N. T., thus again in the Epistle to the Romans iii. 6, 31, vi. 2, 15, vii. 7, etc. To translate γινέσθω δέ, "let it be rather so, God is faithful, &c.," is forced. Reiche justly observes, the imperative is only used to express emphatically the irrefragable nature of the assertion. The words πᾶς ἄνθρωπος ψεύστης are taken from Ps. cxvi. 11. They have so far their perfect truth, that man in his separation from, or even opposition to God, who has alone essential being and truth, becomes untrue and unfaithful; so far as he is good and true, God is it in him. Whenever, therefore, this divine truth takes up its abode in a heart, the man confesses himself to be untrue without God, and with this first truth begins his true life.

(See notes to ver. 10.) For further confirmation, Ps. li. 6 is quoted exactly after the LXX. In this Psalm the struggles by which the soul works its way out of the night of sin are described in an inimitable manner. David wrestles as it were with God, and has a controversy with Him, whilst God, by the operation of His Spirit, convinces him of his sin; the *confession* of David is the victory of the truth in him. On a greater scale the same struggle is going on in this sinful world, and the moment in which any individual emerges into the element of light is that in which he makes the confession here expressed. God is ever the victor, when the creature ventures into a controversy with Him, appearing as just in all His promises. This "judging" of God takes place whenever His guidance is distrusted. *Δικαιοῦσθαι* means here "to be recognized as just." See notes on iii. 21. The parallelism would certainly lead us to suppose that *λόγοι* means here, in the first place, law-suits, as in Acts xix. 38, but according to St Paul's application of the passage, this expression stands parallel to *λόγια*, ver. 2. Accordingly, *κρίνεσθαι* in the Apostle's use of it can only be taken as the passive, although, according to the original text, the active meaning should predominate.

Ver 5. According to the Apostle's view, therefore, God is the only good being, the Good in all good, so that even the best has no merit; sin alone is man's property and his fault; at the same time even this must serve to manifest God's glory and excellence the more brightly. The man who is estranged from God does not recognize this relation of truth to falsehood, of righteousness to unrighteousness; he thinks that God could not punish sin, if it produced what was good. But it is God who works that which is good by means of sin, not sin itself; sin remains notwithstanding what it is, that, namely, which deserves a curse, and has its punishment in and from itself.

Δικαιοσύνη and *ἀδικία* are here to be taken in the most general sense, see the notes on Rom. iii. 21. *Συνιστάνειν* signifies here to represent, and by representation to make anything known in its real nature. Rom. v. 8.—St Paul often uses the formula *τί ἐροῦμεν* especially in objections. Rom. vi. 1, vii. 7, ix. 14.—Reiche has some very happy remarks on this passage with respect to the formula *κατὰ ἄνθρωπον λέγω*. He justly observes, that the meaning of this phrase of such multifarious significations is to be determined solely by the context. It may be used either of the way of all men, or of the majority, or of a certain class of men. Here it may be most properly referred to the natural man as alienated from God, who is without the real knowledge of God, and is therefore incapable of forming a judgment of God's dealings. In the passage Rom. vi. 19, *ἀνθρώπινον λέγω* is used instead, for which in profane writers *κατὰ τὸ ἀνθρώπινον, ἀνθρωπίνως, ἀνθρωπείως λέγω* are found. See the passages cited by Tholuck on vi. 19.

Ver. 6, 7. The unreasonableness of the above question is demonstrated by St Paul from that truth which all Jews acknowledged, that God would judge the *Gentile world;* but this would be impossible, if, from the fact that man's unrighteousness exalts the righteousness of God, it should follow that He could not punish sin. For then the Gentile might also say, "My sin too has magnified God's righteousness, how then can I be condemned as a sinner?" Reiche has proved by convincing arguments, in opposition to Tholuck and Rückert, that ver. 6 is not to be understood of the universal judgment, but only of the judgment of the Gentiles, who from the Jewish point of view were considered as the *κόσμος* in its proper sense, as the *ἁμαρτωλοί κατ' ἐξοχήν.* (Galat. ii. 16.) In fact, it is only in this way of understanding it, that the argument can hold, because that which is uncertain must ever be proved by that which is acknowledged. For it was only considered certain with respect to the Gentiles that God would judge the world, the Jews entertained doubts on this subject as regarded themselves, (ver. 5.) To this may be added, that it is only by this explanation we can gain any distinct notion of the person referred to in *κᾀγώ.* "I also," says the Gentile, "might claim exemption from judgment, for in this case also the same holds true." The only thing which could be urged against this reference of the passage to the Gentile world with any show of reason, is this, that the above Jewish notion of the judgment which shall visit the Gentile world is false, and that St Paul would not argue from an error. But this view of the Jews was not in and of itself false, it only became false in consequence of their supposing that this judgment would concern the Gentiles *only,* and not the Jews also. Now it is just this very falsehood in it that the Apostle combats, and we need therefore surely feel no scruple about assuming his argument to be as stated above.

As regards the meaning "Gentile world" sometimes belonging to *κόσμος*, I cannot say that I agree with Reiche in so rendering *κόσμος* in the passages Rom. iii. 19; 1 Cor. xiii. 31.,* though no doubt the context imperatively demands it in Rom. xi. 12; 1 Cor. i. 21. There can be no doubt but that this meaning may be justly attributed to the word, since the general idea which belongs to it, "that of the creature in its alienation from God," may be confined to the Gentile world, because in it the corruption of the creature was represented in its most glaring colours. *Ψεῦσμα* is found in no other place in the N. T. In opposition to *ἀλήθεια* it denotes that whole state of falsehood, *i.e.*, of alienation from God, from which all the particular utterances of sin proceed. The divine *δόξα* is here the knowledge of God's sublime attributes, which are brought out more distinctly by the contrast of man's sin.

Ver. 8. As at all times, so also even in the Apostle's day, the Gospel was reproached as tending to *promote* sin,† and teaching men to do evil that good might come, but this did not deter him from declaring God's faithfulness amidst our unfaithfulness. St Paul therefore finds himself obliged (vi. 1 etc.,) to refute this error with greater care, and to discover it in all its absurdity. The man who can make such an assertion as this pronounces his own condemnation, in that he makes known, that the nature of divine grace, and of that love which it kindles in the heart, is wholly unknown to him. Doubtless, it was men such as the Judaizers, whom St Paul had to oppose in Galatia, who circulated such blasphemies.

With respect to the construction of the sentence, *καὶ μή* is to be taken as an anacoluthon; the Apostle intended at first to proceed with *ποιήσωμεν* but afterwards connected the principal thought by means of *ὅτι* immediately with *λέγειν* in the parenthesis. The con-

* In his explanation of Rom. iii. 19, this scholar rightly understands the whole human race to be meant by *κόσμος*. His adducing the passage as above, can therefore only be an oversight.

† Of such hypocritical slanderers Luther says, "God grant us grace that we may be pious sinners (that is, poor in spirit, humble), and not *holy slanderers* (that is, outwardly observers of the law, apparently holy, but really proud.) For the Christian is in the state of becoming such, not in the state of having become so; whosoever therefore *is* a Christian, is no Christian, that is, whosoever thinks that he is already a Christian, whilst he is only becoming one, is nought."

jecture ἔτι is therefore just as inadmissible as the omission of ὅτι. Ἔνδικος, that which is founded ἐν τῇ δίκῃ, is only found besides in the N. T. at Heb. ii. 3.

Ver. 9. After obviating these misunderstandings of that important truth, that the unfaithfulness of men does not annul the faithfulness of God, the Apostle could bring forward the concluding thought of the whole argument contained in the first two chapters, and assert, *that all Jews as well as Gentiles are under sin.* He in no way contradicted by this assertion his previous declaration as to the great advantages of the Jews (iii. 1), for to every Jew, who acknowledged his sinfulness, in whom, therefore, the law had accomplished its purpose, in stopping his mouth (ver. 19), and awakening him to a knowledge of his own sin and need of redemption (ver. 20), these privileges were still available in their fullest extent. But to those τινές (ver. 3), who formed the mass of the nation, these advantages were no doubt lost, for in them the truth had so far yielded to the lie, that they did not any longer even retain the fundamental truth of confessing their own sinfulness, but boasted of external things as if they had been substantial privileges. And, therefore, the true inward Jews, amongst Israelites and Greeks, the poor in spirit, the humble, the hungering and thirsting after salvation, and these only, received the promise. But since it was in every one's power to become such an one, in that he only needed to give up his active resistance to the Spirit of truth, which bore witness to him of his sin, no one could complain; God appeared just, as in His promises, so also in their fulfilment.

Τί οὖν; is best taken as a separate sentence. It is found complete Acts xxi. 22. *Προέχω* is found no where else in the N. T., in the active it means " to have advantage over," *præstare.* But in this case the passive form must be derived from the meaning " to prefer," an usage which is completely established even in classical Greek writers; " are we then preferred by God ?" The application of the meaning " to advance as a pretext," so as to make the words signify " have we any thing to urge in palliation," which Meyer and Fritzche have lately defended after the example of Ernesti, Morus, Koppe, &c., is in point of language quite allowable, but not suitable to the context. For the question is not, whether the Jew has anything to defend himself with, to allege in his defence, but whether or not he has any advantage over the

Gentiles. In *οὐ πάντως*, the negative particle could no doubt limit the meaning of *πάντως*, so as to make the whole signify "not in every respect;" but the context plainly demands that *πάντως* be taken as giving emphasis to the negation, *nequaquam*. If persons have demurred about giving to *πάντες* its full signification, and have wished to explain it by *πολλόι*, although the *ὀυδὲ εἷς* which follows leaves no doubt as to the Apostle's meaning, this has arisen from the unclearness of their views as to the peculiar nature of the *ἀκροβυστία νόμον τελοῦσα* (ii. 27), to which however we must of course suppose a *περιτομὴ νόμον τελοῦσα* (xi. 4) to correspond in every age of history. This unclearness has presented a considerable obstacle to a well defined conception of this section in the case of the greater number even of modern expositors. A more detailed explanation of this subject will immediately follow in the notes upon verses 10–18. *Προαιτιάομαι* is found nowhere else in the N. T. In the words *ὑφ' ἁμαρτιάν εἶναι* sin is represented as a tyrannical power from which a *λύτρωσις* is needed. (See the notes on Rom. vii. 1, etc., and vii. 14. *πεπραμένος ὑπὸ τὴν ἁμαρτίαν*.) The two parallel passages, Rom. xi. 32, Galat. iii. 22, throw an uncommon light upon this passage. See the exposition of them.

Ver. 10–18. Since nothing is more intolerable to the high-minded natural man than the confession of his sinfulness, *i. e.*, not only of individual sinful actions, but of sinful corruption in general, and the inability to do anything good of himself, the Apostle justly applies all his power to the proof of this point. By a long succession of passages from the Old Testament, he proves, that the word of God corroborates his doctrine, in that it ascribes to no man, without exception, a true *δικαιοσύνη*. The question now arises, how are the assertions of the Apostle, ii. 14, 26, 27, to be reconciled with the present text. For there individual Gentiles were spoken of who observed the law, and we must of course therefore assume, that amongst the Jews also there were many pious men of whom the same might be said. (See Luke i. 6.) The usual assumptions that the Apostle is only speaking of his contemporaries, or secondly, that the observance of the law is only to be understood of an external observance, and not of that inward law as more strictly defined by Christ in His Sermon on the Mount, or lastly, that the words of the Apostle only refer to the whole mass, and that he is not here concerned with particular exceptions, are yet nothing but ways of escaping from the difficulty, and not of solving it in its foundation, though we would not deny the truth which lies in the second remark. The last view is especially erroneous, namely, that particular exceptions are to be admitted to the general rule of man's sinfulness, for the Apostle's whole demonstration of the necessity which exists for a new way of salvation for all men without exception, rests upon the fact that all, without exception, are sinful. As has already been indicated above, but *one* interpretation of the passage is possible, and by means of this all St Paul's ideas preserve their full harmony. The Apostle namely understands by the faithful men who observe the law, such as unite with earnest endeavours to walk in conformity with their knowledge, the humble insight into their spiritual poverty, and real need of redemption, men of whom the centurion Cornelius (Acts x.) furnishes us with an example. These faithful persons are then so far from being excluded from the general state of sinfulness, that they confess themselves in the most decided manner to be sinners, and acknowledge the justice of the charge which the Word of God brings against them.* Those, in whose minds the earnest endeavour to keep the law is not united with humility, have nothing but a mere apparent righteousness, inasmuch as they grossly violate that law, all whose commandments may be reduced to the love of the truth, in its innermost substance by their want of love, and denial of their alienation from God. To them, therefore, apply the Apostle's words in Rom. ii. 1. All men, therefore, without exception, are sinners; the only difference between them is this, that some give honour to the truth, and acknowledge themselves as such, and in their case the law has accomplished its purpose and they are ripe for the gospel; whilst others are either in a complete state of death, and serve sin without any rebuke from conscience, or if they have been brought by conscience to make certain efforts to observe the law outwardly, still only derive to themselves from these efforts fresh sin, that is to say, proud self-complacency, and contempt of others.

In the Codex Alexandrinus the collection of texts which St Paul here adduces are adopted into Psalm xiv., doubtless only from this

* This confession is the first work in them, which is wrought in God, wherefore they do not shrink back from coming to the light. (See notes on John iii. 20, 21.)

passage.—Vers. 10–12 are cited freely from Ps. xiv. 1–3.—Συνιῶν = מַשְׂכִּיל.—Ἐκκλίνω = סוּר.—Ἀχρειόω is not found elsewhere in the N.T., but frequently in Polybius.—Ver. 13 is from Ps. v. 9. The image is probably derived from beasts of prey.—Ἐδολιοῦσαν is a Bœotian form for ἐδολιοῦν. The words ἰὸς ἀσπίδων ὑπὸ τὰ χείλη αὐτῶν are taken from Ps. cxl. 3.—Ver. 14 is after Ps. x. 7. The Hebrew text has מִרְמוֹת, which does not mean πικρία but deceit. Probably the LXX. had another reading.—Vers. 16, 17 are taken from Isaiah lix. 7, 8.—Συντρίμμα καὶ ταλαιπωρία answer to שֹׁד וָשֶׁבֶר.—Ver. 18 is from Ps. xxxvi. 1, Ἀπέναντι τῶν ὀφθαλμῶν αὐτῶν = לְנֶגֶד עֵינָיו. These passages of the O. T. refer indeed undeniably in their primary connection to more special relations, but in these the Apostle perceives the universal to be depicted; and justly. For every germ of sin contains within it the possibility of all the different forms which it can assume, and no one is without this germ. The more entirely, therefore, the inward eye is opened, the more ready is the man to recognise in his heart the source of every error whatsoever. Even the least leaven leavens the whole lump; and man is in God's sight only either *entirely* holy, or *entirely* a sinner.

Ver. 19. The delineation of sinfulness in the above-cited passages has so objective a character, that it applies not only to the Jews, but just as well also to the Gentiles. The law of nature also forbids such manifestations of sin not less than the written law of Moses. Therefore the Apostle, in conclusion, considers the position of men with respect to the law quite universally, and declares that the law condemns every one who has such sinful notions in himself, and that as no one can entirely acquit himself from these, every one also, without exception, falls under the curse of the law. The connection requires that νόμος be taken in the same sense in vers. 19 and 20; now the conclusions which St Paul derives from the substance of the two first chapters are quite general, and therefore νόμος must also in this place signify in the most general sense the law as such, as well the Mosaic law (and that especially in its moral requirements) as the law written in the heart, (ii. 15.) No reference can therefore be intended in this place to the passages above cited as such, but only a reference to the substance of the thoughts which they express. *Every* law forbids such sins to those who are subject to it. Reiche most inconsistently understands by νόμος the law of the Jews only, and yet proceeds to refer πᾶς ὁ κόσμος to all men. The context indeed imperatively demands the latter reference, but on this very account νομος must also be taken in the most comprehensive sense.

The expressions λέγειν and λαλεῖν are to be accurately distinguished in this place, according to their true conception; the former denotes more the inward aspect of speech, the production of thoughts and the formation of words; λαλεῖν more the outward side, the expression of what is within. The dative λαλεῖ τοῖς ἐν τῷ νόμῳ is naturally to be taken thus, "this it declares for those living under the law," *i.e.*, in order that they may fulfil it. By the expression ὁι ἐν νόμῳ we are led, indeed, to think, in the first place, of ii. 12, where it denotes the Jews; but the context in the present passage is too distinctly general to allow us to retain this meaning here. We must, therefore, understand the thought so that all those who are subject to the sphere of the law may be included in it, without its having particular respect to the wider or narrower sphere of the law, amongst Jews and Gentiles. Στόμα φράσσειν is a strong expression for "to reduce to silence," in this case by convincing of unrighteousness. Ὑπόδικος, to fall under δίκη, is not found elsewhere in the N. T. Most interpreters, even Tholuck and Reiche, erroneously understand ἵνα in this place as denoting the event and not the purpose. The strong delineations of man's sinfulness, in Scripture, have the *object* of excluding every excuse. Calvin rightly said, long ago, "ut præcidatur omnis tergiversatio, et excusandi facultas."

Ver. 20. As the great and decisive result of his whole argument concerning the nature of sin, the Apostle therefore, with a retrospective glance at Rom. i. 16, 17, sets forth this truth, that man in his natural condition cannot attain to true δικαιοσύνη* by means of the works of the law, because the law produces the conviction of sin. And therefore the revelation of a new way of salvation was needed, in consequence of which δικαιοσύνη should be revealed and communicated *without law*; and this way both Jews and Gentiles had to follow in order to obtain salvation. (Ver. 21, etc.) The impossibility of attaining to δικαιοσύνη by ἔργα νόμου is founded, in fact, upon the absolute character of the law, in consequence of which the *smallest* trangression, and that only

* The first half of this verse, like the parallel passage in the concluding words of Galat. ii. 16, appears to be a reminiscence of Ps. cxliii. 2.

*once committed,** constitutes a transgression of the *whole* law and that *for ever.* (Galat. iii. 10.) Human weakness (σάρξ) cannot, without the help of the divine πνεῦμα, satisfy these absolute requirements. It is, moreover, by no means the purpose of the law to realize the true δικαιοσύνη in man (Galat. iii. 19, 21), it is only intended to present moral perfection as the object of man's endeavours, thereby to produce ἐπίγνωσις ἁμαρτίας, and to pave the way for the reception of the gospel. (Galat. iii. 25.) This ἐπίγνωσις ἁμαρτίας is, however, by no means to be regarded as a mere unconcerned *knowledge about sin;* this may be possessed by one who is entirely unawakened, and in whom the law has not at all done its work; it is to be understood as a true acquaintance with sin, a knowledge of its nature and reality. This can only be conceived as existing in connection with deep sorrow on account of it, and a lively longing desire to be delivered from it. The ἐπίγνωσις ἁμαρτίας is, therefore, synonymous with that μετάνοια unto which, as the proper fruit of the Old Testament economy, St John the Baptist baptized those who came to him. (See notes on Matth. iii. 1.) It relates not merely to *particular* unlawful actions and their unpleasant *consequences,* but to *sin itself,* to that sin which affects the whole man, and therefore to the *habitus peccandi.*† But sin in its true nature is always ἀπιστία (John xvi. 9), from which, as their source, all other sinful outbreaks proceed. We may, therefore, affirm that the ἐπίγνωσις ἁμαρτίας, as the λύπη κατὰ Θεόν (2 Cor. vii. 10), has necessarily the germ of faith already existing in it. It is only the truth which can discover the lie in its true character, only πίστις which can fathom ἀπιστία. Although, therefore, the law brings down the *curse* (Galat. iii. 10), and the man who lies under the ἐπίγνωσις ἁμαρτίας bitterly experiences this curse, yet this feeling again always contains within itself a *blessing,* and the deepest repentance is, on this very account, the farthest from *despair,* because the humble and contrite heart,

* The popular feeling has embodied this truth in a proverb; He who has once stolen is, and ever remains, a thief; [Once a thief always a thief?] even if he never steals anything again, yet he remains for ever one who has stolen. Thus the transgressor in the smallest matter retains also for ever the character of a sinner in the sight of the holy God, until the ἄφεσις τῆς ἁμαρτίας and δικαίωσις have erased this *character indelibilis.*

† Stier distinguishes in a very marked manner (Andeut. P. ii. p. 269.) between the ἐπίγνωσις ἁμαρτίας and the mere ἐπίγνωσις τοῦ δικαιώματος τοῦ Θεοῦ (i. 32, ii. 2), which the depraved, as well as the only apparently reformed, may have in their conscience.

as an already believing heart, is well pleasing to God (Ps. li. 19), and because it is only out of that which He has already reduced to *nothing* that the Lord creates *something*, that is to say, the new man created in Christ Jesus unto good works.

SECTION II.

(III. 21—V. 11.)

THE DESCRIPTION OF THE NEW WAY OF SALVATION IN CHRIST.

After having thus laid the foundation for his superstructure of doctrine, by proving the *necessity* that existed for a new way of salvation, the Apostle proceeds in the next place to describe this way itself. In this everything assumes a different aspect from that which it wore under the Old Testament; instead of the demands of the law we hear the voice of grace, instead of works faith is presupposed, and yet the law is not abolished but rather confirmed (iii. 21–31). Of this way of salvation, says St Paul, even the Old Testament itself gave intimations, *especially* in that Abraham, the great progenitor of Israel, was justified by faith and not by works, and only received circumcision as a sign and seal of that faith which he had whilst yet uncircumcised. Faith in Christ, therefore, was truly a *new* way of salvation, but yet, after all, the ancient way, which all the saints had trodden (iv. 1–25). This is therefore the only way which leads to the desired end, and even the sorrows, which are connected with walking in this way, must minister to the perfection of the man. For, instead of the spirit of fear, the spirit of love will be thereby shed abroad in his heart,—of love enkindled by the exceeding abundant love of Christ (v. 1-11).

§ 6. THE DOCTRINE OF FREE GRACE IN CHRIST.

(III. 21–31.)

Before we enter upon the explanation of this important passage, the citadel of the Christian faith, we must give exact definitions of the leading expressions which St Paul uses to communicate his ideas, and throw some light upon the *various points of view* from which these ideas have been considered. To the leading conceptions with which we have to do in the endeavour to comprehend St Paul's doctrine, belongs in the very first place δικαιοσύνη, by which word is denoted the common object as well of the O. T. as of the N. T. dispensation. In the definition of this term, the common mistake has been, either to reckon up too many meanings of it, deduced from a mere superficial view of particular passages (thus Schleusner has noted not less than fourteen significations of δικαιοσύνη), or else, as Bretschneider and Wahl have done, whilst assuming fewer meanings, to neglect to trace them in their derivation from the radical meaning. Notwithstanding several separate treatises on this term, as those of Storr (in his opusc. acad., vol. i.), of Koppe in his fourth Excursus to the Epistle to the Galatians, of Tittmann (de synonymis N. T. i. p. 19, sqq.), and of Zimmermann, we are yet in want of a thoroughly satisfactory development of this important expression from its original meaning. I therefore propose the following essay to the consideration of scholars.

The root of δίκαιος, δικαιοσύνη, and all expressions connected with it, is the word δίκη, whose original meaning, as we learn from Timæus in his Lexicon to Plato, is, "manner and way, right relation," ὁ τρόπος καὶ ἡ ὁμοιότης. This term came to be principally applied in common language to the relations of law, and δίκη therefore denoted the right relation between guilt and punishment, between merit and reward. In its application to earthly concerns, the use of δίκαιος, δικαιοσύνη, according to this original signification, presents no difficulty; but when it is transferred to higher matters, indistinctness arises from the manifold nature of the relations involved. In this case it is best to distinguish two relations, first that of God to men, and secondly that of men to God; from this distinction arises the following difference of meanings. Since in God as the absolute Being all qualities are absolute, we must conceive of the δικαιοσύνη in Him as absolute, so that He orders all relations with absolute justice. The *justitia Dei, quâ justus est*, manifests itself therefore differently according to the differences in men's characters. Towards the *wicked* it manifests itself as *punishing*, towards the *good*, on the other hand, as *rewarding*. Hence δικαιοσύνη, applied to God and His relation to men, has not merely the signification of *punitive justice*, but also that of *goodness, grace.* That צְדָקָה, in the language of the O. T., as well as of the Rabbinical writers, is also used in the same manner, has lately been proved at length by Tholuck (Exposition of the Sermon on the Mount, p. 347, etc.) (Comp. Ps. xxiv. 5; Prov. xxi. 21; with Matth. i. 19, vi. 1; 2 Cor. ix. 10.) But as regards, in the second place, the position of man with respect to God, this is, first of all, in his present condition, a disturbed relation to God, *ἀδικία.* The right relation, the *δικαιοσύνη*, must be sought after by him. But this endeavour can only gradually attain its object. Man, in his alienation from God, commences, namely, with considering that law of God which meets him from without as something *external*, and by sincere endeavours, corresponding to his knowledge, to observe this as an *outward* law, he enters into a relation to God which is relatively true. On this account there is ascribed* to him a *δικαιοσύνη τοῦ νόμου*, or *ἐκ νόμου*, a *δικαιοσύνη ἰδία* (Rom. x. 3; Phil. iii. 9), because the man renders this obedience with, so to speak, his *own* powers, those moral powers which remain to him after the fall, without the operation of grace. But if we consider the matter more deeply, we must of course regard these powers also as of God, and man's own righteousness also as incapable of being produced without God and His co-operation; only grace in its proper and special sense does not yet appear to be operative in this case. But it is not intended that man should remain in this relatively true condition, rather must he arrive at an absolutely right relation; not merely his outward act, but his inward disposition and inclinations must be conformed to the divine law. But this, because it presupposes an inward transformation, the man cannot of himself, and by his own strength, accomplish, on this account it is called *δικαιοσύνη Θεοῦ*, or *ἐκ πίστεως* = *διὰ πίστεως* (Galat. ii. 16), because God gives it, and man receives it in *faith.* In this case it is God Himself in the man, the Christ in us, who satisfies that which God demands of him,† and therefore, that, which on the side of evil exhibits itself not as substance, but

* St Paul also uses, as equivalent to this, the words *δικαιοῦσθαι ἐξ ἔργων νόμου*, or *ἐν νόμῳ, διὰ νόμου*, see Galat. ii. 16, 21, iii. 11.

† Therefore it is termed in St Paul's writings *δικαιοσύνη ἐκ Θεοῦ* (Phil. iii. 9), which is equivalent to *δικαιωθῆναι ἐν Χριστῷ* (Gal. ii. 17), because union with Christ by faith (*εὑρεθῆναι ἐν Χριστῷ* Phil. iii. 9) is the means of obtaining it.

as a mere relation, has on the side of good in its completion passed into *substantiality;* for nothing is really good but God Himself and His influences; but where He works, there He also *is*. From these considerations we may very easily explain the use which is made of the expressions derived from *δίκαιος*. *Δικαιόω* = הִצְדִּיק, denotes the divine agency in the calling into existence *δικαιοσύνη*, which naturally includes in itself the recognition of it as such. *Δικαιοῦσθαι* = צָדַק, denotes, on the other hand, the condition of the *δίκαιος εἶναι*, and of being recognised as such. In both expressions, at one time, the notion of making righteous, or of being made righteous, at another, that of accounting or declaring righteous, or being accounted or declared righteous, comes forward most prominently, but always in such a way that the latter presupposes the former. Nothing can at any time be reckoned or declared righteous by God which is not so. *Δικαίωμα* = *τὸ δίκαιον* signifies that which is right in any particular relation, so that it may be taken as synonymous with *ἐντολή*, מִשְׁפָּט, חֹק. *Δικαίωσις*, on the other hand, denotes the action of *δικαιοῦν* taken abstractedly, the energy of making righteous (Rom. iv. 25, v. 18). Only in two passages, Rom. v. 16, 18, does the signification of *δικαίωμα* pass over into that *δικαίωσις*, which cases are, however, accounted for by the peculiarity of the context, as will be shewn more at length in the exposition of the passage.

From this explanation it is plain, that the common rendering of the word *δικαιοσύνη*, by "virtue or uprightness," proceeds from the Pelagian and Rationalistic view of the subject, and is, therefore, at most, only admissible for the *δικαιοσύνη τοῦ νόμου*. This meaning does not answer at all for that righteousness which is by faith; we shall therefore do best to translate *δικαιοσύνη* by "righteousness," and, indeed, "the righteousness of God,"* since even the expressions "justification," or "righteousness which avails in the sight of God," so far as they are considered as synonymous with "the recognition as righteous," do not, at all events, express the immediate and original meaning of the word, as the phrase *γίνεσθαι δικαιοσύνη Θεοῦ ἐν Χριστῷ*, 2 Cor. v. 21, evidently proves.

* See Augustin (de spir. et litt. c. 9), who observes with great justice: "justitia Dei, non quâ justus est, sed quâ induit hominem, cum justificat impium."

To the common end of δικαιοσύνη, therefore, two ways lead; first, that by the νόμος, secondly, that by χάρις. With both of these, on the part of man, are connected certain corresponding acts, with the νόμος, ἔργα, with χάρις, πίστις. These terms now equally need a closer definition. With respect, in the first place, to the term νόμος, this designates, in its widest sense, the divine will, so far as it meets man with certain *requirements*. The particular expressions of the law, in concrete cases, are termed ἐντολάι or δικαιώματα. But the divine law manifests itself as well amongst the heathen, by the inward voice of conscience (Rom. ii. 25), as in the O. T., by means of the Mosaic institutions (in which, besides moral, ceremonial and political injunctions also are found), and finally, as in the N. T., where Christ, especially in His sermon on the mount, establishes the law in its πλήρωσις. The essence of this πλήρωσις does not consist in imparting altogether new laws, different from that of conscience and that of Moses; but in revealing the nature of these same laws in their inmost depths. It is, therefore, nothing but a development of that one principle, "Be ye perfect even as God is perfect" (Matth. v. 48), which is the same thing as, *Love God above all things*, for it is, in fact, by means of love that the Perfect One communicates Himself, and produces what is perfect. It is, then, quite false to confine the conception of the law to any *one* of these forms of its manifestation, in an exposition of St Paul's view of the way of salvation, as is especially done by those who, considering the subject from the Pelagian and Rationalistic point of view, are accustomed to think only of the *ceremonial* part of the Old Testament law. The Apostle speaks of *all* men, Jews as well as Gentiles, and therefore the law is also to be taken in its widest sense, so that the meaning of χωρὶς νόμου is, "in no form can the νόμος produce δικαιοσύνη in its inward reality; only an apparent, simply outward δικαιοσύνη is possible to a person standing on a legal footing." Further, if we consider more closely the relation of man to the law,* *i. e.*, the ἔργα which the law requires or forbids, we find that *three classes* of them may be distinguished. *First*, ἔργα πονηρά or κακά (Rom. xiii. 3), *i. e.*,

* The general character of the legal position is the prominence of *activity* (the ποιεῖν), whilst that of the New Testament is marked by the predominance of *passivity*, that is, an openness to receive the divine powers of life, by which, however, certainly a new and higher activity is generated.

open transgressions of the commandments, *ἔργα σκότους* (Rom. xiii. 12), or *σαρκός* (Galat. v. 19), also called *ἁμαρτήματα, παραπτώματα, παραβάσεις*, in short, the utterances of *ἁμαρτια*, of the sinful nature of man. *Secondly*, *ἔργα νεκρὰ* (Heb. vi. 1, ix. 14), or *νόμου, i. e.*, works, which outwardly correspond with the commandments, but do not proceed from the absolutely pure disposition; these, therefore, in their extension over the whole life, constitute the condition of *δικαιοσύνη ἰδία*, which is no doubt in itself higher than the state of open disobedience to the law, but yet only in case it is accompanied by a consciousness of distance from the mark, by true *μετάνοια*. If it does not include this, it becomes Pharisaic self-righteousness, which is not less displeasing to God than gross transgression of the law, for it is in fact itself a gross, yea, the grossest transgression of the law, because it sins against that which is the fundamental principle of all the commandments, —against love, which is self-renunciation, whilst the former state implies self-exaltation. (See notes to Rom. ii. 1, etc.) The *third* class of works, lastly, are the *ἔργα ἀγαθά*, or *πίστεως*, also called *ἔργα καλά* (Tit. ii. 7, 14; Coloss. i. 10), *ἔργα τοῦ Θεοῦ* (John vi. 28); in them is realized not merely an outward, but also an inward conformity to the law. They are, therefore, only possible by means of that faith which receives the powers of *χάρις*; for good works are fruits (*καρπόι*), *i. e.*, the organic productions of the inward life, and it is, of course, only the tree which has been made generous that can bear generous fruit; this can, however, never be conceived as without fruit, because the powers of its inward life necessarily produce them. When, therefore, St Paul declares of the works of the law, that they are incapable of leading to *δικαιοσύνη*, he means especially those of the second class; but he does not say the contrary even of those of the third class, because he would rather lay stress upon the *principle*, *πίστις*, than upon the *effects*; St James speaks differently (ii. 24.)

Now, with respect to the *second* way, that of *grace*, this is found also in the Old Testament, in the same manner that the law is recognized in the New; but whilst grace forms the predominant feature of the new covenant, and manifests itself there in its full power, before Christ it only appeared indistinctly revealed. For in its most comprehensive signification *χάρις* is the will of God, as it exhibits itself in communicating, and not in demanding.* Since now justice and grace are the eternal forms of God's revelation of Himself, He worked also under the form of grace amongst Jews and heathen, but grace in these phases of spiritual life could only manifest itself in *consolations* and *promises*, it was not until after the accomplishment of Christ's work that grace appeared in the N. T., really imparting itself and calling forth a new *creation*. All the former operations of divine grace were therefore, so to speak, the breathing of the Spirit *upon* humanity, it was only in the Redeemer that the streams of grace were poured forth. (See notes on John i. 14.) It is to Christ, therefore, that χάρις is especially ascribed, whilst ἀγάπη, *i. e.*, the source of χάρις, resides in the Father. (See notes on 2 Cor. xiii. 13.) But we are by no means to regard grace as the mere heightening of the natural powers of the man from within, but as the communication of a higher, absolutely pure, and perfect principle, that is to say, of the πνεῦμα ἅγιον, to which the human πνεῦμα stands in the same relation as the ψυχή to the πνεῦμα in man. (See notes on Rom. viii. 16.)

Finally, with respect to man's relation to χάρις, *i.e.* πίστις, we have no doubt spoken already several times concerning this term, in our observations on Matthew viii. 2, xiii. 58; Mark ix. 20-27; Matth. xxi. 17; but the importance of the subject demands in this place a fresh and more comprehensive consideration. We start in the first place with the assertion, that this term also has in all the writers of the N. T. but one radical meaning, though it is modified according to certain relations in which it appears. Holy Scripture itself gives us this radical meaning in a formal definition, inasmuch as it designates faith, as ἐλπιζομένων ὑπόστασις, πραγμάτων ἔλεγχος οὐ βλεπομένων (Hebr. xi. 1). Faith, therefore, taken in its most general meaning, forms the opposite to that knowledge of the visible, which appears to the natural man to be the most certain of all, as well as to that *beholding* of invisible things which belongs to a higher state of being, and which St Paul denotes by the ex-

* In relation to the *creature*, therefore, χάρις conveys the idea of that which is undeserved, see Rom. iii. 23, iv. 4. The communication of the life of the Father to the *Son* is not called χάρις, but ἀγάπη. But, inasmuch as the creature is at the same time regarded as *miserable*, ἔλεος, σπλάγχνα are substituted for χάρις. (Comp. the principal passage, 2 Cor. xiii. 13.)

pression περιπατεῖν διὰ ειδοῦς (2 Cor. v. 7, compared with 1 Cor. xiii. 12). Now, man's relation to that which is invisible and eternal may be regarded as *threefold;* it is either entirely founded upon the *thinking* faculty, or it is entirely based upon the *will* and the affections, or lastly, it rests uniformly upon *all* the powers of the man. In the first of these significations, Scripture ascribes πίστις even to the devils (Jas. ii. 19), and supposes the possibility that faith may exist in men,* without a corresponding life (Jas. ii. 17, 20; 1 Cor. xiii. 2). Such a dead *head-faith,* faith in the letter, as this, is not only of no use to men, but even makes them more deeply responsible.† In the *second* relation, it appears as the *faith of the heart, i. e.,* as a living capacity for receiving the powers of the higher world, the soul absorbing, so to speak, the streams of the Spirit as a thirsty land. It was this kind of faith, which, as we showed, in the above quoted passages of our Commentary, was exhibited by those who came to Christ to be healed, as recorded in the gospels. In these persons we could only assume a very imperfect and indistinct knowledge of divine things, but they manifested a heart glowing with love, and were therefore capable of receiving χάρις. We in consequence also designated faith as identical with *receiving love,* whilst grace is *imparting love.* Since now from the heart proceeds life (Prov. iv. 3), such faith as this is ever a living faith, even though it may often be an imperfect faith. For it only shows itself as a complete faith when, in the *third* place, it takes possession of the whole man, when, therefore, it combines a living capacity to receive with clear and comprehensive knowledge. At the same time, we find that it is the practice of the writers of the N. T. to apply the word γνῶσις to such a true knowledge of the divine as springs from participation in the divine reality, so that πίστις and γνῶσις are complementary to one another, representing the life of God in the heart and in the head. But if in the passage in St John xvii. 3, γνῶσις presupposes πίστις, there are many other passages in which, *vice versâ,* πίστις presupposes

* Petrus Lombardus makes the following just distinction between "credere Deum, *i. e.,* credere quod Deus sit, quod etiam mali faciunt," and "credere in Deum, *i. e.,* credendo amare Deum, credendo ei adhærere." The belief *in* God is a dedication, a consecration of ourselves to Him.

† The case of the man who is burdened with such a dead faith is doubtless worse than if he did not believe at all; yet not for those around him. The word which is spoken even by one who is dead, may be the means of awakening others to life.

γνῶσις. Neither can be conceived as absolutely without the other, so long as both retain their true nature; but in order that each may receive an equal and harmonious cultivation, particular circumstances are required; the latter, therefore, is not necessary to salvation, though the possession of πίστις, as heart-faith, is absolutely so; because, without this, it is impossible to take up into one's own being the divine element of life. But if πίστις is not only modified in this way by the *extent* to which it reigns in men, its character depends equally upon the *object* to which it refers. In fact, πίστις is the universal foundation of religion at all stages of spiritual development, so that not only in the N., but also in the O. T. (see the whole 11th chapter of the Epistle to the Hebrews), and, indeed, amongst the Gentiles themselves, the existence of πίστις must be recognised. "Without faith it is impossible to please God." (Heb. xi. 6.) Those faithful Gentiles, therefore, whom God regards as the circumcision (Rom. ii. 14, 26, 27), must have been well-pleasing to God from their faith, in the same way that the true Israelites were. It also appears from the gospel history, that there existed in many Gentiles (the centurion of Capernaum, the Canaanitish woman, and others),* a very powerful faith, and a lively receptivity for the powers of the divine life. What, then, is the difference between these degrees of faith? From the point at which the *noble Gentiles* stood the object of faith was the *Divine* as an undefined and general idea; on which account, in their case it could only manifest itself as a *longing*, testifying of the remains of the divine likeness in man. This longing is not, properly speaking, faith, until the moment when the desired object presents itself and is embraced by it, in the same way that the eye does not see until the sun discovers itself. We might, therefore, ascribe to the noble-minded Gentiles faith *potentiâ*, *i.e.*, the completely developed capacity for believing, which can only come forward *actu* on the revelation of the divine to them, either in doctrine or in life. The condition of ἀπιστία may, on the other hand, be considered as the undeveloped, or even suppressed, capacity for believing, according as the term is taken merely in the negative, or also in the privative sense. Even, therefore, when this Gentile faith, so to speak, was exercised towards the person of Christ Him-

* Worthy of especial remark are the passages with respect to Rahab, to whom, as a Gentile woman, faith and the works of faith are attributed, Heb. xi. 31; Jas. ii. 25.

self. as, for example, in the case of the centurion of Capernaum, &c. (Matth. viii. 1, etc.), it remained still incapable of *recognising* in Him more than something divine, in a general way, although the thirst of the spirit found itself truly quenched in coming to Him, in the same way that the eye of the child rejoices in the sun, without *knowing* what it is. On the other hand, from the position at which the *true Jews* stood, the object of faith appears as the personal Godhead, and of this truth they were also conscious. But the faith of the Jew still conceived of this personal appearance of God as one merely *future*, to be realized in the Messiah, and as something *outward*. It is only Christian faith that is able to raise itself to the conception of the Divine Personality, as having appeared in Christ, as a *present* and *inward* reality. Christ will not merely shine upon men from without by His work and His Being, but He will dwell in them and work in them inwardly, in order that man may become what He is. (1 John iv. 17.) As the human race in general has therefore to pass through these different stages of faith, so also the individual. In childhood, when the personality of man himself is as yet but imperfectly unfolded, he believes only in the divine; in the progress of his life the Divine Personality becomes revealed to him in Christ, but first only as an outward fact, whose full influence upon his heart is yet future; at last he experiences His operation as something present and inward, and then only is his faith completed; it becomes a devotion of himself to God, an espousal of his soul to the heavenly bridegroom, whereby he becomes one with Christ, and Christ's whole work and Being become his own. (Hosea ii. 20.)* In this form, therefore, faith is one and the same thing with *regeneration*, because, whilst faith thus manifests its power, the whole disposition becomes a new creature, the man of earth has become a man of heaven and of God. (2 Tim. iii. 17.) The lower degrees of faith, on the other hand, are as yet without regeneration. (See notes to John i. 17.) In all stages of development, the nature of faith remains the same, the receptivity of the inward life for that which is divine; but the latter reveals itself differently, in the ma-

* When faith is represented as a χαρίσμα (1 Cor. xii. 7, xiii. 3), it denotes the capacity for appropriating the divine power, so as to perform miracles by means of it. Faith, indeed, is requisite for the reception of all gifts of the Spirit (see Matt. xvii. 19, 20), but it appears in a particularly heightened and concentrated form as a special gift of grace in the passages above cited.

nifestation of the Father, the Son, and the Holy Ghost, and on this account that faith which is *one* in its nature presents itself in several forms. Nothing further is needed towards the explanation of πίστις in its *subjective* signification (fides quâ creditur), except to distinguish it from πίστις as used, in an *objective* sense, of the substance of that revelation which is believed (fides quæ creditur), but this need only be briefly alluded to. When used of God (Rom. iii. 3; 2 Cor. i. 18; 2 Tim. ii. 13, several times) it denotes the faithfulness of God in the fulfilment of His promises.

From this unfolding of the various meanings of the terms used, we proceed now to the consideration of the contents of the passage itself, Rom. iii. 21. In the first place, νυνί (= ἐν τῷ νῦν καιρῷ, Galat. iv. 4, and below in ver. 26), is evidently to be referred to the time since the accomplishment of the work of the Lord, so that the ages before Christ appear as the mighty past.* In these, indeed, redemption, as a future blessing, was announced beforehand, and confirmed by witnesses, in the Thorah (Gen. xlix. 10; Ex. xxxiv. 6; Deut. xviii. 15) and in the Prophets (Jer. xxiii. 6, xxxiii. 16; Is. xlv. 17, liii. 1, etc.); but in these and in the symbols of the sacrificial worship, it was hidden under a veil, on which account the saints of the O. T. itself had only an indistinct presentiment of the mode of redemption (1 Pet. i. 10, 11); it was not until the death and resurrection of the Redeemer that the mystery was *revealed.* (Rom. i. 18, xvi. 25, 26.)† Now the subject of this revelation is this: the lofty aim of man, the δικαιοσύνη Θεοῦ, is to be obtained *without law* through faith in Christ. By the χωρὶς νόμου, however, as is self-evident, it is not intended to express a renunciation of the law, for the law is holy and good (vii. 12), and necessary for all phases of life, but to designate the altered position in which man stands to the law. By nature man stands *under* the law, and is impelled by the law to δικαιοσύνη; this relation is to cease; man can indeed never be *above* the law, but can very well

* Fritzsche wishes to take νυνὶ δέ as a mere form of transition, and it is no doubt correct to suppose that no determination of time is indicated in the relation of ver. 21 to ver. 20. But the subsequent mention of the law and the prophets renders it necessary to assert for νυνί the sense of time.

† St Paul does not merely say: The *way* to attain to the righteousness of God is manifested, but *this latter is itself* revealed, for it is personally in Christ, and appears in men only as Christ in us; man has no righteousness of God besides Christ, whatsoever of this righteousness the regenerate man possesses is entirely of Christ.

live *in* the law, and really bear the law *in* his heart. Accordingly, in 1 Tim. i. 9, it is said δικαίῳ νόμος οὐ κεῖται, on which passage Augustin's excellent remarks should be consulted (de spir. et. lit. cap. 10). This condition, in which man is thoroughly *one* with the law, even as our Lord tells us God Himself is (Matth. v. 48), constitutes exactly that δικαιοσύνη Θεοῦ, to which faith brings us, be cause through faith man receives the being of God into the depths of his soul. In this passage, therefore, χωρὶς νόμου is exactly parallel to χωρὶς ἔργων νόμου (Galat. ii. 16), by which it is not denied that good *works cannot* exist in the life of faith, but only asserted that these works form the *foundation* of that right relation to God which is restored under the new covenant, good works being, in fact, merely the *consequences* of this relation. This *foundation* lies positively in the work of Christ, negatively in faith, from which works both outwardly and inwardly conformable to the law necessarily proceed. *Dead* works, in *the sight of God*, do not even constitute a δικαιοσύνη νόμου, these, therefore, cannot at all be meant. The profound meaning of this verse will unfold itself before our eyes most plainly in detail, if we review the false interpretations to which it has been exposed. Of these the coarse Pelagian and Rationalistic view refutes itself. According to this, νόμος is to be understood simply of the ceremonial law, πίστις of the assent of the understanding to the *doctrine* of Christ, and δικαιοσύνη of morality; so that the sense would be, "outward religious exercises avail nothing, but only virtue according to the pure moral precepts of Christ." In this entirely external view, however, one small circumstance has been overlooked, that according to the Apostle's doctrine it is impossible for sinful man to exhibit this pure morality (viii. 3), the question therefore is, whence does the man obtain strength for this work? That which is new in the gospel does not consist in a more excellent system of morality, but in this, that the gospel *opens a new source of strength*, by means of which true morality is attainable. Much subtler is the error of the [Roman] Catholic Church in its doctrine of δικαιοσύνη. The point of difference with respect to this doctrine between her and the Protestant* Church is this, that the latter considers δικαιοσύνη as a judicial *act*

* [*Evangelische Kirche.* The term *Protestant* has been adopted in the translation of this passage, as more suitable than *Evangelical*, according to the common English usage of the words.]

of God (actus forensis), as a recognition as righteous (declaratio pro justo),* whilst the former regards it as a *condition of soul called forth in the man* (habitus infusus), according to which "justificatio" has its degrees; so that on the whole the Protestant view exalts the *objective* side, and the Roman Catholic view the *subjective.* The Protestant Church by no means denies the truth contained in the [Roman] Catholic view; she places the *subjective* side under the name of *sanctification,* immediately on a line with *justification,* and asserts that sanctification is the necessary consequence of justification. The Roman Catholic Church, however, denies the truth contained in the Protestant doctrine, and it is just in this point that her doctrine is erroneous. Considered as a mere question of grammar, *δικαιοῦσθαι* is no doubt more properly interpreted "justus effici" than, according to the Protestant Church, "pro justo declarari;" but since nothing can be *declared* by God to be righteous which *is* not so in fact, it follows that the translation of *δικαιοσύνη*, by "the righteousness which avails before God," is not false but only derived; *δικαιοσύνη Θεοῦ* means in the first place the righteousness which is wrought by God, but that which God produces answers to its idea, and must therefore avail before Him.† The [Roman] Catholic Church, therefore, gains nothing at all by this grammatical advantage; on the other hand, she has not only *let slip* an important element of the truth, but also, when this was proved to her, *opposed* it, an element which the Protestant Church has established with greater grammatical accuracy upon the formula *λογίζεσθαι εἰς δικαιοσύνην,* than upon the expression *δικαιοσύνη Θεοῦ.* This important point is in fact *the purely objective nature of justification,* which the expression *actus forensis* is intended to affirm, so that justification does not depend

* It is quite false to suppose, that the Protestant Church regards justification as something merely outward, because she sees in it a declaration of God, as Möhler misrepresents us in his Symbolik. Justification contains, according to Luther's system of doctrine, not merely *remissio peccatorum,* but also *imputatio meriti Christi,* and the *adoptio in filios Dei.* The divine declaration is consequently to be regarded as an inward *operation* in the consciousness of the man, as is, indeed, necessarily implied in the idea: what God declares, *is* so by His very word.

† Benecke's opinion that *δικαιοσύνη Θεοῦ* in this passage, as well as in vers. 25, 26 means the *justitia Dei quâ justus est,* is just as inadmissible, according to the context, as his view, that *πίστις Ἰησοῦ* denotes the *faithfulness* which Jesus exercises. Faith stands here evidently in opposition to the *ἔργοις* implied in the words *χωρὶς νόμου.* That, however, the grace and faithfulness of Christ produce faith also in men, is brought forward by him with perfect justice.

upon the degree of sanctification, but entirely upon the purpose of God in Christ Jesus; by the passive and active obedience of Christ the sin of all has been expiated, and the obedience of all fulfilled in Him. God now regards men no more as in Adam, but in Christ, from whom in the work of conversion the germ of the new man is transmitted to the individual. Thus only does the gospel become in truth good news, since according to it the salvation of man does not depend upon his own unstable conduct (on which supposition, as the [Roman] Catholic Church desires and requires, a constant *uncertainty* must remain in the man's mind here below whether or not he be in a state of grace), but on the contrary, by the unchangeable purpose of God, which the man apprehends in faith, the instability of his own character is corrected. "If, therefore, the man believes not, yet God abideth faithful, He cannot deny himself" (2 Tim. ii. 13), and the unfaithfulness of man is not removed by the fact that he strives to be faithful (for this very endeavour is unfaithful, and in the best case can only bring presumptuous pride to light), but simply and alone by believing in the faithfulness of God in Christ, by means of which faith he becomes partaker of a higher power. As, therefore, the *mother of all sins* is the *not* believing in Him whom God hath sent, so to believe in Him is the mother of all virtues (John xvi. 9); *beside* faith there can exist no virtue, but all that is true and real in man proceeds *from* it. The [Roman] Catholic Church erroneously understands by faith, fides formata, *i. e.*, fides *cum* aliis virtutibus, arriving at this notion by always regarding faith as a dead assent of the understanding to a thing as historically true, whilst, according to the Protestant view, as well as according to Scripture itself, it is life and blessedness. The doctrine of a meritum congrui, and meritum condigni, has arisen entirely out of the Pelagianizing views of the [Roman] Catholic Church, according to which man in the fall has only lost a *donum supernaturale*, but still possesses all his natural faculties uninjured, and, consequently, the capability of loving God and keeping His commandments. According to my view, the transition from the state under the law to the state under the gospel (of which we shall treat more at length in the notes to chapter vii.), must be conceived of somewhat after this manner. In his state under the law, the man is able, by means of his natural powers, which, however, can never be considered as wholly separated from the influences of the Logos, to perform certain *opera civilia.* But the more powerfully the light of truth works in a man's mind, the more plainly will he perceive that all his endeavours to establish a perfect righteousness are vain, and that his best works, on account of the selfishness which cleaves to them, are, as Augustin says, severely, indeed, but yet truly, but *splendida vitia, i. e.,* the wild fruit of a degenerate tree. With this ἐπίγνωσις τῆς ἁμαρτίας (iii. 20) is connected the longing for deliverance (vii. 24), and if the preaching of the gospel brings the true Redeemer within his reach, faith apprehends this Saviour, and appropriates both Him and His work. On the man's side no merit, no righteousness, is pre-supposed, but simply a living faith in the merits and righteousness of Christ; these faith takes up into itself, and thus everything which is Christ's becomes the man's. This transfer to the sinful man of the being of Christ is denoted by the expression, "righteousness is imputed to him." That work which was objectively accomplished upon the cross, is thus subjectively applied to the individual believer, that germ of the new man which exists in Christ is grafted into and born in the old man. This act of transfer is, therefore, a mysterious occurrence in the depths of the soul, a new creation, which none can effect by his own power, a pure gift of the Spirit, who "breatheth where He listeth." Since, however, in every regenerate man, the old man is still living, and, therefore, sinful motions must still exist, the question arises, how can God, the Omniscient, the Holy, the Just One, regard the imperfectly sanctified man as entirely righteous? The answer is: Because as God judges the man, not according to that which is realized in him, but according to that which is in Christ. As all men have fallen in Adam, so in Christ have they all been raised again; God therefore recognizes all as righteous in Him, even generations yet to come. If the divine declaration of this great fact is made to a man, and he receives it in faith, it produces in him the new life, but inasmuch as this life is derived from another, and can, therefore, also be lost, it does not constitute the decisive point in the divine judgment as to the state of grace. And therefore, also, the believer, in his own judgment, must not found his hopes of salvation upon his inward condition, but upon the merits of Christ; however, as an evidence of being in a state of grace, the inward condition is important, because faith in Christ unto justification cannot be conceived to exist without an inward transformation, and powers received from above, which enable the regenerate man to do that which under the law he could not do. (See notes to Rom. vii. 24, viii. 3.)

Ver. 22, 23. This way of salvation by faith is now equally necessary for all, because the *νόμος* could conduct none to the *δικαιοσύνη Θεοῦ,* in that *all without exception have sinned,* even if not actually in such gross forms as those mentioned in chapters i. and ii., yet inwardly, because the germ of all sins lies in every one.

In the *εἰς πάντας καὶ ἐπι πάντας* we may observe not merely a heaping together of synonyms, but a climax; the image of a flood of grace seems to be at the foundation of this expression, a flood which penetrates *to* all, and even streams *over* all. The words *δικαιοσύνη Θεοῦ* (scil. *ἔρχεται*) *ἔις πάντας* are, however, only to be understood of the divine purpose, " it is intended for all," without any intimation of the actual restoration of all. The expression *πίστις Ἰησοῦ* stands for *πίστις εἰς Ἰησοῦν,* as elsewhere *πίστις Θεοῦ* for *εἰς Θεόν.* (Mark xi. 22; Acts iii. 16; Galat. ii. 20.) In the words *πάντες ἥμαρτον* we are not to think merely of actual sin, the consequence of hereditary sin, but especially of the latter. Even where no *peccata actualia* have been committed, as, *e.g.*, in the case of unconscious children, the power of redemption is still needed. (See notes on vii. 12.) To understand *ὑστεροῦσθαι τῆς δόξης τοῦ Θεοῦ* of the approval of God, as Winer, Fritzsche, and Reiche still wish, or a cause of boasting before God, for which *καύχημα* commonly stands, as Rosenmüller and Tholuck explain it, is plainly feeble. Rückert has decided in favour of the old interpretation, which makes it refer to the image of God in which man was created, and this appears to me also to be alone admissible. There is no difficulty in giving this meaning to the expression *δόξα τοῦ Θεοῦ,* according to the analogy of כְּבוֹד יְהוָֹה (see notes on John i. 1), even though it does not happen to occur again in the N. T. Lastly, the comparison of these words of St Paul in ver. 22, *δικαιοσύνη Θεοῦ διὰ πίστεως* with the parallel passage, Galat. v. 5, *ἐκ πίστεως ἐλπίδα δικαιοσύνης ἀπεκδεχόμεθα* is instructive. The words in the present passage are spoken by the Apostle, whilst taking an entirely *objective* view of the subject; in Christ the righteousness of God exists for believers absolutely complete; but the *subjective* mode of contemplating it has also its truth, although this occurs less frequently in St Paul's writings.

From this point of view δικαιοσύνη is an object of hope, because in this world it can only be imperfectly realized in man. (See the Comm. on Galat. v. 5.)

Ver. 24, 25. Since, then, they cannot become righteous by merit, they are made righteous gratuitously, *i.e.*, without previous works and proper deserts, out of pure grace *through* the redemption of Christ. (Grace is the operative cause, redemption the means by which it works.) We arrive now at another very important point, namely, at the question, How then has Christ introduced the possibility of the δικαιοσύνη Θεοῦ through faith in Himself? The Apostle answers this question by laying stress, not upon the communication of a higher spirit through Christ and upon His divine glory, but just on the contrary, upon His deepest humiliation, His sufferings and His death, by which he declares that *redemption* was accomplished. Now, in the *first place*, with respect to the language of the Bible on this point, we meet with *three* expressions, by which the redemptive agency of Christ is designated. 1°. The term ἀπολύτρωσις, of which we have already treated in the notes on Matth. xx. 28. St Paul generally makes use of this form (Ephes. i. 7, 14, iv. 30 ; 1 Cor. i. 30), inasmuch as the ἀπὸ expresses the idea of making free more strongly than the simple λύτρωσις. The figure of slavery lies at the foundation of this word,* from which slavery man must be redeemed by means of a ransom (on which account ἐξαγοράζω is used, Galat. iii. 13, iv. 5), in order to attain to freedom, in the same way that σωτηρία (Rom. v. 9, 10), implies some great danger or distress, ἀπώλεια, from which he is to be delivered. The λύτρον is the blood of Christ, which constitutes the offering made by love to justice, by means of which objective transaction alone it is that real forgiveness of sins in God, and the appropriation of the same in the individual instance, become possible. 2°. We find the expression καταλλαγή (Rom. v. 11, ix. 15 ; 2 Cor. v. 18, 19), at the root of which lies the idea of an *enmity* which is done away with. The choice of this particular word to express this thought is, however, of the utmost importance ; καταλλάσσω, in fact, means, in the first place, "to change, exchange," and only afterwards "to recon-

* No doubt, therefore, redemption and atonement are *symbolical* expressions, but symbols full of *essential truth*, which cannot find any substitute whatsoever in human language, and are therefore necessary.

cile." (Rom. v. 10; 2 Cor. v. 18, 19.) In reconciliation, namely, those contraries which stand harshly opposed to one another, make, so to speak, mutual exchanges, and form once more an harmonious unity. So Christ takes upon Himself our misery, and imparts to us His glory, in order to reconcile us to God. The distinction which Tittmann assumes between *διαλλάσσω*, to remove a *reciprocal* enmity, and *καταλλάσσω*, to remove an enmity existing on one side only, has been proved by Tholuck to be utterly unfounded (Bergpred. p. 192, etc.)* We find, 3°. and lastly, the expression *ἱλασμός* (1 John ii. 2, iv. 10; *ἱλάσκεσθαι*, Heb. ii. 17), the proper term, even in Old Testament language, for expressing the idea of expiation by sacrifice.† Christ is therefore Himself called the *θυσία* or *προσφορά* (Ephes. v. 2, Heb. x. 12; and *πάσχα*, 1 Cor. v. 7) or else *ἀμνός* (John i. 29, 36; 1 Pet. i. 19), *ἀρνίον* (Rev. v. 6, 8, 12, 13, vi. 1, etc.) With respect to the relation in which these expressions stand to one another, we may, however, further remark, that *καταλλαγή* and *ἱλασμός* always denote the *beginning* of Christ's work, whilst *ἀπολύτρωσις* does not only include the beginning, but the *end* also (see notes on Rom. viii. 23; 1 Cor. i. 30), so that this is the most comprehensive term, comprising even *ἁγιασμός*; itself (it stands parallel to *ἄφεσις τῶν ἁμαρτιῶν*, Ephes. i. 7; Col. i. 14, whilst *μὴ λογιζόμενος ἀυτôις τὰ παραπτώματα ἀυτῶν* stands in opposition to *καταλλάσσων*, 2 Cor. v. 19).

But in the second place, as regards the ideas themselves, designated by these terms, they belong to the most difficult in Holy Scripture. At the same time, the last few years have brought to light such profound views on these subjects, that, in fact, very much has been done towards their solution. We may indeed not only

* In Heb. ii. 15, we find *ἀπαλλάττειν* but = *ἐλευθεροῦν*.

† Nitzsch, in his "System of Christian Doctrine," distinguishes between "Versöhnung" and "Versühnung," *i. e.*, "reconciliation" and "propitiation." This distinction is very serviceable for the maintenance of the difference between *καταλλαγή* and *ἱλασμός*. That a separation of these two expressions has not long ago been established, may be explained from the fact, that the deep meaning which resides in the idea of *propitiation* had entirely escaped the mind of our whole time. It was not, in fact, merely in theology that the importance of this idea was overlooked, but also in the science of law; punishment was degraded into a mere means of man's invention *for deterring men from crime*, instead of receiving its sanctification by means of that propitiation of justice which is manifested therein. In the recovery of this idea, an essential advance has been made towards deeper views of the whole work of Christ.

consider that rationalistic view to be set aside, which wholly misunderstands the essence of Christianity, whilst it reduces the work of Christ to doctrine and example, but also the infinitely deeper mode of representation of Schleiermacher (Glaubenslehre P. ii. p. 252) to be disproved.* The latter theologian, namely, considers the work of Christ as the Redeemer to precede His work of reconciliation, and considers both only from his own *subjective* point of view. Accordingly, redemption is, in his opinion, only the communication to believers of the sinlessness and perfection of Christ, and reconciliation the adoption into that blessed fellowship with Christ, which follows, as a necessary consequence, from that communication. This is, however, an entirely arbitrary definition of the terms. But besides this, in the above view, a most essential point is left out of sight, namely, *the blotting out of the guilt of sin*, which Schleiermacher was obliged in consistency to omit, because he had denied the reality of evil, and was therefore satisfied with a mere replenishment of man's emptiness. This one point, therefore, it yet remains for us to discuss,—how the death of Christ is related to the forgiveness of sins, and whether this fact has reference merely to men, or also to the Divine Being Himself. And here, in the first place, I feel myself constrained to remark, that the views I expressed in my notes on Matth. xx. 28, implying that reconciliation was an act on man's side *alone*, have been modified by some recently published profound researches, as I have also taken occasion to remark in my notes to John iii. 16 (in the second volume of the Commentary, third edition, p. 108, note). For the most profound observations on this subject we are indebted to a man who has deserved well of Theology and Philosophy, no less than of Law, Karl Friedrich Göschel.† In fact, we may say, if reconciliation

* Usteri, in the fourth edition of his "Paulinischer Lehrbegriff" (p. 86, etc.), still adheres to Schleiermacher's view of this doctrine. Amongst the most recent exegetical commentators, Rückert has, in particular, taken a correct exegetical view of St Paul's doctrine, without, however, having been able to adopt the idea of an atonement, not merely on man's part, but also on God's.

† See Göschel's "Zerstreute Blätter aus den Hand und Hülfsacten eines Juristen." Erfurt, 1832. See besides the Essays in Tholuck's lit. Anzeige, 1833. Num. 8–14. An essay of the same in the Evang. Kirchen Zeitung. 1834, January No. Very well worth reading are also the treatises of Stier, which appeared earlier (Andeut. P. i. p. 379. sqq., more accurately defined in the Andeut. P. ii. p. 24. sqq.), of Meyer (in the "Blätter für höhere Wahrheit," vol. vi. 384 etc., xi. 206 etc.), and Tholuck's work "Von der Sünde, und vom Versöhner."

were an act taking place in man only, we could have nothing to do with a "ministry of reconciliation" (2 Cor. v. 18); for then to preach reconciliation would not be to announce an act of *God*, but only an act of *men*, and indeed only of a *few* men, for how many are there who will not be reconciled unto God! Even if, therefore, in the N. T., the expression, "God is reconciled," does not occur (see the note to John iii. 16), because He appears throughout it as the Author and Founder of this reconciliation, yet there is contained in the very idea of sacrifice and expiation (as the O. T. plainly shews), a necessary reference to an altered relation of God Himself. Every sacrifice is intended to *expiate* the guilt of men, and *propitiate* the anger of God, consequently the sacrifice of all sacrifices, in which alone all the rest have their truth, must *effect* that which the others only *foreshadow*. Since now the view of the Scotists (gratuita acceptatio) disproves itself, inasmuch as God can never regard an object as that which it is not, and the view of Grotius (acceptilatio) is erroneous, inasmuch as according to it the law and righteousness are to be considered as detached from the Divine Being and Nature; nothing remains but the highly acute theory of Anselm (satisfactio vicaria), a theory, when rightly understood, just as consonant with the doctrine of Scripture as with the demands of philosophy. The elements of which it is composed are, on the one side, the enormity of sin in itself, and the guilt and liability to punishment which proceed from it; and, on the other side, the impossibility of conceiving in God *one* attribute as active *without* the other, that is to say therefore, in this case love without righteousness, on which account God *cannot* forgive sin on mere repentance, as a man can who is himself a debtor; and between both these elements comes the Person of the God-Man, who is not *a* man, amongst and by the side of many others, but *the* man, the second spiritual Adam of the whole race,* who is just as much connected with sinners by means of His true though most holy humanity, as with the Lord of the world by means of His divine Nature, in whom love is manifested as brightly as righteousness in the Father, and who again reveals the Father's love as brightly as His own

* With respect to the *representative* character, a more detailed explanation will be found in the notes to Rom. v. 12, sqq. We are immediately concerned in this place only with the idea of *satisfaction*, which is quite scriptural, even though the expression is not found in Scripture.

righteousness. That, therefore, which cannot be conceived as united in any human act (in that man can ever only exercise *either* grace *or* justice), the highest act of grace, the absolution of a whole sinful race, and the perfectly righteous punishment of sinners, in the death of Him who bore the whole race in Himself (as the centre embraces the collective rays of the circumference), is all harmonized in the death of Christ; and therefore the giving up of the Son by the Father, and the free sacrifice of the Son, constitute the *highest Act* of God, worthy to form the subject of preaching to the whole human race, because it has power to breathe life into the dead bones, and truly to impart that peace which flows from the forgiveness of sins. It is to this objective act of God that faith attaches itself according to Protestant doctrine, and by the powerful glow of its flame all those half or wholly Pelagian views must be dissipated, which would have the divine life of love to derive assistance from the exertions of man's natural powers. For wnere life is not awakened by gazing on that serpent which is lifted up (an effect just the contrary to that produced by beholding the head of Medusa), there the most exactly defined commands, and the most fakir-like exertions and acts of self-denial, can only produce a bare respectability, or ridiculous conceit. In this fountain thus opened alone flows the water of life, on this altar alone can heavenly fire be obtained;—here righteousness and grace melt into an ineffable unity, as they are one in God himself; for the forgiveness of sins on account of the death of Christ is *οὐδὲ κατὰ νόμον, οὐδὲ κατὰ νόμον, ἀλλὰ ὑπὲρ νόμον καὶ ὑπὲρ νόμον*, *i. e.*, not *according to* the law, for by that man was to bear his own sin, and yet not *against* the law, since in the sufferings of Christ satisfaction was rendered to its demands, but *above* the law, because grace is mightier than righteousness, and *for* the law, because it is itself established thereby. (See Tholuck "von der Sünde," p. 108, 3d edition.)

It is only in this mode of comprehending it that the representation of the Apostle receives also its exact verbal interpretation. He calls Christ *ἱλαστήριον*, a word which is not, however to be taken= *ἱλασμός*, or to be explained with the addition of *θῦμα* of the sin-offering, but which must be understood, with *ἐπίθεμα* supplied, o the *covering* of the *Ark of the Covenant*, in which expression, at all events, the idea of *expiation* is most distinctly enunciated, even according to the etymology of the word. This covering, in fact, made of fine gold, 2½ cubits long and a cubit and a half broad, at whose ends the two cherubim stood overshadowing the ark with their wings, was the throne of the Shechinah, symbol of the presence of God; on this account it is called, Heb. iv. 16, *θρόνος χάριτος*. (See Exod. xxv. 17, etc.) On this mercy-seat the High Priest sprinkled once every year, on the great day of atonement, the blood of a bullock seven times, and the blood of a goat seven times, to make atonement for the sin of the people (Levit. xvi. 18, etc.) This lid is called now in the O. T. כַּפֹּרֶת, from כִּפֵּר, "to cover," *i. e.*, according to the Old Testament view, "to forgive," because sin in this dispensation could not yet be entirely removed, but only remained suspended through the long-suffering of God, until the completion of that true sacrifice which was able to take it away. The LXX. translate it *ἱλαστήριον*. As now the whole form of worship of the O. T. was symbolical, so this institution also represented the real truth in an image. As the mercy-seat of the tabernacle presented itself to the spirits of the people as the place from which the forgiveness of their sins proceeded; so also is the Redeemer solemnly presented, in the Holy of Holies of the universe, as in the true Temple of God, to the believing gaze of the whole of that spiritual Israel, which is gathered out of all nations, in order that they may receive forgiveness of sins through His blood. As He is therefore the sacrifice, so is He also the mercy-seat itself, because all contradictions are harmonized in Him; "God was in Christ reconciling the world unto Himself." (2 Cor. v. 19.) So God Himself was enthroned between the cherubim, above the sacred covering of the Ark of the Covenant, and accepted the offering made for the forgiveness of the sins of the people. (Lev. xvi. 2; Heb. ix. 7, etc.)

On the side of man *faith* alone is required (*διὰ πίστεως* is not to be connected with *δικαιούμενοι δωρεάν*, so as to stand parallel with *διὰ τῆς ἀπολυτρώσεως*, but with *ἱλαστήριον*, only we are not to consider this latter as dependent upon *πίστις*, but must supply as follows, "which must be received through faith in His blood"); but this faith is not by any means to be regarded as a human work, but as the gift of God, and is indeed *πίστις ἐν τῷ αὐτοῦ ἅιματι*. (*Πίστις ἐν ἅιματι* is used according to the analogy of *πίστις ἐν Χριστῷ*, Galat. iii. 26; and several times in Ephes. i. 15;

in which phrases no interchange of prepositions is to be assumed, for the indwelling of believers in Christ, and of Christ in them, and their abiding with Him and His blood is indicated by them.) But with respect to the usual assertion, that ἅιμα denotes the bloody death of Christ, and that this represents the collective sufferings of Christ, it is not indeed untrue, but still does not exhaust the meaning. We *never* find a πίστις εἰς θάνατον spoken of,* it is the *blood* of Christ which is constantly mentioned. (Acts. xx. 28; Rom. v. 9; Ephes. i. 7, ii. 13; Col. i. 14, 20; 1 Pet. i. 18, 19; 1 John i. 7; Heb. ix. 12, 14, x. 19, xiii. 12; Rev. i. 5, v. 9, vii. 14, xii. 11.) The constant use of this language must be founded upon some inward reason, and this Heb. ix. 22 plainly discovers to us, when it says, " without shedding of blood there is no remission of sins." (See Levit. xvii. 11.) For, as we find it expressed in this latter passage, " the life of the body is in the blood." The phrase πίστις εἰς θάνατον would therefore be much less suitable, inasmuch as in it the idea of the forgiveness of sins and of the expiatory sacrifice does not come forward, and θάνατος, consequently, only denotes death as such, the mere dying. But the death of Christ, which is life itself (John i. 3), is the effusion or pouring forth of His holy life, *i.e.*, of His blood, which He also communicates constantly to His people in faith, and in the sacrament of the Lord's Supper. (John vi. 47, 54.) The formula πίστις ἐν τῷ ἅιματι is therefore in the highest degree important, in that it declares, that the shedding of the blood and the death of Christ, who is called the Life itself, is the expiation of the sin of the world, and not something dead, but the most living thing possible, so that in His death, death itself seems to be swallowed up of life. As therefore the vial of balsam, if it is to refresh all those who are in the house by the odour of its contents, must be opened and poured forth, so also did the Redeemer breathe out into the dead world that fulness of life which was contained in Him, by pouring forth His holy blood, the supporter of His life,† and this

* We find in Rom. v. 10, " we are reconciled to God by the *death* of His Son," only because the opposition with ζωή required this expression. In Col. i. 22, θάνατος is more exactly defined in ver. 20.

† No doubt a true and deep idea lies at the foundation of Ackermann's ingenious treatise " On the chemical feature in the Christian conception of sanctification " (in Fichte's Zeitschrift für Philosophie and speculative Theologie. Bonn. 1837. 1 vol. 2d part, pp. 232 sqq.); this namely, that an analogy exists between the operation of Christ

voluntarily, since none could take His life from Him. (John x. 18.) Thus did He, through the Holy Spirit, offer Himself as the most precious sacrifice to God, that He might purge our consciences by the sprinkling of His blood, to serve the living God. (Heb. ix. 14.)

As to the concluding words of ver. 25, *δικαιοσύνη*, in the connection *εἰς ἔνδειξιν τῆς δικαιοσύνης αὐτοῦ*, might no doubt be understood of the *goodness* of God, which manifests itself as plainly as His *strict justice* in the sacrifice of Christ; but the addition of *διὰ τὴν πάρεσιν κ. τ. λ.*, and ver. 31, demand here, in the first place, the adoption of the latter signification. Those sins of the world before Christ, which had hitherto been, as it were, overlooked (Ps. lxxviii. 38), rendered necessary the final manifestation of God's righteousness, and were punished by the righteous God in Christ, the representative of the whole race, who voluntarily gave Himself up for all. At the same time, as is proved by the *πρὸς ἔνδειξιν κ. τ. λ.* in ver. 26 (which is by no means to be considered as a simple repetition of *εἰς ἔνδειξιν*), there is a constant allusion to that *grace* which manifests itself in the work of redemption, and is particularly expressed in the *δικαιοῦντα κ. τ. λ.*; and, in fact, both these attributes, justice and mercy, like the divine and human natures in Christ, can properly only be considered separate *in abstracto* in the work of redemption, inasmuch as they are actually amalgamated into a perfect unity therein.

Πάρεσις does not occur in any other place in the Bible; if it had therefore been intended in St Paul's mind, to be synonymous with *ἄφεσις*, as was grammatically possible, the Apostle would doubtless have chosen, in preference, the latter well-known word. Exod. xxxii. 34, in connection with Acts xvii. 30, is a sufficient explanation of this passage; *ὑπεριδεῖν* = עָבַר there signifies "the overlooking," or "letting alone." The *ἁμαρτήματα προγεγονότα* can, however, according to the following *ἐν τῷ νῦν καιρῷ*, only mean the sins of the world before Christ's coming, in connection, of course, with that original sin of Adam's, which was the source of

and His blood (*i. e.*, of His life) upon the sinful race of man, and chemical agents and reagents; that therefore God has formed Christ by means of the development of His human life into a special source of healing and principle of attraction. But this idea, when carried out into detail, easily gives rise to dangerous errors, and tends to lower the whole process of restoration which is revealed in Christianity into a mere physical one.

[The Translator has thought it expedient to omit the remainder of this note.]

all subsequent transgressions. In the O. T. there was no *real*, but only a symbolical forgiveness of sins;* the former could not then exist (Heb. ix. 12, 13), because it was only through their relation to Christ that the sacrifices of the O. T. received their power of forgiveness.

Finally, nothing can be more erroneous than, as Rückert and Reiche have recently proposed, to confine the redeeming and forgiving power of Christ to those sins only which were committed in the time of *ἄγνοια,* and to deny the possibility of any forgiveness in the case of believers. This view, consistently carried out, would entirely destroy the very essence of the gospel, and convert it into glad tidings for the unbelieving only, but for believers a new and even more hopeless law. The utter fallacy of this opinion will, however, be demonstrated more at length in the notes on vii. 14, etc. Much rather may we regard the time of *ἄγνοια* as belonging not only to the whole race, and to whole nations, but also to *every individual,* at the same time that it must ever be regarded as a state which only gradually disappears. We must, if I may be allowed thus to express myself, conceive of humanity as divided not merely according to its breadth, but also according to its length; and every individual passes through, in his own case, the same stages of development as the race. (The connection of *ἐν τῇ ἀνοχῇ τοῦ Θεοῦ* with what follows is quite unsuitable, it must be construed with *πάρεσις,* of which it discovers the inward ground.)

Ver. 26. As the Apostle had first exhibited the side of severity, he now also brings forward that of grace, which no less displays itself in the work of redemption. If to designate this he likewise uses the expression *δικαιοσύνη*, this arises no doubt from his desire to accumulate expressions of the same kind. As *δικαιοσύνη* itself proceeds from Christ, as He produces nothing but *δικαίους*, so also His work, in every form of its manifestation, has the divine *δικαιοσύνη* as its foundation,

* The expression *ἡ ἄφεσις τῶν ἁμαρτιῶν* or *παραπτωμάτων* (Ephes. i. 7,) must not be confounded with *ἄφεσις ἁμαρτήματος*. The theocratical forgiveness of any *particular* sin was possible even under the O. T., but the forgiveness of *all* sins, actual sins as well as hereditary sin, can only proceed from Christ, and is a divine act. It presupposes, namely, nothing less than the creation of a new and holy man, and the slaying of the old man, inasmuch as it is regeneration itself, on which account the forgiveness *of sins* is at the same time life and salvation. This happens therefore also only *once or twice*, and is only *confirmed* from time to time to the believer, as in the Eucharist; the former, however, is frequently repeated. (1 John ii. 1; Job xxxiii. 29.)

To consider πρὸς ἔνδειξιν as a mere repetition of the foregoing εἰς ἔνδειξιν is not quite suitable ; to be sure, ἐν τῷ νῦν καιρῷ might seem to be in its favour ; but at the same time, δικαιοῦντα κ. τ. λ. is too much opposed to this construction.—In the words εἰς τὸ εἶναι αὐτὸν δίκαιον is implied at the same time the idea of His being recognized as such by men.—Δικαιοῦν can only be understood as a manifestation of grace.

Ver. 27–29. After this explanation of the nature of the new way of salvation, St Paul returns to that question, which he had been treating in iii. 1, etc., whether, namely, there was any advantage in the case of the Jews,* and answers, no ! (Ἐκκλείω, see Galat. iv. 17, means "to exclude, *i. e.*, to make unavailing, inadmissible.") For since in this place the question is not concerning such works as the law could alone produce, but concerning faith, Gentiles as well as Jews had access to this grace, in case they believed. If the Jews had lived in true love, they would have rejoiced on this account, but instead of this, they were offended because God was so gracious.

Νόμος has here the more extensive signification of "divine ordinance or institution." The gospel may therefore be called the *νόμος πίστεως*, in so far as it is that divine ordinance which requires of men faith. And indeed faith *alone* (as Luther rightly translates this passage in the sense of the Apostle), for *in* it is contained every thing, as the collective fruit of the tree in its germ, *beyond* and *besides* it there is nothing which belongs to the same spiritual position. Since, however, Gentiles as well as Jews are here spoken of, the ἔργα νόμου can only mean the works of the moral law, which are derived from the will of God, demanding man's obedience.† These can be, in the most favourable case, but the blossoms of the man's own life, and are therefore transitory like this life itself, but the works of faith partake of the eternal nature of that principle from which they proceed.

* In the conception of κάυχησις is implied that which belongs to self, as opposed to grace ; this iv. 2 shows with especial clearness. To ἐξεκλείσθη we must supply ὑπὸ τοῦ Θεοῦ.

† Glöckler is quite mistaken in his view, that χωρὶς ἔργων νόμου is to be translated, "without the law of works," as the very collocation of the words show. The law, according to St Paul, is only to be abolished in its old form, in which it appears as making requirements upon the man from without ; in the economy of grace, it presents itself again as an inwardly operative law. (See notes to Galat. ii. 16, 18.)

Ver. 30–31. The one God stands in the same relation to all His children, and His different modes of dealing, do not contradict one another,* but afford to one another mutual support.

'Επείπερ, *quandoquidem, siquidem,* is nowhere else found in the N. T. On this account, also, it is not probable, that the reading εἴπερ, which Lachman has admitted into his text from AC and other MSS. etc., of critical authority, is the original one.—'Εκ and διὰ πίστεως do not stand parallel to one another, as designations of the source and cause, as Reiche still supposes; in this case ἐκ τῆς πίστεως must also have been written; rather does διὰ τῆς πίστεως alone refer to the principal thought. 'Εκ πίστεως has a special reference to the Jews. (see iv. 12), who supposed that they were partakers of divine grace, not as believers, but simply as the children of Abraham after the flesh.—The gospel establishes the law, because it is the most sublime manifestation of the holiness and strictness of God. Sin never appears more fearful than at Golgotha, where, on account of it, God spared not His own Son.

§ 7. ABRAHAM JUSTIFIED BY FAITH.

(IV. 1—25.)

In order to demonstrate more exactly the connection between the N. T. and the law, and to vindicate the gospel from every charge of introducing anything strange into religion, the Apostle next proceeds to show, that even the saints of the O. T., amongst whom he mentions Abraham and David, had walked in the path of righteousness by faith. In order rightly to comprehend this whole argument, we must further remark, as was already observed on Matth. xi. 11., that the position of all the pious men in the O. T. was by no means similar. There were some amongst them whose piety wore a purely legal expression, *e. g.* Elijah, others, again, in whom, whilst the legal form retired into the background, the life of faith was predominant. To these last be-

* Calvin has this apt remark on the passage: "Ubi lex fidei opponitur, ex eo statim quandam repugnantiæ suspicionem caro arripit, ac si alterum alteri adversaretur. Præsertim vero facile obtsnet falsa hæc imaginatio inter eos, qui præposterâ legis intelligentiâ imbuti nihil aliud in eâ quærunt quàm operum justitiam, promissionibus omissis."

long in an especial degree Abraham and David, the development of whose spiritual life bears in fact considerable resemblance to that of believing Christians. At the same time, with all this similarity we must not lose sight of the difference between them, for by so doing we should rob the gospel of its specific character (John i. 17). The faith of Abraham and David had indeed, as well as the Christian's, the person of the Redeemer for its object, but then it was directed to Him that *should come*, not to Him who *had appeared ;* it was only after the appearance of Christ and the accomplishment of His work that real power could proceed from him. (John vii. 39.) The very regeneration of the O. T., if we are willing to assume its existence (see notes on Matth. xi. 11), can therefore only be regarded as *symbolical*, a character which the Apostle himself seems to ascribe to it in ver. 23.

Vers. 1, 2. St Paul proves from the O. T. itself, that the righteousness of Abraham had not proceeded from his works. * He names Abraham as being the natural progenitor of the Jewish race, as one whose spiritual character formed the illustrious example to which all Israelites looked.

The phrase *τί οὖν ἐροῦμεν* has here lost its ordinary form ; for *τί* must be connected with *εὑρηκέναι*. If we were to take *τί ἐροῦμεν* in the usual way, we should still be obliged to supply *τί* to *εὑρηκέναι*. (See Æschyl. Eumenid. v. 154.) In fact, St Paul does not wish to ask, *what* has Abraham found or obtained, but *how* has he received that righteousness which we allow him to have? This thought is, however, intimated in the turn, what has he obtained *κατὰ σάρκα*. The answer therefore is also not completely carried out, but only negatively ; ver. 3 contains, on the other hand, the *positive* side though indirectly. The *οὖν* in ver. 1 connects this chapter with *ἀλλὰ νόμον ἱστῶμεν* in the last chapter ; "If then we establish the law by faith, so that the two cannot contradict one another, what can Abraham have obtained by works?" —We can only connect *κατὰ σάρκα* with *εὑρηκέναι* and not with *πατέρα*. According to the sense it = *ἐξ ἔργων*, ver. 2. We may best understand *σάρξ* here of the outward in general (Galat. iii. 3), as contrasted with the *πνεῦμα*, the inward and life-giving. (See notes to Jas. ii. 26.)—*Δικαιοῦσθαι ἐξ ἔργων* = *ἔχειν δικαιο-*

* That it is possible to take another view of the history of Abraham is shown by the epistle of St James, c. ii.

σύνην ἐκ νόμου.—*Καύχημα* denotes the act of boasting and the object of the same, *materia gloriandi.*—The fourth verse discovers plainly the ideas which lie at the foundation of this whole argument. Works give merit, merit justifies a person in making demands or in boasting; no *χάρις* can therefore consist with works, but only a relation of debt. But God can never stand in the relation of a debtor to any creature, therefore St Paul says *ἀλλ' οὐ πρὸς τὸν Θεόν.* For even where a *δικαιοσύνη τοῦ νόμου* is in question, it is only by a gracious condescension on God's part that this becomes possible ; it remains, in fact, always only a righteousness in the sight of men. In ver. 2, *εἰ ἐδικαιώθη*—*ἔχει καύχημα* is to be construed, "if he namely (as is in fact the case), is justified by works, he has indeed some glory, but not before God, only before men." St Paul then says here the same as is found James ii. 21. (With respect to *εἰ* with the indicative, see Winer's Gram. p. 267.) If it meant, "if he had become righteous, he would have glory," we should find *ἔιχεν αν.*

Vers. 3–5. The Apostle then proves from Gen. xv. 6, a passage which he quotes from the LXX., that it was not by his works that Abraham he became righteous, but that his faith was reckoned to him for righteousness. *Works* might have brought him into the relation of a debtor or creditor, but *faith* brought him into the relation of grace, since he relied upon a promise flowing entirely from the divine mercy. This line of argument, taken in connection with chapter vii., in considering which we shall return to it, is most admirably calculated to give us a clear conception of St Paul's doctrine of justification. For it is not *δικαιοῦσθαι* itself, but *λογίζεσθαι εἰς δικαιοσύνην*, which corresponds to the Hebrew וַיַּחְשְׁבֶהָ לּוֹ צְדָקָה, and which forms the centre of the Apostle's statement in this chapter. The two are, however, by no means synonymous, but stand exactly in the same relation to one another as the [Roman] Catholic (so far at least as it contains truth) and the Protestant doctrines of justification, inasmuch as the former is implied in the *δικαιοῦσθαι* (to be *made* a righteous person), the latter in the *λογίζεσθαι* (to be *accounted* as such). Whatsoever is reckoned or imputed to a person, that the person cannot himself possess (see Rom. ii. 26, *ἀκροβυστία εἰς περιτομὴν λογίζεται*), but he is looked upon and treated as if he had it. This now is not predicated in the present passage of Abraham only, who lived 2000 years before the reconciliation effected in Christ, without which the δικαιοσύνην τοῦ Θεοῦ cannot be conceived as existing, but also of *those who lived* according to his example *after* Christ (vers. 11, 24), so that the formula λογίζεσθαι εἰς δικαιοσύνην appears as a general designation of justification, in addition to δικαιοῦσθαι. In order duly to understand the meaning of these expressions, and to perceive their bearing upon the subject before us, we must consider yet more closely than was done at iii. 21, the *transition* from the legal standing point to that of grace, a matter which it is particularly difficult to represent. When the law has accomplished its purpose on the man, *i. e.*, when the ἐπίγνωσις τῆς ἁμαρτίας (iii. 20) or true μετάνοια is produced in him, he regards δικαιοσύνη (which he recognizes as a reality, and in recognizing which he becomes aware of the contrast of his own condition), as something completely *external* to himself. But in the announcement of the Messiah the promise is made to him, that this righteousness shall through His work become an *inward* reality to himself; this announcement he embraces in *faith*, and, although still sinful and far from δικαιοσύνη, yet his faith in that which is outward and future is reckoned to him as righteousness, *i. e.*, he is treated as a righteous person, and therefore as standing in a state of grace.* Now, the difficulty in this view lies especially in the circumstance, that God from His veracity cannot regard a person as that which he is not; if the man is sinful, it seems plain that the True One must look upon him and treat him as a sinner, until he ceases to be such; and if he actually ceases to be such, he can then again only be regarded as a righteous person and no longer as a sinner at all. On this argument rests the opposition of the [Roman] Catholic Church to the Protestant view, an argument which it seems at first sight impossible to refute; but yet on closer examination it proves to be false, and calculated to lead men entirely astray with respect to the way of salvation. In fact, according to the [Roman] Catholic view, it is not the objective purpose of God which forms the irrefragable foundation of man's faith, but the shifting condition of his own heart. If the man thinks that he can discover this condition of righteous-

* Redemption makes the man in the progress of his sanctification free *from* sin; *with* sin no one can become blessed, as is indeed self-evident, for sin itself is the only source whatsoever of misery. But it is quite true that redemption begins *in* sin, that is to say, the man must begin as a sinner, must look upon himself in faith as righteous *for Christ's sake*, not on account of the somewhat improved condition of his own soul.

ness wrought in him, he assures himself of his state of grace, but if in times of temptation he cannot discover it in himself, he is doubtful of it, or despairs of it. The purged eye of the regenerate man can detect even in his best condition much in himself that still needs to be cast out. (See notes on vii. 14.) The [Roman] Catholic Church consequently maintains, and in perfect consistency with her principles, that man in his earthly condition can never be *certain* of his being in a state of grace, but must remain in constant uncertainty; whilst the Protestant Church teaches the exact contrary. The truth of the Protestant conception of this subject is seen most distinctly when we look more closely at that principle on which the [Roman] Catholic doctrine is founded, namely, that God cannot regard any one as different from what he is. If we were to take this thought in its literal sense, since without the work of Christ no forgiveness of sins and no sanctification is conceivable, it would follow that *before* the accomplishment of Christ's atoning sacrifice no holy man could have lived, which contradicts the whole of the doctrine of Scripture. That notion must therefore be modified in the first place, in accordance with that principle, which teaches, that in every action of God all His attributes cooperate. God can therefore no doubt account a man to be something which he is not at present, whilst namely He looks to His own purpose, which is to render the man that which he is to be. As unalterable, therefore, as is this determination, so true also is God's contemplation of that which *is* not yet as already existing (ver. 17). But besides this, it belongs to the very nature of faith, as a living condition, and not the mere assent of the understanding to a thing as historically true, that it already contains within itself the essence of the object of belief; it is an act of the man by which he appropriates the Divine, which of course pre-supposes that the inmost nature of man is akin to the Divine. At the time of Abraham, indeed, Christ Himself and His whole work were as yet future; of Abraham, therefore, nothing more could be said, than that God counted to him his faith for righteousness, inasmuch as He regarded this future work as already accomplished in His omniscience, to which all things are present. But in the case of all those who believe after the coming of Christ, faith does already in itself contain the substance of this righteousness, in that the Redeemer has once for all accomplished the whole work of justification, as well, indeed, as of sanctification and glorification for all men (Rom. viii. 30). But if faith turns itself away from its proper object, the *Christ without* us and the objective purpose of God in man's redemption, and directs itself to the *Christ within us* as the ground, not the consequence of redemption, and if the man only considers himself the object of divine favour because he discovers Him in himself, and only so long as this is the case;—then faith altogether loses its proper nature, and the man falls again under the law, as was once the case with the Galatians. For man, therefore, so long as he is in this world, the λογίζεσθαι εἰς δικαιοσύνην must ever remain the way to true δικαιοσύνη itself; and if he thinks that he no longer needs the *former* because he already possesses the *latter*, he has fallen from faith.* As therefore the forgiveness of sins (that which is vouchsafed *once*, by which man is translated into the state of grace, as well as that which is *daily* needed) is not imparted to the *old* man, who must die, neither to the *new* man, who cannot sin (1 John iii. 9), but to the inmost personality itself, which is conscious of the old man as well as of the new as *belonging to it*, and which in the progress of regeneration must be gradually altogether transformed into the new man; so also does it happen with respect to the λογίζεσθαι. Righteousness is not imputed to the old man but to the true personality, which perceives the presence of the old man as *its own*, but with deep repentance and a lively longing to be delivered from it. The substance of this true personality is, however, nothing else but that *scintilla* of the divine likeness which has remained in man since the fall, and without which sin would form the very substance of the human being. Faith attaches itself to this spark, and then, deriving nourishment from the higher world, elicits once more from this spark the flame of the divine life.

Ἐργάζεσθαι = ἔργα ποιεῖν, and that moreover as a means of attaining to δικαιοσύνη. According to the divine *jus talionis*, man is treated according to the position which he assumes; the man who has recourse to justice alone, is treated according to its stern law, "Cursed is every one who continueth not in *all* that is written in the law" (Galat. iii. 10); but whosoever, on the other hand, clings

* We must not therefore frame the antithesis in this manner, *either* the man is a sinner, *or* he is a regenerate and holy man; the latter also is still a sinner, inasmuch as he retains the old man until death. But in his case God does not look to the old man, but to His own purpose of grace in Christ, and regards him for Christ's sake as altogether righteous.

in faith to grace, is regarded according to its over-ruling law. **Χάρις**, as the opposite to ὀφείλημα, has here accordingly the sense of that which is undeserved, that which depends on no merit.—In ver. 5 the epithet applied to God, δικαιῶν τὸν ἀσεβῆ, does not refer to Abraham *alone*, as Reiche still asserts, nor yet to other men *without* him ; rather is it a general designation of God's relation to mankind. For to suppose that allusion is here made to some particular sin of Abraham's, for instance to his participation in the idolatry of his father Terah, as many commentators on this passage have wished to assume, is quite inadmissible ; the question is entirely about universal sinfulness. And then we have in this way of understanding the passage an important proof, that St Paul does not consider any one as excluded from the general sinfulness of the race ; even Abraham himself, that venerable and holy patriarch, is an ἀσεβής. *All* men in respect of God are in a state of ἀσέβεια, and unable by their own powers to raise themselves into any other condition.* God *alone*, therefore, is the author of δικαιοσύνη, and proves Himself to be such to those who come forward to meet Him in πίστις ; the endeavour to establish one's own righteousness is the surest method of shutting one's self out from the δικαιοσύνη Θεοῦ. (See Rom. x. 3.)

Ver. 6-8. St Paul then corroborates the truth he has advanced by the example of David, from Ps. xxxii. 1, 2, a passage which is likewise quoted according to the LXX. If we find here expressly added χωρὶς ἔργων, it is yet plainly not the meaning of the Apostle that ἔργα should be *wanting ;* on the contrary, these possess in faith, and in that imputation of righteousness of which it is the means, their most plentiful source (Galat. v. 6) ; but however richly and purely works may proceed from this source, the *foundation* of final blessedness does not exist in *them*, but in that *principle* by which alone they become possible, *i. e.*, not in men but in God. As, therefore, it is to God *alone* that thanks are due for the ex-

* The *degrees* of sinfulness are not to be considered in regard of the life of faith in and for themselves, but only the *effect* which is thereby produced upon the inmost condition of the soul. A person in a deeply sunken state may stand quite near to the kingdom of God, if sin has made him of a broken and contrite spirit (Matt. xxi. 31; Luke xv. 30), and a strict observer of the law outwardly may be far from this kingdom, if he has become through his striving hard-hearted, loveless, and arrogant. The most desirable condition is, of course, one of earnest striving and freedom from gross transgressions, combined with humility, a sense of need, and faith. But every one who desires to come to Christ, must altogether, and in everything, recognize himself as a sinner

istence, and creation of man, so also to Him *alone* for man's *goodness;* it is not as if there entered into the latter *two* creative energies, first that of God, and then that of man (such a Dualism makes all true goodness impossible, for this *consists especially in the deliverance from all that belongs to self*); there is assuredly but *one,* namely that of God, because all pure, good, true action on man's part, *is the act of God,* the only true Good, *in him,* so that man has and can regard nothing as *his own,* but sin, unfaithfulness, and unbelief. (See notes ix. 1.)

In the passage, however, adduced by the Apostle, the question appears to be not with regard to the *positive* imputation of righteousness, but only the *negative* non-imputation of sin, whilst at the same time nothing is expressed about faith; we might therefore suppose that the passage did not apply to the present subject; but *forgiveness of sins* is surely not a human fancy, or a human action, in which a man says to himself, "I have forgiveness of my sins," but a divine work, a living *word of God* spoken into the heart, which faith alone can appropriate. But the word and act of God is the most positive thing we can conceive, it is *being* itself; on which account Luther most rightly terms the forgiveness of sins, "life and blessedness," for it contains within itself the imputation of the righteousness of God.

Ἀφιέναι and *ἐπικαλύπτειν* = נָשָׂא and כִּסָּה. In the first expression we perceive more of the New Testament aspect of the forgiveness of sins, according to which it is the real taking away of sin, even though this be but gradual; in the second, on the other hand, as well as in the *ἁμαρτίαν οὐ λογίζεσθαι,* there is more of the Old Testament view, according to which sin *remains,* though under the forbearance of God (Rom. iii. 25), until the completion of the work of Christ, in consequence of which the actual forgiveness of sins was first imparted to those who lived before Christ. Comp. Matth. xxvii. 53, 1 Pet. iii. 18.

Ver. 9, 10. Hereupon the Apostle returns to the consideration of the relation between Jews and Gentiles, and proves that this way of salvation by faith was designed, not merely for the Jews, but *also* for the Gentiles, since the occurrence in Gen. xv. 6 took place *before* circumcision was instituted, at a time, therefore, when Abraham stood on a level with the Gentiles.

In ver. 9, *ἔρχεται* must be supplied. It were better to connect λέγομεν γάρ. κ. τ. λ. with ver. 10, for the sense is, "from the passage concerning David it is not so distinctly to be gathered, whether or not the Gentiles are to be included amongst those to whom faith is counted for righteousness, but this may very well be done from that concerning Abraham, for," etc. In ver. 10 πῶς is to be translated "under what circumstances."

Ver. 11, 12. Circumcision was not, therefore, the *means* of his justification, but only the *sign* of that justification which had before taken place; in the same way, also, that baptism does not beget faith, but presupposes it. On this account also his name, "the Father of the Faithful," does not relate merely to those who are physically circumcised, but to all those, whether Jews or Gentiles, who like him believe.

A C and other documents of critical authority read περιτομήν instead of περιτομῆς; the genitive is, however, to be preferred as well on external as internal grounds.—Σημεῖον = אוֹת, that which points back to something else; σφραγίς the impression of a seal, by which something is confirmed (1 Cor. ix. 2; 2 Tim. ii. 19.) In the same sense is תוֹתָם used in Hebrew.—Δικαιοσύνη πίστεως (ver. 14), the righteousness imputed is treated as a true righteousness.—'Εις τὸ εἶναι is not, as Tholuck supposes, to be understood merely of the consequence, but of the intention, as ver. 16 proves. Abraham received the seal of circumcision first, *in order that* he might be presented as the general *Father* of believers. In the conception of Father the similarity which exists between him and his children, is the point here insisted on; believers are his true children, for the outward circumcision is the unessential part (ii. 28, 29), and these alone receive also the righteousness which he received.—In the words πιστεύοντες δἰ ακροβυστίας, διὰ is not to be understood *causaliter*, but as in ii. 27, "during, under such circumstances."—The transition from the genitive to the dative (τοῖς) was perhaps occasioned by his looking back to λογισθῆναι.—Στοιχέω = περιπατέω, comp. Galat. v. 25, vi. 16; Phil. iii. 16. To understand the Gentiles, again, by the term στοιχοῦντες is inadmissible, and would oblige us to assume that τοῖς οὐκ stands for οὐ τοῖς, an inversion which would be too hard.

Ver. 13. This leads to the more explicit statement, that with Abraham's case *legal* relations had nothing whatsoever to do, but, as in the case of every promise, grace alone. It is remarkable, that it is not merely said, the promise did *not* come by the law for of course all that follows upon this must be regarded as reward, but that there is added, it came through the righteousness of faith. We might expect that it would be said through grace, for it seems natural that the promise should go before, and then faith apprehend the same as an object, and not *vice versâ*. But this difficulty vanishes, if we consider that the promises of God to Abraham form a climax, and that in this, whilst the first promise preceded his faith, all the higher ones followed it. In this place, as Tholuck rightly remarks, reference is made to that promise, which succeeded Abraham's greatest trial of faith (Gen. xxii. 16), and therefore his *κληρονομία κόσμου* does not mean the mere possession of the land of Canaan, in an outward or inward sense, but the incorporation in himself of the whole race, so far as it is faithful, and the spiritual government of the world by his influence proceeding therefrom. At the same time, the idea reaches yet further, as even the Rabbinical writers indicate in that saying, "possidet Abraham pater noster (et nos cum illo) mundum hunc et futurum." In its deepest sense it points to Christ's dominion over the world, which his believing people shall share with him (Rom. viii. 17; Rev. iii. 21), and in which the inward powers of the spiritual world shall manifest their energy outwardly. On this account, also, *τῷ σπέρματι ἀυτοῦ* is added,* by which expression, according to Galat. iii. 16, St Paul considers Christ to be designated, and further, in Christ, as the second Adam, the collective body of believers. (Galat. iii. 28, 29.) A similar promise is not to be found in so many words in any passage of the O. T., but it is given in substance in Gen. xv. 7 (where Canaan is promised) and Gen. xxii. 16.

Ver. 14, 15. If accordingly they which are of the law be heirs, the promise would be of none effect, for they would be able to demand all as *reward*. But since none could so keep the law, as to be able to found any demands upon it, since it rather kindles God's anger against them, the whole assumption is inadmissible. (In ver. 14, *οἱ ἐκ νόμου* are opposed to *οἱ ἐκ πίστεως*, see Galat. iii. 9, 10.—*Κενοῦσθαι* means to be converted into something, *κενόν* empty,

* We must not overlook *ἢ τῷ στέρματι*, instead of which only unimportant MSS. read *καὶ τῷ σπέρματι*. The *ἢ* is to be taken as a nearer definition, in the sense "or much rather," for it was in Christ that Abraham first became actually the heir and lord of the world, and in Christ the human race.

powerless.—Between ver. 14 and ver. 15, we must supply some such expression as, "But it is according to the very nature of the law impossible, that it should make men heirs of the world, for so far from conferring merit, it only awakens indignation.—Ver. 15, *ὀργὴν κατεργάζεται*, not by its nature, for that is holy and good, but through its power in bringing to light the depths of sin. (See more in the notes on vii. 10, etc.) The words *οὖ γὰρ οὐκ. κ. τ. λ.*, are an addition merely intended to give a cursory explanation of *ὀργὴν κατεργάζεσθαι;* it is the law which makes men first appear in their worst condition, how then should it be able to make them the heirs of the world?

Ver. 16. The promise, then, could only come through faith, inasmuch as it thus only could remain a *true* promise, *i. e.*, a wholly gracious assurance; thus only, indeed, could it appear assured to all, inasmuch as by its dependence upon the law the promise of the faithful God would depend for its fulfilment upon unfaithful man, whom the law is intended only to exhibit as exceeding sinful. The contrast intended in the words *τῷ ἐκ τοῦ νόμου*, and *τῷ ἐκ πίστεως*, is not therefore between Jews and Gentiles, but only between men seeking to establish a righteousness by the law, and believers whether amongst Jews or Gentiles. The member of the theocratic nation has not merely as such a share in the promise, if he is not also at the same time a believer. But in these words the expression *ἐις τὸ εἶναι βεβαίαν* introduces us to an idea, which is very important for the understanding of the connection of St Paul's ideas as a whole. Everything, namely, which depends upon the decision, faithfulness, and constancy of such an irresolute and wavering being as man, is, in St Paul's view, extremely uncertain; but that which depends upon God, "with whom is no variableness neither shadow of turning," is firmly established. On this account, the divine promises afford an irrefragable certainty, because nothing can annul them; as God gives the promise, so also does he raise up men to believe it, and thus accomplishes all His works. But so great is the perversity of man, that he will not recognize this most certain foundation of salvation; he wishes to have God's unalterable promises and prophecies considered as *dependent* upon him for their execution, though in this way the fulfilment of a prophecy would tend to the merit of man, and not to the glory of God, which were plainly a blasphemous assertion. According to St Paul's way of looking at the matter, the blessedness of the man is certain, only because God has promised it and firmly intends it, and he only who believes in this decided will of God, has this salvation also wrought in him. (With respect to the mode in which, notwithstanding, man's freedom remains inviolate, and is in fact thus only truly established, see the notes to chap. ix. 1, etc.)

Ver. 17. The citation of Gen. xvii. 5 (which passage is also quoted exactly according to the LXX.), is intended to prove still more decidedly Abraham's right to the title of Father of the Faithful, as a relation extending beyond the limits of Israel, and embracing all nations. (*Τιθέναι* = the Hebrew נָתַן.) But with respect to the latter half of the verse, which presents many difficulties, in the first place the reading *ἐπίστευσας*, which is given by F.G. and the Syriac version, by means of which the following words are connected with the quotation, must be rejected as inadmissible, on account of the preponderance of critical evidence in favour of the usual reading. The construction *κατέναντι οὗ ἐπίστευσε Θεοῦ* must be explained as an attraction of an unusual character certainly, since in this case a dative is affected by it. (See the treatise of Schmidt on this verse in the Tübinger Zeitschrift 1831, part ii ; Bernhardy's Syntax, p. 299, etc. ; and Winer's Gram. p. 155.) But with respect to the sense of the words, it must be allowed that it is difficult to determine it, on account of the *κατέναντι*, whose usual signification, " against, over against," does not seem to suit here. We may, however, take it most simply as = לִפְנֵי or בְּעֵינֵי, so that we obtain the following sense. " Abraham is before the eye of God, *i.e.*, before His omniscience, the father of us all, even before we existed."* To this sense the subsequent description of God, the object of Abraham's faith, as the Creator, answers very well. The words *ζωοποιεῖν τοὺς νεκροὺς* and *καλεῖν τὰ μὴ ὄντα ὡς ὄντα* refer, in the first place, as the context shews, to the begetting of Isaac (ver. 19, 20) by his parents Abraham and Sarah, when their bodies were " dead." The whole history of

* Amongst the many explanations from different sources to be found in Tholuck and Reiche, that of the ancient Fathers, Chrysostom, Theodoret, and others, deserves attention. They take *κατέναντι* after Genes. ii. 18 = *καθ' ὁμόιωμα*, so as to get the sense, " Abraham is the image of God, an image of the true Father, and foundation of that relationship." The meaning is beautiful; but does not agree with the context, because the following description of the creative agency of God, if this interpretation were admitted, would bear an application to Abraham, which is not the case.

Abraham is however here, as also elsewhere (Gal. iv.), *treated as a type*, and thus Isaac, who was born through the power of God, is considered as an image of the whole of the spiritual Israel, and consequently ζωοποιεῖν and καλεῖν as designations of spiritual awakening and regeneration. (vi. 13.) Thus taken, the words καλεῖν τὰ μὴ ὄντα ὡς ὄντα become particularly significant. The expression τὰ μὴ ὄντα is, namely, by no means to be understood of that which is absolutely nothing (nihilum negativum), of which nothing more can be said than that it *is not;* but only of that existence which is not yet fashioned into a concrete form, as it is also to be taken in the language of Plato and Philo. (See Philo de vitâ Mosis. p. 693. de creat. p. 728.) Thus, not only may whole nations, in so far as they have not yet entered into existence, be called μὴ ὄντα, although they already exist in God's sight, and already live potentially in their progenitors, but the natural unregenerate man may also be called a μὴ ὤν, inasmuch as in him the true idea of man, the ἄνθρωπος Θεοῦ, is not yet realized, since this does not take place till his regeneration.

Καλεῖν = קָרָא, is the creative call of the Almighty, by which He, according to the analogy of the first act of creation (Gen. i. 3), calls forth the concrete formations out of the general stream of life. Ὡς is to be taken quite simply as a particle of comparison, "vocat ea, quæ non (nondum) sunt, tamquam (jam) adsint." What a powerful description of that God who beholds all future things as really present!

Ver. 18. The example of Abraham was of too much importance to the Apostle for him to break off his contemplation of it so soon. Every thing, in fact, which is related of him, is a type of the life of faith under the New Testament (ver. 23, 24). As, therefore, Abraham, against all hope believed in hope, and was, consequently, obliged to wrestle in order to hold fast his faith and hope against all the contradictions of the senses and of nature; so also does the fight of faith manifest itself in every child of God.*

* We might accordingly say, that the farther faith stands from the objects of its longing, or hope from its fulfilment, the more intense and powerful it must be, if it asserts itself at all. Abraham's faith may therefore appear to be greater than that of believing Christians, for they have their exercise of it rendered easier, by beholding the effects of that which they believe. At the same time, in considering the degree of faith and its character, we must especially take into account the real substance of the same, and in this respect the New Testament stands far above the Old.

Harder and more deeply agitating than all the struggles between the law and the selfish inclinations is the struggle of faith against unbelief, which would rather have the tender conscience believe anything than its own salvation. It was only in appearance that Abraham's fight of faith referred to anything else than his salvation; for, in fact, Abraham's blessedness depended just as much upon the birth of his promised son, from whom the Messiah should in process of time descend, as the blessedness of every believer upon the birth of the new man in him. But faith itself is already this new man coming to the birth, and, therefore, all depends upon its maintenance and increase.

Chrysostom very justly observes toward the explanation of this Oxymoron, ἐπ' ἐλπίδι τῇ τοῦ Θεοῦ, παρ̀ ἐλπίδα τὴν ανθρωπίνην.—'Εις τὸ γένέσθαι must again be understood of the *purpose*, the exercises of Abraham's faith were appointed not only with the design of perfecting him, but also of laying down in him the germs of perfection for future believers; his life was not merely a foreshadowing, but, if I may be allowed the expression, the fore-*reality*, *i. e.*, the true germ of what was to come. De Wette supposes that, by this interpretation, a distinct intention must be ascribed to Abraham in his believing. But we need not surely assume that the patriarch was conscious of the purpose of these dispensations; the words refer only to God's designs. The new quotation is from Gen. xv. 5, where ὅυτως refers to the stars, with whose multitude God compares Abraham's descendants.

Ver. 19–22. As the object, with respect to which Abraham's faith was especially exercised, the Apostle now names the birth of Isaac. If we regard this event merely as securing to Abraham legitimate issue, there appears indeed to exist an essential difference between Abraham's faith and that of the N. T.; but this mode of understanding it is one entirely opposed to St Paul's view of the subject. From Galat. iv. 22, etc., it appears that the significance of Isaac was no less than this, that he was a *type of Christ*, who was to proceed from his descendants. St Paul, therefore (Galat. iii. 16), treats of the seed of Abraham, *i. e.*, in the first place, Isaac, as of Christ, and contemplates, moreover, in Christ, as the second Adam, all His believing people.

Ver. 19. The usual reading οὐ κατενόησε is certainly preferable to the ὡς, which no doubt arose from a mistake of the copyists in writing *οὐ*, but must yield, as Reiche justly remarks, to the simple *κατενόησε*. For this just brings out the thought that Abraham was well acquainted with all the unfavourable outward circumstances, and yet believed. A.C. 67, as well as the Syriac and Coptic versions, support *κατενόησε*, but it is difficult to understand how *οὐ* can have crept into the text. It is only with the reading, *κατένοησε* that the following *δέ* (ver. 20) receives its proper meaning.—The words *νεκροῦσθαι* and *νέκρωσις* refer here to the deadness of the powers of generation. (Heb. xi. 12.) Concerning Abraham's and Sarah's age, see Gen. xvii. 17.—*Πον* without accent means, in the case of numbers, "about;" this is the only place in the N. T. where it is used in this sense; in Heb. ii. 6, iv. 4, it means "anywhere." *Διακρίνεσθαι* means properly "to be divided, separated," and thereby "to lose one's balance, to waver or stagger." In this way it is several times used of unbelief, as inward spiritual unsteadiness (Matth. xxi. 21; Mark xi. 23; John i. 6; Rom. xiv. 23.) This is contrasted with the inward firmness and strength expressed in *ἐνδυναμοῦσθαι*. As opposed to *πληροφορεῖσθαι*, unbelief might also have been designated by *κένωσις*; for this expression, as well as the substantive *πληροφορία*, represents faith as the replenishment of the inward man with spiritual life (Rom. xiv. 5; Col. ii. 2; 1 Thes. i. 5; 1 Tim. iv. 17). In the *δοὺς δόξαν τῷ Θεῷ* is expressed the practical recognition of the divine omnipoence, which accomplishes that which it promises.

Ver. 23, 24. After this detailed consideration of the life of faith as manifested in Abraham, St Paul declares the *principle* which justifies such a consideration. Abraham's history he does not regard as something dead and past, but as the living history of the believers of every age. This passage, in addition to 1 Cor. ix. 10, x. 6; Galat. iv. 24, etc., contains one of the most important hints as to the manner in which the Old Testament is to be treated according to the doctrine of the apostles. It is not the externals of its history, but that spirit which moves in them, which is to be considered, and in this way it has its eternal truth for the times of the New Testament also. To attribute the whole mode of treatment, which St Paul applies to the Old Testament, in this as well as in other places, to Jewish habits of thought, a view Reiche in particular has once more defended, destroys not only the apostolical character of St Paul, but also the very essence of the O. T., which, as the eternal word of God, is, according to our Lord's own words (Matth. v. 18), to abide when heaven and earth have passed away.

The words μέλλει λογίζεσθαι are to be regarded from the position which Abraham and his generation occupied. But if in this place not faith in Jesus, but faith in the Father who raised Him up, is brought forward, it is accounted for by looking back to the ζωοποιεῖν in ver. 17, which manifested itself most gloriously in the resurrection of Christ. For the physical and spiritual interpenetrate each other in the conception of ζωοποιεῖν, as in that of ζωή (John vi.) God is the awakener of life in every form of its manifestation. Besides this ἐγείρειν presupposes a preceding θνήσκειν, so that a reference to the death of Christ is implied in this verse, as well as distinctly expressed in that immediately following.

Ver. 25. Whilst, however, in iii. 25 δικαιοσύνη is connected simply with the blood-shedding of Christ, δικαίωσις in this verse follows upon the resurrection. The older commentators have found great difficulties in this mode of representation, but if we understand it according to the tenor of v. 10, vi. 4, the thought expressed in the passage is quite simple. For as resurrection necessarily presupposes that death has gone before, so also upon the death of Christ, who is the life, necessarily follows the resurrection, that is the victory over death. These therefore in the life of our Lord stand related to each other as two necessary complementary halves, which it is altogether impossible to conceive as existing without each other. It is not the death of Christ in itself which is important, but only that death which was conquered by the resurrection. But in the same way that the death and resurrection of Christ form an intimate unity, so also in man the death of the old and the rising up of the new, cannot be conceived as existing without each other. It is impossible, that in any individual sins can really be forgiven, and the old man be crucified without the new man arising; and when the new man begins to live, the death of the old man must take place at the same time. In consequence, therefore, of the necessary connection between these two events, only one at a time is commonly mentioned, *either negatively* the forgiveness of sins, *or positively* the communication of the new life. But in some cases both are joined together, as in this place, and in ver. 10, and then the *negative* side, the putting away of the old, is connected with the death, and the *positive* side, the communication of the new, is annexed to and founded upon the resurrection of the Redeemer. In the term δικαίωσις in this passage therefore, we must hold fast the idea of that act, which makes righteous and creates the new man, an act which is expressed in ver. 10, by the word σώζεσθαι; whilst the expression διὰ τὰ παραπτώματα ἡμῶν answers to the καταλλαγή in ver. 10. For the παραπτώματα are the sins which separate man from God, and which need first of all an ἄφεσις, a καταλλαγή, on account of which the Son of God was delivered up to death. In these two complementary halves the whole work of God in the soul of man is complete, and neither can be wanting where this work has truly begun, although no doubt at different crises of the inward life of the individual, now one, now the other side may predominate.

With respect to παραδιδόναι, scil. εἰς θάνατον, see Acts iii. 13, Rom. viii. 32, Isaiah liii. 12. In the passage Ephes. v. 2, it is said, παρέδωκεν ἑαυτὸν προσφορὰν καὶ θυσίαν.—In the life and work of Christ every thing happened *for us, nothing for Himself*, for He already possessed all things with His Father, before He became man (2 Cor. viii. 9.)—Δικαίωσις is not here the same as δικαιοσύνη; for in the same way that διὰ τὰ παραπτώματα ἡμῶν must be understood "in order that our transgressions might be pardoned," διὰ τὴν διακαίωσιν ἡμῶν must also be explained "in order that righteousness might be wrought in us." Δικαίωσις, therefore, denotes the divine act of making righteous, as διὰ τὰ παραπτώματα, the divine act of forgiveness.

§ 8. OF THE FRUITS OF FAITH.

(V. 1—11.)

To this complete exposition of the doctrine of the new way of salvation itself, according to its scriptural foundation, the Apostle now annexes some intimation of the effects of the life of faith, by which the excellence of this way is first brought to view in all its clearness. To be sure St Paul could not in this place do more than cursorily allude to them, because many things needed to be considered before he could enter into such a full description of these effects as is found in the next chapters. It is not until the eighth chapter that we find a complete account of the infinite consequences of redemption, as well for the individual as for the whole creation.

Ver. 1. St Paul includes under one expression the whole fulness of those blessings which accrue to the man who is justified *by* faith (as the receptive cause), *through* grace (as the creative cause), *i. e.*, under εἰρήνη πρὸς τὸν Θεόν. The conception of εἰρήνη = שָׁלוֹם is here distinguished by the addition of πρὸς τὸν Θεόν, not merely from false peace, the εἰρήνη πρὸς τὸν κόσμον, which is destroyed by the operation of Christ (John xvi. 33), in that the latter calls forth a struggle against sin (ver. 3, etc.) ; but also from that higher degree of peace, that inward peace of soul, the εἰρήνη πρὸς σεαυτόν, which St Paul also calls εἰρήνη Θεοῦ (Phil. iv. 7 ; Col. iii. 15), and Christ in St John's gospel εἰρήνη ἐμή. (John xiv. 27.) The two stand, in fact, in the same relation to one another as justification and sanctification ; justification, or the λογίζεσθαι εἰς δικαιοσύνην gives at once καταλλαγή, and with it εἰρήνη πρὸς τὸν Θεόν, the consciousness of being in a state of grace, the contrary to which is the ἔχθρα εἰς Θεόν. (See Rom. viii. 7.) No doubt this state contains within itself sanctification in the germ, but also only in the germ ; because the old man still lives inward harmony of life is only at first partially restored. The completeness of this harmony is only a *fruit* of life in the Spirit (Rom. viii. 6 ; Galat. v. 22), whilst the life of faith *begins* with εἰρήνη πρὸς τὸν Θεόν, because this flows at once from the first act of grace. As the author of peace in every form, God Himself is moreover called ὁ Θεός τῆς εἰρήνης (Rom. xv. 33 ; 2 Cor. xiii. 11 ; 1 Thess. v. 23 ; 2 Thess. iii. 16). The reading ἔχωμεν, which Lachmann and Scholz have adopted from A.C.D.I., must be regarded as inferior to the reading ἔχομεν from inward grounds, for it is a strange idea to call upon men to have peace with God ; for peace with God is the gift of His grace.

Ver. 2. As the second blessed consequence of justification, the Apostle, after a parenthesis, presents to us the exultation felt in the hope of future glory. For the words δι' οὗ κ. τ. λ. cannot be understood to mean, that the προσαγωγή is another result of the δικαιοῦσθαι ἐκ πίστεως, for in that case in the first place the construction with καὶ would have been proceeded with, and then St

Paul would have avoided the introduction of the words εἰς χάριν, which necessarily suggest quite another thought. Tholuck, indeed, has proposed to place a stop after ἐσχήκαμεν, but this the reading, τῇ πίστει, will not permit. These words are no doubt wanting in B.D.F.G. and other documents having critical authority, but it is plain that they have only been omitted to avoid the connection of προσαγωγή with what follows. Besides this, even if τῇ πίστει were away, the placing a stop after ἐσχήκαμεν would be inadmissible, because εἰς τὴν χάριν ταυτὴν would have no right connection with what follows. And further, that St Paul elsewhere (Ephes. ii. 18, iii. 12, the verb is found 1 Pet. iii. 18) uses this word of that access to God which is opened for the soul, can be no reason for giving it this sense in the present passage, since here it is defined more exactly by the addition of εἰς τὴν χάριν τάυτην. The whole sentence δὶ οὗ ἑστήκαμεν must therefore be placed in a parenthesis, expressive of the fact, that the power of the Redeemer not only produces peace at the same time *with* justification, but even introduces the soul into the state of grace itself *before this*, so that the χάρις ἅυτη is the very δικαιοσύνη ἐκ πίστεως itself, to which not our own power, but Christ's grace alone can conduct us.

The allusion to a προσαγωγεύς who, so to speak, introduces the soul to God, is, by the above remarks, proved to be unsuitable; nor has it otherwise any scriptural foundation. The perfect forms an opposition to the preceding present ἔχομεν. St Paul wishes to refer *all* to Christ, to make Him appear as the Author and Finisher of our renewal. The καὶ is therefore to be taken emphatically, "by whom *also already* we have received access." Τῇ πίστει may also be connected with εἰς τὴν χάριν, yet it is better to take εἰς = πρός, to connect it with προσαγωγή, and to regard τῇ πίστει = πιστεύοντες. Ἑστήκαμεν does not denote the mere standing in a certain relation, but leads us to think of the firmness and security of the state of grace, as opposed to all wavering. By the δόξα Θεοῦ Reiche supposes the divine image in man to be meant; this does not, however, suit the context, because ἐπ' ἐλπίδι is added; for the divine likeness is not merely restored to the regenerate man in hope, but in reality. The expression rather denotes the heavenly existence of God, the participation in which constitutes the highest blessedness of the creature. And in the connection of καυχᾶσθαι with ἔλπις is implied the irrefragable certainty of being partaker of the glory of God.

Ver. 3, 4. The Apostle, by a bold contrast, places the *sufferings of the present* in a parallel line with the *glory of the future*, and considers that the former proceed just as necessarily from the δικαιοσύνη τῆς πίστεως, as does the εἰρήνη πρὸς τὸν Θεόν. (2 Tim. iii. 12.) For there resides in the believer a principle which rebukes the sin which is in the world, and by so doing excites it against him, and which will not leave things in a state of indifference with respect to itself, but either attracts or repels them. In these very sufferings of the present, therefore, is contained a source of exaltation* for the Christian, in that they are not punishments to him, but the means of his perfection. (James i. 2, etc.) The three stages of ὑπομονή, δοκιμή, and ἔλπις are considered as proceeding from the sufferings; whilst the former denotes the state of moral earnestness and of faithful endurance, δοκιμή relates to the state of *approval as sterling* proceeding from it, which bears within it *hope* as its blossom.†

Δοκιμή is the act of testing, but also that state of approval as genuine which proceeds from trial. In the same way δοκίμιον unites both significations within itself. (See James i. 3; 1 Pet. i. 7.) Καταισχύνω is to be taken actively, "hope maketh not ashamed," not intransitively, "hope is not ashamed, *i.e.*, is well-founded.

Ver. 5. This hope, thus born in the midst of conflict, contains, however, within itself, the assurance of obtaining the glory which shall be revealed; for, as an earnest of the same, we have already *here below* the love of God shed abroad in our hearts. The ἀγάπη τοῦ Θεοῦ is considered therefore to be only, so to speak, the *secret* presence of God himself in our souls, whilst in eternal blessedness God gives Himself to His saints as the manifested One. Accor-

* Rückert very pointedly remarks on this passage: "We must not pare away any thing from the conception contained in καυχᾶσθαι, unless we wish, at the same time, to detract from the powerful character of the Apostle; he is not only undaunted, not only of good courage, but really joyful, really lifted up in mind, yea, he reckons it *as an honour to himself*, that tribulation befals him, for this is to him a pledge of future glory." But what an advance manifests itself here when compared with the Old Testament! In the book of Job the doubts of the sufferer, on account of his sufferings, wrestle anxiously with his still weak faith, here the believer rejoices boldly in all affliction and even exults in it.

† On the subject of ἔλπις see more in the notes to Rom. viii. 24.

dingly, the love of God is not the inward life of man in a state of exaltation, the life of his feelings raised, so to speak, to a higher power, but it is a higher principle which has been grafted into the man, the *Πνεῦμα ἅγιον ;* the latter words express the *substantial* cause, *ἀγάπη* the *actual* effect; but in reality they are both identical, for the *ἀγάπη Θεοῦ* cannot be regarded as separate from the essential being of God in its highest *manifestation, i.e.*, the Holy Ghost. God's love is there only where He Himself is, for He *is* love, and does not *have* love as something in or beside Himself.

Καταισχύνω = בּוֹשׁ "to make ashamed, to disappoint by want of success." Rom. ix. 33, x. 11. In ἡ δὲ ἔλπις the article is not to be taken = ἄυτη, for there is but one true hope, rather is this sentence to be regarded as the fourth member in the sense, "but hope works its own accomplishment, or has its fulfilment in itself," so that the colon must be placed after καταισχύνει. The words ὅτι. κ. τ. λ. (ver. 5) are not in fact to be connected with καταισχύνει alone, but with καυχώμεθα (ver. 3), and indeed the whole passage in vers. 3, 4. According to that Pelagian and Rationalistic view, which is opposed to the doctrine of the communication of the Spirit, ἀγάπη Θεοῦ means the love of man to God; in the Apostle's meaning it is the love of God to man, which however awakens in him reciprocal love (1 John iv. 19), not indeed proceeding from his own mere natural powers, but from the higher powers of the Divine Spirit. Only when thus taken can it be properly said, concerning love, that it is shed abroad, for it is identical with the element of the Spirit, and only contained in His manifestation. The expression εκκέχυται is founded upon the image of a spiritual stream which spreads itself out over men; no doubt an image, but in which there is this reality, that a higher power takes possession of man's being. (See John vii. 38, 39; Acts ii. 16; Is. xxxii. 15; Ezek. xxxvi. 25; Joel iii. 1.) The movement, by which the Spirit is shed abroad, is considered to be connected with the μένειν of the same in the inner man, therefore we find ἐν not εἰς. The καρδία is, moreover, regarded as the receptacle of the Spirit, as the centre of the disposition and of the inclinations; for instance, νοῦς could not be used here. (See Olshausen opus. theol. p. 156 sqq.) The addition of τοῦ δοθέντος ἡμῖν is not pleonastic by the side of ἐκκέχυται, the relation of the two expressions may be thus stated. The Spirit was given at the day of

Pentecost once for all to mankind as a whole, but it is not therefore shed abroad in every individual heart, for this the personal appropriation of the work of Christ is first needed. The addition of *τοῦ δοθέντος ἡμῖν* is not therefore unnecessary, but expresses the *possibility*, which is provided for every one, of receiving the Holy Spirit poured forth into his heart. See John vii. 39, xvi. 7.

Ver. 6. The nature of divine love is then exhibited by the Apostle, in the most illustrious proof which it could give of its power, in the sacrifice of the Son of God. It manifests itself therefore in the same self-sacrificing character in the hearts of believers also, to whom it is imparted by that Holy Spirit which Christ obtained for men by His death. (John vii. 39.) The leading thought in this verse presents no difficulty, after what has been said on iii. 25, but the different readings of the text demand a more exact consideration. The *ἔτι* at the commencement of the verse has probably occasioned all the variations with which it abounds.* In the first place, for *ἔτι* several MSS. read *ἔιγε*, others *ἐι γάρ* or *ἔι τι*. Semler, followed by Usteri, concludes, therefore, that *ἐι* is the right reading, and supposes that in the original letter of the Apostle an anacoluthon existed, to avoid which, some transcribers wrote *ἔτι*. This hypothesis has certainly something to recommend it at first sight, but at the same time, the singular position of *ἔτι* affords a sufficient explanation of the origin of the different readings; and then, if we carefully examine the passage, the reason for which *ἔτι* was prefixed to it appears to have been the emphasis which this particle gives, on which account the ardent soul of the Apostle could not pronounce it too soon. But besides this, several MSS. of considerable authority, A.B.C.D.F.G. and others, repeat *ἔτι* after *ἀσθενῶν*. Griesbach has even admitted this reading into the text; but it was soon rejected by Knapp, and, in fact, it appears only to have been adopted from those MSS. which had erased *ἔτι* at the beginning of the verse, and were determined by

* Compare on this point the critical essay of Professor Franz Ritter of Bonn, in the "Zeitschrift für Philosophie and Kathol. Theologie," Heft 19. (Cologne, 1836.) p. 46, &c., who reckons this passage amongst the few in the N. T. to which conjectural criticism must be applied. In fact, according to Ritter we should here read, *ἔτι γὰρ ὄντων ἡμῶν ἀσθενῶν κατὰ καιρὸν Χριστὸς ὑπὲρ ἀσεβῶν ἀπέθανε*, according to the analogy of ver. 8, in which the same collocation is found. But the exercise of conjecture where so many critical appliances present themselves, appears justly to most modern critics to be altogether inadmissible.

the parallel passage in ver. 8. If we retain the double ἔτι, we must explain the repetition by the strong feeling under which St Paul wrote, just as in vii. 21. No doubt the whole stress in this thought (as in iv. 5) is laid upon the fact, that men did not amend themselves *before*, and do not now receive the blessings of Christ, as it were, for their reward, but that He died for them, even whilst they were *yet* godless and estranged from God, so that this highest act of love was the very *means* of their transformation. The difficulty, that God, from His very holiness, cannot love the ungodly, so long as they remain what they are, is obviated if we remember, that evil does not surely manifest itself absolutely in any man, but always in such a way, as to attach itself to the remains of the image of God in him. Inasmuch, therefore, as God loves the proper substance of man, his true though now darkened and oppressed self, He hates only that element of sin in or about man which impedes his free development.—With respect to the transposition of ἔτι, see Winer's Gram. p. 509. The term ἀσθενῶν is not merely explained by ἀσεβῶν, but also in ver. 8, by ἁμαρτωλῶν, and in ver. 10, by ἐχθρόι. At the same time, it is not personal transgressions which are referred to, which are only derived from something deeper, nor some few particularly sinful men only (iv. 5), but the *condition* of moral weakness in which *all* men are without exception. (See Galat. iv. 9, 13; Heb. iv. 15, v. 2.) *Κατὰ καιρόν*= εὐκαιρῶς, at the time appointed by God. (Galat. iv. 4; 1 Pet. i. 20; Heb. ix. 26.) On the signification of ὑπέρ, when the subject is the death of Christ as the representative of man, see Rom. v. 15.

Ver. 7, 8. In order to display in the fullest light the excellency of the divine love, it is compared with the most noble utterances of natural human love, which, however, remain far below it. But in the communication of the love of God to men through the Holy Spirit (ver. 5), is also given the possibility of imitating Christ in the point of loving our enemies (Matth. v. 44, 45; 1 Pet. ii. 21). Particular difficulties have been discovered, strange to say, in ver. 7, though, as Reiche justly remarks, the passage is quite simple. Semler even regarded vers. 7, 8, as interpolated; Grotius wished to read ἀδίκου for δικαίου, and others asked, whether δικαίου and ἀγαθοῦ were substantives or adjectives, masculines or neuters. Since the whole question is about persons, in the first place both expressions must naturally be also referred to persons.

And further, as regards the terms δίκαιος and ἀγαθός, the context plainly leads us to assume, that δίκαιος designates the character of the righteous man, who performs whatever can be *required* of him, ἀγαθός the character of the benevolent man, who does *more* than others venture to ask.* The first man we may esteem and respect, the second, on the other hand, we can love, and even earthly love can lay down its life for the object of its affection; but divine love dies for its enemies.

Ver. 7. The first γάρ must be explained by a thought which is to be supplied, "but this is something noble, something unheard of!" The word ταχα = ἴσως is only found again in the N. T., Philem. v. 15.—Τολμᾶν serves to denote the highest degree of self-sacrifice.—Συνίσταναι, "to prove, announce." See iii. 5.

Ver. 9, 10. Just as in iv. 25, St Paul now again places parallel with the *first operation* of Christ, the δικαίωσις, which was brought about by means of His death *the other* part of His work, which is here designated as σωτηρία, and is referred to His *life* as its source. These two, as already remarked upon the former passage, are by no means to be *separated*, but, at the same time, in their very connection they must also not be *confounded*. The *first* is always absolute, for although the first forgiveness of sins, by which man enters into a state of grace, is daily repeated, on account of continual transgressions (1 John ii. 1), yet it is always vouchsafed *total and entire*, for a *partial* forgiveness is none at all; the *second*, on the other hand, is the subject of a gradual *development*, and is only complete with the ἀπολύτρωσις (1 Cor. i. 30, Rom. viii. 23), in the more confined sense of that word. On this very account, therefore, as has already been remarked, the state of grace cannot have its foundation in the new life in man, because this is never more than relative, and therefore can never give peace (ver. 1); where this is notwithstanding done, as according to the doctrine of the [Roman] Catholic Church, there exists continual insecurity (*i. e.*, an uncertainty as to one's being in a state of grace), as its consequence, and this is a condition which the doctrine of truth rejects, because no effort can be successful, which does not proceed from a heart altogether reconciled, and living *at peace with*

* The same relation subsists in Latin between *justus* and *bonus*. See Cicero de offic. iii. 15. "Si vir bonus is est, qui prodest quibus potest, nocet nemini, recte *justum* virum, *bonum* non facile reperiemus."

God. In this difference between forgiveness of sins and sanctification, according to their inward nature, lies the Apostle's justification for having represented them *as standing parallel to each other*, and drawing from one a conclusion with respect to the other.

Δικαιοῦσθαι and *καταλλάσσεσθαι* are here used as quite synonymous; the proper substance of both is the *ἄφεσις τῶν ἁμαρτιῶν*, the negative side of the way of salvation, the removal of the old, of the barrier. (With respect to *καταλλαγή*, see the notes to Rom. iii. 24, 25.) This transaction, *an act of God*, occurs whilst man is yet in the condition of an enemy to God; since then by means of this act the man becomes a *φιλός Θεοῦ*, and *ἠγαπημένος* (Ephes. i. 6), how much more easy is it to be assured that the work He has begun He will also complete in the *σωτηρία*? Neither is this last, however, according to the Apostle's view, *a work of man*, as if God began indeed the new life in him, but the man himself is to continue it and complete it (see notes to ix. 1); He who is the Author is Himself also the Finisher of our faith (Hebr. xii. 2), and indeed by means of His *ζωή*, *i. e.*, His glorified life at the right hand of God. But it is just this climax, indicated by the *πολλῷ μᾶλλον*, which is expressly repeated in ver. 10, which is peculiar to the present passage (compared with iv. 25). The thought is not to be understood *objectively*, as if Christ had more power in His exaltation than in His humiliation, but only *subjectively*, according to the way in which it is comprehended by man. The power of Christ is equal in all stages of His life, but in His state of humiliation He restrained Himself from the utterance of His power, and on this account after His resurrection it presents itself to our human comprehension as an increasing power. We may therefore realize to ourselves the thought in this manner; if God has regenerated the man, it is to be hoped that He will maintain and perfect him in his regenerate state, and the conceivableness of a falling away gradually diminishes till it reaches a minimum. The term *σωτηρία* here, as well as *ἀπολύτρωσις* in 1 Cor. i. 30, is to be taken in the narrower sense; in its wider signification this word may also include that *δικαιοῦσθαι*, in which lies the pledge of the further development of the inward life. *Σωτηρία*, moreover, stands commonly alone, as the mere contrary to *ἀπώλεια*, but in this passage it appears in a connection which we could never have expected, and this shows us how careful we ought to be in supplying words to complete the sense of Scripture. If ἀπὸ τῆς ὀργῆς had not stood here, certainly no one would have supplied just these words, but probably some such as ἀπὸ τῆς ἁμαρτίας. For it appears as if the δικαιοῦσθαι had already relieved us from the wrath, and that therefore in the further development of the life the only question could be about our entire deliverance from the old man of sin. But however true this may be, it is not less true that every, even the least sin, has the divine ὀργή for its necessary accompaniment. We may therefore say of the man who is δικαιωθείς or καταλλαγείς, on the one hand, that he as such is already delivered from wrath, inasmuch as the centre of his personal being is saved (John iii. 36), but, on the other hand, that he remains yet under the ὀργή, inasmuch as the totality of his being is not yet sanctified, and he needs continual forgiveness; the latter mode of representation is that here chosen, whilst the former is the more usual.

Ver. 11. However, with this σωτηρία, which is only to be attained *hereafter*, the Apostle once more contrasts, as in ver. 2, that joy already *present*, which is to believers the earnest of the divine glory (viii. 24). The present blessing of reconciliation here below, with which is connected the gift of the Spirit (ver. 5), is to them so sure a pledge of their future inheritance, that they feel as if they possessed it already.

To σωθησόμεθα is opposed καυχώμενοι sc. ἔσμεν (for which later MSS. read καυχώμεθα and καυχῶμεν).—The climax οὐ μόνον—ἀλλὰ καὶ raises καυχᾶσθαι above the preceding σωθησόμεθα; the latter contains in fact only the mere conception of ἔλπις, whilst καύχησις goes far beyond this. There is no reference here to a new and higher object. Fritzsche and Winer wish to keep strictly to the participle in καυχώμενοι, and co-ordinate it with καταλλαγέντες so that both participles may depend upon σωθησόμεθα, and the following sense arise, "not only reconciled, but also rejoicing in God, we shall be saved." But the thought "we shall be saved rejoicing" is not very suitable, either in itself, or in relation to "we shall be saved being reconciled." We therefore prefer to take the participle as *temp. fin.*, so that St Paul proceeds from the subject of redemption to the new subject of καύχησις.

SECTION III.

(V. 12—VII. 6.)

OF THE VICARIOUS OFFICE OF CHRIST.

After this description of the nature of the new way of salvation, and its effects, Paul might at once have proceeded to set forth how the individual man is developed upon it, which at chap. vii. 7, &c., he does, but that a thought mediating this, which then presented, as it does now, especial difficulties to men, *the vicarious office of Christ,* required a further deduction for the foundation of the doctrine itself. Without the idea of His vicarious office the whole work of the Saviour would remain something isolated, a beautiful act of self-sacrifice by an individual, without any real power for the totality, a power which first made it the object of a sermon to the world, and the turning-point of the world's history. The apostle proves, therefore, this important point most carefully, and does so *firstly,* by bringing Christ as the second Adam into parallel with the first, and shewing, that, as from the first *sin,* so from the second *grace* issues, like streams from different well-springs (v. 12–21). *Secondly,* Paul sets forth, how accordingly all that was done in Christ was fulfilled in the faithful themselves, who are in Him as they were in Adam (vi. 1–11.) And, *lastly,* he infers, that no one, consequently, who is in Christ, can serve sin, for that by his very being in Christ he has died to sin and become free, in order to his entering a higher state (vi. 12, vii. 6.)

§ 9. PARALLEL BETWEEN ADAM AND CHRIST.*

(V. 12–21.)

According to the tenor of the epistle in the whole, the Apostle's primary object here was nothing more than to set forth Christ as

* Compare upon this important section of the epistle Rothe's Monographie (Leipzig, 1836), and the Essays of Finkh (Tübing. Zeitschrift 1830. H. 1.), and Schmid (Ibid, H. 4.)

the representative of the whole race, and as the originator of righteousness for all; in order, however, to make this relation perceptible, he sets out from the position of Adam to the human race, which he presumes as acknowledged; and so gains occasion to trace as well in its inward *ground* the *fact* of general sinfulness, which he had brought out in chapters i. and ii. Accordingly the following weighty section forms the foundation for two doctrines of truth equally important, and each supporting the other; for the *doctrine of original sin*, that is, the *proclivitas peccandi*, which diffuses itself over the race, in the way of generation from Adam, independently of the proper *personal* sin of men, and for the doctrine of *the vicarious office of Christ*. As Paul's exposition sets out from the former as a thing presumed, we also take it first into consideration that the latter may follow upon it. Meanwhile both rest upon a *common basis*, to which, therefore, we must previously make reference. In a treatise I mean, like that in which we are now engaged, it is quite impossible to arrive at any satisfactory result, if we are divided in the fundamental views. The hope of uniting all expositors in the view of this passage must be entirely given up, for the very reason that there is no prevailing unity upon its principles. No one, however, with the best intention, can make any other exposition, than such as shall comprehend the ideas of the holy writer, with which he wishes himself to agree, in one harmony, that is in accordance with *his* principles; but this process is certainly far from producing a likeness of result. Of the truth of this assertion with regard to this passage, every one may be convinced by the treatise of Reiche (Comment. ad. loc. p. 409–446.) This learned man treats the difficult and important passage with great industry, and certainly with unbiassed mind, notwithstanding he arrives at results which are in direct contradiction to the express words of the Apostle, and the sum of scriptural doctrine; and this for no other reason than because he sets out from an entirely different basis from that on which Paul stands. From this his different station all the expressions of the Apostle present themselves to him in a false light, so that he must necessarily fail in comprehending the whole. The dispute upon the differing conception of single parts is now an endless one, and therefore most unsatisfactory and to no purpose; yet something may surely be hoped for from a conference upon the *common basis*—to this, therefore, we chiefly apply, and according to our plan shall touch only upon what is most important in particulars.

Antiquity knew only two different stations from which to consider this passage, and although under altered names and forms with shades of distinction and modifications, the same have continued to the present essentially like what they were, since the time when they were first keenly expressed ; the *Augustinian* and the *Pelagian.* The difference between these two carefully considered is not in *some*, but in *all* points, and they deviate specifically upon all the great problems ; any reconciliation, therefore, between them is out of the question ; they run, like parallel lines, constantly beside, without getting nearer to each other. For our purpose, the following observations upon the interpretation of this passage result from these two directions. The Pelagian (whether *half* or *whole,* it makes no difference here) can never conceive of mankind otherwise than as a sum of free, intellectual individuals, standing by one another ; in virtue, as in sin, every person stands and falls by himself.* The Augustinian can just as little conceive of mankind otherwise, than as an united whole, in which the separate individuals are by no means disengaged substantial entireties, but integrating parts of the totality. If now the expositor sets out from

* Whether the fall of individuals be said to occur in this world, or, according to Origen, in a former, is in the main all one ; each individual ever stands or falls by himself according to this theory. See thereon the admirable exposition in the Phil. des Rechts by my honoured colleague, Prof. Stahl, vol. 2, part i. (Heidelberg 1833), p. 99, &c., where he says, " Adam is the *original matter,* Christ is the *original idea* in God, of mankind, both personally living. Mankind is one in them, therefore Adam's sin became the sin of all, Christ's sacrifice the atonement for all. Every leaf of a tree may be green or wither by itself, but each suffers by the disease of the *root,* and recovers by its healing. The shallower the man so much the more isolated will everything appear to him, for upon the surface all lies apart. He will see in mankind, in the nation, ay even in the family mere individuals, where the act of the one has no connexion with that of the other. The deeper the man is, so much the more do these inward relations of unity proceeding from the very centre force themselves on his notice. Yea, the love of our neighbour is itself nothing but the deep feeling of this unity, for we love him only with whom we feel and acknowledge ourselves to be one. What the Christian love of our neighbour is for the heart, that unity of race is for the understanding. If sin be through one, and redemption through one be not possible, the command to love our neighbour is also unintelligible. The Christian ethics and the Christian faith are therefore of a truth indissolubly united. Christianity effects in history an advance like that from the animal kingdom to man, by its revealing the essential unity of men, the consciousness of which in the ancient world had vanished when the nations were separated." Even so ; man comes not truly to himself until he comes to God in Christ ; without Christ he remains in the element of animal life !

the *first* station, he has only the choice between two ways; *either* to take the words of the Apostle, in this place, to mean, that the effect of Adam's sin and the effect of Christ's righteousness are to be understood merely as the operation of doctrine and example, but in no respect as really inwrought, which indeed, according to his principles, they cannot be, *or* to say, that Paul doubtless proposes a different view, but that this view is false. Whoever, on the other hand, interprets the words from the *second* station, finds himself according to their nearest, simplest meaning, in perfect harmony, not merely with the Apostle Paul, but with the whole Scripture. That the *advantage*, therefore, is on this side, needs no proof; yet that alone certainly cannot determine any one to incline to it; but independently of this, the deeper truth lies in the contemplation of mankind as a comprehended unity, since the substantiality and separateness of individuals is but a very relative one, and in this relativeness is comprised in that unity, just as the relative substantiality of the members of a body is comprised by the absolute unity of life of the whole animal organism. (Comp. further at xi. 1.) However, this is, of course, not the place to enter more particularly into this extensive inquiry; suffice it here to notice, that the voice of the Scripture itself accords with this conception by the images of the body (1 Cor. xii. 20), of the vine (John xv. 1, etc.), and olive tree (Rom. xi. 17, etc.), whereby it marks the unity of life of the whole. But in these images, consecrated by scriptural use, the idea is expressed in a singularly illustrative manner; as, namely, in a tree not every little branch is of any essential importance to its whole growth, but as many may be broken off, without causing any damage to the entire tree, so also in the human race. But in two respects the destruction even of the smallest twig brings all the tree to nothing. First, at the sprouting of the seed, secondly, at the grafting of the tree. By breaking off the apparently insignificant sprout, or the feeble graft, the whole tree is destroyed. Even so, mankind has *two poles of life* in its development, the condition of which decides the state of the whole. *Firstly*, Adam, the bud, out of whom the whole race was developed; his death immediately after his creation would have annulled mankind, the injury he suffered damaged all the coming race, as a bruised bud makes the whole tree grow scant and crooked. *Secondly*, Christ, whose relation to the race derived from Adam is like that of the noble graft to the wild tree [Jer. ii. 21];* could it be thought, that Christ had been taken away before the completion of His work, mankind would then have remained in their natural rudeness, just as a tree, whose graft was destroyed, and which now puts forth mere water-shoots. But if the noble graft abide, it makes the whole tree noble; all juices, which are guided through it, change their nature, and are no more wild. Men are wont to say, that parables prove nothing; nevertheless, comparisons often teach by depth of meaning infinitely more and better than all abstract arguments, seeing they are derived from nature, the mirror of the glory of the unseen God, living demonstrations, as it were, of the Most High God Himself. It follows of course, that, according to the principles of these different views, the notions also, which properly fall under consideration here, respecting the *origin of souls*,† must be modified. The Pelagian can only consistently follow *Creatianism*, or what leads to the same isolating of men, *Præ-existentianism*, for which Benecke has again attempted to plead. But according to the Augustinian principle we are led to *Traducianism*, which alone has any agreement with Scripture and experience, and, *kept clear of Materialism*, is able to satisfy all requisitions of the Christian consciousness. The consequence, therefore, is, that, as the *existence* of this passage, with its precise explanations, effected no more for the Pelagians of all centuries, but their trying by subtleties to evade its import so opposite to their system; so even if the passage were *not* there, the Augustinians would be no further from their principle, since it rests by no means merely on these words, but upon the coherent doctrine of Scripture and its inward necessity.

A totally different position, however, regarding the questions which come under consideration in this passage, from that occupied

* As to how far it can be said that Christ represents also the sinful tendency in mankind, see the observations at Rom. viii. 3.

† The discussion of this subject at large we defer to Hebr. ix. 7, &c. I have only now to remark, that it would not be very difficult to get rid of the objections, lately made by Tholuck (lit. Anz. Jahrg. 1834. Num. 23), against the traducian view, from the experience of bad children being often begotten of good parents, and *vice versa;* since the old man still lives even in the best, and germs of nobler life are resting in the worst; but individually we cannot trace, without prejudicing in some degree the main view, by what law the one element or the other gains predominance in the moment of generation. The assertion, however, that every traducian view has materialism in it, is decidedly false, and will meet its refutation at the passage referred to.

by antiquity, has been adduced by the latest theology,* and from this station Usteri (Paul. Lehrbegr., 4th edit. p. 24, &c.) gives his exposition. The latest theology is far from that *mechanical* contemplation of the world, upon which the Pelagian method of isolation rests ; on the contrary, in respect to the relation of the individual to the whole, it takes entirely the side of the *dynamic* view of the world, which forms the basis of the Augustinian theory. But it deviates, nevertheless, in the result, because it sets out from a different view of *evil.* As Schleiermacher's doctrine of predestination could not but be quite different from the Augustinian, since he openly avowed the restoration ; so also the doctrine of original sin could not but take a different form, if evil, as he and the Hegel School assert, is to be held as *mere negation.* Adam's fall could be no loss to him, for he had nothing to lose, but only the manifestation of that deficiency which clave to him as creature ; the sinfulness of the race could not proceed from Adam's act, because all bear in themselves the same imperfection which made Adam's fall necessary, and they just as much as Adam must have been brought into that opposition, of which it is no advantage not to know ; Christ, accordingly, worked only so far in redeeming and atoning, as by His divine fulness of life he made up the created deficiency in the creature. Infinitely more full of spirit and depth of meaning, however, as this doctrine of modern theology is, than the flat Pelagian rationalism, we feel ourselves nevertheless unable to make it our own, since evil, according to the Scripture, is by no means represented as *mere* negation. It is not, indeed, like good in its complete manifestation, *substance,* as Manichæism holds, yet surely something *real* and *positive ;* it has, that is, without substantiality its positive reality in the *actually disturbed symmetry.* As such real disharmony in the relations ordained by God, Holy Scripture removes evil in its origin and its operative power into the spiritual world ; from hence it continues to diffuse the effects of its

* The mode in which Benecke has proposed the passage should be understood, needs but a brief notice, since it proves itself at once to be untenable. He supposes, namely, as Origen, that every man has sinned by himself, not however in this world, but in a state of *præ-existence.* The Scripture, however, does not acknowledge any personal præexistence, it teaches rather merely a præ-existent state of being in the divine mind, since God beholds the future as present. (Comp. thereon Ephes. i. 4.) The farther defence of præ-existence by Benecke in a letter to Lücke (Stud. 1832. H. 3. p. 616, &c.), brings forward no new matter.

disharmonious nature, until it finds its barrier at the element of good. Therefore is the fall of Adam set forth in the Bible as *the opening of a gate* that leads to the spiritual world, so that it is not his act, outward and isolate, which is efficient, but that act in connexion with the frightful element to which it conceded entrance. So that, as a spark thrown into inflammable matter can enkindle a fire, to consume the greatest wood, or one stone taken from a protecting dam causes a whole stream to pour away; so also Adam's sin which might appear so trifling. Spark and stone, without touchwood and stream, could do no essential harm, so without the existence of a kingdom of darkness Adam's sin could not have caused such hurt. In relation to this kingdom Adam stood, like the porter, holding also as he did then in his hand the keys of the kingdom of light; he opened *that* door and the lot was cast for ages. In the same position we behold the Saviour. According to the history of the temptation the key to the kingdom of this world's prince was offered also to Him, but He refused it and opened for mankind Paradise instead, whereby the stream of light then breaking in had power to scare off the shades of former night which ages had been gathering. Thus comprehended, Adam and Christ alone appear in their complete central meaning, as the Scripture sets them forth. They are the hinges, round which the doors of the powers of the universe move; the poles, from which life and death, light and darkness stream, which reveal themselves as well in the totality, as in every individual, in the power which they exercise on the world. The life of the great collective body, which we call mankind, oscillates between Adam and Christ, ay the life of the whole universe, for Adam's fall and Christ's resurrection are turning-points for the development of it all. (Comp. at Rom. viii. 19, &c.) And even so the being touched by the life-stream of Christ is for individuals greater or less, for nations and men, the turning-point of their existence. If, therefore, the latest theology and philosophy are to attain to a complete appropriation of the substance of the gospel, which they are trying for as a task of highest worth, a revision of the doctrine of evil and a deeper foundation for it will be of urgent necessity. (Comp. the observations at Matt. viii. 28.)

Ver. 12. The Apostle now clearly, while connecting by διὰ τοῦτο the foregoing exposition of the efficacy both of the death and life of Christ, presumes by the comparison with ὥσπερ the relation of

Adam to the sinfulness of the whole race as acknowledged. The question however is, how far Paul could do this? For we certainly do not find among the Rabbins any common agreement upon the doctrine of original sin. They term the general sinfulness קלקול, that is, "confusion, desolation," or as original sin יצר הרע, that is, "the imagining* of evil." (Comp. Buxtorf. lex. talm. pag. 973 and 2041.) At one time, however, they refer the origin of sin in man to Adam's fall, at another they represent it as created with man by God.† Meanwhile Tholuck observes justly, that the latter of these conceptions could proceed only from the theory of cabbalistic emanation, which makes evil appear as mere negation; now since no trace is to be found among the Jews of the properly Pelagian view, that every one is himself the originator of his own sinfulness by personal abuse of free will, we may so much the more consider the doctrine of Adam's sin, as the *causa efficiens* of the sinfulness of his race, to have been the prevailing Jewish doctrine, for the cabbala kept constantly in narrower circles and the Apocrypha clearly shew, how much the doctrine of original sin at the time they were composed was formed. (Comp. Wisd. Sol. ii. 23, xii. 10, xiii. 1; Sirach xxv. 24.) Most decisive, however, is the collective

* [Sinnen. See note, where יצר seems to be translated by "Concupiscentia;" its original meaning is "bilden, *fingere*, form." Gen. vi. 5. comp. Van Ess.]

† Compare Schöttgen and Wetstein ad loc. Tholuck and Reiche also have given copious extracts in their commentaries; the views of the Bible Dogmatists may be seen in Usteri, Paul. Lehrbegr. s. 25, note. Among the passages which refer sin to the fall of Adam, besides the interpretations of later Rabbins, to which certainly less is to be conceded, and the Targums on Eccles. vii. 30, Ruth. iv. 22.—Jalkut Rubeni, fol. 18. 1, has considerable weight, where it is said: "nisi Adam peccaset, fuisset nudus et coitum exercuisset et concupiscentia prava neminem induxisset; postquam vero peccavit et concupiscentia prava יצר הרע adest, nemo nudus incedere potest." The יצר הרע on the contrary appears as created by God in Succa fol. 52, 2. "Quatuor sunt, quorum poenitet Deum, quod illa *creaverit*, nimirum captivitatem, Chaldæos, Ismaelitas et concupiscentiam pravum." It may be questioned notwithstanding, whether *creare* here, like *plantare* in Aben Ezra *ad Psalm.* li. 7, ought not to be otherwise interpreted, namely, to be understood of the negative operation of God, permission. Nothing tells more for the correct apprehension of the doctrine of the Rabbins than the circumstance that they had also conceived correctly the parallel between Adam and the Messiah as his antitype. So in Neve Schalom, fol. 160, 2. "Quemadmodum homo primus (Adam) fuit אחד בחטא (that is, the first or rather only one in sin, the representative of the whole sinning race of man) sic Messias erit ultimus ad auferendum peccatum penitus." The doctrine of the Messiah alone, in the complete form in which the Jews already had it, could not, indeed, consistently followed out, lead to any other view upon the origin of the sinfulness of the race, than that the whole must have fallen *in* Adam and *through* him.

import of the Old Testament with its doctrine of the Messiah and His sacrifice, which, as the Epistle to the Hebrews proves at large, necessarily presupposes the sinfulness of the whole race through Adam. For were all men born with the same moral powers as were created in Adam, and did they all sin by the mere abuse of their own free will; neither regular expiatory sacrifices could have been *beforehand* ordained for all, since every moment some one might have proved himself to be quite pure, and at all events children who died in infancy must have been excepted, who nevertheless were just as unclean according to the law as all the dead were, nor could so thorough an influence have been derived from the appearing of *One Person,* as is connected with the Messiah. As far as regards passages like Ezek. xviii. 1, &c., they are only apparently contradictory, for the doctrine of original sin on no account excludes the responsibility for particular sins nor a faithful use of the proffered means of salvation spoken of in that chapter. The doctrine of original sin does not say, that any one *must* steal, commit adultery, or such like, on the contrary man possesses even after the fall, according to the doctrine of Scripture and the Symbolical Books, power enough to perform *opera civilia* and to abstain from positive transgressions of the law; it only teaches, that man is unable by his own power to get rid of the *prava concupisentia,** the evil desire that swells up in the heart, and the *proclivitas peccandi,* into which the mere *possibilitas peccandi* created by God in the first man passed, when by the first sin he made room for the influence of darkness.

Now, in what manner the Apostle could have put it, in order more clearly and decidedly to express his doctrine of the sin of Adam being causative of the sinfulness of his race, than by saying: *δι' ἑνὸς ἀνθρώπου ἡ ἁμαρτία ἐις τὸν κόσμον ἐισῆλθε,* cannot certainly be conceived, notwithstanding artifice enough has been employed upon his simple words. For instance it is attempted to evade the apostolic idea, by taking *ἁμαρτία* to mean independently sinful actions (*peccata actualia*), while it designates the sinful habit (*habitus peccandi*), the expressions of which are termed *ἁμάρ-*

* Luther: "Original sin is not *done* like all other sins, but it is, it liveth and *doeth* all other sins."—And in another place: "Thou canst do nothing but sin do as thou willest, all which thou settest about is sin, and abideth sin, let it show as fine as it may; beginning, furthering, and finishing is all *God's.*"

τημα, παράπτωμα, παράβασις. So far as the sinful habit must be necessarily presupposed from these expressions of it, ἁμαρτία *may* certainly denote the sinful act, but even the following exposition of the Apostle shews, that, where a sinful act is to be expressly mentioned, he makes use of one of those words. Besides, supposing that ἁμαρτία might be so taken here, the δι' ἑνὸς ἀνθρώπου (which thus occurs again 1 Cor. xv. 21), would be sufficient to forbid that the passage should be interpreted: "Adam opened the line of sinful acts," whereby alone it can be brought near to the Pelagian view. But the modern theory of sin being create in man is contradicted not only by the διὰ but the εἰσῆλθε. Sin existed already *with* and *in* Adam, it did not come first by him. According to that theory Paul must have written, "as sin in the first man first also manifested itself."—The εἷς ἄνθρωπος is moreover, as ver. 14 shews, *Adam*. If it is said, 1 Tim. ii. 14, of *Eve*, that she, not Adam, was deceived, this form of exposition refers merely to the relation of woman and man, the former being certainly the half the more accessible to sin. But where mention is made of the race collectively, and the relation of man and woman is not brought forward, Adam is named as the head of the first human pair, which is to be comprehended as unity.—As consequence of sin *death* only is made prominent, in which as the head of all evil every other form of it is comprised. Here indeed θάνατος signifies principally the death of the *body*, as also Gen. iii. 3, 4, but this had not been possible without the spiritual death, which entered with sin itself.* For it is the nature of death to disturb and separate that which belongs together; in the first state indeed men had no more the *impossibilitas moriendi* than the *impossibilitas peccandi*, but both the *possibilitas non moriendi* and *non peccandi* he had, and this passed by sin into the *necessitas moriendi* and the *proclivitas peccandi*. Thus, while the *bodily* death is the separation of the *soul* from the *body*, the *spiritual* death is represented as the separation of the *spirit* from the *soul*. This latter, however, was not a *total* separation, as sin did not de-

* Comp. Augustine's treatise hereon, in the first chapter of the thirteenth book, *de civitate Dei*; particularly in cap. 5, upon the question: "Quod sicut iniqui male utuntur lege, quæ bona est, ita et justi bene utuntur morte, quæ mala est." Adam's life after his fall was even as a slow dying, that reached its completion in his physical death: Christ's ζωοποίησις of mankind is also gradual, the height of which is in the glorification of the body.

velope itself, as with the fallen angels, in man himself, but was brought to him from without, as in the temptation of Christ. The *necessitas peccandi* appears therefore first as the θάνατος δεύτερος, as the highest point of sinful development. The reciprocal operation of the spiritual and physical, which finds expression in this, is not however limited according to the Pauline doctrine merely to man, but its disturbance reacts also upon the κτίσις generally, as at Rom. viii. 17, &c., will be further shewn.* But no sooner has the expression εἰς κόσμον εἰσῆλθε been used of Adam's sin (where κόσμος does not signify the universe, for sin was already in the spiritual world, but the world of man), than this sin is set in death, as its bitter fruit, as a principle penetrating through (διῆλθεν) the whole of the race, and, as is the course with every development, increasing and terminating in itself. (The οὕτως must be taken therefore "according to the connection of sin and death.") Although therefore Adam's act was not the act of an isolated individual, but the act of the race, since he is not to be considered as *one* man by the side of and among many others, but as *the* man;† yet the continuing progress of sin is not so denied by the sin of his posterity, but most decidedly established with it. Only sin itself is ever to be considered as punishment of sin, so that the sinning of the descendants became the very saddest consequence and punishment of the first sin. Had it been possible for the nearest descendants of Adam, for instance Abel or Seth, by perfect righteousness to stop the stream of corruption that came breaking in, to stand in the gap (Ezek. xxii. 30), Adam's act would then have been of no greater importance than any other sin, and it would then have been not merely fitting for the Apostle to mention any other, in order to make the antitypical comparison with Christ's act, but it would have answered even better, for instance, Cain's *killing* would seemingly have formed a far stronger contrast with Christ *being killed*. But every one feels that such a thing would,

* Glöckler (p. 84) says very appropriately: "Sin has the power of reproducing itself in the next neighbour, and that to the full extent, with all its consequences, unless it be subdued by the mightier power (derived from Christ) of that neighbour's life. Especially must this be the case with *that* neighbour, who owes his whole existence to a living organism, which is penetrated throughout by the power of sin. Here, conception is already a conception in sins, the first germ of life receives already the whole shape of sin."

† Rightly says Augustine: "In Adamo omnes tunc peccaverunt, quando in ejus natura adhuc omnes ille unus fuerunt." (De pecc. mer. et rem. iii. 7.)

according to St Paul's way of thinking, have been quite untenable, for Adam's sin is to him the *mother of all the rest*, and therefore, however insignificant in outward seeming, in its essence the sin of all sins, because the greatness of the sin depends on the situation which the sinner occupies, and no sinner ever yet stood where eternal love had placed Adam.

After these observations, it is clear what ought to be thought of the ordinary Pelagian-rationalistic view, that the addition ἐφ' ᾧ πάντες ἥμαρτον, signifies that the sinfulness of men is not caused by *Adam's* act, but by their *own* sins. For it is evident that the Apostle is thinking of that sinning of all as being the *consequence* of Adam's sin, and makes this addition only in order to show that if any one could have been supposed who sinned not, as the case was afterwards with Christ, then indeed a bound had been thereby set to death, provided that he occupied as central a position as Adam and Christ. Excepting this, it could only be said that the Apostle intends to intimate that the unfaithfulness of men, in not resisting sin even *to the extent* that they might have done, according to the moral powers still left to them, diffused the common sinfulness more *quickly* and *generally* than otherwise it would have been. Surely, therefore, if ἐφ' ᾧ is not to be translated with the Vulgate *in quo*,* and so this *expression* forms no *proof* in favour of the representation of the race by Adam; still it forms no weapon against this doctrine itself, which, in the *connexion* of the whole argument, is sufficiently established. Grammatically, ἐφ' ᾧ can only be taken as conjunction, as no antecedent can be fully traced, to which the relative could be easily applied.† As such, ἐφ' ᾧ answers to our "indem" (in that), = בַּאֲשֶׁר, and signifies the being at the same time, or together‡, with another.§ As to ἥμαρτον, many are

* How little ἐν ᾧ would be contrary to Paul's meaning, is shown by 1 Cor. xv. 22, where it is said: ὥσπερ ἐν τῷ 'Αδὰμ πάντες ἀποθνήσκουσιν, οὕτω καὶ ἐν τῷ Χριστῷ πάντες ζωοποιηθήσονται.

† Glöckler and Schmid (ad loc. p. 191, &c.) would refer ἐφ' ᾧ to θάνατος, "even unto which all sinned," that is, to make death the τέλος of sin; but this has something extremely forced.

‡ [Zugleichseyn.]

§ In passages like 2 Cor. v. 4, Phil. iii. 12, ἐφ' ᾧ is the conjunction also, not merely ἐπί with the relative, but it cannot be admitted to be so here. According to Rothe's explanation, who takes ἐφ' ᾧ = ἐπὶ τούτῳ ὥστε, the sense would also be: "in such wise that, under the certainty that." But he assumes that all sinned *themselves*. Now this was not so; death struck many without their having themselves sinned, *e.g*, all infant children. But of opinion that Paul is thinking of actual sins in using the word sins which proceed from the *proclivitas peccandi;* but if the πάντες, as the representation of the whole chapter requires, is to be understood in its properest sense of the totality, and so to include children dying in unconsciousness, this view naturally gets involved in extreme perplexity, and can only fall back upon the assertion that Paul is only speaking of individuals capable of sin; an assertion, however, which assuredly draws on the difficult argument, where the capability for sin begins.* How entirely untenable this view is, appears by this its own principal support in the most glaring light! Augustine's theory, on the contrary, although his translation of ἐφ' ᾧ by *in quo* is wrong, is here in thought impregnable. For the ἥμαρτον signifies "*being* sinful," together with "*committing* sin," and it is only casual in individuals that the latter does not issue from the former, the *being* sinful remaining nevertheless; the sense of the words therefore is: "in that (in Adam) all (without any exception) sinned, and with the greater number as consequence thereof the original sin expressed itself besides in further sinful acts, therefore did death also, the wages of sin, pierce through to all." Taken so the *imputatio in pœnam et reatum* of the sin of Adam has its truth; taken so the efficiency of Christ, in whom all in fact rose again just as they had in fact fallen in Adam, forms with that truth a true parallel. The question how in Adam all who were not yet in existence could sin with him, has difficulty in it only so long as the isolation of individuals is maintained. If this be given up, all takes a simple form,

it is just on πάντες that all the emphasis in the argument is laid. According to the Apostle's meaning, therefore, ἐν ἀυτῷ is doubtless to be supplied, and the passage to be taken thus: since they had all (collectively) sinned, namely, in Adam. This sense, too, alone agrees with what follows, where even the difference of the sinning, of those, for instance, who lived before the Mosaic law, from Adam's sinning, is set forth. Adam acted as person, and transgressed a positive command of God, the collective body sinned only in him; yet the punishment of death fell upon all together, as a proof, that even the participation in the general sin is of itself sin before God, although certainly in another sense than purely personal sin. (Upon the classical usage of ἐφ' ᾧ in the signification ἐπὶ τούτῳ ὥστε, comp. Matthiæ's Gr. § 479, p. 1063; Bernhardy's Syntax, p. 268; Fritzsche ad loc. p. 299, &c.—Upon the use of the synonymous ἐν ᾧ, comp. at Rom. viii. 3.)

* The manner in which Meyer (in his comm. ad loc.) tries to solve the difficulty, why children should die in infancy, if death is the consequence of actual sins only, is too meagre; he supposes (p. 120): "Paul entirely forgot this necessary exception (!)" Elsewhere surely the memory of the great Apostle is not wont to fail him in any respect.

and in Adam every one of his descendants must have sinned with him, just as in the act of one man, all his members and every drop of blood co-operate; and in an army not the general only conquers or is defeated, but every warrior of the host conquers or is conquered with him.*

As concerns the structure of the whole sentence ὥσπερ has no apodosis. To consider ver. 13–17 as parenthetic digression, in favour of which Reiche, after Grotius, Wetstein, and Flatt, has again pronounced, is harsh, because in this digression the substance of the thought proper to the conclusion is already anticipated. It is better therefore to suppose an anacoluthon here also, and to consider ver. 18 as recapitulating resumption of the discourse in ver. 12. So Rothe explains it, as also Winer, Rückert, and others. Besides this conception of the passage as anacoluthon, De Wette's view is the only one which can claim any attention, that the second member is introduced with ὥσπερ, and the first presupposed from what has been said before, as ὥσπερ occurs Matt. xxv. 14. But it is decidedly against this interpretation, that in what has been said before the preceding member has not been sufficiently expressed, to be immediately understood by the words: διὰ τοῦτο ὥσπερ. Moreover, with this acceptation it seems as though the principal reflection intended to be brought in view by the Apostle were, the connection of sinful man with Adam; but it is quite the reverse, for the chief object with Paul is to set forth the connection of the faithful with Christ. Hence this principal idea must also be considered as resting upon the bythought,† supposed to be taken for granted, the sinfulness of men since Adam, and therefore an ὄυτως follow the ὥσπερ. But as it was Paul's intention to shew the difference as well as the similarity between Adam and Christ, and further to draw the attention to the relation of the law to these two poles of the life of man, and the parallel resulted of itself from the line of argument; he let go the conclusion, and returned, ver. 18, to the leading thought.—In the Codd. D.E.F.G., and other critical au-

* Rückert's explanation of ver. 12 is quite correct. He says, p. 218, "According to this verse, therefore, Adam is the *originator* of human sinfulness, and so far the first cause of death; but men have *withal* by their own sinning deserved it." Only the last part of the sentence is not quite strictly expressed, for Paul does not intend to allege *two* causes, the sinning of men rather is itself founded in Adam's sin: their unfaithfulness has only enhanced sin the higher.

† [Nebengedanken.]

thorities, ὁ θάνατος is omitted before διῆλθεν. Much may certainly be said, as well critically as exegetically, in favour of the omission; as θάνατος for instance is only subordinate,* it *seems* more fitting to refer διῆλθε to ἁμαρτία the principal idea, out of which the presence of θάνατος follows of course. But the reading ὁ θάνατος διῆλθε appears the more preferable on account of ver. 13 being connected with the former by γάρ, since the mention of ἁμαρτία after wards requires θάνατος to be immediately preceding, which as mere consequence presupposes the *cause,* and as the head is named for *all* consequences.

Vers. 13, 14. This general dominion of death, even in the time before the promulgation of the positive Law of Moses, when therefore men *could* not by *personal* transgression of the law incur guilt as Adam did (vii. 7), proves the presence of sin in mankind, through the influence of the first sin, for the righteous God cannot suffer *punishment* (that is, θάνατος here) to come, where there is no guilt. These two verses are commonly considered as a passing observation; but such is not the case, according to the connexion of the subject, which has been indicated. The Apostle uses them rather, immediately to corroborate the principal thought in ver. 12. That sin was in the world *after* the law he presumes as a matter of course, but even *before* it, he says, sin was there, as death proves, although it might have been supposed, there was no sin, because there was no commandment to transgress. Paul therefore clearly infers the *imputatio reatus* from the *imputatio pœnæ peccati Adamitici.* As far as regards the supposition of many of the most distinguished expositors and dogmatists, as Origen, Augustine, Thomas Aquinas, Melanthon, Beza, that the sinfulness of *children* is intended here, this view, although inadmissible of itself, has somewhat of truth, in that the period from Adam to Moses is in fact the time of the *childhood of mankind.* Adam himself *before* the fall occupied indeed a higher station of consciousness, but *after* it he sunk with his descendants to a childish consciouslessness, in which not even a law could be given to men. Every individual has a similar period in his own life, during the twilight consciousness of childhood (comp. at vii.

* Rothe (p. 36) protests against θάνατος being subordinate, but the διὰ τῆς ἁμαρτίας ὁ θάνατος clearly enough makes death to be conditioned by sin; it is subordinate, therefore, although it becomes especially prominent afterwards.

9, &c.) ; nevertheless man, like the race in the whole, ay the very child in the cradle, is even during this period in sin, and suffers the punishment for sin, even death ; so that here it is perfectly clear how the Apostle in the use of ἁμαρτία would not be understood to mean sinful independent actions, but the *state* of *inward* disharmony, from which *outward* disharmony, whose head is death, takes rise. This state of disharmony is found also in the beast, ay in the physical creation (Rom. viii. 17, &c.), but it is called ἁμαρτία only where the *possibility* of conscious development is given, elsewhere φθορὰ only.

Ver. 13. Paul does not mean any *absolute* absence of law, as Rom. ii. 14, 15 shews ; where, however, there is no outward law, it is only by very indistinct warnings that the inward law gives indication of itself, especially in the twilight life of childhood. Personal *imputation* (ἐλλογεῖσθαι) of personal acts (the unconscious one shares only the burden of the many's guilt), is therefore out of the question during such a state.* Yet a βασιλεία θανάτου found place (opposed to the kingdom established by Christ, the βασιλεία ζωῆς), *even* (καί) over those who had not, like Adam, transgressed a positive command ; death therefore has naturally no less dominion over those who, arrived at a state of consciousness, have by their *own* guilt increased the sin which they *inherited*.—The μή before ἁμαρτήσαντας is omitted in some of the Fathers. But as all MSS. have it, and the context properly understood requires it, the omission can only proceed from misinterpretation.—The ἐπὶ τῷ ὁμοιώματι answers to כִּדְמוּת (Daniel x. 16.) With an entirely new thought : ὅς ἐστι τύπος τοῦ μέλλοντος, Paul now passes to that statement to which the representation of the efficacy of Adam's sin is intended merely to be a foil. Christ and Adam bear the relation of antitype to type, or as a Rabbin says:

* The acceptation of ἐλλογεῖσθαι proposed by Usteri (fourth edit. of the Paul. Lehrbegr. p. 42) and Glöckler (p. 82), instead of the explanation given here, and correctly put forth by Rückert also, is quite inadmissible. They would have it to be understood not of the imputation of God, but of the self-imputation of men, so that the sense should be : "Without law, man does not impute sin to himself, that is, he is not conscious of it as such, heeds it not, therefore, and does not take it duly to heart." This, however, does not agree with the context, because it is not the subjective judgment of man which is there treated of, but the judgment of God. God indeed allows death admission to all men, because it is the consequence of the collective guilt contracted through Adam, but the individual guilt of men is not yet punished, as is shown by the instance of Cain and Lamech, the law being wanting. (Comp. upon the πάρεσις at Rom. iii. 25.)

סוֹד אָדָם הוּא סוֹד הַמָּשִׁיחַ—that is: "the mystery of Adam is the mystery of the Messiah." The elements of forgotten typology are becoming more and more recognised, and cannot, consistently with truly historical exposition, be overlooked in the New Testament. The Old Testament is a μόρφωσις τῆς ἀληθείας to all the writers of the New Testament, and according to this principle Christ must naturally appear as the *second* Adam (1 Cor. xv. 45), the whole race being represented by him after a spiritual manner, just as by Adam after an outward manner. Now the point of comparison between Adam and Christ here is manifestly the passing of sin and of righteousness from them upon all. Accordingly this passage must present great obstacles to Benecke's doctrine of præexistence; he is obliged therefore to have recourse to the forced interpretation, that μέλλοντος must be taken as neuter, scil. γένους, so for Adam to be called a type of the race to come, because all sinned like him. How arbitrary this construction is, is evident.

Ver. 15. The relation between the efficacy of Adam and that of Christ is however with all similarity still a different one; the power which appears in Christ is one of incomparably greater might.* But this preponderance is not, with Grotius and Fritzsche, to be referred to a mere logical More of possibility and certainty, but to the intensive power of grace. *First of all* (ver. 15) it shews itself stronger, in that in Adam's sin the principle of righteousness merely is manifested, but in Christ the overflowing element of divine grace. *Next* (ver. 16) Adam produced mere negative effect, but Christ positive, forgiving the many sins by His sacrifice. Ay, not by forgiveness merely does He operate, but also (ver. 17) by communicating a new and higher life. Then follows, in vers. 18, 19, an antithetic repetition of the whole thought. Here accordingly Paul asserts the idea of the *vicarious office* of Christ, with which the doctrine of the satisfaction expressed Rom. iii. 24, 25, is so closely united. For were Christ *one* man beside and among many others, it were indeed inconceivable, how His doing and suffering could

* The whole exposition given here may be used in favour of the doctrine of the restoration. Since namely Adam's sin came in fact to all, its power would appear greater than the power of Christ, if the wicked could resist the latter, and it penetrated all. That would, however, lead to the *gratia irresistibilis*, which Paul does not teach, as will be shewn at ch. ix.; we must, therefore, with regard to the greater power of grace, la emphasis only on those points which are brought forward.

have any essential influence upon collective humanity ; He could have worked only by doctrine and example ; but He is, besides His divine nature, to be conceived of as *the* Man, that is, as realising the absolute idea of mankind, and therefore potentially bearing mankind in Himself *spiritually,* just as Adam did *corporeally.* This character of the human nature of Christ is designated in dogmatism by the term *impersonalitas,* and Philo, anticipating the profound idea, described the Logos as *τὸν κατ' ἀλήθειαν ἄνθρωπον,* that is, as the idea of man, the human ideal. According to this His universal character, the Redeemer becomes in twofold respect *vicarious ;** first, in that standing in the stead of sinful men, by His own suffering he takes their suffering on Himself, as sacrifice for the sins of the world ; then, in that He perfected in Himself absolute righteousness and holiness, so that the believer does not generate them afresh, but receives their seed in the Spirit of Christ. The former is the *obedientia passiva,* the latter the *obedientia activa.* The latter will be further treated of at ver. 19 ; of the former it is to be remarked, that it is commonly said of Christ in the language of the New Testament: *ὑπὲρ ἡμῶν ἀπέθανε.* Meanwhile it has been already noticed at Matt. xx. 28, that *περὶ* also, *διὰ,* and even *αντί* is used. The most of these prepositions certainly can signify no more than " for, in behalf of," but in *αντι* the signification "in the place of, instead," is clearly prominent, which, according to ver. 7, and 2 Cor. v. 20, *ὑπὲρ* also undoubtedly bears. But according to the antithesis here carried through of Adam and Christ, it becomes perfectly evident that the Apostle conceives the life and death of our Lord as *vicarious,* so that what took place in Him, in fact went on in all (2 Cor. v. 15.) Now the reason for putting the expression *χάρισμα* here (ver. 15) in opposition to *παράπτωμα* (the sin of Adam), as also ver. 16 parallel with *δώρημα* is, in order that the circumstance of its having been done *once for all* may be marked in the act of Christ's love, in opposition to the sin committed once for all by Adam ; the effect of the termination *μα* being to denote this.† Long intervals decide

* In both relations the power of Christ in its transition into mankind is to be compared with a movement proceeding from a centre, concentrically diffusing itself. Christ brings His *death* and *resurrection* to every individual, the former for the old, the latter for the new man.

† Compare Buttman's large Gram. B. ii. p. 314. The syllable *μος* denotes the ab-

not on mankind's destinies, but moments ; even so also in the life of individuals and nations there are precisely-limited moments in which the determination to better or worse for long periods is at stake, parting-ways which for long spaces condition the development to come.

Οἱ πολλοὶ (with the article) is equal to *πάντες* above ver. 12. As Augustine cont. Jul., vi. 12 says : omnes revera sunt multi. Without the article, indeed, a part only of the race could be meant,* but *with* it the expression has regard to the preceding *πάντες*.

Χάρις is general, the love of God in its utterance towards sinners, *δωρεά* its special utterance in the mission and the work of Christ. *Περισσεύω* is not to be taken transitively, as Paul certainly uses the word (2 Cor. ix. 8 ; Ephes. i. 8 ; 1 Thess. iii. 12), but, as ordinarily, intransitive. The aorist is put, that grace in its historical manifestation in the work of Christ may be set in the balance against *ἀπέθανον*, the operation of justice.

Vers. 16, 17. But there is a further distinction between Christ's efficacy and that of Adam, in that it operates not merely *negatively* but *positively*, justifying mankind from the infinitely many transgressions, yea even imparting to them a new and higher life.

Ver. 16. The reading *ἁμαρτήματος* is found instead of *ἁμαρτήσαντος*, arising doubtless merely from the seeming incompleteness of the antithetic member. *Δι' ἑνὸς δικαίου* must certainly have been added to *δώρημα*, if the sentence were to have been filled up. *Κρίμα* is the operation of the divine justice objectively considered, which could but shew itself as *κατάκριμα* after Adam's, the first man's sin. According to the antithesis *ἐκ πολλῶν παραπτωμάτων*, the only word that can be supplied after *ἐξ ἑνός* is *παραπτώματος*. In the *ἐκ πολλῶν παραπτωμάτων, πολλῶν* is not to be taken as masculine ; the *many* sins rather are opposed to Adam's *one*. The preposition, however, is not to be construed in either case in the sense of "proceeding from," but is to be understood "on account of, in consequence of;" so that the sense is : "in consequence of one sin the operation of God's justice passed into condemnation, in con-

stract, *μα* the concrete, *μη* fluctuates between both. This with reference to Rothe's opinion, who thinks this conception of *χάρισμα* and *δώρημα* capricious.

* Glöckler's observation is wrong, when he says that *πάντες* could not be used, because the one is taken out. For it is the same thing at ver. 18, and yet *πάντες* is used there. Besides the one continues to belong to the whole, nay he *is* the whole.

sequence of the many sins among mankind the operation of God's grace passed into justification."* The use of δικαίωμα here and ver. 18 is peculiar, as was observed at Rom. iii. 21. Commonly it signifies that which in a particular case is δίκαιον, therefore "statute, ordinance, ἐντολή." But here it is used, as δικαίωσις ζωῆς in ver. 18 shews, like δικαίωσις = τὸ δικαιοῦν, הַצְדִּיק. This deviation from the common use in the passage before us is founded in the structure of the whole sentence. The Apostle's point was, to contrast the *act* of Christ's efficacy to the *act* of the fall; now δικαίωμα expressed the momentary better than δικαίωσις.—Ver. 17. The dative παραπτώματι denotes the *causa efficiens* of death, διὰ τοῦ ἑνός designates Adam as the organ, through whom the cause became operative. So was God also through Christ the *causa efficiens* of His work (2 Cor. v. 19). The δικαιοσύνη is that which is worked in man by the δικαίωσις = δικαίωμα of Christ.—By an easy turn of the parallel, instead of putting ζωή itself as the reigning power in opposition to the reigning θάνατος, the ζῶντες are represented with Christ as those who reign ἐν τῇ βασιλείᾳ τοῦ Θεοῦ.

Vers. 18, 19. Finally the Apostle once more comprises in these verses this great contrast between Adam and Christ, and in so doing not only lays the emphasis upon the efficacies being each *universal*,† but indicates also, that the δικαιοσύνη and ζωή, which he had just before treated abstractedly as separate moments, in the concrete fall into each other, only with this distinction; that the δικαίωσις constantly appears as absolute, no degrees being conceivable in the forgiveness of sins, the ζωή on the contrary is represented as gradually growing perfect.—In ver. 19, the idea which grounds this whole passage is expressed in altered terms, and with a distinctness, which renders Paul's real meaning more perceptible

* If ἐξ ἑνός and ἐκ πολλῶν are to form an antithesis, it might be supposed whether the many sins did not designate those merely which brought Christ to the cross; truly, but this was done not merely by the sins of those who lived at the time, but of all men of all times, so that it comes to the same thing. The emphasis in this verse, moreover, is laid on δικαίωμα, God did not only forgive the sins, but he made the sinners righteous.

† As οἱπολλοί is said as well of Christ as of Adam, *i.e.*, πάντες, it must be said, to evade the restoration, that mention is made here of the divine *purpose* in the work of the redemption, not of its *result*. (Comp. upon the restoration more particularly at ix. 1 and xi. 25.)

than all he has said before.* Not the personal transgressions of individual men, but the *disobedience* of Adam, was *alone* the foundation of all being sinners; and just so the reverse; the personal striving of individuals could not make them righteous (for the very best effort of man's own powers remains powerless and defiled without Christ's support), but the obedience of Christ is the only effectual cause of the righteousness of all. No expression can be imagined by which Paul could have himself more distinctly defined vers. 12 and 15, and protected his meaning from erroneous conceptions; if notwithstanding he has not succeeded in preventing them, the cause of the failure can only at last be found in the heart's resistance to this doctrine, bringing as it does to nothing all man's selfsufficiency, a resistance which even unconsciously asserts itself while interpreting such passages.—The expression *ὑπακοή* applied to Christ deserves a closer consideration here, as the question regarding the *obedientia activa* and *passiva* is connected with it. (Comp. Phil. ii. 8.) Now we must certainly allow, that the doctrine of the *obedientia activa* cannot be proved from this passage, for the nearest signification of *ὑπακοή* in contrast to *παρακοή* (Adam's eating of the fruit) must be the obedient surrender of Christ to death, as the once done act of love, to which Phil. ii. 8 also has reference. Nevertheless the doctrine of the *obedientia activa* has foundation in the Scripture, only it must be laid on other passages, for instance Rom. viii. 30. The whole life of Christ as such is His work, and even His death, as the summit, receives its significance only from its connexion with the perfect life of our Lord. As death and resurrection, so are even in this whole life the active and passive obedience of Christ related, it being however borne in mind, that the distinction is not an absolute one, since the highest passivity cannot be imagined without activity, nor the latter without the former.

Ver. 18. *ἄρα οὖν* is according to Bible use placed at the beginning of the sentence, which certainly is not conformable to classic use. (Comp. Rothe ad loc. p. 136.)—In ver. 18 also, *κρίμα* and *χάρισμα ἔρχεται* are to be supplied after ver. 16. As to *κατα-*

* Yet Usteri says (p. 27) even of this passage, that it says no more than: "that in the sinfulness of Adam, which first made itself known as actual conscious sin in the transgression of a positive command, the sinfulness of the whole human nature was brought *to light*. How the words *διὰ τῆς παρακοῆς τοῦ ἑνός* could be chosen to express such a thought as this, the foundation of which is the false assumption that sinfulness belongs to the character of the creature, is inconceivable."

σταθήσονται in ver. 19, καθίστασθαι certainly signifies "to be set forth as somewhat, and by the setting forth to be pronounced to be somewhat," so that the expression is parallel with λογίζεσθαι ἐις δικαιοσύνην. But as the discourse relates to the operation of God, it must be borne in mind, that God cannot pronounce any one to be what he is not; so far καθίστασθαι, like καλεῖσθαι, ὀνομάζεσθαι, coincides with εἶναι.

Ver. 20. The Apostle's readers must naturally after this exposition have felt it requisite to ascertain, in what relation then the law, which is also a divine institution, stood to the principal turning-points of the world's history.* Paul therefore briefly touches upon this question although in chap. vii. he discusses it at large. His view is briefly this: the import of the law is in its being a *preparatory step* of the life of faith, it comes in between Adam and Christ, to awaken the consciousness of sin, and thereby to sharpen the longing for redemption. (Comp. at iii. 30, and vii. 24, 25.) The chief object, therefore, in its being given is not that it may be fulfilled, for no one exists, who could keep it in its intrinsic meaning, as it is set out in the Sermon on the Mount, and a half or improperly fulfilled law is before God a law not kept at all (Gal. iii. 10), although the prevention of *gross* sins is before man not unimportant (Gal. iii. 19); but it is to be the παιδαγωγὸς εἰς Χριστόν (Gal. iii. 24). In so far, however, as it is of divine, eternal nature (vii. 12), it continues even for the faithful the absolute rule of the development of life.

In the παρεισῆλθεν not only its coming in between is indicated, but also that it was something beside, and not absolutely necessary, for in the efficacy of Christ the law is given also; its antecedent promulgation by Moses was only to facilitate man's way in getting to Christ.—The παράπτωμα is remarkable, for the law was certainly to enhance sin *inwardly*, but the *outward* bursts of sin were to be checked (Gal. iii. 19) and not increased by it; yet παράπτωμα cannot signify the sinful state.† Doubtless therefore the expres-

* The treatise, Gal. iii. 19, &c., is quite a parallel to this; the commentary upon it may be compared here.

† Rothe's supposition must be considered faulty, according to which the παράπτωμα is to mean Adam's παράπτωμα more and more developing itself, and diffusing itself according to its effects. In treating of the operation of the law upon the sinful state, the actual sins of single individuals only, but not the collective act of Adam, can be intended.

sion here must be taken thus; the law indeed is not purposedly to multiply the outbreaks of sin, but they are notwithstanding the inevitable consequences of it (vii. 8); now, inasmuch as the consciousness of sin is awakened by it, the transgression itself may be also regarded as an object of the law. It is inappropriate to take *ἵνα* merely *ἐμβατικῶς*, it is clearly contrary to the Apostle's meaning to consider it as mere consequence, as chap. vii. 8, &c., will further shew. He regards the law as a beneficial medicine, which forces outwards a disease, which is raging undiscerned in the noble parts within.* On account of the aorists *οὗ* is taken better with Grotius and De Wette in the signification "as," instead of "where:" the Apostle is speaking of the regulations of God quite in their objective character, the subjective conception of them does not come into play. The aorist *ἐπλεόνασε* goes on, therefore, to the fact of the killing of the Son of God, in which sin actually reached its summit, but at the same time grace set forth her over-measure, in that the salvation of the world was gained and made sure by the highest sin. Rothe endeavours to explain the aorists from the circumstance, that the sentence, in his opinion to be taken as parenthesis (*οὗ — χάρις*), contains a thought expressed as an axiom or proverb. But this is contradicted by the peculiar constitution of the thought, which has its place entirely within the Pauline theory, but has nothing at all of a proverbial character in it.—*Ὑπερπερισσεύω* is to be taken like *πλεονάζω* intransitively, in the signification "being rich beyond." In the passages 2 Cor. vii. 4; 1 Tim. i. 14, the parallel *ὑπερπλεονάζω* occurs.

Ver. 21. The absolute reign of grace, therefore, to eternal life (vi. 22, 23), is the final aim of redemption through Christ, while till then sin reigned to death.

The strict antithesis would have required *ἐις θάνατον* or *ἐν ζωῇ*, but *ἐν* denotes expressly, that sin itself is spiritual death, *ἐις* makes the aim more prominent.—The *δικαιοσύνη* is taken as the means by which grace exercises her dominion. But at the very founda-

* Augustine correctly expresses himself upon the relation of the law: "Data est lex ad ostendendum, quantis quamque arctis vinculis peccatorum constricti tenerentur, qui de suis viribus ad implendam justitiam præsumebant." Equally so Calvin: "Erant quidem homines naufragi ante legem, quia tamen in suo interitu sibi videbantur natare, in profundum demersi sunt, quo illustrior fieret liberatio, quum inde præter humanum sensum emergant. Neque vero absurdum fuit, legem hac partim de causa ferri, ut homines semel damnatos bis damnet; quia nihil justius est, quam modis omnibus adduci homines, imo convictos trahi, ut mala sua sentiant."

tion Christ Himself is considered as the holy Instrument, through which the reign of life is realised; inasmuch namely as the Father, who sends the Son into the flesh, is acknowledged as the First Cause of the decree of grace.

§ 10. THE BELIEVER IS DEAD TO SIN.

(VI. 1—VII. 6)

It is not likely that the passing notice of the law and its relation to grace (v. 20, 21), induced the Apostle Paul in what follows to proceed to refute the error, that we might continue in sin that grace should abound. It answers far better to connect as Rothe does (p. 49), the subsequent words with the leading thought of chap. v. in this manner: " What shall we say, then, in this state of things? Namely, seeing that justification through faith in the redemption by Christ according to its specific operation is essentially the sanctification of believers. Shall we, therefore, yet think of continuing in sin?" The Apostle then prosecutes the refutation of this error in such a manner, that the principal idea of the section, *the vicarious relation of Christ* to the collective whole, always continues in the foreground, and forms the main of the argument. Although, however, according to the tenor of the epistle in the whole, the treatise that follows can form no more than an accessory part, it is notwithstanding of the highest importance for the *practical application* of the Apostle's doctrine of justification by faith without the works of the law; and this indeed not merely at that time, but in every time, and especially in the present. For *firstly*, there are never wanting persons who, in fact, *misunderstand* this holy doctrine, and through misunderstanding *misuse* it. Whether it be that stupidity, or which is perhaps more common, more or less unconscious impurity is the cause, certain it is that many construe the doctrine of justification as though they now had leave to live on quietly in sin, as if Christ would make a man blessed with sin, which is itself unblessedness, and not *from* sin. No one has ever consciously taught such doctrine, because it is in fact too absurd for the lowest grade of spiritual development not to acknowledge the perverseness of it; but insincerity of heart makes the consciences of many dull, and in such a state they apply the doctrine falsely, and turn grace to wantonness. (Jude ver. 4.) But, *secondly*, this treatise is no less important, because the opponents of the doctrine of justification regard this abuse of it as one necessary to it, and essentially founded in it, and think themselves obliged therefore to combat the doctrine as an extremely dangerous one. In this error are found not merely all thorough rationalistic-pelagian theologists, but others also, who with no living experience of the nature of faith and of justification, are animated by a kind of legal jealousy, and flatter themselves that by their own effort they can soon attain, if they do not already exhibit the type of absolute perfection. For every one, however, who is willing to see, the apostolic doctrine may, under the guidance of this section, with very little pains be perfectly justified; on the other hand, indeed, no help is to be found against impurity of heart, or against the conceit of self-righteousness, unless grace itself reveals to hearts their secret sins; at least the statement of the Apostle has not itself been able to prevent the errors either of the former or of the latter. Meanwhile the Scripture fulfils even by this inability one of its purposes, that, namely, of becoming, like Christ himself, the *fall* of many (Luke ii. 34), not to destroy them, but by revealing to them their most secret sins of impurity, or of conceited self-confidence, to save them.

Ver. 1, 2. Without noticing any particular party—such as Jews or Jew Christians only—the Apostle proposes the question quite generally, as one proceeding from impurity of heart in general,—whether according to what had been said the meaning be, that sin could be continued in, in order to let grace have its full power? He answers this question most decidedly in the negative, by designating the faithful as those who are dead with respect to sin, who cannot therefore live in it any more.* This idea of the faithful being dead, Paul carries through to ver. 11, and that in such a manner as to regard the death of Christ not merely as a symbol of the death of the faithful, but as a *real event* in themselves, of which they are partakers, as they are also of His resurrection

* So Calvin, when he justly observes: "Plusquam igitur præpostera esset operis Dei inversio, si occasione gratiæ, quæ nobis in Christo offertur, peccatum vires colligeret. Neque enim medicina morbi, quem extinguit, fomentum est." Yet man can hardly believe in the power of Christ without law; hence Luther says well: "The multitude will have a Moses with horns;" that is, the law with its frightening power.

through faith. Here then is manifest, how keenly and with what thorough decision Paul conceives and applies the vicarious office of Christ. *He* is mankind; what came to pass in Him, in fact went on in all, in Him *are* all dead, have all suffered death for sin, in Him *are* all risen again and have received the new life. The history of Jesus therefore is a living continuing history, since it is livingly repeated in every one. (1 Pet. ii. 24.) According to the Pelagian interpretation, this passage is understood only of the *resolve* or the *vow* of abstaining from sin, which was entered into at baptism. But Paul would clearly contradict himself by such a thought, for down to iii. 20, he had shewn at large that man is incapable, by mere resolve, to renounce sin. According to such an acceptation, moreover, even the δοξάζειν in the passage, Rom. viii. 30, could not be conceived as a thing already past, but it is put in the aorist, just as all the other moments are. The Pauline idea doubtless is, that our Lord in those words upon the cross, "it is finished," declared the work of atonement and redemption to be accomplished not merely for himself, but also for all believers of all times, so that whoever believes in Him as surely died with him,* as with Him rose again. Such a postulate, too, is not merely *admissible* or the like, but *necessary* [as a consequence] from the idea of the vicarious office, that as in Adam all fell, so must all die and rise again in Christ, for *He* was *themselves*.

Griesbach is right in putting the reading ἐπιμένωμεν into the text, and Lachmann also; while other codd. read ἐπιμείνομεν, ἐπιμένομεν, ἐπιμενοῦμεν. The last is the reading of the *text. rec.*, and has distinguished critical authorities also in its favour; it must, notwithstanding, be considered inferior to the first. Ἀποθνήσκειν, like ζῆν τινι (ver. 10), is, even in profane authors, the usual figurative mode of expression for "entertaining or breaking off connection with any one." But the following exposition shews, that Paul does not merely mean the expression figuratively, but conceives it inwardly indeed, yet quite really. ἀυτῇ by itself might have stood for ἐν ἀυτῇ.

* The old man is not to be gradually sanctified, but must die as sinner, as Luther aptly says: "Flesh and blood abideth ever and ever unclean, until they fetch shovel strokes upon it;" that is, until it is dead and buried. And in another place: "We must scourge the old man and strike him on the face, pain him with thorns, and pierce him through with nails, until he boweth his head and giveth up the ghost."

Ver. 3, 4. In proof of the affirmation above, Paul appeals to the conscience of his readers with regard to their own experience. They had gone through, he says, *in baptism* the death, nay, the burial of Christ with Him, as also the awakening up unto a new life.* In this place, also, we must by no means think of their own resolutions only at baptism, or see no more in it than a figure, as if by the one half of the ancient rite of baptism the *submersion*, the death and the burial of the old man—by the second half, the *emersion*, the resurrection of the new man—were *no more than* prefigured; we must rather take baptism in its *inward meaning*, as spiritual process in the soul. That which was already *objectively* fulfilled on and in the person of Jesus, the same is appropriated *subjectively* through him in faith to man; he experiences the *power* as well of the sufferings and of the death, as of the resurrection of the Lord (Phil. iii. 10). Accordingly this efficacy can only be ascribed to the baptism of grown persons, and in their case it coincides with regeneration; in the baptism of infants a spiritual influence certainly is already wrought upon the child, but the personal *appropriation* of the power of Christ does not take place before that later awakening and conversion, the necessity of which confirmation prefigures.

The *συνετάφημεν* is only a stronger expression for *θάνατος*. The burial withdraws the dead person entirely from view, and is, therefore, like annihilation. (Comp. Rom. viii. 17, Col. iii. 1, 2 Tim. ii. 11.) The *βαπτισθῆναι ἐις Χριστὸν*† (comp. at Matth. xxviii. 19), is only more clearly defined by the *βαπτισθῆναι ἐις τὸν θάνατον ἀυτοῦ*, as by the *συνταφῆναι ἀυτῷ ἐις τὸν θάνατον*. The baptized person vows himself to the *whole* Christ, and Christ himself wholly to him, consequently death and resurrection become equally man's. The *ἐις θάνατον* is not to be understood therefore = *ἐις πίστιν θανάτου*, but of death itself, the participation of which surely is mediated by faith. The *δόξα τοῦ πατρός* appears as the awakening power, that is, the whole fulness and majesty of His Being, for even in the creation of the world the divine properties shew not such splendour, as in the redemption and raising up

* Rückert's observation ad loc. is quite just; that the Apostle is not saying here, what Christians have done at their baptism, but what has *been done* to them in baptism.

† Against Bindseil's observations upon this formula (Stud. 1832. p. 410, &c.), comp. the striking refutation of Fritzsche ad h. l. p. 359, not.

of Christ. *Περιπατεῖν* means the abiding continuance and living in the *καινότης ζωῆς* (2 Cor. v. 17, Galat. vi. 15, Ephes. ii. 15, iv. 23), which forms the contrast with the *old*, sinful state, which is in itself properly a death, so that in the regeneration death, which has in itself a positive power, is, in truth, itself killed, that is the life of pure spirit is born.

Ver. 5. Upon the necessary connection of the one with the other, the Apostle then grounds the proof, that where the death of Christ shews itself effective, His awakening life must be also powerful (comp. 2 Cor. iv. 14), for it is life only that kills the old man.

Σύμφυτος is only found in this passage in the N. T.; in profane authors it occurs, like *συμφυής*, very often in the signification, "grown to, grown together, thence united, bound together." This sense is perfectly suitable here; the faithful are considered as grown together with Christ to one unity.* Instead of Christ himself, first *ὁμοιώματι θανάτου* only (that is, *ὁμοίως*, or *ὅμοιοι θανάτου*), and afterwards *ἀναστάσεως* is used, because the efficacy of Christ is represented by these two halves. It is inappropriate to take the dative as *instrumental* here, and to found *σύμφυτοι γεγόναμεν* upon it. Tholuck asserts, that according to the acceptation proposed here the *ἀνάστασις* must then be applied not merely to the spiritual, but also to the bodily resurrection. But we need not hesitate at that (comp. at Rom. viii. 11), since the bodily *ἀνάστασις* is but the height of the expression of the *ζωή* of Christ in man (comp. at John vi. 39.) *Ἀλλὰ καὶ* is not to be taken as merely inferring, as Rückert and Reiche correctly observe, but to be explained rather from an *ὀυ μόνον* latitant in the first part of the sentence, since the resurrection, as the life, is more powerful than death (comp. at v. 10, 11.) The reading *ἅμα καὶ* has arisen merely from a correction.

Ver. 6, 7. But at all events the service of sin must be out of the question with one that is dead; for death, the sum of all punishment, necessarily frees every one from sin, on account of which it is suffered.

* Calvin observes rightly on the passage: "insitio non exempli tantum conformitatem designat, sed arcanam conjunctionem, perquam cum ipso coaluimus, ita ut nos spiritu suo vegetans ejus virtutem in nos transfundat. Ergo ut surculus communem habet vitæ et mortis conditionem cum arbore, in quam insertus est, ita vitæ Christi non minus quam et mortis participes nos esse consentaneum est.

Τοῦτο γινώσκοντες = *ὀυκ ἀγνοοῦντες*, "since we know *for certain.*" *Συνεσταυρώθη*, a stronger expression than *θάνατος*, which is partly chosen to point at the death of Christ, partly to describe the death of the old man as a painful and ignominious one. The *παλαιὸς ἄνθρωπος* forms the contrast with the *καινός* (Ephes. iv. 24), answering to the בְּרִיא חֲדָשָׁה, by which the proselytes were designated. In consequence of the doctrine of regeneration this name was assigned in a higher signification to the faithful. In the passage Rom. vii. 21, &c., the relation of the two will be treated more at large. I only observe here, that this contrast is by no means identical with the *ὁ ἔξω* and *ὁ ἔσω ἄνθρωπος* (Rom. vii. 22), for this latter has place as well in the *natural* man, but the first only in the *regenerate*. *Καταργεῖσθαι* = *συνταφῆναι*, to be entirely done away, annulled in its efficacy. The opinion, that *here* in the *σῶμα τῆς ἁμαρτίας*, the body as the seat of sin in and by itself is intended, in favour of which De Wette has again determined, is sufficiently refuted by Reiche.* After the *συνεσταυρώθη* the *καταργήθη* cannot have any weaker meaning; according to De Wette it is no more than "to make inactive." In the stronger and proper acceptation, the thought however is untrue, for the body subject to sin is not to be annihilated in the process of regeneration, but to be glorified. It were a forced expression to say, that in its very glorification the sinful body is actually annihilated and absorbed by the spiritual body. Here therefore perhaps the Hebrew usage of עֶצֶם or גוּף might be compared, by which the reality and substance of a thing is denoted. Meanwhile it is simpler to interpret *σῶμα* by carrying out the complete image of the crucifixion of sin, so that it is itself considered as embodied. Thus Theodoret, later Koppe, Flatt, Benecke. Reiche. Ver. 16, &c., the service of sin is described at length as *δουλεία*.† The whole of ver. 7 is wanting in some of the Fathers, but it is without doubt genuine, and omitted only as being merely explanatory; as such it cannot have reference immediately to the spiritual, but to the phy-

* We shall express ourselves more at large at the close of the 7th chapter, as to the relation which, according to the Pauline conception, the bodily substance bears to sin.

† At the words *τοῦ μηκέτι δουλεύειν* Calvin observes: "unde sequitur, nos, quamdiu sumus Adæ filii ac nihil quam homines, peccato sic esse mancipatos, ut nihil possimus aliud, quam peccare; Christo vero insitos a misera hac necessitate liberari; non quod statim desinamus in totum peccare, sed ut simus tandem in pugna superiores."

sical death. The latter, however, is certainly comprehended in its analogy with the spiritual death. In thinking of the physical death notwithstanding, we are not so much to consider that the sinner is free from sin, that is, that he cannot sin any more, for the expression δεδικαίωται has too decidedly a judicial relation. We are to consider rather a *sentence of punishment* to which Christ's death also leads; whoever died in consequence of this, he, even although he returned to life, is acquitted from sin on account of which he was condemned,* for he has expiated it. (Guilt before men, I mean, is the only thing spoken of in this sentence, and the satisfaction which is made to civil justice; not the divine eternal justice.) So is man also dead in Christ, and as a dead man, incapable of serving sin. So, therefore, justification stands in no contradiction with the law. According to the law the sinner must die, and even so he dies, who is justified through Christ; only in the dying of the old man the new gets life. Upon δικαιοῦσθαι ἀπὸ comp. Acts xiii. 39.

Vers. 8, 9. In the certainty, therefore, of death with Christ lies the certainty also of life with Him, that is, of His life in us, for in Him dwelleth the fulness of infinite, immortal life. Entirely the same train of thought is found 2 Cor. v. 14, &c., from which repetition may be perceived what deep root it had in the Apostle's mind. (When the believer in his immediate consciousness is certain of his death with Christ, the *living with Him* [συζῆν], although its germ is likewise present in him, is yet so far something future, as its complete development extends into the ζωὴ αἰώνιος. But the firm ground which this faith has, is in the unconquerable life of Christ, which he sheds without ceasing on His own.—In the ὀυκέτι κυριεύει it is signified, that death certainly had dominion over Christ,† in that he really died, but not by the necessity of nature, but by freely giving up Himself in love (John x. 18; Phil. ii. 7). Yet even in death life could not be holden of death.)

Ver. 10. The relation which Christ, the ζωή (John i. 4), bore to

* In entirely the same sense the Talmud says: postquam mortuus est homo, cessat a praeceptis. Schabb. fol. 151. 2 (comp. Menschen, N. T. e Talmude, illustr. pag. 170.

† If theologians of the Reformation believed, that death had dominion over Jesus until the resurrection, their opinion rests upon a false conception of the descent to hell and its import. (Comp. at 1 Pet. iii. 18.) Our Lord appeared among the dead as already conqueror over death; God is not a God of the dead, but of the living, may also be said of Him.

death, on which our hope of life rests, is yet more nearly defined, namely, that *His* death, the once-suffered death, came to pass only for our sins; but what* he liveth, he liveth to God. There is no difficulty in the first half of the verse; the idea of κυριεύειν (ver. 9) leads the Apostle to a closer description of the death of Christ. He died not for Himself, but *for* men, that is, for the doing away of their sins, not often and for ever, but once. (Hebr. ix. 12, 26, &c., x. 10.) The greatness of His sacrifice outweighed by His dying once mankind's eternal death. In the second half, however, the ζῇ τῷ Θεῷ causes a difficulty, some antithesis being looked for to ἐφάπαξ, or at least to ἁμαρτία, but to neither does the ζῃ τῷ Θεῷ seem to afford any. Now the antithesis to ἐφάπαξ may lie in the present tense by its expression of continuity. The τῷ Θεῷ is not so easy. For if the words are to be construed: "He liveth *for* God, with regard to God," this did Jesus even on earth, and in His heavenly Being He lives again not less for men, than on earth. The whole thought then appears somewhat irrelevant; δικαιοσύνη might, as it seems, have been better opposed to ἁμαρτία. The only tenable acceptation of the passage seems to many to be that of the Fathers. Chrysostom, and after him Theophylact, take τῷ Θεῷ as ἐν τῇ δυνάμει τοῦ Θεοῦ, that is, *through* God; taken so, the idea certainly of eternal and imperishable life, which the context requires, comes clearly into view, for God it is who only hath immortality (1 Tim. vi. 16). But even so, there arises no antithesis to ἁμαρτία, and then too ver. 11 does not come right, where ζῆν τῷ Θεῷ is said of men, and where notwithstanding it can have no other sense than ver. 10. Accordingly we can only say, that to live to God is the same as "to live to righteousness," namely for the purpose of furthering it among men, whereby this sense results: Christ died once for sin, that is to extirpate it, and lives eternally for God, that is, to further righteousness. Death is then as at v. 10, 11, understood as working forgiveness, and the resurrection, righteousness. So in ver. 11 this is applied to the human standard, and understood as a dying off from sin and a living for God.

The ὅ is best taken as accusative of the object in the sense, "in as far as, in respect that," so that in the first member the σάρξ, in the

* [Or *in so far as, in respect that.* Eng. V. "in that." B.]

other the πνεῦμα, is to be understood. Thus the passage becomes quite parallel to 1 Pet. iii. 18. θανατωθεὶς μὲν σαρκί, ζωοποιηθεὶς δὲ πνεύματι (comp., too, the parallel 2 Cor. xiii. 4). Reiche takes it so only in the second member, but the antithesis requires the same in the first as well. To complete the antithesis, some would construe τῇ ἁμαρτίᾳ also : "*through* sin" (comp. upon the ablative use of the dative Winer's Gram. p. 194). But the parallel νεκροὶ ἁμαρτίᾳ, ver. 11, forbids this, just as we observed upon ζῇν Θεῷ, which cannot be to live *through* God.

Ver. 11. Hitherto Paul had conceived and set forth the relation of the faithful to sin quite *in the abstract,* and accordingly said that what came to pass in Christ, in fact came to pass in all believers. As Christ died and rose again, so are also all, who are incorporate in him through the laver of regeneration, really dead in the old man, can therefore, as being dead, serve sin no more, and live really in the new man. But the relation does not so purely shew itself in the *concrete case.* As doubtless the kingdom of God, which has peace, righteousness, and happiness in its train, exists on earth, yet peace, righteousness, and happiness, have not yet *dominion* upon earth; so may also the new man, Christ in us, truly live in an individual man, without having yet the *absolute* dominion. Rather does the process of the dying of the old man extend itself over the *whole* earthly life, as well as that of the new man's growth in living; each of them is the condition to the other, and their consummation is reserved for *that* life beyond, since without the glorification of the body (Rom. viii. 11), it is impossible. Therefore the life of the believer exhibits itself as an oscillating between two poles of life; its result, the final completion of the new man, as well as the complete death of the old, reaches beyond this present life. To this relation, as it appears in the concrete, the Apostle passes with the: λογίζεσθε ἑαυτοὺς νεκρούς. For even as iii. 21, &c., he had represented abstract δικαιοσύνη, and then iv. 1, &c., in the λογίζεσθαι ἐις δικαιοσύνην considered it in its concrete growing in man, so it is repeated here. This passage is therefore most highly important to the comprehension of the Pauline doctrine of the old and new man, which is especially treated of vii. 8, &c., in the description of the course of development in the new man. The common view already spoken of, vi. 2, that the Apostle is treating here of purposes and vows merely, to forsake sin, and to practise righteousness, as they were promised at baptism, has its apparent support in the circumstance that in what follows the discourse assumes an imperative form. Paul *exhorts* to forsake sin and to serve righteousness (ver. 13, 18, 19), he presumes consequently, it is said, that such is by no means the case yet, but had only been promised in good purposes. Thence it is inferred, that no *real* vicarious power is ascribed to the dying and rising again of Christ, but that it has only the weight of an influential *example.* But the conception of the true relation between the old and the new man, gives a perfect insight into St Paul's mode of expression. Where by regeneration an ἄνθρωπος καινός is born, there the man is certainly no more *sub lege* (ver. 14), though yet by no means *in lege,* since even the new man needs for this a full development, in which he first gets absolute dominion ; he must rather walk constantly *cum lege,* and by no means suffer his own will to loose him from the law, for against this, vii. 1, &c., he is warned, as against a spiritual adultery. Just as little, however, may he fall back again into a legal state, which is the Apostle's censure among the Galatians, for so fear rules him instead of love, and his works do not flow forth of thankful love for love, but are the *means* to him to merit blessedness. Yet the aspect of the old man still mighty in him tempts him continually to such relapse into the state *under* the law; therefore the Apostle gives here that wise precept, preventing equally both stray paths, so continually in faith to *regard* ourselves, as being absolutely dead to sin, that is, in other words, constantly to appropriate Christ in faith, as Him who makes sin dead, and gives the new man life. By this continual action of faith the new man is constantly nourished by powers from above, and the I* is engaged in a continual Exodus from the Babel of sin. *This considering ourselves as dead for sin,* however, is no comforting self-deceit, but it is a spiritual operation fully true, answering throughout the aim of Christ, without which altogether no real sanctification, that gaining above all of thorough humility and divesture of all selfishness, is possible. For it has its truth in this—that the germ of the new man created in regeneration in fact is absolutely pure (1 John iii. 9), and *salvation* is not to be considered as depending on its de-

* [*Das Ich*, τὸ ἐγώ.]

velopment, but the *degree of glorification* only. (Comp. more particularly thereon at 1 Cor. iii. 11, &c.) Therefore may the believer, although he knows that he is capable of a greater development of the new man, look towards death without anxiety for his salvation, because this depends not upon the degree of individual development, but upon the faithful laying hold of God's objective decree of grace, which can neither be increased nor diminished, but abides unchangeable, as God himself. This λογίζεσθε ἑαυτοὺς νεκροὺς τῇ ἁμαρτίᾳ, ζῶντας δὲ τῷ Θεῷ is besides so much the more an urgent admonition for all, as it is in the very life of the most advanced that often times of heavy combating set in, in which their new life in God is quite hidden from themselves, and they seem left with sin. These are the sifting times to hold up and keep the victory, through that faith, that does not see, that against hope believes in hope, (iv. 18.)

The addition τῷ κυρίῳ ἡμῶν is wanting in the oldest and best Codd. Perhaps the words have found way into the passage from liturgical use. Whether the stop be placed after ὑμεῖς or after ἑαυτούς makes no difference to the thought; after ὑμεῖς is the more simple as to grammar.

Vers. 12-14.* Sin, therefore, (with retrospect upon ver. 1) is no more to have *dominion* over him, who does not live under the law, but under grace, than death over Christ (ver. 9); for him there is access to the higher power of life in Christ, which is stronger than sin (v. 15.) But the Apostle purposely chooses the words βασιλεύειν, κυριεύειν here, to signify the relation of the believer to sin. For the *law* is able to check gross outward transgression of it (ἔργα πονερά), and in it a man, even without grace, can perform *opera externa* and *civilia*; but even under grace a man may not entirely avoid and check finer expressions of sin, hastinesses in words and deeds, sinful desires and impulses, since the old man at times represses the new, and checks him in his efficacy. Hence there is need of the constant cleansing and ever renewed intercession of Christ (1 John ii. 1), of daily repent-

* From ver. 12 the principal ideas of sin, unrighteousness and righteousness have assumed almost personal forms; in order that this personification may be distinguished, Fritzsche has had them not unsuitably printed with capital initial letters. [As Fritzsche wrote in Latin, the capitals would have a significance in his work, which they have not in German. B.]

ance and forgiveness, as they are expressed in the Lord's Prayer, and symbolically represented by the washing of the feet. (Comp. at John xiii. 11, &c.) From this state, however, the *dominion* of sin must be distinguished, that is, its free unresisted sway in the life of the man; this in the regenerate is utterly inconceivable. (Comp. at vii. 25.) The whole representation in this passage (as in the following 16–21) is so managed that the man never appears as *absolutely independent*, as the natural man is disposed to consider his state, but as constantly *governed by an element*. As any one, who is swimming in a powerful stream, notwithstanding his wilful exertions, finds himself compelled to follow the course of the current; even such is the condition of the unregenerate man in this world's sinful stream; he receives his course from the ἄρχων τοῦ κόσμου τούτου, and is incapable of freeing himself out of this stream, however he may be able, by applying his powers in true practice of law (which affords him the attainment of a *justitia civilis*,) to prevent his sinking deeper and deeper into the mud. But if the higher and redeeming power of Christ has drawn him from this sinful stream (vii. 24), he stands not then, as it were, absolutely isolate and independent; but a new stream receives him, though a holy, blessed stream of divine light, by which it is the highest freedom to let himself be governed and swayed. *In service, therefore, man is always;* and there is no middle state between the service of sin and the service of God. Man has either *justification*, or forgiveness of sins, (and with it life and salvation,) *entirely*, or he has it *not at all*.* *Sanctification* only, which springs from living faith, as fruit of love returned, has its degrees, may be pursued more earnestly and lukewarmly; but this does not determine, as was observed before, the state of grace, salvation, but only the *degree* of glory in salvation (1 Cor. iii. 12–15). This is the apostolic and evangelic doctrine, which no force and no prudence can protect from *misunderstanding* (whether it come undesignedly from ignorance, or designedly from insincerity of heart,) but which nevertheless remains the way which *alone* leads to God, and upon which the sincere and humble cannot err. The erring of the insincere upon it, as well as the offence which the proud take

* Rightly says Luther: "Where this article is gone, the church is gone, and no error can be withstood. If we stand to it, we have the true, heavenly sun, but if we let it go, we have then nothing but hellish darkness."

at this way of God, is most properly, as was observed before, on among the aims which the Lord pursues in having this word of reconciliation preached (2 Cor. v. 18, &c.), for Christ is to be as well the rock on which the proud are shattered, as on which the humble stay themselves. The key, however, to this mystery, that the doctrine of reconciliation, without exacting works, begets in the mind the purest works, lies here; that love awakens love again and strong desire for holiness. Thereby the striving of the man leaves off being a heavy, bitter toil;* he no more struggles *that* he may be saved and please God, but *because* he is become, without deserving, saved, and acceptable to God in the Beloved (Ephes. i. 6), he works for love as if the matter were his own. So there are but *two states* of the man (ver. 14); he is either *ὑπό νόμον*, or *ὑπὸ χάριν*. Under the scourge of the law he deals in works, and serves for hire (iv. 4), but according to the strict right of retribution he fares by it but very badly; if he is tempted he falls, and sin *has rule*, even though the better conquers now and then. On the other hand, under grace, the man indeed is tempted, but he *conquers*, even if now and then sin for once tells upon him.

As regards the expression *ἐν τῷ θνητῷ ὑμῶν σώματι*, *θνητὸν σῶμα* is used entirely = *σάρξ* (vii. 18), or *τὰ μέλη* (vii. 23–25). But this is by no means to say that, according to Paul's view, sin is to be sought for in the body, and its sensual impulses *alone;* it is intended rather to be signified only, that it commonly makes itself known in the body by the excited sensuality. (Comp. more particularly thereon at Rom. vii. 17.) By the *σῶμα*, however, the character of mortality is put forward in order to contrast the sinful body, and, as sinful. especially exposed to all temptations, with the sanctified organ of the glorified one (viii. 11). The words must not therefore be construed, "let not sin reign in your body," as though the body were distinguished as the place where it should not reign, for in vii. 25 the body is described as still subjected to sin, even in the regenerate; but they are to be connected thus: "let not the sin revealing itself in your mortal body reign, so that ye yield to it, but oppose strong resistance to it from the spirit." *Ἐν τῷ θνήτῷ ὑμῶν σώματι* may therefore be supplied by *οὖσα* or

* [*Schaärwerken*,—a word which we cannot profess to translate, except conjecturally. —B.

οικοῦσα. At the close of ver. 12, the Codd. vary much. Some have only *ἀυτῇ*, others only *ταῖς ἐπιθυμίαις ἀυτοῦ*, others both together. *One* dative only can be received, for the blending of the two in the *text. rec.* by an additional *ἐν* is certainly inadmissible. Göschen has declared for the reception of *ταῖς ἐπιθυμίαις ἀυτοῦ*; notwithstanding, the addition of a dative might be more easy of explanation than its omission, as the mere infinitive seems somewhat bare. *Παριστάναι*, to present or exhibit one's self forth, that is, to give up or offer for disposal. The choice of the word *ὅπλα* proceeds from the image of a contest, which lay at the foundation of the Apostle's exposition. (Comp. Ephes. vi. 12, &c.) The addition *ὡς ἐκ νεκρῶν ζῶντας* refers to the fact that the service of sin is only possible in spiritual death; where life is, there is its longing for the fountain of life.

Vers. 15–16. After this statement, the Apostle expressly resumes the question from ver. 1, only with this modification, that he draws the Christian's relation to the law more decidedly, with regard to the last-mentioned contrast of *ὑπὸ νόμον* and *ὑπὸ χάριν* into consideration. For as the decree of God in Christ is so hard to be comprehended, not merely to the Jew, but to the man generally, since he does not easily get rid of the conceit that righteousness and salvation must be *his* work, not God's act; so also does the opposite Antinomian error lie very near him, that, if then man is not saved by the law, but out of grace, sin is something indifferent, the law something useless. To this error the Apostle, in what follows, opposes the reasoning, that if the man be no more *ὑπὸ νόμον*, he on no account lives *without* the law, or *above* the law, but *in* and *with* it. The man's state is *under* the law, when it meets him, like a strange thing, from without, and, by its rigid commandment, checks and confines the life that resists it; this is not in itself a false, though a subordinate state, which is to bring on the higher one of the life *in* and *with* the law. For in this state, the law establishes itself as the inward principle of life itself; it appears as written on the tables of the heart, and as one with the will of the man. *Without* law, or altogether *above* the law, the man can never be, for the law is the expression of the divine essence itself. Upon this deeper conception of the nature of the law, Paul also founds his argument, in which, although he does not use the terms *ἐν νόμῳ, σὺν νόμῳ*, he, in fact, expresses the idea which they denote. He refutes, namely, the question, whether we shall sin, because we are not under the law, but under grace? by saying, we are in the very state of grace made free from sin, and become servants to God (δουλωθέντες Θεῷ, ver. 22), and therefore can serve it no more. This thought of the *service of God*, or, which is the same thing, of righteousness, must not, however, be again understood as an *outward* relation of a servant towards God, as under the dominion of the law, for this is just what grace has overcome (viii. 15); but as an *inward* one. The soul of him who is living in the state of grace serves God, inasmuch as He makes abode in it by His Spirit, which is His own Being (John xiv. 23; Rom. v. 5), and so becomes the determining principle of its life. Now, as the divine Being has the law not *in* itself or *beside* itself,* but, being divine, is the law itself, so also the regenerate man has the law itself essentially in himself, in the indwelling of the divine Spirit, as the moving, governing power within him (Rom. viii. 14), and cannot, *as such*, act otherwise than perfectly (1 John iii. 9). But this state, indeed, appears, as such, in no one here on earth; for as in every regenerate man the old man is living still, so also moments occur in the life of every one in which it pushes back the new (1 John ii. 1). The service of God in Christ still appears to the old man as a yoke (Matt. xi. 30), because he feels that it leads him into death; yet if he is loosed from the divine law, he feels his state undisciplined. So understood, the whole of the following passage gains the strictest consistency with itself, and with what precedes it; to the false ἐλευθερία (Galat. v. 13; 1 Pet. ii. 16) is opposed the true, which is the very dependence upon God himself.

The reading ἁμαρτήσωμεν has certainly weighty authorities; for instance, the Codd. A.C.D.E. and others. Notwithstanding it is probably only a correction of ἁμαρτήσομεν, because the future seemed unusually applied here. But it is to be understood here of the possibility or admissibility of being ignorant† of the law. The conjunctive of the future, besides, is not found in the N. T. except in various readings. (Comp. Winer's Gr. p. 69.) The first half of ver. 16 seems pleonastic, but the δοῦλοί ἐστε ᾧ ὑπακούετε is to be understood as the *consequence* of παριστάναι, so that the sense is: "to whom ye yield yourselves to obey, to

* [*An* sich oder *neben* sich.]

† *Ignoriren*—rather, perhaps, *a shutting one's eyes against it.* B]

him ye *must* then pay obedience." Thus the dependence of man as creature is held to view; he serves always, if not God, then sin and its prince. (John viii. 44.) He cannot, however, at any moment he would, release himself from his service, to whom he once yielded himself; but the power of that element, to which he gave in, either of good or evil, binds him. If the sinner feels the heavy yoke of sin, often would he be quit of it; but as he hates only the evil consequences, and not sin itself, he continues bound, and sin becomes punishment of sin. If the Christian feels the bitterness of the Cross and of the world's contempt, which befalls him, the wish may at the same time rise within him, Could'st thou be again as thou wast before! but the power of grace holds him to his good, and so becomes its own reward. Ver. 16. the antitheses *ἁμαρτία* and *ὑπακοή, θάνατος* and *δικαιοσύνη*, are not strictly chosen. However, as it is clear, according to v. 19, that the very nature of *ἁμαρτία* is *παρακοή* (comp. 1 Sam. xv. 23. Rebellion is as the sin of witchcraft), its contrast may be *ὑπακοή*. And to *θάνατος*, as spiritual and bodily death, as consummated fruit of sin (ver. 21) not less aptly is opposed *δικαιοσύνη* = *δίκαιος εἶναι*, the essential internal state of righteousness, as in germ identical with the *ζωὴ αἰώνιος* (ver. 22), which is not merely to be hoped for hereafter, but begins already here.—The omission of *εἰς θάνατον* in D.E. and other authorities may doubtless be accounted for by *θάνατος* not appearing to the copyists to form an antithesis to *δικαιοσύνη*.—The *ἤτοι* is = *ἤ*, the earlier writers usually put *ἤτοι* once only, the later also use it twice.

Ver. 17. This salutary turn then, Paul continues, has, God be thanked (vii. 24), taken place with his readers, they have felt the service of sin, and are become obedient to the truth. The same holds good of all the truly converted; the old is passed away, and a new life is begun. In the passage vii. 24, 25, this transition will be more particularly represented in its peculiar character.

In the *ἦτε δοῦλοι* the preterite has its full force, so that the former state is understood as past; for even if sin is not thoroughly removed from the believer, yet it has no *dominion*, but is *under dominion* to the man.—The *ὑπακούειν* is = *δοῦλος εἶναι τοῦ Θεοῦ*; in order, however, to distinguish it from a mere show of life in faith, the Apostle adds *ἐκ καρδίας* (= בְּכָל לְבָב Deut vi. 5), where by the entrance of the whole being, with the centre of the personality, into the gospel, is intended to be marked.—The expression τύπος διδαχῆς is peculiar for ἐυαγγέλιον. The signification "form, type," namely, does not suit the verb ὑπακούειν, it should have been said seemingly: "Ye have shaped yourselves to the form of doctrine." But in the ὑπακούειν this idea, in fact, is latitant, for as the servant of sin accepts its image in himself, so also does he who obeys the truth receive her form within him. Commonly, indeed, the O. T. is called τύπος, as type of the New (1 Cor. x. 6; Hebr. viii. 5), but the N. T. itself may also be called τύπος, inasmuch as the life of the faithful is formed after it.—As to the construction, ὑπακούειν is never construed in the N. T. with ἐις, but always with the dative; it is more appropriate, therefore, to connect ἐις with παρεδόθητε, which has an equal signification with ὃς παρεδόθη ἐις ὑμᾶς or ὑμῖν, so that by παραδιδόναι the guidance of divine grace, which leads men to the gospel, becomes marked. This certainly uncustomary use of παραδιδόσθαι has induced Van Hengel, drawing his analogy from Rom. i. 24, 26, 28, to think of a being-given-over to errors, which however cannot possibly be meant by τύπος διδαχῆς. The accusative τύπον stands according to the proposed solution of the construction by attraction for τύπῳ.

Ver. 18–20. To the *false* freedom, which the natural man is wont to find without the restraint of the law, the Apostle opposes the *true*, which consists in the deliverance from the yoke of sin and in the service of God and of righteousness, which His Spirit creates in man. This conception of δικαιοσύνη as a new δουλεία, Paul justifies by the necessary condescension to the standard of his readers. The notion of ἐλευθερία (John viii. 36) might have been conceived by them as absolute and unbounded licentiousness, therefore he describes it as a new and nobler bondage,* as the Redeemer also Himself (Matt. xi. 29, 30) represents it as the taking on of a yoke, of a burden. The earthly life of the believer, since the real ἐλευθερία never comes completely to view, is represented with perfect truth as the going under a ζυγός or φορτίον, only it is easier than that of the O. T. For although God's commandments are not grievous to the *new* man who lives in love (1 John v. 3), yet the I† continues still bound up with the old man, and so far is sensible of a δουλεία of δικαιοσύνη. Not until with the *impossi-*

* [Gebundenheit.]

† [Das Ich.]

bility of sin the absolute perfection comes, and God in Man is become all in all, does the ἐλευθερία τῆς δόξης τ. Θ. (Rom. viii. 21) appear. Yet there is notwithstanding even in the earthly life of the believer a specific difference from the natural state to be observed ; in the latter, although with some good, the man expressly and unresistingly served sin ; in the state of grace, although he sometimes fall,* he serves as expressly† righteousness to his becoming perfect.

The parenthesis : ἀνθρώπινον λέγω κ. τ. λ. has reference not merely to the figure generally, but also to the constitution of the figure, as Rückert rightly observes. The ἀνθρώπινον therefore can only be = κατ' ἄνθρωπον (comp. iii. 5), but on no account signify, as Origen, Chrysostom, Wetstein, Semler propose, " what is to be performed by man, possible for man," for Paul requires, what no man can perform, absolute righteousness.—The ἀσθένεια τῆς σαρκός, however, cannot be understood with Reiche of mere weakness of intellect, which we have no warrant whatever for attributing to the Christians of Rome ; there is intelligence, indeed, treated of here, but the circumstance to which it refers, is of that kind, that the comprehending of it is hard even to men of *strong* intellect, if they are wanting in the inward experience, and easy to those of *weak* intellect, if they possess it. Σάρξ, therefore, is the whole sinful nature of man, whereon more particularly at vii. 18.—Paul again calls the μέλη as ver. 12 the σῶμα, in order to denote the coming of the evil desire into act, in which sin, when it is finished, bringeth forth death (James i. 15).—'Ακαθαρσία and ἀνομία signify the more passive and active side of sin, where enjoyment or violence prevails. In the ἐις τὴν ἀνομίαν the idea of ἀνομία is extended and becomes the entire contrast to ἁγιασμός, so that thereby the nature of sin is designated as that of opposition to law.‡ But the Apostle with profound perception makes this as the bloom to be born of sin itself, *for sin continually brings forth sin*, only

* [Ps. xxxvii. 24, P. B. vers.]

† Excellent are the words of Anselm, ad loc., which Tholuck quotes : " Sicut ad peccandum vos nullus cogebat timor, sed ipsius libido voluptasque peccati, sic ad juste vivendum non vos supplicii metus urgeat, sed ducat delectatio justitiæ. Sicut ergo ille iniquissimus, quem ne poenæ quidem temporales deterrent ab immundis operibus ita justissimus ille, quem ne poenarum quidem temporalium timore revocatur a sanctis operibus."

‡ [Gesetzwidrigkeit.]

she produces figures ever more frightful from her teeming womb. Even so does δικαιοσύνη also generate by degrees more gloriously, until she becomes ἁγιασμός. (Comp. upon ἁγιάζειν at John xiii. 31, 32.) This expression denotes here, as 1 Thess. iv. 3, 4, 7, the state of *being* holy, which arises in the holy God's communication of His holiness to man (1 Pet. i. 16); but so far as the being holy proceeds from a gradual development of the new man, ἁγιασμός is used also for the becoming holy (2 Thess. ii. 13; 1 Cor. i. 30; 1 Pet. i. 2). Δοῦλος is only found here in the N. T. used as an adjective.

Vers. 21, 22. In order that the difference of the two stations under the law and under grace may be brought still more decidedly forward, the Apostle points, in conclusion, to the final result of their development. He designates it as *fruit*, according to the image pervading the whole Scripture, according to which man in his moral constitution is compared with good or bad trees. (Ps. i. 3; Is. lxi. 3; Matt. xii. 33; John xv. 1, &c.; Rom. xi. 16, &c.; Jude v. 12.) This image, therefore, is most highly significant; because it comes most powerfully in opposition to the Pelagianism so convenient to fallen human nature. The natural man, without knowledge of himself, of God and of sin, fancies that he will by his own power and able exertion produce a virtue, which shall be able to stand before God's judgment; he knows not, that necessarily and naturally he *can* bear no other than evil fruit, as the wild tree can only bring forth woody, bitter fruits. For, if he succeeds most perfectly in his striving after virtue, it brings in its train lovelessness and conceited presumption, and so has just as much death for its reward, as if fleshly transgressions defiled his life. The beginning of that truth,—whose fruit is holiness, and, being no less conformable to nature, proceeds from inward organic necessity, with which true freedom is one,—is for man ever the confession, that the principle of death rules in him, and that life must first be brought into him. (vii. 24.)

Τότε and *ὅτε*, ver. 20, answer to the *ὑπὸ νόμον*, as *νῦν* does to the *ὑπο χάριν εἶναι*. Paul does not name the fruit of sin itself, as no expression parallel to ἁγιασμός presented itself to him; hence arises the inexact connexion by ἐφ' οἷς, which is retrospective to καρπός taken collectively, and so refers to the ἔργα πονηρά, the consciousness of which fills the better part in man with shame.* The note of interrogation, therefore, is without doubt better placed after τότε, than after ἐπαισχύνεσθε. Τέλος is by no means to be taken in the same signification with καρπός, but to be understood as denoting the final use of the fruit which proceeds from its nature. *Death* therefore signifies here the being rejected as of no use and worthless ; *eternal life* the being acknowledged as useful, essentially answering its end. This is naturally not to be understood as if θάνατος and ζωὴ αἰώνιος had other significations here than elsewhere, but only that by the image made use of, and from which these expressions properly issue, they acquire a modified relation. The acceptation of καρπός in the signification "advantage, gain," does not, as Reiche has well proved, suit so well here ; especially as vii. 4, 5, καρποφορῆσαι τῷ θανάτῳ is spoken of. In the ἔχειν καρπὸν εἰς ἁγιασμόν, however, holiness is again taken to mean as vi. 19, the result of the life of faith gradually proceeding from its development.

Ver. 23. In the closing verse it is not so much that a new thought is expressed, as that the thought stated in ver. 21, 22, is only more closely defined. Although, namely, both courses of life bring their fruit, and their different disposition decides their final event, yet their respective circumstances are by no means exactly alike. Sin is altogether man's ; Death therefore, the wages of it, must also devolve upon him according to the law of strict justice ; but righteousness and holiness is altogether not of man, but the work of God in him (Ephes. ii. 8–10) ; he cannot, therefore, as holy, demand, and, according to the law of justice, receive, anything ; but the mercy of God adds to the gracious gift of forgiveness of sins and sanctification the new gift of eternal life beside, so that the lost one must confess, that through himself he has lost *all*, the saved one that through himself he has gained *nothing*, to the glory of the justice and grace of the Lord. Thus did Augustine rightly comprehend the passage (Epist. 105), while he writes : "adversus elationis pestem vigilantissime militans, *stipendium*, inquit, peccati mors. Recte stipendium quia debetur, quia digne retribuitur,

* From deep experience Calvin says : "Sola est lux Domini, quæ potest oculos nostros aperire, ut prospicere queant latentem in carne nostra foeditatem. Ille igitur demum Christianae philosophiae primordiis imbutus est, qui sibi serio displiceri ac suae miseriae verecundia bene confundi didicerit."

quia meritum redditur; deinde, ne justitia de humano se extolleret bono merito, sicut humanum malum non dubitatur esse peccatum, *gratia*, inquit, Dei vita aeterna."

'Οψώνιον properly signifies provisions, then pay of soldiers (Luke iii. 14; 1 Cor. ix. 7; 1 Macc. iii. 28, xiv. 32), finally merited, earned wages (2 Cor. xi. 8). So here, equal to *μισθός*, contrast to *χάρισμα*, comp. iv. 4. How Reiche in such passages as 2 Cor. iv. 17, v. 10; 2 Tim. i. 12, iv. 8, 18 (Phil. iv. 5 is wrongly cited), can find to the contrary, namely that eternal life is merited reward, not the gift of grace, is to me inconceivable.

Chap. vii. 1–3. Now although the question which, vi. 1, was brought on as to the relation in which one living under the gospel stood with regard to sin, might appear sufficiently discussed by the exposition hitherto made, the Apostle Paul notwithstanding thinks fit once more concisely to demonstrate his thoughts in a fresh similitude, in order that no uncertainty may remain with regard to this important and difficult point. This similitude is taken from *marriage*, by the laws of which the wife is bound to the husband until he dies. His death allows her the freedom to form another connexion; and she would not on that account be considered as an adultress. This relation of the wife to the husband is one generally human, any predominant bearing, therefore, to Jews or proselytes is here inadmissible. Even with nations, among whom polygamy prevails, the *wife* is the property of the husband, and is not free of him until he dies. Rückert, therefore, is right in observing that neither the address *ἀδελφοί* relates to Jew-Christians, nor the addition: *γινώσκουσι γὰρ νόμον λαλῶ*. Baur, therefore, seeks here in vain a support for his opinion, that the Christians of Rome had a Judaising tendency. For as the article is used neither with *γινώσκουσι* nor with *νόμον*, no contrast can be found here, to others, who do *not* know the law (and such indeed could hardly be supposed),* but this addition is to be taken like the *ἀνθρώπινον λέγω*, vi. 19. *Νόμος* signifies here the regulation existing among all nations, that the wife is bound to the husband, not the Mosaic law. The Apostle reasons from premises common to mankind; in writing, therefore, to his first readers, he writes for all intelligent men without excep-

* Glöckler would have those understood, who *will* not know the law, that is, the unruly; however, if this contrast had been intended to appear, another expression would probably have been chosen for *γινώσκειν*.

tion. The way of applying this parable, however, to the relation of man to sin has its difficulties. The figure of marriage as significant of the relation of the soul to God is certainly not unusual either in the Old (Is. liv. 5; Hos. ii. 16, &c.) or in the New Testament (John iii. 29; Ephes. v. 22, &c.); but here a *second* marriage is spoken of, which is entered into, the first being considered as dissolved by the death of the husband. Now unless it be said, that we are not to press the dying of the husband, which of course cannot be admitted, inasmuch as it is on this very point that the whole argument turns, the question then is, who is to be considered as the dying husband? Rückert, indeed, asserts that no comparison at all is to be seen here, but a mere example; that the Apostle could not have found any instance, in which the party *in subjection* should die, and therefore notwithstanding the inconvenience chose this one of marriage, in which the *ruling* party should die. Paul, however, might only have reversed the same similitude, to say that by the death of the wife the husband is free of her, if that had served his purpose better. But taken so he could have made no use at all of the comparison of marriage to make his thoughts perceptible. De Wette dispenses entirely with the solution of the difficulty by asserting, that the Apostle has not chosen his example accurately, and in this, instead of bringing in the death of the party bound to the law (ver. 1), has brought in the death of the one to whom the law binds, and has continued this mistake in the application (ver. 4). As we may safely assume that Paul knew how to choose his instances with exactness and precision, we must ascertain with more carefulness who the dying husband is. Two opinions prevail upon this; according to *one*, which Origen, Chrysostom, Ambrose, and Hilary proposed, and afterwards Calvin and Bucer defended, as lately Tholuck also has done, the *law* is the dying husband. But first of all it is manifestly unfit to consider the law, holy, just, and good (vii. 12), as abolished; it is in fact not abolished for the believer (Matt. v. 17), but only gains a different position towards him; he is no more *under* the law, but lives *in* it. In the next place, according to this view, a leap into another similitude must be assumed at ver. 4, for there it is said, "ye are dead;" such a change, however, has at all events something extremely awkward in it, and could only be assumed in extreme necessity. The *other* opinion is proposed by Augustine, and afterwards especially defended by Beza. According to this, the lust of sin is at first the husband, and the old man, the wife; but in the second marriage, the new man is the wife, and Christ, the principle of righteousness, the husband. Against this there is less weight in Tholuck's objection,—"that in what follows (ver. 7, &c.), it is not the relation to lust, but to the moral law, that is treated of;" for the law excites (according to ver. 11) even lust (vii. 8, &c.)—than that then a second wife seems to be supposed, while, according to the comparison, the wife continues the same. This difficulty will only be radically removed by the following conception of the passage. As in Christ himself, without prejudice to the unity of his personality, the mortal is distinguished from the immortal Christ (comp. ver. 4, with 1 Pet. iii. 18), so in man also the old man is distinguished from the new, without prejudice to the unity of his personality, which Paul subsequently (ver. 20) signifies by ἐγώ. This true personality, the proper self of man, is the wife, who, in the natural state, appears in marriage with the old man, and, in intercourse with him, generates sins, the end of which is death (vi. 21, 22.) But in the death of the mortal Christ, this old man is dead with him; and, as the individual man is grafted by faith into Christ, his old man dies, by whose life he was holden under the law. As, however, with the death of Christ, the immortal Saviour of the world also arose, even so with the death of the old man, the new man becomes living; and with this, the Christ in us, the I* enters upon a new marriage, from which the fruits of the spirit are born. But here it might be asked, whether such a distinction of the I from the old and new man has warrant from other passages of Scripture? I refer with regard to this question, besides the explanation already given at Matt. x. 40, to the following illustration of Rom. vii. 7, &c., for the distinction lies at the foundation of this passage throughout; and I have only to remind further of the forgiveness of sins, the nature of which necessarily leads to this difference; for sin cannot be forgiven to the old man, that must die, not to the new, for this is sinless, but certainly to the I,* who is the bearer, as well of the old as of the new man, and by whom the man can speak of *his* old and *his* new man. There is only one more seeming inexactness in the Apostle's statement, with reference, namely, to the νόμος; but this indeed is

* [*Das Ich*, throughout the passage.]

inseparable from the use of similitudes, since the thing compared can never be even with the object, to which it refers. In ver. 2 and 3, which contains the similitude itself (ver. 1 expressing the thought which forms its general basis), the *νόμος* is only the marriage law, or the precept, that the woman may only be the wife of one man, to whom she belongs. But in the three following verses (ver. 4–6), *νόμος* is the law generally, and indeed not merely the ceremonial law, but the law in every expression of it, and therefore the moral law also; wherefore Paul's statement possesses its truth for all times and every state of things, because the moral law is given with the essence of man itself.

Ver. 1. comp. upon *ἢ ἀγνοεῖτε* the passage vi. 3. The *ὁ νόμος κυριεύει τοῦ ἀνθρώπου* expresses the general thought, from which, ver. 2, the special case of marriage and the precepts relating to it is deduced. The thought exactly answers to the passage vi. 7. Hence *ἄνθρωπος* must not be explained of the wife, for the same thing holds good of the husband; as it does also with the slave. Death make every one free from every law.—Ver. 2. *ὕπανδρος* signifies subject to the power of the husband, according to Numb. v. 29. אִשָּׁה תַּחַת אִישָׁהּ (comp. Eccles. ix. 9, xli. 21).—The construction *κατήργηται ἀπὸ νόμου* is peculiar. The verb *καταργεῖσθαι* commonly refers to *things*, especially to law, but not to persons. Besides this passage it is found vii. 6, and Galat. v. 4, used in the same way, = *ἐλευθεροῦσθαι*. The Chald. בְּטֵל מִן, Ezra iv. 21, 23, v. 5, vi. 8, is used in exactly the same manner, for which the LXX. have always *καταργεῖν*, though without the following *ἀπό*.—*Νόμος ἀνδρὸς* not the law, which the husband gives, the *imperium domesticum*, but which protects the husband in his right over the wife, and determines it.—Upon *χρηματίζω* in the meaning "to be, to be called," comp. at Acts xi. 26.—*Γίνεσθαι ἀνδρὶ ἑτέρῳ* = הָיָה לְאִישׁ אַחֵר, Deut. xxiv. 2.

Ver. 4. The Apostle now applies this comparison by representing the faithful themselves as dead in their old man, and thereby freed from the yoke of the law (Acts xv. 20), so that the freedom is acquired for them to devote themselves to another husband, even Christ (2 Cor. xi. 2.) But the death of the faithful in the old man is again, as vi. 2, 4, 6, connected with the death of the Redeemer, so that *his* death was *their* death, and did not merely prefigure it; for no one by his own power or resolution can die in the old man, because no one can generate the new man, by whose birth the death of the old is conditioned. Christ is therefore the living type both of the old and new man; of the old, according to the ἀσθενεία τῆς σαρκός (2 Cor. xiii. 4, 1 Pet. iii. 18), which was in him, and because he bore the sin of the world; of the new, according to the power of the Eternal Spirit, which filled him. From this spiritual union, then, spring spiritual fruits (Galat. vi. 22), begotten to the honour of God. According to this representation, it is clear that the liberation from the law must not be an act of *self-will*. As little as the wife may wantonly separate from her husband, since his death is requisite for her liberation; so little may the I free itself from the law, as long as the old man is living. If this is done therefore, as is always the case where a mere seeming faith prevails, it is a spiritual adultery, the lust after false freedom, that is, licentiousness, lawlessness. The liberation from the law rightly takes place only where the new man arose in the stead of the old, where therefore Christ is truly living in the man. There is no licentiousness, for Christ brings with him the strictest law, wheresoever he works; but the *yoke* of the law is removed by that love, which is shed into the hearts. This love urges to do more than the law requires, and to fulfil every act with purer intention than the most threatening law can demand. For love is insatiable, she never satisfies herself and the Beloved; she burns on, till with her fire she glows through the whole heart and being, and has sacrificed her all to the Beloved. After this manner works the gospel *all* in man without law (iii. 21) although it exacts *nothing* from him, but only promises and gives to him. But because it gives all of grace, and even loves and blesses enemies, it wins the inmost self of man, and therefore all his powers. As on the one side, however, there is the danger lest a man should liberate himself from the law, and persuade himself that he has faith and is regenerate, a way that seduces to false freedom; so, on the other side, there threatens a danger equally great, which leads into new, and indeed still more galling slavery, than the former was.* A false zeal for sanctification, proceeding from vanity, and striving only to see itself perfect as soon as possible in

* [The author here quotes, in a note, a forcible saying of Luther (Leipz. edit. vol. xi. p. 83).]

an image of its own design, often fancies, that the long, but certain way of sanctifying grace in Christ does not lead quick enough to the goal, and so draws back, when the life in grace has scarce begun, under the law again. What God in man has begun, the man himself (in contradiction to Phil. i. 6, Heb. xii. 2) would complete; he will not become blessed *through* Christ, but with and beside him through himself, but so destroys the delicate tracery of the new man in him. This is, then, not merely to wake up the old dead man again, but even to despise the new true husband, to rate his power low, yea, to count the blood of the covenant unholy, and to do despite unto the Spirit of Grace. (Heb. x. 29.) Hence it is, that Paul so emphatically warns the Galatians, who had entered on it, from this dangerous byeway. (Galat. ii. 16, &c., iii. 3, &c.) And yet it is so tempting, and just to the more earnest, zealous men, to fall into this error, that even the Apostle Peter, Barnabas, and others, could be for a moment seduced from the way of grace! (Galat. ii. 12, &c.) Ay, the sectarian history shows that most of the founders of sects made use of a self-willed striving after sanctification as their motive, to collect their followers, and, with the guidance of that striving, to exercise an often frightful spiritual tyranny. Therefore does the Apostle Paul teach the true middle way, which just as little suffers a man of his own will to loose himself from the law, as that he should bring himself under it again, since Christ continues to him both the Beginner and Finisher of Faith. (Heb. xii. 2.)* This completion, however, Christ, of course, does not perfect *out of* and *without* the man, but *in* the very depth of his own self, since he takes in full possession the noblest thing the man possesses, even his love, and fills it with the powers of his higher love, which makes him mighty enough for all, even the weightiest requirement. If he sees, therefore, that the old man still is stirring, he draws in faith unceasingly fresh power from Christ's fountain, and so is more than conqueror in him who loved us.

Ὥστε is here particle of inference, "accordingly;" comp. Winer's

* Of the contrast between true and false righteousness, Luther speaks profoundly in his exposition of the 38th Psalm: "It is a wondrous thing; whoso hath no sin (because of faith) he [it is who] feeleth and hath it (in true penitence and humility); and whoso hath sin, he [it is who] feeleth it not, and hath none" (after the conceited blindness of his heart). And at the 143d Psalm: "Satan is such a dexterous master [meister], that he can make even the very best works (by admixture of conceit) the very biggest sins."

Gr. p. 277. The expression διὰ τοῦ σώματος τοῦ Χριστοῦ can, of course, only form the antithesis to the ἐγερθεὶς ἐκ νεκρῶν. Σῶμα is distinguished here, as 1 Pet. iii. 18, the σάρξ, in order to signify the mortal side of the Redeemer, to which the immortal, the πνεῦμα, of the risen Christ, is opposed.

Vers. 5, 6. That he may once more offer to his readers a distinct perception of the difference between the two states, Paul sets them out in their principles side by side. In the legal state, the sinful *impulses* (τὰ πάθηματα τῶν ἁμαρτιῶν, the individual utterances of the spiritual members of the old man,) work with absolute sway in the whole nature of man, even to the periphery of the physical life, so that they become act. In the state of grace, the old man dies with all his sinful impulses, and the man can then, free from the fetter of the law, which could only bind the old man, serve God in spirit and in truth. The dying of the old, and the rising of the new man, however, are, of course, not completed in him all at once, but through the earthly life they continue *beside* each other in the believer, (comp. more particularly at vii. 25,) although the former is to be constantly decreasing, the latter ever growing. Therefore the problem is, because the old man still continues to exist, and may become strong again, never to be *secure*, yet for the sake of the ever efficacious and accessible grace never to despond, but to fight most zealously against all doubts of God's grace and power against sin.*

Σάρξ can only signify the old man here, as viii. 8, 9 ; it forms indeed the antithesis to the νυνί, κ. τ. λ. (ver. 6.) Theodoret,

* The observation of Melanthon, ad loc. is very pertinent : "Hic locus diligenter observandus est, ut *discamus dubitationes de gratia Dei esse peccatum*, ut repugnemus et erigamus nos evangelio et sciamus, *esse cultum Dei in illis terroribus repugnare dubitationi et diffidentiæ.* Surely the beloved man of God says right, that it is not permitted only, but a duty, ay, *holiest service of God,* to contend to the utmost *against all doubts of God and of his grace,* for those never spring from a good source. Yet, on the contrary, it is very wrong to smother *the doubts of himself and his own virtue,* which God's Spirit of grace calls forth, in order to convert the man ; it is to contend against God, and hinder regeneration. The [Roman] Catholic Church, however, with which all sects, that proceed from Pelagian principles agree, deters from the certainty of the state of grace, and desires uncertainty towards God. Such uncertainty of *hearts* is then a convenient means to keep men in the leading-strings of the priesthood or ambitious founders of sects; for since they are not allowed to have any certainty themselves respecting their relation to God, they can only rest upon the judgments of their leaders about it, who thus rule souls with absolute dominion; the true evangelic doctrine makes free from such slavery to man.

Grotius, and others, would have it to be understood of the O. T., which in and by itself might certainly be admissible, but still only where the contrast of the πνεῦμα clearly stands out. *Τὰ διὰ τοῦ νόμου* can only be supplied, according to ver. 11, with *κινούμενα*, it is intended, namely, to be signified that the law is the inducing, provoking cause of sin. It altogether misleads to take ἐνηργεῖτο passively, for the μέλη = σῶμα, appear then to be the proper seat of sin, whereas it really manifests itself outwardly from within. To be sure its blossom is in this manifestation upon the periphery of life, for a repressing power of the spirit must be presumed, if at least the outward eruptions of sin are hindered. *Θάνατος* appears again as the τέλος (vi. 23), inasmuch as the sins collectively work, as it were, for him and his kingdom. In ver. 6, a variety of readings are found. For the ἀποθανόντος of the *text. rec.*, A.C., and many other Codd., and the Greek Fathers as well, have ἀποθανόντες, while D.E.F.G. and the Latin Fathers read τοῦ θανάτου. This latter reading, however, looks very like a correction of the copyists, in their not understanding how the Apostle could speak of a dissolution of the law itself. The genitive of the singular proceeded from that conception of the passage, according to which the law is considered as the dying husband, but the ἐθανατώθητε, ver. 4, speaks against this. *Ἀποθανόντες*, therefore, is certainly the only correct reading, for which Lachmann also has decided. In the κατέχεσθαι, the binding, compulsory power of the law is signified. The ἐν ᾧ refers to νόμος, and is on no account to be taken, "in as far, in as much as." *Καινότης πνεύματος* is = καινότης ζωῆς in the passage vi. 4. The πνεῦμα is considered as the principle from which the new life issues. The old, therefore, is a spiritless, merely physical life (1 Cor. ii. 14). The substantive παλαιότης is found in the N. T. only in this passage. *Γράμμα* forms here, as ii. 29, an antithesis with πνεῦμα, as σάρξ elsewhere, to denote the outside, as the form in which the life manifests itself. The choice of just this expression is founded in this passage upon the reference to the law, which, in its most complete form, the law of Moses, appears to be compassed in the letter, but in this form is for the sinful man a heavy, killing yoke. (2 Cor. iii. 6, 7).

SECTION IV.

(VII. 7.—VIII. 39.)

OF THE STAGES OF THE DEVELOPMENT AS WELL OF INDIVIDUALS AS OF THE UNIVERSE.

The properly dogmatical exposition has at length completely finished the foundation of the new way of salvation upon the vicarious character of Christ and the indication of its relation to the law. The Apostle forthwith most fitly proceeds to indicate all the stages of development, as they are exhibited themselves immediately in individual men, whereby all he has said before gains first its proper light. He shews namely, *first of all* (vii. 7–24), how the man rises from the state of undeveloped childishness into that of the life *under the law*, in which the sin that awakes by the resistance of the law calls up that inward conflict, by which he first becomes truly conscious of the contradiction in himself and how he is held bound by sin. The result of this conflict is the need of redemption, out of which the faith in the redemption brought to pass in Christ developes itself; and in the power of this faith the believer is enabled, what of his own effort he could never do, to serve the divine law in spirit, albeit the old man in him remains still subjected to the law of sin. *Then* follows (vii. 25—viii. 17) a description of the development of the new life itself received through Christ. This penetrates not merely the inward man, but sanctifies and glorifies by degrees the bodily substance also, so that the *whole* man becomes like to Christ, and thereby heir of God and co-heir of the glory of Christ. But since man is a member, the most essential member of the creation, his life must react upon the universe for glorification no less than his death has acted upon it for *destruction*. The participation of the totality in the perfecting of humanity in Christ, Paul treats of *lastly* (viii. 18–39), and this contemplation of the endless power, which lies in Christ, as the germ of the whole great, glorified creation, gains such hold on the Apostle. that he closes with a bold song of triumph, in which he utters with glad assurance the unconquerableness of the life of Christ in all His faithful.

§ 11. OF THE DEVELOPMENT OF THE INDIVIDUAL UNTIL HIS EXPERIENCE OF REDEMPTION.

(VII. 7–24.)

Before we treat of the particulars of this remarkable, and, both theoretically and practically, so highly important section, some general questions are to be taken into consideration, upon the answer to which its illustration in great measure depends. Is Paul speaking in this section *of his own state or not?* and are the experiences of the *regenerate or unregenerate* its subject matter? As regards the first question, it is clear, that the Apostle could not possibly have chosen to carry through this representation in the first person, if *no* analogy at all for his description had been discoverable in his own life, if he had intended himself to be considered as expressly *excepted.* On the other hand it is equally clear, that Paul cannot be so speaking of himself, as if the subject related to him *alone,* for his desire is, to enlighten his readers upon their own necessities; in his experiences those of the generality must the rather be reflected. Hence it can only be said that the Apostle is certainly speaking of himself, but simply according to the experience he had in common with mankind, not according to his own individually. Little, however, is gained by this, unless it be determined in what period of his life the experiences, of which the Apostle speaks, were felt. This determination coincides with the other highly important question, whether the description given by the Apostle has reference to the state of the regenerate or unregenerate. The passage 7–13, indeed, according to the opinion of *all* expositors, applies to the state *before* regeneration, as the Apostle also sufficiently indicates by the *aorist* that the state described is gone by; but whether ver. 14–24 is likewise to be considered as before regeneration, seems very uncertain, since in this section Paul makes use of the *present* only, while viii. 2, &c., the *aorist* again appears. It is in fact difficult to answer this question, as in the *first* place the events treated of are purely internal, and require thoroughly analogous experiences and a definite consciousness of these experiences, in order to be rightly estimated; in the *next* place, the influence of many false tendencies has confused the inquiry. Pela gian blindness as to moral states, as well as Donatist rigorousness, must have found it easy to assert, that ver. 14–24 could not have reference to the regenerate, for that sins in these must be henceforth quite out of the question. Moral laxity or hypocrisy again have found it very convenient to say, that Paul is describing the state of the regenerate, fancying so, that they might, notwithstanding their moral degradation, consider themselves as regenerate. But beside these decidedly false tendencies, even the most faithful and learned members of the church have held different conceptions of the passage, according as they were accustomed to consider the sinfulness of man to be greater or less, and so to rate differently the effect of regeneration. Accordingly we are not surprised to find the easterns always inclining to Pelagianism, as Origen, Chrysostom, Theodoret, on the side of those who refer the passage to the state before regeneration. Even Augustine followed them at first; as he carried out his system, however, he was induced to defend the opposite view, that Paul is describing the state of the regenerate themselves. He was followed not merely in the middle ages by the most esteemed theologians, especially Anselm and Thomas Aquinas, but the reformers also, Luther, Melanthon, Calvin, Beza, interpreted the passage as Augustine did. After Spener, Franke, Bengel, Gottfried Arnold, Zinzendorf, the words of the Apostle were again begun to be explained of the state before regeneration, and Stier, Tholuck, Rückert, De Wette, Meyer, follow them in their interpretation. These learned men nevertheless quite rightly acknowledge, that the Augustinian representation has also something true in it, since that in the life of the regenerate moments occur, in which they must speak entirely as Paul expresses himself here; and, moreover, as it is only by degrees that the transforming power of the gospel penetrates the different tendencies of the inward life, congenial phenomena extend through the whole life of the believer; and this leads to the thought, that the two views might admit of being united in a higher one. For it is little probable beforehand, that men like Augustine and the reformers should have *entirely* erred in the conception of so important a passage. It may perhaps become perceptible from the following mode of laying out the context, how such a difference of views could be formed in the interpretation of the passage, and what in such difference is right and what erroneous.

First of all, it is evident that the Apostle's purpose is, to sketch a description of the inward process of development from its first beginnings to the highest perfection. He sets out, vii. 9, from a state in which the man is living entirely without law, and closes, viii. 11, with the glorification of the bodily substance. The question occurs here, how many stages of development are properly distinguished? *Four* clearly present themselves. *First*, a life without law, in which sin is dead; *next*, a life under the law, in which sin becomes alive and has dominion; *further*, a state in which, by the power of Christ, the spirit has dominion, and sin is mastered; *finally*, the state of the entire separation of sin by the glorification of the bodily substance. If by *regeneration* all is to be understood from the first stirrings of grace, the whole of the Apostle's description may then be applied to the regenerate, because the very heedfulness of the law is called forth by grace But it is surely more correct and scriptural to call regeneration that inward process only, by which, after the need of redemption is awakened, the power of Christ becomes mighty in the mind; so that a new, spiritual man enters into being, and exercises his ruling power. According to this acceptation, the state under the law cannot co-exist with regeneration, and without question therefore—as vii. 24 is to express the awakened need of redemption, and ver. 25 the experience of redemption itself—vers. 14–24 is to be referred to a position *before* regeneration, and to be understood as a description of the conflict within an *awakened person*. As, however, the Apostle makes use of the present for this section, while before and afterwards he applies the aorist, we are led to the idea, that he does not intend to have this state of conflict regarded as concluded with the experience of redemption. In the description, vers. 14–24 itself too, as will afterwards be more particularly shewn, an *advance* in the conflict with sin is clearly observable, the better I stands out in the man more and more, and the pleasure in God's law grows gradually in him. To this, vers. 17 speaks, especially the νυνὶ δὲ ὀυκέτι, and ver. 20, ὀυκέτι, which indicates a bygone state. In a far higher degree, as ver. 25 expresses, is this the case *after* the experience of the redeeming power of Christ, where the conflict with sin is described as for the most part victorious on the side of the better part in man. But a conflict remains still, even *after* the experience of regeneration; and that even the regenerate man does not *always* hold it victoriously, that even for him times of temptation, of very hard temptation, come on, the Scripture sanctions in express declarations (comp. at 1 John ii. 1), and in communications upon the life of the Apostles, even as the experience of all saints of all times sanctions it. If we add to this consideration, that in proportion with the true advance in the life of faith, the spiritual glance into the stirrings of sin sharpens, the conscience refines and censures strictly even the smaller deviations, which had else on lower standards remained unnoticed ; it is clearly right that Augustine and the great doctors of the church who followed him, should have declared, that even the regenerate man can and must say of himself all that the Apostle, vers. 14–24, utters. The best manner, therefore, in which we can express ourselves upon the question, whether Paul is here treating of the regenerate, is, that in the passage, vers. 14–24, he *immediately* describes the state of the man *before* regeneration, since his purpose is, to set forth coherently the whole course of development ; in the consciousness, however, that phenomena entirely similar present themselves within the regenerate man, he makes the description applicable to the regenerate also. The opinion, therefore, on the *one* side, that the Apostle *immediately and directly* intends the regenerate, is as absolutely wrong, as on the *other* side the assertion, that in the regenerate man *nothing* like what is described, ver. 14–24, can or ought to be found. The distinction between the conflict and the fall of the unregenerate and the conflict and fall of the regenerate remains, notwithstanding the subjective feeling of their near affinity, objectively so great (as at vii. 24, 25 will be proved), that the anxiety, lest by the view proposed, regeneration should be robbed of its essential character, must appear to be quite unfounded.* If we now look back again to the first question, of which period of his life the Apostle could say such things as he utters, vers. 14–24, it is clear that he cannot be immediately describing the state of his soul after the Lord's appearing to him by Damascus,

* Reiche has strikingly failed in his acceptation of this passage; he holds that the Jewish humanity, comprehended in the Apostle's person, is speaking here. The one-sided reference of the νόμος merely to the Jewish ceremonial law, is the immediate cause of this clearly false acceptation; that one-sided reference itself, however, is founded in the dogmatic principles of this learned man.

but that he is speaking of his inward conflicts under the yoke of the law; but the transition into the present certainly indicates, that even in his state at the time he wrote, sensations were still sounding, which made him exclaim with perfect truth, although with incomparably finer application to more delicate circumstances than in his former state (comp. at vii. 24, 25): What I would, I do not, and what I would not, that I do; wretched man that I am, who shall deliver me from the body of this death! (Comp. at 2 Cor. xii. 7, &c.)

Vers. 7, 8. The two first verses of this section contain the general fundamental thought briefly expressed, which ver. 9, &c., further carries out. The Apostle namely pronounces in these the relation which sin bears to the law, and describes the latter as the power* which brings sin to sight. Sin *is* in human nature, even without regard to the law, but by the law only it comes to the *sight* and so to the *conscience* of man. Hence also, notwithstanding this provocation of sin by the law, the law itself is no sinful formation, but rather is it holy, just, and good (ver. 12), as the expression of the holy will of God, of whose eternal, unalterable nature it even therefore partakes (comp. Ps. cxix. 96), and is to lead to life; only sin misuses it to *death*. (Ver. 10 and the observations at John xii. 50, compared with Levit. xviii. 5, Deut. v. 16, 33.) What the Apostle pronounces here, therefore, holds also, not by any means merely of the Mosaic ceremonial law, but of the *moral law* generally, in all forms of its manifestation among heathens, Jews, and Christians. It is the entirely universal character of the law, that sin breaks and swells up against it (comp. at ver. 13), since it checks the stream of sinful desire in a concrete case by a positive command (ἐντολή), and by this check urges to a transgression of the commandment, whereby his inward state then becomes perceptible to the man. The relation in which Paul places the ἁμαρτία and the ἐπιθυμία is peculiar in these verses. At first sight namely, it seems, as though Paul considered the ἐπιθυμία as the first, the ἁμαρτία as derived from it. In the sinful *act* the two are really so related, the evil desire is the mother of the evil deed (James i. 15); but ἁμαρτία denotes here the sinful state generally, which comes to sight in the concrete case only, and for this relation the position is exactly reversed. The ἐπιθυμία, *prava concupiscentia*,

* [*Moment.*]

issues from the general, sinful nature of man, as its first utterance and then the act follows. Upon nearer consideration of the Apostle's words, however, it becomes evident, that he intends the relation of ἁμαρτία to ἐπιθυμία to be exactly so understood here. Sinfulness causes the evil desire in all its forms (πᾶσαν ἐπιθυμίαν), to rise up at the law in the inward man (κατειργάσατο ἐν ἐμοί); and the divine commandment against the desire reveals now to man his corruption. A permission of the desire to proceed into *act* is not at all in question. *The desire itself is sinful,* and forbidden in the law, and the man may become conscious of his sinfulness, even by the greatness of the lust, although it should not break forth into outward evil deeds, which indeed is commonly the case. Hence, too, the ὀυκ ἐπιθυμήσεις (Exod. xx. 14; Deut. v. 8) is not to be taken, according to Tholuck, with an "and so forth," as though Paul put forward *one* only of the *many* commandments; but it is to be understood as the comprisal of the whole law. Positively, all laws say: love God above everything; negatively, they all say: suffer not thyself to covet; that is, cleave not with thy love to any created thing, not even to thyself, but to the Eternal only.* The nature of ἐπιθυμία is not the desire of itself, the joy at this or that, for the perfect man might have the highest, purest pleasure in all creatures of God; but the desire, when it is separate from God, the selfish love, estranged from God. The command ὀυκ ἐπιθυμήσεις, therefore, is nothing less than that the man has to give himself up with all his own desire and joy; this giving-up, however, is not possible without regeneration, therefore the man can never, as the following discourse demonstrates, arrive at peace by the law; he is in need of a Redeemer from himself (ver. 24.) (Ver. 8. the διὰ τῆς ἐντολῆς, as afterwards ver. 11, is better connected with ἀφορμὴν λαβοῦσα than with the following words, because the peculiar operation of the law is thus most decidedly marked.)

Vers. 9, 10. The Apostle now, after having expressed the general

* The Apostle takes no notice of the circumstance which is the rarer case, that even the *fright*, the terror of sin, may hurl into sin, if the shield of faith is wanting. Evil thoughts, that fill the heart with horror, may by this very terror, which takes away the presence of mind, draw men down into sin. The histories of criminals often afford proof of this. Notwithstanding, in order to explain such cases, we might assume, perhaps without exception, either previous moral corruption, or spiritual weakness as well as disease.

thought, proceeds in the description of the course of development in the man from its first beginnings; he describes a state in which sin is as yet *dead,* and the man is living *without law.* This state of childish unconsciousness is disturbed by the law with its commandment in the case in question. There is a question, however, how we have to suppose such a state of life *without law,* for the Apostle cannot mean the state of proper *infantia;* yet, except this, there is no time in the life of man, of which it may in the proper sense be said that the man is in it without law and sin without motion.* To explain this difficulty, it may be of essential service to remark, that the Apostle, during his whole exposition, is not supposing crimes and such like outbreaks of sin, which even the magistracy resents, and which drew after them the contempt of the world; for the law surely is able to repress sins of this kind, and the man can by the guidance of the law fulfil of his own power so called *opera civilia* or *justitiae externa.* But in such a state of legal action all laws and ordinances appear to the man as *political,* or at least as merely human statutes, and his whole effort is without reference to God; he avoids the sins, not for God's sake, but for the sake of their disagreeable external consequences, which to be sure is better than that impudence which does not even shun the consequences, yet it does not satisfy absolute righteousness; with such a spiritual standard, the Apostle has nothing at all to do here. He is speaking rather of that moment, when the man becomes conscious of his relation to God, not as mere proposition, but in essence and power, and he learns to regard all the commandments and ordinances of the law as *divine,* that is, as absolute commandments. The whole time before this moment he calls the life without law, *when sin was dead.*† With this acceptation results also, what is to be equally remarked upon

* Usteri (in the Paul. Lehrbegr. 4th edit. p. 39) supposes this state to be like that of Adam before the fall, which is surely against the Apostle's meaning, who considers this state of the deadness of sin itself as a *consequence* of the fall.

† The ἡ ἁμαρτία ἀνέζησεν (ver. 9), is not, as Rückert still holds, to be construed "sin revived," as though it had once been alive (from which conception the reading ἔζησεν, which must certainly be set aside, proceeded); ἀναζάω is rather "to come to life," (aufleben), as ἀνίστημι (in its intransitive tenses) is "to arise (aufstehen), stand up." The coming to life, however, presupposes no antecedent living of that which comes to life, but a slumbering only of the life in it. Thus the slumbering germ of a grain of seed comes to life, which had not as yet independently lived. The expression, "to come to life again," or, "for the second time," is here quite inappropriate.

all subsequent stages of development, that we are not to suppose this first stage as instantaneously got over. Certain it is that with most men the discernment of the law, as being the will of the absolutely holy God, takes place in a moment, and the former and after life may be clearly distinguished; but it is only by degrees that the risen light diffuses itself into the different regions of the inward life, and even those who have made progress may have still to experience on isolated departments, that they were living there without law, since the necessity of applying the divine law in this or that individual case had been a long time in becoming to them a matter of living consciousness. Thus it may be perceived, what is meant by the expression *χωρὶς νόμου ἁμαρτια νεκρά.* The deadness of sin is not to imply that it has no motion at all, for it is the very disordered *life,* and must constantly utter itself as such, even though often negatively only by deficiency in fear and love of God; but it is so far dead *without law,* as it is not at first discerned in its nature and in its whole magnitude, without the light of the law to enlighten its darkness. With that knowledge, however, the sin itself increases; first, because from the insight a resistance now unfolds itself, by which the wild power of the natural life rises (ver. 13); next, because the sin, which has got so far into the consciousness, is like a germ awakened from slumber, that strives to develope itself more and more. The self-will of the man rears against being broken, the lust of knowledge perverted to curiosity burns for eagerness to taste the forbidden thing, and so by the law sin finishes itself in itself by the increasing of the desire; supposing that it does not also, which however will always rarely be the case, break forth into openly criminal actions. This phenomenon is so consonant to experience that it is acknowledged before in the O.T., Prov. ix. 17, and even by profane authors. Comp. the noted passage in Ovid. Amor. iii. 4, "Nitimur in vetitum semper cupimusque negata." To the quickening of sin the Apostle immediately attaches the *dying of the I,* the better self;* it seems. therefore. as though the latter had been

* I believe it may be said, that the development of the conflict assumes in many men a different shape. Sin is with many alive from the beginning, and the better I seems to sleep. The course of conversion with such persons then takes shape, the conflict is first developed, when the *I awakes* from its deep slumber in the inner man, and opposes itself to the unresisted dominion of the sinful element. The Apostle's descrip-

alive before the moment of the law's coming in, that is, that the better had prevailed, and that accordingly this moment would not appear to be the foundation of any advance to the better, but of a retreat to the worse. And indeed this is Paul's meaning, as ver. 13 clearly shews; but the retreat is but a seeming one, like the full, open coming-out of a disease hitherto lurking in secret. As no cure is possible without this, so unless sin be thus forced to shew itself, there is no deliverance from it. The relatively better state of a kind of good-nature and freedom from violent desires is also but a seeming one, that has no true foundation, and therefore vanishes as soon as the hour of temptation approaches. The coming forth of sin, however, is not, as was before noticed, to be understood of outrage and crime, which man *on any standard* can and must by his own power leave, but of those inward motions of sin and its finer utterances, which are beyond the cognizance of human judgment Meantime it is certainly possible, even for the gross offender, when the law becomes alive in him, forthwith, by penitence and faith, to enter into redemption, only he may not misuse this passage for the purpose of exculpating himself. The *actual* thief or adulterer may not appeal to the sinfulness, in consequence of which [as he might pretend], he *must* have sinned so; he could very well have omitted the *deed;* but the *inward* lust no man can of his own power do away; and it is of the overpowering of this that the Apostle immediately treats here.

Ver. 11–13. Paul lingers awhile by these thoughts,* and brings forward the holiness of the law, as expressing the will of the holy God, so that it is indeed sin itself which is the *cause* of its effect in increasing sin. The law is but the innocent occasion, the *conditio sine qua non;* the *causa efficiens* is the sinfulness of man. The

tion, therefore, is not to be understood, *as though every course of conversion must necessarily assume the shape which he describes;* experience indeed shews, that in the life of many converted persons, *e.g.*, Spener's and Zinzendorf's, no such decisive moment occurred, as Paul describes in the passage, vii. 24. But such as theirs naturally are only to be supposed in the church; with heathens and Jews, as those of whom Paul was immediately thinking, the conversion must necessarily have shewn itself, as Paul represents it; because with them any *abiding in the grace of baptism* is out of the question, and consequently in them conversion must reveal itself as moment [*qu.* a momentary thing?] namely, as entrance into the communion of the faithful.

* The delineation of the state under the law begins fundamentally at ver. 9 with the ἐλθούσης δὲ τῆς ἐντολῆς, the description itself does not properly follow until ver. 14, while ver. 10–13 regard more immediately the moment of transition

latter therefore appears as something in itself foreign to the man, deceiving himself, with a glance at the narrative, Gen. iii. This relation of the ἐγώ to ἁμαρτία is of the highest importance for understanding what follows, and for the scriptural anthropology generally. Sin is not the nature, the substance of man himself (as evil generally is nothing substantial, but disharmony only, the disturbance of the relations originally ordained by God), rather has the germ of the divine image remained even in fallen man, to which grace knits on her work of bringing back to God. (Comp. at Rom. ii. 14, 15.) This better germ of life, however, appears in the natural state, when sin has quickened, as suppressed by a foreign power, troubled and obscured in its nature, and hence the operation of grace finds expression in striving to draw it upwards, and to make it prevail. Sin therefore is not to be considered as a sum of evil actions standing separate, any more than good as a sum of good deeds standing separate, but both, *good and evil, are elements of life;* wherefore, where good or evil has place in one person, the one or the other element, light or darkness, the Lord of the kingdom of light, or the prince of darkness, exercises his dominion. Therefore it is said also, 1 John iii. 8, *ὁ ποιῶν τὴν ἁμαρτίαν ἐκ τοῦ διαβόλου ἐστίν.* But the dominion of sin, when it is allowed, takes the form of *ἀπατή*, because the I fancies it will find in sin true joy and abiding satisfaction, in which, however, it deceives itself. Sin, as disharmony, is never able to still that thirst for eternal joy which is planted in every being, for she brings ever in her train the loathing of herself. The law fulfils, then, one of its important aims in bringing this *deceit* home to the conscience of the man; it manifests the secret hidden nature of evil (*ἵνα φανῇ ἁμαρτία*), it increases it in its nature, in order the more surely to awaken the disgust at it, and to convert all the desire and love of the man to that good, which as the internal harmony stills the longing for eternity. The words *ἵνα γένηται καθ' ὑπερβολὴν ἁμαρτωλὸς ἡ ἁμαρτία*, therefore, are not to be refined on; they are intended to state, according to their simple sense, that *the commandment increases sin.* As a rapidly flowing stream rolls calmly on, so long as no object checks it, but foams and roars so soon as any hindrance stops it, just as calmly does the sinful element hold its course through the man, so long as he does not stem it; but if he would realize the divine commandment, he begins to feel the force of the element, of whose dominion he had as yet no boding.

The construction of the sentence is not without difficulty. To Ἀλλὰ ἡ ἁμαρτία the words ἐμοὶ γέγονε θάνατος are evidently to be supplied from the preceding, but the following ἵνα φανῇ ἁμαρτία seems to stand unconnectedly, and some expositors would therefore have bracketed it as parenthesis, which however is without doubt wrong. It is better to draw from ἵνα the idea of the divine purpose, and consequently to supply: "whereby (namely that sin becomes the cause of death to men) God purposes that." Καθ' ὑπερβολὴν = ὑπερβαλλόντως, is frequently used by Paul. (Comp. 1 Cor. xii. 31; 2 Cor. i. 8, iv. 17; Gal. i. 13.) The formula is found also in later profane writers. The second ἵνα is to be taken as standing quite parallel to the first; the second clause only illustrates and enhances the thought of the first.

Ver. 14. Hereupon, the carnal state of man is opposed to the purely objective divine nature of the law (the πνευματικός is to be interpreted as emanation of God, of the πνεῦμα, John iv. 24.) Spirit and flesh lust against each other. (Galat. v. 7.) Therefore, the I also and the law are against each other, the I would be autonomous. There is certainly no break to be made here at ver. 14, the Apostle does not pass to any new representation; but the alteration of the tenses,—the present keeping on so constantly to the end of the chapter, and preterites having been hitherto used—can not, as has already been observed, be overlooked. We find a generalization of the relations signified in this; Paul regards in what follows the man in himself, upon all stages of development, in conflict with the law, and in as far as the old man remains even after regeneration, so far the following description, as has been shown above, has its truth also for the regenerate man himself. But the question occurs, what conception are we to form of σάρξ, and its derivative σαρκικός? Schleusner counted no less than sixteen significations of σάρξ, which Bretschneider and Wahl have, to be sure, reduced to seven; notwithstanding even the exposition of these learned men is not calculated to make it perceptible, how one of these meanings proceeds from the other. The following observations may perhaps afford an easy survey of the course of the formation of the different meanings which the word takes in. Σάρξ, בָּשָׂר, immediately signifies the substance of the flesh, as far as it belongs to the living organism; as dead, it is called *κρέας*. In this meaning, as substance of the *σῶμα,* flesh and bones are often connected (*e.g.*, Luke xxiv. 39; Ephes. v. 30), in order to mark as strongly as possible the material. This nearest meaning, founded on the perception of the senses, becomes then applied in holy writ to spiritual things in two ways. *First,* the flesh is understood as the visible veil of the spirit, and so far *σάρξ* appears in equal signification with *γράμμα,* the veil of the spirit in the Scripture, or with *φανερόν* in contrast to *κρυπτόν* (Rom. ii. 28, 29; Col. ii. 1, 5; Heb. ix. 10), and denotes the outward, the outside, the form in contrast to the essence; *next, σάρξ* signifies the decaying, perishable part of man, in contrast to the eternal, imperishable spirit dwelling in him. This sense appears especially in the forms *σάρξ καὶ ἅιμα,* (Matt. xvi. 17; 1 Cor. xv. 50; Ephes. vi. 12) and *πᾶσα σάρξ* (Luke iii. 6; John iii. 6; 1 Pet. i. 24) as signifying the decaying, perishable race of man generally. The notion of *sinfulness* is, then, necessarily given with that of decay, for the former is the cause of the latter; death penetrated into mankind with sin; and decay is but that death gradually diffusing itself. Accordingly sinfulness itself is also, especially in the Epistles to the Romans and Galatians, directly called *σάρξ*, and *ἐπιθυμίαι σαρκός* (Ephes. ii. 3; 1 John ii. 16; 2 Pet. ii. 18), a *νοῦς σαρκός* (Col. ii. 18), *σῶμα σαρκός* (Col. ii. 11. compared with Eccles. xxiii. 16), and such like are spoken of. Yet this usage is not to be understood, as though the writers of the Bible considered sin to be grounded merely in the bodily impulses, as preponderating sensuality. The *σάρξ* is rather to be understood, as embracing the whole *psychical life,* with all its will and mind; for without the animating *ψυχή,* the same being distinguished from *πνεῦμα,* the *σάρξ* alone cannot so much as commit sin. It is certainly correct, however, that *σάρξ* can only be used to denote *human* sin, the sin of the world of evil spirits having quite a different character. In this it is of a spiritual nature, and, therefore, incurable; in the natural man sin has only penetrated the nature of soul and body; the spirit, by being oppressed or troubled by sin, may be defiled, but it has no sin in its nature. When in man sin occupies the spirit itself, and proceeds from it, he is then on his way to the sin against the Holy Ghost.*

* Compare more particularly hereon at the important passage, 2 Cor. vii. 1. Very striking observations upon this subject are to be found in Vitringa obs. sacr. (Jenæ

The use of the adjectives σαρκικός and σάρκινος may now be easily explained. The latter (2 Cor. iii. 3, is the only place where it is quite ascertained) answers to the German *fleischern*, or "fleischig," fleshy; the former is our *fleischlich,* carnal. In the later Greek, the two adjective forms were confounded, and hence many variations are found in the readings; in the N. T., however, excepting the passage adduced, σαρκικός might be everywhere read. This form, then, designates as well the merely outward (Rom. xv. 27; 1 Cor. ix. 11), as the perishable, and, therefore, sinful, which latter meaning prevails in the passage before us. The ἐγώ, namely, is so far called σαρκικός, as it is governed by sin; not, in as far as it has sin essentially in itself, for in the course of the following exposition of the Apostle it appears as again freed from that foreign dominion, as it was relatively free from it before sin became alive (ver. 9). The expression πεπραμένος ὑπὸ τὴν ἁμαρτίαν also points to the same relation; the image of one sold for a slave, who is in need of being ransomed, is the foundation of it. For the *free* man only can come into bondage, and becomes free again with his liberation from it. Surely, however, he cannot loose *himself* from it, but needs a ransomer, and to this point the deduction of the Apostle leads (ver. 24). Therefore, even the regenerate man may say the σαρκικός ἐιμι of himself, in that he, albeit for moments only, has yet to experience the dominion of sin.

1723) pag. 560, seqq. Comp. also my opusc. theol. (Berol. 1833), pag. 156, seqq. Müller, in his excellent work upon sin (Breslau, 1839. B. i. s. 182), thinks my illustration of the notion of σάρξ more satisfactory in the treatise upon the Trichotomy than here. I am not aware, however, that I have expressed myself otherwise in the commentary, than in that treatise, only I have here developed my view more fully. The scriptural explanation which Müller himself gives of σάρξ I certainly cannot acknowledge to be the right one, and it is impossible for it to gain credit. Müller, namely, is of opinion, that the expression σάρξ does not signify the sinful side in man, but "*all* that is merely human, the human as denuded of its relation to God and in contrast to this relation" (p. 184.) That πνεῦμα, in opposition to σάρξ, is not the human, but the divine spirit; that νοῦς or ὁ ἔσω ἄνθρωπος is used in contrast to σάρξ. But νοῦς is acknowledged to be a function only of the πνεῦμα, and how the ἔσω ἄνθρωπος is to be otherwise understood than of the πνεῦμα, is not to be conceived. But even setting aside this identity of the πνεῦμα with both the notions which Müller recognises as opposite to σάρξ, the assumption of such contrast itself contradicts the notion of σάρξ which he has proposed. Paul states here a conflict in the man between the σάρξ and the νοῦς, it cannot be that all which is merely human is called σάρξ, for that includes the νοῦς itself. Σάρξ is the human nature, *so far* as it is separated from God, and becomes subject to the power of darkness, that is, σῶμα and ψυχή, in the πνεῦμα, on the contrary, or, taken as faculty, in the νοῦς, the light has remained to him, a light still in his darkness; the good impulses proceed from it, as from the σάρξ the evil ones.

The reading οἴδαμεν is without hesitation to be preferred to the other οἶδα μέν, as the latter has no manuscript authority at all, and has evidently proceeded merely from the observation, that the singular stands elsewhere in the whole passage. But for the very purpose of indicating that the Apostle is not expressing merely individual experiences, but such as are at the same time experiences of the generality, the employment of the plural was necessary here at the turning-point of the whole disquisition.

Ver. 15–20. The thought just now generally put, ἐγὼ σαρκικός εἰμι, the Apostle carries out experimentally in the following verses, and describes in the most vivid manner the fluctuation of desires and thoughts both tempting and fighting against the temptation. The repetition of the same words (ver. 15 comes in ver. 19, and ver. 16 in ver. 20, word for word again) gives in the most touching manner the impression of *a dreary uniformity* of this inward struggle, before a higher power of peace has revealed itself in the mind. Meanwhile, however, this repetition is by no means to be considered as entirely without purpose, it is intended rather to lead to even stronger consciousness of the sinful state, and thereby to ever livelier longing for redemption. In the course of the conflict, too, more conscious separation of the better I from sin bespeaks that progress, which the Apostle afterwards indicates not merely by the stronger expression, which marks in the advance (ver. 23) the joy in the divine law, but also by the even more perceptible parting of the old man from the new man who is in process of formation, and of the law of sin from the law of the spirit. It is yet to be observed, that here again the Apostle's representation is not to be applied to such offences, as human authority punishes, that no murderer therefore, or adulterer, or any one who commits anything else, which is generally considered as a criminal act, can say, I do what I would not, but I cannot help it. Such an one the Apostle would answer: thou hypocrite, thou canst well forbear committing the *act*, if thou only appliest the natural powers which God has bestowed upon thee. The whole representation regards the inner man, and finer transgressions of the divine commandment, *e. g.*, by an overhasty word. Hence, it has also its perfect truth for the regenerate man,* who is open to impressions from the more subtile

* The boundary, how and wherein a regenerate person can still sin, and how and wherein not, is to be defined by men upon the extremities only. We may say, a regene-

temptations only. But the conscience being also more acute in him, his situation is *for his feeling* quite similar to that represented here, and he is as much in need of *daily* repentance and renewed forgiveness of sins, as the unregenerate is of the *first* repentance. Some consideration is now requisite in this passage of the relation of the *one* and the *other* I, of which respectively Paul speaks, to the *unity of the personality*. The one I would the good, gives assent to the law (ver. 16, σύμφημι τῷ νόμῳ), nay has its pleasure in it (ver. 22, συνήδομαι τῷ νόμῳ); the other notwithstanding does sin, that is, nourishes desire, the evil concupiscence, albeit the other I can withhold it from breaking out into act.* In quite a similar manner our Lord also speaks (Matth. x. 39) of a *twofold* ψυχή, one of which must die, if the other is to be kept. According to the ordinary notion of the soul, as being a thing of itself closed in itself, that breeds of itself at pleasure good as well as evil, this mode of expression is hard to be explained; but, as has been already observed at Matth. x. 39, it becomes quite intelligible, when the soul is considered as receptive nature, penetrated by the powers of light and darkness, that contend in it for the mastery. In the better I, light gets predominant, in the sinful one, darkness, and the man thus perceives in the unity of his life the duplicity of the fighting elements, that reflect their nature in him; he has not two souls, but the oneness becomes twofold by the powers that are operative in it. By total surrender to the one or the other of these elements, he passes entirely into their nature. Even before Christ experience led rightly to such a duplicity in the inner man. Besides the well known: "video meliora proboque, deteriora sequor" of Ovid (Metam. vii. 19), and beside the expression of Epictetus: ὁ ἁμαρτάνων ὃ μὲν θέλει ὀυ ποιεῖ, καὶ ὃ μὴ θέλει ποιεῖ (Enchir. ii. 26), the passage of Xenophon (Cyrop, vi. 1, 21) is remarkable, in which two souls are expressly

rate person, who should commit a premeditated murder or the like, was entirely fallen from faith; but if a believer should be faulty in a word or a similar small matter, it would naturally not be considered as in itself apostacy. Notwithstanding even *one word* may in the divine judgment be a very heavy sin, if *e.g.*, it is intended to wound a neighbour deeply; and circumstances, which often God only knows, may exceedingly mitigate a seemingly very heavy sin. The greatness of the temptation, the degree of consciousness and the like, which are beyond human judgment, are instances in point.

* Bengel says very aptly upon this: "Assensus hominis legi contra semet ipsum praestitus, illustris character est religionis, magnum testimonium de Deo."

distinguished, with the entirely correct remark, that the phenomenon of the inward conflict, and of the attraction to good as well as to evil, cannot be satisfied by the explanation, that the same soul addresses itself at one time to the good, at another to the bad, for that in the choice of the one, the draw towards the other manifests itself *at the same time.** Naturally, however, the willing of good before regeneration can only be considered as the free will gradually developing itself, as *disposition* to true freedom, as mere *velleitas.* For this θέλειν can only express itself negatively, in as far as it checks the outbreak of sin into the gross act; but as soon as the man becomes conscious that the evil desire as such is sin, he feels that mere willing is not sufficient to remove it, even as it is incapable of calling forth in the heart holy motions and desire for holiness.

The ὀυ γινώσκω, ver. 15, is not to be construed with Augustine and Grotius, "I approve not," as Reiche still maintains. For although the conceptions "know," and "approve," or "be inclined towards," pass into each other, the context forbids the application of the meaning "be inclined to, like," here, because a tautology thereby arises, θέλειν expressing the same thing. One is led to construe the expression so, only because the speaker seems to know well what he does, as at ver. 18 too it is said: ὀιδα γὰρ κ. τ. λ. But then it is overlooked, that although the Apostle does know well the *fact* of the inward conflict, he does not comprehend the *cause* of this phenomenon, or at least in the described moment of inward development he pictures the speaking subject as perplexed in his view of it. Like as it is said, John iii. 8, of the regenerating Spirit, "a man hears and feels its sound indeed, but knows not whence it cometh and whither it goeth."—Ver. 16. σύμφημι is weaker than the following συνήδομαι, ver. 22; this is to be distinguished from ἐφήδομαι, by which mischievous joy is designated. The two expressions are only found here in the N. T. Vers. 17 and 20, the νυνὶ δὲ ὀυκέτι is important; Paul indicates therein, as has been remarked above, a progress; he is supposing that the man at first himself performs the evil, till the parting of the ἐπιθμία and

* Reiche, in a strange manner, explains these words of the Apostle, expressing so profoundly the general experience of all more earnest men, of the ideal and real Jew! The conformity of profane writers with the Apostle's expression might surely have taught him better!

the *νοῦς* is completed in him, and the evil afterwards stands opposed to him as a strange thing, molesting his true I. *Νυνὶ* is not to be understood of time, but to be construed as inferring on' The temporal progress is indicated only in the *ὀυκέτι*. Ver. 18. Upon the *ὀικεῖ ἐν τῇ σαρκί μου ἡ ἁμαρτία*, and the *θέλειν παράκειταί μοι*, comp. at 21, 22. Ver. 18. A.B.C. and several critical authorities leave out *ἑυρίσκω*, and read only : *τὸ δὲ κατεργάζεσθαι, ὀυ.* The omission of the verb might be more difficult to explain than its addition, and therefore I prefer the shorter reading. Ver. 20. The most important authorities, namely the Codd. B.C.D.E.G., omit the first *ἐγώ*, while the second remains quite undisputed; the omission seems certainly very proper, for the following *ἐγώ* together with *ἁμαρτία*, goes back to *θέλω* and *ποιῶ*, there was therefore no ground for putting *ἐγώ* at the beginning of the verse; notwithstanding the very reason for the omission might have been, that the so putting it was unaccountable.

Ver. 21–23. That duplicity within the man, already notified in the foregoing verses, is now more closely described.* Paul namely distinguishes the *ἔσω ἄνθρωπος* (Ephes. iii. 16), from the *ἔξω ἄνθρωπος* (2 Cor. iv. 16); parallel with the first expression he uses *νοῦς*,† with the second *σάρξ* or *μέλη*. Considered in and by themselves, these expressions are *not* of equal signification with *καινὸς ἄνθρωπος* (Eph. ii. 15, iv. 24), or *καινὴ κτίσις* (Gal. vi. 15; 2 Cor. v. 17), and *παλαιὸς ἄνθρωπος* (Rom. vi. 6; Eph. iv. 22; Col. iii. 9). For the three latter formulæ refer only and solely to the birth of the new man in regeneration (John i. 13); whereas every natural man has an inward man, a *πνεῦμα* or *νοῦς*, or as Peter says (1 Pet. iii. 4), a *κρυπτὸς ἄνθρωπος τῆς καρδίας*. But as far as the transformation in regeneration begins in the *πνεῦμα* or *νοῦς* of the natural man, and the *inner* man is the condition, we may say the mother of the *new* man, so far the meanings reach one another, and although therefore in the passage before us the state of the regenerate is not *immediately* the subject of discourse, yet the description, with the modifications above directed, has its truth for *this* state also. The relation, however, of *πνεῦμα* or *νοῦς* to

* Comp. hereon, and upon the connection of ch. vii. and viii., Knapp's treatise in the scriptis var. arg. p. 429. sqq.

† In 2 Cor. iv. 16, however, there is reference also in *ἔσω ἄνθρωπος* to the glorified body.

σάρξ or μέλη will be only properly understood from that trichotomy of human nature, which serves as basis to the Apostle's representation.* According to the acuteness of the contrast, in which Paul places the two above-mentioned parts of man, his unity would be entirely annulled, if we might not upon the authority of other passages of Scripture (especially 1 Thess. v. 23, and Hebr. iv. 12) supply the ψυχή as the third part, and indeed as that part, in which the man becomes conscious both of the νοῦς and of the σάρξ, as *his,* and which therefore must be considered as the proper centre of his personality. In the πνεῦμα (which is only comprehended in the νοῦς as ability, as capacity) the connexion of the ψυχή with the higher world of the spirit is represented, in the σάρξ the connexion of it with the creature. In the natural state certainly, the spiritual potency of the νοῦς is dimmed (2 Cor. vii. 1) ; the νοῦς of itself is in ματαιότης, having no power or capacity to conquer (Ephes. iv. 18), as even the conscience may be defiled (Tit. i. 15) ; wherefore the man is in need of the *πνεῦμα ἅγιον,* of the absolute, pure, the highest Spirit, for his perfection ; meantime, however, the νοῦς, even although obscured, forms for the natural man an inward light, that gives him a sort of insight. This light is never quite extinct but by a continued resistance to it, and then all spiritual power vanishes. (Matt. vi. 23 ; Jude ver. 19.) Accordingly the Apostle speaks of a νόμος τοῦ νοός, that is, of a law coming to the consciousness of man by the νοῦς. This law, which the man feels himself unable to satisfy, is not however given to him autonomously, but God gives it him *by* the νοῦς, as the organ susceptible of the divine operations. The two laws therefore are not to be held apart, as Tholuck still holds them ; they are thoroughly identical, only regarded according to their nearer or farther sources. So for the νόμος τῆς ἁμαρτίας, or νόμος τῆς σαρκός, the νόμος τοῦ διαβόλου might be put, since the ultimate cause of the expressions of sin in man cannot be supposed without incitement from the kingdom of darkness and its prince. When, however, *a law* is assigned to sin itself, which is in its nature opposed to law, it is with a view to indicate, that in the sinful development, no less than in good, there is a constant advance, an incessant urging and assertion of itself. It may be said, that in the department of sin the law of good is re-

* Comp. hereon my treatise: de trichotomia humanæ naturæ N. T. scriptoribus recepta, which is printed in my opusc. theol. pag. 143 sqq.

versed; as in good a constant law of attraction upwards reveals itself, so in evil a constant law of the attraction downwards. Nothing, as has already been remarked on another passage, is more dangerous and erroneous than the opinion, that one evil deed can stand isolate, that a man can commit one or another and then stop. Rather does all evil hang like a chain together, and every sin multiplies the weight of the indwelling evil in frightful progression, until, quicker than the man forbodes, it turns him dizzy and drags him into the deep. But even so the good grows also in itself, and every little victory furthers its elasticity, which has its impulse upwards. These two potencies, therefore, fight against each other in the *ψυχή*, as their arena. The I has the insight into the better, has the *θέλειν* even, a sort of *velleitas* to do it, but the *κατεργάζεσθαι* is wanting (ver. 18); thus the inward power of action in the man, that which proceeds from the *πνεῦμα*, is crippled. Sin makes a prisoner of the I (ver. 23), it is a slave in its own house.

No emphasis is to be laid on the expressions *ἡ ἁμαρτία οἰκεῖ, τὸ θέλειν παράκειται* (ver. 18, 20, 21), as though *οἰκεῖν* were to express the constant inhering, *παρακεῖσθαι* the more distant attachment, for ver. 21, *παρακεῖσθαι* is used likewise of evil. The expression *οἰκεῖ ἐν ἐμοὶ ἁμαρτία* (ver. 17), is more nearly defined, ver. 18, by *οὐκ οἰκεῖ ἐν τῇ σαρκί μου ἀγαθόν*. The *οὐκ ἀγαθόν* = *κακόν*, ver. 19, answers to *ἁμαρτία* considered as a state; sin is removed out of the nobler, higher potency of the man, the *νοῦς* into the lower, the *ψυχὴ σαρκική*, or the *σάρξ ψυχική*. (Comp. at ver. 14.) The lower potency defiles the higher also, and presses back its operation; but the latter has not in itself the law of disharmony; this is the case with the evil spirits only, and with men, when they have by continued personal sin killed the spirit itself. *Καλόν* is used entirely as the hellenic *καλὸν κἀγαθόν* in a moral-æsthetic meaning. יָפֶה is similarly used in a moral view, Eccl. iii. 11. Ver. 21. Touching the difficult construction of the verse, it is not entirely cleared by any of the attempts to solve it (Reiche's comm. ad loc. may be referred to for them); it seems that an anacoluthon must be assumed in it. With this supposition one must be guided by the leading notion *νόμος*, which must then in ver. 21 be understood as in ver. 22, 23, and therefore of the law of God. With regard to the grammatical construction, *τὸν νόμον* might be annexed to *ποιεῖν*. But in this way of taking the passage, especially maintained by Knapp, not only is the τὸ καλόν* harsh, for which Knapp would improperly read τὸν καλόν, but also the repetition of ἐμοί. If it be further considered that Paul never † uses the form νόμον ποιεῖν; it is only found Galat. v. 3; that in fine an ἕτερος νόμος is spoken of in ver. 23, which is explained as νόμος ἁμαρτίας; the simplest mode seems to be, to take τὸν νόμον as accusative of the object in the sense: "I find, then, the law, that evil is present with [or besets] me, while I am yet wishing to do good." The placing τὸν νόμον before suits this sense very well. Ver. 23, αἰχμαλωτίζω, as well as αἰχμαλωτεύω (2 Tim. iii. 6) belongs only to the later Greek, and especially to the Alexandrine dialect. Comp. Phrynichus by Lobeck, s. 442.

Ver. 24. So, then, Paul had arrived at the proper turning-point in the interior of the spiritual life, to the complete development of the need of redemption, to the parting of law and gospel. The law has fulfilled its work, when it has awakened repentance, and the despair in a man's own power to set forth true holiness within and without him (Rom. iii. 20), and is thus become the παιδαγωγὸς ἐις Χριστόν (Galat. iii. 24). It seems surprising only, that he who in the deepest longing cries for redemption, longs for this redemption not from sin, or from the law of sin, but from the σῶμα τοῦ θανάτου = σῶμα θνητόν.‡ All explanations of this expression, which abstract from corporeity,§ must necessarily founder on the two decided declarations of the Apostle, in the preceding part of the discourse, which constantly speaks of the σάρξ, nay of the μέλη (comp. vi. 12, vii. 18, 23, 25.) Paul is not, however, supposing (as was remarked at ver. 14) in a Manichæan manner, the σάρξ or the σῶμα to be in and of itself sinful, the Apostle says rather, that as far as the σῶμα is necessarily connected with

* The τὸ καλὸν can only be taken as redundant, unless with Homberg νόμον, or with Hemsterhuis καλόν is to be struck out, but for which there are no critical authorities. (Comp. Knapp, scr. v. arg. p. 437.)

† [This seeming contradiction is the author's.]

‡ If a moment could be pointed out earlier, which might be considered as the experience of the redemption of Christ in the spirit, and could this whole section be explained immediately of the regenerate, one might believe that ver. 24 might be taken thus: "Would that I might, now that I am spiritually redeemed, be glorified in body also!" But so the redemption would appear totally done with spiritually, and only remain to be completed corporally; while, according to scriptural representation, it needs, as well for the spirit as for the whole man, constantly renewed repetition.

§ [Leiblichkeit.]

the psychical life of man, and as a member of the material world is exposed to its wild powers, so far ἡ ἁμαρτία οἰκεῖ ἐν τῇ σαρκί. He wishes, therefore, to be redeemed, not from the body in itself (he longs rather to be clothed upon with the true heavenly body, 2 Cor. v.), but only so to be redeemed from the *mortal* body, that is, the body subject to corruption, that the Spirit may give it life. (Comp. at Rom. viii. 11.) Accordingly, it may clearly be perceived from this passage also, that Paul, as we already intimated, teaches the sinfulness of man's nature, and recognizes in him* the remains of the divine image, which restoring grace knits on to. Man is become by original sin no πνεῦμα ἀκάθαρτον, such as the evil spirits are; but from the disobedient will of the ψυχή, man's *corporeity* is immediately become subject to the mere natural life and its rude powers,† hence by a reaction the πνεῦμα also is become grieved and hindered; howbeit the πνεῦμα has retained a certain light and grade of beneficial influences, whereby even in the heathen world phenomena relatively noble are bred. (Comp. at Rom. ii. 14, 15.) Meantime the natural life suffices not, the natural power of the will to boot, to do away with sin and rear true inward holiness, as the divine law requires; man needs a Redeemer, therefore, through whom his spirit may receive again the whole fulness of its original power, which hereupon first sanctifies the ψυχή and glorifies at last the σῶμα also. As, therefore, the lusts of the flesh war from beneath against the ψυχή; so does the impulse of the spirit sanctify it from above; hence sanctification must, before all things, be directed to the crucifying of the flesh (Galat. v. 24; 1 Cor. ix. 27), because the spirit comes to have dominion, when the predominance of the flesh is suppressed. But if sin were founded immediately in the πνεῦμα or νοῦς, so that Paul might have said: ἁμαρτία οἰκεῖ ἐν τῷ πνεύματι, atonement could then have been as little spoken of for men, as it is in the case of the evil spirits, for

* [*In ihm.* There is no masculine word in the sentence to which *ihm* can relate. Perhaps it may be a misprint for *ihr*, *i. e.*, *der menschlichen natur;* or the author may have put *ihm* to agree with *dem menschen*, forgetting that this was not the expression which he had used. B.]

† Only, Holy Scripture certainly knows nothing of the heathen view of the body, as a prison of the soul; it is rather a necessary organ to her of herself, wherefore, even upon the highest stage of perfection, the body again appears, only in glorified form. Without body, the state of the soul is an imperfect one. (Comp. upon the relation of the body to the soul, Seneca [epist. 65] who expresses himself thereon in a manner nearly approaching the Christian doctrine

there had been no connecting point for grace in the inner man. Since, then, even *with the regenerate man*, the body of death and the old man is living still, he also has occasion to exclaim : *ταλαίπωρος ἐγὼ ἄνθρωπος ;* more in a partial sense, however, the exclamation being here intended in its full compass, as liberation from the whole former state, and longing for a thoroughly new life, whose property the subsequent representation describes. (The expression *ταλαίπωρος*, from *τλάω*, to suffer, and *πῶρος*, a rock, a heavy stone, is very suitable for describing the hard pressure under which the man is suffering during the dominion of sin. It is found besides at Rev. iii. 17. The choice of the word *ῥύομαι* is also very significant ;* that powerful, energetic pulling-out lies in its meaning, which is looked for not from any circumstance, but from a *person* only, spiritually superior in might, therefore, *τίς με ῥύσεται.* That in the *ῥύσεται*, moreover, not merely the communication of a new principle of life, but the forgiveness of sins, atonement is intended, the expression *κατάκριμα ὀυδὲν τοῖς ἐν Χριστῷ* testifies. In the words, *ἐκ τοῦ σώματος τοῦ θανάτου τούτου*, the pronoun belongs to *σώματος*, since it is placed according to the known Hebrew use where two substantives are connected, after.†)

§ 12. OF THE EXPERIENCE OF REDEMPTION UNTIL THE PERFECTION OF THE INDIVIDUAL LIFE.

(VII. 25—VIII. 17.)

To the question uttered in ver. 24 : who shall redeem me ? the Apostle answers by a deep but eloquent silence. He points namely

* The whole expression: *τίς με ῥύσεται*, expresses, moreover, not merely the thought: who *will* at last sometime *deliver* me out of this cheerless state of conflict, but also the thought: who *can*. The feeling finds vent, that no *human* help avails anything here.

† The Hypallage with pronouns in Greek is certainly unusual (comp. Winer's Gr. p. 519, and Meyer ad loc.); but the context speaks decidedly here for the adoption of a Hebrew idiom. (Comp. Gesenius Gr. p. 741.) For the thought, "body of this hitherto described death," does not suit the context, since *θάνατος* last occurred at ver. 13, and the following description from ver. 14, contains no point at all, which could lead to the notion of death in a physical sense. The putting *σῶμα θανάτου* together, however, suggests immediately the physical death, as the final expression of the corruption which has dominion of the whole man. *Σῶμα τοῦ θανάτου* cannot certainly be : body, which is the *cause* of *θάνατος*, but it may be : body which bears in itself the *nature* of death, = *σῶμα θνητόν* [viii. 10]. The meaning "mass, whole," according to the analogy of גֵּו is quite inapplicable here.

by it to that invisible and unspeakable act of *regeneration*, when the man sees heaven open, and perceives the whisper of the Spirit, and therein the presence of God (I Kings xix. 12), without knowing whence the breathing cometh and whither it goeth (John iii. 8.) To signify, however, that here the experience of redemption in his own heart is to be considered as attained, he utters his thanksgiving for this grace to the originator of the work of redemption, God the Father, through Christ, whom he can now from his heart call his Lord.* With this experience an entirely altered state commences within the man, the nature of which the Apostle proceeds to describe, unto entire perfection, even of the body (viii. 11.) While namely in the former state the divine law reflected itself indeed in the νοῦς and the *wish* was stirring in the inner man, that he could keep it, nay his joy in it notified itself, yet the main thing still was wanting, the κατεργάζεσθαι (vii. 18). The νοῦς could not in freedom serve the law of God,† the very inner man was taken prisoner by the resisting law of sin. But by experience of the redeeming power of Christ, whereby the νοῦς is strengthened, the man sees himself enabled, at least with the highest and noblest potency of his being, to serve the divine law, and thus we find no more in him the θέλειν merely, but the κατεργάζεσθαι also. Meantime the head only as it were is as yet lifted up from the raging sea, there is but the ἀπολύτρωσις τοῦ πνεῦματος or νοὸς, to which afterwards, viii. 23, the ἀπολύτρωσις τοῦ σώματος must join; the σάρξ, and the ψυχή necessarily to be considered as united with it, the whole inferior region of life therefore, remains yet subject to the law of sin. Hence even in the regenerate the conflict lasts on, but it has lost its cheerless uniformity; in the power of Christ he knows he shall usually conquer in this battle, and if he sometime fall (in lesser things), he knows he shall soon get up again

* Should the act of regeneration be supposed to have come to pass earlier, it would appear strange, that from ver. 9 to 25 *the name of Christ* should not occur; this just entirely agrees with our acceptation.

† Stier erroneously understands this of a mere *delight* in the divine law in the thought of man, of equal signification with συνήδεσθαι above; it is, however, more than that, it is the *doing* of the law according to its *inward sense*, for in its coarser *exterior* the man may keep it even without grace. Such *doing* only can rightly be called δουλεύειν νόμῳ Θεοῦ, the δουλεύειν νόμῳ ἁμαρτίας which happens merely with the σάρξ, is no doing of sin, but a mere remaining exposed to the motions of the sinful flesh. (comp. Galat. v. 17.)

(1 John ii. 2); so that εἰρήνη governs now in that higher sphere of human being, where once the contest was most violent, because there the opposition to sin revealed itself most determinedly. Accordingly they, who belong to Christ, are quit of the condemning conscience, since the living spirit of Christ has made them free from sin and death (viii. 1, 2.) This new principle of life, however, is gradually to diffuse itself through the being of the man, until the ψυχή, nay the σῶμα, is glorified by it, and Christ becomes the ζωή for the whole man, that He may raise him up at the last day (Comp. Rom. viii. 11, with John vi. 44, &c. At both passages my commentary may be consulted.)

Notwithstanding that a most simple consistency results from this conception of the passage, it has been mistaken by almost all the older and later expositors,* nay Reiche would have the whole of ver. 25, which is so essential a member in the Apostle's description, considered as a gloss. Most of the others refer the ἄρα οὖν to the whole description of vii. 14–24,—so that ver. 25 is to represent the same state, which that section describes,—and the ἄρα οὖν (viii. 1), either to ch. v., or even as Tholuck would, to ch. iii. If no other acceptation of the passage could be made good, I would rather with Reiche strike out the verse, than determine upon so forced an interpretation. Perhaps the false division of the chapters may have prevented the right sense of the words from being found, for it is indeed as improper as it can be. The seventh chapter ought surely to close with ver. 24, and all would then go on in connexion; the strict particle of inference ἄρα and the γάρ following at viii. 2, 3, on no account allows the thread of the discourse to be broken here. But what can have induced the expositors so with one voice to find the same thing in ver. 25, as is expressed vii. 14–24, while the words are so palpably a declaration of something quite different? It was believed that because the νόμος τοῦ Θεοῦ was spoken of above also (ver. 23), that the νοῒ δουλεύω νόμῳ Θεοῦ was identical with the συνήδομαι τῷ νόμῳ τοῦ Θεοῦ (ver. 22), and again the δουλεύω σαρκὶ νόμῳ ἁμαρτίας identical with the before (ver. 15, 18, 23) described dominion of the νόμος ἁμαρτίας. But that is clearly not the Apostle's meaning.† In the

* Glöckler only *seems* to have conceived it rightly; he is, however, too brief in his explanation of the important words for his view to be clearly perceived.

† It might be said, it is not: ἡ σάρξ δουλεύει νόμῳ ἁμαρτίας, but ἐγὼ τῇ σαρκὶ

state of which first the need of redemption was a result, the *whole* man, the νοῦς therefore with him, was unable to serve the law of God, the better I itself was taken captive by the law of sin. But here the νοῦς appears as freed, and in this freedom serving the law of God, and only the lower sphere of life remains subjected to the law of sin. The νοῦς, however, being the ruling principle in the whole man, the law of God rules in it, and by it also in the whole man, albeit something indeed remains still to be got the better of and brought under, namely the flesh itself yet captive in the sinful element.*

For ἐυχαριστῶ τῷ Θεῷ the reading χάρις τῷ Θεῷ is found, which must however yield to the usual one, as having less critical foundation. The διὰ Ιησοῦ Χριστοῦ is not to be taken elliptically, with ἐσώθην for instance supplied, but to be connected with ἐυχαριστῶ. The thanksgiving offered to God *through* Christ testifies the redemption wrought by God *through* Christ. The ἀυτὸς ἐγώ is not to be construed "I myself," but *ego idem*, "I, the one and the same, have in me a twofold element." To be sure ἀυτός in this signification commonly has the article, but the ἐγώ supplies it here.

Chap. viii. 1. As the ἄρα οὖν, according to the acceptation given

δουλεύω ν. ἁ., and therefore the I, just as from ver. 14–24, might be supposed as serving sin. But ἐγώ in ver. 25 is not, as ver. 9 in the ἐγὼ ἀπέθανον, to be understood as denoting the better part in man, for this is signified by the νοῦς, which is distinguished from it, and which can now serve the law of God; but as denoting the personality in general. Now in the regenerate man the flesh is not the flesh of another, but *his own* flesh, *his* old man, consequently he also remains, the flesh merely considered, still as regenerate subjected to the law of sin. Galat. v. 17 is especially important for understanding the whole passage, and there principally the words: ἵνα μὴ, ἃ ἂν θέλητε, ταῦτα ποιῆτε. So also here Paul supposes in the believer that possibility of κατεργάζεσθαι, which is wanting in the merely awakened.

* Meyer makes the following objections to my acceptation: 1. "If Paul had intended to express the thought in this signification, he must have reversed the sentence: ἄρα οὖν ἀυτὸς ἐγὼ τῇ μὲν σαρκὶ δουλεύω νόμῳ ἁμαρτίας, τῷ δὲ νοῒ νόμῳ Θεοῦ." By no means; it was necessary that after the thanksgiving the progress should be immediately brought forward, of being now able with the νοῦς to serve the law of God; the suffering in arrear ought only to be mentioned afterwards. 2. "According to viii. 2, 3, the redeemed is *entirely* freed from the law of sin;" that is not so; the regenerate conquers in the conflict with sin, he has dominion over it, but he is not rid of it; this entire riddance is not effected until the glorification of the mortal body. 3. "If the redeemed still with the σάρξ remained subject to the law of sin, Paul could not say, viii. 1, ὀυδὲν ἄρα νῦν κατάκριμα." Answer; Paul can say so with full right, because the man is not free from condemnation, on account of his subjective condition, but for the sake of the objective work of Christ, which he lays hold of in faith.

above, is closely connected with the thanksgiving for the experienced redemption, so again is the ἄρα νῦν with the description of the state of the regenerate, in whom the conflict indeed has not altogether ceased, but is become a *victorious* one. Those, who have experienced redemption, are now in Christ (ὁι ἐν Χριστῷ Ἰησοῦ); that is, by real spiritual communion, by the indwelling of the Spirit of Christ, they are become spiritually united with him, members of His body, and as such they are freed from the κατάκριμα, from the sentence of God's justice that rejects sinners. And this, too, not merely in subjective feeling, so that they now *feel* the peace of God instead of the curse, but objectively also, so that their relation to God, and God's position towards them, is become another. The righteousness of Christ is *imputed* to the believer, so that he is *regarded* as though he were Christ; he is precious to God for the Beloved's sake, to whom he belongs, and whose life dwells in him. In thorough misconception of the passage, De Wette remarks, "The doctrines of satisfaction and justification are not to be intermixed here;" as if an exposition of the Christian religious development were possible, unless those doctrines formed the turning-points in it!

It only seems to strike one here, that this alteration commencing with the experience of redemption (νῦν) is derived in this passage from the *state of the sinner*, not from the objective act of Christ's redemption and atonement, as it was, iii. 25. But this difference of representation is easily explained from the different points of view taken here and there by Paul for his descriptions. There he was viewing the relation quite objectively, here he contemplates the subjective appropriation of that objective process. It is not, therefore, in any way his meaning, that forgiveness of sins and deliverance from condemnation is *effected* by the state of the man; rather that comes to pass by the sacrifice of the death of Christ alone; he would only say, that the subjective appropriation of this act of Christ is now first *acknowledged* and ensues with the actual experience of His redeeming power. The cause (Christ's death) and the effect (the regeneration of man) are, therefore, in the life necessarily together, they can only be separated and conceived in their different relations when they are considered abstractedly. Should it however be said, that a κατάκριμα remains still even for the regenerate, since their σάρξ (and the ψυχή united with it) is still subject to the law of sin (vii. 25); it is assuredly right, that where sin is, condemnation is, and that even the regenerate, therefore, is in need of *constant repetition* of forgiveness of sins when transgressions occur, be they in the eyes of men of ever so little importance. (1 John ii. 1.)* But as a tree once grafted is called a more generous one, although it may yet shoot water-sprouts below the graft, which may itself as yet be little developed; so is the regenerate man called perfect, pure, holy, without sin, free from all condemnation, for the sake of the divinely pure nature of the new element that is come into him, although this element, whose new course of development is in itself,† may as yet be taken up with the first beginnings of this development (1 John ii. 13, 14), and at times be repressed by the stirring powers of the σάρξ. Thus the seeming contradiction is reconciled, that whosoever is born of God doth not commit sin, because he *can* not sin, and yet sin still befals in the old man of the regenerate, which sin, because the old man is *his*, must be called *his* sin also. Nay, even if a regenerate man falls away from faith, the regenerate man, as such, has not sinned, but the old man, again grown mighty by that man's fault, has again thrust out the germ of the new man from his nature. That the new man, however, the *Christ in us*, is not, even in the most advanced development of the regenerate, the *ground* of favour, but the *token* of it only, must ever be maintained, as he withdraws himself at times entirely from the man; the ground of acceptance to favour with God is and remains the *Christ for us*. (As to the state of the text of viii. 1, the mistaken interpretation of vii. 25 could alone have suggested the alteration of the import-

* Upon the sins of the regenerate, Luther thus aptly expresses himself: "If the regenerate had no sin, he would not come so well off. For if I felt not sin, the evil life and conscience, I should never relish so the power of the divine Word." Sin itself must therefore be the means, for evermore urgently seeking the power of Christ. It may be said that this is a dangerous doctrine, for so a man might make light of sin and abuse grace! It is certainly possible; but upon this possibility it has nevertheless seemed good to God to free the faithful from the yoke of sin. Such knavery of sin, that makes an abuse of the holiest gift of God, must surely come to light. The truly regenerate, if he trace any sound of it in himself, will only so much the more zealously abhor sin; if he did not so, he would be in process of apostacy from faith. The man who only in self-deceit holds himself as regenerate, will, if uprightness be in him, thereby be frightened out of his error. The insincere hypocrite, however, who can calmly carry on such a wanton abuse, fancies indeed he can deceive God and man, but is properly only deceiving himself, and has his reward that way.

† [*Or*—"which contains in itself his (*i.e.*, the man's) new course of development." B.]

ant νῦν into οὖν. It is the very note of the new state of regeneration, and is entirely necessary here. On the contrary, the addition : *μὴ κατὰ σάρκα περιπατοῦσιν, ἀλλὰ κατὰ πνεῦμα*, [the first half of which only is found in some critical authorities], is wanting in the best Codd. B.C.D.F.G., and betrays itself, moreover, so evidently as a gloss borrowed from ver. 4, in order to guard against a misconception of the *ὀυδὲν κατάκριμα*, that it is at all events to be struck out. The words are intended namely to attach a *condition*, and are to be translated : if so be they walk according to the Spirit, &c. For if they were merely to signify the character of the regenerate, they would run : *τοῖς ὀν κατὰ σάρκα περιπατοῦσιν κ. τ. λ.*)

Ver. 2. The following representation then describes, as is generally acknowledged, the way and manner of the formation of the regenerate state. The man draws not himself, but a Power that makes free, that looses the bond, draws him from the *αἰχμαλωσία* of sin (comp. vii. 23), namely *ὁ νόμος τοῦ πνεύματος τῆς ζωῆς*. As (John viii. 36) the Son appears as the only one who indeed makes free, so here also it is said : *ὁ νόμος τοῦ πνεύματος ἐν Χριστῷ Ἰησοῦ ἠλευθέρωσέ με*. It is only that the contrast with the law of sin and of death proceeding from sin may stand more clearly to view, that Christ is here comprehended in the law of the spirit of life founded by Him. For in the aorist *ἠλευθέρωσε* is signified here not the once-done act of Christ, but, as De Wette rightly observes, the laying hold of the work of Christ's redemption in faith. The possibility of this laying hold is, then, ver. 3, grounded on the act of Christ. Both life and death, however, are comprehended in their absoluteness, as Christ himself is called the Life and the Resurrection, being the conqueror of death. If, further, the name of a *νόμος* is assigned to the *πνεῦμα τῆς ζωῆς*, this is with regard to vii. 22, where the *νόμος τοῦ Θεοῦ* was spoken of, and in contrast with the *νόμος τῆς ἁμαρτίας*. The expression has its inward truth ; the divine is in itself the legal,* only it so represents itself in Christ to man, that it brings with it the power to satisfy the very claims which it establishes. That the faithful, therefore, fulfil the law is not their *own work* (and consequently gives no

* [*Das Gesetzmässige*, that which is according to law.] The law, the inward impulse of the Spirit, is to be holy and to make holy ; the law of the flesh is, to be unholy and to make unholy. Both lust constantly against each other (Galat. v. 17.) Comp. at iii. 27, *νόμος τῆς πίστεως*.

merit) but God's work in them (Ephes. ii. 8–10) by His Spirit that giveth life. Whether, moreover, the expression *ὁ νόμος τοῦ πνεύματος τῆς ζωῆς* is construed like *πνεύματος καὶ τῆς ζωῆς*, or as *πνεύματος ζωοποιοῦντος* is essentially the same thing as far as regards the thought. For the Spirit is the true life, and, therefore, alone capable of imparting it, of animating death itself.

Ver. 3. The incapacity of the law (as a divine institution for salvation) to deliver man from sin, made, as Paul had set forth at large in the beginning of the Epistle, the other way necessary, namely, the sending of the Son of God in the flesh, to attack sin in its root.

Τὸ ἀδύνατον is to be taken as absolute accusative, "touching the incapability of the law."—*Ἐν ᾧ* = בַּאֲשֶׁר "in that, in as far as," of like signification with *ἐφ' ᾧ*, comp. at v. 12 (used also classically, comp. Bernhardy's Syntax, p. 211). Thus *ἐν ᾧ* is found, Heb. vi. 17, but not, as De Wette thinks, Heb. ii. 18, 1 Pet. ii. 12, nor John xvi. 30 ;* in these passages it is the relative with the preposition.—The law might perhaps avail somewhat with the perfect, but the sinfulness of human nature hinders its efficacy. (Comp. at vii. 12, 13.)

In the description of the sending of the Son of God, all stress is laid upon the *identity of the human nature*, in which he appeared, with ours. The incapacity of the law, to bring forth true holiness, lay not in itself (vii. 12), but in corrupted human nature, which robbed the divine law of its strength (*ἠσθένει*).† Hence this sinful nature was to be in Christ's person destroyed in the divine judgment (*κατέκρινε τὴν ἁμαρτίαν ἐν τῇ σαρκί*). It seems remarkable, however, that the Apostle uses here the expression, *πέμψας τὸν ἑαυτοῦ υἱὸν* (*υἱός* is used in its strictly proper sense of the eternal, divine nature of the Son, and the greatness of God's love is intended to be set forth by the *ἑαυτοῦ*), *ἐν ὁμοιώματισαρκὸς ἁμαρτίας*, for by this the human nature of Christ himself seems to be described as sinful. But had Paul meant to say, that Christ's human nature (for *σάρξ* signifies here, as Rom. i. 4, by synecdoche

* [A wrong reference.]

† When Hebr. vii. 18, an *ἀσθενὲς καὶ ἀνωφελές* of the law is spoken of, the expression is not to be understood of the *nature* of the law but of its *working*, which is powerless on account of the sin of men. Therefore Paul calls it, Galat. iii. 21, *μὴ δυνάμενος ζωοποιῆσαι*.

the whole humanity of spirit, soul, and body) was sinful, as fallen human nature is; he must then have written ἐν σαρκὶ ἁμαρτίας, not ἐν ὁμοιώματι σαρκὸς ἁμαρτίας. Adam's nature, too, before the fall, was the ὁμοίωμα of man's nature now; he became not by the fall specifically another, *the same man* merely became corrupt. Here it lay in the Apostle's course, to bring forward more immediately the *affinity* of Christ's nature with ours; he is silent, therefore, upon the *difference* between them. This difference, however, must be so conceived, that the Redeemer, certainly before the resurrection, wore no σῶμα τῆς δόξης, but a σῶμα ταπεινώσεως (Phil. iii. 21), that was affected with an ἀσθένεια τῆς σαρκός (2 Cor. xiii. 4); but his humanity, notwithstanding, was *free from positive sinfulness*, as begotten of the Holy Ghost. That ἀσθένεια has then the aim, to mediate the possibility of temptation (comp. at Matt. iv. 1, &c.), which our Lord had to suffer, in order to become the conqueror over evil (Heb. ii. 14, 17, 18, iv. 15). Thus the two equally necessary moments were united in Christ; connection with mankind unto one true unity of life, and the exaltation above mankind, that he might lift them out of their misery.

Ὁμοιότης is properly, analogously as ἁγιότης, the being like, and ὁμοίωμα, the made like, an image. Paul uses it, however, also like ὁμοιότης. So Rom. i. 23, v. 14, vi. 5, and, besides, Phil. ii. 7. James iii. 9, ὁμοίωσις is found. So also in the LXX., Gen. i. 26. Now if the sinfulness of human nature were nothing but a mere deficiency, the filling of mankind with the life of the Son of God would have sufficed to scare it away. But since beside this deficiency in spiritual life there is a real disturbance of the harmony in the inner and outer man, more than the mere incarnation was requisite, namely the extirpation of the guilt and the restitution of the disturbed order by the founding of a centre, from which harmony might pour forth through all the spheres of life, even as from Adam disharmony had been diffused (comp. at Rom. v. 12, &c.). This thought however is not to be pressed upon the καὶ περὶ ἁμαρτίας, which words are rather to be connected with the preceding in the simple sense, "on account of sin," "by reason of sin," as ground for the sending of the Son of God; but it lies in the κατέκρινε τὴν ἁμαρτίαν ἐν τῇ σαρκί.* There is no foundation whatever for finding

* Neander (apost. Zeitalt. B. ii. s. 544, note), explains the κατέκρινε τὴν ἁμαρ-

in the *περὶ ἁμαρτίας* a reference to the sacrifice of Christ's death, so that *ἁμαρτία* = אָשָׁם should mean sin-offering (comp. at 2 Cor. v. 21). The closing words of the verse, on the contrary, express most decidedly the vicarious and atoning death of the Saviour. For the *κατέκρινε* evidently has retrospect to the *οὐδὲν κατάκριμα* (viii. 1), so that the sense of the words is this: no *κατάκριμα* falls on *them*, because *He* took it on Him; He stands, therefore, in the stead of mankind, bears what should fall on them, and so effects all which the law could not effect, which all comprises in itself the reconciliation of God. As therefore in the *sending* of the Son the *love* of God expressed itself, so in the *giving of Him up* His righteousness did, while the Son represents *compassion*, in that of *His own accord* He let Himself be sent and given up to death. Thus is the divine righteousness, as its nature requires, thoroughly satisfied, and at the same time a sinful world is saved by love. For the sin condemned in the death of Christ is not the sin of some, but the sin of the world, which the Lord bore in His flesh (ἐν τῇ σαρκί scil. *αὐτοῦ*), so that the words are equal to the saying of Peter (1 Pet. ii. 24): *τὰς ἁμαρτίας ἡμῶν ἀυτὸς ἀνήνεγκεν ἐν τῷ σώματι ἀυτοῦ ἐπὶ τὸ ξύλον*. How Christ's suffering and Christ's death can be the suffering and death of the collective whole (so far as they are one with Him in faith), became perceptible to us by the idea of the representation (comp at v. 12, &c.), according to which Christ is not *a* man, but *the* man, the real comprisal of the totality, It is difficult, however, to suppose the sin of the collective race in the Holy One, so that they could be condemned in Him; for it may be conceived, how the Redeemer could be the representative of the *holy* part of mankind, but it is not so clear, how He was able to represent the *unholy* also, which nevertheless seems to follow from that sentence. As this consideration was not entered into at the passage v. 12, &c., the following notice may perhaps help to remove the difficulty in making such relation perceptible. As there is but one personality in the regenerate man, and yet this one person *distinguishes* in itself the old and new man, and at the same time acknowledges both as *its own*,

τίαν by: "he took away sin, broke its power," and appeals to John xii. 31, xvi. 11, where, however, *κρίνειν* is quite properly condemn. Neander chooses this explanation, because he thinks that he must refer *ἀδύνατον τοῦ νόμου* to the *κατακρίνειν τὴν ἁμαρτίαν*, which is by no means necessary.

so Christ represented in the divine and human unity of His person the collective members of a race that form one whole. In this race the oppositions of the old and of the new man are set forth as tendencies of the good and of the evil, and so far then as Christ represents the inseparable and indivisible sum, He represents also in Himself the tendency of sin. Spiritually, indeed, His holy Being was totally separate from sin, and even bodily he was connected with the world of sin but loosely, since the indwelling Spirit was ever raising even His σῶμα, while yet His earthly sojourn lasted, from the ταπείνωσις of the natural life to the δόξα of the divine; but loose as this His bond with the sinful world was in itself, so intimate did it become through that *love*, that fills the foreign to it with its own being.* And in the power of this love the Lord identified Himself essentially with sinful men, His relation being to them, as their new man to the old. As therefore the new man in the regenerate thrusts not from him the I, that still bears in it the old man, but even identifies himself essentially with it and bears all which the old man brings dragging after it; neither did the Saviour in His sojourn upon earth thrust mankind from Him, for having in it still its old man, the evil tendency; but He penetrated even its inmost centre, identified Himself entirely with it, and though, indeed, he bore the whole pressure of the world's sin and all its consequences, even thereby He won His very adversaries, and so converted the whole into Himself. Whilst He then first became like mankind, afterwards mankind became like Him! Accordingly neither the taking upon Himself the sin of the world on the part of the Son, nor the laying of the sin upon the Son (as the Lamb of Sacrifice) on the part of the Father, is, consistently with

* The mystery of love, which allows a transition into a foreign being, and becomes like it, without giving up its own nature, is treated of at large by the Apostle Paul under the *figure of marriage*, especially Ephes. v. 25, &c. By the power of love Christ became entirely as the sinful world, so that He, as Luther's expression is, could say with truth, "poor sinner that I am," and remained notwithstanding, by his nature, specifically separate from sin. He only changed with mankind, took their sin upon himself, and gave them His righteousness and holiness. The possibility of such an exchange becomes perceptible from the nature of evil. Christ could not love sinful humanity as His bride, if it were substantially sin; but as sin only cleaves to it, he loves the germ of the divine left in it. If now sin were a mere μὴ ὄν, it could not well be seen how the essential union with this divine germ of life could prepare suffering and death for Christ; but if sin is taken to be real disturbance of the original harmony of life, such an union must necessarily have had as its consequence, that the Redeemer was smitten by the whole violence of that disharmony which sin had generated upon earth.

this representation, to be considered as a mere act of the will, which must always retain something arbitrary in it; but as something given with the incarnation itself. Then has this event its analogy in every act of compassionate love. Whoever would help another panting under a heavy burden, must go under it and bear its whole pressure himself; or, to give an example from spiritual things, whoever would bring the salvation in Christ to the Negroes or any other rude people, must enter into their necessity, must bear all the burden of their corrupted sinful nature, must, as it were, first become like them, to form them like himself. Thus also does the Lord from heaven lower Himself into sinful humanity, and bears essentially its sin, with all its consequences, of which death is the heaviest.

The reference of ver. 3 to the active obedience of Christ can forcibly only be traced in the words. The connection namely is simply this. What the law could not do, Christ can. The law was not able to take away the *κατάκριμα*, it served rather only to increase it; but Christ takes it away, in that He takes it upon Himself; this comes to pass by the vicarious, atoning sacrifice of His death. It certainly implies as well, that Christ founded absolute righteousness, else the *κατάκριμα* would ever again have generated in man; but that is not the chief thought *here*, it is in ver. 4 that the active obedience decidedly appears. The most that can be said is, that as it must constantly be affirmed of the life of Christ, that passive and active obedience every moment penetrate each other in Him, so even here His *surrender* into death presupposes the highest *activity*. There is no necessity for supplying *ἀυτοῦ* exactly at *ἐν τῇ σαρκί*, but certainly *τῶν ἀνθρώπων οὖσαν* ought not to be supplied. The expression embraces rather the flesh of Christ and of men together. He represented the totality; what therefore came to pass in Him, was essentially the event also to all. However, the prevailing idea requires, that the sentence should immediately be understood as completed thus: *Θεὸς κατέκρινε τὴν ἁμαρτίαν ἀνθρώπων ἐν σαρκὶ Χριστοῦ.*

Ver. 4. Now immediately next in order to the description of the way of God in sending Christ follows the delineation of the efficacy of Christ; what the law could not, the gospel is able to do, in that it condemns sin, namely, to call forth in man the state of true holiness. Evidently, then, it is not according to the context the Apostle's meaning, that this state is the *condition* of partaking in Christ's word, but the *consequence.* He presupposes already the περιπατεῖν κατὰ πνεῦμα, and this again the experience of the redeeming power of Christ (vii. 25). But so surely as the Catholic acceptation is wrong, as surely is the exaggeration of the Evangelical interpretation to be rejected, according to which sanctification is considered as quite parted from the forgiveness of sins. According to the genuine doctrine of the Reformers, which rests upon this apostolic passage, sanctification of life necessarily (although at first in germ only) comes with the appropriation of Christ's work, not however as stated condition, but rather as consequence of the forgiveness imparted in free grace without condition.

The πληρωθῇ ἐν ἡμῖν distinctly indicates, that sanctification of life is none of man's own work, but that God in Christ perfects it in man; hence δι' ἀυτοῦ only need be supplied. *We* do not fulfil the law, but the work of Christ is our work; by His Spirit He imparts His righteousness and holiness unto us. The perfection of every individual therefore in Christ's life is to be considered as already completed, entirely according to viii. 30; as in His death the sin of every individual appears condemned. The expression δικαίωμα τοῦ νόμου comprises all, which the law can in any respect whatever require; it is the absolute δικαιοσύνη considered as command of God. The addition τοῖς μὴ κατὰ σαρκὰ κ. τ. λ. is to define the ἡμεῖς more nearly, so that the sense is: the effect of Christ's appearing applies to those only who walk after the Spirit, have therefore experienced in themselves, vii. 25. Christ's work indeed is reckoned for all, but it first reveals itself in its sanctifying efficacy, when the man appropriates it personally.

Vers. 5, 6. This state of κατὰ πνεῦμα περιπατεῖν Paul now describes more nearly by its contrast. It is that, namely, in which the believer tarries* here below, until his bodily glorification (viii. 11), for if the state be capable of a heightening in itself, yet man can never get beyond it in this earthly life. Its proper character, however, is best perceived by the κατὰ σαρκὰ περιπατεῖν = τὰ τῆς σαρκὸς φρονεῖν, = φρόνημα τῆς σαρκός, = ἐν σαρκὶ εἶναι (ver. 9), and = κατὰ σαρκὰ ζῆν (ver. 12). All this is consequent on κατὰ σαρκὰ εἶναι, which expression is of like signification with γεγεννημένον ἐκ τῆς σαρκός (John iii. 6). The Apostle, certainly,

* [Ps. xxvii. 15, 16, Prayer-book version.]

would have no life of vice to be understood by this; but the very state described vii. 14–24, in which the νοῦς is taken captive by the law of sin in the σάρξ. To this the οὐδὲ γὰρ δύναται (viii. 7), in connection with the ἀδύνατον τοῦ νόμου (viii. 3), most distinctly points. But then the περιπατεῖν κατὰ πνεῦμα = φρονεῖν τὰ τοῦ πνεύματος = φρόνημα τοῦ πνεύματος = ἐν πνεύματι εἶναι (ver. 9), and = πνεύματι ἄγεσθαι (ver. 14), (all this is consequent on κατὰ πνεῦμα εἶναι, which expression is of like signification with γεγεννημένον ἐκ τοῦ πνεύματος, John iii. 6) is the very state described vii. 25, in which the νοῦς can serve the divine law, and the σάρξ only remains subjected to the law of sin. The walking after the Spirit does not, therefore, exclude attacks on the part of sin, temptations of the flesh, even single smaller transgressions are not thereby denied (1 John ii. 1); but the *direction of the whole inner man* to God and the *victory over sin essentially* and in the whole is thereby asserted. The advance in the new man, the development in the walking in the Spirit, is altogether not to be considered as a *gradual transition* of the old man into the new, or as a constantly progressing conversion of the former into the latter; but as in the sum of mankind, the tares are developed *beside* the wheat, and good and evil come to their full in parallel rows, so does the old man continue to the last beside the new man; and it may not be that, the further the spiritual development advances, so much the nearer an approximation takes place between them, but the reverse; as spirit and flesh lust continually against each other, so must the Christ in us lust more and more against the old Adam. The right conception of this relation is, therefore, of the highest importance, because, according to the light in which the regenerate man beholds it in himself, his whole effort at sanctification is formed. If he seeks gradually to improve the old man in him, and to wash it clean, he not only undertakes a labour utterly in vain, but he is also in constant danger of falling back under the law, as it happened to the Galatians; nay, this very striving is properly the retreat already beginning. The old man cannot be sanctified, but he must be crucified, that is, *be given unto death in self-denial.**

* In this spiritual death of the old man the law of the Old Testament keeps its full right, when it requires the death of the sinner. But the *gracious* and *righteous* God so fulfils His strict justice, that he makes life itself the killer, so that he who dies in the old man first finds in this very death the true life.

From the Spirit, therefore, a constant war must be kept up against the flesh and its lusts. This conflict, however, is but the negative side in the life of the regenerate; the positive activity that furthers his new life is the constant keeping up of intercourse with the originator and the abiding well-spring of this new life. Thereby he receives on and on the πνεῦμα from above, and the man born of grace lives and grows, too, on and on, in grace and by grace, So the man shares rightly law. and gospel; the new man lives in the gospel, the sharpest law is given to the old man by the new, and the man is not *without* law by not being *under* the law, but is living *with* the law of God, of which, certainly, the old man only is in need, for the new man has it in his very nature, he *can* not sin (1 John iii. 9), as little as the sun can darken. Regarded from a human point of view, moreover, the possibility of apostacy remains still for every regenerate man upon every standard of development, even upon the highest, that is, that the new man may be thrust aside by the old; but just as decidedly we must say, that, regarded from the divine point of view, it is impossible for the elect of God to be overpowered by sin. Were it possible, namely, with one, it would be so with all, and then God's plans would be dependent upon man's fidelity; it might happen, that the whole world fell away. This is, of course, inconceivable, and impossible (Matt. xxiv. 24)! Hence, as in Christ's temptation, freedom and necessity penetrate each other in the regenerate; their relation will be treated more at large at chap. ix. and xi.

In the φρονεῖν, φρόνημα, the *constant* direction of the whole inward being towards something is expressed; this alone determines the true constitution of the man. (Comp. my opusc. theol. pag. 159.) At viii. 6, comp. the parallel, vi. 23, where ζωή stands alone, while here εἰρήνη is united with it.

Vers. 6–8. The reason why carnal mindedness works death, is no other than this; because this disposition separates from God (the Fountain of Life). That which is akin to Him alone can please the Holy One, but the carnal mind is unable to generate anything well-pleasing to God; even its good works are an abomination to Him, because they come from impure, selfish motives. No one, however, can set himself free from himself, a higher love must come, that attracts him more than his own I. The notion of ἔχθρα must not be softened. The carnal man hates God, for he sees in Him the robber only of his lust; and God hates him according to His holiness; the two are thoroughly and irreconcileably against each other. But so God hates not *man* as such, He loves him rather, but He hates the sin in him. This holy hate passes to the regenerate; he hates in himself and others sin and carnal mindedness, without hating men.

The inability in the νοῦς to submit to the divine law (viii. 3), is the cause of the conflict (vii. 23), and so of the want of peace. The ability to fulfil the law (viii. 4) God is well pleased in, as His own work, and it gives the soul the taste of peace with God. Ver. 8, δέ forms no antithesis, but only carries on the same thought.

Ver. 9. Here then the Apostle makes the transition to his readers, whom he naturally treats as regenerate, who walk after the Spirit. For if ἔιπερ seems to express a doubt, it is only seeming, as it is not to be construed here like *si modo*, but as *siquidem*, as sure and certain presupposition. (Comp. thereon Hartung's Partikellehre, Part i. p. 327, &c., 344, &c, where πέρ in its relation to γέ in its fundamental meaning is excellently displayed.) The Being of the Spirit in the believer is conceived as an ὀικεῖν of Him, like vii. 18, where the ὀικεῖν of sin in the flesh was spoken of. The divine Spirit dwells, of course, in that part of human nature most kindred to Him, in the πνεῦμα or νοῦς. The ὀικεῖν, however, is opposed to that fleeting passage and breathing-through of the Spirit, as it appears in the O. T. in the prophets, for which the word φέρεσθαι is used (2 Pet. i. 21), as contrast to the ἄγεσθαι of the N. T. (ver. 14, Galat. v. 18), by which the constant, unbroken operation of the indwelling Spirit is signified, the life of Christ in us, Galat. ii. 20. The ὀικεῖν is therefore like the μένειν of John (comp. at John i. 33, in the comm.) and the ἔχειν πνεῦμα, which occurs in the verse before us. In the latter expression, the man appears as though he were the possessor and governor of the Spirit, that yet, however, possesses him, and governs his inmost being, by which idea the ἔστιν ἀυτοῦ at the end of the verse is to be explained; *to be Christ's*, namely, is to be a member of Him, to be governed, guided by Him. The opposite would be ἔιναι διαβόλου, comp. at John viii. 44. But in fact the man also possesses the Spirit within him (as the husband indeed is the lord of the wife, but yet the wife also possesses the husband), in so far, namely, as he may drive Him away by unfaithfulness, nay in so far as he has the privilege of conducting this Spirit according to the intended aim (1 Cor. xiv. 32). The words *ἐι δέ τις πνεῦμα Χριστοῦ οὐκ ἔχει* point to this possibility of apostacy, for the question here cannot be of entire unbelievers ; either therefore the recreant must be meant, or at least those who are in conflict indeed against sin, but have not yet experienced the redeeming power of Christ (vii. 25). At all events the words are to contain the warning, that the benefits of Christ are then only to be appropriated when a man is conscious by faith, and the Spirit received in faith, of being a member in the body of Christ. The possession of this Spirit of Christ, however, is naturally not to be measured according to the mere *feeling* (the agreeable sensation of the nearness of God, of comfort, of spiritual joy), for this is too fleeting, and the state of grace may be entirely unimpaired, even in great barrenness and dryness,* nay, in the progress of the inward life, the sweet sensations of the first young love are almost ever disappearing, but according to its real *effects* and *fruits*. If the man observes not these in himself, and temptations at the same time increase and strengthen, then at all events he is in a suspicious, assaulted state.

It is to be observed that the Apostle, from ver. 8–11, uses *δέ* six times one after the other. The expressions *πνεῦμα Θεοῦ* and *Χριστοῦ* alternate (comp., besides, ver. 11, 14) ; *πνεῦμα ἅγιον* might have been said (comp. ver. 16). For Father, Son, and Spirit are *One*,† although not *One Person* ;‡ "I am in the Father and the Father is in me," saith the Lord. (Comp. the Commentary at John x. 30, xiv. 10.) The background of the whole representation before the soul of the Apostle is, that whosoever is not Christ's belongs to the kingdom of darkness. Independent man cannot be, according to his whole constitution ; he cannot stand *between* light and darkness ; he must ever incline to the one or the other. (Comp. at John viii. 44.)

Ver. 10, 11. The Apostle, in a conclusion, points at last to the highest stage of the perfection of the individual life, to the glorification of the body. As it was said in Paradise, "if thou eatest of the tree of knowledge of good and evil, thou shalt surely die," so does the enjoyment of the true tree of life, of Christ, bring again to perfect life, even of the body.§ This passage has its commentary

* [Ps. lxiii. 2, P. B. version.] † [*Eins*, ἕν.] ‡ [*Einer*, εἷς.]

§ [Leiblichkeit.] De Wette's remark ad loc. is pertinent: "*An inward bodily-spi-*

in John vi., where Christ represents himself as the ζωή in all respects, even of the body. Whatever, therefore, at the transition into the state of regeneration (vii. 25) was left behind, the δουλεύειν τῇ σαρκὶ νόμῳ ἁμαρτίας, is here likewise considered as overcome; even the body has experience of redemption (viii. 23). As σῶμα stands here instead of the former σάρξ, it is clear that the Apostle means decidedly the material side of human existence, naturally however in union with the whole psychical life, without which there is neither σῶμα nor σάρξ, but κρέας. But if the σῶμα is here called νεκρόν, it is self-evident that this expression is not to signify absolute deadness, for it is intended to describe the very living body in its natural constitution; it is to be taken rather as ἁμαρτία νεκρά, vii. 8. The ἁμαρτία is called dead, because it does not yet express and make itself known in its true nature, so neither does the body, which, according to its original destination, is something far more glorious than it now appears. Hence it cannot be said that νεκρός is = θνητός; the latter expression is used in its proper physical sense, according to which the living only can be mortal; but the former is used in a figurative sense. Therefore the passage would be entirely perverted, if, instead of νεκρόν, θνητόν should be put. For this sinful state certainly the deadness of the body is so far good, as it lessens the susceptibility for the disturbing and painful impressions, of the outward world (wherefore the nobler bodily nature of Christ must have enhanced His suffering), but it remains still a most imperfect state, which must be overcome. Sure pledge then for the glorification of a man's own body is given by the consciousness of that awakening power dwelling in the Spirit of God, which has verified itself in the waking of Christ from the dead. It may yet be remarked, that the Apostle represents the resurrection as though it were merely something imparted to the holy, as though there were no resurrection of the wicked. It might certainly be said here, that Paul is treating only of the course of the development of the faithful, that the wicked are

ritual process is here spoken of, not an event occurring from without, as the resurrection is usually understood." Even so; without this conception the scriptural doctrine of the bodily glorification, which is constantly represented as going on already here below (comp. especially at 2 Cor. iv. 10, 11), would be thoroughly unintelligible. But this life of bodily glorification forming itself in gradual process, comes in many as if by a flash of lightning, at once into appearance (1 Cor. xv. 52), and so is the resurrection of the dead represented.

out of the question; but by the similar representation, 1 Cor. xv. 22, where the glance of the Apostle seems to comprehend all men, and by the circumstance, that he never makes mention of the resurrection of the wicked, and once only of eternal damnation (2 Thess. i. 9), the matter becomes more difficult. The difficulty however must be reserved for further discussion at the passage adduced from the Epistle to the Corinthians.

Upon the doctrine of the glorified body comp. more particularly at 1 Cor. xv., 2 Cor. v. It was preliminarily spoken of at John vi., and at the history of the resurrection. By the readings ζῶν, ζῇ, the contrast to *νεκρόν* is intended to be more distinctly shewn; for that very reason, however, ζωή is surely the original reading. *Δι' ἁμαρτίας* and *διὰ δικαιοσύνης* might have been said; but the accusative brings forward not so much the means as the presence, " on account of the sin present in the body, on account of the righteousness communicated by the *νοῦς*."—*Δικαιοσύνη* is here also the state of *δίκαιον εἶναι*, the *δικαιωθῆναι*.—*Ζωοποιεῖν* is used of the bodily awakening according to 1 Cor. xv. 22. At the close of ver. 11, also, the *text. rec.* has the lighter reading of *διὰ c. genit.* D.E.F.G., however, several translations, and many of the Fathers, have the accusative. Lachmann has decided on the usual reading, as Knapp has; Griesbach, Koppe, Rückert, Reiche, on the other hand, decide for the accusative. This I too hold as more appropriate, but not so much because I consider, as Reiche does, that the genitive has arisen from dogmatic principles (in order to represent the Holy Ghost as operating more independently), but simply for the sake of the context, in connection with the stronger critical authorities, and because by taking the genitive the sense appears lightened. The accusative represents the indwelling of the Spirit as *pledge* of the glorification which shall be of the body; and that enters best into the train of Paul's ideas. *'Ενοικέω* is found besides at 2 Cor. vi. 16, Col. iii. 16, of the spiritual penetrating of the human spirit by the divine. All the *material* is here naturally to be excluded, but the *real* nevertheless to be maintained; such expressions are not to be reduced to mere Oriental phrases, since they have life and being. As surely as the spirit is immaterial, yet really dwells in the material body, so surely does the Divine Spirit penetrate and unite with the human, without annulling His essence, or confounding His inward laws; for the human spirit is the very organ for the divine, and that is a perverse state (sin) if He is not working in it. We have too little knowledge of the substance of the spirit to get a clear insight into such penetration of spirit by Spirit, meanwhile nature offers analogies not to be rejected in the material, for instance, the penetration of electric or magnetic streams.

Ver. 12, 13. These verses seem to interrupt the chain of the discourse, which proceeds again, in strict connection with the foregoing part, at ver. 14. They give the impression of an onset to a parænesis, which is not completely carried out. A very strict connection, however, might result, if the *μέλλετε ἀποθνήσκειν* and *ζήσεσθε* were only definitely referred to the glorification of the body, so that the sense would be formed as follows : " Since such glory (of bodily glorification) awaits us, we are so much the more obliged to live according to the spirit, that we may not lose such glorification, but receive it." Then " the mortifying the deeds of the body " would very fitly denote the advancing bodily sanctification, which is considered as means to bodily glorification. And in the dying and living not merely the general states of misery and happiness would be indicated (which, according to the special glorification of the body, would be something very feeble), but the obtaining and losing this grace of bodily glorification be made prominent. Now that *ζῆν* should signify glorification, can make no difficulty, for this is in fact the *summit of life*, and therefore, at John vi. 40, and frequently, *ζωὴν αἰώνιον ἔχειν* is used in equal signification with the capacity of being raised up at the last day. It might however appear more difficult, that *μέλλετε ἀποθνήσκειν* should be : " Ye will not obtain the resurrection." Notwithstanding if it be considered, that at John vi. 50, *μὴ ἀποθανεῖν* also is used in equal signification with the *ἀνάστασις ἐν τῇ ἐσχάτῃ ἡμέρα*, consequently, that dying is taken equal to not attaining to the resurrection, and that, further, the Apostle supposed the time of our Lord's coming again to be near, and was hoping still to be while in the body clothed upon (2 Cor. v. 2, &c.) ; then the bodily dying of the carnal may, without hesitation, be taken synonymously with the loss of bodily glorification, and it cannot here be conceived otherwise, if a strict connection is to unite this verse with what precedes and follows. The mere general observation, that those who walk after the flesh die, would be, according to the special thoughts immediately preceding and following, altogether too feeble, and nothing but a repetition of what was said at viii. 6, &c.

Comp. upon ὀφειλέτης at i. 14. The condition of debtors has reference to the union entered into with Christ. (Comp. vi. 18.) The πράξεις denotes here the individual sinful tendencies of the old man, his members as it were, which must be crucified (Gal. v. 24). The life of the regenerate, therefore, as already observed, is to be a gradual *crucifying* of the old man, not a *bettering* of it; the holy, but granted life, is in the new man only. So the man becomes perfect, and yet continues poor in humility, for what he has is God's work, not his property. The reading σαρκός is seemingly more conformable to usage than σώματος, but on that very account it is certainly a mere correction. Paul uses σῶμα also in such combinations; comp. vii. 24.

Vers. 14, 15. Most unconstrainedly now, after the proposed acceptation of the words of the preceding verse, the subject continues. The mortifying of the deeds of the flesh is a being led by the Spirit, and therefore not (like the former striving described vii. 14–24) an anxious task of law, but a working in joyous spirit, as if owning the cause, as the sons of the house work for themselves in their Father's business. We do not deny ourselves, in order *to be saved thereby*, but because *we are saved in hope* by grace. The communion in the pains of the Son of God κατ' ἐξοχήν, secures then, too, the communion in His glory, that is, in the entire perfection, the glorification even of the body (viii. 17–23.) Those who are born of the flesh are flesh, those born of the Spirit are spirit (John iii. 6.) All πνευματικοί therefore, in the true sense of the word, are children of God, of the absolute πνεῦμα (John iv. 24.) Thus Paul arrives quite consistently at the idea of υἱοὶ Θεοῦ, which he maintains as the thread of his argument until ver. 17, and still pursues in the following weighty section (from viii. 18.) The ἄγεσθαι πνεύματι Θεοῦ, accordingly, is not to be understood of the influence of a foreign power, giving as it were its impulse from without, but it is to be considered as the element of life, as deciding the tone of character and being, so that the Spirit of God generates also, where He works, a higher, heavenly consciousness, a man of God, a son of God.* This sonship of God, how-

* Comp. as parallel the expression of Olympiodor (Comm. in Plat. Alcib. p. 123, edit. Creuzer): κρεῖττον τὸ θεόθεν ἄγεσθαι, ἢ ὑφ' ἑαυτοῦ.

ever, men receive merely as one derived from the original Son, the Logos, the μονογενής and πρωτότοκος (viii. 29.) The difference of ἄγεσθαι (Galat. v. 18) and φέρεσθαι (2 Pet. i. 21) was spoken of above at ver. 9. But here Paul is not contrasting the abiding of the Spirit's operation in the N. T. to its alternation in the Old, but bondage to freedom or sonship. In the O. T., namely, God meets man as the holy, righteous principle, foreign to the sinner, living outward to mankind, opposing to him His strict requirements and awakening the φόβος τοῦ Θεοῦ, the *beginning* of Wisdom (Ps. cxi. 10); in the N. T., on the contrary, God appears in Christ most intimately connected and allied with mankind, awakening therefore that love, which in its perfection drives away all fear (1 John iv. 18), and not only requires, but gives also what it requires. But God gives nothing of less value than His own being and nature, because nothing is enough for Him, but Himself; therefore is the state of freedom in love identical with sonship. As spirit born of Spirit, therefore, the faithful of the N. T. are greater than the greatest, that are born of women (Matt. xi. 11), children, namely, of the heavenly mother, the Jerusalem above (Galat. iv. 26.)

Upon υἱὸς Θεοῦ comp. the observations at Luke i. 35. The phrase differs from τέκνον Θ (ver. xvi. 21) only by expressing more exactly the developed consciousness of being a son, while τέκνον denotes only the origin itself. The latter name, therefore, does not occur as applied to Christ. The poor reduction of the state of being God's children to the favourable inclination of God towards the faithful is thoroughly untenable; such inclination is to be considered as mere *consequence* of the essential transformation, the birth from the Spirit; God loves the faithful, because He has made them accepted in the Beloved (Ephes. i. 6.) 'Εις ἀγάπην should be contrasted to ἐις φόβον, but the saying Abba is to be construed as the very expression of love. The reading δειλίας came perhaps into the text merely from the parallel of 2 Tim. i. 7, where πνεῦμα δειλίας is opposed to the πνεῦμα δυνάμεως καὶ ἀγάπης. Πάλιν is to be connected with εἰς φόβον, the omission of the word in some unimportant Codd. arises perhaps from the false application of it to ἐλάβετε, which must have made πάλιν appear strange, because no actual communication of the Spirit is spoken of in the O. T. The word υἱοθεσία is used only by Paul

(Rom. viii. 23, ix. 4; Galat. iv. 5; Ephes. i. 5.) It signifies acceptance to the state of children, and presupposes, therefore, that those accepted had not been children. Hence it is clear that the expression has no reference to physical existence, by which all natural men also are children of God, but to the inward life only. In reference to this, natural men are without God in the world, strangers and enemies to Him (Ephes. ii. 12); in Christ they are first ordained to the state of children (Ephes. i. 5.) The expression of a child's consciousness is the cry of Abba, which naturally is only to be understood of the true expression of the inward life. Ἀββᾶ, אַבָּא, Chald. form of אָב. The ὁ πατήρ is the Hebrew vocative, wherefore the conjecture, ὦ πατήρ, is untenable. The choice of the Chaldaic word is not to be referred to the prayer of Christ (Mr. xiv. 36), as Reiche thinks, nor with Winer (at Galat. iv. 6), to be explained from the circumstance that well-known prayers of the Jews began so; but to be derived from the form of the word. Abba, like papa, can be spoken by the mouth even of the babbling child, and properly, therefore, characterizes genuine child-like disposition and manner.

Ver. 16. In this state of being children, then, the witness of our own spirit with that of the divine Spirit penetrate each other in a peculiar manner. The one that properly *gives* witness in this *testimonium spiritus* is the divine Spirit; the human spirit is more the *receiver* of the witness from Him, as it is said: Spirit witnesseth that Spirit is truth (1 John v. 6); that is, the Spirit needs no witness but Himself for His truth, He has it wholly in Himself; as the light is not and cannot be testified by ought but by itself. But as the physical light needs an eye, a faculty of receptivity, in order to be perceived, and as this is itself light, so is the spiritual light, the νοῦς (the human πνεῦμα) the eye for the divine Spirit. It was observed before (at ver. 9) that this witness of the Spirit is not to be placed merely in the feeling (1 John iii. 19), but His whole inward and outward efficacy must be taken together; for instance, His comfort, His incitement to prayer, His censure of sin, His impulse to works of love, to witness before the world, and such like more. Upon the foundation of this immediate testimony of the Holy Spirit, *all the regenerate man's conviction of Christ and His work* finally rests. For the faith in the Scripture itself has its basis upon this experience of the divinity of the principle which it promises, and which flows into the believer while he is occupied with it. This passage is, besides, important as one of the most striking in which the *human spirit* is represented *as not in and by itself identical* with the Divine.* We cannot certainly conceive the difference as a specific one; as image of God man must be in his spirit *kindred* to the Divine (Acts xvii. 28, 29.) But the human spirit may be defiled by sin (2 Cor. vii. 1), the Divine not; He may be grieved only (Ephes. iv. 30), or driven away; but as the absolute principle of holiness, He is himself incapable of spot. By communication of this highest principle of all life, man therefore first becomes one spirit with the Lord Himself, as it is said 1 Cor. vi. 17. (*Συμμαρτυρεῖν* here, as at ii. 15, is not of the same import with the simple verb; a twofold witness rather is here spoken of, that actually indeed blends again to *one,* wherein, however, a positive and a negative side may be distinguished.) Moreover, the expressions *πνεῦμα δουλείας*, *πνεῦμα υἱοθεσίας* are not to be taken, as though the Apostle assumed a double *πμεῦμα*, or a twofold form of the operation of the Spirit, one of which effects a servile, the other a filial mind; nor is *πνεῦμα* to be taken subjectively in the meaning "mindedness;" the idea is rather to be understood thus: We have received the One true Spirit, this Spirit leaves us not in a state of bondage, nor calls forth such a state again, but He begets a filial consciousness. For the state of bondage and fear is, not that of castaways, but subordinate only to that of children; the utterly dead man alone is without fear and without the feeling of bondage (ver. vii. 9); with the awakening (vii. 10—24.) Fear begins, with the regeneration (vii. 25, &c.) love.

Ver. 17. The idea of the state of children leads the Apostle, in conclusion, to the conception of *δόξα* as an inheritance, the proper possessor of which, indeed, the Only-begotten is, but in which His brethren (ver. 29) are to have share. All that glory, therefore, which the Lord from eternity had with the Father, and which he took possession of again after His return to the Father, (John xvii. 22) is imparted to the faithful also (Rev. iii. 21.) The condition, however, presupposed as known and acknowledged of participation in the glory of Christ is the previous participation in His sufferings, that is, in the conflict with sin in ourselves and

* The assertion of the *identity* of the human and divine spirit would lead to the consciousness of God in man being the consciousness of God of Himself, which is thorougly unscriptural. Christ himself prays to the God without him, to the Father in Heaven!

in the world, whereby alone the new man attains to the full growth in God. Even so are sufferings represented as the condition of participation in glory, in the passages Col. iii. 4; 2 Tim. ii. 12; 1 Pet. iv. 13; not as though for the extraordinary glory something extraordinary also must be endured, as equivalent, but in so far as the old man must be crucified with Christ, since the new man only is and can be capable of the reception and the thankful enjoyment of the glory to come. (Comp. 1 Pet. iv. 1.) Upon the idea of *κληρονόμος*, compare more particularly at Gal. iv. 1, &c.

Εἴπερ has the signification *si modo*, "provided that;" comp. at ver. 9 and at 2 Cor. v. 3. *Συμπάσχω* is found besides at 1 Cor. xii. 26. *Συνδοξάζεσθαι* does not occur again in the N. T.

§ 13. OF THE PERFECTION OF THE WHOLE CREATION WITH THE CHILDREN OF GOD.

(VIII. 18—39.)

With a very free and beautiful turn, the Apostle leads over from the idea of the suffering of the faithful with Christ to a description of the glory which awaits them. The peculiar character of this glory is in its being a perfection of the individual together with the whole. Thus the following statement gives the reason why the individual cannot alone attain to bodily glorification; every individual, namely, is only part and member of the whole, and as one member of the body cannot, without disturbance in its harmony, be completed alone, neither can the individual believer without the totality. Here below, therefore, the life of the believer is a constant walking in hope; to behold what is hoped for is not for this world. Only the Lord himself was excepted from this law, because He was Himself the whole, in that He essentially included in Himself the totality of the life, which unfolded from Him, as the germ does the whole tree to be developed from it. Sufferings appear therefore here (albeit they remain still consequent on sin, without which every development might have gone on without disturbances and distractions) as a blessing, as a means to perfection; and it is naturally to be understood that this is not meant of self-made sufferings—for instance, of false ascetic exercises and denials of a man's own choosing—but of such only as the Lord himself sees good to lay upon him. If now the perfection of the individual were attached in the passage before us merely to the perfection of the whole Church, or even of the whole human race, doubtless far fewer difficulties would have been found in it; but the Apostle extends his look over the *whole creation*, and this has not unfrequently been thought too bold an idea. It has been attempted, therefore, to say nothing of the utterly unfit conceptions which at one time have suggested *angels*, at another *animals*, at another the *dead* (comp. thereon Reiche's excellent observations in his comm. B. ii., S. 215, &c.), gradually to narrow the mighty compass of the Pauline contemplation, according as the [expositor's] particular view was more or less stinted. Now κτίσις was to mean Christians merely, then only a *part* at most of Christendom, and that either Jew or Heathen-Christians; then again the expression was to apply to the *people Israel*, or to the *Heathen magistracy;* then it was extended to the *whole Heathen world*, or to the *whole of mankind*. The wider the reference is made, the nearer naturally it comes to the truth, notwithstanding the most comprehensive of the explanations adduced, that of the whole of mankind, is not sufficient, since the Apostle spans with one mighty glance *the whole creation* in all its parts. That even the inanimate creation was not excluded from his thought, has been set forth so with one consent, and with such striking reasons, by the latest interpreters, (by Tholuck, Stier, Rückert, Reiche, Usteri, Schneckenburger,* Köllner), that I feel excused from the repetition of those reasons, with leave to refer to the well-known writings of these learned men, (especially to Reiche's copious discussion upon this passage, compared with his two Festprograms of 1830 and 1832.) Meanwhile, this remarkable and important idea of glorification to be looked for of the whole creation, demands still a somewhat more exact consideration, to which we hope to contribute by the following reflections.† The

* Comp. Schneckenburger's Beitr. S. 118, &c., and Ullman's and Umbreit's Studien Jahrg. 1832. H. 4. S. 835, &c. Of Usteri the 4th Edit. of the Paul. Lehrbegr. appendix H. In the three first editions he explains κτίσις of mankind.

† The Greek fathers explained the passage, almost without exception, of the creation. Augustine's Polemics against the Manichees, for whose hylozoistic view of the world this passage must naturally have been very welcome, induced him to consider it merely of the extra-Christian part of mankind, and his influence in the middle ages decided

question then is, first of all, how far the Apostle, if he would speak of inanimate and unconscious nature, can ascribe to it a waiting, yearning, and groaning for the revelation of the children of God? Just because this did not seem probable, even men, who were not averse from the idea of a glorification of nature in itself, have believed themselves forbidden to find it *here*; and, therefore, explained the κτίσις of the heathen world, or of all men apart from Christianity, who are longing yet to become partakers of the salvation in Christ. Or, in referring the κτίσις to inanimate nature, its representation as of a waiting, yearning creature, has been conceived merely as allegory, for which even Reiche still decides; but in no way can we accede to this latter view. Holy Scripture throughout conceives nature, in its relation to the world of spirits, like the human body in its relation to the soul and spirit, as filled and borne by their living breath. As, therefore, in the individual, the spiritual life operates either with a distracting or glorifying effect upon the bodily substance, so does the life of the regenerate, considered as a whole, upon the totality of the creation. The conscious life in man is but the bloom of the life that sways in the sum of the creation. If we observe, then, the unconscious creation more narrowly, we must acknowledge that an impulse to glorification, a yearning for perfection, appears in it also.* The whole bent of the plant urges it to bring all its powers to perfection in the blossom and the fruit, and if checked by circumstances in its development—for instance by want of light—an effort of all its powers may be perceived to surpass the hindrances, and outset the default; so that a plant often presses through narrow clefts to get at the element of life, and produce its bloom. The same impulse for glo-

many to follow this view. The reformers first unanimously returned to the reference of the κτίσις to the whole creation, for which even Grotius too determined. The Socinians and Arminians again adduced other acceptations, which, since the last century, many Protestants followed. The latest commentators upon the epistle since Tholuck have returned, notwithstanding, to the ancient explanation; only many of them, even Tholuck, Reiche, Meyer, de Wette, err from the truth in this respect, that they would altogether capriciously have the extra-Christian men excluded from the κτίσις. Köllner has given quite the right interpretation, as also Krabbe has. (Of Sin, p. 115, 184.)

* Beautifully, says Schubert (Handb. der Kosmol. Nürnberg. 1823. p. 5): "Even in the things of the world of bodies which surrounds us, there is an element of life, a yearning of what is bound, which, like that Memnon-statue, unconsciously makes symphony, when the ray touches it from above." The Genevese philosopher, Bonnet, represents the striving of nature after a more perfect state in his palingenesie philosophique.

rification shows itself also in the animal. In this impulse of life that creates life again, the life enclosed in the animal would press as if beyond itself, but naturally can produce nothing better than what itself contains. Inasmuch, however, as the animal sensibly suffers from the sin of men, the yearning and waiting for redemption is expressed far more distinctly and perceptibly in it; * the eye of a suffering or dying animal speaks a language to which every feeling mind is sensible; it sighs and yearns for redemption, or rather the general life in it yearns to get free from its confinement. The waiting and yearning of the creature, therefore, cannot possibly be admitted to be mere allegory, neither is there any obvious reason, after what has been said, to think it applicable *only* to men living out of the Christian principle. These certainly are not to be considered as excluded, for, as the children of God (ver. 19) can only be those regenerate by the Spirit of Christ, there would be a total silence (if the κτίσις were to signify the inanimate creation *exclusive* of men) upon the ultimate bringing in of the extra-christian world, nay, it would be almost denied, which in every respect is untenable. It is also entirely indemonstrable, that κτίσις signifies the creation *without* man. The children of God, on the contrary, may be considered as separated from the general creation, and are here expressly distinguished by the Apostle, because they form, as it were, a new creation different from the old. If it should be said, however, that the Apostle does mean by these children of God all mankind, so far, namely, as it is destined to be received into the community of Christ; then the men who lived before Christ would still be omitted, or supposing them to be included as children of God, (but which ver. 23 decidedly contradicts, since the first fruits of the Spirit cannot possibly be ascribed to them), then thus much, at least, must be allowed, that men, *as much and as far* as they yet belong to the old life, are also reckoned as κτίσις, for, ver. 23, the same yearning is mentioned of the children of God, as ver. 19 is ascribed to the creature. The separation, therefore, does not admit of being so much outwardly as inwardly effected; the κτίσις

* Göthe's correspondence with a child affords proof of how a spirited contemplation of nature still leads to this apostolic idea. Bettina writes (B. i. S. 38): "When I stand all alone at night in open nature, I feel as though it were a spirit and begged redemption of me. Often have I had the sensation as if nature, in wailing sadness, entreated something of me, so that, not to understand what she longed for, cut through my very heart."

is everywhere, even in man, in the regenerate himself, so far as the transforming Spirit of Christ has not yet wrought his change; but, at all events, mankind out of Christianity cannot be considered as excluded from the *κτίσις*.* It would be much easier, and far more natural, if the *κτίσις* were to be understood only of men, who are still ever the nearest object of redemption, exclusive of the inanimate world; an acceptation of the passage, which, on the whole, is the only one that can have a place in our consideration, beside the explanation proposed by us. But 1, it is against this that *all* men cannot be meant by *κτίσις* here, since the regenerate *as such* (ver. 19) are expressly excepted from it, but in no way are they treated as part of the *κτίσις*. Then 2, the simple thought, that there is a yearning for redemption in the men, who are yet far from the covenants of the divine promise, would clearly have been expressed quite differently from the tone of this passage. Lastly, 3, the idea of a glorification of the universe does not at all belong to the Apostle alone, but it pervades the whole scripture; it is, therefore, in thorough keeping with the connexion of the whole passage, which advances from the individual to the whole, for Paul to demonstrate, how, with the perfecting of the Church of Christ, the world itself will receive its perfection.† Accordingly, then, we must say, that Paul contrasts Christ, and the *new* creation called forth by Him, to all the *old* creation, together with the unregenerate men, as the flower of this creation. The whole of this old creation has one life in itself, and this is yearning for redemption from the bonds which hold it and hinder its glorification; this one yearning has forms dif-

* For the acceptation that Paul, in this passage, would have merely unconscious nature, excluding unconverted men, to be understood by the expression *κτίσις*, the passage, ver. 21, *καὶ αὐτὴ ἡ κτίσις* seems to speak. The Apostle has most certainly conceived the life of nature in its extreme form, as unconscious, nay, as lifeless nature; but it does not follow that he did not conceive the natural man, the *μὴ ὄντες* (Rom. iv. 17), from whom true men are yet to be born, as grown with the most remote formations of the natural life. The *πᾶσα ἡ κτίσις*, ver. 22, speaks decidedly for this, and the manner in which the *κτίσις* is described as willing and longing, for which the supposition of a mere personification is not sufficient.

† Rosencranz, in his Dissertatio de corrupto naturæ statu, (Regiom. 1834), denies altogether the *disturbance* of the harmony of life in unconscious nature; but to say nothing at all of the clear declarations of Holy Scripture thereon, this acceptation, since the actually apparent monstrous disharmonies in nature cannot be denied, would lead, consistently carried out, to Lucretian doubts in God's love and wisdom. Comp. Lucret. de natur. ser v. 196, &c., where it is said: "Ausim confirmare, nequaquam nobis divinitus esse paratam naturam rerum, tanta stat prædita culpa."

ferent only upon the different degrees of life, and is naturally purer and stronger in unregenerate men than in plants and animals; in them the creation has, as it were, its mouth, by which it can give vent to its collective feeling. Yet the most of these men *know* not what the yearning and seeking in them properly mean; they *understand* not the language of the spirit in them; nay, they suppress it often, though it is, meanwhile, audible in their heart, and what they do not understand themselves, God understands, who listens even to prayers not understood.* So decided, notwithstanding, as the contrast is between the old and new creation, yet they may not be considered as separated thoroughly. Rather as the new man, in all distinctness from the old, still is *in* the old, so is the new creation (Christ and the new life proceeding from Him) in the old world. The old creation, therefore, is like an impregnate mother (comp. at ver. 23) that bears a new world in her womb—a life which is not herself, which neither springs from her, but which, by the overmastering power that dwells in it, draws her life, with which it is connected, on and on into itself, and changes it into its nature, so that the birth (the completion of the new world) is the mother's death (the sinking of the old.) As then there is a regeneration of the individual, there is a regeneration † also of the universe (Matt. xix. 28), and as the former is completed gradually, so is the latter also. For as Paradise at first vanished from the earth with sin (Gen. iii. 18), and in man's inward being the νοῦς was subjected to sin; so does the restoration through Christ begin first with the liberation of the νοῦς (Rom. vii. 25), and in the creation with the restoring of Paradise at the resurrection of the just, the representatives of the νοῦς for the totality (Rev. xx. 4, &c.). To this time the prophecies of the prophets point, that the deserts shall blossom again (Is. xxxv. 1, &c.), the lamb and the lion shall feed together (Is. xi. 6, &c.; xxxv. 9; lxv, 25.) As, however, in the individual

* Accordingly Luther quite justly says: "Albeit the creature hath not such speech as we have, it hath a language still, which God and the Holy Spirit heareth and understandeth, how it groaneth for the wrong it must endure from the ungodly, who misuse it so."

† Acts iii. 21, ἀποκατάστασις πάντων has a like signification, answering the Rabbinical חִדּוּשׁ עוֹלָם, renovatio mundi. Luther naively designates this glorification of nature as the putting on of God's Easter robe, instead of the present workaday dress; the foundation of which expression is the comparison of the course of the world with the week of the creation (Gen. i.), upon which a new Sabbath is still to follow. (Comp. Tholuck's fifth appendix to his Treatise on Sin and the Atoner, where the universality of the longing for a paradisiacal time is proved.)

even after the experience of redemption, the flesh remains still subjected to the law of sin (comp. at vii. 25), so with the restoration of Paradise in the kingdom of God upon earth, the animal life in nature, ay, even in man (Rev. xx. 7, 8), is not yet quite overpowered; hence, as the individual needs the bodily glorification, so does the whole creation need a total transformation—the passing away of the old heaven and the old earth (2 Peter iii.), and the birth of a new heaven and a new earth (Is. lxv. 17; Rev. xx. 11, &c.; xxi. 22), at the general resurrection. Here the animal life, that adverse middle step between matter and spirit-conscious life, is quite overcome, and the glorified matter become the pure bearer of the spirit. So then it is clear also, that, by the *κτίσις*, not merely our earth or our solar system, but the totality of all creation, (*οὐρανὸς καὶ γῆ* = הַשָּׁמַיִם וְהָאָרֶץ, the spiritual and material world), must be understood. Whether the ancient world had such a perception of the greatness of the universe as the telescopes give us, does not signify in this respect; the Spirit of God in the Apostles understood explicite what they themselves took implicite only; even if they *thought* the universe smaller than we are accustomed to consider it, they, nevertheless, *meant* the universe as well as ourselves in every expression that denotes the totality; just as a drop of water is meant by every one who utters the word, whether he know or not, that it contains a world of animalcula. Just as little can the smallness of the earth, in relation to the universe, and the many vast globes in it, withhold from this acceptation; for *either* it may be said that, as in the human organism, little members (the eye for instance) are more important than great ones, the leg for instance—so in the whole system of the worlds (to us, indeed, yet quite unknown) the earth occupies a far more important place than the largest fixed stars; *or*, the diminutiveness of the earth might be admitted with the remark, that it is the very method of the Lord to choose the little and to make something out of that which is nothing.* At all events, the earth never ap-

* Beautiful as this thought, which does not, however, belong to me, appears, it must notwithstanding, on nearer consideration, yield perhaps to the other alternative; God namely chooses indeed for His most sublime purposes, what is little and despised *in the eyes of men*, because they look to the form, and not to the substance, but still not what is in and of itself little and contemptible. God beholds the things according to their true essence, and accordingly uses them also; what is little for little purposes, what is great for great ones.

pears in holy scripture as a pitiful speck of rust on the great clock-work of the creation, but as the point where the great conflict between light and darkness is most decidedly carried on; therefore, it is, that what is going on upon the earth may have the most thorough effect upon the universe.

Ver. 18. The Apostle passes from the foregoing part of his discourse to the glory awaiting the faithful, by bringing the sufferings in this temporal state of the world into immediate parallel with it. The *λογίζομαι γάρ* namely, is so connected with the *έιπερ συμπάσχομεν*, that the mediating thought: " which we easily may," is to be supplied. Ver. 18 then contains an indirect encouragement not to withdraw from these sufferings.

Ὁ νῦν καιρός = *ἀιὼν οὗτος*. Comp. in the comm. part i. at Matt. xii. 32. *Ἄξιος* has here its closest meaning, that which draws down the scale, outweighs anything. The *παθήματα* are not merely physical sufferings, but the spiritual sufferings also, which proceed from the sins of *others;* the consequences of men's *own* sins, known and express, are naturally to be excluded. Even therefore the *δόξα* also is the comprisal of all that, which inwardly and outwardly blesses and glorifies the man. The principle of blessedness and glory is operative indeed in man already here below (Col. iii. 3, 1 Cor. xii. 12), but only in a manner hidden and ever in conflict with the sin in the old man; hence its *ἀποκάλυψις* is something future.

Ver. 19. How very incapable the sufferings of this time are of being compared with the glory to come, Paul proves by this that the children of God and their glorification are an object of yearning for the universe. In this thought mankind is raised to a height which as much surpasses all poor human conjectures upon its development, as the humiliations which the Scripture awards to the natural man, to the unenlightened, seem little suitable. The Word of God measures out depth and height to the very uttermost, and shocking as it is, when human pride would make itself great, as adorable is the mercy of God, by which he, whom it first lowered beneath all, is then as made humble exalted over all. In this sense, as the centre, round which the purposes of God conduct their movements, Paul calls the faithful " a spectacle to the world, to angels, and to men." (1 Cor. iv. 9, comp. also thereon at 1 Cor. vi. 2). As ver. 18 the *δόξα*, so here now the *υιοὶ τοῦ Θεοῦ* are considered as present, already existing, but not become perceptible as being what they are.* It follows, of course, that no such members of the Church are meant, as only outwardly belong to her, but those, who as truly regenerate, bear Christ's life in them. Hence it is ever properly Christ alone that is glorified, rules and governs in the faithful; and for this very cause alone the least in the kingdom of God, as born of God, is greater than the greatest born of women, because Christ is his life (Galat. ii. 20.) As, however, Christ's glory was first revealed at the resurrection, so too the glory of the regenerate at their resurrection. This revelation then the waiting creature yearns for, in the feeling that it is to share the glory of it.

Ἀποκαραδοκία, which is found once more in the N. T. at Phil. i. 20, from ἀποκαραδοκέω, καραδοκέω, signifies *exserto capite prospicere*, as the *Etymol. magn.* says: τῇ κεφαλῇ προβλέπειν. Hence "urgently to long for something, to wait for." (Comp. *Eurip. Rhes.* 144, *Diod. Sic.* xiv. 60.) The connection with the synonymous ἀπεκδέχεσθαι enhances the idea in this passage.

But as regards the principal idea κτίσις, the prevailing signification of the expression (as was observed at i. 20), in the N. T. is, what is created (= κτίσμα), in i. 20 only it extends to the *act* of creating. Hence it frequently signifies (usually in connexion with ὅλη or πᾶσα, but without this addition also, though not without the article† the universe, the whole world. (So ver. 22, Mr. xvi. 15, Col. i. 15. Further Wisd. xix. 6, Judith xvi. 14.) Doubtless now κτίσις might figuratively, as with most nations similar expressions are so used, *e.g.*, בְּרִיָּה by the Rabbins), signify men only; but it does not so occur in the N. T. The passages Mr. xvi. 15 (which Reiche still maintains), Col. i. 23 are to be taken otherwise; in the former κτίσις is mankind only so far as it is regarded as the flower of the creation in general, as appears from the use of πᾶσα also with it; in the latter κτίσις is taken locally of the extent of earth, equal to κόσμος. Κτίσις, however, occurs in the N. T. of

* The difference of the inward life of the faithful from their exterior, which is not different from the world, is incomparably represented by the well known song:—

"Es glänzet der Christen inwendiges Leben."—("All glorious within is the life of believers.")—[Comp. Ps. xlv. 14.]

† Yet compare Mark x. 6, xiii. 19, 2 Pet. iii. 4, where the formula ἀπ' ἀρχῆς κτίσεως occurs; in this formula, however, the idea of the beginning already leads necessarily to the totality, which therefore does not require to be further especially marked by the article.

single created things, as Rom. i. 25, viii. 39, Heb. iv. 13, and therefore it cannot still be denied that it is possible it *might* mean mankind. Only this must be denied in the passage before us, because, to say nothing of the reasons already adduced above, *πᾶσα ἡ κτίσις* occurs ver. 22, which cannot possibly signify a *part* of the creation, yet *κτίσις*, ver. 19, may not be taken in a sense different from that in ver. 22. The rabbinical usage, however, (on which compare the remarks at Mr. xvi. 15), according to which בְּרִיּוֹת signifies the heathen, cannot be of any assistance here, because surely not the *heathen* only are longing for the revelation of the sons of God, but the *Jews* also. Accordingly the *κτίσις*, as has been deduced already, can only signify here the totality of the universe, as the first creation, in contrast to the *new* one in Christ, and that not *without* men, but *with* even the extra-Christian men. When Reiche (B. ii. S. 191), mentions, on the contrary, that judgment awaits those who are without Christ, that they therefore cannot long for the revelation of the children of God ; this is true only of those who, having become acquainted with the life in Christ, have rejected it ; but all those, to whom it has not come at all, who could not therefore refuse it, are naturally to be considered as the members of mankind before the birth of Christ. The same longing therefore is to be supposed in them, which constitutes the character of this race before Christ. Of the circumstance, however, that there are men who refuse the salvation in Christ, the Apostle could so much the less take notice here, as an unconscious longing for well-being is still even in them, and they are only deceiving themselves, if they hope to find it *out* of Christ. (Upon the particular use of *κτίσις* in Hebr. ix. 11, 1 Pet. ii. 13, we shall treat when we come to the explanation of these passages.)

Vers. 20, 21. As ground for this expectation of the creature the Apostle assigns first of all its subjection to perishableness, but then at the same time observes that this is not nor is to be absolute, but that the creature itself must become free from it, as the children of God are already (in hope, v. 24) become free from it. In these verses the *ματαιότης* (or *φθορά*) and the *δόξα*, which is to be considered as *ἀφθαρσία*,—the *ὑποταγή* (or *δουλεία*) and the *ἐλευθερία*, form antitheses. Both parallel members stand in necessary connexion ; the bondage is as little to be supposed without perishableness, as the freedom without glory ; nay, the one is, necessarily and of itself, the other also; wherefore too at the close of verse 21 freedom and glory could be blended to the one conception of *ἐλευθερία τῆς δόξης*. Now the aorist (*ὑποτάγη*) leads in a manner not to be mistaken to an historical event; originally the creature too was free, but it ceased to be so. That here the fall of man and the curse attaching to it is alluded to (Gen. iii. 17, &c.,) cannot be doubted; we have accordingly in these verses a highly significant commentary upon the Old Testament hieroglyphics. We perceive from it, that the transition of the curse from the conscious creature to the unconscious is no arbitrary one, but one of internal necessity. The Apostle, namely, connects the two here, the conscious and unconscious life of the creation, in such a manner with each other, as to predicate the same event equally of both. The *ὀυχ ἑκοῦσα* leads principally to the conscious or at least animated creation, whilst the *καὶ α υ τ ἡ ἡ κτίσις* immediately refers to the extreme points of the creature in its unconscious existence, whose participation in the great process of liberation in the redemption is wont to be the latest perceived. But, as was before observed, there is the same relation between the conscious and unconscious life of the creature in the whole, as that between soul and body in the individual; mankind is the bearer of the consciousness of the world in the creation, as the children of God are the bearers of the consciousness of God, and are even therefore, as *καινὴ κτίσις*, taken from the old. Accordingly, as the fall even of the creature began with man, so does the restoration of that creature begin also with him. The notion of being subjected to *ματαιότης* or *φθορά* presupposes however naturally a germ of better life, which, bound only by alien power, is held in *δουλεία*. This alien power is no other than that of the prince of this world, of the kingdom of darkness. As the light is the life of the world (John i. 4), so is the darkness the death, the disturbing element; but death is only the head of *φθορά*. The words of the Apo stle consequently are not to be limited to any special corruption, such as the abuse of the creature for idolatry, but they mean this together with all other consequences of sin. In as far, however, as there is left in every creature a germ of nobler life, which forms the fount of yearning for redemption, so far also a constant combat of nature against the *ματαιότης* and *φθορά*, and the head they come to, *θάνατος*, may be observed. This is signified by the *ὀυχ ἑκοῦσα ὑπετάγη*. Every natural man, ay every animal, every plant struggles to get beyond itself, to realize an idea, in the realization of which it has its ἐλευθερία, that is, the being perfectly answering the divine harmony; but the nothingness (הֶבֶל, Ps. xxxix. 6, Eccl. i 2, 14), pervading its nature, that is, the life failing in its fulness, and the transitoriness grounded therein and death its end, lets no created thing attain its aim; every individual of the species rather begins the circle of its course again, and struggles cheerlessly against the impossibility of perfecting itself. And even the history of mankind would be nothing more than such a cheerless beginning over again, were not the element of hope in it, and that the hope on Him who is to bring back all that is lost. Through this fount of life alone the life of man receives being by Him, who has that power of endless life (Hebr. vii. 16), which gives all nature being also. For this whole ὑποταγή under the bondage of death is indeed for *punishment* of sin, but it is at the same time a *blessing* too and a means for God to complete His works; therefore the Apostle says, ὑπετάγη διὰ τὸν ὑποτάξαντα. That the ὑποτάξας can only be God, not the devil, nor Adam, nor Nero (as Semler thought, who understood κτίσις of the Jews, whose conversion Nero hindered), needs no proof; Gen. iii. 17, &c., where God pronounces the curse, is decisive for it. But the ordinary acceptation of the διά in the meaning "by or through" is not so certain. *Διά c. acc.* may doubtless be used of means (comp. at John vi. 57, and Winer's Gr. p. 378), and this acceptation might here be thought preferable, because ἑκοῦσα precedes it, so that the sense should be: "not by its *own* will, but by God's will." But the observation, that God is the originator of this ὑποταγή, and not man, is something too idle to have any place in this grand development. God is acknowledged to work all, and man nothing but by God. There is signified however besides in ἑκοῦσα not the mere will, but the willingness (1 Cor. ix. 17);* the κτισίς sub-

* The conception of the ὀυχ ἑκοῦσα as contrast, not to the children of God but to the natural man, who with and by his will became subject to vanity, which is not the case with the unconscious creature, is quite untenable. It was in man's first sin by no means his will to become subject to vanity; probably indeed he subjected himself *with inward repugnance* to this curse, which becomes a blessing, so soon as the resistance yields. Hence all divine preaching begins with *repentance*, for this deadens the resistance and makes the cross to be willingly borne. But that, if this be the sense of the words, the creature cannot be meant without man, is clear. Should the conception of the ὀυχἑκοῦσα, which we have disputed, be tenable, the ὑπο-

jected itself *with resistance* (only repentance and faith effect in man the willingness to subject himself to this order), because it did not perceive the *purpose* of this divine management; but this purpose was no other than the fulfilment of the divine plans of the world, which after the entrance of sin could only be completed by surrender of the creature to death, wherefore Christ's death took away again all consequences of the fall. The διὰ τὸν ὑποτάξαντα is intended to express this reference to the plans of the divine government of the world; for God's sake, to His honour and final glory even this seeming destruction of His creation served. On this account the only begotten Son of God also subjected Himself to it, and all His saints with Him share this subjection to the φθορά and the θάνατος, for as man fell by *willing to be high*, he rises again by the *love to lowliness*, for God dwells only with the lowly.

Vers. 22, 23. Into the more general idea of the *yearning* of the κτίσις (ver. 19), that of *pain* is admitted now, which since the eating of the fruit of the tree of knowledge is the inheritance of the creation. In the νῦν of Christ's appearance there is, *beside* the fountain of pain, an inexhaustible fountain of joy first opened also, which the world before Christ looked for in hope, whereby its pain was hindered from turning to despair, but which to the faithful of the New Testament already vouchsafes enjoyment; albeit only a partial enjoyment. The συνωδίνει defines still more nearly the *nature* of the pain; it is compared to that anxious, woful pain of a woman in travail, which is peculiar, in that those who are in labour feel together with the pain the secret joy of giving existence to a new being. The Apostle ascribes this character also to the conflicts and sorrows of mankind, and of the whole creature in her travail of thousands of years. The συνωδίνει therefore indicates indeed on the one hand the greatest height of pain, but on the other it contains the intimation also, that it brings with it the secret cheer of not being purposeless. The birth-pangs of the creature give

τάξας must then be man, which the context does not admit of. Calvin understood the words quite properly, in saying: "Invita et repugnante natura vim patitur, quidquid detinetur sub corruptione." Life has a natural horror of death, which can only be overcome by a higher power, that of love. (The words are not with Griesbach to be enclosed in brackets, but to be connected thus: ἡ κτίσις ὑπετάγη ὀυχ ἑκοῦσα, ἀλλὰ διὰ τὸν ὑποτάξαντα ἐπ' ἐλπίδι. 'Αλλά namely forms no antithesis to ὀυχ ἑκοῦσα, but with ἐπ' ἐλπίδι the antithesis to the entire half of ver. 20. "With repugnance was the creature subjected to vanity, but not for ever."

life to a new and fairer world! (The rabbinical expression חֶבְלֵי הַמָּשִׁיחַ for denoting the great conflicts before the Lord's coming again, is to be taken from the same profound image; comp. thereon at Matt. xxiv. 6, &c.) In this general struggle for a perfect state the children of God themselves, so long as they sojourn here on earth, still take share; for in their *σάρξ* they carry the *κτίσις* still, and in it even they still remain subjected to *φθορά*. As therefore the regenerate has a conflict similar to that of the merely awakened (comp. at vii. 14, &c.), he also has the groaning and waiting of the creature, but with this difference that in his *νοῦς* he has the consciousness of God already present, and his *σῶμα* only tarries still for the *ἀπολύτρωσις*, which comes to pass so soon (according to ver. 11) as the mortal body is made living.*

Ver. 22, the *συστενάζει, συνωδίνει* is not to be referred to the children of God; the transition *ὀυ μόνον δέ, ἀλλά,* does not admit of this. I would not however regard the *σύν* as mere strengthening of the simple form. It is best without doubt to resolve the *κτίσις* into the totality of the individual formations, which constitute it, and then to take the sense of the words to be that everything in nature yearns *one with another* for the freedom of the children of God. The *ἄχρι τοῦ νῦν* applies to the time of the completion of the work of Christ, and the birth of the children of God connected with it, to which the yearning of the creature looked. Ver. 23. Many different readings are found in the words *ἀλλὰ καὶ ἀυτοί κ. τ. λ.*, which however have no influence on the thought. The reading proposed by Griesbach is very natural, but it is just on that account questionable, whether it is the original one. Lachmann would read *καὶ ἀυτοί* merely, and encloses *ἡμεῖς* in brackets. But perhaps Paul wrote *ἡμεῖς ἀυτοί* twice, without its being at all necessary to suppose an enhancing at the second, such as any special reference to Paul or the Apostles. The *στενάζειν ἐν ἑαυτοῖς* is to be considered as opposed to something like *στενάζειν ἐν ἄλλοις*, and applies to the groaning for their own perfection, which does not exclude a sympathy praying for the perfection of others and of the whole. The expression *ἀπολύτρωσις τοῦ σώματος* is only found here: it gives the redemption in its absolute completion (1 Cor. i. 30), while the expression used elsewhere with-

* Upon the *ἀπολύτρωσις τοῦ σώματος* comp. more particularly at 1 Cor. xv. and 2 Cor. v. The latter passage has especial affinity with the one before us.

out the addition σώματος denotes the beginning of the redeeming operation of Christ. Applied to the body, the formula contains at the same time the indication, that there is a nobler germ, a body of light as it were, dwelling in it, which being bound at present, shall some time be free through Christ.

The description of the proper character of the υἱοὶ or τέκνα τοῦ Θεοῦ is remarkable. They have the πνεῦμα υἱοθεσίας (ver. 15), but yet are longing for the υἱοθεσία itself. The Spirit namely is only the principle, which both begets that υἱοθεσία and at the same time grants the pledge for it. The υἱοθεσία is not perfect until the bodily glorification, for it is the state of absolute perfection, in which the man as microcosm is a pure image of the μακροκόσμος, the πᾶσα κτίσις. Without bodily glorification, however, the being of man is imperfect, therefore even the souls under the altar long for bodily perfection (Rev. vi. 9.) As possessors of the Spirit, the faithful, from whom there is no ground at all for separating the Apostles or Paul alone, are said to be τὴν ἀπαρχὴν τοῦ πνεύματος ἔχοντες. Upon the idea already touched upon, that the regenerate is called a possessor of the Spirit, so that the Spirit seems to be subject to him, comp. more particularly at 1 Cor. xiv. 32. The expression ἀπαρχή (= רֵאשִׁית, Levit. xxiii. 10, Deut. xxvi. 2) refers to the figure of a great harvest of the Spirit, which awaits mankind, and whose first fruits were allotted to the Apostolic church in all their glory. The ideas both of the early ripe, and of the excellent, are equally to be maintained therein, and on this account those are by no means to be understood here, according to the supposition which has been again maintained by Glöcker, who are just come into Christianity, and the Apostles to be contrasted with them by the second ἡμεῖς. This expression, however, naturally leads to an inferiority of the Old Testament life, in which all, as well regeneration as communication of the Spirit, existed as type only, not as substance.

Vers. 24, 25. By this participation of the regenerate in the groaning of the creature, the Apostle would not have the reality of the redemption denied or limited; this is rather objectively fulfilled (ἐσώθημεν), though not in perceptible possession of it, but in *hope.* This passage is especially important to determine the notion of ἐλπίς. First of all it is opposed to βλέπειν (= διὰ εἴδους περιπατεῖν, 2 Cor. v. 7), to the being able to behold as outwardly existing; but next it forms as strong a contrast to the complete absence and separateness of the object; it is rather identical with the *inward possession* of the thing hoped for, so far namely as it is spiritual goods. Man can only believe and hope for eternal things, so far as they are inwardly present to him, and on this account the Christian hope stands so high; she is the daughter of *experience* (Rom. v. 4), and as such maketh not ashamed, and sister of faith and love (1 Cor. xiii. 13). Good wishes, desire, longing, all this therefore is not ἔλπις, for there is wanting therein the inward essential possession of the thing longed for.

Ver. 24. Lachmann leaves out the καὶ, which too is more burdensome than advantageous to the sense. Hermann's remark upon the use of καὶ (ad Viger. p. 837) is not applicable here, as τί is not "what," but "why;" καὶ therefore, if it is not to be rejected from the text, could only be translated here, "also, besides."

Ver. 26, 27. As we thus have what we *do not see* (says Paul in the name of the faithful), so are we able in that groaning in us (ver. 23), to pray for what *we do not know*, namely by the spirit that guides us. Even in the creation it is alone the universal Spirit filling it, that is yearning for the eternal magnet; in the faithful it is that higher spirit that makes them children (ver. 16.) This spirit upholds the human weakness, and leads it aright in the gloom of its longing, which suffers it not to bring before God the necessities it feels in the frame of definite prayers. The στεναγμοὶ ἀλάλητοι are therefore (with reference to ver. 23), stirred by the Spirit himself; they are called ἀλάλητοι,* inasmuch as the man can only speak out what he knows and apprehends, but in this instance he only knows *that* he wants something, but not *what* he wants. The knowing *generally* that the ἀπολύτρωσις σώματος is wanting, is of course not enough; the Apostle means that the *special* need in every moment (which is signified by the καθὸ δεῖ), and the way that it can be appeased, is hidden from the believer; only an unutterable secret yearning thrills through his being, a draught to his eternal origin, that finds its vent in sighs. The Apostle's words are gathered from such deep experience, that they make good their truth in every heart that ever felt this yearning; it makes itself

* Ἀλάλητος is not to be distinguished from ἀνεκλάλητος (1 Pet. i. 8), or ἀνεκδιήγητος (2 Cor. ix. 15): it signifies the unuttered, because it is (for the time or for ever unutterable.

known however there especially, where that sweet feeling, companion to the first love, has disappeared, and now the conflict with the wicked one (1 John ii. 13) begins. Then the soul often feels anxiety, without being conscious of any decided sin, and in her anxiety groans for redemption.*

In the συναντιλάμβανεσθαι (comp. Luke xviii. 40), the σύν is not to be understood of the co-operation of the divine Spirit *with* the human; the Spirit of God does not work *beside* the human spirit, but *on* and *through* it. Still, however, not so as to annul it, but by sanctifying and glorifying it. The word is used for the simple ἀντιλαμβάνεσθαι in the meaning *adjuvare, opem ferre*. The reading ἀσθενείᾳ is marked partly by the Codd. A.B.C.D. and many other critical authorities, partly by its intrinsic worth as the preferable one. Lachmann has also, according to his principles properly received it into the text. In the τὸ γὰρ τί κ. τ. λ. the τό applies to the whole sentence. Ἐντυγχάνειν ὑπέρ τινος is to intercede for any one, κατά τινος (xi. 2) to work, pray against any one. The verb in its immediate sense is "to meet with any one," so Acts xxv. 24 only. The composition with ὑπέρ, as the passage before us has it, does not occur again. The formula with ὑπέρ τινος is used also of the Son, Rom. viii. 34, Hebr. vii. 25. Now the *intercession* of the Son is naturally as distinct from that of the Spirit, as the *efficacy* of the Son and the Spirit in general differ. The former is atoning, the latter sanctifying and perfecting. The words of the Apostle are to be understood accordingly, that the Spirit, what he teaches to pray for also Himself fulfils and creates. The Spirit's intercession is not merely, as De Wette holds, "He teaches us to pray aright;" the thought is rather implied that nothing human as such holds good before God; only God Himself can satisfy God; so the Son in the work of redemption; as the Holy Ghost in the work of sanctification. As the divine principle He naturally ever works in accordance with God's will (κατὰ Θεόν), who as knowing the depths of the heart can perceive the most secret wishes of men. In this relation of the Spirit to God entirely the same thing appears, which we observed in the relation of the Son

* Meyer has remarkably misconceived this passage; he thinks namely, that it is not the groaning of men that is spoken of, which the Spirit incites, but the groaning of the Spirit itself. As if groaning could be a predicate of God, and unutterable groans might in any sense whatever be spoken of as to God

to the Father, and the prayer which the former suggests (John xvi. 23, &c.) All true emotions of life in man, and therefore prayers among the number, have their foundation in God Himself, and this alone gives them their fulfilment ;* whether the incitation shall be referred to the Son or the Spirit, depends upon its relations to the work of the one or the other. In the expression *φρόνημα τοῦ πνεύματος*, the *πνεῦμα* is not to be understood of the divine or Holy Spirit, but of the human ; *φρόνημα* can only be said of man, never of God. But then either the divine Spirit is to be supplied at *ἐντυγχάνει*, or, which seems more suitable, we say, Paul does not clearly distinguish here the divine and human spirit, since they have most intimately penetrated and wedded each other.

Ver. 28, 29. The waiting for the redemption of the body (ver. 23), even as all sufferings (ver. 18), so little, however, keep back the perfection of the children of God, that with the elect, who as such love God, they are the direct means of perfecting them, for

* Quite justly Augustine says (Tract. vi. in Joan.) "Non Spiritus S. in semet ipso apud semetipsum in illa trinitate gemit, sed in nobis gemit, quia gemere nos fecit." This observation, which makes itself known in the experience of every one of the regenerate, even the extra-Christian world expresses in its more profound members, as the excellent passages of Dschelaleddin show, which Tholuck has adduced here ; in one of them it is said:—

Sagst du: Herr komm! selber heisst das: hie mein kind!
Deine gluth und seufzer Gott's boten sind.
Sayst thou: Lord come! that says: come, child to me!
Thy glowing sighs God's message bring to thee.

[Is. lviii. 9, lxv. 24.] The following anonymous lines from an English mind, composed undesignedly within the last fifteen years, may contribute something to the reflections upon this beautiful subject; at least may bear some testimony to that great Master's hand, who, amidst His whole creation, wakens the deep music of the human heart. —(Acts xvii. 26.)

* * To me they seem,
Those far, sad streaks that reach along the West,
Like strains of long, full yearning from the chords
Of nature's orchestra. Weary, yet still
She sinks with longing to her winter-sleep,
Dreams ever of that birth, for whose bright dawn
The whole creation groans. Fair, sad companion!
I join my sigh with thine; yet none can be
Our sigh's interpreter, but that great Good,
Who breathes eternal wisdom; made, redeemed
O, loves us both: and ever moves as erst
On thy dark waters' face.
* * * *

November.

this their perfection and assimilation to the image of Christ, is the very predestination of God, and therefore immutably firm.

Ver. 28. πάντα applies especially to the sufferings; these embitter or deter all who do not love God, but further all who love Him. The εἰς ἀγαθόν denotes just this inward ripening. The conception of συνεργεῖν in the sense that several co-operate in the work of sanctification, is entirely contradictory to the Pauline doctrine: 1, God; 2, man himself; 3, sufferings and all circumstances in general. According to Paul, man effects *nothing*, God *everything*, and that *too* by circumstances. The συνεργεῖ is therefore, as συστενάζει above (ver. 22), to be taken as resolving the idea of πάντα: "for furthering the perfection of man all must, according to the will of God, co-operate one thing with another, but so, that He is the fundamental cause of all these effects." Paul does not found the certainty of perfection upon good purposes, or upon fidelity, but upon the election of God's grace, which itself first transforms the bent of the man's mind from faithlessness to truth. Christ, the prototype of holiness, is in this the model, to which God assimilates the faithful. Σύμμορφος occurs again Phil. iii. 21, and there certainly of the body only, which neither here (according to ver. 23) is to be considered as excluded. The will of the decree of love is to unite the regenerate mankind to one great *family of God*, in which Christ is the πρωτότοκος. Rev. i. 6, Christ is called the πρωτότοκος τῶν νεκρῶν, as first become alive from the dead; so too Col. i. 18. But the resurrection is not immediately and expressly the subject here; the expression therefore is to be taken in a wider sense, namely, like בְּכוֹר, as the first perfected, and at the same time pre-eminent in every sense. So it occurs too Col. i. 15; Heb. i. 6. Πρωτότοκος, however, is by no means of the same signification with μονογενής, it does not, I mean, refer, like μονογενής, to the divine nature of the Redeemer only, but to the *whole* historical Christ, with whom therefore men even may be compared. The name of honor, "Brethren," Christ himself moreover gives to His own, Matt. xii. 50; Mark iii. 35; John xx. 17. Comp. also Heb. ii. 11, 12; Ps. xxii. 23. The expressions in these verses, which refer to the doctrine of election by grace, as κατὰ πρόθεσιν κλητοί, προγινώσκειν, προορίζειν, will be further explained at Rom. ix. I observe here, by way of preliminary merely, that, according to Pauline doctrine, a *prædestinatio sanctorum*, in the proper sense of the words, exists; that is, God does not know beforehand that they will, by their own decision, be holy, but He creates this very decision in them. In the προγινώσκειν the property of the divine *knowledge* only, in προορίζειν that of the *will* alone is marked, both of which appear combined in the πρόθεσις. Nevertheless there seems to be no difference here between προέγνω and προώρισε, while, too, Acts ii. 23, 1 Pet. i. 2, Rom. xi. 2, πρόγνωσις is used directly for the divine will. In the verse before us it is only συμμόρφους τῆς εἰκόνος κ. τ. λ. that forms the advance in the thought.

Ver. 30. The attention was drawn to the importance of this passage for the doctrine of the *obedientia Christi activa*, at v. 19.* The circumstance that Θεός is here the subject and not Christ, does not influence it at all; the whole work of Christ is God's work through the Son, and what is said here of God, therefore, holds just as good of Christ, because God has fulfilled it through Him. The essential moment in the doctrine of the *obedientia activa* is however this, that the efficacy of Christ is not merely a *negative*, but just as much a *positive* efficacy also. Christ does not merely root out the sins of men, and then leave it to them to produce holiness *themselves*, but he has likewise brought this forth for Himself and all His own by His holy life, so that in the work of regeneration both the annulling of the old, and the creation of the new, are equally the work of *Christ*, and both were fulfilled already in His life on earth; wherefore they are immediately only imputed to individual believers, and then gradually communicated. It is just this which, in the passage before us, is most decidedly expressed by the ἐδικαίωσε καὶ ἐδόξασε. In the former expression the real communication of the δικαιοσύνη Χριστοῦ lies already indicated (comp. at Rom. iii. 21); but in the ἐδόξασε even that entire sanctification and completion of the δικαιοσύνη is expressed, which Paul had above (ver. 23) denied of himself and his brethren, namely as being yet to be found in their actual possession. Accordingly, as in *Adam* the whole natural race of man rested, and all history is but a development of that which is set forth* in him, so is *Christ* the real bearer of the whole Church, of the new creation,

* Comp. here the important parallel, 2 Cor. v. 14, &c., in which likewise all is conceived as for all already finished once for all in Christ.

† [*Gegeben*, seemingly *given* as the terms of a proposition are. B.]

the sanctified mankind, in that, as by His atoning power he annuls the old, He just as much creates the new, and deposits His holy image in every faithful soul. After this acceptation it first becomes clear, how faith is the one and all in the Christian life; the Christian has neither *before* nor *after* his conversion to generate *an independent sanctification of his own,* but he has only constantly to receive the stream of the influential powers of Christ's life upon him, and this *receiving* is faith itself. Just so the tree, when the development of its germ is begun, has only to suck in water, air, and light, in order to unfold itself from within, and all the drawing of a stupid gardener at the branches, all his working at the buds, to coax forth blossoms, can only disturb, but never further its development. And yet this utmost *passivity* is at the same time the utmost *activity,* since Christ does not work *out of* the man, but *in the very innermost depth of his most secret self,* and then pours the stream of His whole active power through the will. But the believer remains ever conscious of this active power as of one *given* him, and can so preserve the deepest humility with the highest perfection; *he* does not work, but Christ liveth and worketh in him (Gal. ii. 20). After this it is sufficiently evident also, how in the passage before us the *aorists* are chosen to convey its essential meaning, wherefore every attempt to alter them must be thoroughly set aside.* They are not to be *Futures,* for with the word: "it is finished!" the Lord had negatively and positively completed His whole Church, together with the κτίσις for all ἀιῶνες. No mortal could add to it even the very least; all which presents itself in the individual members of the Church, after the course of centuries, is mere development of that already given† in Him; the Church, and every individual in her, together with the κτίσις, which necessarily forms her basis, are "God's workmanship created in Christ Jesus" (Eph. ii. 10); the redemption is a new glorified creation, and the prerogative of creation is and continues God's alone. The context leads imperatively to this reflection, for it is the very *certainty* of salvation, which nothing earthly can disturb, that Paul intends to shew. But the divine act only has any true certainty. Salvation would be the most uncertain of all un-

* [The peculiar power of the aorist seems to be, that it is an indefinite past formed from the future, and combining or involving it: a prophetic past.]

† [*Gegeben*, as before.]

certain things, if it rested not on the objective act of God in Christ, but on the wavering subjectivity of man. Only by this its objectivity is the gospel a true glad tidings, which *nothing can remove;* even unbelief can merely refuse it. (Comp. upon δοξάζειν the remarks at John xvii. 4.)

Ver. 31–34. This profound and colossal thought, which indeed divine power alone could generate and reveal to men, inspires the Apostle to a dithyrambic of faith, which even in a purely formal consideration, must be acknowledged to equal any of the most sublime creations of human language; wherefore even Longinus, it may be too principally for the sake of this passage, ranks the Apostle with the greatest orators.* The absolute power of God makes every thing earthly vanish: "if God be for man, what can be against him?" But the greatest possible act of God's love is the giving up of His Son; in that all else which can be thought and wished for lies enclosed.

Ver. 32. *ἴδιος* has reference to the merely adopted children of God (viii. 19). The *ὀυκ ἐφείσατο* is chosen with regard to Gen. xxii. 12, the history of Isaac being typically conceived. For *τὰ πάντα* D.F.G. read *πάντα* only, which I rather prefer; it comprehends the idea more absolutely, while *τὰ πάντα* has respect to ver. 30. Inasmuch, however, as in the moments there enumerated, especially in the *δοξάζειν*, all is absolutely included, it comes back to the same thought. Ver. 33, &c. I prefer, with Augustine, the interrogative form throughout; the vividness of the language gains much by it.—*Εγκαλέω* = *κατηγορέω,* comp. Acts xix. 38, xxiii. 28, xxvi. 2.—Upon *ἐκλεκτός* comp. at Rom. ix.—Upon *εἶναι ἐν δεξίᾳ* comp. in the Comm. Part ii. p. 488, 3 Edit.—Upon *ἐντεύξις* comp. at ver. 26. Used of Christ intercession signifies the continuing *communication* of His atoning and redeeming power to men; it is, like all which proceeds from Christ, to be understood not verbally merely, but really. Comp. more particularly at Heb. vii. 25; ix. 24.

Ver. 35–39. As God and Christ can neither contradict themselves in their efficacy, nor alter, but as they are throughout and constantly *for* Christians, so neither can any thing earthly draw the faithful away from them. Man only has the sad prerogative

* Erasmus observes of this passage quite justly: "quid usquam Cicero dixit grandiloquentius!

of being able to draw himself away from the eternal Pitier* by *unbelief*, the mother of all sins. (Comp. at John xvi. 9.) The whole world, indeed, with all its powers, its enticements, and its threatenings, is against the believer; but what is the world against God, who does what He will with its powers in heaven and on earth!

Ver. 36. The parenthetic citation describes the Christian's constant danger of life; it is taken from Ps. xliv. 23. The expression πρόβατα σφαγῆς describes the adversaries' contempt, who regarded the Christians as devoted to death.—Ver. 37. ὑπερνικᾶν is found only here in the N. T. The preposition strengthens the meaning; Josephus uses ὑπεραγαπᾶν, ὑπερισχύειν, and similar expressions in like manner, as corroborations of the *simplicia*.—The reading διὰ τὸν ἀγαπήσαντα has important authorities, especially D.E.F.G., notwithstanding the genitive evidently gives an apter thought, since the power is thereby more decidedly referred to God, as the origin of it.—The farthest contrasts are placed together, in order rhetorically to mark the idea of allness. That which is common to all is the idea of the created (the κτίσις, ver. 39), which is opposed to the divine as the eternal. No creature can do any thing else than what God wills, for He holds them all in his hand; now it is not God's will to destroy the saints by sufferings, but to perfect them, consequently every creature must serve to bring the saints to their object.

As to the text, in some Codd. ἐξουσίαι is added, in others, which the *text rec.* follows, δυνάμεις is placed before ἐνεστῶτα and μέλλοντα. The latter reading is evidently founded merely in the desire to rank the δυνάμεις immediately with the ἄγγελοι and ἀρχαί, from which they seem to be separated by ἐνεστῶτα and μέλλοντα. The addition of ἐξουσίαι, however, may be derived from the passages 1 Cor. xv. 24; Eph. vi. 12; Col. ii. 15. (At these passages comp. more particularly upon the different degrees of angels.) It is by no means entirely necessary by angels to suppose *evil ones*, because unless they were so they could not wish to draw away from the gospel, for Gal. i. 8, Paul puts the case even that an angel from heaven may preach another gospel. All the terms are to be taken here in their most general sense, and do not need any closer definition, as life and death, height and depth; the

* [Ps. ciii. 13.]

indefinite expressions are to denote all that can be thought of, and are only a rhetorical paraphrase of the conception of allness.—Ἐνεστῶτα = πάροντα, "what is present," occurs also Gal. i. 4; 1 Cor. vii. 26.

SECTION V.

(IX. 1—XI. 36.)

THE RELATION OF ISRAEL, AND OF THE GENTILE WORLD, TO THE NEW WAY OF SALVATION.

After this explicit exposition of the new way of salvation, (ch. iii. 6), and after the portraiture of the manner in which the development both of the individual and of the whole (ch. vii. 7) is conditioned by the same, the Apostle Paul might naturally have brought the doctrinal part of his Epistle to an end. But, in the meanwhile, the song of triumph with which he terminated that exposition, awakened powerfully his feelings for his own nation, for whom all glory in Jesus Christ had more immediately been promised and designed. For this very people, to which he belonged, the Israel of God, had forfeited the divine promises the moment they were fulfilled, and they were entrusted to the heathen. This unexpected issue, this peculiar relation of the two great portions of mankind to God's new way of salvation, reversing, as it did, their positions with regard to the covenants of God, Japhet coming to dwell in the tents of Shem (Gen. ix. 27), held back the pen of the Apostle, and before St Paul attains the close of the Epistle, he expresses himself in words full of mystery upon God's election by grace (ix. 1–29); with a view of evincing, not that God had proved unfaithful to his promises, but, rather, that the Jews had, wilfully, maintained the righteousness which is by the law, while they rejected the righteousness by faith which God had revealed unto them (ix. 30—x. 21.) Before, however, he concludes, he points to a time when the remnant of holy seed remaining in the nation of Israel shall again be grafted into the olive tree and so all Israel shall be saved; and this gives him an occasion of terminating with praises of the love, the wisdom, and the knowledge of God.

§ 14. OF THE ELECTION OF GRACE.

(IX. 1—29.)

The ninth chapter of our Epistle belongs to those passages of Holy Writ in which the unfathomable nature of its contents, and the colossal character of its ideas, are exhibited in a more than usually conspicuous light.* On this account, it has ever been, since the time of Augustine, a hinge around which the prevailing tendencies within the Church have moved, and such is it even now. The [Roman] Catholic Church, in striking upon this rock, fell under the dominion of a Pelagianizing view, and daily experienced all the injurious consequences which are wont to accompany this tendency; while, on the other hand, in the Protestant † Church, at the present moment, in their endeavour to master the import of this chapter, men have either fallen down the precipice of the absolute prædestination of the evil to evil, or have been betrayed into the gulf of an universal restoration;‡ of which errors, the former leads at one time to desperation, at another to security,

* Luther very truly says, on the reading of this section, "Who hath not known passion, cross, and travail of death, cannot treat of foreknowledge (Election of Grace) without injury and inward enmity towards God. On this account must Adam be first fairly dead, before he may bear this thing, and drink this strong wine. Wherefore, take heed that thou drink not wine, while thou art yet a sucking babe. Each several doctrine had its own season and measure and age." A noble instance of the wisdom of the great reformer. On the subject of the following investigation, see the treatise upon Rom. ix. by Steudel, in the Tubigen Journal, 1836, No. 1, p. 1–95, and by Haustedt in Pelt's Theol. Mitarb., No. 3. In the same work will also be found an essay by Meyer, upon the line of thought in Rom. ix.–xi. Ruckert, in addition to his commentary, gives a separate treatise upon the doctrine contained in Rom ix., in the first number of his Exegetic Magazine. In this section, Ruckert discovers the rigid doctrine of Prædestination.

† *Evangelisch.*

‡ Schleiermacher's doctrine upon the subject of the Election of Grace (in the journal conducted by himself with De Wette and Lucke, No. 2) is an entirely anti-Calvinistic one, since he maintains the restitution of all things. Glöckler, Benecke, and Höllner, also adopt the Apocatastasis. Reiche altogether questions the objective truth of the Apostle's statements.

while the latter, as the Scripture plainly declares, must have moral indifference for its inevitable result. In the meanwhile, the symbolical books of the Lutheran Church, especially the Formula of Concord, as well as the "Confessio Marchica"* among the reformed confessions, have already, in all essential points, delivered the true scriptural definition; and many of their commentators have, in the main point, adhered to them.† The causes which have, notwithstanding, led men so frequently, and on different sides, to depart from it, were probably, first, the inward one, of the want of a real experience of grace, and, in the next place, the outward one, of taking up with insulated passages, without having regard to their connection with others, and with the general teaching of Scripture. The want of experience leads to Pelagianism; the upholders of the absolute predestination of the evil to evil take the ninth chapter of our epistle apart from the eleventh; the defenders of universal restoration take the eleventh without the ninth. In order to avoid this one-sidedness, let it be our first endeavour to make ourselves acquainted with the connection which this momentous chapter has with itself, and with the whole of the Epistle, and teaching of Holy Scripture, before we examine more closely the particular points in it.

The fifth section (ch. ix.–xi.) of the dogmatical portion of our epistle exactly corresponds with the first section of it (ch. i. 18—iii. 20.) In this first section, the Apostle had considered the relation in which both Jews and Gentiles stood to the first way of salvation, the law; in the fifth, he considers the relation of the Jews and the Gentiles to the new way of salvation, the gospel. We are not, however, by any means to look upon the ninth chapter as a resumption of the same subject which was treated ch. i. 18—iii. 20; the Apostle is speaking, on the contrary, of a very dif-

* Compare Augusti's "Corpus libr. symb." (Elberfeldi, 1827), page 382 and following.

† Especially, among more recent commentators, Flatt, and Beck, in his "Pneumatico-Hermeneutical development of the ninth chapter of the Epistle to the Romans, Stuttgart, 1833." Only Beck's paper, which contains so much that is excellent, would have been greatly improved, if, in connection with this chapter, he had at the same time elucidated chapters x. and xi. Tholuck (whom my respected colleague, Professor Höfling, in his "Beleuchtung des Daumerischen Sendschreibens," Nuremberg, 1832, follows in essential points) takes the middle course, and explains some insulated passages very well, but he has neither delivered himself with sufficient precision upon the remarkable passages, ch. xi. 25–32, nor has treated ch. ix. enough in connexion with ch. x. and xi., to give entire satisfaction.

ferent matter; at the same time the contents of either section have a close affinity one to the other, since the relation of the Jews and of the Gentiles to both of God's dispensations were very similar. For, with regard to the law, their situation was this. By far the greater number of the Gentiles had transgressed it in the grossest manner, and so were sunken in an abyss of misery; while some few among them really fulfilled it, according to their relative measure of knowledge. In consequence of these opposite conditions, both divisions of them were fitly disposed for the reception of the gospel, the new way of salvation. For those gross transgressors had experienced the dreadful consequences of sin which in them had become exceeding sinful, and so grace was able in them to be all powerful; while the more virtuous heathen had likewise attained, by their noble endeavours, to the true blessing of the law, the conviction of sin (Rom. iii. 20); and, on that account, they also were led to embrace the gospel as a remedy. And with regard to the Jews, although a small portion of them might be in the last mentioned condition, yet the relation of the greater number of them to the law was such that they gave it an outward obedience, but inwardly transgressed it—a case which might occur with individuals among the Gentiles also, though it was a very rare one. And so arose the melancholy consequence, that the law was unable to work its blessing on Israel, it could not, that is, effect any conviction of sin; they confidently looked upon themselves as righteous, and yet were no less sinful than the most degraded among the heathen, if not in the outward, yet in the inward man; and this relation of the two parties to the law would naturally regulate their respective attitudes, with regard to the new way of salvation in the gospel. The great mass of the Jews who were inaccessible to the faith, were sure to reject it, only those few availed themselves of the proffered way of salvation; while with the heathen, on the contrary, it was precisely the great mass of them who were disposed to receive salvation in Christ; and so the truth of the word (Rev. iii. 15, 16), "I would thou wast either hot or cold, so then, because thou art lukewarm, I will spew thee out of my mouth," was established both in the Jew and in the Gentile. The Gentiles, viewed as grievous transgressors of the law, were cold, as sincerely fulfilling the law they were warm, and so, in both capacities, they were susceptible of grace, whereas the great mass of the Jews came between these two conditions. They strove in an hypocritical manner after the fulfilling of the law, but they had no inward hatred against sin, nor any fire of true and divine love. And so fell Israel from his vocation, and the heathen world stepped into his place.

By this means was brought about a strange complication. Mankind had the appearance of being more powerful than God, since they were able, through their sins, to make void what God had promised. To show, however, that this is not the case, but that God observes justice in all His ways, this is the great object of the Apostle in the present section; on which account also, xi. 33, he exclaims, "Oh, the depth of the riches, both of the wisdom and knowledge of God!" He proves, I say, that, from the beginning, the promise of God was spoken not to the Israel after the flesh, but only to that which was after the Spirit (comp. ix. 7 with ii. 28);* but, among these last, the promise had already found its fulfilment, namely, among the Israel of God, whether they were Jews or Gentiles. The contradiction, therefore, was only an apparent one (ix. 30), when the Gentiles, who sought not after righteousness, attained to it, while the righteousness-seeking Jews received it not, because the endeavour of the Jew after righteousness had been one that appeared so only in the sight of men, but in the eye of God had been a real transgression of the law; and, on the other hand, what, in the case of many a Gentile, would appear to human eyes, a non-seeking after righteousness, had, in fact, been an inward fulfilment of the law. And thus there had been in God's dealings a strict consistency, which manifested itself no less in the adoption of the true spiritual children of Abraham, than in the rejection of his merely fleshly issue; and which is apparent from other things, and especially from this, that the heathen, if they fall from their vantage ground of faith (xi. 17), might again, on their part, be deprived of the gospel (which has already, in some degree, been verified in the Oriental church), while, in like manner, there is a possibility for the Jews, on their becoming ready to receive the faith, to enter again into their calling; yea, the Apostle expressly announces that, with regard to Israel, an uni-

* Compare also Deut. xxxii. 5, where it is said of the rebellious Israelites, "they are blemishes and not His children." [Their spot is not the spot of his children, Eng. vers.]

versal conversion really impends (xi. 25.) So far the connexion of thought is plain enough; and it necessarily follows from this, that the Apostle neither intends by the grace of God to take away from man the free determination of the will, nor by means of the latter to question the all-sufficiency of grace—his only object is to establish both together. The manifestation of the grace of God is always made to depend upon the more or less of fidelity with which men employ that knowledge of divine things which they already have. (Ezek. xxxiii. 12.)

In the meanwhile, it must be allowed, this simple connexion of ideas would not have been misunderstood as often as it has been, if it were not for an intervening discussion (ix. 14–29), which appears to lead to a very different result; namely, the declaration of St Paul, that "God hath mercy upon whom he will have mercy, and hardens whom he will harden." This declaration, viewed in itself, might very conceivably lead those who believe in the eternal damnation of the wicked, to the doctrine of absolute predestination, as, on the other hand, in the case of those who do not uphold the former tenet, it serves just as easily to establish that of the restoration; the compassionating and the hardening presenting themselves only in the sense of an earlier or a later election; and the close of St Paul's argumentation (xi. 23), while it is directly opposed to the doctrine of the predestination of the wicked, which loses all semblance of truth as soon as ch. ix. 14 is viewed in connection with ch. xi., furnishes a very plausible ground for the last-mentioned interpretation, because the whole question there appears to be about the final reception of all, without one word being spoken of the damnation of any, and the whole reasoning issues in the great thought, "God hath concluded them all in unbelief, that He might have mercy upon all," (xi. 32); and thus the earlier or later disobedience, together with the unbelief which is necessarily connected with it, is just as much attributed to all as the earlier or later experience of the mercy of God. Consequently, as ch. i.–iii. teaches the universality of sin, so ch. ix.–xi. would appear to indicate the universality of redemption, and so, in *this* point of view also, both sections would correspond one with another. But, although perhaps we may not be able to point to any passage in St Paul's Epistles, with the exception of that in 2 Thes. i. 9, which expressly teaches the doctrine of eternal damnation*—nay, it must be admitted that they contain expressions, such as 1 Cor. xv. 28, which rather seem to lead to the opposite conclusion—yet the New Testament, in those portions which do not belong to St Paul, and notably in the discourses of Jesus Christ Himself (Matt. xxv. 41, &c.), and that not merely in parabolic language (Matt. xii. 32; xxvi. 24; John xvii. 12), contains such decisive passages for this opinion, that we should be very cautious how we place the Apostle Paul in contradiction with them. The business of the expositor is certainly to find the true sense of the passage before him, and not to allow himself to be diverted in his operation through fear of a contradiction of other places; still he would do well to reflect whether his operation have reached the true meaning of the words, if it issue in an open contradiction with other passages of Scripture; and even such is the case here. For, granting that by admitting the doctrine of a restoration, the passage receives a consistent meaning, it by no means follows that this may not be obtained without this admission; and if this be the case, the last-mentioned sense must be preferred, as the one which was really in the Apostle's contemplation, since, at all events, it must be allowed that St Paul, though he does not bring it prominently forward, is far from combating the doctrine of eternal damnation, or preaching explicitly the doctrine of the restoration. The following considerations may serve to indicate the practicability of such an explanation of the passage in question, as may avoid both the one and the other of the two extremes.

The difficulty and obsurity of the whole section before us are diminished when we reflect that it by no means contains any thing peculiar, since the same ideas which so startle us in reading it, are also expressed throughout the whole of the Old as well as the New Testament. It is only their conciseness, their bold and powerful utterance, that lends them, as it were, an unprecedented appearance here. There are two series of apparently conflicting representations of the relation of mankind to God, which pervade to the whole of the sacred writings. According to one series, all appears to depend upon man, his earthly position as well as his eternal position in the world to come. Already, in the Old Testament,

* The doctrine of eternal damnation is implicitly given in the passage Rom. ix. 4, upon which compare the commentary. In Rom. ii. 8, 9, 16, the eternity of the punishment of the wicked is not expressly marked, and the same applies to 1 Cor. v. 13; xi. 32.

laws were placed before man, accompanied with blessings and with curses: if he observed them, he was bid to expect welfare and peace both here and hereafter; if he observed them not, the contrary portion awaited him. In this point of view, man is represented as responsible for all his actions, and for the development of his whole life; he appears as the absolute master of his destiny. And in the New Testament, a similar series of expressions presents itself. "Believe and be baptized," is the command given to man: it is their own affair; it rests with them to receive or not receive it. The most arduous commandments are imperatively laid upon them, "Be ye perfect," or "Be ye holy!" Of the impenitent and unbelieving, it is pronounced, "Ye would not!" It is the Lord Himself who calls with deepest sorrow; it is the Creator who cries with tears before his creature, "how often have I desired to gather you, as a hen gathereth her chickens together, but ye would not!" (Matt xxiii. 37; Luke xiii. 34.) But, by the side of this view, there is another series of representations which apparently constitute a complete contradiction of the first.* It is expressly said that it is "God that worketh both to will and to do in man of his good pleasure," (Phil. ii. 13), while immediately before occur the words, "work out your own salvation with fear and trembling." Christ Himself says, "All that the Father giveth me is mine; no man can come unto me except the Father draw him." (John vi. 37, 44.) "No man can come unto me except it be given him of the Father," (John vi. 65); and, "without me, ye can do nothing." (John xv. 5.) Moreover, it is said, "a man can receive nothing (and therefore neither truth nor untruth) except it be given him from Heaven." (John iii. 27.) According to this view, man no longer appears as the lord of his destiny, but Almighty God alone, who worketh all in all. And on this account do all saints acknowledge, with the Apostle Paul at their head, "through the grace of God, I am what I am;" everything, the truth, the belief, the reception of grace, is God's work in man, and man may as justly call his conception, and birth in his mother's womb, his own work, as he can call the life of faith his own work. The believer is God's work, created in Christ Jesus unto good works. (Ephes. ii. 10.) "He

* Compare my remarks in the earlier volumes of this Commentary, viz. vol. i., Matt. xiii. 10, 17, 36, 43; xxv. 34, 36. Vol. ii., Matt. xxvii. 3, 10.

that glorieth, let him glory in the Lord." (2 Cor. x. 17.) Now, on the side of the good, this statement of the exclusive operation of God, as delivered in Scripture, is easily understood and admitted. He who has abandoned the Pelagian point of view finds no difficulty in conceiving that the good are not good *beside* God, in such sense that He is acquainted with their good thoughts, resolutions, works only from without, rather will he feel that no man is good but the one God, who Himself both is the good that is in them, and works the good that he discerns in them. But, if such be the relation of man to God, then it further plainly appears that man cannot reserve any good for himself, even though the greater portion be of God, as, for example, the free continuation of the work of regeneration, which God has begun (for what God begins God alone can continue), or belief in grace, or the apprehension and appropriation of the same ;* for this apprehension is precisely the capital point in the whole work of conversion, and this would reserve to God only a secondary part, or, at any rate, man would admit God only to an equal share in the production of the new man, which is certainly altogether inadmissible. It is God who makes the beginning, the middle, and the end in the work of conversion. He gives grace, and empowers man to embrace it at the beginning, and hold it fast to the last ; all, in short, is God's, and nothing is man's of his own. Meanwhile, although we maintain the operation of God in man in its fullest extent, this will yet combine very well with the first series of expressions which apparently attribute all to man, so long as we keep to the side of the good. For the working of God by no means takes away the freedom of man, but rather perfects it. God works in the good and holy not externally to their wills, but rather within them, and fills them with that energy from a higher world which they experience in themselves. Hence it is, that he is able to create in them to will and to accomplish, without their ceasing to be free, nay, by this operation it is that they just become truly free, since so long as they are able to will any thing, other than what God works, they have not the *libertas*, but rather, at the best

* Compare the subjoined passages in which conversion, belief, fidelity, are expressly referred to God, and nothing of his own left to man. Jerem. xxxi. 18 ; Heb. xii. 2 ; Luke xxii. 32 ; 1 Cor. iv. 7; 2 Thess. iii. 2 ; 1 John v. 4.

(as Adam before he fell), the *libera voluntas*, or (as is the case with fallen men, in whom exists a predominating inclination to what God willeth *not*), the *liberum arbitrium*. The whole world of good angels, as also the just men made perfect,* will nothing and can do nothing of themselves, but only through God, and yet are they free, yea, among the creatures they alone are free, since in them God works as in beings whom He hath constituted in independence and freedom. Moreover these imperative addresses to men, "Be ye perfect," &c., are intelligible, notwithstanding the fact that man is not able to make himself perfect, but only God, when understood with reference to the good, since this divine command is no other than that creative word whereby they become perfect, according to that deep saying of Augustin, *Da quod jubes, et jube quod vis.*

The whole weight of the difficulty falls thus upon the side of the evil. God is in Himself, substantially, The Good. He wills and creates only the good; and so it is conceivable, how in good men who are known to him, he operates all that is good. But then He is absolutely separate from the evil, which, otherwise, has no substantial being, by virtue of his holy nature he is not able to will it;† and yet the Scripture says that God, according to his eternal foreknowledge, not only knows all evil, but that He works it too. The former assertion alone might at first suffice, since in consequence of the unity of operation in all His attributes, the knowledge of God cannot be conceived apart from his operation; but then the Scrip-

* Meanwhile no created being has this freedom innate within it. It is the result of establishment in the war against sin. So that we cannot say that God might have so made all conscious beings that it should have been impossible for them to sin. It is necessary for the creature to retain the possibility of prevaricating from the law of life implanted in it by God, in order that it may not hold its perseverance therein as somewhat merely mechanical.

† The difficulty which many find in this whole cycle of doctrine, is aggravated by the want of a distinct conception of the fundamental ideas, good and evil. The good may, it is true, in a subordinate sense, signify a relation, but even then only where it is a question of a merely legal righteousness. In its true and highest meaning, it is to be taken as a substantial thing. God's essence alone is good, and where good is, there is God. On which account no man can generate good, it must be imparted unto him. On the other hand the evil is nothing substantial (to affirm which is Manicheism), and yet it is not without reality (a mere μὴ ὄν); it is a real but inwardly, and by consequence also an outwardly disturbed relation. And therefore all the powers of the evil are in substance good, only their employment has been perverted. And from this it is that God may be operative, in and with all the evil, and yet from the evil, as evil, remain absolutely separate.

ture adds to this the explicit declaration, that God worketh evil, both here and in other passages as well. In the prophecies of the Old Testament, from Gen. ix. 27, downwards, God's knowledge of evil is decisively enough proclaimed. "Japhet shall dwell in the tents of Shem," but then the descendants of Shem are to fall from their vocation. Again, in Deut. xxxi. 16, 17, 20, 21, and Deut. xxviii., xxix., xxx., the fall of the people of Israel is predicted in the distinctest manner, and no less clearly is it signified (precisely as in Rom. xi.), that after this fall Israel will be converted and inherit the blessing. The passion of the Messias is foretold in the clearest manner, and this involves also the knowledge of those by whom He was to suffer. (Comp. Ps. xciv. 11, 1 Cor. iii. 20.) In like manner Jesus knew who it was that should betray him (John vi. 64, &c.), and yet chose Judas to be one of his disciples; He knew beforehand that Peter would fall, He warned him, and it came to pass as Jesus had already foreseen and spoken. In consequence of this God's absolute knowledge of evil, it is also said (Is. xlv. 7), "I form the light and create darkness, I make peace and create evil," and (Amos iii. 6), "Shall there be evil in the city, and the Lord hath not done it?" He hardeneth Pharoah, He awakeneth Nebuchadnezzar, in short He worketh what He will, good as well as evil. To say that these are merely Oriental phrases is evidently inapplicable to the solution of this difficulty, nor again would any man be disposed in the face of these and similar passages to maintain that God does not foreknow the free actions of man, or at least if he foreknow the good, because the good has a being, to deny that he knows the evil, since evil is a nonentity. For the world's history developes itself as well by evil actions as by good, even as the crucifixion of the Son of God, which was brought about by actions perfectly free, is the turning point of the old and the new world; and if there be any thing that God does not know, then it becomes impossible to admit any true foreknowledge in God, and consequently any personal God at all. Since, therefore, as we remarked before, it is found impracticable, upon deeper considerations of the subject, to separate the foreknowledge from the predetermination of God, nothing remains but to take the thoughts of holy Scripture as they are presented to us, and to enquire in what way it would have them understood. That it should mean that God wills the evil as evil, and hath wrought it Himself in His creatures, is so manifestly contradictory to innumerable passages of it, and also to its entire spirit, that none of the elder partizans of the rigid doctrine of predestination, Augustine, Gottschalk, Calvin, ever ventured to maintain it; they only said that, whereas by the fall of Adam, which took place without the predetermination of God, mankind had become a *massa perditionis*, God, out of them, by an absolute decree of grace, and by means of *gratia irresistibilis*, hath elected some to happiness, and (as Gottschalk and Calvin infer), by a decree of reprobation, hath appointed others to perdition. The later supralapsarians were the first who went so far as to maintain that the fall of Adam himself was predetermined, in which, indeed, the doctrine of a *gratia irresistibilis* being once admitted, they were more consistent than Augustine and his followers; nay, in consequence of their principles, they were obliged to derive even the fall of the devil and his angels from the decree of God, and not from the misuse of their own free will. Still, as surely as we see it to be the doctrine of Scripture, that God does not work evil as evil, it being the melancholy privilege of the creature, in virtue of the free will created within him, to be able to generate evil, so surely is it equally impossible to exclude evil, viewed as a phenomenon, from the divine operations. The abstract evil never appears in history, it is but evil personalities, who, with their evil deeds, ever appear on the scene; these, however, exist in necessary combination with the world of good, because, in every evil being, and even in the devil and his angels, the powers themselves with which they act are of God, who bestows on them at the same time both the form in which, and the circumstances among which, they may come into manifestation.* With reference to this latter agency of God *in* evil, He is said in Scripture to be the originator of evil itself, considered as a phenomenon in history, and this was what the ancient dogmatical authors† intended to express by the canon,

* Without this infinitely consolatory doctrine, the man whom hostile elements assail, would be obliged to believe himself abandoned without hope to their savage power. Consider the martyrs of the early church in presence of the shocking wickedness of their persecutors; what could have inspired them with courage, if they had not been upheld by the sure conviction that God, in his wisdom, had ordained even this way, in order to their perfection and happiness, and therefore had summoned up such forms of evil as those which they saw opposed to them.

† Nor has the most recent science been able to produce any thing more satisfactory upon the relation of human freedom to the divine omnipotence, than the old theory of the *concursus* contains. Only this must not be so understood as if God contributed one

Deus concurrit ad materialè, non ad formale actionis malæ. Certainly, after this method of understanding it, the great and perhaps ever insoluble problem still remains, namely, the ability of a created being to act contrarily to the will of God.* Meanwhile we must proceed upon the supposition of this ability as upon an axiom, even as we lay it down as an axiom that the world was created out of nothing, without forgetting that of the *how* the world came to be from out of God, and through God, does not on that account cease to be a problem. What has been said, however, will serve to elucidate the various expressions used in Scripture, regarding the relation of free beings to God, and solve, at the same time, in essential points, the difficulty of the passage under our consideration. We thus avoid the predestination of the evil to evil, as well as the restoration of all things, and maintain, on the contrary, an election of grace in the case of the holy,† in pursuance of which God not only knows who will be holy and happy, but also effects that they may be holy and happy, without abolishing their own free self-determination. This, as the *confessio Marchica* very pertinently says, is "one of the very most consolatory articles," for, whereas no man is acquainted with the mind of God, and God excludes no man from happiness (1 John ii. 2; 1 Tim. ii. 4), although God knows who excludes himself, so each one can and may hold himself as elected. This belief that we are elect, can injure none but him who inwardly is so impure as to dream it possible for a man to be happy without becoming holy, nor, on the other hand, without this belief can any one be made perfect; for, upon what shall a man found the certainty of his happiness, if he may not presume to rest it upon the unalterable decree of

half to the execution of the free deed and man the other, but rather that God alone and exclusively is the creator as well as the upholder of the whole man, and of every deed he does.

* The assertion that, as the possibility of a thing is already the thing in the germ, if God have created man with the possibility of sinning, he must have also created the germ of sin in him, is not tenable, because it is only in the case of substantial realities that there can be any question of a germ at all. But evil is not any substantial reality, the evil is the deflection of created will from the will of God; this originated in a free deed, which was in fact the beginning of an entirely new series, but it draws its ground or cause for and in itself alone.

† Although, therefore, man is free, it is impossible that all should become evil and oppose God's way of salvation; for, were this possible, man would be more powerful than God, and able to defeat God's plan. Comp. the words of Christ, Matt. xxiv. 24; 1 Cor. x. 13.

God ? Nothing remains but to rest it upon himself, his own will, his own integrity, which, of all conceivable foundations, is the most insecure. Yet we do not by any means conceive this election of grace as a *gratia irresistibilis*, which necessarily draws after it the whole doctrine of predestination, with its most extreme consequences, but only, as we do not attribute to the holy and the happy the smallest part in that by which they become such, for that is the mere work of God, so man, certainly, in every stage of his earthly development, reserves the negative ability of resisting grace, he may fall at any time from it. So that the whole merit as entirely belongs to God, as the whole of the guilt belongs to man alone.* Though the whole development and historical formation of the evil in the world depends upon God, so far as it is He who causes the evil to be evil in that particular form in which it is so, yet the being evil, in itself, is the simple consequence of the misuse of man's own free will. Taken in this scriptural point of view, history becomes no stiff necessity, no fatal physical evolution, nor, on the other hand, are mankind exhibited as a number of little gods, each one of whom makes of himself even whatsoever he may please. The truth is, that in God all is necessary, as in man all is free—not, however, in mere supposition, but in living truth ; and it is only thus that the ideas of guilt and judgment have their deep and awful significance. All evil, in God's hand, serves but for a foil and for the promotion of the good, and yet His wrath burns with justice against it, because it originates only in the wickedness of the creature which receives its punishment from righteousness. The possibility of this punishment

* The non-resistance of grace in the holy does not signify the same thing with the receiving of grace. The former is the pure negative, the latter is positive, and presupposes an energy in the will, which is first wrought in man by God. Man, therefore, hinders God's work, but he is not able to promote it, in the same manner in which man is in a condition to destroy created objects in the world, and yet is unable to make a single blade of grass. Nor is there any inconsistency, when we are told in the Bible that in the work of regeneration, man can do nothing of a positive nature, and yet we are directed to pray, for prayer is simply this non-resisting towards that attitude of preparation to the progress of the human mind which is requisite in order to receive the workings of grace. For the rest, it stands to reason, that there is no moment of human existence, nor any conceivable act of men, in which the negative and the positive portion of it can be entirely separated; rather they are continually interpenetrating one another. In the meanwhile, one or the other always has a decisive predominance; the *positive* activity predominates in the natural man, but in the work of regeneration the *receptivity* must prevail, in order to leave the positive side to the Holy Spirit.

being an eternal one, does not depend upon God, but is in the creature alone, which, as it has the power to resist God's will once, may also continue to persevere in its resistance.* The doctrine of the restoration appears inconsequent in admitting the possibility of resistance for a time, and making it cease in as arbitrary a way at a certain point, for there is no point at which the resistance of the evil may not be considered as possible to be continued. Moreover, as this doctrine does not deny the reality of sin, it gains little by having recourse to a final restoration of all the evil, because, if God knew beforehand that a being would be evil for thousands of years, and yet created that being, it might justly be said, that, since evil is so awful a thing, that it would appear better never to have been born than to have sinned but once with no more than the glance of the eye, God should have preferred never to have created such a being at all. The only doctrine consistent with itself, is that which denies the reality of evil, but this leads to a consequence which rests upon a πρῶτον ψεῦδος; for, according to this, the quality of all actions is alike. Whereas, if we assume the reality of sin, and admit only the problem of the ability of the creature to resist God, the whole doctrine of Scripture follows in order, and both divine and human interests are perfectly secured. And the principles here laid down furnish at the same time the following simple connexion of the passage in question: "I behold with deep sorrow the unbelief of Israel; but God's word is not on that account made of none effect; the All-knowing and Almighty One rather permits both good and evil to have their manifestation according to His will, even as He has long ago predicted the fall of the Jews, and the election of the Gentiles, in the prophecies of the Old Testament" (ch. ix.) But the guilt of this apostacy is not, on that account, at all the less chargeable upon the Jews alone, since by resisting grace, they went about to

* According to the theory of the unreality of sin, and the perpetuation, not of the individual, but only of the race, it might be said that there is neither a restoration, nor yet an eternal damnation. Those who have become entirely evil would perish when they die altogether, and come to nothing, as the withered leaves fall from the tree, while the sanctified alone would continue to live. But it is scarcely necessary to observe that the Bible is far from asserting the personal immortality of some persons only; not to mention, also, that upon this supposition, the grief of St Paul, Rom. ix. 1, &c., would be without adequate motive, "for he who is dead is free from sin," (Rom. vi. 7), and no longer an object of lamentation.

establish their own righteousness, instead of the righteousness of God (ch. x.) Moreover, even in the fallen nation itself, God hath reserved a holy seed, and in this will the fulfilment of the divine predictions one day be realized (ch xi.)

If we now proceed to consider the cycle of expressions employed by the Apostle Paul to expound his doctrine of election, we shall find that the circumstance of earlier or later, which are merely human modes of thinking, and which cannot be thought to have any place in the mind of God, are implied in all of them. The terms *προείδω* (Acts ii. 31 ; Gal. iii. 8), *προγιγνώσκω* (Rom. viii. 29, xi. 2 ; 1 Pet. i. 20), *προορίζω* (Acts iv. 28 ; Rom. viii. 29, 30 ; 1 Cor. ii. 7 ; Ephes. i. 5–11), *προτίθημι* (Ephes. i. 9), and the substantive *πρόγνωσις* (Acts ii. 23 ; 1 Pet. i. 2), and *πρόθεσις* (Rom. viii. 28 ; ix. 11 ; Ephes. i. 11 ; iii. 11 ; 2 Tim. i. 9) express the knowledge and the will of God, before the object of His knowledge comes into outward manifestation. And as all the expressions applied in Scripture to God have been selected not on His account, but only for the sake of man, so too it is only for man that they hold perfectly good. Considered from the human point of view, God does in fact foreknow, although, as far as regards Himself, the whole co-exists in one eternal present. So that, in the expressions in question, there are evidently two distinct classes, first those which express knowledge or discernment, then those which apply to the will. It may be objected that, albeit the will always presupposes the knowledge of that which a man wills, yet our knowledge need not always be combined with the volition of the thing known. God, for instance, knows the evil as such, not simply as a phenomenon, he discerns in the evil deed what it is that makes it evil, in short, God possesses the thought or the knowledge of evil, but not the will. Still, however accurate this statement is, it has nevertheless no relation to the phraseology of St Paul. The Apostle never speaks but of God's knowledge of the evil phenomenon, but this God wills as well as knows ; and it is only and solely because He wills it that it comes into manifestation. We must, therefore, altogether reject the Pelagian distinction of a *prævisio* and *prædestinatio* when we view the question in relation to the good, since it is only with regard to evil that it has a certain degree of truth, and is of no service at all in solving the difficulties in the Apostle's writings. In

St Paul, God's foreknowledge always implies a fore-working and a fore-determination, just as His fore-determination is never without foreknowledge. Now this fore-determination, as has already been demonstrated, does not destroy the freedom of the will, but rather presupposes it. God creates and works in free beings as free, and in beings not free as not free. Now, one remarkable expression of the divine *πρόθεσις* is the term *ἐκλέγειν* (John xv. 16–19; Acts xiii. 17; 1 Cor. i. 27, 28; Ephes. i. 4), equivalent to which is *ἀφοίρζειν* (Gal. i. 15), or the *ἐκλογή* (Rom. xi. 5–7; 1 Thess. i. 4), also *πρόθεσις κατ' ἐκλογήν* = *πρόθεσις ἐκλέγουσα* (Rom. ix. 11), by which the *ἐκλεκτοί* (Matt. xx. 16; xxii. 14; Rom. viii. 33; Col. iii. 12; comp. comment. on Matt. xxii. 14; xxiv. 22) are designated, and which is manifested through the *κλῆσις* to the human consciousness. (Rom. xi. 29; 1 Cor. i. 26; Ephes. i. 18; iv. 1; 2 Thess. i. 11; Heb. iii. 1.) This election of the holy and the blessed (since it is to blessedness alone that *ἐκλογή* in St Paul's language refers, and not, as will be shortly shewn, to subordinate advantages) has nothing compulsory in it: the possibility of resisting still remains in every one of the elect, only with God, in virtue of His omniscience, neither this possibility obtains nor any other possibility whatever. (Matt. xxiv. 24.) Nor does the *ἐκλογή* at all involve in itself the positive rejection of the non-elect. Humanly considered, they also are elect, since God wills the happiness of all; but since they resist this divine will, and God knows it so will be, before Him they are non-elected or rejected, but not through any decree of reprobation, but only through their own rejection of the universal decree of grace.

After these observations, we may now proceed to consider the particulars with some hope of a prosperous issue out of the labyrinth of the Apostle's discourse, which seems, like the sixth chapter of St John, calculated for the express purpose of sifting the Church of Christ.

Vers. 1, 2. St Paul expresses his sorrow for the unbelief of his people with the most earnest protestation; his use of the phrase *ἀλήθειαν λέγω, οὐ ψεύδομαι*, indicates an apprehension that some might not give him credit for these sentiments. It is clear that in the case of the hostile Judaizers, this was so; we have, however, no particular ground for looking for these in Rome; the habitual feelings of the Apostle exerted an involuntary influence upon his immediately present ideas; and he had the less inducement to repress it, inasmuch as he must needs have expected to meet with the counteraction of these his opponents also in Rome.

Tholuck is certainly right in not allowing the words *ἐν Χριστῷ, ἐν πνεύματι ἁγίῳ* to amount to forms of swearing; after these words, we ought rather to understand *ὤν*; but he overlooks the fact that there is the resemblance of swearing in these vehement protestations, which are so heightened by the words *ἐν Χριστῷ* that they come very near in meaning to an oath. There is no kind of ground for Griesbach's proposal to inclose the words *συμμαρτυρούσης μοι τῆς συνειδήσεώς μου* in a parenthesis. Lachman rightly connects them with those following.—Ver. 2. *ὀδύνη* is the stronger expression for sorrow, grief of soul.

Ver. 3. To shew how great his grief is, the Apostle exclaims, *ηὐχόμην αὐτὸς ἐγὼ ἀνάθεμα εἶναι ἀπὸ τοῦ χριστοῦ ὑπὲρ τῶν ἀδελφῶν μου.* The whole passage loses its meaning and its deep earnestness, if we suppose that Paul was really aware that every single individual of the Jewish nation, all mankind indeed, would in the end be blessed. These words, therefore, indirectly contain a strong proof of this conviction, that there is a state of eternal damnation; as he expressly declares, 2 Thess. i. 8, 9, that those who obey not the Gospel shall suffer punishment, even everlasting destruction from the presence of the Lord. See John iii. 36. The words have no meaning unless we understand him to wish to be banished from Christ and so miserable for ever, in place of his brethren (*ὑπέρ* = *ἀντί*, not merely for their advantage, comp. Comment. Rom. v. 8, 12, &c.) This wish, it is true, is an impossible one, since neither does love admit of unhappiness (rather where true love is there must needs be happiness), nor can one brother suffer in place of another (Ps. xlix. 8); Christ alone is able to do that, because He is the representative of all.* But the love of Christ which had been shed

* To maintain the objective possibility of any one giving his soul to be anathema for another, leads by direct consequence to Gichtel's doctrine of the Melchizedekian priesthood, according to which, the Christ within us is able to suffer for sins, in the same manner in which Jesus himself suffered. But this doctrine evidently contradicts the all-sufficiency of the merits of Christ, who, by His once offering of Himself, hath perfected all them that are sanctified (Heb. x. 14). No doubt Christ pours his love into the hearts of the faithful, and they willingly undergo whatever portion of temporal suffering the sin

abroad in the heart of Paul, made him also cry, as the same spirit of Christ had already bid Moses say: "forgive them their sins, if not, then blot me out of thy book" (Ex. xxxii. 32, 33), in which place, also, the sense of the whole passage ought, certainly, not to be completed by the words, "for a certain time," but "for ever." The words may also be taken for an intercession of Paul with Christ,* who was able to do what he was only able to wish, and what, in the form of a wish, he utters of and for himself. Meyer's view will not hold (v. Pelt's Theology, Mitarb. Pt. 3, p. 71), according to which, the imperfect tense is intended to indicate the merely momentary rise of this wish. The imperfect here, as Winer has already rightly remarked (Gram. p. 259), has no narrative force, it only stands, as it often does, for the conjunctive, "I could wish."

'*Αναθέμα* was originally the same with *ἀναθήμα*, but in more recent times, and in the N. T. also, the latter form was used for what was consecrated, devoted to the gods, while *ἀνάθεμα* came to signify any thing accursed, or devoted to the gods in an evil sense, like the Latin *sacer*. It corresponds with *κάθαρμα*, *περίψημα*, *περικάθαρμα* (1 Cor. iv. 13), that is, a victim for a community, a

which is in man brings with it for them; but the undertaking of the burthen of sin for another upon one's self, together with its eternal consequences, is a thing not to be conceived of any man except in the person of Jesus alone. The partizans of the so-called pure love, as Fenelon and Madame Quion, often quote these words; meanwhile, if the doctrine of pure love mean any more than that man ought not to love God on account of his gifts alone, it cannot certainly lay claim to any countenance in Scripture. In the rest, the words of Bengel are worth considering: "de mensurâ amoris in Mose et Paulo non facile est existimare; non capit hoc anima non valde provecta." Such passages as Eph. iii. 13, Col. i. 14, 1 Thess. iii. 10, which are apparently related to the present, require another interpretation, as will appear when we come to explain them. [Gichtel, mentioned at the beginning of this note, was a German enthusiast, born 1638, died 1710.]

* Similar sentiments are of frequent occurrence in the mystics, both of former and of modern times, which are to be viewed as the offspring of their overflowing love. So Angelus Silesius, in his "Cherubinical Pilgrim," No. 28, says:—

> Kein Tod ist seliger als in dem Herrn sterben,
> Und um das ew'ge Gut mit Leib und Seel 'verderben.
>
> "No death is more blessed than to die in the Lord,
> And for the eternal good with body and soul to perish."

[Angelus Silesius was the name assumed by John Scheffler, a physician of Breslau, born 1624. He became a convert to the Romish faith, and published several works of mystical poetry. He died in a convent at Breslau in 1677. His Cherubinisher Wandersmann is described as having enjoyed great popularity in Germany. See Conversations Lexicon.]

man upon whom, in the case of a pestilence or other national calamity, the guilt of the community, which is supposed to be the cause of the visitation, is laid as upon a victim. This meaning would be applicable here by reading *ὑπὸ*, which is supported by D.E.G.; but *ἀπό*, which, upon critical grounds, merits the preference, does not admit the application of this figure of speech. On this account, it is more to the purpose to compare the Hebrew חֵרֶם, by which we obtain the notion of extrusion, exclusion, banishment. We need not be reminded that the ban here spoken of is not to be understood as an outward exclusion from the communion of the church, or of merely physical death; the depth of the thought points to the spiritual and eternal exclusion from the communion and life of Christ, in which alone Paul had found happiness (viii. 33, &c.) We may supply here *ἐι δυνατόν*, which occurs in a similarly hyperbolical passage of Gal. iv. 15.

Ver. 4. In order to set the depth of the fall of Israel in the plainest light, Paul brings forward all their prerogatives, the exercise of which, nevertheless, was bound up with their obedience (Deut. xxviii.), and which are kept in reserve by God for the people, until the stipulated condition, the obedience of faith, should have been realised in them, just as a throne is withholden from a kingly race overthrown by their own culpability (xi. 29.) In most of all their privileges he places the sacred name *Ἰσραελῖται*, by which the theocratic people were characterized as the soldiers of God (2 Cor. xi. 22, Phil. iii. 5). But in the days of Christ they were no longer victorious in the struggle, as was Jacob of old (Gen. xxxii. 29); on the contrary, they were fallen. The *υἱοθεσία* belonged to the nation as the type of the true Israel of the N. T., for, considered in itself, Israel was yet in bondage (viii. 14), yet the people is already called in hope the first-born son of God. (Ex. iv. 22, Jer. xi. 3.) The *δόξα* here cannot well be applied to the general glory of Israel, since that could not, properly speaking, be mentioned among its especial privileges, nor is the supposition of an Hendiadys more tenable, since the object of the Apostle evidently is to enumerate, one by one, the greater prerogatives of Israel, and on this account *καὶ* is constantly repeated. The best way, undoubtedly, is, to compare it with the Hebrew כְּבוֹד יי (see John i. 1), and to understand the pillar of cloud and fire which lead the people through the wilderness, and was the symbol of the presence of God. To find the reason why the διαθῆκαι are distinguished from the νομοθεσία, we must remember the covenants of God with the patriarchs Abraham and Jacob. The λατρεία specifies the νομοθεσία with reference to the several theocratic institutions of the temple worship. Under ἐπαγγελίαι are included all the prophecies, especially the Messianic ones. *Πατέρες* denote especially the patriarchs, the first ancestors of the race, of whose possession the Israelites were so proud, and by whose blessing they were blessed. The reading ἐξ ὧν would restrict what follows to πατέρες alone, and καὶ ἐξ ὧν reckons the natural descent of Christ among the privileges of the nation. Critical authorities are decisive for καὶ, only F.G. omit it, as also the following τό.

Ver. 5. In the treatment of this famous doxology, interpreters have differed down to the most recent time, according to the dogmatical view which they have taken of the person of Christ. All those who have maintained the divinity of Christ, have understood this passage also of Him ; all those who have denied it, refer it to the Father. Glöckler alone is in favour of referring it to God, though he is far from denying the divine dignity of Christ. On the contrary, he expressly acknowledges it. This impartiality is laudable in itself, and it must be admitted that the momentous dogma of the divine nature of Christ cannot suffer from the loss of a single text; and, moreover, Christian antiquity made but little use of this passage as a proof, properly so called, from an apprehension that too much might be proved thereby, namely, the Sabellian indifference of the persons.* I should, on that account, determine myself, without hesitation, in favour of Glöcker's view, if his reasons were more solid than they are. For he takes the words from ὁ ὢν unto ἀμήν together, and considers the first half, with ἔστι or ἔστω understood, as the subject, and the latter half as the predicate. The words are thus intended to fit into the context in such a way, that Paul praises God for the many tokens of His grace exhibited to the Jews; but as the Apostle had just been afflicted by the thought that all these favours had been forfeited by the people of Israel, Glöckler supposes that these words are only to be viewed as a transient smile called up on the countenance of one in sorrow, by the remembrance of happy moments of his life. But this is obviously a forced construction, and it is much more

* Compare Reiche's Comm. vol. ii. p. 268, note.

simple to say that Paul's intention is to place the human nature of Christ in contraposition to His divine nature. The observation that, by referring it to Christ, the sentence falls into two parts, an apposition, that is, and a doxology, whereas this is not the case if it be referred to God, is entirely insignificant. Only two objections of any moment remain, first, that εὐλογητός does not occur in application to Christ (comp. Luke i. 18, Mark xiv. 61, 2 Cor. xi. 31, Rom. i. 25, Eph. i. 3, 1 Pet. i. 3), but to God alone;* and, secondly, that ὁ ἐπὶ πάντων Θεός can only be predicated of the Father. To the former of these remarks no weight is to be attributed, since it is only so far true that εὐλογητός cannot be applied to mere man, or any creature whatever, nevertheless, but in as far as Christ is God of God, so far does this divine predicate also belong to Him, as much as any of the remaining ones, so that it must be looked upon as matter of mere accident that it has not been assigned to Him in more numerous places. The second observation, on the other hand, is not without its weight, and it is, upon the whole, the only one which can perplex the expositor in his treatment of this doxology. For not only does the expression ἐπὶ πάντων Θεός not occur with respect to Christ (if that were all, the argument would have force, since there is no need that all His names should often occur), but it appears as though it could not be assigned to Him. For, notwithstanding the consubstantiality of the Son with the Father, the latter remains ever the Unbegotten, and so God over all, and the former the Begotten One. If, then, this name could, without violence, be reconciled with the scriptural doctrine regarding the Son of God, the reference of the doxology to Christ must then be abandoned, although every thing else is in its favour, since critical authorities in favour of the omission of Θεός are unimportant to the last degree, being no more than a few citations of the Fathers; and the inversion of the words Θεός ἐπὶ πάντων. does not at all affect the sense. It must, however, be

* In Matt. xxi. 9, Luke xix. 28, ἐυλογημένος is certainly applied to Christ, but it occurs in a quotation from the Old Testament. But if we remember that, with the exception of 2 Tim. iv. 18, the New Testament in general contains no formal doxologies to Christ (see, however, Rom. xvi. 27, Rev. v. 12, vii. 10), the want of places in which the term ἐυλογητός is applied to Christ, is very simply accounted for. But after such passages as John v. 23, the almost total absence of formal doxologies to Christ can be the result of accident alone. The doxology in 2 Peter iii. 18, cannot well be brought to bear, as the genuineness of this epistle has been called in question.

acknowledged, upon a nearer survey of the words *Θεός ἐπὶ πάντων*, that we cannot take *πάντων* as the masculine with *ανθρώπων* or *Θεῶν*, or some such word understood (as is the meaning Lord of all Lords, God of all Gods, Deut. x. 17), since there is here no reference to the Gentiles; it can only be taken in the neuter gender, so that our passage will then be parallel to the words in Rom. x. 12, and Acts x. 36, where it is said, *οὗτός ἐστι πάντων κύριος*. And if we further consider that in John i. 1, &c., the name *Θεός* is applied to the Logos, and, at the same time, the universe is represented as dependent upon Him, it is difficult to see why the Son should not be called *ἐπὶ πάντων Θεὸς*. The expression would only be an improper one in case the Father were conceived as included among *τὰ πάντα*, but it is self-evident that this is not the case, as Paul says, 1 Cor. xv. 27: *ὅταν δὲ εἴπῃ, ὅτι πάντα ὑποτέτακται, δῆλον, ὅτι ἐκτὸς τοῦ ὑποτάξαντος αὐτῷ τὰ πάντα.* I therefore understand the passage in the usual manner with Tholuck, Ruckert,* and other recent expositors, as relating to Christ. Among the various punctuations on record since Erasmus wrote, the one which has found the most favour, is that according to which the words *ὁ ὢν ἐπὶ πάντων* are referred to Christ alone, and the last words taken as a doxology to the Father. But in that case the doxology stands without any connection, and *ἐπὶ πάντων* has no regular position, and, therefore, this can satisfy only those who have an insuperable objection to apply the name *ἐπὶ πάντων Θεός* to Christ. The conjecture of *ὧν* instead of *ὢν*, is certainly an acute one, but it is destitute of any critical authority from manuscripts.

Vers. 6–9. After this introduction, the Apostle proceeds to the argumentation itself. In the first place, he shews how the fall of the Israelites from their vocation does not make void the word of God, and the promises contained in it, since among the descendants of Abraham, to whom these were to be referred from the beginning, were to be understood not the fleshly but only the spiritual progeny. He might even have said that the Word of God had

* The last mentioned scholar's remark, that *εὐλογητός*, when applied to God, must, according to the idiom of the Old and New Testament, always precede the noun, is of no importance. Köllner rightly observes, that the position of the words is altogether not a mechanical thing, but is rather determined, in each particular conjuncture, by the connection, and by the mind of the speaker.

been established by the fall of Israel, since he shews by the quotations from the Old Testament in Rom. ch. ix. 24, &c., that the fall itself had already been predicted in it. St Paul founds the idea of a spiritual Israel, which he had already broached, Rom. ii. 28, 29, upon that passage in Gen. xxi. 11, where Isaac is denoted as the seed to whom the promises belonged, and upon Gen. xviii. 10, 14, which contains the words of the prophecy itself. Isaac is represented as the antithesis to Ishmael, who was born indeed before the former, and yet was not the heir, and therefore stress must not be laid upon the merely natural descent, but rather upon the spiritual affinity with the faith with which Abraham lived. (Compare the detailed treatment of this antithesis between Isaac and Ishmael, Gal. iv. 22, Heb. xi. 1, 9.) The primary object of this demonstration is indeed only to shew that the Word of God remained unshaken, but this would not make the notion that the Apostle had no positive intention of exhibiting Isaac as the figure of the faithful, and therefore of the happy, and Ishmael as the type of the unbelievers, at all the less assuredly false. It is true St Paul does not here express the idea, but it sleeps in the depths of his soul, as appears from Galat. iv. 22, and as will be made more evident by the sequel of the argumentation in this chapter. Only we must not conclude that because St Paul represents Ishmael as the typical representative of the unbelievers, that is, of the non-elected portion of mankind, he therefore viewed Ishmael himself and his descendants as actually condemned; since we ought, on the contrary, to reserve to Ishmael and all the Ishmaelites, the power to cease in the Apostle's sense, to be that which they are, and also to pass over into the spiritual family, just as respecting Israel we must assume for them the power of excluding themselves from the spiritual family. St Paul is not here intending to offer any decision upon the secrets of the divine judgment, as to whether Ishmael in person should be eventually blessed or not, but only wishes his spiritual position, as it occurs in Scripture, to be conceived as symbolical.*

The phrase *οὐκ οἷον ὅτι*, in ver. 6, is elliptic for *οὐ τοῖον ἐστιν, οἷόν ἐστιν ὅτι*, meaning, at the same time, I do not mean to

* As the meek Isaac, who gave his life for a willing sacrifice, is the symbol of the gospel in its peculiarity, so Ishmael, the wild man, whose hand is against every man (Gen. xvi. 12), symbolises the peculiarity of Islam, which was born of the people descended from him. For as the seed already contains the character of the plant which is to be developed from it, so in the ancestors of nations are found those peculiarities which characterise their descendants.

say, or it does not however follow from that. [v. Winer's Gram. p. 282.] Lobeck on Phrynichus, p. 427, adduces similar figures of speech from ancient writers, but a precisely parallel idiom is nowhere found. A similar use of ὡς ὅτι occurs in 2 Cor. xi. 21. 2 Thess. ii. 2. *Λόγος Θεοῦ* refers to the whole of the Old Testament, which would be altogether shaken by the annihilation of so very important a portion as the prophecies.—*Ἐκπίπτειν* answers to נָפַל, the opposite to *μένειν*, and signifies to fall away, to lose power or significance; here in reference to the fulfilment, it means to remain unfulfilled. Israel denotes not the person of the patriarch, but the nation, with reference however first to their physical existence, and secondarily to their spiritual character. No one can possess the latter who wants the natural descent, and *vice versa*. Ver. 7. In like manner *σπέρμα* = זֶרַע is first the physical *soboles*, and then the spiritual; the former are the *τέκνα τῆς σαρκός*, the latter the *τέκνα τοῦ πνεύματος* or *Θεοῦ*. The same distinction between *σπέρμα* and *τέκνα* occur in John viii. 37, 38. *Καλεῖσθαι* here, as frequently in the Old Testament (see Comm. on Luke i. 32), has the signification of being, with the secondary idea of being recognized as such; it can by no means be equivalent to *ἐκλέγειν*, as Tholuck proposes. The quotation, ver. 9, is the substance of Gen. x. 18 and xiv., given freely from memory. The word *ἐλεύσομαι* refers as it were to God's foresight of the accomplished fulfilment, with regard to the phrase *κατὰ τὸν καιρὸν τοῦτον* = כָּעֵת חַיָּה, compare Reiche's letter, p. 15. In the Septuagint, instead of the usual form, we find *εἰς τ. κ. τ.* together with *εἰς ὥρας*, and I agree with Reiche in thinking it probable that originally this last phrase alone stood in the text of the LXX., and the phrase *κατὰ τ. κ. τ.* was first introduced into it from Rom. ix. 9. The expression signifies "this time year," the year being taken as a thing which perishes and again produces itself.

Ver. 10–13. But the history of the holy patriarchs furnishes in the relation of Esau to Jacob a still more decisive proof of the principle that the blessing does not depend upon the fleshly descent. For Ishmael was the son of a bondmaid, which makes it more easily conceivable that the child of the lawful wife should be preferred to him; but Jacob and Esau were both sons of a free woman, nay, they were even twins, and yet as soon even as they were born, and without regard to any act of theirs whatever, their respective positions were assigned, by the predestination of God, according to the passages in Gen. xxv. 22, Mal. i. 3. Here again, then, Jacob corresponds with Isaac, and Esau with Ishmael. Every attempt, however well intended, to mitigate the harshness of the idea, and to avoid viewing Esau as the representative of the reprobate, must here be abandoned, as contrary to the intention of St Paul ,especially as Esau is presented as such elsewhere in Scripture. (Heb. xii. 17.) In this place the Apostle already adopts into his argument the leading idea which he follows out in the 14th and succeeding verses, namely, that God summons evil creatures as well as good into the historical order of the world (not certainly as evil, but as evil beings in this or that definite shape), and therefore these last do not avail to defeat his purpose and system of governing the world, which are made known by the prophecies.

The construction of ver. 10 is elliptical, not inconsecutive ; as Rebecca is named, the most natural word to supply is Sarah, when the sense would be, and not only " Sarah shews this, but also Rebecca." The other ways which have been suggested for completing it, are forced. ***Κοίτη***, bed, an euphemism for cohabitation, where *κ. ἔχειν* is said of the woman who conceives in consequence of cohabitation with any one, *κ. διδόναι* of the man.—Ver. 11. The words *πρασσεἰν ἀγαθόν* points evidently to Jacob, *κακόν* to Esau, so that the meaning is, that although they had neither done either good or evil, yet God spoke of them as if they had. It is doing great violence to the meaning to refer the *πρόθεσις κατ' ἐκλογήν*, which did not depend upon the works which were not in existence, but rested upon the holy will (*μένειν* = עָמַד, remain unalterably fixed), alone of Him who calleth whom He will, Jacob only, and not Esau, with Beck, simply to the right of primogeniture, or with Tholuck to the occupation of the theocratic land. For in St Paul's view, Esau's possession of the primogeniture and the theocracy involved his election to eternal life; as therefore he proves in Galat. iv., that Israel was to be rejected, so in his view Esau is also the rejected son, and the type of all the rejected in general. —Ver. 12. The thought is not materially affected, though we should, as Tholuck does, understand the terms *μείστον* and *ἐλάσσων* of the nations which sprung from Jacob and Esau, since, according to the sense of St Paul and the Scriptures, these latter participate in the character of their fathers, not indeed in every individual, but in the great mass of them. But δουλευέιν need not be understood of political servitude, it must be referred to a state of spiritual dependance into which Esau was brought by throwing away his birthright, while the stream of grace flowed away to Isaac.—Ver. 13. All the assurances that μισεῖν here does not mean to hate, but only to love less, to bestow a less advantage, cannot satisfy the conscientious expositor, since he cannot overlook the fact that St Paul has advisedly selected a very strong and repulsive expression from the passage of Scripture in question. Nor does it make against this, that in the passage of Malachi the immediate question is of outward circumstances, since these also are to be viewed as expressions of the wrath of God.

Ver. 14. It is only in this severe manner of interpretation that the question has any meaning, μὴ ἀδικία παρὰ τῷ θεῷ; and the thrilling answer in ver. 15 suits. The mitigating construction of the passage from ver. 6–13, affords no occasion for such thoughts at all; and, therefore, the interpreter cannot in any way evade the stringent connexion of thought. Only he must not forget at the same time the principle, *Scriptura Scripturæ interpres*, and therefore many to whom the observations which have been already made (ch. ix. 1), have clearly shown that God does no injustice when He hates the wicked, because God is not the cause of his being wicked, but only of his wickedness coming into manifestation in such a form as is most salutary both for himself and for the universe, might demand how are those other passages in which the universality of grace is asserted, to be reconciled with this doctrine of the πρόθεσις κατ' ἐκλογήν. But we have already given this a brief consideration in ix. 1, in treating of the twofold manner in which the subject is represented in Scripture, according to which the whole process in the work of renewal is attributed at one time to God, and at another to man; nevertheless this doctrine forces itself so strongly upon us in every verse of the following passage, that it stands in need of a fresh consideration. The Scripture declares in the most explicit words, that God wills that all mankind should be saved, and come to the knowledge of the truth. (Ezek. xxxii. 11, 1 Tim. ii. 4, Tit. ii. 11, 2 Pet. iii. 9.) This universality of grace would seem, however, to be done away by the πρόθεσις κατ' ἐκλογήν. But, evidently, this could only be the case were we to attribute the activity wherewith man resists grace also to God, in the way in which this is done by the rigid doctrine of predestination. for in that event God would call those who were not elected as it were in mockery, only to put men all the sooner and more surely to confusion ; a representation which can only be described as one of the most remarkable aberrations of the human mind that has ever been revealed. Whereas, if we will only put down the power of striving against grace, and, in short, all that is evil in man, as his own melancholy property, the two manners of expression may easily be reconciled one with another in the following method. God's all comprehending love excludes no man from salvation, whosoever is excluded is himself the cause of his own exclusion. But, on the other hand, God compels no man to be saved, and knows, in virtue of his omniscience, who it is who will exclude himself, even, as in virtue of His omnipotence he is the author of every form of sinful development. In reference, therefore, to this latter consideration, God's will is styled a *πρόθεσις κατ' ἐκλογήν*, in reference to the former God's grace is universal. Though, therefore, in virtue of His attributes of omniscience and omnipotence, God assuredly both foreknows who they are that will resist His grace, and also permits them to appear in definite forms in history, He knows them only as persons who, by misuse of their own free will, have become evil and continued so, and if there exist beings possessing the possibility of resisting God, the relation of God to those in whose case this possibility may have been realized, can be represented no otherwise than as the Bible exhibits it.

Vers. 15, 16. St Paul does not meet the question with a direct answer, he only replies by quoting God's words in Exodus xxx. 19. The question indeed envolves a self-contradiction, and could only have been hazarded by human blindness or temerity, and accordingly, at ver. 20, it meets with its merited censure. God's will is the eternal rule of right (Deut. xxxii. 4.) How then can unrighteousness be in Him ; there is no abstract right to which God is as it were subordinate, but his free and holy will alone is for the creature the rule of right. The circumstance, however, that in the passage here quoted, the mercy of God alone is spoken of, is but an apparent alteration of the difficulty, since, according to the intention of Paul, we must also add, "and whom He will he hardeneth" (ver. 18). The words only agree with the context when taken in the following sense: God's will is absolute, He does what He will, and there is no one who may call him to account, and say, "What doest thou?"* It is self-evident that in God the will cannot be an arbitrary one, but must ever work in union with love and wisdom; but since man is not able to comprehend the ways of God, his duty is humbly to submit himself to His will.

Ver. 15. No distinction need be sought between ἐλεεῖν and οἰκτείρειν חָנַן and רִחַם, both are used only in opposition to the idea of merit, ἐξ ἔργων, ver. 11. But they certainly refer to the election to happiness, not, as Tholuck thinks, to the exhibition of any extraordinary proofs of love. The immediate context of the passage, in the original, gives us here no clue; St Paul treats this as well as the following from a more extended point of view, and we must therefore follow him to his point of observation. Ver. 16. θέλειν and the stronger word τρέχειν, which needs not to be exclusively applied to running in the race course, signify here the positive activity of man, which has no existence in relation to God. Every, even the least portion of good in man, is from God alone.† It is not however here pretended that man is not able to exert a negative power of resisting God. On which account the Scripture continually urges upon him, *ye* would not, *ye* have been unfaithful, disobedient, but then on the other hand it says: it is *God* who hath wrought both the will, and the faith, and the obedience in you.

Ver. 17. Although in ver. 15 the question was only of the gracious operation of God, the example in the present verse is taken from an instance of a directly opposite character, which clearly shews that Paul intends this notion to be supplied in the former verse also. In the passage of Exod. IX. 15, 16, the Scripture expresses itself in such a manner with regard to Pharaoh and his opposition to Moses, the messenger of God, that God would seem to be himself the author of this sinful phenomenon.‡ Every attempt to explain

* It stands to reason that the notion that Paul intends in this place to oppose the Pharisaic doctrine concerning fate, as Herman especially, following Origen and Chrysostom, has construed it, is altogether untenable.

† Glöckler's view of this passage is quite mistaken. He translates it, "It depends not upon man's willing and running, that is, it is not according and subservient to human willing and running, but yet not contrary thereto. St Paul is treating of the causality of the spiritual life, and this must be denied to man, and awarded to God alone.

‡ Glöckler understands ἐξεγείρειν of the elevation of Pharaoh to the throne, and

away the force of these thoughts is altogether contrary to exegetical principles. According to the manifest drift of St Paul, the conceptions denoted by ἐξήγειρα and ὅπως ἐνδείξωμαι, are not to be taken in a diluted sense, but in the full power of their import. It by no means follows from this high view of the subject, that St Paul intends to say that God has made Pharaoh evil by any positive operation, but he only means that God permitted that evil person, who of his own free will resisted all those workings of grace which were communicated in rich measure even to him, to come into manifestation at that time, and under these circumstances, in such a form that the very evil that was in him should even serve for the furtherance of the kingdom of The Good and the glory of God.* Even so, St Paul means to say, must the apostacy of Israel also glorify the name of God, for it too has been brought into manifestation by God in this very form.

St Paul has intentionally sharpened the language of the LXX., who had expressed the thought in milder terms. He renders הֶעֱמַדְתִּיךָ by ἐξήγειρα, whereas the LXX. have ἕνεκεν τούτου διετηρήθης, according to which the idea will be that Pharaoh had made himself evil. But St Paul's translation entirely corresponds

maintains that ἐνδείξωμαι should be taken in a passive sense, "in order that I might be manifested as to my power." The first proposition is altogether untenable, and needs no refutation, and the second does not mitigate the thought, as Glöckler seems to think it does. Moreover, there is a decided predominance of the middle form in the New Testament idiom, and there is no ground whatever to depart from it here.

* It is quite horrible when Gomarus, and the other Supralapsarians say, that when God will condemn a man, He first creates sin in him, in order that after he has been plunged into sin, he may be justly damned. But, in the Apostle's view, the ἐγείρειν of the evil themselves, is an act of the love of God, not only for the members of the kingdom of God and the pious, but even for the wicked. For the evil is in man without having been created by God; when therefore he causes what is lying concealed to come to sight in the concrete appearance, this is just the most powerful mean to bring the wicked into a sense of their condition, and, if possible, to effect their conversion. (See Comm. xi. 8.) If, however, any one should rejoin, before men, this may be true, because they may always hope that the wicked may be converted, but not before God, who, by virtue of his omniscience, knows who they are who will not be converted, for in such persons as should not be converted, their guilt would be even aggravated by every attempt to convert them: the answer must be, that it certainly is the very curse of the evil that they turn even what is good to their own injury, but that God, when he willed the possibility of sin, thereby established also the possibility of persevering in sin, and of misusing His grace. There only remains the matter of fact, which furnishes the ultimate problem, viz., "How came God to create a being with power to withstand Him the Almighty One?" And here nothing is left for man but to be silent, and say: it is God's doing, whatever God does is well done.

with the original text. The interpretation, "permit to stand," "permit to continue," for which Tholuck decides, is no doubt admissible in itself, but in the first place, it is not the nearest to the Hiphil of עָמַד, and next, it is contrary to the sense and intention of the writer, as the following verses clearly shew, and Reiche, Kölner, and Glöckler rightly acknowledge. Ὅπως must be taken strictly τελικῶς; *in order that* Pharaoh might become a monument of the penal justice of God, God provided that the evil actually existing in him should be manifested in this definite form. The last words of the quotation, which in no way affect the main idea, agree with the LXX., only they have ἰσχύν instead of δύναμιν. St Paul therefore substituted ἐξήγειρα with express design, as his argument required, a circumstance which puts all mitigation of the thought out of the question.

As a sequel to the preceding quotation, the Apostle now plainly discovers the previously suppressed antithesis, according to his bold method of pursuing an idea to the very limits of the truth contained in it; for he says, God also hardeneth whom He will. Here, also, the θέλειν of God is obviously not to be understood of mere arbitrariness, which cannot in any way be imagined in God, but of His will, as directed by wisdom and love. But it is objected that the notion of σκληρυνειν (equivalent to which is πωρόω from πῶρος, *callo obducere, obdurare*, Rom. xi. 8, John xii. 40), appears to be in itself inapplicable to God; certainly the usual form is σκληρύνεσθαι or σκληρύνειν ἑαυτόν (see Acts xix. 9, Heb. iii. 8, 13, 15, iv. 7. Occasionally also in the Old Testament and the Apocrypha. Ex. vii. 22, viii. 19; Ps. xciv. 8; Sirach. xxx. 11). But here the hardening, as in Rom. xi. 8, is referred to the will of God. In the Old Testament, on the other hand, הִקְשָׁה ,חִזֵּק (v. 2 Sam. xvi. 10, 1 Kings xxii. 22, Is. lxiii. 17, Deut. ii. 30, Ps. cv. 25), is more frequently found, denoting the positive operation of God against the wicked. The notion of its standing, as Ernesti and Schleusner prefer (like μισεῖν in ver. 13), for a mere equivalent to ὀυκ ἐλεεῖν, is evidently inadequate. They refer to Job xxxix, 16, where it is said of the stork, ἀποσκληρύνει, τὰ τέκνα ἑαυτῆς, *i. e.*, she *neglects* her young. But even there it is a hard thought to say that God neglects one of His creatures. On the other hand, it is not incorrect to refer to the divine presence in the case of evil, provided this be not extended also to good, so as to make the sense, that God will have mercy upon those of whom He foresees that they will, of their own accord, determine themselves to good, and He hardens those of whom He has foreseen the contrary. For the very determination of himself to good in the good man is God's work, but the resisting of good in the evil is no work of God. Meanwhile, this appeal to the prescience of God, even though it be not incorrect in the case of evil, creates more difficulty than it clears up, in that it makes the divine will appear dependent upon the will of man; whereas, the express object of the Apostle, in this place, is to set in clear light the absoluteness of the will of God. The best method, therefore, will be to consider more attentively what is implied in the notion of hardening. In the first place, this hardening is not the beginning of an evil state, it rather presupposes this as being already begun. Accordingly, St Paul does not say that God awakens the beginnings of evil in men. He considers these notions as already in being, first as a consequence of original sin, and then on account of man's own unfaithfulness, which does not suppress the already existing sinfulness, but only gives it sway. This hardening, therefore, is not an aggravation of sin, but, so far at least as it is partial, it is rather a method of checking its aggravation. It is essentially the withdrawal of the capacity of receiving the operations of grace; God renders man, under certain circumstances, incapable of receiving grace, in order to mitigate his guilt; for if the man in question had the eyes of his spirit open, were he aware what was offered to him, and yet resisted, in that case he were a far greater subject of punishment than without this capability he could be. Thus one might say of the cotemporaries of Noah, that God had hardened, had indurated them so that they obeyed not the preaching of Noah (2 Pet. ii. 5), and yet, by reason of this very obduracy, they were not rejected for ever (1 Pet. iii. 18). Finally, the total induration is a manifestation of the simple punitive justice of God, when the sins of man have reached that degree of intensity in which they constitute that which is called the sin against the Holy Ghost. If this be the import of St Paul's conception, no objection can be made, on any score, to the proposition, ὃν θέλει σκληρύνει. The divine will, tempered as it is with wisdom and love, applies this hardening, be it a partial or a total one, only in those cases, and in that degree in which His holiness requires that it should be applied. God neither makes the hardened person evil, nor the evil more evil than they are; all He does is to cause the evil that is already in him, and must at any rate accomplish its development, to come in such a way, and no other, into outward manifestation; this, however, he does, as Calvin says, not merely *permittendo,* but also *intus et extra operando.*

Ver. 19–21. The Apostle now introduces* anew the unwise enquirer of ver. 14, in order to find an apology for himself in this operation of God, even in the forms of evil. St Paul abashes this arrogance with an appeal to the absolute character of God, for whose ways the creature must render an unconditioned submission, even where it is not able to comprehend them. The similitude which he introduces of a potter, and his relation to the clay which he fashions, exhibits this dependency in the most striking manner. Nothing, however, but the same want of sense which suggested that question, could understand the comparison as though St Paul's intention was to represent God as resembling, in all respects, an human artizan. The difference between the two, which the Apostle nowise intends to deny here, but which he has no inducement to bring especially forward on this occasion, is this: man maketh what he will of his own weak and often unholy and loveless will, whereas God createth with his almighty will, but which is yet ever holy, ever full of love. In consequence of this, God can certainly form beings with different talents, and impart to one more, and to another less of these talents, and, consequently, determine their several vocations to a greater or inferior agency, but He cannot make one evil and the other good, because His holy will is unable in any case to produce evil. But here the question arises, whether

* The whole tone in which Paul here exhibits the remonstrances of the Jews, is characterised by a kind of familiarity which we often find, in the Old Testament, in all its simple dignity, and especially in Job, where, towards the close of the book, God himself acknowledges the truth that it contains. When, however, nobility of sentiment is lost, this familiarity then assumes the form of rashness, and, therefore, this defect also belongs to the darker side of the Jewish character, in the days of its degeneracy. The consciousness of the divine election, which, in an objective view, was a well-founded one, instead of producing an humble adoration under such unmerited favour, imparted to many individuals among the Jews an unblushing temerity, a vaunting of their own righteousness even in the sight of God, the like of which was never found in any other nation. Paul's present object is to abash this tendency, and hence the form which his argument assumes, which, however, is not carried to a vicious extreme, but observes the limits of the truth.

the *σκεῦος εἰς τιμήν* and *ἀτιμίαν* in the present passage, do not exactly denote these two degrees of vocation which God dispenses of his own free determination, without their having any relation to morality or a life of faith, and therefore to the bliss dependent upon them? In the first place, the comparison might be employed to show that no potter ever makes entirely unserviceable vessels, but only such as are destined for some more or less honourable use. Next, this view is apparently favoured by the circumstance, that, in the following verse, the *σκεύη ἐλέους* and *ὀργῆς** may be so discriminated from the vessels of honour and dishonour, that the vessels of honour should not necessarily be vessels of mercy, nor the vessels of dishonour vessels of wrath, but only so that, according to the good or bad use of their free will, the Jews, who were the vessels of honour, might become vessels of wrath, whereas the heathen, who were the vessels of dishonour, should become vessels of mercy. And this would contain this admonition for the Jews: do not imagine that you, although you be vessels of honour, must necessarily become and continue vessels of mercy; you may become vessels of wrath, and the heathen, who are vessels of dishonour, may become vessels of mercy! And no doubt this yields a very beautiful meaning, and we must unquestionably admit that Paul might have followed out this thought; but his line of argument, upon the whole, does not authorise the notion that this was what he really meant to deliver here, or why should he have come so suddenly upon the investigation into the dispensation of gifts? The words from ver. 19 onward refer, I admit, to the thought in ver. 18, but then *ἐλεεῖν* and *σκληρύνειν*, in this verse, refer to moral conditions alone, not to gifts of grace, and verses 24–29 also point to the same. There is not a word to indicate any difference between the *σκεύη τιμῆς* and *ἀτιμιάς*, and the *σκεύη ἐλέους* and *ὀργῆς*; according to St Paul's intention, they correspond one with another throughout, just as in the parallel passage of 2 Tim. ii. 20, the wooden and earthen vessels stand, not for those who are more less endowed, but for the wicked. These latter, indeed, are called vessels of God, inasmuch as God knows how to make even them available to his purpose, and

* The expression *σκεύη ὀργῆς* seems to be formed after the Hebrew כְּלֵי זַעְמוֹ (Is. xiii. 5), although its signification in the passage from the Old Testament varies a little from that in which Paul employs it.

in this respect also the similitude of the potter holds good.* God not only permits the wicked to come into the world, but he also causes them to become as they are, although He does not cause the evil that is in them (ver. 19.)

'Αι θέστηκε is not a hebraism for the optative aorist, as Tholuck supposes, but is to be understood thus, "Who hath ever been able to resist His will?"—Ver. 20, μενοῦνγε is wanting in D.E.F.G. In A. it comes after ἄνθρωπε, but we doubt it was only left out on account of the difficulty; it occurs elsewhere in the New Testament only in Luke xi. 28, and is to be viewed as a particle implying at the sametime concession and limitation, and to be rendered ' certainly it may so seem." (Com. Hermann ad Viger. p. 541, who translates it by *quin imo*, *enim vero*.) Upon the image of the potter. comp. Job x. 8; Isaiah xlv. 9; Eccles. xxxvi. 7; Wisdom xv. 7. But the passage which appears more particularly to have been in the Apostle's mind in this comparison, is Jerem. xviii.—Ver. 21. πῆλος is the clay in its raw state, φύραμα the mass of clay kneaded for work, the *dough* as it were.

Ver. 22, 23. After this may now be mentioned the respective relations in which the phenomenon of the evil as well as of the good in the world's history stand with regard to God's designs: the latter furnishes occasion for the revelation of His grace, as the former does for his power and his justice. On this account, it is impossible

* Glöckler groundlessly refuses to recognise any similitude here, but only a simple conclusion from the less to the greater, as if the meaning were, if a vessel cannot question the potter, how much less can man question God? But evidently this will not hold. since it might be answered, that it is the very property of a man that he is able to do what the lifeless vessel cannot. The parallel instances of the Old Testament sufficiently prove that it is intended to be a similitude. But the reader has already been reminded, on Matt. xiii. 1, that no comparison holds good in all its relations, otherwise it were identical with the object which is to be illustrated by it. Rückert and Usteri are of opinion that the proof is defective in this place, but the exposition which has been just given of the connection of thought here will have made it evident that the proof is conducted in the most stringent manner, if only we do not encumber the Apostle with the proposition that God creates evil itself. If, however, it be rejoined, why then does not Paul give the question τί ἔτι μέμφεται the direct answer, "because thou makest the evil thyself, and God only determines the shape in which it shall come out in manifestation?"—it will be sufficient to answer, that the Apostle does, in point of fact, expressly make this observation in the 30th and following verses of this chapter; only here he will not allow himself to be diverted from his immediate train of ideas, which is of the highest importance with him, because it might be the means of impressing upon the Jewish mind. that they must first abandon their claims upon God, before any mention could be made of a participation in the kingdom of God, because it was the advancement of these pretensions that entirely stood in the way of an humble reception of grace on the side of the Jews.

to deprive ἵνα of its intentional sense, and the phrase θέλων ἐνδείξασθαι καὶ γνωρίσαι must be considered as equivalent to ἵνα. On the side of the good, God's operation is altogether to be considered as ubiquitous though not compulsory, on which account, in ver. 23, it is said, θεὸς προητοίμασεν σκεύη ἐλέους εἰς δόξαν. According to which the word προητοίμασεν signifies God's foreknowledge as well as his working and creation of the good, both in its commencement, continuation, and end. But of the evil, on the other hand, Paul will not consent to say that God creates the evil in them, but only the form which the evil assumes. Therefore, he does not use προητοίμασεν of them; moreover, instead of the active, he uses the middle form κατηρτισμένα,* by which the production of evil itself is transferred to the side of the creature.

Ver. 22. A few unimportant MSS. omit ἐι δέ or δέ alone, in order to relieve the construction; but the words are evidently genuine, though the sentence is an anacoluthon. The usual supplements, τί ἐροῦμεν or τί μέμφεται, do not suit, because they only go back again to the question in ver. 19; it is better to suppose that after the words ἐι δέ κ. τ. λ., the subsequent member of the proposition, which with its present form, καὶ ἵνα γνωρίσῃ, denotes the construction with which it set out, ought to have followed with some such words as ὅυτως καὶ γνωρίζει κ. τ. λ. or γνωρίζει καὶ κ. τ. λ. At any rate this is more natural than Meyer's most violent supposition, according to which, at the conclusion of ver. 23, an Aposiopesis takes place. The manner in which ver. 24 joins on to ver. 23 is quite incompatible with this interpretation.—Τὸ δυνατόν = ἡ δύναμις with the idea of avenging power implied—φέρειν ἐν μακροθυμίᾳ can only apply to the

* Here also Reiche and others would supply ὑπὸ τοῦ θεοῦ. Were this in the text, even then it might be explained of the operation of God in the wicked considered as a phenomenon. But since it is not found there, I cannot consider such an addition warranted by the intention of St Paul, but am much rather disposed to believe that we must assume that the Apostle intended by this method to signify the different relation in which God stands to the good and the evil, since he employs such different terms for the one from what he does for the other. And I am the more readily determined in favour of this sense in the present case, (although, otherwise, I observe, as an exegetical cause for the interpretation of this passage, the rule of taking every expression in its entire force) because the ἤνεγκεν ἐν πολλῇ μακροθυμίᾳ will not accord with the prominence thus given to the divine activity. There is something not only discordant but absolutely contradictory in the idea that God endures with much long suffering what He has Himself prepared.

ripening of the evil in evil. God endures the wicked in their evil until they become manifest to themselves in their evil fruit, in order that, even by these means, they may yet be brought to repentance, or else be involved in utter destruction. In St Paul's intention *ἀπώλεια* in this place is that which is *αἰώνιος* (2 Thess. i. 9), even as *δόξα* must be taken as equivalent to *ζωὴ αἰώνιος*.—*Σκεῦος ἐλέους* = *σκεῦος ἐκλογῆς*, Acts ix. 15. The choice of expressions here is strictly governed by the already used image of the potter. Moreover, in the Hebrew כְּלִי has the more extended meaning of utensil, or mean. Comp. Is. xiii. 5 ; Jerem. l. 25.

Vers. 24–26. The principles which have just been developed are also openly propounded in Scripture. The passages of Hos. ii. 25, i. 10, are a comment upon *ὃν θέλει ἐλέει* (ver. 18.) These prophecies were realised in the calling of the Gentiles, which is so far from evacuating God's word, that it fulfilled it (ver. 6.) God's prophecies, being the utterances of the All-knowing and Almighty one, must needs be fulfilled, not, however, by destroying the free will of the creature, but rather through that very free will.

In ver. 24, with the word *ὅυς*, the figurative expression *σκέυη* is dropped for terms peculiar to man. *'Ον μόνον—ἀλλὰ καὶ* is a mitigated expression ; for St Paul might have said, few Jews and many Gentiles. It is of the latter alone that there is any question in the first quotations, yet so that the fall of Israel is there already intimated. Since, according to the analogy of the sons of Isaiah (Isaiah vii., &c.), the daughters of Hosea also wear a typical character, in particular, the *οὐκ ἠγαπημένη* (לֹא רֻחָמָה) represents the kingdom of Israel. St Paul, however, takes the name in a wider sense, and comprehends under it all the heathen down to whose level the kingdom of the latter had sunk. (1 Pet. ii. 10.) In the rest, the translation does not exactly correspond with the original text ; but as the difference does not at all affect the thought, it must only be ranked among those incidental to quotations from memory.

Vers 27–29. The following quotations from Is. x. 22, 23 ; Is. i. 9, form the comment on the second half of ver. 18, which constitutes the middle point of the whole of the Apostle's argument, namely, the words, *ὃν δὲ θέλει σκληρύνει.* According to these predictions, the people of Israel, taken in the mass, is represented as rejected, while a holy remnant alone is to remain to later times. The extension of the Jews does not on this account evacuate God's word, but rather establishes it (ver. 6.)

St Paul might have produced many similar prophecies, *e. g.*, Is. vi. 13; Amos ix. 9; Zachar. xiii. 9.; Zeph. iii. 12. But he selected these, because, in connexion with the rejection (which, for the rest, in the former of the two passages, is only expressed in a negative and indirect manner), they also make mention of an holy remnant. In contrast with the little troop of the true soldiers of God, St Paul places the innumerable mass of the fleshly unbelieving Israelites. Though the number of the children of Israel be as the sand of the sea, nevertheless the remnant only shall be blessed. Israel has its old and its new man, the old man must be slain and put off. God's wonderful providence is seen in the dreadful judgments which fell upon the people, while those escaped destruction who were to constitute the *κατάλειμμα* = שְׁאֵרִית, שְׁאָר, as seed for the future; a thought which already points to ch. xi.—Ver. 28. The words here quoted follow exactly the LXX., until *ἐπὶ τῆς γῆς*, for which the latter read, *ἐν τῇ οἰκουμένῃ ὅλῃ*. St Paul probably chooses the former expression, because it more decidedly declares the universality of the judgment. The passage portrays the judgment of God visiting the Israelites, which began on them, with the appearance of Christ (which here, as so often elsewhere, is conceived as one with the last times); they ought then to have brought forth fruits worthy of repentance, but no such were found among them. In the original, the quotation, accurately rendered, runs thus, "God executeth his fixed decree with righteousness, since God will make, that is, accomplish, a decisive decree in the whole land." On which account, the participles must be completed by the words *θεὸς ἐστι*; but *λόγος* corresponds with כִּלָּיוֹן, fulfilment, decision, word; that is, will of God. *Συντελεῖν* stands for שֹׁטֵף, which properly means stream forth, then fill, fulfil. *Συντέμνειν* is used in a peculiar sense, to which the Hebrew חָרוּץ corresponds. This word signifies to cut. cut off, and then to decide. To decide, to shorten, to hasten, are all contiguous conceptions; and the Apostle, following the LXX., has brought the last especially forward. The words therefore, according to the disposition of the text in the passage before us, must be translated thus, "God is speedily fulfilling His decree, for He will make a rapidly completed decree on the land." Ver. 29 entirely agrees with the LXX. The Hebrew, כִּמְעַט שָׂרִיד "a remnant, how small, *i. e.*, a small remnant," is translated by the LXX, σπέρμα, to signify that out of this remnant, as out of a grain of corn, the nation shall, as it were, flourish again. By means of this remnant, life was preserved in the whole,* and, without them, all Israel had come to destruction; and then indeed the promises of God had been made void; but God, in his omnipotence and compassion, was always able to preserve this holy seed in the nation of Israel.

§ 15. ISRAEL'S GUILT.

(IX. 30—X. 21.)

The Apostle has hitherto confined himself to the distinct consideration of the *divine* agency; he now with a like precision exhibits the *human* side of the subject. Although it was not without the knowledge and will of God that the Jews fell from their calling, yet the *guilt* is solely and entirely their own, notwithstanding all the warnings of God in the Old Testament. For every prophecy is at once an act, and, when it relates to sin, is at the same time a warning to man against the accomplishing of that act, *e g.*, the Saviour's words to St Peter, "Before the cock crow, thou shalt deny me thrice."†

* Just as Abraham, at the destruction of Sodom, prayed that God would not destroy the city for the sake of the righteous persons that were within it. At the same time, the life-giving power of the holy must ever be considered as standing in some relation to the number of those who are to be preserved. Ten may serve to preserve a city, but not a nation.

† The remark of Bacon, quoted by Beck. (loc. cit. p. 104), is here in point, "Prophetia historiæ genus est, quando quidem historia divina eâ polleat super humanam praerogativâ ut narratis factum *praecedere* non minus quam *sequi* posset." Prophecies are to no purpose, unless on the presupposition of St Paul's doctrine as to predestination: it is not man that causes their fulfilment, but God by means of man, and that precisely by his free act. Hence it is no illusion if God warns against a sin, and yet that sin must needs be committed; for it is precisely as the free act of the creature that God foreknows it; although doubtless such a sin heightens the guilt of the sinner. But according to the comprehensive love of God, the deed of sin is always meant to lead to repentance and regeneration, as the history of St Peter clearly shows; and on this account even the evil are not to be rooted out (comp. on Matt. xiii. 30.)

The Jews opposed the long-desired Messiah when He came, nay, they nailed him to the cross (as is intimated in ix. 33), because he did not answer to the idea which they had formed of Him. Before the Babylonish captivity, the people had been addicted to idolatry and gross sins; even in those days it was rejected in the mass; only a small σπέρμα returned into the Holy Land, and from this remnant the nation derived a new youth. From that time it appeared entirely cured of idolatry and heathenish vices; but it now fell into the opposite error of proud self-righteousness. This became quite as great a hindrance to laying hold on Christ as the former state (comp. Rom. i. 18, iii. 20, where these two forms of sinful perverseness are described as those generally prevailing among men); for it is humble repentance alone which fits for a reception of Christ and His power, and to bring himself to such repentance is still harder for a self-satisfied, self-righteous person, than for one who has grossly sinned, and therefore our Saviour promises the kingdom of heaven rather to publicans and harlots than to such persons, (Matt. xxi. 31.)

Ver. 30, 31. St Paul by an oxymoron expresses the idea, that the Gentiles who were degraded and took no thought about any righteousness, laid hold on that which was offered to them in Christ as a free gift, while the Jews, who followed after righteousness, did not attain to it. These words are an authoritative commentary on ver. 16; all θέλειν and τρέχειν of the Jews were unavailing; while they anxiously avoided fleshly sins and idolatry, they fell into so much the greater spiritual sins—into self-conceit, hard-heartedness, and want of love—and thus the second deceit became worse than the first; they only departed farther from the goal which they sought to reach. But, on the other hand, while God punished the sin of the Gentiles by sin, so that they became exceedingly sinful, these came into the condition of true repentance; they conceived a longing for aid from above, and were now able in faith to lay hold on Christ. Thus, then, all depends on God's ἐλεεῖν, not on man's τρέχειν. *Positively*, man cannot produce the least of what is good; he must, therefore, always place himself in a passive position towards God, never in an active; his whole productive power is *negative*, and its fruit is evil, of which the essence is opposition to the will of God. Hence no sin is so difficult to cure as self-righteousness; for this is want of love; and love alone is the fulfilling of the law, for God is love, and it is only through his power that the creature can love purely.

Glöckler is for connecting τί οὖν ἐροῦμεν with ver. 22, and considering all that intervenes as a continuation of the first clause of the sentence; but this is clearly very unsuitable. Nor is the question to be regarded as a subsumption of the whole preceding argument (vers. 6, seqq.), and to be translated, "What shall we now say after all this?" (It is so taken by Koppe, Rückert, Beck, De Wette, who make the answer to begin at ὅτι ἔθνη κ. τ. λ.) The following διατί (32), is in favour of the continuation of the question to ἔφθασε. Vers. 30, 31, contain the problem to be solved, but not the solution of it, τί οὖν ἐροῦμεν, therefore, must relate only to what follows, not to the preceding words.

Vers. 32, 33. The cause of this strange phenomenon is their unbelief—*i. e.*, their resistance to the grace which would work belief in their heart; for this reason it is that the rock of salvation became to them a stone of stumbling, as had been foretold long before in the Old Testament (Is. xxviii. 16, viii. 14.) The nature of πίστις, therefore, is the key to the mystery; as it is impossible to pour anything into a vessel which is stopped up and full, in like manner is a soul full of pride and devoid of love incapable of receiving the streams of the Spirit. Man cannot, indeed, by his own deed, empty and open himself, but doubtless he can hinder God's accomplishing this work on him, and on this resistance, which is within the power of man, his guilt rests as its final cause.

In ver. 32, ὡς ἐξ ἔργων νόμου denotes the subjective fancy of the Jews, that they might attain to righteousness through works (comp. Winer's Grammar, p. 497). On λίθος προσκόμματος comp. note on Matt. xxi. 42 seqq., where there is a similar citation from Ps. cxviii. 22. For σκάνδαλον, see note on Matt. xviii. 6. St Paul accommodates Is. xxviii. 16 to his purpose, by an addition from viii. 14 (on this proceeding see note on Luke iv. 18–19). The same union of texts is found in 1 Pet. ii. 6, in combination with Ps. cxviii. 22. Neither of these passages relates to the Messiah in its immediate connection, but they had been typically applied to Him as early as the Chaldean and Rabbinical paraphrases, and St Paul with propriety so applies them. The Old Testament is one great prophecy of Christ; all isolated and particular relations of men to God, have in Him and by Him become universal and comprehensive truth.—*Πᾶς* is here spurious; it is wanting in the MSS. A.B.D.E.F.G., and in several versions; it was perhaps adopted from xi. 10.—*Καταισχυνθήσεται* would correspond to יָבִישׁ, but the text has יָחִישׁ, which primarily means *festinavit*, and then is commonly taken in the sense of *fugit*, *expavit*. Perhaps the LXX read יָבִישׁ.

Chap. X. 1, 2. There was, after all, a true side in the legal striving of the Jews; it arose from a deep earnestness and a lively zeal, which, however, were without a true insight into the nature of the old covenant, as well as of the new. This, then, the Apostle explains more exactly in what follows. (The *μέν* presupposes an omitted *δέ*, by which the guilt of Israel should be marked. Compare Winer, Gr. p. 500.) *Εὐδοκία* and *δέησις* do not harmonise with reference to *ὑπὲρ αὐτῶν*, if the usual sense of "good pleasure" be retained; but the connection is enough to shew that it is here inapplicable; the word is rather to be taken in the sense of *longing, wish*, as רָצוֹן is also used. *Εἰς σωτηρίαν* signifies the object of the prayer for Israel. In ver. 2, *ζῆλος Θεοῦ* does not denote the greatness of the zeal (as if it were *a divine zeal*), but zeal for God and His cause. Josephus, Philo, and the profane writers of the first centuries of the Christian era, are full of examples of the zeal which the Jews shewed for their religion; but it was a raging, fanatical zeal, and hence was full of conceit, without higher aspirations, love, and the tender virtues of the spirit which truly seeks God. The words *οὐ κατ' ἐπίγνωσιν* are meant—not, indeed, to *acquit* the Jews of all guilt (for they might have had the knowledge from the word of God), but yet—to *soften* their guilt, and render visible the possibility of the conversion promised in c. xi.

Ver. 3, 4. The ignorance of the Jews relates to sin and righteousness. The law had not wrought in them any *ἐπίγνωσις τῆς ἁμαρτίας*, and therefore they did not lay hold on the new way of salvation, which offered them that which the law could not bring. They clung to the law, although it had reached its end in Christ.

In ver. 3, *ὑπετάγησαν* bears a middle sense. The aorist points to the act of proffering the gospel to them. De Wette wrongly understands *τῇ δικαιοσύνῃ τοῦ Θεοῦ οὐχ ὑπετάγησαν* to mean, "They have not submitted to the righteous ordinance of God, the *νόμος πίστεως*." *Δικαιοσύνη* never occurs in such a sense. The meaning is: They have not penitently submitted themselves in faith to the righteousness which has been won by Christ, and which was offered to them, but they have wished to originate a righteousness of their own. . . . In ver. 4, Christ is to be understood in combination with His whole work; but it is a peculiarity of the gospel, that in it every thing is referred to the person of the Redeemer Himself, not to any thing *in* Him or *from* Him. Agreeably to the connection, and to the usage of language, τέλος νόμου can only mean the *object*, the *end*, as our Lord says (Luke xvi. 16), ὁ νόμος καὶ οἱ προφῆται ἕως Ἰωάννου. But this, of course, is not to be understood of a portion of the law only (the law of ceremonies alone, for instance), but of the whole law; nor must we conceive of it as an abrogation, but as a higher and real fulfilment. (Matt. v. 17.) Everything in the Old Testament is, in its enduring import, transferred into the New, and is only done away with in such a sense that there it remains preserved. Hence we learn from the fate of the Jews, that man must not depend on any momentary operation of God, but on God Himself, so as to be able to follow the changes of His dealings. The Jews strove against the Lord by the very circumstance that they wished to maintain an institution which unquestionably originated from Him, at the time when He did away with it. True piety fixes its love on God, not on His gifts.

Ver. 5–8. The Apostle proceeds, as if by way of supplement to the argument in iii. 21, seqq., to exhibit the difference between these positions of men under the law and under the gospel, by passages from the Old Testament, and that from the writings of Moses. from the law itself; whence it appears that the Jews had not understood the writings of Moses, inasmuch as they fancied that they were adhering to them when they opposed themselves to faith. He shews from Lev. xviii. 5, that *doing* is the character of the law, and from Deut. xxx. 12, 13, that *believing* is that of the gospel; the former presupposes an *active*, the latter a *passive* position of the soul. That St Paul intends here to found a formal argument upon the passages which he quotes, has been well maintained by Reiche, in opposition to Tholuck and Rückert, who had followed earlier interpreters in questioning it. The difficulty in the second quotation is the only thing that could suggest such an assertion; for the passage from Leviticus (which is also referred to in

Ezek. xx. 21, Neh. ix. 29, Matt. xix. 16, Gal. iii. 12), is excellently adopted to the Apostle's line of proof. "No one can live (*i. e.*, ζωὴν αἰώνιον ἔχειν) by the law, but he who keeps it; but no one can keep it (Rom. i.–iii.); consequently, another way of salvation is needed."

The reading ὅτι before τὴν δικαιοσύνην in ver. 5 is merely an attempt at correction on account of the construction of γράφει, with the accusative. It is not suitable to take γράφειν as meaning "*to describe, to represent.*" We shall do better to take the accusative absolutely "with respect to the righteousness." Αὐτά and αὐτοῖς refer to ἔργα, understood in the idea of νόμος. On this passage compare the remarks on Gal. iii. 12.

There is, however, unquestionably a difficulty as to the second quotation (Deut. xxx. 12–13) in which the righteousness of faith is conceived of as if personified, or God, as its author, speaks to man, in whom it is produced, with the intention of directing his mind from that which is outward to that which is inward—to deep self-contemplation and heedfulness to God's working in him. In the first place, the passage in St Paul does not agree either with the original text or with the LXX. The clauses τοῦτ' ἔστι Χριστὸν καταγαγεῖν and τοῦτ' ἔστι Χριστὸν ἐκ νεκρῶν ἀναγαγεῖν are, indeed, to be regarded as explanatory additions of the Apostle, which he did not at all intend to be reckoned as part of the question; and thus, leaving out of sight unessential omissions and abbreviations, the variation certainly does not appear so very considerable. Still, it is here said τίς καταβήσεται εἰς τὴν ἄβυσσον; instead of which, the LXX. have τίς διαπεράσει ἡμῖν εἰς τὸ πέραν τῆς θαλάσσης; which, with the other alterations, is enough to cause perplexity to the defenders of literal inspiration. According, however, to the principles which we have throughout maintained, such a free use of the Old Testament text does not occasion any difficulty which can affect us; St Paul made use of the Old Testament in the same Holy Spirit in which it was composed, and therefore could not charge its import with anything foreign to it. But, besides this, the sense of the passage is itself obscure. The connexion in Deut. xxx. is as follows:—In ch. xxix., Moses had threatened the people with ejection from the land of promise in case of unfaithfulness, but afterwards, in ch. xxx., foretells that they will return to themselves, and will at last be gathered again by God into the land of their fathers. "Here God will circumcise their heart, that they may love Him with all their heart, and keep His commandments. For God's commandment is not far from them, neither in Heaven, that they should say, *Who shall go up for us to Heaven, and bring it to us?* neither is it beyond the sea, that they should say, *Who shall go over the sea for us, and bring it to us?* it is nigh unto them, in their mouth, yea, in their heart." Thus the passage refers, in a way which cannot be mistaken, to the dispensation of the Messiah; it points to the circumcision of the heart—to a state in which man will be able truly to love God, and to keep the commandments. The only possible difficulty is from the circumstance that, in xxx. 11, it is said—*ἡ ἐντολὴ, ἣν ἐγὼ ἐντέλλομαί σοι σήμερον*; by which it would seem that the passage which follows is referred to the law of the Old Testament, and not to faith. But if we consider that the law is by no means wanting in the New Testament—that it is only regarded as no longer something merely outward, but as inward—as the voice of the eternal Word in man's heart (John xii. 50), nay, that this reception of the divine into itself is the very essence of the New Testament, and of the life of faith which belongs to it—it will be clear how the Apostle might, with perfect justice, interpret those words of the Old Testament as relating to the circumstances of the New.* He conceives of Christ in His person, and as the object of preaching, not merely according to His historical appearance, but as the eternal Word, which is dormant in every man, and which preaching from without only wakens and renders active. This Word, then—the living law itself—has also in itself the power and energy whereby man is placed in a condition to keep it, and to love God above all things.† The

* Some (as lately Reiche) have falsely designated the Apostle's explanation in this place as *allegorical*, such as that in Gal. iv. 22, seqq. The only proper name for it is *spiritual; i e.*, it is such an explanation as penetrates through the letter of the Old Testament into its spirit. The whole passage (Deut. xxix.-xxx.) points most properly on the New Testament dispensation, and in this inner sense it is understood by the Apostle.

† Christ is active in the Old Testament (1 Pet, i. 11; Heb. xi. 26) also; but rather as an operation (*ῥῆμα*) than as a person (*λόγος*) (comp on John i. 1; also my Opusc. Theol. p. 123 seqq., and the essay on the Word of God in the *Christoterpe* for 1835, p. 1. seqq.) But, in the preaching of the Apostles, the subject was not the doctrine *concerning* Christ, but He Himself, in His life and power. (Comp. 1 Pet. i. 23-25, which forms the most perfect parallel to ver. 8.)

course of thought, therefore, in St Paul takes this form. "The Scripture saith of the righteousness of the law, that whosoever shall fashion himself conformably to the law which meets him from without, shall live; but this no man can do; consequently, no man attains life thus; all that he can attain by this way is the knowledge of sin (iii. 20.) But, in the New Testament, he hath, by the operation of the Spirit, the law within himself; it is written on his heart; therefore, he need no longer seek it from afar, but only become aware of this treasure within him, and follow the power of the Spirit."* The words, "*say not in thine heart, Who shall ascend or descend*" (with which those in vii. 24. "*Who shall deliver me?*" are parallel) are a negative expression of an idea which would be positively expressed as follows:—If in the Old Testament doing was required, so now it is faith; for all has been done through Christ. The words *ἀναβαίνειν εἰς οὐρανόν* and *καταβαίνειν εἰς τὴν ἄβυσσον*, therefore, are merely symbolical expressions to signify a seeking in the remotest quarters.

The latter phrase is stronger and bolder than that of the LXX. —*διαπερᾷν εἰς τὸ πέραν τῆς θαλάσσης*; for the word *ἄβυσσος*, which corresponds to שְׁאוֹל, is not to be understood as meaning

* If the connexion of the words, both in the Old Testament and in the passage before us, had been more carefully attended to, it could not have been possible that so many *single* applications should have been brought forward—as, that the intention was to prove that Christ is omnipresent (Origen)—or, that the gospel is not hard to fulfil or to discover (Flatt, Morus, Rosenmüller)—or, that the reality of the appearance and the resurrection of Christ is the subject (Reiche, Rückert, Usteri.) These applications, it is true, all lie in the words; it is not, however, as *isolated* truths that they are there, but in as far as they belong to the essence of faith generally. Bengel, Knapp, and Tholuck suppose that St Paul is representing to the anxious heart, which knows not how to enter into heaven or to escape hell, that Christ can effect this in it. The context in this place, however, evidently does not point to the distresses of penitent hearts, although it is true that, where there is faith, penitence is presupposed. Rather the Apostle contrasts the law and the gospel with each other *in their most general character*, and shews that this is already recognised and exhibited in the Old Testament. The nature of the law is represented *directly*, as requiring the *doing* of the law: the gospel *indirectly*, as the life of faith. The indirect form of the proof, however, is of such a nature that faith is indicated in its origination [Genesis]; faith personified, on one who already believes, is represented as speaking to unbelieving mankind, or to an individual unbeliever. Unbelief has for its characteristic a turning to what is outward. It regards God as a distant being. From this outward direction, the spirit is called back into its inward depths, in which it finds God's eternal Word present; and this finding is faith itself. But St Paul, of course, conceives of the eternal Word as that which has become incarnate; and hence he brings forward the consideration that *Christ* is neither far off nor dead, but intimately nigh to every one and living.

the sea, but the regions of the dead.* In making choice of it, the Apostle had, no doubt, Ps. cxxxix. 8 before his eyes. Ἄβυσσος is properly an adjective, *bottomless*. from βυσσός, the Ionic form of βυθός; thus Euripid. Phoen. 1632, ταρτάρου ἄβυσσα χάσματα. Comp. Luke viii. 31; Revel. ix. 1, 2, 11; xi. 7; xvii. 8; xx. 1. After what has been said, it only remains to be explained how St Paul could apply the ἀναβήσεται and καταβήσεται to *Christ*, as if they related to bringing *Him* down from heaven, or up from the dead. As in Christ, the eternal Word had been made flesh (John i. 1–14), and this Word forms the very object of the preaching of faith in the gospel (ver. 8), every seeking after the Truth, as if it were something distant, which had not yet appeared among men, is to be looked on as an ignoring of Christ and His almighty presence; by such seeking, men act as if Christ had not yet come down from heaven into the flesh, or as if He were still among the dead, and not long ago risen again.

Instead of ῥῆμα πίστεως, 1 Tim. iv. 6 has λόγος πίστεως. It is not the business of preaching to introduce the word originally into man, but only to arouse its dormant life as a spark does fire. There is in all things a word of God, for God upholdeth all things by the word of His power. (Heb. i. 3.)

Vers. 9–11. This having of the Divine Word within ourselves, in unspeakable intimacy, so that it is nearer to us than we are to ourselves, is the essence of faith, in which profession is included; whosoever, then, possesses faith, obtains, through the power of the Divine principle in it, the salvation which he could not have attained to without it. This power of faith, which leads to salvation, is, moreover, owned in the Old Testament also. (Is. xxviii. 16.)

The distinction between ὁμολογεῖν στόματι and πιστεύειν καρδίᾳ is caused simply by the foregoing quotation; for the two are correlatives. No true belief remains without confession, any more than fire without light; and every confession presupposes belief. for a hypocritical confession is no confession at all, but a

* The opinion of some writers (as Bolten and Koppe), that εἰς τὸ πέραν τῆς θαλάσσης also signifies *Scheol* [Hades]—this being imagined, as by Homer, to be situated at the boundary of the ocean—is inadmissible. The Hebrews supposed the region of the dead to be beneath the earth (comp. note on Ephes. iv. 9); the expression in question denotes merely a distance which it exceeds man's power to reach. And this idea has only been expressed more pointedly, but not altered, by St Paul.

counterfeit of it. A dumb faith is no faith. "I believed, and therefore have I spoken." (2 Cor. iv. 13.) The reason why the resurrection of Christ is especially brought forward as the object of faith, is that it is the moment of victory, the figure of the spiritual resurrection of all men. *Σωτηρία* and *δικαιοσύνη* are not to be distinguished as Glöckler supposes; for in ver. 9 *σωθήσῃ* stands by itself. As this distinction, then, cannot be pressed, and as, moreover, ver. 11 also relates to one thing only, ver. 10 seems tautological after ver. 9. The emphasis, however, is to be laid on *καρδία* and *στόμα*, so as to yield the sense—In order to the attainment of salvation, what is outward must be united with what is inward. On the quotation of Isaiah xxviii. 16 in ver. 11, compare the remarks on ix. 33.

Vers. 12, 13. The distinction made under the Theocracy between Jews and Gentiles, therefore, no longer appears in the New Testament; *all* men have one access to the Lord of all, namely, faith, of which calling on Him is the expression. This is again confirmed by a passage of evangelical prophecy. (Joel ii. 32.)

As to *οὐ γάρ ἐστι διαστολή* (ver. 12), compare iii. 22. *Ὁ αὐτός* is the subject, and *κύριος* the predicate. According to the context God is primarily meant, as the quotation indicates, but according to St Paul's way of thinking, it is of course God *in Christ*. *Πλουτεῖν* relates to the riches of grace and mercy, from which no one is excluded. By *εἰς* is signified the direction in which the stream of grace pours itself forth. *Ἐπικαλεῖσθαι*, like *ὁμολογεῖν* above, presupposes a lively faith. We need not therefore supply, "If the calling be sincere and honestly intended," for unless it be so, it ceases to be a *calling*, it only *appears* to be that which it really is not.

Ver. 14–21. If, however, this new way of salvation is to be for all, it is necessary that to all—Gentiles and Jews alike—the opportunity of becoming acquainted with it should be given. This St Paul sets forth in four questions, which depend one upon the other, and then he shews how God, agreeably to His promise (Is. lii. 9), has sent His messengers to preach. But men, especially the Jews, have been inattentive to the preaching, as God had foretold (Is. liii. 1); they have not listened to it or acknowledged the preaching.*

* This is not to be understood as if the preaching alone were of God, and faith were of man; rather, as God creates both the light and the eye, so also the preaching and faith

The sentences in vers. 16–19, therefore, answer exactly to the several questions in ver. 14, and carry out the idea that God has done what was to be done on His part—He has sent messengers and has set them to preach—but men have not laid hold on God's word (John i. 5). The reference to Israel peeps through in the whole passage, but is not expressly brought forward until ver. 19, seqq.

In ver. 14, to which ver. 17 is a necessary supplement, we meet with the important idea that preaching is the only way by which the gospel is propagated among mankind. In ver. 17 *ἀκοή* is to be taken as = שְׁמוּעָה, *κήρυγμα.*) It cannot be produced by some immediate operation of the Spirit, scattered as seed here and there, but in order to its propagation there is constantly required an imparting from the centre of the Church. The Church of Christ partakes in the nature of every self-contained* organization, which cannot develop itself save on the condition that all the members remain in connexion with the whole. Not only is it impossible that a community of Christians should come into existence without connexion with the whole body of the Church, without having the history of Christ preached to it,† but, moreover, without this living connexion, it cannot subsist for a length of time without changing its nature—as is proved by the history of the Ethiopian Church This is to be accounted for, first, from the *historical* character of Christianity, which essentially rests on the *facts* of the history of Jesus; and, next, from the Spirit, which is the power that operates in preaching. This principle is connected with the person of Jesus (John vii. 39), and is diffused from Him in continuous operation. Hence in ver. 17 *ῥῆμα Θεοῦ* is certainly to be referred to the *doctrine* of the revelation which forms the basis of the preaching, but in such a way that this doctrine is conceived of as one animated and quickened by the Spirit of God, so that the expression might also have been *ἡ δὲ ἀκοὴ διὰ πνεύματος Θεοῦ.* Missionary ac-

are both of Him. *Unbelief*, however, is man's fault, as, without being able to *produce* the light, he can certainly close his eye intentionally against light, that he may not see.

* [Geschlossen.]

† No people ever has been or can be converted, nor can a church be formed, by means of the Holy Scriptures alone, without an interpreter and the living word [of preaching]; otherwise the first member would have to begin by baptizing himself. Wherever there arises a really lively feeling of the need, thither God sends messengers of the faith; the Bible, however, may certainly awaken the need.

tivity, therefore, is an essential property of the Church, and the charge in Matt. xxviii. 19 is of force for her to the end of time. Next, however, comes the question, what ought to be supplied after ἐὰν μὴ ἀποσταλῶσι? First of all, evidently ὑπὸ τοῦ Χριστοῦ. He Himself, the Lord of the Church, sends forth all the messengers, and by His Spirit arouses them for his service. But that the order of the visible Church may be preserved, this inward calling requires the addition of an outward sanction. Therefore the inward call must have recourse to the constituted ecclesiastical authorities, in order that it may be able, through their confirmation and recognition, to co-operate in a regular manner towards the edification of the Church. An opposite course would introduce a tumultuary and separatistical manner of working, in which all superintendence of the teachers, and consequently all prevention of enthusiastic and fanatical efforts, must become impossible. St Paul, who was called from the world in the most immediate manner, nevertheless by his example most strikingly confirms the reality and necessity of this mutual operation with the established organs of the Church. Although baptized with the Spirit by the Lord Himself, he yet receives baptism from Ananias at Damascus (Acts ix. 19); and, although expressly set apart by the Lord for the ministry of the Gentiles, he yet does not formally enter on his ministry among them until the Church of Antioch chooses him, and sends him forth as a messenger to the Gentiles (ch. xiii 1). The subordination of the individual* to the needs and regulations of the whole body, is a necessary condition of the Church's dev loping itself with a blessing.

The passage from Is. lii. 7, does not exactly follow the LXX. St Paul keeps nearer to the Hebrew text, and gives the passage in the form which was most suitable for his purpose. The feet are mentioned as the organs which are most characteristic of the messengers, and of their itinerant office.† The parallel with the angels, as spiritual messengers of God, forces itself on us; the incarnate God sends forth human messengers also to fulfil His commands. The passages from the second part‡ of Isaiah, which are quoted in this section, are all to be considered as most properly evangelical; all other applications—*e. g.*, to the people of Israel, the prophets, or the better members of the people—are not excluded by

* [*Subjectivität.*] † [*Wandernden Wirksamkeit.*] ‡ [cc. xl.—lxvi.]

this, but by a typical interpretation lead us back to the evangelical sense. In ver. 15, Göschen renders ὡραῖοι by *veloces*. The speed of the messengers, and the zeal from which it proceeds, are certainly included in the idea, but yet it is because of the delightful tidings which they bring, that the feet of the messengers, *i.e.*, they themselves, are especially styled ὡραῖοι. In vers. 18 and 19, μὴ οὐκ are not to be joined together; μή is the interrogative particle, and οὐ belongs to the verb. (Comp. Winer's Gr. p. 427.) Ps. xix. 5 is quoted according to the LXX. The passage relates, in the first instance, to *nature*, which tells the glory of God; which is the reason that φθόγγος, corresponding to קוֹל, is used, whereas in the application to *persons*, λόγος or κήρυγμα would be more suitable. St Paul, however, considers the Church as a new work of the creation of God, the creatures of which—the saints—penetrate the world with their song of praise, and draw all things to join in the general ecstacy. Whatever opposes this movement (as the Jews did), shuts itself out from the joy of the new world. Hence ἐξῆλθε is to be understood as prophetically spoken; that which is begun is viewed as if already completed, and therefore we need not seek for any further explanation, how it is that St Paul can represent Christ's messengers as spread all over the earth, whereas, when he wrote these words, they had not so much as carried the preaching of Christ through the whole of the Roman empire. Ver. 19. The unbelief of Israel had been expressed as far back as Deut. xxxii. 21, in terms which also indicate the pressing forward, in faith, of the Gentiles, who are designated by οὐκ ἔθνος, ἔθνος ἀσύνετον, to get before them. The idea that even in those days there was a possibility of the gospel reaching the Gentile world, pre-supposes its rejection by Israel. *Παραζηλόω, παροργίζω, to excite jealousy*, are expressions taken from the figure of the marriage between Jehovah and Israel; by bestowing His love on others, God designs to awaken in them a consciousness of their infidelity. Bretschneider and Reiche wrongly take Θεός as the nominative to ἔγνω, making the sense to be, "Does God then no longer know (*i.e.*, love) Israel?" It is not until xi. 1, seqq. that this idea is brought forward; to supply Θεός here is too hard, and is quite unnecessary, as the connection is plain. Οὐκ ἔγνω is parallel with οὐκ ἤκουσαν in ver. 18, and in this place as in that, we ought to supply κήρυγμα πίστεως, which is agreeable to the bearing of the whole passage.* The object of ver. 19, then, is merely to apply the general question to Israel in particular. There is no reason for apprehending that the quotations which follow would not accord with this way of taking it. For St Paul could not again answer that messengers had been sent to them, since he had just before declared, in the words of Ps. xix. 5, that messengers had been sent into *all* lands, even into the distant regions of the Gentiles; he therefore answers indirectly; in shewing that the Gentiles believe, he implies—How, then, should Israel have been unable to believe, if only it had been *willing!* The same idea is repeated by Isaiah lxv. 1, "I am found of them that sought me not;" how much more might Israel have found me if it had been willing; but it is in vain that God stretcheth forth His arms to the unfaithful people; they *would* not (Matt. xxiii. 37.) *Πρῶτος* in ver. 19 refers to the later prophecies of Isaiah. In ver. 20 δέ is not to be taken as marking opposition but continuation. Ἀποτολμᾷ denotes the boldness of the prophet's speech in representing the heathen as called. The idea in ver. 20 is parallel to that in ix. 30, and the contrast which is there expressed (ix. 31), is to be supplied in this place also.—*And those who* (*in appearance*) *sought me have not found me.* Ver. 21. For πρὸς λαὸν ἀπειθοῦντα καὶ ἀντιλέγοντα the Hebrew has only אֶל־עַם סוֹרֵר; perhaps the LXX. found added in their copies וּמוֹרֶה, which occurs in connection with סוֹרֵר in Jer. v. 23.

§ 16. ISRAEL'S SALVATION.

(XI. 1–36.)

After having shown the guilt of Israel, St Paul proceeds to teach prophetically that this apostacy of the people is neither total nor perpetual—that God has preserved in Israel a holy seed, and in this all Israel is to be blessed. For the understanding of this sec-

* Köllner follows Koppe and Rosenmüller in understanding—"Did not Israel know *that it was to stand below the Gentiles?*" But ver. 21 does not agree with this, and, moreover, a subject is thus anticipated which St Paul does not begin to treat before ch. xi. It is only by taking the first two quotations (19, 20), apart from their main connexion, that this way of supplying the ellipse could be suggested.

tion, however, it is necessary to consider more particularly an idea without which it must be obscure, namely, the relation of individuals to the whole body—which has already been cursorily touched on in vol. i. p. 865,* and in the note on Rom. v. 12. Doubtless the whole race of men forms one unity, in which the nations are lesser wholes, and these in their turn are composed of individuals; but yet the degrees of development of the collective body, and of the several nations, is very different, and consequently so is their responsibility. At the moment of Christ's appearance, when the fulness of time was come, and mankind had attained the age of maturity (Gal. iv. 4), yet all the nations were not equally advanced, but many were still in the lowest grades of development, as continues to be the case at this day. But as to the question of a nation's guilt, everything depends on its degree of development. In the wilderness the people of Israel incurred guilt, so that it was necessary that the elder generation should die there; the like happened in the captivity, where the greater number of the exiles remained behind among the heathen, and were mingled with them; but because the development of the people was not then so far advanced as in our Lord's day, their guilt in those earlier times was also less. (Comp. on Matt. xi. 20, seqq.) And in the same way do individuals in the greater or smaller aggregations of people stand relatively to each other. True it is that all the members of a nation without exception are influenced† by the same spiritual atmosphere—the spirit of the nation, as we commonly call it. The lower the condition of the whole people, the greater is the dominion exercised over individuals by this spirit of the generality; as development advances, individualization increases in a nation. But yet the condition of all the individuals who compose the nation is not alike, whether in the higher or in the lower degrees of development. Rather, as different nations in the unity of mankind stand at different stages in the same period of the development of the whole, so too do the various individuals in the unity of a nation. When, therefore, we speak of the guilt of a people at a particular period, this guilt is distributed in very vari-

* [*i. e.*, of some German edition earlier than the third, to which the reference is not suitable. The passage intended would seem to be a part of the commentary on the warnings in Matt. xxiv.]

† [*Getragen.*]

ous measures among the individuals of that people. Now, in every people there may be distinguished *active* and *passive* individuals; in acts of sin, the latter are merely drawn along in the train of the former class, but the active are those who, in the critical moments, determine the tendency of the whole to sin. Thus, in our Lord's time, it was the Pharisees and Priests who produced the sin of the apostacy; the mass of the people was only carried along by them; if the leaders had taken another direction, it might have been differently guided. Thus, then, in a case of national guilt, the *degree* of guilt is variously determined in such a way that the active members especially bear it. In the mass, which is only swayed by them, the guilt of many may be very slight in such a proceeding as the rejection of Christ was, inasmuch as an exact knowledge of the circumstances is often not even rendered possible for them. Those, then, who thus have loaded their conscience but little, may form the seed of a new generation. Hence the great *judgments* which befel Israel, (in the wilderness, in the captivity, under Titus, and under Hadrian)—in which those members of the people who had fallen wholly under the dominion of sin, were removed—appear, at the sametime, as *restorations*, inasmuch as the remnant of the people, like a living root which is set free from the dead tree, was in a condition to put forth new shoots. There are, therefore, *three* classes to be distinguished in the people of Israel; *first*, the few who had the energy, in opposition to the corrupted spirit of the mass, to recognise and apprehend the Messiah in Him who was crucified; these passed over into the spiritual Israel of the Church. *Next*, those members of the nation who, with more or less clearness of knowledge, strove against God; these fell off from Israel, and, although circumcised in the flesh, became in spirit of the heathen uncircumcision (ii. 28–9), for which cause God caused them to perish in the great judgment under Titus which followed. *Thirdly*, those who were not strongly enough actuated either by sin or by grace; so that they neither became so deeply guilty as the second class, by their not believing, nor, on the other hand, did they attain to the same perfection as the first. This third class remained over as a seed, and out of it was developed the Israel after the flesh, which we see descending through the course of the Christian ages, and which sojourns among ourselves, as a living miracle of the Lord, scattered over all the world, yet faithfully adhering to the customs which it has inherited. Japheth indeed now dwells in the tents of these children of Shem; *i.e.*, they are bearing the guilt of their fathers, and have ceased to be the centre of the divine system of salvation; yet they are not cast off for ever, but their prerogative is only withdrawn from them for a time, and still remains in store for them. They are like a royal race excluded from the throne through the fault of its ancestors, but for which the crown is reserved until the time when it shall please God to restore it to its dominion.

After these remarks, the following statement of the Apostle as to the various classes of individuals, and the aggregate of the people of Israel, will be more easily intelligible.

Ver. 1. In accordance with what has been said, the question *μὴ ἀπώσατο κ. τ. λ.* is not to be understood of the individual members of the nation who lived in the days of our Lord and the Apostles; for they were, in truth, for the most part rejected, and in ch. ix. St Paul expressed that deep sorrow over them that they did not belong at all to that Israel for which the promises were intended (ix. 6, seqq.); it relates to the people as a body. This depended on the λεῖμμα (xi. 5); *i.e.*, on the better disposed among the people, who either already believed, or, at least, did not intentionally strive against faith. For these the promise *remained*, according to God's prescience (*ὃν προέγνω*) which also involves the operation of grace, and therefore cannot be in vain. Those, on the contrary, who had fallen away, were never in God's sight members of the true Israel; for he foreknew their unfaithfulness, and had not elected them; just as the dry branches of a tree are cut away by the gardener, without his thereby giving up the tree itself—nay, rather the pruning is a proof of his continuing care for it. As an *example* of this holy seed in the nation, the Apostle mentions himself; but with St Paul we are also to think of all those who had at that time already attached themselves to the Church; for by these it was visibly manifest that God had not forsaken his people.

Ver. 2–4. He proceeds, however, further from the *visible* to the *invisible* nucleus* of the people of God. The history of Elijah (1 Kings xix. 10, 14, 18) offers him an excellent opportunity of il-

* [*Kern.* The term must be retained in this place, because the figure is afterwards carried out.]

lustrating this truth as to the existence of a hidden handful of true believers in an apostate people. It is evident that St Paul cannot here mean those Jews only who had passed over to the church—for they were discernible—but those, unknown to every human eye, who bore in their heart, without being themselves conscious of it, the hidden treasure of faithfulness and uprightness. These stand in the same relation to the bulk of the people as the remains of the Divine image to the old man in the individual; or as in the regenerate person the new man, undeveloped, and often repressed by sin, stands towards the sinful man which encompasses him. As this latter must die in order that the other may dominate, so too must the λεῖμμα be set free from the alien husk in which it dwells, in order that it may be in a condition to extend itself. It is always the people properly so called (ix. 6, seqq.), to which all promises relate, as the new man which makes no show is alone the true man in the rude mass of the old man.

In ver. 2, ἐν Ἡλίᾳ means the section in which the history of that prophet is told. In like manner Thucydides i. 9, uses ἐν τῇ σκήπτρου παραδόσει to denote the second book of the Iliad. Ἐντυγχάνω κατά τινος does not occur elsewhere, except in the Apocrypha, 1 Macc. x. 60. In ver. 3 the quotation is freely made, and does not exactly follow either the LXX. or the Hebrew. Χρηματισμός, the answer of an oracle; the substantive occurs in this place only; as to the verb compare note on Matt. ii. 12. Ver. 4. The form ἡ βάαλ is chosen by St Paul after the example of the LXX., who most commonly use this form, although in the story of Elijah (1 Kings xix. 18) it is ὁ βάαλ. The feminine for בַּעֲלָה does not occur in the Old Testament as meaning the goddess, who is there spoken of by the name of Queen of Heaven or Astarte. The circumstance that the LXX. represent the male god as also female, is to be traced to his androgynous character, and is not to be regarded as intended in mockery.

Vers. 5, 6. Having in ch. x. decidedly characterized the want of faith as guilt, he now as strongly denies that the superiority of the better kind is their desert; this, like all other good, is not to be ascribed to any works whatever, but solely to grace.

In ver. 5 λεῖμμα = κατάλειμμα, comp. on ix. 27. The words ἐκλογὴ χάριτος do not require ἐκλογὴ κρίσεως by way of opposition, for the Divine operation produces only what is good. The idea, however, of the election of grace doubtless includes this—that God perfects those whom He chooses. The election is in itself as comprehensive as the love of God itself; but through His fore-knowledge of those who by resistance make themselves evil, it becomes *partial*. In ver. 6 A.B.D.E.F.G. omit the addition *εἰ δὲ ἐξ ἔργων, οὐκέτι ἐστὶ χάρις· ἐπεὶ τὸ ἔργον οὐκέτι ἐστὶν ἔργον*. There is evidently something superfluous in it; and moreover, the last words, *τὸ ἔργον οὐκέτι ἐστὶν ἔργον*, are in their form quite out of character with St Paul's manner. *Ἐπεί* is to be taken in the sense of "otherwise," comp. iii. 6.

Vers. 7–10. Israel, therefore, considered as a people, is divided into two parts—the *λεῖμμα* or *ἐκλογή*, the people in the true theocratic sense (ix. 6), and the hardened. In the former class the grace of God accomplishes everything; in the latter it produces the *form* in which they appear in history. In order to establish this idea of the division of Israel into a believing and an unbelieving half, as an act of God, the Apostle again appeals to the Old Testament, where the unbelief and the sinful development of many Israelites (always, of course, in respect of the manifestation only, and not in that it is sin itself), is not only foretold according to God's omniscience, but is also ascribed to His omnipotence. Thus the ideas of ix. 17, are here repeated, only with a definite application to Israel.

Reiche is for extending the question to *ἐπέτυχεν*, but it is better to understand *τί οὖν* only as interrogative. The words refer back to ix. 30. Here, however, as in ix. 6, *Ἰσραήλ* is to be understood of the physical posterity only; the *ἐκλογή* alone is the spiritual Israel. But it is God alone, as omniscient, that can distinguish between the spiritual and the physical Israel *before* the event; man cannot do so until *after* the event.—*Πωρόω* = *σκληρύνω*, comp. note on ix. 18. The only words that can be supplied, agreeably to the quotation which follows, are *ὑπὸ τοῦ Θεοῦ*. But God hardens only those whom He *will*; and He only wills to harden those who, to a certain degree, have given themselves over to sin. Such an one He intends to restrain from deeper guilt by the *πώρωσις*, if it is but temporary, or to punish by it, if it is permanent. It is evident from the words *ἕως τῆς σήμερον ἡμέρας*, that the Apostle has in view, in the first instance, only a temporary hardening, and hopes that it will soon be possible to remove the spirit of slumber from them, without being obliged to apprehend that they will afterwards, when awake, continue to resist, and only incur heavier guilt. The received text reads τούτου, but A.C.D.E.F.G. have τοῦτο, which reading is to be preferred, as the most unusual; ἐπιτυγχάνειν usually takes the genitive, comp. Heb. vi. 15, xi. 33; James iv. 2. The reading ἐπηρώθησαν (*they were hurt*, or *maimed*), has no considerable authority in its favour. The quotation in ver. 8 is freely made up from Is. xxix. 10, and Deut. xxix. 4. The unbelief of Israel is the proper subject of both passages; but in the first πεπότικεν stands instead of ἔδωκε, and in the second the turn of the sentence is, "God gave you not eyes to see and ears to hear;" whereas St Paul refers the negative to βλέπειν and ἀκούειν. The word κατάνυξις signifies in the LXX. *deep sleep*, תַּרְדֵּמָה, from νύω, not, as in profane writers, *pricking*, from νύσσω. The expression, *spirit of slumber*, is meant to denote the reality of the divine operation—the outpoured element which produced the same effect in all. Vers. 9, 10 are from Ps. lxix. 23, 24. In this passage Israel is not the subject; rather David is speaking of his enemies and curses them. Here, however, as in other Psalms, these are not his personal enemies, but the enemies of God's cause in him; his curses are the expression of God's righteous judgment, the effect of which was the only thing that could avail to lead the adversaries from their evil way and convert them. This quotation also is freely made from memory; θήρα is neither in the original nor in the LXX. The sense of the first verse is—*Where they least expect it, let the snare of destruction come upon them by way of recompense;* of the second—*Load them with misery, let their eyes become dark, bow down their backs for ever.* The original has, in the first verse, לִשְׁלוֹמִים *for those who are at rest, the secure*; as the LXX. translate εἰς ἀντοπόδομα, they no doubt read לְשִׁלּוּמִים. The *darkening of the eyes*, and *bowing down of the back*, cannot well be understood here of age and its troubles, because διαπαντός, equivalent to תָּמִיד, is joined with them; we shall do better to understand *subjection*, perhaps with blinding of the eyes.

Ver. 11. The subject of ver. 1 is now resumed, and carried further—how that God has by no means rejected the people as such, but rather salvation has come to the Gentiles, through the fall of the

Israelites, in order thereby to incite these to the recovery of their prerogative. Thus (as in ver. 8) the hardening of Israel would appear as merely transitory, out of which God, according to His wisdom, knows how to bring forth some good effect. If, however, this idea were understood of *all* the individual members of the outward body of the nation, then, as has been already remarked at ver. 1, in the first place the grief which St Paul expressed in ch. ix. seqq., would be merely affected; for in that case the calamity would be nothing more than that some reached the goal later than others; and as, moreover, the salvation of the Gentiles was hereby brought about, all cause of complaint would substantially disappear. And further, in that case the Apostle would contradict himself; for in ix. 6, seqq., he had said that not all those who were physically members of the Israelitish people were such inwardly also, but that to these latter alone the promise belonged; consequently he cannot here intend to speak of all who are Israelites by fleshly descent. If we should choose to suppose (which, however, according to the subsequent discussion, is not probable) that St Paul imagined the coming of Christ to be immediately at hand, and hoped that it would effect the conversion of the Israelites; still, there had been an interval of more than twenty years since our Lord's ascension, and during that time many Jews, who might have become believers in Christ, had died in unbelief; and therefore, even on this supposition, the Apostle could not mean *all* the individuals who had ever belonged to the nation. We must rather, according to the principles laid down at the beginning of this chapter, make a clear distinction between the individuals and the essential part* of the nation. Many individuals "stumbled at Christ that they should fall"—*i.e.*, in punishment of their own sin they utterly forfeited the salvation which is in Christ; but these were such as in nowise belonged to the people of God, properly so-called, being only members of the fleshly Israel; the *λεῖμμα,* on the other hand (ver. 5), which is the proper essence of the nation, was, through this very stumbling of the others, and the calling of the Gentiles, to be saved, and hereafter to become a great blessing to the world. The sense of the words is consequently this—to the elect all things must serve for good, even the sin of their neighbours; to those who are not elect, all things serve for their hurt, even the divinely-appointed means of salvation; for their inward perverseness causes them to pervert everything from its proper purpose. (Comp. Ps. xviii. 27; Revel. xxii. 11.) Of course, however, as has already been often remarked, this election of God is not to be thought of as arbitrary, but as directed by Divine wisdom and holiness, and consequently as leaving no one unchosen but such as resist the operation of grace. After what has been said, the only thing in the passage under consideration that strikes us as a difficulty is, that the Apostle does not distinguish these two classes, but speaks of the whole mass as if it were of uniform quality. The cause of this appearance, however, is only to be sought in the circumstance, that St Paul views the people as a definite unity, and attributes to it collective actions. The two wholly different classes contained in this unity—those of genuine and false Israelites, of elect and non-elect—can be separated by God alone; it is only in the generations which have quitted the earthly scene that man begins to perceive their difference, and even in these it is but partially and uncertainly, while in the living he cannot discern at all. One who to the last moment is an unbeliever, may yet, with his latest breath, turn and become a believer. And it is with the whole of mankind as with the people of Israel. In God's sight there are two wholly distinct classes among mankind, but for man this distinction is not perceptible. In the living and in future generations, man sees a great mass destined to salvation; it is only in the generations which have passed away that he sees the difference; and even among these, again, he sees it but imperfectly, since no human eye penetrates into the depth of the soul, and we can seldom be entirely assured as to the happiness or misery of another.

We must not attempt at all to refine on the relations of πταίειν and πίπτειν to each other; the former means simply *to stumble against* (with reference to ix. 33), the latter the *falling*, which is the consequence of stumbling, with the result of this fall, viz., the ἀπώλεια which may follow from *such* falling. The tendency of the Apostle's argument in this place, is to prove how God's wisdom can turn the fall of Israel, in the sense which has just been more particularly defined, to the good of others in the first place (as had *already* been seen), and eventually to that of Israel itself also.

Ἵνα is, therefore, to be understood *τελικῶς*, as it is also in ver. 19, which is a passage very similar to the present. *Ἐγένετο* is to be supplied to *ἡ σωτηρία*. Salvation, doubtless, would have come to the Gentiles, even in the case of Israel's having believed; but, in the first place, it would not have been until later, and moreover, if Israel had remained true to its calling, the Gentile world would not have become, as it has, the transmitter of the ordinances of salvation.* As to *παραζηλῶσαι*, compare note on x. 19. As in the individual, a deep fall is often necessary in order rightly to kindle the new life in him to a flame (as, *e. g.*, in the case of St Peter), so too are the fall of the Jews among mankind, and the sight of the Gentile world enjoying their prerogatives in consequence of this fall, the means in God's hand of bringing the Israel of God to the true life.

Ver. 12. St Paul goes on to shew, by an argument *a minori ad majus*, how powerful an influence Israel exercises on mankind—like the heart, by the motions of which the life of the whole organic system is regulated. If even their *fall* has had the power *per contrarium*, to operate for blessing, how much more will their *rising again*, when it takes place! The Apostle, however, forthwith defines more precisely the idea of the *παράπτωμα*; for, in another view, this fall of Israel was the acceptance of some members of the people. If it had been possible that the Apostles also (who were all children of Abraham), the Seventy, and all the Israelitish friends of our Lord, should have continued in unbelief, or have become apostate (which certainly was impossible, according to Matt. xxiv. 24), then neither would the gospel have reached the Gentiles; it would have utterly failed. St Paul's idea, therefore, is properly this:—If so small a number of Israelites has been able to effect so much in the Gentile world (*κόσμος* = *ἔθνη*, comp. note on iii. 7), what will Israel effect when the whole body comes to act! The expression chosen for this idea, *ἥττημα καὶ πλήρωμα*, is as difficult as the idea itself is simple. *Παράπτωμα* would require, by way of contrast, some such notion as *ἀνάστασις*; but this is wanting, and is absorbed in *πλήρωμα*. *Ἥττημα*, attic for *ἥσσημα*, is used by profane writers like *ἧσσα* or *ἧττα*, in the sense of *overthrow, hurt, loss;* in that sense it would be synony-

[* Träger der Heilsanstalten.]

mous with παράπτωμα, but if so taken it would not, seemingly, form a contrast with πλήρωμα. The only other place where it occurs in the New Testament is 1 Cor. vi. 7, where it means, like ἐλάττωμα, *a moral defect, degradation.* The expression πλήρωμα, which is used of the full complement of a ship, the whole population of a city, and the like, points to the idea of a *part* as its opposite; but it cannot be certainly made out that ἥττημα can bear this sense. [Olsh. would render it by the word *Ausfall* ("abatement, deficiency"), which, he says, "is used to signify that portion of a connected multitude which is not filled up."] The Apostle, no doubt, had in his mind the idea of a definite number, which, in the course of its development, the people of Israel must make up—an idea which also appears in a modified form in Revel. vii. 4. This number had, in our Lord's day, an important deficiency [*Ausfall*], in consequence of the unbelief of many; and yet, if the faithful few already had such powerful influence, what, St Paul means to say, may we infer that the effect will be, when the number determined by God shall be full !* The passage was rightly explained in a similar way as far back as Origen. Beza and Grotius in later times, and most recently De Wette, also agree in this explanation, of which ver. 25 is a further confirmation.

Vers. 13, 14. St Paul proceeds to say that, actuated by a knowledge of what is in store for Israel, he, although especially an Apostle to the Gentiles, yet always keeps his own people also in view, in the hope that his labours among the Gentiles may react beneficially on Israel. As, however, he says σώσω τινὰς ἐξ αὐτῶν, it is clearly a mistake to suppose that the Apostle continued,

* The passage Gal. iv. 24, seqq., is very instructive as to the Apostle's whole view of the relation between the aggregate of Israel and the individuals who compose it. The nation is the mother, who constantly represents a *possibility* of bearing; but she is long barren (Galat. iv. 27); and when she bears, as Sarah bore only Isaac, she bears but few children. But the time will come when the forsaken, aged, barren one, shall bear more children than she that hath an husband. Israel, scattered among all nations, and forsaken of God, is like to such a declining and barren woman; individuals alone here and there separate themselves from the people, and enter into Christ's Gentile Church, which at present has the husband—*i. e.*, in which God and His grace are in operation. But this barren widow will in her age hereafter bear children, as the dew is born from the dawn (Ps. cx.), [where the latter part of ver. 4 is rendered by Luther, "Thy children are born to thee as the dew from the dawn."] Israel's growing-old is a continuous process of purgation; the refuse gradually falls away, the pure gold remains behind.

at the date of the Epistle to the Romans, to imagine our Lord's second coming to be as near as he had thought when he wrote to the Thessalonians. For, as appears from ver. 25, he expected the conversion of πᾶς Ἰσραήλ at the advent; consequently, if he had still regarded this as so near, he would have chosen some more comprehensive expression instead of τινές. It might indeed be said, that St Paul left the conversion of the mass of the Jews to the Twelve, and himself only hoped to convert some Jews in addition to his proper work. And if so, no conclusion could be drawn from this passage as to St Paul's views respecting the nearness of Christ's coming. Still, however, the Epistle to the Romans gives the impression, that St Paul no longer considered the advent so near. (Comp. note on xii. 11.) But in any case, he hoped by his conversion of some, to hasten greatly the restoration of all.

Ἐφ' ὅσον is to be taken in the sense of *in so far as, inasmuch as* (supplying τρόπον), not *so long as*, (supplying χρόνον). The conversion of some Jews appears to the Apostle, who always keeps in view the great prerogatives of his nation, as a δοξάζειν of his office. Σάρξ μου = בְּשָׂרִי (comp. Gen. xxix. 14), in the sense of *kindred, persons of the same nation, fellow-countrymen.*

Ver. 15. Now, from this conversion he expects a beneficial effect for the whole kingdom of God, according to the principle of ver. 12, that if even the deficiency* of so many conduced towards the salvation of the world, the accession of these would have a yet far more powerful effect. Here καταλλαγὴ κόσμου explains the more general expression πλοῦτος (ver. 12). The Gentiles were in a state of natural enmity to God (Eph. ii. 1, seqq.); the removal of this enmity, by their calling unto Christ, is the καταλλαγή. Here too the Gentiles are conceived of as a collective body, standing in contrast to the Jews as another collective body. Although so many Gentiles were still in unbelief, it is yet already said of them in altogether general terms that *they are called,* inasmuch as the Gentile world, *as such,* was destined by God's decree to be, instead of the Jews, the transmitter of the divinely-appointed ordinances of salvation; and although individual Jews became believers, and in the course of ages many more continually joined the Church, it is yet said of them that *they are rejected,* because, regarded as a people, they had ceased to be the centre of the

* [Ausfall.]

ordinances of salvation. Ἀποβολή is used as equivalent to ἥττημα in ver. 12. The rejection of Israel is at the same time the reception of some, and it is only on this positive side that it is the blessing of the Gentile world. The πρόσληψις, however, is that reception of the whole body which is to be expected (according to ver. 25), and of which the operation will be so much more potent for all mankind, because already so small a number had been able to work on them so powerfully. The term τίς—ἐι μή (which corresponds with πόσῳ μᾶλλον in ver. 12), is intended to give prominence to the greatness of this influence. Ζωὴ ἐκ νεκρῶν (sc. κόσμου), is equivalent to ἀνάστασις, which is to be regarded as that still higher result which arises out of the καταλλαγή, exactly as in Rom. v. 9, seqq., the two are mentioned together as the lower and the higher. The *resurrection* is here to be primarily understood in a *spiritual* sense (as in Ezek. xxxvii.) The enmity of the Gentiles was, indeed, removed by the fall of Israel, but the spiritual life was still weak in them; from the assumption of Israel, on the other hand, St Paul expects the most powerful excitement of life for them. The two divisions of mankind, therefore, Jews and Gentiles, operate reciprocally on each other. The life which is in the Gentiles arouses the emulation of the Jews; and the life of the Jews, in its turn, heightens that which is in the Gentiles. But inasmuch as, according to ver. 25, it is not until the end of the world's development that the πρόσληψις is to take place, and then also the physical resurrection of the saints follows, thus far the idea of the ζωὴ ἐκ νεκρῶν has reference at the same time to the *bodily* resurrection also—as the two, indeed, always properly imply each other. (Comp. on John vi. 39, seqq.)

Ver. 16. Again continuing his argument with εἰ (a particle which begins six sentences between ver. 12 and ver. 21), the Apostle employs figures of which the sense is in itself plain, although there is an obscurity as to their connexion with the course of the reasoning. The object of both figures is to affirm that the part bears the nature of the whole, or the derivative that of the original. The ἀπαρχή is the general*—the holy first fruits which were offered to the Lord,

* There were two kinds of firstlings—רֵאשִׁית בִּכּוּרִים, the first ripe fruits, and רֵאשִׁית תְּרוּמוֹת, the parts offered to the Lord of that which was prepared. To suppose. with Tholuck and Reiche, that the latter are meant, is a needless increase of the difficulty; for so the two images would stand in an opposite order. The *root* is the general, out of which

from which the *φύραμα* is prepared as a derivative; in like manner, the *ῥίζα* is the original, out of which the *κλάδοι* grow. The nature of the tree is shown also by the branch which shoots forth from it. St Paul holds fast to this second image, and uses it as a substratum throughout the argument which follows. But how does he light on the idea at all? and what does he intend by it in this place? The sentence which must be supplied in order to restore the connection, is this:—*But that πρόσληψις which has been spoken of may be expected with certainty, for that which is derived must needs have in it the nature of its original, and consequently the Israel that now is—(the branches)—must also have the nature of the root from which it grew.* Now these *roots* are, of course, the patriarchs, Abraham, Isaac, and Jacob (ver. 28); because they are holy, their seed must also be holy; for the blessing of the righteous descends to thousands (Exod. xxxiv. 7). Then the connexion is quite simple between this and the further statement (ver. 17, seqq.), that the Gentiles indeed were grafted in instead of the branches which were cut off, but that, notwithstanding, Israel was not rejected for ever. If it be objected that too much would follow from this idea, viz., that the Jews could not have fallen at all, whereas the Apostle had just been representing that they had fallen—it is to be considered that St Paul does not mean to deny the possibility of a good tree putting forth unprofitable shoots; the only inconceivable thing is that it should not produce *any* fruitful branches at all. The apostacy of many, therefore, nowise proves that all hope is given up for ever; rather generous branches must yet be put forth from the generous root. De Wette's explanation, which makes *ῥίζα* to denote the ideal theocracy, founded in the patriarchs, and *κλάδος*, on the other hand, to mean the mere external relation to it, fleshly descent and outward membership—exactly coincides with our interpretation; for

the *branches* grow; and by analogy *φύραμα* must also have stood first, and *ἀπαρχή* have followed. But, that St Paul should have intentionally chosen the one position in the first comparison, and the other in the second, is utterly unlikely, since his argument requires that the derivative should follow from the original, as existing before it. Ἀπαρχή means the first fruits which are consecrated to the Lord, *φύραμα* the dough which is prepared from them. Reiche tells us that we nowhere read of dough being prepared from the first fruits, but it is not necessary that a thing which is understood as a matter of course should be specially related. If St Paul had wished to express the other idea, he would have had to say, *εἰ δὲ τὸ φύραμα ἅγιον, καὶ ὁ ἄρτος*. Moreover, the distinction altogether is of later origin. Comp. Winer's Real-lexicon *in voc.*

outward membership is designed to include an invitation to enter into that which is inward also.

Vers. 17, 18. The figure of the *tree*, which has been chosen, is more exactly defined by its being characterized as a generous *olive tree*. From this branches have been cut off—(the Apostle gently speaks of them as τινές, whereas he might have styled them *the greatest part*); and instead of these, wild olive-branches have been grafted into the generous parent-stock. St Paul, of course, means by this the children of Japheth who dwell in the tents of Shem, and who are thus, consequently, admonished to preserve a humble consciousness of this benefit as a *favour* shewn to them. The circumstance that St Paul makes choice of the olive-tree for the illustration of his idea, while our Lord chooses the vine, arises from the character of the former tree; its πιότης is symbolical of the spiritual fulness of Israel. Hence the holy anointing-oil (Exod. xxv. 6, xxx. 31, xxxvii. 29) was a symbol of being filled with the Spirit. And whereas, according to the image in this place, the wild branches are engrafted into the generous tree, reversing the usual process by which good branches are grafted into wild trees—we are informed by both ancient and modern writers that such a process is practicable in this very tree, the olive, and is often practised in the East—a circumstance which is fully sufficient to account for the representation in the text. (Comp. Columella de Re Rust. v. 9; Palladius de Insit. xiv. 53; Schulz, Leit. des Höchsten, vol. v. p. 38.) Still the main idea in these verses—the *engrafting* namely—has itself an appearance of difficulty. What is the idea which it is intended to express when the figure is explained? The converted Gentiles will after all not become Jews, as might be said of a proselyte [to Judaism], inasmuch as he is quite absorbed into the nationality of the Jews, and joins them in their manners and way of life. Still, it is said that the Gentile Christian is grafted, not only into the root, but into the very branches which are cut off (ἐν αὐτοῖς.) These words are by no means to be considered pleonastic, but denote the place where the branches grew on to the tree, the wound (as it were) which was produced by their removal, and into which the Gentiles are engrafted. The Apostle's whole representation of the case can only be understood by premising the following fundamental ideas. St Paul conceives of the true Israel, *i.e.*, the community of all true believers—

as an articulate organization which has in it its own proper life. Whoever does not stand in connection with this body has no share in the life which animates it. Now, this organization has been developed from Abraham, as the Father of the Faithful (Rom. iv.), until Christ, who was, in his humanity, the absolutely perfect fruit of this organization; its influence did not extend beyond the bounds of the fleshly Israel, inasmuch as the Gentiles whom it received into itself were always proportionately few, and these, moreover, became at the same time nationally Jews. But with the appearance of Christ arrived the hour of salvation, and at the same time of judgment on the fleshly Israel; the power of life in this holy self-contained organization broke forth, attracted the kindred natures in the physical Israel, and repelled the uncongenial multitude. As the latter preponderated, and formed, properly speaking, the mass of the nation, the physical Israel now ceased to be the centre of that spiritual organization, the *true* Israel. The Gentile world now became this centre, and the gaps left by the unfaithful members of the fleshly Israel were filled up by the faithful Gentiles. We must, therefore, consider the idea—that if members in this organization fall away, others must fill the gap,—as the basis of the argument. This is typically shown in the body of the Apostles; when Judas had fallen out of it, his place was filled, another was to take his bishopric (comp. note on Acts i. 20). This idea leads us to apprehend the powerful realistic manner in which St Paul conceives of this spiritual body, which is no other than the true ἐκκλησία, extending through all mankind—the new man coming into being within the great old-man of the human race, who was even from the beginning filled with the breath of the Eternal Word, although it was not until the fulness of time (Gal. iv. 4) that this Word personally incorporated Himself in it,* and so brought Him to the knowledge of himself.

'Αγριέλαιος is less usual than the feminine form, *ἀγριέλαια*; *καλλιέλαιος*, ver. 24, is its opposite. *'Εγκεντρίζειν, to insert into anything by pricking*, from *κέντρον*, Acts ix. 5. *Κατακαυχᾶσθαι* here means *selfish exultation over another*, as opposed to the humble consciousness that whatever has been received is of grace. *Εἰ δέ* in ver. 18 requires us to supply "then know—then thou must know."

* [*Derselben*, fem. seemingly the ἐκκλησία, or perhaps *menschheit*, mankind.]

Vers. 19–22. Notwithstanding that the Apostle's statement *appears* in certain parts to subject every thing to a rigid necessity; yet other passages, on the other hand, clearly show how firmly he at the same time holds free-will; and to this latter class the following verses belong. He reminds the Gentiles of the possibility of their falling away, and of the restoration of the people of Israel. St Paul, therefore, is far from teaching a doctrine of *irresistible grace.* It is, indeed, through God alone—as well through His election as through His operation—that the good man does any good thing; but yet he retains the power of *resistance* as long as he lives on earth; hence the continual possibility of falling away. And, on the other hand, the worst of men, so long as he sojourns in the body, retains the possibility of ceasing from his resistance, and hence the continual possibility of conversion. God, indeed, knows the event beforehand, but he knows it precisely as one that is brought about through the free-will of the individuals. This possibility St Paul states in the passage following; and we must acknowledge in consequence the *possibility* that the candlestick of the Gentiles might be removed. History presents us with partial appearances of this kind, especially in the Eastern Church; but, according to ver. 25, it is not to be conceived that, as to the Gentiles as a whole, this *possibility* should ever be *realised* *

In ver. 20, *faith* and *unbelief* are specified as the tempers which fundamentally determine the mind, by which the man stands or falls. The former means, as it always does, the inward openness to receive the influences of a higher world; the latter, the self-sufficient self-isolation and limitation to its own powers, which consequently cannot lead to anything above itself. Ὑψηλοφρονεῖν is again found in 1 Tim. vi. 17, and is the opposite to φοβεῖσθαι, which is not meant to denote a slavish fear, but a tender carefulness—not a fear *of* God, but a fear *for* God and His cause, a fear *of* one's-self and sin. In ver. 21, φοβοῦμαι is to be supplied before μήπως. The received text has φείσηται, which is indeed more suitable than

* The adherents of the well-known fanatical preacher, Irving, in London, hold that the whole Gentile Church has already become apostate, and that now, at the end of the development of the Church, a Jewish Church will again be formed. This idea, however, has evidently no foundation in Scripture, and must therefore be reckoned among the many errors of that party. It may, however, not impossibly be in the scheme of Divine Providence, that in the last days a Jewish Church may again arise, *by the side of* the Gentile Church, as was the case in the apostolic age.

φείσεται to the usual construction of *μήπως*; there is, however, no lack of examples of the construction with the indicative also (comp. Winer's Gr. p. 471.) In ver. 22 the meaning of *ἀποτομία* is sufficiently determined by the opposite, *χρηστότης*; it is equivalent to *ὀργή*, but is preferred on account of the figure of the cut-off branches. By *ἐὰν ἐπιμείνῃς* it is not intended to ascribe to man an independent power of action of his own, as if without the help of grace he could preserve himself from falling away by his own strength and faithfulness; but *τῇ πίστει* is to be understood (comp. ver. 23), and it is intended to signify the continual preservation of the receptivity for that grace which protects from falling away. *Ἐπεί, else, otherwise*, as in ver. 6.

Vers. 23, 24. The possibility of the restoration of rejected Israel is now placed by the side of the possible apostacy of the Gentiles; the condition of it is, that they no longer continue to resist the divine grace, by which resistance the omnipotence of God itself is hindered, inasmuch as it cannot be His *will* to put constraint on a being which was created free. The whole, however, continues thus far to be on the footing of a hypothesis, as it is not until vers. 25, 26, that the *certainty* of such a restoration is expressed; further observations on this idea are therefore reserved for the following verses.

In ver. 23, *δυνατός κ. τ. λ.* denotes the divine omnipotence, which, however, is never to be thought of as separate from wisdom; hence God *cannot* again engraft those who continue in *ἀπιστία*, since His wisdom does not admit of His *willing* it. The opposition of *κατὰ φύσιν* and *παρὰ φύσιν* must by no means be regarded as an unmeaning part of the image; rather it has the important signification that the Jews, considered as a people, have in their whole tendency and qualifications, a higher call than all other nations to employ themselves on the things of God. This calling of theirs is not taken away by their unfaithfulness, but only suspended; the consciousness of it, consequently, can very easily be reawakened in them, while a very long time was required to bring the Gentile world into its proper relation to the divine ordinances of salvation.

Vers. 25, 26. In order, then, to bring the Gentile Christians, whom he seems in this place to regard exclusively (or quite predominantly) in the Roman church, to the proper estimate of their position (*ἵνα μὴ ἦτε παρ' ἑαυτοῖς φρόνιμοι*), the Apostle points with prophetic emphasis (οὐ θέλω ὑμᾶς ἀγνοεῖν, comp. note on i. 13), to the mystery of Israel's restoration, when the πλήρωμα τῶν ἐθνῶν shall have first come in (to the community of the faithful, or of the kingdom of God.) That this remarkable passage contains a prophecy, properly so called, respecting the people of Israel, is acknowledged by the great majority of expositors, both ancient and modern; and the context so positively requires us to understand Israelites *after the flesh*, that a different interpretation of the passage will never be able to gain a permanent footing. It was only from a mistaken opposition to the Jews, and from apprehensions of fanatical abuse of the passage, that Chrysostom, Theodoret, and Jerome long ago, and in later days the reformers especially, were led to explain the Apostle's words as relating to the *spiritual* Israel. The correct application, however, was again established as early as Beza in the reformed* Church, and in the Lutheran by Calixtus and Spener. How forced the sense of the words is, according to that interpretation which refers them to the spiritual Israel, is apparent from the translation of the passage to which this leads, *Israel has been in part affected with hardness, throughout the whole time that* (ἄχρις οὗ) *the fulness of the Gentiles is entering into the kingdom of God*, i.e., *while the Gentiles are entering in a body, individual Jews only will become Christians;* there is no help to be expected for the Jewish people as a whole.†) *But then* (viz., when all the Gentiles shall have entered), *will the whole spiritual Israel, made up of Jews and Gentiles, be blessed.* The utter irrelevancy of this last sentence must be apparent to every one; it is only when applied to the fleshly Israel that it acquires a meaning. Ammon, Reiche, and Köllner acknowledge this, indeed, but suppose that the prophecy has remained unfulfilled;‡ as if the history of the people of Israel to this day did not preach aloud that it is yet to receive its fulfilment. Benecke, without any ground, transfers this fulfilment

* [*i. e.*, Calvinistic.]

† The positiveness with which Luther asserts the impossibility of the conversion of the Jews is remarkable. He says, among other things:—"A Jewish heart is so stock-stone-devil-iron-hard, that in nowise can it be moved; they are young devils, damned to hell; to convert these devil's-brats (as some fondly ween out of the Epistle to the Romans), is impossible." From this, as from other expressions, it is manifest that the knowledge of the last events of the world's history was a province closed against the great Reformer.

‡ [*i. e.*, apparently, that it is utterly void.]

wholly into the next world; the portion of truth which may lie in this idea will forthwith come out more distinctly. The first question which occurs, on our attempting to ascertain more exactly the sense of this remarkable prophetic expression, is—what does the Apostle wish to be understood by πᾶς Ἰσραήλ? Does he mean all the individuals who ever belonged to the fleshly Israel? and consequently, among them, Judas Iscariot, Absalom, and all the cut-off branches? It might seem so, according to vers. 15 and 23, where the possibility of engrafting is declared with respect to those who have been cut off, *i.e.*, the reprobate. This is also strongly favoured by ver. 11, where it is expressly stated that the design was not that they should utterly fall, but that they should be stirred to emulation. Still, the κᾀκεῖνοι only means the Jews regarded as a whole, in opposition to the Gentiles, but not the single individuals of the nation who had contracted especial guilt. If all individuals were one day to be made blessed, there would, as has been remarked already, be an inward untruth in St Paul's grief (ix. 3); and so too in the separation between the spiritual and the fleshly Israel (ix. 6), since in that case the whole of Israel would be spiritual, only that this character would not be developed in some until a later time. Or (2), does πᾶς Ἰσραήλ signify only those Jews who live in the last days, so that we must suppose all earlier generations of the people of Israel excluded from bliss? If so, the history of Israel since Christ's coming would be like the forty years in the wilderness, only that, as the space of time is greater, the repetition also would be on a larger scale. In the one case, it was necessary that the old generation should utterly die out, in order to make room for a new; in this case, it would be necessary that a whole series of generations should die off, in order more and more to gather together the scattered seeds of a better life, and at length to exhibit them united in the last generation, as in a matured fruit. In like manner, as we see in the patriarchs of the nation, that of Abraham's descendants his son Isaac alone (and not Ishmael) could be regarded as the transmitter of the holy life, and of Isaac's in turn, only his son Jacob, not Esau; while, on the other hand, of Jacob's, all his twelve sons form the pillars of Israel. But the Christian spirit is opposed to this representation, on the ground that, according to it, the *one* saved generation would not stand in any proportion to the many who perished, while yet the loss of salvation would not appear as caused by any personal guilt of the latter, by their resistance to grace. Rather the Apostle unquestionably means, that the λεῖμμα κατ' ἐκλογὴν χάριτος (xi. 5), is to be conceived of as existing in the nation at every period of time. Israel would have ceased to be Israel if this had been utterly wanting in any generation. Consequently, we can only understand the prophecy in such a sense that all those members of the Israelitish people who ever belonged to the true λεῖμμα attain σωτηρία; at the end of the world, assuredly, the people will enter in a mass into the kingdom of God, but even then too there will be no want of such individuals as are Israelites after the flesh only. But all the better persons of the earlier generations, who remained in ignorance of Christ without guilt of their own, and yet led their lives in sincere fulfilment of the law, true repentance, and firm faith in the Messiah, whom they had been taught to look for —(as is doubtless to be supposed of many Jews in all ages)—these will be dealt with like those who lived before the coming of Christ, and who learn in the next life to know that which here they knew not; in like manner as pious heathens also, who here had no means of becoming acquainted with Christ, will there find a possibility of laying hold on Him as their Saviour. Thus the fulfilment of the prophecy is of a truth to be partly placed in the next world, and this is the truth which is contained in Benecke's view. But in this sense St Paul could with propriety speak of πᾶς 'Ισραήλ, since those who forfeit salvation do not really belong at all to the Israel of God. (ix. 6.) It is indeed certain that the Apostle did not imagine the fulfilment of this prophecy to be so distant as experience has shown it to be; still, it has been already observed (on ver. 14) that neither did St Paul conceive it to be quite close at hand, as if it might take place in his own lifetime; he did not know the time of Christ's second coming (Acts i. 7), but hoped that that which he longed for would soon come to pass. The greater or less length of the interval, however, does not in any way affect the substance of the view; if there were but a single generation between, still the question always arises how this is to be regarded; and it cannot be answered otherwise than as it has been, since there is nothing to warrant us in supposing that the generation either attains salvation without exception or perishes without exception. The expression ἄχρις οὗ, consequently, is meant merely to indicate the term at which the σωτηρία of Israel will come to pass, without more particularly defining the time. The εἰσέρχεσθαι of the πλήρωμα τῶν ἐθνῶν (viz., εἰς τὴν βασιλείαν τοῦ Θεοῦ), is, however, no less a difficulty than the definition of πᾶς Ἰσραήλ. Are we, under this phrase, to understand *all* Gentiles who ever lived or will live, without exception?* This, again, cannot possibly be the Apostle's meaning, since in chap. i. he had represented them as so deeply sunk, and nowhere intimates that *all* will allow themselves to be brought to repentance. Or is it only all the Gentiles who shall be alive at the time of Christ's second coming? If so, how should the better-minded of the earlier heathens (ii. 14, 26, 27) have offended, who, without guilt of their own, knew nothing of the way of salvation? And how can we reconcile with this the statement, which is continually repeated in Scripture (comp. on St Matt. xxiv.), that just at the time of the second advent, sin will be exceedingly powerful among men? That *every individual* should be won to the truth by the preaching of the gospel among the Gentiles, is in itself unlikely, and contradicts Scripture, which represents the gospel as preached to them for a *witness* unto them. (Matt. xxiv. 14.) The elect among the Gentiles, therefore, can alone be meant. But why does St Paul choose for this meaning the word πλήρωμα, which may also signify the whole aggregate body? (Comp. on ver. 12.) It is in order that here again he may hold fast the idea of the supplying of a deficiency.† The gap caused by the unfaithfulness of many Israelites will be filled up by a corresponding number of the Gentiles, who enter on the higher calling of those who have fallen out from their places. In God's kingdom, all is rule and order; and thus even the number of His saints is counted! (1 Cor. xiv. 33.) The explanation of ver. 32 will show that that verse is to be reconciled with this interpretation.

* According to Revel. xx. 8, there are still heathens even in the kingdom of God, who are led astray by Gog and Magog; thus all heathens cannot become Christians.

† It is similarly taken by Bengel, who rightly renders it *supplementum*. So, too, Stier, who refers to John x. 16, xi. 52; and remarks that the conversion of the Gentiles will not fully flourish until forwarded by the activity of the converted Israelites. (Comp. Is. ii. 3, lxvi. 19, seqq.; Zechar. viii. 20, seqq.; Mic. v. 6.) Compare, also, Justin Martyr, Apol. ii. p. 82, ed. Sylburg., who in like manner expresses the idea of a number of the Gentiles which is to be filled up by degrees.

Μυστήριον does not mean something which in itself cannot be known, but something which (as being the free counsel of God) cannot be discovered by man. In like manner, the calling of the Gentiles is also called *μυστήριον*. (1 Cor. xv. 51; Ephes. i. 9; iii. 3.)—*Παρ᾽ ἑαυτῷ φρόνιμος εἶναι* answers to חָכָם בְּעֵינָיו (Prov. iii. 7.) The *πώρωσις* (comp. on ver. 7) here appears in so far as an act of grace, as it withdraws the knowledge from the people until the suitable moment for their conversion. If the Jews had resisted salvation with their eyes open, their guilt would have been far greater than in the actual case. *Ἄχρις οὗ* can, of course, signify only the *term*, until the entrance of the Gentiles shall be complete, not the *duration* of their entering through all ages. *Ἀπὸ μέρους* is not to be joined with *πώρωσις*, as if the *hardening* were partial, but with *Israel;* as many Jews became believers, this addition was necessary. Glöckler is mistaken in his interpretation of the passage—"Hardening came on the people of Israel from a portion of it," viz., from those who lived in our Lord's day—(*i. e.*, a part brought guilt on the whole); *ἀπὸ μέρους* mus be the opposite to *πᾶς Ἰσραήλ*.—*Οὕτω* is to be taken as meaning "Such circumstances having arisen."

Vers. 26, 27. For the confirmation of the hope which he had expressed, St Paul now again refers to a prophecy of the Old Testament. He quotes freely, from memory, and thus, as he had before done, mixes up two passages (Isaiah lix. 20 and xxvii. 9.) Hence no stress is to be laid on the variations from the original and the LXX. The Apostle was concerned only with the leading idea, that, according to the Old Testament, a deliverance is to be expected for Israel—an idea which is indeed expressed in both passages. That St Paul regards Christ alone as the person who accomplishes this deliverance of Israel, and does not suppose (as some enthusiasts have fancied) that at the end of time a further *special* Redeemer is to come for Israel,—this point requires no proof. The circumstance that here His coming is represented as future, whereas Jesus had already performed His work at the time when St Paul wrote, is easily explained by considering that the intention is hereby to express that the *experience* of this redemption through Christ, before which it cannot be said to have acquired its reality for them, is *future* for the Israelites.

Instead of *ἐκ Σιών*, the LXX. have *ἕνεκεν Σιών*, from the

Hebrew לְצִיּוֹן. St Paul probably had in his mind such passages as Ps. xiv. 7, where מִצִּיּוֹן is found. The title ῥυόμενος answers to גּוֹאֵל, a well-known Jewish designation of the Messiah, which is the same in idea with σωτήρ.—*Διαθήκη παρ' ἐμοῦ* points to the fact that the covenant proceeds from God, and is founded in His grace.

Vers. 28, 29. After this full statement, the Apostle is now able to recur to the fundamental idea, that the Israelites, consequently, although by resistance to the gospel they had put themselves into a position of enmity, must yet ever continue to be regarded as friends by the believer, for the sake of their fathers, in whom they were called—a relation which cannot be done away with by their unfaithfulness. In these verses there is an opposition between εὐαγγέλιον and ἐκλογή, and again, between δι' ὑμᾶς and διὰ τοὺς πατέρας. The former of these oppositions is, of course, to be so understood that the gospel is taken in connexion with the resistance to it which proceeds from the Jews, and the ἐκλογή with the grace of God which keeps them upright. In the word διά the signification "with respect to" is primarily to be kept to. The ὑμεῖς, consequently, are to be conceived of as Gentiles, the *fathers* as the true Israel, so that in these words are signified the two divisions of mankind according to the fundamental idea of the Theocracy. But when the election is traced back to the fathers, the idea comes out that the posterity are regarded as included in the ancestors. (Comp. the more particular remarks in note on Rom. v. 12; Heb. vii. 9.) If the individuals were absolutely isolated, the children would have no connexion with the fathers. The important point in these verses, however, is the question whether here (ver. 29) the doctrine of *gratia irresistibilis* do not appear to be expressed. We must indeed allow that Holy Scripture does not contain any passage from which that doctrine might be deduced with greater plausibility than from this, taken in combination with ver. 32. But even here it is easy to show the unsafeness of such an inference. The divine κλῆσις is not to be thought of except as united with God's omniscience, by which He knows the non-resistance of the elect; He does not, therefore, force the resisting will, since there is no such will, but He does according to His pleasure in those hearts which give themselves up to Him. But if it should be said that there is in all men a certain resistance to grace, forasmuch as they are sinful beings, and therefore it can only be the power of grace that overcomes this resistance in the elect; that hence, we must either suppose, if there be any eternal damnation, that God by a decree does not suffer grace to become powerful enough in the damned to overcome their resistance, or else we must suppose an universal restoration, as many of the later writers have been led by ver. 32 to imagine; but that, in any case, the Divine grace is to be conceived of as irresistible, since it is the working of the Almighty: —if, I say, such a conclusion were proposed, it may be met as follows, from a scriptural point of view and on scriptural principles. The Almighty and Allwise God, who has once created man with a capacity of resisting His will, cannot contradict Himself, as would be the case if He wished to *force* the resisting will of the creature to a conformity with His own. Hence results the operation of grace for every man according to the measure of the position in which he stands, so that there always remains for *every one* a possibility of resisting the operations of grace which come to him. This agency of God is in the passage under consideration understood only in combination with His *omniscience*, by means of which God knows from everlasting those individuals who compose the true Israel as persons who do not hinder the power of creative grace which visits them.

The χαρίσματα are the several manifestations of χάρις, which word would suit the place equally well; we are, of course, not to think of the extraordinary gifts of the Holy Spirit. Κλῆσις, on the other hand, is the Divine agency by which the grace which dwells eternally in God visits man in time. And from this relation of the two expressions, the circumstance that κλῆσις stands second is to be explained; if the extraordinary gifts of the Holy Ghost were meant, κλῆσις must of course stand first. The only other passage of the New Testament where the form ἀμεταμέλητος is found is 2 Cor. vii. 10. In profane Greek it is of very frequent occurrence.

Vers. 30, 31. The general principle which has just been declared is now established equally with respect to Gentiles (who are again exclusively and expressly addressed), and Jews, so that the divine grace forms the Israel of God alike from Jews and Gentiles. But if the unbelief of the Jews was the occasion of the calling of the Gentiles, it yet will not in turn be the apostacy of the Gentiles that is to cause the restoration of Jews; for an *universal* falling away of the Gentile world is, according to ver. 25, inconceivable; but, on the contrary, the Gentile world's experience of God's mercy will soften the heart of Israel also to emulation of its example. (Comp. on x. 19; xi. 14).

In ἀπειθεῖν and ἀπείθεια the notions of *disobedience* and *unbelief* interpenetrate each other; the latter is properly the deviation from true obedience towards God.* The dative, τῇ ἀπειθείᾳ, is naturally to be taken in the sense of "by occasion of their unbelief." The attempt to connect ὑμετέρῳ ἐλέει with ἠπείθησαν is quite inadmissible, if there were no other reason than that the unbelief of the Jews did not *follow* but *preceded* the reception of the Gentiles. In ver. 31, ὑμετέρῳ ἐλέει is to be taken passively "*through God's showing you mercy*," not actively "*through your practising mercy*." For, according to ver. 11, St Paul means to say, "Your reception is intended to provoke Israel to jealousy, in order that it also may lay hold on the salvation which is in Christ."† The insertion of νῦν or ὕστερον before ἐλεηθῶσι is a mere correction of the transcribers, which varied according as they imagined the future conversion of the Jews to be nearly or more remote.

Ver. 32. The whole statement is at length concluded with a deeply significant declaration, in which the whole history of the world is represented as the *act of God*, without prejudice to *the freedom of man*. Sin itself must become a foil to that which is good and beautiful; it turns love into grace, and grace into mercy. Sin (in its outward determinate form), no less than mercy—all is the act of God, the All-sufficient. The limits, however, which in the Apostle's mind are set to this sublime declaration, are exceeded by those among the later interpreters (especially Reiche, Köllner, and Glöckler), who understand the words οἱ πάντες to relate to all in-

* St Paul does not intend in this place to treat of the *origin* of unbelief among the heathen, but only of the *fact*. Hence there was no need for Bengel's observation, "Incredulitas cadit etiam in eos qui ipsi non audivere verbum Dei; quia tamen primitus id in patriarchas, Adamo, Noacho, susceperant." It is simpler to say that, as through their fall in Adam they were sinners, so too were they unbelievers.

† [The German has "in order that *you* also, &c.," which does not appear to make sense.]

dividuals of the Jews and Gentiles. This word stands in direct contradiction to the plain statements of St Paul, that all are not the children of faith (ix. 6); moreover, the article before πάντες* forbids us to suppose so, showing, as it does, that we are not to think of the absolute total of the individuals who compose mankind, but of that aggregate of the elect among Jews and Gentiles, which had previously been indicated. And lastly, the words, ἵνα τοὺς πάντας ἐλεήσῃ ought in any case to be understood as signifying the divine *purpose* only, like other passages which declare the universality of grace (1 Tim. ii. 4; 2 Pet. iii. 9; 1 John ii. 2), without giving us to suppose that this purpose takes effect in the case of every individual. Since, then, St Paul teaches in the strongest terms that salvation is not in fact attained by every individual of mankind (2 Thess. i. 9), the interpretation of this passage which has been noticed, can only be regarded as erroneous. Stier, among later writers, rightly declares himself to the same effect. The parallel passage, Gal. iii. 22, speaks decidedly in favour of our interpretation. It is there said συνέκλεισεν ἡ γραφὴ τὰ πάντα ὑπὸ ἁμαρτίαν, ἵνα ἡ ἐπαγγελία ἐκ πίστεως Ἰησοῦ Χριστοῦ δοθῇ τοῖς πιστεύουσι. Thus, although the Apostle had in the former part of the verse taken a more extensive conception of the whole, so that even the κτίσις may be understood as comprehended in it,† still in the latter part he restricts the salvation to *those who believe;* but that all the individuals of mankind, without exception, will believe, is assuredly not St Paul's meaning, since in 2 Thess. iii. 2 he says expressly, οὐ γὰρ πάντων ἡ πίστις, and in 2 Tim. iii. 1, seqq., he particularly describes the manner in which very many give themselves wholly up to sin, and fall away again from the faith which they had acknowledged.

The expression συγκλείειν is based on the metaphor of a *prison*, in which those whose guilt is alike are shut up together. In εἰς

* Comp. the commentary on John xii. 32. I would remark, further, that in the exposition of that passage I have not given prominence to the circumstance that there too it is the *purpose* and not the *effect* that is spoken of. We may say that in that place the subject is the universality of the *operations of grace*, but not the *blessedness* of all; *i. e.*, not the actual result.

† D. and E. read τὰ πάντα, and F.G. read πάντα, in Rom. xi. 32 also, but these variations are seemingly to be regarded only as corrections from Gal. iii. 22, which passage, as being an important parallel, might easily influence the text of the other.

ἀπείθειαν is signified the element to which men are thereby made over; while in Gal. iii. 22, ὑπὸ ἁμαρτίαν denotes sin as the hard master, to whose service sinners must be subject. The whole passage, however, represents God, not as the author of sin, through whose influence and counsel it is generated, but as one who distributes in equal measures the evil which has been generated by the misused free-will of the creature, in order to afford a possibility of salvation to all who do not resist.

Vers. 34, 35. This whole contemplation of the wonderful ways of the Lord, who knows how to gather His flock unto Himself out of all languages, kindreds, and tongues, was assuredly fitted to excite a feeling of amazement and admiration.* To this feeling, then, the Apostle gives vent in an exclamation which is indeed short but deeply felt, and full of great ideas. If, however, βάθος πλούτου be taken as *one* notion (according to the usual explanation), then that very attribute of God is wanting which, from the context, we must expect to find mentioned before all others—the attribute of compassionate love. There is something so distressing in this want, that we decide with Glöckler in favour of understanding πλοῦτος to mean *riches of mercy—of love.* In this there is no difficulty whatever, since St Paul speaks directly of πλοῦτος Χριστοῦ (Eph. iii. 8; Phil. iv. 19), which can only be understood of His *grace;* and since, besides, in the idea of love there is involved an intimation of its overflowing, rich character, which establishes a natural connexion between *love* and *spiritual riches.* Add to this, that the clauses which follow correspond exactly, in a reversed order, to the three attributes. The words ὡς ἀνεξερεύνητα κ. τ. λ. refer to γνῶσις; τίς γὰρ ἔγνω, κ. τ. λ. to σοφία; and, lastly, τίς προέδωκεν αὐτῷ to the mere grace, which gives where there is no desert. Nay, further, in ver. 36, the three prepositions ἐξ, διά, and εἰς point back to the three characteristics mentioned in ver. 33. Reiche's remark, that if three genitives were to be connected with βάθος, there ought also to be καὶ before πλοῦτος, or that which stands before σοφίας should be wanting, is insignificant.

* This bold and powerful flight seems, however, to have a foundation only on the supposition of an entire restoration. If only some, or but a few in all, are blessed, how is God's wisdom to become manifest in the result? but if all become blessed, without prejudice to free-will and justice, this, assuredly, appears as a miracle of God. The doctrine of a restoration has very many passages of St Paul's epistles apparently in its favour.

For, to say nothing of the fact that the *καὶ* before *σοφίας* is wanting in some MSS., we have no ground for supposing that there must necessarily have been a triple *καὶ* in this place; it would be necessary only if it had the sense of *as well . . . as also*; but here we may take it as merely a connecting particle, like the Hebrew וְ, so that the passage resembles Matt. xxvi. 59, Ephes. iv. 6.

Σοφία is God's knowledge of the *purposes*, *γνῶσις* His knowledge of the *nature* of things. *'Ανεξερεύνητος* is not found elsewhere in the New Testament, but Aquila uses it, Prov. xxv. 3, for אֵין חֵקֶר. *'Ανεξιχνίαστος* occurs again, Eph. iii. 8, and in the LXX. version of Job v. 9, ix. 10. *Κρίματα* and *ὁδοί* signify the utterances of God's will in as far as they give things their nature and subsistence, while in ver. 34 is described the agency of God in determining ends.

Vers. 34, 35. The Apostle enlarges on the unsearchableness of God in words taken from the Old Testament (Is. xl. 13; Job xli. 2). The meaning, of course, is only that no creature can *penetrate* into the counsel of God; but, doubtless, God Himself may, by revelation of Himself, give glimpses into His ways. The words *τίς προέδωκεν αὐτῷ*, however, are in every respect to be taken absolutely, inasmuch as the giving powers of the creature are themselves only derivative; the creature has nothing of its own but what is evil. God's gift is always a grace, for it can never be deserved.

The passage, Job xli. 2, is in the LXX., xli. 11, and runs thus —*τίς ἀντιστήσεταί μοι καὶ ὑπομενεῖ.* In the Hebrew, on the other hand, it is מִי הִקְדִּימַנִי וַאֲשַׁלֵּם, which exactly agrees with the sense of St Paul's words. Perhaps, therefore, the Apostle translated immediately from the original. In the Alexandrian MS. of the LXX., the words are placed at Is. xl. 14, but as they are there altogether wanting in the Hebrew, they must, no doubt, have been written by some copyist in the margin of xl. 13, and so have found their way into the text of some MSS.

Ver. 36. St Paul at length closes his great doctrinal investigation with a doxology, in which God is described as embracing all things*—as the beginning, middle, and end of all things, and, consequently, of the believing Israel as a whole, and of every indi-

* Tholuck aptly compares with this Dante's address to God—"Thou in whom all good things begin and end!"

vidual. That these references are what is intended by the prepositions ἐξ, διά, and εἰς, is no longer questioned by later writers. But, on the other hand, they continue blind to the fact that these references also express the relation of Father, Son, and Spirit. In an exactly similar way it is said of God, Eph. iv. 6, ὁ ἐπὶ πάντων καὶ διὰ πάντων, καὶ ἐν πᾶσι. Of the Father as the *source* of all being, ἐκ or ὑπὸ is always used in the New Testament, and ἐπὶ with respect to His absolute power; of the Son, always διά, as the Revealer of the Father, the organ of His agency (comp. on Joh. i. 3); of the Spirit, εἰς, inasmuch as He is the End to which the divine agency leads, or ἐν, inasmuch as He is the element which penetrates and supports all things. 1 Cor. viii. 6 is decisive in favour of this interpretation; as there St Paul himself explains ἐξ οὗ and δι' οὗ of the Father and the Son, and if so only by accident that he does not also mention the Holy Ghost. The only objection which might be advanced is, that the passages, thus understood, might favour Sabellianism. It is. indeed, unquestionable that the personality of Father, Son, and Spirit, cannot be deduced from these passages, which witness only to the unity of Essence; but if the personality be warranted elsewhere, such passages as these are no argument against it, affirming, as they do, nothing more than that one divine Being manifests itself as Father, Son, and Spirit.—Again, Col. i. 16, might seem to bear against our interpretation, as there the predicates of the Spirit (εἰς and ἐν), although not those of the Father, are transferred to the Son. This, however, may be got over by the consideration, that the agency of the Son and that of the Spirit are, in the New Testament, not unfrequently represented as blended together,—the Spirit receives every thing from the Son (John xvi. 14); hence also that which belongs to the Spirit may be ascribed to the Son, without our having any reason thence to conclude, that the difference of personalities in the Divine Being, as indicated by prepositions, is not to be maintained. . . . Πάντα εἰς αὐτόν might also be referred to the *restoration* of all things; but in this aphoristic clause there is not so much the declaration of a fact,—that all things shall be brought back,—as that all are designed to be brought back to Him; but whether all things have attained this destination, this, it may be said, is a different question. Still, in this place, as in others, there is a very strong *appearance* in favour of the restoration. (Comp. the remarks on 1 Cor. xv. 26, seqq.)

PART III.

(XII. 1—XV. 33.)

THE ETHICAL EXPOSITION.

SECTION I.

(XII. 1—XIII. 14.)

EXHORTATIONS TO LOVE AND OBEDIENCE.

The Apostle most suitably follows up his detailed *doctrinal* statement with an *ethical part,* as is the case in almost all his epistles. As blossom and fruit grow only from a sound root, so too it is only from faith in Christ, and in the redemption wrought by Him, that the true moral life proceeds. But from this faith it must indeed *of necessity* be produced, as surely as light and warmth must be diffused where there is fire. But if from this it should be argued, that therefore there can be no need of particular moral admonitions, we should overlook the perverseness of human nature. If indeed the life of faith had its thoroughly right course in every individual, then, certainly, it would not be necessary to call attention particularly to the fruits which ought to proceed from it, even as there is no need of any special precautions in order to make a generous tree bring forth generous fruits. But in man, changeable as he is, the life has no such physically regulated course. The disordered relations of head and heart often lead him to persuade himself that he has the life of faith, without really having it. Hence it is necessary to point to the fruits of faith, inasmuch as the defect of these is a decisive token of the defects of the inner man. The object of the ethical admonitions is not, therefore, immediately through them to produce fruit; for of this the law altogether is not capable, not even in its New Testament form. Still neither is their object the purely negative one of merely forming a mirror, in which the reader may be able to discern what he has not and is not. Rather the ethical admonitions of the New Testament have a *positive* character, which consists in this, that, although they do not work *productively* (which nothing can do but faith, or the power of the Spirit accompanying the admonitions), yet they are meant to arouse the consciousness how far the power of faith must work into all circumstances of life, even the minutest. The advanced members of the Church, therefore, and above all, the Apostles, have to shew others the way how to attain by degrees to the estate of being penetrated on all sides by the Christian principle.

In the ethical development before us, we must first direct our view to the plan which the Apostle follows in it. For I can by no means accede to the assertion of the majority of expositors, that St Paul has no plan at all here, and merely strings his exhortations together without regard to order; rather we should adhere to the deep saying of Hamann—"In the Bible there is the same regular disorder as in nature."* In the first chapter of this portion, the Apostle starts from the idea which is the foundation of all Christian morality,—an absolutely-embracing consecration of the whole life. This has *humility* for the principle which gives the tone to the inner man (xii. 3), and out of it are rightly shaped, *first*, the relation of the individual Christian to the *Church of God* on earth (xii. 4-13), according to faith (4–8), love (9–11), and hope (12 13); and also, *further*, his relation to the *world* (xii. 14–21), inasmuch as the principle teaches him even to love and bless his enemies. And this general relation of the Christian to the world finds its especial application in his position towards the *ruling power*, which *as such* always stands *without* the Church, inasmuch as, from the character of the community, it can only represent the law and not the gospel. In submitting to the ruling power, therefore, the believer submits to the Divine law itself, and his submission to both is equally without exception (xiii. 1–7.) But, again, this obedience to the divine ordinance has its root in nothing else than love, which is the fulfilling of the law, to which the time of the Messiah urgently warns us to devote ourselves, since now the night is past† and the day has dawned; for which cause, also, the believer is bound to walk as a child of light,

* Compare the Essay by Stier,—"Die geheimere Ordnung" (in his "Audeutungen für gläubiges Schriftverständniss." Königsberg, 1824, p. 83, seqq.), which well deserves a reading.

† ["Is far spent."—Eng. V.]

and has before him the task of quelling all the works of the flesh (xiii. 8–14.) The Apostle takes this last turn with a prospective regard to what follows in ch. xiv., where he has to deal with an error opposite to the indulgence of the flesh, viz. with erroneous asceticism

§ 17. OF LOVE.

(XII. 1-21.)

The Apostle sets out with the idea of an entire devotion, *i. e.* offering up of one's-self to God, as the fundamental moral principle of the Christian: (renunciation of vice being the fundamental moral principle of the man who lives under the law.) The motive of this is the mercy of God (manifested in Christ), which must call forth a return of love; and the devotion is represented as absolute, inasmuch as it extends even to the body—thus presupposing the devotion of spirit and soul. It is only in this absolute entireness that devotion to God has a meaning and significancy or is a *λατρεία λογική;* the Lord of all requires every man to give his all.

The *οὖν* is immediately connected with xi. 36, but, in so far as this verse is a summing-up of the whole preceding deduction (especially from ix. 1), it is also connected with the whole of what precedes. *Σῶμα* is not chosen because it suits better with the notion of a sacrifice, or even because it stands by synecdoche for the whole of man (according to the analogy of the Hebrew עֶצֶם), but in order to extend the idea of the Christian sanctification even to the lowest power of human nature. In the idea of the sacrifice is indicated the *spiritual priesthood* of the Christian (comp. note on 1 Pet. ii. 9), which has no relation to the outward Church, but rather to the inward life; the unceasing praying devotion of the faithful is the continual sacrifice which they present to God. The predicates *ζῶσα, ἁγία,* and *εὐάρεστος*, characterize the nature of the Christian sacrifice; even the Old Testament required for sacrifice animals free from blemish (Levit. xxii. 20, Deut. v. 21); how much more must the New Testament require a pure mind! The epithet *ζῶσα,* however, is peculiar. For every sacrifice only becomes what it is when the animal dies and sheds its blood; but the Christian life is an unceasing spiritual devotion of self, a *living* sacrifice or self-offering. The only other place where *λογικός* occurs in the New Testament is 1 Pet. ii. 2. It is equivalent to νοερός which, however, is not found at all in the New Testament,* although the substantive νοῦς is the usual expression, and λόγος does not occur as synonymous with νοῦς. This service of God is here styled "reasonable," as alone answering to its idea. The opposite to it is not that which is false (for the outward sacrifices of the O. T. were not false), but only that which is subordinate; the O. T. institutions are sensible forms for the ideas. There is a hardness in the construction of the accus., as it does not suit well with παραστῆσαι; it should have been ὅ ἐστι λογικὴ λατρεία.

Ver. 2. The negative idea is opposed to the positive:—Be not conformed to *this* world, in which good and evil are mingled, but form yourselves after the pattern of the absolutely pure *heavenly* world. The idea of man's capability of formation, the reception into his inward part of a holy or an unholy pattern, is, according to scriptural principles, closely connected with the doctrine of the [divine] image, and of the essential character of the soul. The ψυχή has no active, creative nature, but is passive in its character; it cannot of itself produce a form, a shaping of the being, but the influences which it receives impress a form on it. It has, however, the power of warding off unholy agencies, and of giving itself up without reserve to those which are holy; and this self-abandonment is the way of sanctification.

On αἰὼν οὗτος comp. Comment. vol. i. p. 411, seqq.;† αἰὼν μέλλων, *i. e.* οὐράνιος, is here to be understood as its opposite. Συσχηματίζεσθαι is also found at 1 Pet. i. 14; its meaning is, to take the σχῆμα of something else. It is substantially equivalent with μεταμορφοῦσθαι; the latter expression, however, bears more on what is inward, while the former relates more to the outward part. The ἀνακαίνωσις τοῦ νοός here denotes the progressively transforming operation in the believer. The νοῦς itself is the first object of this operation; but from it as a beginning, the whole man, even to his body, is renewed. Tit. iii. 5 is the only other place where the substantive occurs; the verbs ἀνακαινόω (2 Cor. iv. 16, Col. iii. 10) and ἀνακαινίζω (Heb. vi. 4–6) are more frequent. The *renewal* is not different in kind from *regeneration;* the latter term, however, regards the matter more as an act, the former,

* The parallel νουνεχῶς occurs Mark xii. 34.

† i. 404 of Ed. 3; ii. 108 of the Translation.

more as a consequence of this act. Renewal coincides exactly with *sanctification*—in which expression, also, the gradual prevalence of the new life is especially marked. In εἰς τὸ δοκιμάζειν it is signified that the natural man cannot truly prove the will of God; he is without the higher light and the delicacy of the moral feeling; he can, consequently, discern God's will only in that which is most palpable.*

The first particular to which the Apostle passes from speaking generally, is *humility*, the especially Christian virtue, the supporter of all the rest. Through this it is that each man acknowledges the place and the gift allotted to him,† and thus makes possible a joint operation of the whole. The Apostle utters this and the following exhortations, however, not as his personal good wishes, but by virtue of his apostolical authority; and this for the faithful alone, since it is only for the position of the life of faith that the instructions which follow are suitable. Where the principle itself is yet wanting, no directions can be given how it shall diffuse itself through and impregnate all the circumstances of life; or, at the utmost, they can only effect that which is all that the law altogether can effect—the knowledge of sin. (Rom. iii. 20.)

Χάρις denotes primarily the apostolic office, but of course in connexion with the gifts imparted for discharging it. The words παντὶ τῷ ὄντι ἐν ὑμῖν are intended, unquestionably, to make the exhortation quite general; but the εἶναι ἐν υμῖν is meant to mark especially that the exhortation is addressed to believers, to members of the Church. Ὑπερφρονεῖν = υψηλοφρονεῖν, comp. xi. 20. In παρ᾽ ὃ δεῖ φρονεῖν, it is indicated that there is also a false humility, which will not own to itself what God has done. True humility is fully conscious of the grace which it has received, of the call which has been addressed to it, yet not as if this were anything of its own, but as of God. This true humility is the σωφρονεῖν = τὰ σῶα φρονεῖν, the right and healthy view of ourselves and our position. God's creation knows no absolute equality; as among the angels there is subordination, so too in the

* Augustine aptly says—"Tantum videmus quantum morimur huic saeculo; quantum autem huic vivimus, non videmus."

† Reiche supposes that the Apostle is led away from the chief idea, humility, to a subsidiary consideration, the gifts; but the two subjects are most closely connected. It is precisely the consciousness of our own limited gifts that teaches the necessity of co-operation with others, who possess other gifts.

Church of God the measure of faith, and consequently also the measure of the Spirit, is variously dealt out. And this is not as if according to individual faithfulness, but according also to the free ordering of God. *Πίστις* is here taken quite generally, as denoting the subjective disposition of soul, in which man is capable of receiving into himself the objective working of the Spirit—the grace spoken of in ver. 6. This expression *μέτρον πίστεως* has, as is well known, given rise to the dogmatic term *analogia fidei*; but it is needless to remark that the sense of the phrase is here quite different. On the trajection *ἑκάστῳ ὡς* comp. Winer's Grammar, pp. 508, seqq.

Vers. 4, 5. After the figure of the human organization, the Apostle regards the faithful as an organized whole, in which the individuals, as members, are mutually supplementary; the visible Church, therefore, like the invisible, cannot be conceived without members respectively leading and led; and hence follows the necessity of government for the visible Church.

Comp. as to the figure of the *σῶμα* what is more particularly said at 1 Cor. xii.—As to *ὁ δὲκαθ' εἷς*, comp. on Mark xiv. 19, John viii. 9, where *εἷς καθ' εἷς* occurs, as here, in the sense of "each." (Comp. Winer's Gr., p. 227.) *Every one* is regarded as a collective notion, and is construed with the plural *μέλη*. In order to the completion of the parallel, there should immediately have been added—*and these members have also diverse operations;* but this is more fully set forth in ver. 6 and what follows.

Vers. 6–8. Having hitherto regarded the persons themselves, as the members of the body of Christ, the Apostle in the sequel makes use of the figure in such a way as to represent the various gifts of the Divine Spirit (who, if regarded in His operation, is the same with grace), as giving the law to the various operation of the members. St Paul here only names some gifts by way of example—and indeed only three; while in 1 Cor. xii. 7, seqq., a much greater number is reckoned up. To the *Charismata* properly so called—*i. e.*, to the extraordinary and miraculous gifts which were peculiar to the apostolic age—there are then added (ver. 8) other points, which might either be taken as merely expressions of the three Charismata, or as appearances of the Christian life in general, such as are enumerated in the 8th and following verses. As expressions of the three Charismata, they might perhaps be taken in a reversed order, so that *παρακαλεῖν* should be applied to the *διδάσκαλος*, *μεταδιδόναι* to the *διάκονος*, *προΐσ-τασθαι* and *ἐλεεῖν* to the *προφήτης*, with reference to the severe and to the gentle sides of his office respectively. For in the three gifts there seems at the same time to predominate a reference to the three principal offices in the Church, inasmuch as the *προφήτης* answers to the bishop, the *διδάσκαλος* to the priest, and the third gift to the *διάκονος*. There seems, however, to be one objection to this supposition of the three gifts, viz., the *εἴτε* before *παρα-καλῶν*. But, as appears from the evidence of D.E.F.G., and other critical authorities, this is spurious, and has found its way into the text only from the analogy of the preceding *εἴτε ὁ διδάσ-κων*. St Paul knows nothing of a special Charisma of *παράκλη-σις*. . . . As to the structure of the sentence, Meyer would erroneously connect *ἔχοντες* with *ἔσμεν* (ver. 5) ; but the *δὲ* of ver. 6, by which, in opposition to the already concluded sentence, vers. 4, 5, the discourse is begun afresh, and carried onwards, is decidedly against this. Rather the sentence has something of an anacoluthon in it ; the verb is wanting to *ἔχοντες*, and the most natural words to supply would be—"Let each use his gift according to its purpose." Moreover, St Paul also leaves the accusative, and in ver. 7 puts the nominative, and the concrete instead of the abstract. It is, however, remarkable that, in the clause about prophecy, there is put, not, as in the case of other gifts, *ἐν τῇ προ-φητείᾳ*, but *κατὰ τὴν ἀναλογίαν τῆς πίστεως*, which is evidently synonymous with *μέτρον πίστεως* above, and, consequently, as being quite a general expression, would seem applicable, not to the prophecy alone, but to all gifts. It is, indeed, impossible to draw from the *πίστις* any special and exclusive reference to prophesying, and therefore we must say that the Apostle, by an inexact way of expressing himself, especially connects with the chief Charisma, the general idea which is to be understood in the case of every gift, and thus comes to leave out *ἐν τῇ προφητείᾳ*. For *πίστις* is here, as in ver. 3, the fundamental disposition of the soul, without which it is altogether impossible to conceive any working of the Spirit, and consequently also any gift in man.

On *προφητεία*, the gift of teaching as to the things of God with full consciousness in the power of the Spirit ; on *διακονία* = *κυ-βέρνησις*, and on *διδασκαλία*, comp. the more particular observations at 1 Cor. xii. 28. Ἀναλογία is not found elsewhere in the New Testament; in profane usage, it is especially employed of mathematical proportions. Here it answers to μέτρον, ver. 3. In ver. 8, ἁπλότης excludes all mixture of purposes in giving; it ought to be the expression of pure benevolence, and it is only as being such that it has any real value.

Vers. 9–11. The Apostle now leaves the subject of the extraordinary operations of the Spirit, and turns to other exhortations, especially the exhortation to make love, in its true nature, the regulating principle in all circumstances. In the most general way, love manifests itself in hatred of what is evil (a hatred necessarily implied in love itself, which loves the sinner), and in cleaving to what is good; and next, in more particular workings. Even the honour shewn to our neighbour is beautifully referred to love; without love it is mere hypocrisy or flattery.

On ver. 9 comp. Amos v. 15, where the same idea is found. In the general clause, ἡ ἀγάπη ἀνυπόκριτος, it is better to supply ἔστι than ἔστω, as the latter is very rarely supplied. (Comp. Benhardy's Syntax, p. 331.) In ver. 11, the two clauses, τῇ σπουδῇ μὴ ὀκνηροί and τῷ πνεύματι ζέοντες, express the same idea, first negatively and then positively. They both describe the nature of love—"The coals thereof are coals of fire, which hath a most vehement flame." (Cantic. viii. 6.) In addition to many earlier commentators and critics, some of the moderns, especially Tholuck, Rückert, Lachmann, and Reiche, have decided in favour of the usual reading, κυρίῳ, which has certainly by far the greater support from authorities, as only D.F.G., and some Latin Fathers, read καιρῷ. But the internal reasons appear to me so weighty, that I decide unreservedly for καιρῷ. A charge so entirely general, to "serve the Lord," is out of place among such altogether special exhortations. The form κυρίῳ δουλεύειν is so well known, that it might easily have been substituted for the unusual καιρῷ. In Latin, indeed, *tempori servire* occurs (Cic. Epist. Famil. vi. 21), but it is not found in Greek before the second century. To serve the time in a right manner, however, is an expression of love which perfectly suits the context, and is, moreover, a thought which easily arises out of the Pauline circle of ideas.

Vers. 12, 13. Lastly follow the expressions of the third great Christian virtue—*Hope*. The manifestation of this in endurance of sufferings and in prayer is simple; but acts of kindness and hospitality seem not so much to come under the head of *hope* as of *love*, especially of the φιλαδελφία mentioned in ver. 9. Both these virtues, however, have also an essential connexion with hope, inasmuch as they point to the recompense which is to be expected; and here, without doubt, St Paul had a view to this side of the subject, which is also touched on in other passages of Scripture. (Comp. on Matt. x. 40, 41, and on προσκαρ τερέω, Acts i. 14; ii. 42; vi. 4, &c.) In ver. 13 the reading μνείαις instead of χρείαις is remarkable; but it undoubtedly originated in a later time, when the invocation of saints became customary. The same MSS. which read καιρῷ support also the various reading μνείαις—a circumstance which, as must be allowed, is favourable to the maintenance of κυρίῳ.

Vers. 14–16. From the relation of the Christian to the members of the Church, the Apostle now turns to his position relatively to the unbelievers.* Faith and hope must now retire; it is love alone who here celebrates her triumphs; she blesses the enemies, she weeps with them that weep. The Christian is always accessible to the universally human feelings of joy and grief, from whatever quarter they meet him; he never in stoical indifference or insensibility holds himself above such sympathy, but willingly condescends to the wretched. The words τὸ αὐτὸ εἰς ἀλλήλους φρονοῦντες (ver. 16), however, do not seem to suit with this connexion. An exhortation to Christians to unity among themselves is certainly quite out of place here; but it fits easily into the connexion if we take it as follows:†—Paul exhorts all believers to be alike *in this love towards the unbelievers* (and that for the very purpose of converting them), not arrogantly to place themselves at a distance and above them, but to enter into their needs.

Ver. 14 refers to the words of Christ, Matt. v. 44. Chrysostom's

* It might be said that even in the Church itself there is room for the application of the precepts of love towards enemies (comp. on Matt. v. 43, seqq.), and that, consequently, we cannot conclude from their occurrence that they form a transition to the relation of Christians to unbelievers. But, in so far as these precepts still find their application in the visible Church, the αἰὼν οὗτος also still exists in the Church itself; the admonitions which follow regard the relation to those who are still moving wholly or partially in the element of this αἰών.

† The sense in which the Fathers take it—that we should enter into the circumstances of another, in order to understand his feelings,—is hardly justifiable in point of language.

remark, that it is harder to rejoice sincerely with the joyful than to weep with the sorrowing, is very true; but this, doubtless, has its foundation in the remarkable and deep-seated temptation of pleasure at the misfortunes of others, which it is difficult to extirpate. In the misfortunes of our best friends, says Kant,* there is something which is not altogether displeasing to us. In ver. 16 the ταπεινοί are, of course, not the humble or poor in spirit, but those who are outwardly or inwardly unhappy. The word here answers to the Hebrew עָנִי or עָנָו. Reiche, without sufficient grounds, is for taking it as neuter. *Συναπάγω, to carry off with, συναπάγεσθαι, to carry off with one's-self, i. e.*, to put one's-self into connexion or communion with a person. Luther rightly says—Let yourselves down to the wretched, nay (since there is nothing to restrict the words to the communion of believers with one another), withdraw not thyself from the poor and despised who as yet know not the gospel. Self-withdrawal and exclusiveness belong to the religion of the Old Testament; that of the New Testament bids us remain in communion even with those in whom the life of Christ dominates not as yet. The proverb, "Tell me what company you keep, and I will tell you who you are,"† is therefore true only for the Old Testament, where exclusiveness is a duty because the power is too little to master the opposition. The Son of God teaches the faithful to consort with publicans and sinners, in order to win them for his kingdom.

Vers. 17, 18. The words *μὴ γίνεσθε φρόνιμοι παρ' ἑαυτοῖς* again do not seem suitable to the connexion, which is otherwise very exact as far as ver. 21. This clause, however, must be taken as parallel with *μὴ τὰ ὑψηλὰ φρονοῦντες* above; it is the worst form of high-mindedness—*i. e.* of lovelessness—to think highly of self; by this a man's view is limited to himself, and the loving care for others is checked.

The words *μηδενὶ κακὸν κ. τ. λ.*, are merely a negative expression of the same idea which is positively contained in *προνοούμενοι κ. τ. λ.* The latter words are taken from Prov. iii. 4. With the second half of ver. 17 compare Is. v. 21, which appears to be referred to in the Apostle's words. *Προνοεῖν* is used with the genitive, 1 Tim. v. 8: with the accusative, 2 Cor. viii. 21. The words ἐνώ-

* [The sentiment is Rochefoucauld's.]

† Answering to the Latin—Noscitur ex socio qui non cognoscitur ex se.

πιον ἀνθρώπων are to be explained according to Matt. v. 16. *Universal* peace is not possible except where sin does not exist; therefore the Apostle says *εἰ δυνατόν*; but yet Christians may on their part (*τὸ ἐξ ὑμῶν*), often by endurance mitigate the sharpness of opposition, and gain even their enemies.

Ver. 19. Even in the worst case, however, the Christian must not avenge himself, but must, according to Scripture (Deut. xxxii. 35), leave vengeance to Him with whom alone it is always holy.

In the phrase *δότε τόπον τῇ ὀργῇ*, most expositors have rightly supplied *Θεοῦ*, so that the sense of the words is—Do not anticipate the ways of God, allow time and space to His righteous retribution. Reiche wishes to understand it of human anger, and takes the words to mean—Allow space to wrath, that it may not at once break out into act.* But the quotation does not agree well with this, since it forbids not only the wild anger of a moment, but also that anger *of man* which is deferred, and thereby mitigated. It is quite unsuitable to understand the anger of the person wronged, in the sense—Do not expose yourselves to anger, give way to it. On *τόπον διδόναι* comp. Eph. iv. 27. The quotation is free; in the LXX. version the words are—*ἐν ἡμέρᾳ ἐκδικήσεως ἀνταπαδώσω*. St Paul is nearer to the Hebrew—לִי נָקָם וְשִׁלֵּם.

Ver. 20, 21. Instead of the wrath of the natural man, the Apostle recommends the love of the spiritual man, which, at the same time, is of the most potent influence in overcoming evil; it not only gains something from the adversary or on him, but it even gains his most proper self.

The passage is borrowed, word for word, from Prov. xxv. 21, 22. The image of coals heaped on the head is to be explained especially from 2 Esdras xvi. 53; it can only mean—Thou shalt prepare for him a sensible pain, yet not in order to hurt him, but to lead him to repentance and improvement. The Oriental style, which delights in strong expressions, contains many kindred forms of expression. (Comp. the passages in Tholuck and Reiche *in loc.*) Glöckler thinks that the figure is taken from laying coals

* In other respects, the Latin *Spatium dare irae*, would suit well with this interpretation. Perhaps Lactantius had an eye to the passage before us when he wrote, *Laudarem, si, cum fuisset iratus, dedisset irae suae spatium, ut haberet modum castigatio.* De Ira. c. 8.

on pots in order to soften hard meats, and, consequently, that the meaning is—Thou shalt soften his hard heart; but this is quite erroneous.—Σωρεύω, from σωρός, *a heap*, is also found in 2 Tim. iii. 6.

§ 18. OF OBEDIENCE.

(XIII. 1–14.)

Without any apparent connexion, there follow exhortations to obedience towards authority. According, however, to the manner which we have indicated of understanding xii. 14–21, the dissertation which follows is very naturally connected with those verses. The hostile element, against which Paul had hitherto directed the behaviour of the Christian in his *private relations*, met the Church of the apostolic age in a concentrated form, as it were, in the *civil power of the Roman empire*. A wrong conception of the idea of Christian freedom might, therefore, easily have misled the Christians to place themselves in a false relation towards the heathen authorities; as it is well known that among the Jews the party of Judas the Galilean made it an article of faith that it was unlawful to pay tribute to heathens, inasmuch as the genuine Jew could recognise Jehovah alone as the king of the Theocracy, according to Deut. xvii. 15. (Comp. note on Acts v. 37, and Josephus Antiq. xviii. 1, 1, Bell. Jud. ii. 9.) In the statement of Suetonius (Claud. c. 25), that the Jews of Rome made a commotion under the leadership of one Chrestus, there is perhaps an indication that a portion of the Roman Christians, in their lively feeling of Christian liberty, may not have quite rightly apprehended their relation towards the authorities. If, now, we consider that the Epistle to the Romans was written under Nero, after Tiberius, Caligula, and Claudius, with their abominations and madnesses, had already passed over the scene, there appears in the following exhortation a greatness and purity of thought strikingly contrasting with the malice and baseness which were manifested in the ruling power of the Roman empire. This purity and truth could not but at the same time carry in it the power of renewing the youth of the whole old and corrupted world, and of restoring it for a series of ages. At present we look forth into a world which has in like manner passed into corruption, in which "the people are become wild and desolate because prophecy is nothing heeded;"* in such a case, the object is that the law should be again "kept," as coming from above, and that the doctrine of holy Scripture respecting the magistracy, as God's representative on earth, should be anew established.

Ver. 1. The precept of obedience towards the magistracy is one of universal extent, so that no one may suppose himself released from it by attaining a high degree of spiritual advancement, or the like; hence it is said, *πᾶσα ψυχὴ ὑποτασσέσθω* = כָּל־נֶפֶשׁ, *i. e.*, *ἕκαστος*. By the term *ἐξουσίαι*, St Paul designates the magistracy in the widest sense, and under it we must understand not only the emperor and the highest official authorities, but also the inferior authorities which act only in his name. The predicate *ὑπερέχουσαι* designates them as *actually existing*, as having the power in their hands, and answers to the following *αἱ δὲ οὖσαι*. The *δὲ* in *αἱ δὲ οὖσαι* is to be understood as explicative, not as adversative. By this the believer is exempted from all investigations as to the *rightfulness* or the *origin* of an actually subsisting power; in that which subsists he sees the ordinance of God, although it may be only provisional.† Notwithstanding, however, this unconditional subjection to the human magistracy, there is no one further removed than the Christian from the service of men; in the magistracy, as in all other relations, he serves his God alone. Every authority by the grace of the people, leads to frightful tyranny of man, even under the mildest rule; the magistracy, regarded and conceived of as by the grace of God, is a ministry of God, even if a Nero sits on the throne. Thus the believer is servant of none save his God, and yet is subject to every one who has power over him; thus only is true freedom compatible with order; the

* Prov. xxix. 18. [*Wenn die weissagung aus ist, wird das Volk wild und wüste: wohl aber dem der das Gesetz handhabet.* Luther's version. The translator has left his version of the words derived from the latter clause of this verse—"*dass das Gesetz wieder gehandhabt werde von oben*"—as he originally wrote it; but he has little confidence in its correctness. A. would render—"It is then necessary that the law should again be administered as by Divine commission," and has kindly procured translations from two eminent German scholars. (1), "It is necessary that the law should again be exercised from above (by those in authority.)" J. C. H. (2), "It imports that the law be again maintained (or affirmed) as from above." R. C. T.

† The question how the believer ought to act in the perplexing *transitions* from one government to another, *e. g.*, in revolutions, especially at what point a newly-arisen government is to be regarded as *de facto* subsisting, is not referred to by the Apostle; because, on account of the multiplicity of circumstances which are conceivable in such cases, it is impossible to lay down any objective rules on the subject.

freedom which is independent of God has within it the element of the most fearful confusion. In this representation, however, the Apostle's idea, οὐ γάρ ἐστιν ἐξουσία εἰ μὴ ἀπὸ (or, according to another. and perhaps more correct reading, ὑπὸ) Θεοῦ, appears very remarkable. Was a Nero of God? But of course the person of the ruler ought to be separated from his office, and then we must certainly say that Nero's office was of God; even the worst government is better than anarchy, and whatever such a government still contains of the elements of order, that is of God. But are there not absolutely ungodly powers, which come into being by sedition or other evil means? Are these also of God? Certainly they are so, in as far as they really come to appearance and subsistence.* We must here apply the same principles which were laid down in ix. 1, with respect to the phenomena of evil generally. All evil which comes into existence has been willed by God, not as evil, but as a phenomenon; and thus too it is with powers which originate through sin. The Christian, who as such knows himself to be the citizen of a higher world, has not (*unless he be also obliged thereto by his civil relations*), to go into investigations as to the rightfulness of the subsisting power, which besides are generally of great difficulty, and hence cannot possibly be devolved on each individual; he belongs to that power to which God has given the sway over him. Evil governments have their judge in God alone, not in men.

Ver. 2. Hence the act of resistance to the magistracy—independently of the motives which at the utmost may render it less criminal, but never can excuse it—is as such a resistance to God's ordinance, and whosoever has been guilty of it falls under the divine judgment. But here arises the question, Why does not the Apostle mention that the magistracy may also require something contrary to God's command, and that in this case it is not to be obeyed (according to the saying in Acts iv. 19; v. 29, that "we ought to

* Reiche is altogether wrong in his understanding of this passage, inasmuch as he thinks that the recognition of every *de facto* government, as of God's willing, is erroneous, and that we must only extend what is predicated to *good* governments. For according to this principle every one is left to consider the power above him as good or bad at pleasure, and thus an opening is made for any revolutions. The Apostolic principle alone wholly prevents them, since by it both good and evil governments are warranted in demanding obedience. But the moment *when* a government is to be regarded as *de facto* subsisting, cannot (as has been already observed) be determined by objective rules.

obey God rather than men," on which the observations in the commentary are to be compared), since surely such cases were of very frequent occurrence, in the Apostolic age especially? The reason of his silence is, undoubtedly, because it is in the nature of the thing itself, that, as God's ordinance is to be recognized in the magistracy and in its will, the will of God has precedence of the magistrate's command, where the one is against the other; inasmuch as in such cases the latter has ceased to be what it was meant to be. Unquestionable, however, as is the abstract principle—that we must obey God rather than men, even than the magistracy—it is no less difficult to reduce to definite rules the application of it in the concrete circumstances. The Mennonite finds a conflict between the order of the magistrate and God's commandment in the requisition to become a soldier; the Quaker and other parties in other points. Holy Scripture, therefore, has not gone into any definitions on the subject, because it is always a question of the most particular inward and outward circumstances, to decide what is the right course in the case which occurs. This only it maintains without reserve—that the fundamental character of the Christian must always be *endurance,* and that no force and no injustice can justify him in opposing the subsisting authority by *act,* whether in a negative or in a positive shape.

Κρίμα λαμβάνειν is according to the analogy of the Hebrew נָשָׂא מִשְׁפָּט, comp. James iii. 1. Under *κρίμα* it is best to include outward and inward, temporal and eternal detriments, inasmuch as these are all regarded as the punishment of disobedience, which God lays on us.

Vers. 3, 4. Without allowing himself to be in the slightest degree prejudiced or embittered by the state of things which was before him in the Roman empire, the Apostle Paul holds exclusively to the idea of *authority,* which is indeed never wholly realised, because the authority is represented by sinful men, but which yet may be recognised even in the worst magistracy, inasmuch as this is under a necessity, for the sake of its own existence, of upholding social order in essentials. Hence the magistracy appears as a blessing for every one, even for such as should suffer from it through individual acts of injustice which proceed from it. Hence results, then, the simple exhortation to do that which is good, which is at the foundation of all laws in idea; for only he who does what is evil need fear the magistrate.

In ver. 3, very many considerable critical authorities, instead of the genitive plural, read the dative singular—τῷ ἀγαθῷ ἔργῳ ἀλλὰ τῷ κακῷ. To me, also, as to Reiche, this appears to deserve the preference over the usual reading, since the collective use of ἔργον might easily be mistaken. In ver. 4, the phrase μαχαιρὰν φορεῖν denotes the power of punishment in general, not merely the right over life and death, which is but the highest exercise of that power. The expression is commonly understood of the dagger which the emperors were in the habit of carrying as an ensign of the judicial power. (Sueton. Galba, c 11, Tacit. Hist. iii. 68). The punishments inflicted by the magistracy, therefore, are God's punishments, since it is His minister; as to which it must again be kept in view that St Paul argues from the *idea* of the magistracy, which cannot be done away with by individual exceptions.

Vers. 5–7. Hence, consequently, fear alone cannot be the motive of obedience, but the consciousness of the good itself which results to every one from the orderly arrangements of the state. For this reason are to be fulfilled even those duties which appear more trivial, and, therefore, are very readily neglected; the trivial is closely connected with the great—with the fundamental tone of the mind.

Ver. 5. ἀνάγκη does not denote any outward force, but that inward moral control which the truth exercises. The two terms ὀργή and συνείδησις are to be differently referred; the former belongs to the magistracy, the latter to the faithful.—Ver. 6. τελεῖτε must, on account of the preceding γάρ, be the indicative, not the imperative—"For this cause, *i. e.* inasmuch as ye recognize this right of the rulers, it is that ye pay tribute." In the words which follow, the λειτουργοί might be the officers who gather the tribute, who must be active for this very purpose (εἰς αὐτὸ τοῦτο, for the collection of it). But in that case, προσκαρτεροῦντες must be taken as the *subject*, and with this the want of the article does not agree. It is better, therefore, to supply, with De Wette, the leading notion of the whole sentence, ἄρχοντες and to translate, "for they, the rulers, are God's ministers, who attend upon this very thing," viz. the λειτουργεῖν. This construction, indeed, is not without difficulty; for there is a hardness in taking the notion of the λειτουργεῖν out of the λειτουργοὶ Θεοῦ εἰσι, and then connecting the εἰς αὐτὸ τοῦτο with προσκαρτερεῖν, which also does not suit perfectly with it; but yet it seems to me preferable to the other.—In ver. 7 it is a mistake to refer the ἀπόδοτε πᾶσι to all men indifferently, as Reiche does; the ideas which follow relate undoubtedly to the authorities, and therefore we must think only of the gradations among the authorities. The extension of the idea in the 8th and following verses, must not be supposed to have an influence so early as ver. 7.* The only question is, for what reason St Paul may have chosen this very position for the sentences. Perhaps, as has already been hinted, it is intended that the special should be represented according to its foundation in the general; whosoever fears and honours the prince, will also pay scot and toll to his officers. Φόρος denotes taxes on persons, τέλος, on things. Ἀπόδοτε is to be supplied with the datives. How careful the early Christians were even in this point, which is so often treated with disregard, appears from Tertullian's Apolog. c. 42.

Vers. 8–10. With a remarkably spirited turn St Paul, in the following verses, again passes to the subject of love, as that which contains the security for the fulfilment of this, as of all other commands of God. The Apostle keeps to the idea of *debt*, and characterizes love as the only debt which can never be cleared off, which the Christian may owe with honour. The whole ethical part of this epistle is in substance as much a representation of the nature of *love* as the doctrinal part is an exposition of the nature of *faith*, and the supplement to that part (cc. ix.–xi.) of *hope*; hence the Apostle can from any point revert to love, which is the fulfilling of the law. In the first verses the Apostle probably had in his mind the word of Christ, Matt. xxii. 40, as to which the observations in my commentary may be compared.

In ver. 8, ὀφείλετε is to be taken imperatively—"ye should not, must not owe anything!" Μηδέν is used, and not οὐδέν, in order to give prominence to the *subjective* application; according to the various degrees of inward enlightenment and development the notion of guilt contracts or expands—love alone has the wonderful quality that the more it is practised the more amply it unfolds itself, and rises in its claims. While, therefore, in other circum-

[* The original erroneously reads 9th and 8th, for 8th and 7th respectively.]

stances a man stands better in proportion as he owes less, love is in the best condition the more that it feels itself in debt.* Reiche's objections to this idea are altogether mistaken. The ground of his error is, that he conceives of love as a commandment, which is true only for the position of the Old Testament; whereas, according to the apostolical view, it is an element, a power, namely, the life of God in man. Hence love is as inexhaustible as God himself, and is the absolute fulfilment of the law. In man, however, love is growing, and, consequently, is only the fulfilment of the law in process of approximation. Ver. 9. It is not intended that any exact order should be observed; hence the sixth commandment stands first. The addition *οὐ ψευδομαρτυρήσεις* is spurious, according to the best critical authorities. On λόγος comp. note on ix. 6. *'Ανακεφαλαιοῦσθαι* to comprehend under one chief idea (*κεφάλαιον*); it also occurs in Ephes i. 10. As to the quotation comp. note on Mark xii. 31, Levit. xix. 18. Ver. 10. *πλήρωμα* is chosen merely on account of *πεπλήρωκε*, ver. 8, and denotes perfect observance.

Vers. 11, 12. The exhortation to love is indeed one of universal force, and it is already found in the Old Testament; yet under the New Testament dispensation it has a peculiar meaning.† For in the Old Testament the precept of love is intended chiefly to awaken the consciousness of the want of it; whereas in the New Testament, on the contrary, it is present as a real source of power. To this character of the New Testament the Apostle refers, by way of giving point to his exhortation. The time before Christ is in his view the period of night, of men's unconsciousness as to their higher origin; the time since Christ, on the other hand, is the day, since the Sun of Righteousness sheds forth His beams, since the true consciousness has become awake in man. With this figure, of day and night, light and darkness, sleep and waking, St Paul proceeds to mix up a second, of putting on armour, for a more particular notice of which the notes on Ephes. vi. are to be compared. The man who has awaked goes also into the fight which is appointed for him, and arms himself for it with the armour of

* Augustine says, with equal beauty and truth, *Amor cum redditur, non amittitur, sed reddendo multiplicatur.*

† Vers. 11-14 are historically remarkable, inasmuch as they were the means of the conversion of Augustine, that greatest teacher whom the Church had until the Reformation.—[Confess. viii. 29.]

light or of the Spirit. (Comp. Rom. vi. 13.) The only difficulty which can be felt here is in the words *νῦν γὰρ ἐγγύτερον ἡμῶν ἡ σωτηρία, ἢ ὅτε ἐπιστεύσαμεν.* These evidently point to the second coming of Christ, and the perfecting of humanity which will then take place, and which is here denoted by *σωτηρία.* Consequently the *νῦν* and its relative* *ἢ ὅτε* apply to the time when Paul wrote, as opposed to the time of the first conversion, "Salvation is nearer to us than at the time when we embraced the faith." We need not, however, conclude from this passage that the Apostle, at the date of this epistle, continued to expect the second advent in his own lifetime; he says, indeed, no more than that they have advanced *nearer* to this great concluding act of the world's history. (Comp. on xi. 13, 14.) The exhortation to the faithful, to put off the works of darkness, is rather a reminding of the resolution already embraced at their baptism, and which ought to be daily renewed.

Ver. 11. *Τοσούτῳ μᾶλλον* is is to be supplied after *καὶ τοῦτό.* Comp. Heb. x. 25.—*Καιρός* is the *nature* of time generally, *ὥρα* that which is properly chronic in time. The parenthesis is not to be placed (as Griesbach has it) after *ἤγγικεν*, but after *ἐπιστεύσαμεν*; the words *ἡ νὺξ κ. τ. λ.* are a more exact description of *καιρός.*—Ver. 12. On *προκόπτω*, comp. Luke ii. 52. Here the idea of growth, increase, has combined with it the sense of being completed, passed by. Reiche erroneously derives *ἀποθώμεθα* from *ἀποθέω*, instead of from *ἀποτίθημι.*

Vers. 13, 14. In the admonitions which here follow, we must not think of gross manifestations of fleshliness, such as even the law punishes, so much as of more delicate spiritual manifestations in evil thoughts and inclinations, which may be quelled by a careful discipline of the body.

Ver. 13. *Εὐσχημόνως* is also found in 1 Cor. xiv. 40; 1 Thess. iv. 12.—*Κῶμος, commessatio,* properly *roving about in villages,* thence *roving, dissoluteness,* in general. Gal. v. 21; 1 Pet. iv. 3. *Κοίτη, bed,* is euphemistically put for *unchastity.*—Ver. 14. The phrase *Χριστὸν ἐνδύσασθαι* is derived from the figure of *a robe of righteousness* (Is. lxi. 10); it occurs again in the N. T. at Gal. iii. 27. Profane writers also use *ἀποδύεσθαι* and *ἐνδύεσθαι* in like manner, in the sense of *fashioning one's self unlike or like*

* [Gesetz.]

a person. (Comp. Dion. Halic, xi., p. 689, Lucian in Gall., c. 19.) *Πρόνοιαν ποιεῖσθαι = προνοεῖσθαι,* comp. xii. 17. The negative is, on account of the connexion with what follows, to be so taken as not to censure the care of the body as such, but only in the excess, when it excites the lusts of the flesh. Hence we may supply *οὕτως ὥστε* after *ποιεῖσθε*, since the *εἰς* denotes that operation which alone is intended to be forbidden.

SECTION II.

(XIV. 1—XV. 13.)

OF BEHAVIOUR AS TO THINGS INDIFFERENT.

By the transition which the contrast suggests, the Apostle comes from the improper care of the body to the opposite error of *improper asceticism,* and shows in what manner love ought to bear itself towards the maintainers of this tendency. The precepts which St Paul gives with reference to this breathe the deepest truth, and real freedom—*i. e.,* impartiality—of spirit. The following section is the more important in proportion as the errors of believers have been, and still are, more frequent in respect of the so-called *Adiaphora;* errors which might have been avoided if men had been at pains to apprehend the apostolic counsels more deeply in their inward meaning. For there are two classes of intermediate things; (1) those connected with moral laxity, and (2) others which are connected with moral strictness. It is only in respect of the latter that Holy Scripture contains express admonitions, and especially in the passage before us; respecting the former, there are only the general observations as to keeping ourselves unspotted from the world. (2 Cor. vi. 14, seqq.) There is nowhere a direct prohibition of sharing in dancing, theatrical amusements, and the like. This is, doubtless, in part to be explained by the circumstance that, in the apostolic age, the severe tone of feeling tended much rather to exaggerated strictness than to laxity. But assuredly this absence of directions has also its foundation in the whole manner of dealing of the sacred writers. They do not begin with outward things, but first change, through God's grace, the ground of men's hearts, convinced that with this inward change that which is outward will also be spontaneously changed. In the later ages of the Church, as also at the present day, this course has often been reversed ; outward things are treated as that by which all is decided, and from a forsaking of these a change of the inward man is expected. No heart, however, is regenerated by forsaking dances, plays, and other such indifferent things, but rather the heart which is renewed by regeneration will of itself lose its relish for such trifles. The cause of this unwise and unscriptural proceeding is chiefly to be sought in this — that men confound such indifferent things with positive divine commands, and treat the former like the latter. It is, indeed, true that nothing is morally indifferent, and that the most trivial thing may be good or evil according to the mind with which it is done ; but, nevertheless, the notion of *Adiaphora* is correct, and is necessary in ethics. For that which is denounced by divine laws must never be done under any conceivable circumstances ; thus we must never steal, commit adultery, or abuse the name of God. But with the *Adiaphora* it is otherwise. In these it is not the act, as such, that is sin, but the circumstances under which, the manner in which, it is done. Now, because in these matters the question is usually about *subjective conditions,* on which their moral worth or unworthiness depends, Holy Scripture wisely avoids defining as to things indifferent by *objective commands,* but seeks always to influence the *subjective conditions,* in order thereby to sanctify the whole. According to these principles St Paul proceeds here as elsewhere. He does not command—*Ye shall eat flesh, ye shall drink wine*—although, in an objective view, he held the asceticism in question to be wrong, but he exhorts to treat with forbearance those who maintain it, and expects their deliverance from that error to be the gradual result of the gently transforming power of the Spirit of God.

§ 19. OF BEARING WITH THE WEAK.

(XIV. 1–23.)

Vers. 1, 2. The particularity with which St Paul treats these ascetics leads us naturally to suppose that they lived in Rome, and that the manner of behaving towards them had been a subject of discussion there. It is, however, difficult to determine of what spiritual tendency these ascetics were, since what St Paul adduces respecting them does not seem to agree either with rigid Jewish Christians, with Essene, or with Gentile ascetics. For the first of these classes kept, indeed, the precepts of the Old Testament as to food, but they did not wholly avoid the use of flesh and wine,* as St Paul reports of these Roman ascetics (xiv. 2, 21); for there is nothing to afford a foundation for the assumption that in the passages in question the subject is only the partaking of flesh offered in sacrifice to idols, and of wine used in libations. The Essene ascetics, on the other hand, whose life was similar (comp. Josephus Vit. § 2, in the description of the ascetic Banus), never lived in towns, but in the wilderness. And, again, Gentiles, who in the apostolic age also often practised a rigid asceticism, did not observe days in the manner related in xiv. 5 of the persons here described. It is, therefore, most correct to suppose that in these ascetics we have before us persons in whom Jewish principles mainly prevailed, indeed, but in combination with Gentile elements. This conclusion is especially supported by the passage, xv. 7, 8, where the "strong" are designated as Gentile, and the "weak" as Jewish Christians. Such mixtures of elements, in themselves heterogeneous, are not inconceivable in a time of such excitement as that of the Apostle's was. Among the Neopythagoreans and other philosophical sects of the first century of Christianity, there had been developed a sort of religious-moral eclecticism, which might easily call forth appearances of this kind. Seneca describes, in his 108th

* Still such a form of asceticism might easily be developed in Jewish Christians out of the Nazarite rule, as appears, among other instances, from that of St James, the Lord's brother, which Hegesippus relates (in Eusebius, Hist. Eccl. ii. 23)—*οἶνον καὶ σίκερα οὐκ ἔπιεν, οὐδὲ ἔμψυχον ἔφαγε.* (Comp. my *Monum. Hist. Eccl.* i. p. 11.) Jewish ascetics will be spoken of more particularly in the Introduction to the Pastoral Epistles.

Epistle, how he himself had for a time been engaged in a similar endeavour; in opposition to the prevailing immorality and voluptuousness, many of the nobler spirits had recourse to rigid self-denial. Such a tendency must, indeed, have been repulsed by Pharisaical Judaism, but it might very readily amalgamate with Essene elements. Eclectics of this kind, then, when they had become Christians, still persevered in their accustomed way of life; and St Paul desires that they may not be disturbed in it, since they did not insist on it as necessary to salvation, as the Jewish Christians of Galatia insisted on circumcision. In any case, these ascetics must be altogether and most carefully distinguished from the pharisaical Jewish Christians, who every where persecuted St Paul, and against whom he wrote the Epistle to the Galatians. (Comp. Introd. § 3. These Jewish Christians were fanatics who carried on attacks against the Apostle; whereas the Roman ascetics appear to have been quiet, anxious persons, who were only unable from scruples of conscience to disengage themselves from their accustomed observances, but did not affect to lay down rules for others.

In ver. 1, *προσλαμβάνεσθαι* signifies forwarding, helpful, support.—*Μὴ εἰς διακρίσεις διαλογισμῶν* sc. *ἔλθωσι*. *Διάκρισις* is opposed to *πίστις*, as the condition of inward wavering or uncertainty. The *ἀσθενεῖν πίστει* brings forward not so much the wavering itself as the source of it—the powerlessness of the principle of faith.—The conjecture *διὰ λογισμῶν* is unnecessary; for the thoughts are represented as brought into a state of uncertainty in the weak.—Ver 2. The form *λάχανα ἐσθίειν* indicates not only the refraining from the use of sacrificial flesh, or of animals forbidden in the law, but the avoiding all use of flesh—an abstinence which did not exist in the Jews as such. *Λάχανα* denotes all sorts of vegetables, as opposed to flesh.

Vers. 3, 4. Both parties, as well the weaker as the stronger, are then warned against one-sided judging of others; the decision is to be left to God, who alone can begin and complete the work of regeneration.

Ver. 3. *κρίνειν* has the sense of *κατακρίνειν*. It is not the judgment as to the objective ground or want of ground that is forbidden, but the determination as to the personal guilt in the matter—the condemning.—*Προσελάβετο* has reference to ver. 1, but is used in a modified sense, as it here relates to reception into the Church.—

Ver. 4 proves this idea from the circumstance, that no believer is lord over another, but all are God's servants, and to Him, consequently, the case of His servants is also to be left; by judging, we place ourselves above the servants, of whom, however, we ourselves are; it is, as it were, God's own affair to keep His servants for Himself, and if man thinks to assume the care of it, he invades God's province. The form *στήκω*, formed by aphaeresis from *ἕστηκα*, is very often used by St Paul. Beyond his writings, it occurs in the New Testament only in Mark xi. 25.

Vers. 5, 6. It might be supposed that a new class of persons is here spoken of; but, from the manner in which the eating is mixed up with the observance of days in ver. 6, this is not probable. It accords, also, with the whole tendency of such anxious religionists, that, where the one scruple exists, the other developes itself likewise. For such points of difference also the Apostle recommends forbearance towards the weak, and that each should act faithfully according to his own subjective conviction. If this be observed, and that with an entire reference to God, He by His Spirit guides to the objectively right view also. Ver. 5. By the forms *ἡμέραν κρίνειν* or *φρονεῖν* is expressed the attaching a value to days, such as Sabbaths, new-moons, and the like. ***Κρίνειν*** signifies examination and selection; *φρονεῖν*, careful consideration, valuation. In the words *κρίνειν πᾶσαν ἡμέραν* is expressed the original apostolic view, which did not distinguish particular festivals, because to it the whole life in Christ had become one festival. As, however, the season of the Church's prime passed away, the necessity could not but at the same time have again made itself felt, of giving prominence to points of festival light in the general current of everyday life. An Old-Testament-like observance of the Sabbath, such, for example, as prevails in England, is, according to this passage, assuredly not that which is objectively correct.* The requisite for each of these positions—neither of which alters the essence of the gospel—is an assured conviction, *ἕκαστος ἐν τῷ ἰδίῳ νοῒ πληροφορείσθω*. For *πληροφορεῖσθαι*, which is the opposite of *διακρίνεσθαι*, see on Rom. iv. 21. In ver. 6, the words *καὶ ὁ μὴ φρονῶν —φρονεῖ* are omitted by very many important MSS; the context,

* [The reader may be referred to Mr Vansittart Neale's Essay on "Feasts and Fasts," London, 1845, for information as to the degree in which the view here censured is countenanced by the authority of the English Church and Legislature.]

however, imperatively requires them, and it appears, consequently, that they have been omitted only because the copyists were misled by the homoiotelenton.

Vers. 7–9. An unreserved devotedness to the Lord is that which must ever be the essential of the Christian life; whatever can consist with this may be willingly borne with in a brother. It is not until something is remarked in a brother, which might interfere with this devotion, that love acquires a right to be jealous. The opposition of living and dying is not meant merely to denote absoluteness, but, as ver. 10 shews, to point to the idea of the divine judgment, by which all human judgment is excluded. Ver. 7. The Christian is neither another's nor his own; he is wholly God's; as in marriage the wife devotes herself wholly to the husband. The presential forms, *ζῇ, ἀποθνήσκει*, express the ideal, which, indeed, is not always actually realized. The believer, however, must always keep before him the ideal in its absoluteness; he must always regard it as his task to bear himself as betrothed unto the Lord, in order that by degrees he may realize it to the full. Ver. 8. The conjunctive *ἀποθνήσκωμεν* is not to be explained (as it is by Reiche) by the apostolical view as if Christ might come again before the death of many who were then alive—an opinion which we are convinced that St Paul had ceased to entertain at the date of this epistle—but by the uncertainty of the *moment* of death. The indicative, which is found in many MSS., is assuredly to be rejected. This union of the faithful with the Lord for death and life, is then, in ver. 9, regarded as the essential object of His work. The life and death of Christ were, so to speak, an acquisition, a purchase, a conquest of the living and the dead; with this His property no one may interfere. A profound and forcibly practical idea! Whosoever knows himself to be thus bound to the Lord of the world, will not wish to belong to any other, and will loose all ties which might still hold him! The readings vary greatly in the words of ver. 9, *καὶ ἀπέθανε καὶ ἔζησεν*. The first *καὶ* is decidedly to be rejected; it would seem to have been added only on account of the *καὶ νεκρῶν*. The variations in the verbs undoubtedly arose from the position; it seemed that *ἔζησεν* ought to stand first, or, if it were meant to denote eternal life, it seemed that the present was required. Hence *ἔζησεν* was taken in the sense of *ἀνέζησεν* or *ἀνέστη*. It is probable that sometimes one, sometimes the other, of these expressions, was at first written in the margin, and that from it sometimes one, sometimes both were adopted with the text. The explanation of ἔζησε, which is in any case the right reading, as an aorist and in this position, is indeed not free from difficulty. To take it without scruple as equivalent to ἀνέζησε is altogether inadmissible; even where the resurrection is referred to, the tense which is used of the simple verb is always the present, and never the aorist (comp. Rom. vi. 10, 2 Cor xiii. 4), even although an aorist preceded. But to explain the aorist, as Meyer does, by supposing that it is intended to mark the *beginning* of the condition, is altogether a perversion; for, in the first place, there is no motive for marking the beginning; and further, this suits only with states in time, not for those of eternity. The simplest way is to assume a hysteron-proteron for the explanation, and to understand ἔζησε of the earthly life of Christ, since ζῶντες also denotes those who are alive on earth.* By His perfect participation in the life of earth and its necessities, the Lord has won for Himself the right of dominion over man. (Comp. Heb. ii. 17, 18.) This transposition was no doubt caused by the circumstance that the idea of dying immediately preceded, and that Paul wished to connect with it the parallel with the Saviour.

Vers. 10–12. The universal equality of all believers, notwithstanding their inward differences, admits, then, no judgment of one respecting another; each has to give account for himself in the general judgment. If, however, believers, as well as others, are here represented as appearing before the judgment-seat of God, whereas in John iii. 18 it is said that "whosoever believeth on Him is not judged,"† the seeming difference is to be explained by the consideration that the Divine declaration of exemption from judgment may itself be regarded as an act of judgment. The fundamental idea of judgment is the separating from the mass, the joining together of what is akin; where this separation has already taken place, as in the case of believers (1 Cor. xi. 31) it cannot, of course, be again executed in the proper sense; God, however, may recognize it as executed, and thus the judgment is to be understood in this passage.

[* Olsh., therefore, would read ἀπέθανε καὶ ἔζησεν, and he translates *hat gelebt und ist gestorben, i. e.*, "lived and died."]

† Eng. Vers. "He that believeth on Him is not condemned."

Ver. 10. On $\beta\tilde{\eta}\mu\alpha$, compare note on Matt. xxvii. 19, and 2 Cor. v. 10. For *Χριστοῦ*, I follow the reading of Lachmann and Reiche, supported by the authorities A.D.E.F.G. *Θεοῦ*, since the substitution of *Χριστοῦ* might easily have taken place or account of the preceding words.—Ver. 11. The quotation is from Is. xlv. 23, and is very free. It expresses, indeed, the idea of adoration only, but this is one with the consciousness of dependence, which is here the subject. Reiche wrongly applies *ἐξομολογήσεται* to confession of sins—which, occurring to the parallelism, cannot possibly be meant.

Vers. 13–15. The Apostle follows up the negative side with the positive. He does not suppress the fact that the ascetics in question did not hold the objectively correct view; but, as their subjective error was not one of essential importance, he exhorts other Christians not merely to abstain from condemning them, but even to accommodate themselves to them. These verses (with which the parallel verses, 1 Cor. viii. 9, seqq., are to be compared) furnish a commentary on the apostolic saying as to becoming "a Jew to the Jews, and a Gentile to the Gentiles," (1 Cor. ix. 20, seqq.) For this idea may easily be misunderstood, as if the Apostle allowed us to accommodate ourselves to *all* weaknesses; and then an inference might be drawn, that the Reformers did amiss in refusing to keep the fasts with the [Roman] Catholics. There was, however, the difference, that with these the question was not merely of fasting, but of fasting as a means to salvation and as a meritorious work; whereas the ascetics of Rome had no such idea of their fasts; and it was on this account only that the Apostle could, without injury to the truth, advise accommodation to them.* Next, however, the idea in ver. 14 is difficult—*οὐδὲν κοινὸν δι' αὐτοῦ*, compared with ver. 20. For by this the laws as to food in the Old Testament appear degraded to merely capricious ordinances—which is unsuitable to their Divine origin. The Apostle, indeed, does not here refer immediately to the rules of the Old Testament; for the Roman ascetics did not adhere closely to

* This is most clearly shown by 1 Tim. iv. 1, seqq., where St Paul reckons among doctrines of devils the forbidding to marry and the *abstaining from meats which God has created.* This, however, applies only to such as make it a *principle of doctrine* that, for the sake of salvation, men must not eat this or that kind of food.

these, but went far beyond them; but yet they doubtless presupposed these rules, and only thought to do an *opus supererogatorium* if they ate no flesh whatever, and abstained from all wine. There is, therefore, good ground for inquiring into the relation of these apostolical declarations to the laws laid down as to food in the Old Testament. Now these laws cannot be merely capricious orders; we cannot conceive that God might have declared other animals to be unclean than those which He has declared. In the creatures which were declared unclean, the sin of nature must be supposed to have been most remarkably concentrated; and in any case it seems that, since all nature is defiled by the Fall (comp. note as to the *κτίσις*, on viii. 18, seqq.), it might rather be said that *nothing* is clean than that *all things* are so. Farther, we must say that St Paul would have assuredly disapproved of it if any one under the law had allowed himself in not observing the regulations as to food; which yet would have been objectively right, if none of the forbidden animals had been in itself unclean. We can and may, consequently, understand the Apostle's idea only in this sense—that *through Christ and His sanctifying influence* the creation has been restored to purity and holiness. If it should be said that this influence does not manifest itself as yet, but (according to viii. 18) only at the end of the world, and that nature still appears as unholy and unclean—the answer is, that this is certainly true, but that (1), as is often the case, the inchoate work of Christ is already regarded as complete, and (2), the superior force of Christ's power in the faithful neutralizes the slighter effects arising from nature in such a way that they become as if null. The passage before us is therefore to be taken exactly as 1 Tim. iv. 4, 5, where it is said that "every creature of God is good, *for it is sanctified by the word of God and prayer*."

Ver. 14. We might be inclined to connect ἐν κυρίῳ Ἰησοῦ with what follows, rather than with πέπεισμαι, but that the position of the words is against it. Still, from the mention of the *Christian* conviction the idea must be drawn that Adam's fall and its consequences are not to be thought of as removed, until removed by Christ. Ver. 15. ἐκεῖνον ἀπόλλυε refers of course to the shaking the person in his persuasion, and the consequent wavering and doubting as to everything, so that ἀπώλεια αἰώνιος is indicated as a pos sible result of it. The value of even the poorest and weakest brother cannot be made more strongly prominent than by the words, *ὑπὲρ οὗ Χριστὸς ἀπέθανε.*

Vers. 16–18. Consequently the point is, to distinguish between what is and what is not essential, for which purpose indeed the distinguishing principle, the Holy Ghost, is necessarily required. Ver. 16. *Βλασφημείσθω* is of course to be understood as meaning—Do not by your conduct give occasion that the good which has been manifested in you be slighted.—Ver. 17. *Βασιλεία τ. Θ.* is the community of life which Christ has brought in and founded, conceived in the widest sense, both as outward and as inward. (Comp. Comment. on Matt. iii. 2.*) *Βρῶσις καὶ πόσις* is a short expression for the attaching importance to eating and drinking, whether by abstaining from certain things or by eating of everything. We might have expected that the *ἐλευθερία* should be brought into prominence; but since this might itself be also carried to a faulty extreme, St Paul puts the general idea, *δικαιοσύνη*. The words *ἐν Πνεύματι ἁγίῳ* are to be extended to all the three points named; for it is intended precisely to exclude the *self*-righteousness to which a mistaken asceticism so readily leads. Hence also *ἐν τούτῳ* and not *τούτοις* is to be read in ver. 18; for with the principle of the Holy Ghost all individual virtues are implied.

Vers. 19, 20. From this fundamental principle of the Christian life the Apostle proceeds to deduce an exhortation to strive after peace, and to edify God's building, not to destroy it by unwise and unseasonable instruction. The persuasion of liberty in such matters must be organically developed from within.

After *ἀλλήλους*, D.E.F.G. have *φυλάξωμεν*, which, however, cannot well be more than an addition of the copyists.

Vers. 21–23. "All things are lawful for me, but all things are not expedient" (1 Cor. vi. 12); to this Pauline principle the following exhortation reverts. In cases where any one out of personal conviction does or refrains from a certain thing, without making his own practice an objective law, his conviction is to be honoured by the stronger believer through voluntary abstinence; for in such *things of intermediate character* the subjective conviction is the

* [This is, no doubt, the passage intended. The author's reference is to "vol. i. pp. 150, seqq.," which does not agree with the edition before us—the third.]

rule of action. For that so important moral principle, *πᾶν ὃ οὐκ ἐκ πίστεως, ἁμαρτία ἐστίν* is throughout to be taken with this necessary restriction, if it is not to lead to the grossest errors. Where positive commands or prohibitions of God are in question, the subjective conviction has no voice.* As has been already remarked on ver. 1, no conceivable grounds can be a sufficient motive for the suspension of a positive command of God. But in Adiaphora, *i.e.*, not in morally indifferent cases (for such have no existence). but in cases for which *no positive rule can be laid down*, because through circumstances they may at one time be morally good, at another time wrong, and in which the greater or less development of the subjectivity has an influence—for Adiaphora, the personal conviction of the moment, *i. e.*, the *πίστις*, is the decisive ground of determination. Hence, also, we cannot say that *true* faith, *correct* conviction, alone may be the decisive ground which determines our action; on the contrary, even that which is objectively false may be so. The conviction of these ascetics at Rome was of this objectively false nature, and yet St Paul advises them to go on according to its dictates, until the Christian life should have developed within them to a purer conviction. This, however, applies only in the case of such *Adiaphora;* never in cases which are immutably fixed by appointments of God.

In ver. 21, A. and C. omit the clause *ἢ σκανδαλίζεται ἢ ἀσθενεῖ*; and indeed both these verbs appear to be merely supplied from what goes before. In vers. 22, the reading *σὺ πίστιν ἣν ἔχεις κατὰ σεαυτὸν, ἔχε κ. τ. λ.* only interferes with the idea; yet it is supported by A.B.C.

§. 20. CHRIST AN EXAMPLE OF BEARING WITH THE WEAK.

(XV. 1–13.)

That the insertion of the concluding doxology (xvi. 25–27), between the xivth and xvth chapters, is altogether unsuitable, has been

* An addition to Luke vi. 4, which is contained in the MS. D., is very highly instructive for the understanding of this passage. It is, indeed, unquestionably spurious, and probably belongs to an apocryphal gospel; but the idea is genuinely Christian, and perhaps the whole incident related may have really taken place. It is there told that

already fully shown in the Introduction (§ 1.) The connexion of the following passage, (xv. 1–13), with the preceding is so close, that the division of chapters ought to have been different. It is not until ver. 14 that an entirely new subject comes in. The earlier verses are merely a setting-forth of Christ as a pattern of the conduct towards the weak recommended in chapter xiv.

Ver. 1, 2. St Paul here clearly distinguishes two classes among the Christians of Rome (and the same may be assumed as to all churches); the one includes the strong (*δυνατοί*), the other, the weak (*ἀδύνατοι, ἀσθενεῖς*). The distinction between the two is to be sought in the degrees of spiritual development, especially of the *γνῶσις*, which gives insight into the peculiar connexion of doctrines and laws. Among these classes it is the duty of the stronger towards the weaker not to live after their own pleasure, but lovingly to bear with the infirmities of the others.

On *ἑαυτῷ ἀρέσκειν* and *τῷ πλησίον ἀρέσκειν*, comp. 1 Cor. x. 33, Galat. i. 10. It is the nature of love to go out of itself, to live not in itself but in others.

Ver. 3. This love towards the weak manifested itself in perfect purity in the Saviour (Phil. ii. 7), who left all His glory to enter into the deepest ignominy for man. According to this conception, the quotation from Ps. lxix. 10 stands in exact connexion with the course of the Apostle's ideas. The living not for one's own pleasure but for that of our neighbour is always a self-denial, which grieves the flesh; this self-denial Christ practised in the purest form, as is manifested in His course of suffering. He loved those who hated Him, and out of love willingly endured all the ignominy which they heaped on Him, and all this for the building up of the work of God.

On quotations from the same lxixth Psalm, compare Matt. xxvii. 39, seqq.; John ii. 17, xix. 28; Rom. xi. 9. The words are quoted exactly from the LXX.

Vers. 4–6. Exactly as in the passage, Rom. iv. 23, 24 (on which compare the comment), St Paul again announces the important canon of interpretation—that the whole substance of Scripture is

Jesus saw a man working on the Sabbath, and said to him, *εἰ οἶδας τί ποιεῖς, μακάριος εἶ, εἰ δέ μὴ οἶδας, ἐπικατάρατος καὶ παραβάτης εἶ τοῦ νόμου.* In these words, the *εἰδέναι* expresses the same which is here signified by *πιστεύειν*, namely the settled subjective conviction.

designed for man and for his instruction. It is not, therefore, to be understood according to its outward letter, but rather according to what is inward; *i. e.*. according to the Eternal Spirit which pervades its whole substance, and which renders it a mirror of truth for all times and for all circumstances. This external purport of the Scriptures, however, is recognized by the πνευματικός alone; it is Spirit alone that discerns and understands the Spirit. The reason why St Paul here gives especial prominence to the ideas of patience and consolation is, because the relation to the weak members of the Church of God itself has in it something especially trying,* and for this the believer requires above everything consolation and strength to endure. The Apostle then expressly wishes his readers the communication of these gifts, in the hope that in their power all such differences may be overcome, and unity may be preserved.

Ver. 4. On account of the chief idea—of Scripture and its significancy for men, the words τῶν γραφῶν are to be referred (as by Reiche) to both the preceding genitives, ὑπομονῆς and παρακλήσεως, not (as by De Wette) to the latter only. The intention here is, of course, to characterize Scripture as the channel of grace which God employs in order to work patience and comfort in men. Ver. 5. The expression Θεὸς τῆς ὑπομονῆς καὶ παρακλήσεως denotes the all-sufficient God as the real source of these gifts; He may be designated according to all that is good and beautiful, because He includes all in Himself. Similar expressions occur, Rom. xv. 13, 33; 1 Thess. v. 23; 2 Cor. i. 3. On the former Θεὸς καὶ πατὴρ Ἰησοῦ Χριστοῦ. comp. note on 2 Cor. i. 3. For ὁμοθυμαδόν, comp. Acts i. 14.

Vers. 7, 8. By a peculiar turn, St Paul further sets forth the person of the Lord as an example of merciful love towards the weak, in that out of mercy He called the Gentiles into His kingdom. It is evident that the Gentile Christians are here conceived of as the strong, and the Jewish Christians as the weak; whence it

* The Christian does not make any claims on the world, since he knows that in it the Spirit of God is not; but so much the more does the believer, in the beginning of his life of faith, make claims on the Church. Every neophyte is a born Donatist; he requires that the Church should be the perfected kingdom of heaven! The continual striving with the weaknesses of the brethren is the most difficult self-denial for the faithful, even as in the Saviour's life it was one of the most trying necessities that he had unceasingly to contend with the perversities and weaknesses of his disciples.

results that the Roman ascetics cannot possibly have derived thei views from Gentile sources alone. But it has been fully shewn in the Introduction (§ 3), that these Roman Jewish Christians are not to be regarded as judaizers in the same sense as the Galatians were so. In a peculiar manner the Apostle now represents the relation of Christ to the Jews as a matter of *duty;* because of the promises made to the fathers, it was in a manner necessary, for the sake of His *truth,* that God should send Christ to the Jews. It was therefore out of mere *mercy* that the gospel was preached to the Gentiles, inasmuch as they had no right to lay claim to the fulfilment of promises. The whole manner of representing the matter is, of course, to be understood κατ' ἄνθρωπον; for in a preceding part of the epistle (ch. x.), St Paul had reproved the Jews for the very fault of supposing that God *owed* them His favour. His object here is, to impress upon the Gentiles the advantages of the Jews, and, therefore, he makes use of this particular form of stating the case.

Ver. 7. On προσλαμβάνεσθαι comp. note on xiv. 1.—Ver. 8. λέγω δέ, "Now I mean—I intend to say." The title διάκονος περιτομῆς, used of Christ, occurs only here. So strong an expression is intentionally chosen, in order to represent Israel in its exaltation. Baur has, without ground, (comp. Introd. § 1.) declared the expression unpauline, and characterized the following ὑπὲρ ἀληθείας Θεοῦ as containing too great a concession to the Jewish Christians. For in the διάκονος there is only a reference to the devotedness of Christ, which is represented as a *serving* in Matt. xx. 28 also; and that the salvation in Christ is primarily intended for the Jews, was clearly declared by the πρῶτον in i. 16, and in like manner in ix. 5, xi. 16, 28, as it is by Christ himself, Matt. xv. 24. All that it implies, therefore, is, that Israel is the people of the covenant, and that the truth of God requires the fulfilment of his promises on it.

Vers. 9–13. The calling of the Gentiles, as the idea which actuates the Apostle, is again represented by means of quotations from the Old Testament as purposed by God. The passages are taken from Ps. xviii. 50; Deut. xxxii. 43; Ps. cxvii. 1; Is. xi. 10. Paul almost entirely follows the LXX. in his citations.

Ver. 10. Ἡ γραφή is to be supplied to λέγει. In the quotation, ver. 10, the Hebrew text varies from the LXX., who perhaps read it differently.—Ver. 12. Ἰεσσαί, Jesse, the father of David. The root of Jesse or David is Christ, as branch or son of David. Comp. Revel. v. 5, xxii. 16; Ecclus. xlvii. 26.—*Ὁ ἀνιστάμενος ἄρχειν*, "He who is born or destined for rule;" for *ἀνίστασθαι* is here to be taken in the sense of "to appear, to announce one's self as."—Ver 13. The triple *ἐν* gave occasion for alterations; some MSS. wholly omitted *ἐν τῷ πιστεύειν*, others the *ἐν* before *τῇ ελπίδι*. But the not altogether proper accumulation of prepositions is itself an evidence for the correctness of the usual reading.

SECTION III.

(XV. 14—33.)

PERSONAL COMMUNICATIONS.

The following section is really only a sort of appendage to the ethical part, which properly ends at xv. 13. The Apostle begins by apologizing for the free admonitions which he has ventured to give to the Romans, and then gives information as to his intended travels, at the same time expressing a wish that he may be able to visit the Christians of Rome, (xv. 22–33.)

§ 21. APOLOGY.

(XV. 14–21.)

It seems at first sight somewhat strange that the Apostle apologises for his serious admonitions. It looks, as it were, worldly, that he, the Apostle clothed with divine authority, speaks as if he might possibly have been too bold in what he had said. Ver. 20, however, shews what induced him to this turn. Even although disciples of his might have been at work at Rome (comp. Introd. § 3), still St Paul could not altogether regard the Church in Rome as his own, since he had not been its founder. According, then, to his principle of never invading another's field of labour, there arose in him the apprehension, that his free-spoken language to the Romans might be made a crime by the Jewish opponents who everywhere followed in his track, and that by their insinuations the Romans might be prejudiced against him. This possible danger the Apostle seeks to avert by the following *captatio benevolentiæ*, in which he places himself as a brother on a level with them (as in i. 12), without asserting his dignity as a teacher and an Apostle of the Lord. Baur and Kling have altogether groundlessly taken offence at this. It is naturally understood that here the question is not of any hypocritical or flattering *captatio benevolentiæ*, but of one which is pure and true, and such St Paul often makes use of. In 1 Cor. i. 4, seqq., he praises the Corinthians, although he had much to blame in them. To this kind belong also the passages, 2 Cor. vii. 4, seqq.; vii. 12, seqq.

Vers. 14–16. If there had indeed been contentions among the Romans like those in Galatia, ver. 14 would contain an untruth. The Roman Church was really in a good condition (i. 8); hence St Paul could praise it with truth. His boldness in admonition he excuses on the ground of his high calling, which (he says) makes the Gentile world his especial care, and makes it his task to prepare it as a holy sacrifice, well-pleasing to God.

Ver. 14. *καὶ αὐτὸς ἐγώ*, "I as well as others," even although in appearance my admonitions indicate the contrary.—*Ἀγαθωσύνη* is also found Ephes. v. 9, 2 Thes i. 11. It belongs to the later Greek. As this denotes the condition, so does *γνῶσις* the knowledge respecting it; these two elements constitute the capacity for *νουθετεῖν*.—Ver. 15. On account of the *ἀπὸ μέρους*, the *τολμηρότερον* cannot apply to the writing itself, but only to the manner of writing in some parts, especially from chap. xi. onwards. The words *ὡς ἐπαναμιμνήσκων* suppose every thing to be before known to the Romans, and are, consequently, a mitigating expression.—*Χάρις* signifies again, as in xii. 3, the *apostleship*.—Ver. 16. St Paul by a grand figure represents himself as an officiating priest, and the Gentile world as a great sacrifice to be consecrated to God (*προςφορά*), which he had to offer to God through the gospel (*ἱερουργεῖν*), so that the whole Christian process of sanctification appears as an adorning of the sacrifice which is to be consecrated to God. *Λειτουργός* properly signifies one who administers business of the state, and secondarily often stands as equivalent to *διά-*

κονος (Rom. xiii. 6); by the LXX. it is commonly used of priestly servants. This is the only place in the N. Test. where *ἱερουργεῖν* occurs; it is the proper term for sacrificing. Hesychius explains *ἱερουργεῖ* by *θύει, ἱερὰ ἐργάζεται.*

Vers. 17–19. The mention of his apostolic calling very naturally leads the Apostle on to speak of its blessed effects, which are such as to give him an apparent warrant for administering admonition to the Romans. The whole of this blessed efficacy he humbly refers to Christ, without claiming any part of it for himself. The help of the Lord, however, manifests itself quite as much through ordinary as through extraordinary supports.

Ver. 17. *Καύχησις* is to be taken as in iii. 27, in the sense of "occasion for boasting."—*Τὰ πρὸς τὸν Θεόν* is to be taken as an accusative absolute—"as regards the cause of God."—Ver. 18. The transition is somewhat obscure, and so is the term *λαλεῖν τι ὧν οὐ κ. τ. λ.* If, however, we only take in its positive form the idea which is here negatively expressed, it is quite simple; instead of saying—"I shall not venture to bring forward any thing which Christ hath not done by me," the same idea may be thus expressed: "I shall never venture to glory in my deeds, but will proclaim the glory of Christ alone." Reiche's objections to this way of taking it are not to the point. He supposes the negative to apply, not to the manner of the operation, but to the operation itself; and, moreover, that St Paul could not intend here to disclaim the conversion of the Gentile world, inasmuch as in the preceding and following parts of the epistle he ascribes it to himself. According, however, to the way of understanding the words which we have indicated, both these objections are needless. He does not disclaim the conversion, but regards himself wholly as Christ's servant, and hence refers it wholly to the Lord. Consequently the idea is meant to refer precisely to the operation itself, and not to the manner of it, to which the interpretation here given in nowise constrains us.—*Λόγῳ καὶ ἔργῳ* signify the ordinary operation of grace; *ἐν δυνάμει σημείων καὶ τεράτων,* that which is extraordinary—through *charismata,* for fuller details as to which the comment. on 1 Cor. xii. is to be compared. In the words *ἐν δυνάμει Πνεύματος ἁγίου,* the common source of both is named.—Ver. 19. *Πληροῦν εὐαγγέλιον* is certainly not a Chaldæism, according to the Chaldee גְּמַר, which means, first, *to fill,* and secondarily, *to teach;* but like the form λογον πληροῦν, to bring a discourse to an end, to speak completely to an end (Col. i. 25), it has the sense of "to publish in its whole compass," = κηρύσσειν. That St Paul visited Illyria itself, is nowhere related; probably he only proceeded as far as the boundary of this province during his residence in Macedonia.

Ver. 20. St Paul feels himself further induced to mention the principle of his action as an apostle (Gal. ii.), according to which he wrought only where no one had before preached, in order to avoid building on another's foundation. If indeed the passage οὐχ ὅπου ὠνομάσθη Χριστός were literally taken. St Paul would have been obliged to refrain from preaching at Rome also; but, 1, no other apostle had preached there, and this was the very point of his determination, in order that the spheres of operation might not come into any conflict; and, 2, the population of Rome was greater than that of many a province, and, consequently, as several apostles might labour in different parts of the same province, so also Peter and Paul might preach together in Rome.

Ver. 20. Φιλοτιμεῖσθαι, properly *to strive after honour*, and thence *to strive with zeal* in general. The accusative of the participle refers to με, ver. 19 Ὠνομάσθη means more than simply *to be preached*, viz., *to be named as Saviour*, *i.e.*, to be acknowledged as such. Ver. 21 is quoted from Is. lii. 15, closely according to the LXX. In the quotation περὶ αὐτοῦ is, according to Paul's intention, to be taken as masculine, and referred to Christ.

§ 22. NOTICE OF JOURNEYS.

(XV. 22–33.)

Ver. 22–24. In this principle of his, then, St Paul also finds the ground of his never having as yet visited Rome, because the gospel was already spread there. It was not until after it should have been diffused in the eastern provinces of the Roman empire that he could hope to be at liberty to gratify his wish to see Rome. Even then, however, it would not be so that Rome should be the proper mark of his travels in the West, but he only hoped that he might be able to touch it in passing on towards Spain. The only thing which seems surprising here is, how St Paul can say *μηκέτι τόπον ἔχων ἐν τοῖς κλίμασι τούτοις*, since he was yet far from having preached every where in Greece and Asia Minor. We see him always labour in the great chief towns of provinces, and then devolve on his assistants, who were fixedly stationed there, the further diffusion of the gospel from these points. Moreover, he undoubtedly did not believe that every individual was to be received into the Church, but only those who, according to God's gracious election, were ordained unto eternal life. His task, therefore, ap peared to him to be that of every where breaking ground and preaching the gospel to all nations for a witness concerning them; and this he might regard as fulfilled in the eastern provinces.

Ver. 22. The *διό* refers to ver. 20, "by reason that I always found much yet to be done in the East." The *ἐνεκοπτόμην*, sc. *ὁδόν* is to be taken thus—"The way was cut off for me, I was hindered." (Comp. Acts xxiv. 4; Galat. v. 7; 1 Thess. ii. 18; 1 Pet. iii. 7. *Τὰ πολλά = πολλάκις*.—Ver. 23. *κλίμα*, from the *inclination* of lands towards the pole,—a geographical term of the ancients. Paul's wish to visit Rome is no doubt to be explained from the circumstance that in that city he saw the centre of the heathen world. He wished to preach in the seat of the prince of this world the kingdom of the Lord of heaven. —Ver. 24. This passage is certainly insufficient to prove that St Paul executed his plan, which is here merely represented as possible, of going into Spain. But yet the necessity of supposing a second imprisonment,* combined with the statement of Clement of Rome (Ep. i. and Cor. ch. v.), that St Paul penetrated *εἰς τὸ τέρμα τῆς δύσεως*—(an expression which, when written at Rome, can only be understood of Spain)—render it in the highest degree probable that the great Apostle of the Gentiles was also preserved by God for the complete fulfilment of his vocation. He does not speak of Rome as the proper object of his journey, because Christ was already known there (xv. 20); he only wishes to salute the Roman Christians in passing. He was, however, afterwards involuntarily detained there for a long time. The reading *ἐλεύσομαι*

* Compare Introd. to the Pastoral Epistles.

πρὸς ὑμᾶς, ἐλπίζω γάρ is opposed by so many and important critical authorities that it ought undoubtedly to be rejected.* Rink and De Wette, however, endeavour to assert the genuineness of the words against Lachmann, because A.B.C. have the *γὰρ*, and with this conjunction the whole clause stands or falls. It is more correct to suppose, with Meyer, that the words were early interpolated, and that when the original text was restored in A.B.C., the *γὰρ* still remained.—*Προπεμφθῆναι* relates to the convoy usually given to apostles on their leaving a place; comp. Acts xv. 3, xvii. 14, seqq.; xx. 38; xxi. 5.—*Ὑμῶν ἐμπλησθῶ, until I be filled with you, satiated;* the addition of *ἀπὸ μέρους* is intended to signify the insatiableness of the Apostle's longing.

Vers. 25, 26. In the first place, however, he remarks, he has before him a journey to Jerusalem, whither he has to convey a collection† for the poor Christians of that city. How on this journey he was arrested at Jerusalem, afterwards remained two years in prison at Cæsarea, and at length was taken to Rome as a prisoner, is (as is well known), fully related in the Acts of the Apostles. On the *κοινωνία* or *διακονία* for the poor of Jerusalem, compare more particularly the notes on Galat. ii. 10; 1 Cor. xvi.; 2 Cor. viii. 9; Acts xix. 21; xxiv. 17.—Ver. 26. The expression *εἰς τοὺς πτωχοὺς τῶν ἁγίων* shews that not *all* the Christians of Jerusalem were in poverty; hence the community of goods cannot have produced the poverty, or at least it cannot itself have been long in force.

Vers. 27–29. In the observation that the believers of Macedonia and Achaia had regarded themselves as debtors to the Jewish Christians, there is implied a delicate hint for the Romans, that they should also do so, and consequently should contribute to the collection. After accomplishing this business, the Apostle continues, he hopes to go to Spain by way of Rome, and he knows that he shall not come to them without a blessing.

Here again, as in verses 8 and 9, the Jews are regarded as the first rightful possessors of the gospel, the priestly nation for mankind, as it were, to which earthly things are to be given for heavenly, in like manner as to the individual spiritual pastor (1 Cor. ix. 13, 14).—Ver. 28. *Σφραγίζεσθαι* denotes *securing, making*

* [Thus the reading will be *ὡς ἐὰν* (or *ἂν*) *πορεύωμαι εἰς τὴν Σπανίαν, ἐλπίζω διαπορευόμενος θεάσασθαι ὑμᾶς.*]

† On St Paul's purpose as to the collections, comp. the remarks on 1 Cor. xvi. 1.

fast, in general. Here the personal conveyance is the means of the secure delivery. The explanation of this passage which has been attempted by Böttger (*Beitr.* Part. iii. pp. 67, seqq.), can hardly be regarded as other than an utter failure. He wishes to illustrate it by the Roman laws, which prescribed in what manner contracts ought to be sealed, and to be secured against falsification. Ver. 29. *οἶδα* is more than subjective conjecture; it is certainty of conviction, because he had a word of the Lord for his warrant. (Comp. Acts xxiii. 11.) *Πλήρωμα εὐλογίας* = *πλοῦτος εὐλογίας*, *rich, full blessing*. The reading *πληροφορία* for *πλήρωμα* has indeed D.E.F.G., in its favour, but Paul uses this expression not in the sense of *πλοῦτος*, but for "firm conviction," which is not applicable in this place.

Vers. 30–33. The Spirit of the Lord, however, signified to the Apostle, at the same time, the sufferings which threatened him from the enmity of the Jews; hence he recommends himself to the intercession of the believers at Rome, for deliverance from their hands. The knowledge of the Divine plans, therefore, was not in St Paul of a fatalistic nature; he does not say—I know that I must surely go to Rome, and therefore I have no need of any precaution or of any intercession; rather it was a lively, free acquaintance with the plans of the free personal God, which are fulfilled through the working together of the free actions of free beings.

Ver. 31. The *εὐπρόσδεκτος* indicates, that St Paul supposes even the Christians of Jerusalem to be prejudiced against him, as is confirmed also by Acts xxi. Instead of *ἀναπαύσωμαι*, D. and E. read *ἀναψύξω*, and F.G. *ἀναψυχῶ μεθ' ὑμῶν*. The Oriental MSS., however, unanimously support the usual reading.—Ver. 33. As the ethical portion is here ended, St Paul concludes it with a short doxology. It is, however, in the nature of the case, that for so rich a letter he reserves a more full-toned conclusion; this does not follow until quite at the end, after the greetings.

PART IV.

(XVI. 1–27.)

SALUTATIONS AND CONCLUSION.

It has been already shewn in the Introduction (§ i.), that there is no ground whatever to warrant us in denying that this concluding chapter was written by the Apostle, or belongs to the epistle. The great number of the salutations is certainly striking, when it is considered that Paul had not yet been at Rome. As, however, this city formed the central point of the then world, where people from all countries met, and from which journeys were taken into all parts of the vast Roman empire,* it is intelligible that St Paul may even in it have had a particularly numerous acquaintance. And, moreover, it is nowise necessary to suppose that St Paul knew them all personally; he had, doubtless, heard of many of the Roman Christians through Aquila and Priscilla, and now greets them as acquaintances known not in person but in the spirit.

§ 23. GREETINGS.

(XVI. 1–20.)

Vers. 1, 2. First, St Paul recommends to the Christians of Rome the deaconess Phoebe, who was no doubt the bearer of the epistle. She did not serve the Church in Corinth itself, but in Cenchrea, to which place also it thus appears that the gospel had already spread. Ver. 1. *Ἡ διάκονος*, afterwards *ἡ διακονίσσα,* denotes the female ministers of the Church, whom the rites of the early Church, especially in baptism, and the position of the

* On this compare the passage from Athenaeus, Deipnos i. fol. 20, quoted by Neander, *Apost. Zeitalter*, vol. i. p. 343, note. Τὴν *Ρωμαίων πόλιν ἐπιτομὴν τῆς οἰκουμένης, ἐν ᾗ συνιδεῖν ἔστιν πάσας τὰς πόλεις ἱδρυμένας—καὶ γὰρ ὅλα τὰ ἔθνη ἀθρόως αὐτόθι συνῴκισται.* With especial reference to Christendom, Irenæus, as is well known, says of Rome and the Church there—"Ad hanc enim ecclesiam propter potiorem principalitatem necesse est omnem convenire ecclesiam, h. e. eos qui sunt undique fideles." (*adv. Haer.* II. iii. p. 201, edit. Grabü.

female sex in the East, imperatively required. For more particular information, compare the commentary on 1 Tim. iii. 8. Cenchrea was the name of the eastern port of Corinth; Lechaeus of the western.—Ver. 2. ἐν κυρίῳ, in the mind and in the name of Christ, because she is a Christian, and as befits such an one. Grotius rightly observes, that St Paul does not say παράστατις, *i. e.*, a *helper*, but προστάτις, *i. e.*, *a chief*, a *patroness*. By this title of honour Paul intends to raise her consideration, and to make his recommendation more complete.

Vers. 3, 4. For an explanation how Aquila and Priscilla could already be again at Rome, whereas 1 Cor. xvi. 19 represents them as still being at Ephesus, the observations in the Introduction, § 1, may be compared. It is not known to what occurrences Paul here refers. As to this celebrated family in general, see note on Acts xviii. 19. In Rome, as well as at Corinth and Ephesus, it appears to have had in its dwelling the place of assembly (ἐκκλησία κατ' οἶκον), for a division of the city. A city of such extent as Rome must naturally have very early had places of assembly in various parts of it.

Ver. 3. *Πρίσκα* is the original form of the name, but *Πρίσκιλλα* is more commonly used for the wife of Aquila. The phrase τράχηλον ὑποτιθέναι is figurative, and means, *to expose one's self to the most evident dangers.*

Vers. 5–7. The persons here named are not further known. The title ἀπαρχή denotes the first convert of a city or province. Instead of Ἀχαΐας, we should read, agreeably to the best critical authorities, Ἀσίας, *i. e.*, *Asia proconsularis.* For according to 1 Cor. xvi. 15, Stephanas was the first fruit of Achaia. De Wette, however, has observed, in favour of the former reading, that that passage may itself have been the very cause of an alteration, and further, that ἀπαρχή need not be precisely limited to an individual, inasmuch as several persons might have been named together as the first converts. But in that case it would probably be "*one* of the first fruits."—Ver. 7. Junia appears to have been the wife of Andronicus; it is not known where they were fellow-prisoners with St Paul. Their relationship to him is probably to be understood only of national connexion. The title of *Apostles* is of course to be taken here in the wider sense of the word. Comp. Acts xiv. 4, 14.

Vers. 8–12. The names which follow are also unknown. The

formula in ver. 10, τοὺς ἐκ τῶν Ἀριστοβούλου is to be filled up like τοὺς ἐκ τῶν Ναρκίσσου, τοὺς ὄντας ἐν κυρίῳ in ver. 11—those among the slaves of Aristobulus or Narcissus who have become believers. Narcissus, the well-known favourite of Claudius (Sueton. Claud. 28), had been some years dead at the date of the epistle, and therefore cannot well be meant here.

Vers. 13-16. It is of course only in a figurative sense that St Paul styles the mother of Rufus *his* mother, from her having shewn motherly love towards him. The expressions in vers. 14 and 15, οἱ ἀδελφοὶ σὺν αὐτοῖς are to be explained like ἡ ἐκκλησία κατ' οἶκον in ver. 5—the brethren attached to their community or circle, so that the persons named are to be regarded as the presbyters and deacons of this church.—Ver. 16. As to the kiss of peace, comp. 1 Cor. xvi. 20; 2 Cor. xiii. 12; 1 Thess. v. 26; 1 Pet. v. 14. The Christians regarded themselves as members of one family of God, and expressed the consciousness of this spiritual unity by the symbol of the kiss. The addition ἀσπάζονται ὑμᾶς αἱ ἐκκλησίαι πᾶσαι τοῦ Χριστοῦ is omitted by some authorities; perhaps because it was supposed that the greetings were not in place before the section xvi. 21, seqq. In the common text, πᾶσαι alone is wanting, doubtless because it was supposed that Paul could not know whether all churches on earth saluted the Romans. But no doubt πᾶσαι is to be understood only of the various churches of Corinth and its ports.

Ver. 17, 18. It is not until here, quite at the end of the epistle, that we find a short admonition against divisions, couched in altogether general language, which may be referred to the Judaizing party which persecuted Paul everywhere, but which wrought in Galatia especially with so pernicious effect. The circumstance of its being conceived and introduced so abruptly, and in such general terms, is most decisive evidence that the erroneous teachers in question did not actually exist in Rome, but that St Paul only wished to give a warning against them, with a view to the possible, and unhappily only too likely case, that they might make their appearance there also. The edict of Claudius, which still continued in operation, and only by degrees fell into oblivion, was no doubt the only cause which had until then preserved Rome free from these opponents of St Paul.*

* De Wette and Meyer also acknowledge, that the passage cannot prove, as Baur as-

The term διδαχή, ἣν ὑμεῖς ἐμάθετε, is an indication not to be mistaken that it was disciples of St Paul who had first preached at Rome.—Ver. 18. The charge of serving their belly is not to be so understood as if Paul meant to represent them as persons of grossly sensual habits; for this is precisely what the Pharisaical Jewish Christians usually were not; the meaning is only to describe them as working for themselves and their own advantage, not for Christ. (Comp. on Matt. xxiii., and Phil. iii. 19.) Χρηστολογία usually includes the bad subsidiary meaning, of kind and gentle speech without deeds to correspond. In exactly a similar way εὐλογία is here used in its properly classical signification; it stands for words fair and well put together, but of deceptive appearance. The omission of εὐλογίας originates only with such as understood the word in the sense of blessing, which it usually bears in the New Testament, and which they naturally, according to the context, regarded as unsuitable in this place.

Vers. 19, 20. With respect to this danger, however, St Paul trusts to the obedience (ὑπακοή) of the Roman Christians, and therefore expresses the hope, that they may be found no less wise and prudent than free from falsehood; with God's help they then would soon overcome all evil, together with the prince of darkness.

Ver. 19. Ὑπακοὴ εἰς πάντας ἀφίκετο, as is said in i. 8, of the faith of the Romans. The τό has wrongly been omitted before ἐφ' ὑμῖν; it is intended precisely to bring out a particular feature in the Romans as a subject of joy. The reference to Matt. x. 16, is not to be mistaken in the end of the verse.—Ver. 20. The God of peace is placed in contrast with the author of all strife, who works by his instruments here on earth. The power of God in the faithful—Christ in them—bruises the head of the serpent. The words συντρίψει ὑπὸ τοὺς πόδας contain an allusion to Gen. iii. 15. The form of conclusion, ἡ χάρις κ. τ. λ. is undoubtedly genuine, although it is wanting in D.E.F.G.

serts, that there had already been disputes with Jewish Christians at Rome, but only that the Apostle is anxious to provide against their breaking out there as in other churches. In addition to the Epistle to the Galatians, compare especially 2 Cor. ii. and Phil. iii.

§ 24. CONCLUSION.

(XVI. 21—27.)

The verses 21–24 cannot but seem somewhat strange if one ascribe them to St Paul. For ver. 22 is, in any case, an addition by the penman of the epistle, Tertius himself; but how singular it would be if ver. 21 were by St Paul, ver. 22 by Tertius, and vers. 23, 24, by St Paul again! There is, too, the circumstance, that St Paul had already concluded his salutations before the exhortation in vers. 17–20, with the comprehensive form *ἀσπάζονται ὑμᾶς αἱ ἐκκλησίαι πᾶσαι τοῦ Χριστοῦ*. Is it then to be supposed that, after this, he added some others by way of supplement? It is far simpler to assume, that the great doxology, vers. 25–27, was immediately connected with the blessing in ver. 20, but that (according to the hypothesis of Eichhorn which we have adopted, comp. Introd. § 1), it was written on a small separate parchment, as the larger was already full. The back of this small parchment remained empty, and this the writer Tertius then employed for writing in his own name, ver. 21–24, including the blessing. The only objection which may be made to this is, that Timothy is styled *συνεργός μου*, and Gaius *ξένος μου*, which seems to point to St Paul rather than to Tertius. There is not, however, any discoverable ground why Tertius also might not have styled himself a fellow-labourer of Timothy, or connected by hospitality with Gaius. But even if this were an inconvenience, it will bear no comparison with the difficulties in which we must entangle ourselves if we refer the verses to St Paul.

Vers. 21, 22. As nothing further is known of Tertius, some have wished to identify him with Silas, the well-known companion of St Paul, and to regard his name as merely the Latin translation of the Hebrew שְׁלִישִׁי, "the third." There is, however, no historical ground that can be adduced for this conjecture. The addition *ὁ γράψας* denotes the penman, as St Paul was in the habit of dictating his epistles. (Comp. 1 Cor. xvi. 21, Col. iv. 18, 2 Thess. iii. 17, and Galat. vi. 11.)

Ver. 23, 24. Gaius is undoubtedly the person named in 1 Cor. i. 14, whom St Paul himself had baptized. In Acts xix. 29, xx.

4, 3 John 1, other persons of this name are spoken of. The expression ξένος τῆς ἐκκλησίας ὅλης, signifies that Gaius had at Corinth the assemblies of a congregation in his house. Erastus occurs perhaps in Acts xix. 22, 2 Tim. iv. 20; but if so he must have resigned his office as manager of the city funds. The blessing in ver. 24 is also best referred to Tertius, as St Paul had already used the same words in ver. 20. It is precisely on account of the repetition that the MSS. A. C. and other critical authorities have omitted it.

25–27. On the position of the great concluding doxology, and on the variations of MSS.,* and the learned hypotheses connected with it, compare the remarks in the Introduction, § 1. As we cannot adopt Reiche's hypothesis of the spuriousness of the doxology, on account of its internal nature, and as Glöckler's view—that Tertius was the author of this doxology, as well as of the preceding verses—is also improbable, inasmuch as Tertius would assuredly not have written κατὰ τὸ εὐαγγέλιόν μ ο υ, Eichhorn's hypothesis, although in itself somewhat farfetched, is yet the most deserving of commendation, viz. that the variations in this section are to be explained by supposing a transposition of the different pieces of parchment on which the epistle was written. The similarity of the conclusion of the Epistle of St Jude, which is not to be mistaken, I should regard as arising from imitation of this in the Epistle to the Romans rather than the reverse. As to the internal structure of the doxology generally, Reiche, in his effort to prove it spurious, has very considerably exaggerated its difficulties. The ᾧ in ver. 27 certainly raises a difficulty; but Glöckler has already rightly shewn how this may be got over by the simple means of supplying συνίστημι. The form of the doxology will thus become perfectly regular—"To God, who alone can stablish you in the faith, to the only wise God, *I commend* you through Jesus Christ, to whom be glory for ever." It is consequently nowise necessary to suppose an anacoluthon, as Tholuck would do. And in other respects the doxology fits most appositely into the connexion, and by means of the ideas introduced,† agrees very well with the purpose of the whole epistle. For, according to our view, the doxology is immediately connected with the exhortation against giving into any divisions. With this, then, the notion of the στηρίξαι perfectly agrees.

* [*Kritische Erscheinungen.*] † [*Zwischengedanken.*]

In order that they may be secured against the assaults of the seducers, St Paul wishes the Christians of Rome *establishment* in the life of faith. With respect, next, to the intervening clauses,* they relate exactly to the substance of the epistle; they bring forward the two leading ideas which the Apostle has developed in it:—*first,* the mystery of the gospel, which was long hidden but now is made manifest; and *secondly,* its transition to the Gentiles. Hence we must not allow ourselves to be misled by the triple κατά into supposing three parallel members; there are but two oppositions in the passage, and these ought to be so connected as that the second point shall be introduced by the τε. The following would then be the rendering of the passage:—"*To God, who alone is of power to stablish you, according to my gospel and the preaching of Christ*—(these representing God as the source of all strength) —*which* (gospel and preaching) *are agreeable to the revelation of the mystery which was kept secret from eternity, but now is made manifest, and which, according to the commandment of the everlasting God, by the scriptures of the prophets, is made known to all nations for the obedience of faith;—to this only wise God I commend you through Jesus Christ, to whom be glory for ever, Amen!*" The mention of the prophetical scriptures, and the name αἰώνιος Θεός, which apparently do not suit the context, had the object, which we have already seen manifested in the epistle, of marking out the transition of the gospel to the Gentiles as not a new or unheard-of thing, but as something already announced beforehand by the unchangeable God in the scriptures of the Old Testament. And with relation to this it is, too, that in the end of the doxology God is designated as the only *wise,* while in the beginning of it he had been designated as the *Almighty.*

+ [*Zwischensätze.*]

THE END.

1983-84 TITLES

No.	Author	Title	Price
0104	MacDonald, Donald	Biblical Doctrine of Creation and the Fall: Genesis 1-3	18.95
1401	Bennett, William H.	An Exposition of the Books of Chronicles	17.50
1903	Cox, Samuel	The Pilgrim Psalms: An Exposition of the Songs of Degrees	9.50
2703	Wright, Charles H. H.	Studies in Daniel's Prophecy	13.95
3202	Kirk, Thomas	Jonah: His Life and Mission	12.95
4503	Olshausen, Hermann	Studies in the Epistle to the Romans	16.50
8803	Westcott, Frederick B.	The Biblical Doctrine of Justification	15.25
8804	Salmond, S. D. F.	The Biblical Doctrine of Immortality	26.95
9516	Harris, John	The Teaching Methods of Christ: Characteristics of Our Lord's Ministry	16.75
9517	Blaikie, William G.	The Public Ministry of Christ	13.25
9518	Laidlaw, John	Studies in the Miracles of Our Lord	14.75

TITLES CURRENTLY AVAILABLE

No.	Author	Title	Price
0101	Delitzsch, Franz	A New Commentary on Genesis (2 vol.)	30.50
0102	Blaikie, W. G.	Heroes of Israel	19.50
0103	Bush, George	Genesis (2 vol.)	29.95
0201	Murphy, James G.	Commentary on the Book of Exodus	12.75
0202	Bush, George	Exodus	22.50
0203	Dolman, D. & Rainsford, M.	The Tabernacle (2 vol. in 1)	19.75
0301	Kellogg, Samuel H.	The Book of Leviticus	21.00
0302	Bush, George	Leviticus	10.50
0401	Bush, George	Numbers	17.95
0501	Cumming, John	The Book of Deuteronomy	16.00
0601	Blaikie, William G.	The Book of Joshua	15.75
0602	Bush, George	Joshua & Judges (2 vol. in 1)	17.95
0603	Kirk, Thomas & Lang, John	Studies in the Book of Judges (2 vol. in 1)	17.75
0701	Cox, S. & Fuller, T.	The Book of Ruth (2 vol. in 1)	14.75
0901	Blaikie, William G.	First Book of Samuel	16.50
0902	Deane, W. J. & Kirk, T.	Studies in the First Book of Samuel (2 vol. in 1)	19.00
0903	Blaikie, William G.	Second Book of Samuel	15.00
1101	Farrar, F. W.	The First Book of Kings	19.00
1201	Farrar, F. W.	The Second Book of Kings	19.00
1301	Kirk, T. & Rawlinson, G.	Studies in the Books of Kings (2 vol. in 1)	20.75
1701	Raleigh, Alexander	The Book of Esther	9.75
1801	Gibson, Edgar Charles	The Book of Job (available December)	10.00
1802	Green, William H.	The Argument of the Book of Job Unfolded	13.50
1901	Dickson, David	A Commentary on the Psalms (2 vol.)	32.50
1902	MacLaren, Alexander	The Psalms (3 vol.)	45.00
2001	Wardlaw, Ralph	Book of Proverbs (3 vol.)	45.00
2101	MacDonald, James M.	The Book of Ecclesiastes	15.50
2102	Wardlaw, Ralph	Exposition of Ecclesiastes	16.25
2201	Durham, James	An Exposition on the Song of Solomon	17.25
2301	Kelly, William	An Exposition of the Book of Isaiah	15.25
2302	Alexander, Joseph	Isaiah (2 vol.)	29.95
2401	Orelli, Hans C. von	The Prophecies of Jeremiah	15.25
2601	Fairbairn, Patrick	An Exposition of Ezekiel	18.50
2701	Pusey, Edward B.	Daniel the Prophet	19.50
2702	Tatford, Frederick Albert	Daniel and His Prophecy	9.25
3001	Cripps, Richard S.	A Commentary on the Book of Amos	13.50
3201	Burns, Samuel C.	The Prophet Jonah	11.25
3801	Wright, Charles H. H.	Zechariah and His Prophecies	24.95
4001	Morison, James	The Gospel According to Matthew	24.95
4101	Alexander, Joseph	Commentary on the Gospel of Mark	16.75
4102	Morison, James	The Gospel According to Mark	21.00
4201	Kelly, William	The Gospel of Luke	18.50
4301	Brown, John	The Intercessory Prayer of Our Lord Jesus Christ	11.50
4302	Hengstenberg, E. W.	Commentary on the Gospel of John (2 vol.)	34.95
4401	Alexander, Joseph	Commentary on the Acts of the Apostles (2 vol. in 1)	27.50
4402	Gloag, Paton J.	A Critical and Exegetical Commentary on the Acts of the Apostles (2 vol.)	29.95
4403	Stier, Rudolf E.	Words of the Apostles	18.75
4502	Moule, H. C. G.	The Epistle to the Romans	16.25
4601	Brown, John	The Resurrection of Life	15.50
4602	Edwards, Thomas C.	A Commentary on the First Epistle to the Corinthians	18.00
4603	Jones, John Daniel	Exposition of First Corinthians 13	9.50
4801	Ramsey, William	Historical Commenatry on the Epistle to the Galatians	17.75
4802	Brown, John	An Exposition of the Epistle of Paul to the Galatians	16.00
4901	Westcott, Brooke F.	St. Paul's Epistle to the Ephesians (available December)	10.50
4902	Pattison, R. & Moule, H.	Exposition of Ephesians: Lessons in Grace and Godliness (2 vol. in 1)	14.75
5001	Johnstone, Robert	Lectures on the Book of Philippians	18.25
5102	Westcott, F. B.	The Epistle to the Colossians	7.50
5103	Eadie, John	Colossians	10.50
5104	Daille, Jean	Exposition of Colossians	24.95
5401	Liddon, H. P.	The First Epistle to Timothy	6.00
5601	Taylor, Thomas	An Exposition of Titus	20.75
5801	Delitzsch, Franz	Commentary on the Epistle to the Hebrews (2 vol.)	31.50
5802	Bruce, A. B.	The Epistle to the Hebrews	17.25
5803	Edwards, Thomas C.	The Epistle to the Hebrews	13.00
5901	Johnstone, Robert	Lectures on the Epistle of James	16.50
5902	Mayor, Joseph B.	The Epistle of St. James	20.25
5903	Stier, Rudolf E.	Commentary on the Epistle of James	10.25
6201	Lias, John J.	The First Epistle of John	15.75
6202	Morgan, J. & Cox S.	The Epistles of John (2 vol. in 1)	22.95
6501	Manton, Thomas	An Exposition of the Epistle of Jude (available December)	14.00
6601	Trench, Richard C.	Commentary on the Epistles to the Sever Churches	8.50
7000	Tatford, Frederick Albert	The Minor Prophets (3 vol.)	44.95
7001	Orelli, Hans C. von	The Twelve Minor Prophets	15.50
7002	Alford, Dean Henry	The Book of Genesis and Part of the Book of Exodus	12.50
7003	Marbury, Edward	Obadiah and Habakkuk	23.95
7004	Adeney, Walter	The Books of Ezra and Nehemiah	13.00
7101	Mayor, Joseph B.	The Epistle of St. Jude & The Second Epistle of Peter	16.50
7102	Lillie, John	Lectures on the First and Second Epistles of Peter	19.75
7103	Hort, F. J. A. & Hort, A. F.	Expository and Exegetical Studies	29.50
7104	Milligan, George	St. Paul's Epistles to the Thessalonians	12.00
7105	Stanley, Arthur P.	Epistles of Paul to the Corinthians	20.95
7106	Moule, H. C. G.	Colossian and Philemon Studies	12.00
7107	Fairbairn, Patrick	The Pastoral Epistles	17.25
7108	Cox, S. & Drysdale, A. H.	The Epistle to Philemon (2 vol. in 1)	9.25

TITLES CURRENTLY AVAILABLE

No.	Author	Title	Price
8001	Fairweather, William	Background of the Gospels	17.00
8002	Fairweather, William	Background of the Epistles	16.50
8003	Zahn, Theodor	Introduction to the New Testament (3 vol.)	48.00
8004	Bernard, Thomas	The Progress of Doctrine in the New Testament	9.00
8401	Blaikie, William G.	David, King of Israel	17.50
8402	Farrar, F. W.	The Life and Work of St. Paul (2 vol.)	43.95
8403	Jones, John Daniel	The Apostles of Christ	10.00
8404	Krummacher, Frederick W.	David, King of Israel	20.50
8405	MacDuff, John Ross	Elijah, the Prophet of Fire	13.75
8406	MacDuff, John Ross	The Footsteps of St. Peter	24.25
8602	Shedd, W. G. T.	Theological Essays (2 vol. in 1)	26.00
8603	McIntosh, Hugh	Is Christ Infallible and the Bible True?	27.00
8701	Shedd, W. G. T.	History of Christian Doctrine (2 vol.)	31.50
8702	Oehler, Gustav	Theology of the Old Testament	22.50
8703	Kurtz, John Henry	Sacrificial Worship of the Old Testament	16.50
8801	Lidgett, John Scott	The Biblical Doctrine of the Atonement	19.50
8802	Laidlaw, John	The Biblical Doctrine of Man	14.00
8901	Fawcett, John	Christ Precious to those that Believe	10.00
9401	Neal, Daniel	History of the Puritans (3 vol.)	54.95
9501	Schilder, Klass	The Trilogy (3 vol.)	48.00
9502	Liddon, H. P. & Orr, J.	The Birth of Christ (2 vol. in 1)	15.25
9503	Bruce, A. B.	The Parables of Christ	15.50
9504	Bruce, A. B.	The Miracles of Christ	20.00
9505	Milligan, William	The Ascension of Christ	15.00
9506	Moule, H. C. & Orr, J.	The Resurrection of Christ (2 vol. in1)	20.00
9507	Denney, James	The Death of Christ	12.50
9508	Farrar, F. W.	The Life of Christ	24.95
9509	Dalman, Gustaf H.	The Words of Christ	13.50
9510	Andrews, S. & Gifford, E. H.	Man and the Incarnation & The Incarnation (2 vol. in 1)	15.00
9511	Baron, David	Types, Psalms and Prophecies	14.00
9512	Stier, Rudolf E.	Words of the Risen Christ	8.25
9513	Innes, A. T. & Powell, F. J.	The Trial of Christ (2 vol. in 1)	10.75
9514	Gloag, P. J. & Delitzsch, F.	The Messiahship of Christ (2 vol. in 1)	23.50
9515	Blaikie, W. G. & Law, R.	The Inner Life of Christ (2 vol. in 1)	17.25
9801	Liddon, H. P.	The Divinity of Our Lord	20.50
9802	Pink, Arthur W.	The Antichrist	12.00
9803	Shedd, W. G. T.	The Doctrine of Endless Punishment	8.25
9804	Andrews, S. J.	Christianity and Anti-Christianity in Their Final Conflict	15.00
9805	Gilpin, Richard	Biblical Demonology: A Treatise on Satan's Temptations	20.00
9806	Ironside, H. A. & Ottman, F.	Studies in Biblical Eschatology (2 vol. in 1)	16.00